THE BOOK OF
THE CAT

THE BOOK OF
THE CAT

Edited by Michael Wright and Sally Walters

Designed by Celia Welcomme

Original paintings by Peter Warner

Consulting editors

Dr Barbara S. Stein
President of the American Association of Feline Practitioners

Sidney R. Thompson
Former publisher of Cat World magazine

SUMMIT BOOKS
New York

Published by SUMMIT BOOKS
A Division of Simon & Schuster, Inc.
Simon & Schuster Building
Rockefeller Center
1230 Avenue of the Americas
New York, New York 10020

SUMMIT BOOKS and colophon are trademarks
of Simon & Schuster, Inc.
Manufactured in the United States of America

2 3 4 5 6 7 8 9 10

6 7 8 9 10 pbk.

Library of Congress Cataloging in Publication Dat

Main entry under title:
The Book of the cat.
    Bibliography: p.
    Includes index.
    1. Cats.   I. Wright, Michael, 1941-   II. Walters,
Sally.
SF442.B66   636.8   80-23570

ISBN 0-671-44753-X
        0-671-41624-3 pbk.

This book was conceived and created by New Leaf Books Ltd, 38 Camden Lock, Chalk Farm Road, London NW1 8AF, with the assistance of many people, including the editorial and design team listed on the right and a large number of outside advisers and contributors. Grateful acknowledgement is given to them all.

Director Michael Wright

Project editor Sally Walters

Sub-editors Neil Ardley
Martin Bramwell
Vivianne Croot

Editorial research; index; proof-reading Trevor Dolby
Jill Girling

Art editor Celia Welcomme

Designer Jill Della Casa

Design assistant Viv Quillin

Picture research Jackum Brown

General assistance and admin Margaret Hall
Sue Wright

Consultants and contributors
Ronald S. Anderson, BVMS, PhD, MRCVS; head of the Animal Studies Centre, Pedigree Petfoods Ltd;
Alison Ashford; cat breeder and judge; vice-chairman of the Rex Cat Club;
Gareth Clayton Jones, BVetMed, MRCVS, DVR; lecturer in veterinary surgery, Royal Veterinary College, London;
Angus M. Dunn, PhD, MRCVS; senior lecturer in parasitology, University of Glasgow Veterinary School;
Michael Findlay, BVMS, MRCVS, MIPR; veterinary surgeon; honorary secretary of the Feline Advisory Bureau; central information officer, British Small Animal Veterinary Association; cat breeder and judge; vice-president of the United Chinchilla Association;
Paul Flecknell, MA, VetMB, MRCVS; member of the scientific staff of the Medical Research Council; member of the advisory council of the Feline Advisory Bureau;
Christopher J. Gaskell, BVSc, PhD, DVR, MRCVS; veterinary surgeon; lecturer in veterinary medicine, University of Bristol; scientific editor, Bulletin of the Feline Advisory Bureau;
Tim J. Gruffydd-Jones, BVetMed, MRCVS; lecturer in clinical pathology, Department of Veterinary Medicine, University of Bristol; chairman of the Feline Advisory Bureau Central Fund for Feline Studies;
Sophie M. Hamilton-Moore; boarding cattery officer of the Feline Advisory Bureau; boarding cattery proprietor;
Jorun Ryden Jensen, breeder of Norwegian Forest Cats;
Joan O. Joshua, FRCVS; emeritus reader in veterinary surgery (small animals), University of Liverpool; author of Clinical Aspects of Some Diseases of Cats;
J. Geoffrey Lane, BVetMed, FRCVS; lecturer in veterinary surgery, University of Bristol; surgeon, University of Bristol Veterinary Hospital;
John G. Loxam, MRCVS; assistant chief veterinary officer, Ministry of Agriculture, Fisheries and Food (UK);
David W. Macdonald, MA, DPhil; research fellow in animal behaviour, Department of Zoology, Oxford University, with particular interest in the behavioural ecology of cats;
Judith and Terry Moore; education officer and vice-chairman, respectively, of the Cat Survival Trust;
Roger Mugford, BSc, PhD; consultant in animal behaviour;

Catherine M. Orr, BVSc, MRCVS; veterinary surgeon; former Feline Advisory Bureau scholar;
John Rivers, BSc, MIBiol; lecturer in nutrition, London School of Hygiene and Tropical Medicine;
Roy Robinson, NDR, FIBiol; research geneticist; author of Genetics for Cat Breeders and Colour Inheritance in Small Livestock; president of the Havana, Foreign and Oriental Cat Association;
Anthony D. Self, MRCVS; veterinary surgeon; head of veterinary clinical services, Royal Society for the Prevention of Cruelty to Animals;
Geoffrey C. Skerritt, BVSc, MRCVS; veterinary surgeon; lecturer in veterinary anatomy, University of Liverpool; committee member of the Feline Advisory Bureau;
Geoffrey Startup, PhD, BSc, MRCVS; veterinary surgeon specializing in ophthalmology;
Rodney Steel; technical journalist; former member of scientific staff, British Museum (Natural History);
Barbara S. Stein, BS, DVM; veterinarian and director of the Chicago Cat Clinic; lecturer in feline medicine and surgery; president of the American Association of Feline Practitioners; consultant to two Chicago zoos;
Moira Swift, breeder of Burmese and former secretary of the Burmese Cat Club;
Sidney R. Thompson, BSEd; co-founder and former publisher of Cat World magazine; breeder of several breeds of cats;
Patricia Turner, DesRCA; cat breeder; director of the Cat Genetics Investigation Centre; chairman of the International Society for the Advancement of Developing Feline Breeds; officer of several other cat breed clubs;
Michael I. Wilson, BA, DipEd; senior research assistant, National Art Library, Victoria and Albert Museum, London;
Alan I. Wright, BVSc, MRCVS; senior lecturer in clinical veterinary parasitology, University of Bristol.

Specialist breed advisers
Caroline Andrews; breeder of Angoras and Oriental Shorthairs;
Claire Betts; breeder and judge of British Shorthairs; breeder of Burmese and Birmans;
R. Elizabeth Brown; breeder of Birmans and Colourpoint Longhairs;
Mary Dunnill; breeder of Siamese, Havanas (Oriental Chestnuts) and Foreign Blacks;
Margaret K. Kidd; breeder of Burmese, Abyssinians, Russian Blues and Siamese; international judge;

Daphne Negus; editor of Cat World magazine; importer and breeder of Korats;
Marjorie D. Nelson; former breeder of Abyssinians;
Rosemonde S. Peltz, BFA, MD; breeder of various breeds, including Burmese; member of the executive board of the Cat Fanciers' Association; chairman of the CFA Research Committee;
Angela Sayer, BA; breeder of Oriental Shorthairs; manager of Kensington Kitten and Neuter Cat Club annual show; photojournalist and author of nine cat books.

Other assistance
Detailed acknowledgements of the sources of illustrations are given at the end of the book. Special thanks for assistance of various kinds are due to the following: American Cat Fanciers Association; Dr Everette Baker Jr of the US Dept of Health, Education and Welfare; Professor Ken Baker; Arthur Bradshaw; Bob Brodie of Pitman-Moore International; Burmese Cat Club (GB); Canadian Cat Association; Cat Fanciers' Association Inc; Cat Fanciers Federation; Colourpoint Society of Great Britain; Warren Cox of the American Humane Association; Pamela Cross Stern; Crown Cat Fanciers Federation; Madalyn Dakin; Jane Dards; K. Doyle of the Dept of Health, Canberra, Australia; Ann Ellis; Professor Robert Fagen; Feline Advisory Bureau; Mrs J. E. Felthouse; Clement Fennell; Governing Council of the Cat Fancy; Dr Ray Guillery; J. T. Hadley; Jenks Bros Foods Ltd; Barrie C. Jimmieson of the 1 Deutscher Edelkatzenzuchter-Verband eV; Korat Cat Fanciers Association; Barbara Kuhn of the American Genetics Association; the late Frank Manolson; Michael McGuinness; Jaqui Murphy; Willie Newlands of the Scottish National Zoological Park; New Zealand Cat Fancy Inc; Susie Page of Cats Magazine (USA); Pedigree Petfoods Education Centre; Pet Care Information and Advisory Service (Australia); Pet Foods Institute (USA); Dr Pittler of the West German Ministry of Agriculture; Mrs Pruce; Royal Society for the Protection of Cruelty to Animals; Dorothy Richards of Catac Products Ltd; Ralston Purina Company; Vicky Sanders of the Chinchilla, Silver Tabby and Smoke Cat Society; Professor Patricia Scott; Siamese Cat Society of America; Society for Prevention of Cruelty to Animals (New Zealand); Dr J. M. Sokolowski of the Upjohn Company; Jack Stevens (Australia); Miranda von Kirchberg; Alison Weare of the Mars Group Information Centre; Doris Wurster Hill of the Dartmouth-Hitchcock Foundation.

Contents

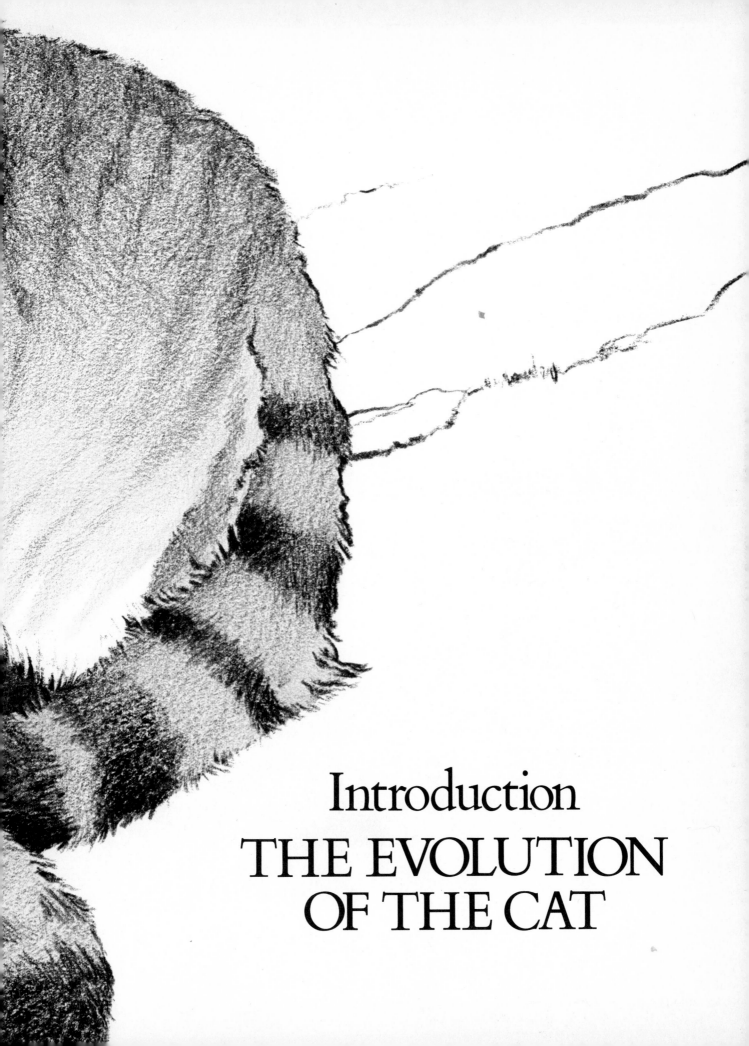

Introduction
THE EVOLUTION
OF THE CAT

The cat's prehistoric ancestors

The forces of evolution have resulted in an astonishing diversity of animals. Almost everywhere, life in some form has gained a purchase, producing an ever-changing pyramid of creatures that range in size from the humblest single-celled organisms to the mighty dinosaurs of the past and the whales of today. At the summit of this pyramid is the human species, currently the most successful of all animals. But not far below come the cats. Over a million species (distinct kinds) of animals live on the Earth today, but none excite more respect and admiration than the members of the cat family. Comprising only about 40 out of the million species, they represent the most supremely efficient muscular machines. How did nature come to produce such a marvel of co-ordinated power?

The theory of evolution suggests that the kinds of animals that survive have gradually changed and developed to take advantage of the varying conditions on the Earth. Life began in the sea, and only later spread onto land. Among animals with backbones, there developed fishes, amphibians (represented today by frogs, newts and toads), reptiles (including snakes, lizards and dinosaurs), and then birds and mammals, all suited in their own ways to life in the various habitats in the sea, on land or in the air.

They ate plants or other animals (or both), and in the complex webs of relationships that developed, certain animals always ruled – creatures that had no fear of suddenly falling prey to another. Towards the top of the pyramid of life, there evolved creatures so large or well-armoured that no attack on them could possibly succeed – at least when they were in the prime of life – among them today's elephant, rhinoceros, whale. Alongside these came the best hunters – animals graced with keen senses of sight, hearing and smell to find and stalk their victims, strong legs to pursue or spring on them and sharp claws and teeth to kill and tear them apart.

On the land, this ecological niche – this vacancy in the great scheme of things – has for some 40 million years been filled by the cats, at least until the rise of ourselves and our weapons. This may seem far in the past, but it must be compared with the formation of the Earth 4,600 million years ago and the appearance of the first living organisms more than 3,000 million years ago, from which the cats and all other living things can trace their descent.

Ancestors of the cats

Cats belong to the animal group known as mammals – warm-blooded, hairy creatures that suckle their young. They evolved some 200 million years ago from reptiles, which in turn trace their origins back to the amphibians and fishes. The first mammals were small creatures, and it was not until after the great dinosaurs mysteriously met

Sabre-tooth tigers, seen in a reconstruction **above**, were fearsome hunters and died out only in the latter part of the Ice Ages. Their place was taken by the more agile and larger-brained modern felines, whose rise is charted **opposite**. (Figures indicate millions of years.)

their doom about 70 million years ago that the mammals gained the chance to take over the world. Since then they have become the dominant animals, and the most accomplished hunters among them make up the group known as the Carnivora, or carnivores. They include dog-like animals such as wolves and foxes, bears,

pandas, weasels, badgers, skunks and otters, and cat-like animals such as civets, genets, mongooses, hyaenas and true cats. These last comprise big cats such as the lion, tiger, leopard, jaguar and cheetah, and small cats like the lynx, ocelot and margay.

Although termed carnivores, many of the Carnivora can and do turn to food other than meat. The panda, for example, is now almost totally vegetarian, and the cats are the only group that depend almost wholly on live vertebrate animals as a source of food. One of the distinctive features of them all, however, is a set of teeth well adapted to cutting and tearing meat. Such teeth are to be found in the fossilized remains of primitive fish-eating mammals known as creodonts, which flourished about 50 million years ago. Some creodonts were fearsome beasts like today's wolves and bears, but their line was not to last and they have no direct descendants today. Another early carnivore group, the miacids, outlived them. These also had teeth for cutting and tearing, though arranged differently (and more efficiently). This specialization, together with their larger brains and more athletic bodies, made the miacids better hunters than the creodonts.

The first miacids lived in forests and were small creatures that resembled today's martens. They clambered easily through the trees, and probably had paws with retracting claws like those of modern cats. From about 45 million years ago, the miacids evolved into the various families of carnivores alive today – among them, members of the cat family.

The genet is not only very cat-like in appearance, but is also about the size of a domestic cat. It is one of the dominant small carnivores of the forests of tropical Africa. Nocturnal and an agile climber, it feeds on insects, birds, mice and the like.

CATS AND THEIR RELATIVES

Similarities in skull structure link the mongoose and civet family, the hyaena family and the cat family. All these animals have short jaws that confer great biting power, and most are formidable predators. Apart from the true cats, they are mostly found only in Africa and southern Asia.

Civets (sometimes called civet cats) and genets are remarkably cat-like in appearance, with cat-shaped heads and bodies but generally longer tails than cats of the same size. They live in forests and feed on invertebrates and fruit as well as small mammals and birds. The closely related mongooses are more ferret-like, while the hyaenas are also quite close relatives although they are more dog-like in appearance. Their jaws are strong enough to crack thick bones, and they live on carrion as well as on prey that they catch for themselves.

The true cats are almost exclusively hunters, neither their teeth nor their digestive systems being suited to anything other than an all-meat diet.

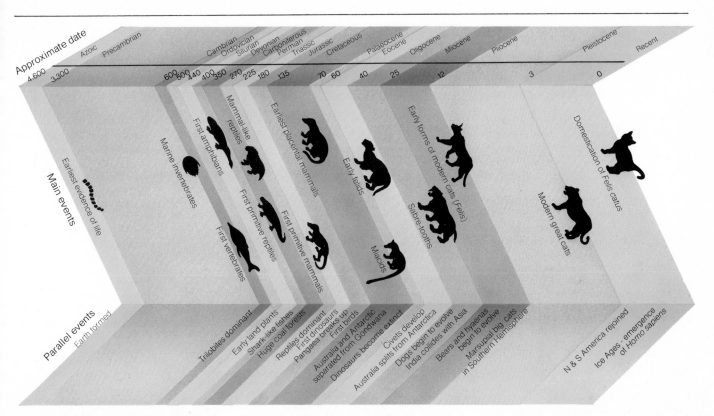

Approximate date

Azoic | Precambrian | Cambrian | Ordovician | Silurian | Devonian | Carboniferous | Permian | Triassic | Jurassic | Cretaceous | Palaeocene | Eocene | Oligocene | Miocene | Pliocene | Pleistocene | Recent

4,600   3,300   600 500 440 400 350 270 225 180 135 70 60 40 25 12 3 0

Main events

Earliest evidence of life

Marine invertebrates

First vertebrates

First amphibians

Mammal-like reptiles

First primitive reptiles

First primitive mammals

Earliest placental mammals

Early felids

Miacids

Sabre-tooths

Early forms of modern cats (Felis)

Modern great cats

Domestication of Felis catus

Parallel events

Earth formed

Trilobites dominant

Early land plants

Shark-like fishes

Huge coal forests

Reptiles dominant

First dinosaurs

Pangaea breaks up

First birds

Australia and Antarctica separated from Gondwana

Dinosaurs become extinct

Civets develop

Australia splits from Antarctica

Dogs begin to evolve

India collides with Asia

Bears and hyaenas begin to evolve

Marsupial big cats in Southern Hemisphere

N & S America rejoined

Ice Ages – emergence of Homo sapiens

Development of the cats

The early 'prototype' cats began to spread out through the world, settling in places that suited them and moving on if conditions made hunting difficult. As they did so, various kinds evolved, each suited to a particular habitat and the prey to be found there. Few of these have survived. Among

The marsupial 'cat' of Australasia looks rather like a cat, and occupies a similar ecological niche, but is pouched like the kangaroo.

the casualties were several fearsome beasts, including the huge cave lion of Europe and a giant tiger in Northern Asia.

Most renowned of all extinct wild cats are the sabre-tooth 'tigers', named for their dagger-like upper canine teeth. These formidable weapons were probably capable of felling young adult elephants, something no present-day animal can do. From about 35 million years ago, the sabre-tooths were widespread in Europe, Asia, Africa and North America (and subsequently also in South America), evolving as a separate line from the cats that survive today. They used their teeth to stab their prey and not to bite as modern cats do. Their relatively small brains, heavy bodies and cumbersome jaws may have helped to push them into extinction, though they are not long gone. Remains dating back only 30,000 years have been found in Derbyshire; and in California, sabre-tooths may still have been alive only 13,000 years ago.

For some millions of years before their demise, the sabre-tooths shared mastery of the land with the smaller-toothed, faster modern felines. The oldest fossils that show close similarities with modern small cats are about 12 million years old. By about three million years ago, when the great Ice Ages began and our own primitive ancestors were well established, there lived a variety of felines similar to those of today, though even more diverse. They included members of the three modern cat genera (see p 14): *Acinonyx* (cheetahs), *Felis* (smaller cats) and *Panthera* (great cats). All of these except the cheetahs occurred in both the

Old and New Worlds, though with the exception of the lynx (which is found in both Asia and North America) the actual species living in the two hemispheres today are different. This shows that members of the cat family were able to cross from one hemisphere to the other (via a land 'bridge' across the Bering Sea) at various times over the last few million years, but could then evolve into distinctive species in isolation.

Two continents – Antarctica and Australia – have never had any native cats, however, and they reached South America for the first time only about two million years ago. The reason is to be found in continental drift: These southern continents began to split away from the huge supercontinent that comprised the whole of dry land some 180 million years ago, long before the cat family – and in fact before any other modern placental (live-bearing) mammal – evolved on the northern land mass. South America rejoined its northern neighbour some two million years ago, allowing the cats to invade, but nature had not been idle in the meantime. The most advanced creatures to evolve in the southern continents were the marsupials (pouched mammals), and these included a variety of remarkably cat-like creatures. They were no more closely related to true cats than a kangaroo is to a reindeer, but they filled the same ecological niche and developed very similar characteristics – some even had 'sabre' teeth. They are a remarkable example of environment forcing evolution – as if to prove that if the cats did not exist, nature would have to 'invent' them.

The cat's wild relatives

All cats, from the savage hunters of the tropical plains and forests to the domestic pet curled up in front of your fire, are recognizably related. The rounded head and agile, light-footed body immediately identify a cat, whatever its size or markings, and suggest that all cats evolved from a common prehistoric ancestor. There are also certain characteristic internal anatomical features and a particular cell structure – almost all cats have 38 chromosomes in each cell (see p22), though a few exceptional species have only 36.

Cats therefore make up a well-defined family, called the Felidae, within the order Carnivora (carnivores) of the class Mammalia (mammals). Within a family, animals are further classified into groups called genera (singular, genus), and within each genus into separate species – the basic unit of classification. Animals are assigned to separate species if they do not normally interbreed and produce fertile offspring.

Zoologists disagree on the exact number of cat species, though most recognize 38, including the domestic cat. Classification of these species into genera is not easy. One important feature is the structure of the hyoid bone, at the base of the tongue. In the lion, leopard, tiger, snow leopard, clouded leopard and jaguar, this is partly made of cartilage. As a result, the vocal apparatus is able to move freely, enabling these cats to roar. The big roaring cats are therefore usually grouped in the genus *Panthera*.

In all other cats, the hyoid bone is fully ossified and rigid, so that they cannot roar. All but one of these species are generally grouped together in the genus *Felis*, and commonly called small cats, even though the puma is as large as a leopard. The exception is the cheetah, which has claws that do not retract fully; it is placed in a genus of its own, *Acinonyx*.

However, some authorities break the Felidae down into more genera. The clouded leopard has very long upper canine teeth, and is sometimes placed in its own genus, *Neofelis*. The lynxes, with their short tails and tufted ears, may be grouped in the genus *Lynx* instead of *Felis*, while the ocelots and Geoffroy's cat, which have 36 chromosomes, may be classed as *Leopardus*. Similar marginal differences account for further division of the small cats (see the listing of species on page 14).

Body and behaviour

In general, the size of wild cats and the detailed characteristics of their body structure are the result of evolution to take advantage of a particular kind and size of prey. However, there are very many similarities, and many of the features can be clearly seen in the domestic cat (see chapter 2). Apart from the male lion's mane, cats show little difference between the sexes, though male cats are usually slightly larger.

Hunting is a way of life for all members of the cat family, but only the cheetah **left** is fast enough to chase its prey. After the kill **above**, a lynx uses its carnassial teeth to slice the meat for swallowing.

Climbing cats inhabit many forest areas, among the most beautiful and agile being the ocelot **left**. Its spotted coat gives excellent camouflage in the deeply contrasting light and shade of the jungle. In the flat, brilliant light of the savannah live many plain, unpatterned species of cats, while striped cats like the tiger are often inhabitants of tall grasses.

Variant cats may result from mutations, as in the case of the white tiger **right above**, which is probably a semi-albino, or from hybridization between two distinct species, as in the case of the leopon **right**, which is a cross between a leopard and a lion. Such hybrids normally occur only in captivity, and are usually sterile except with very closely related species.

Cats walk on their toes, which effectively lengthens the legs and enables them to run faster than if they were flat-footed. But although they are swift, cats cannot keep up a high speed for long; they therefore lie in ambush to catch their prey. The body is very flexible and powerful, so that the cat can creep up on its victim and then suddenly leap upon it (see p122). The cheetah is the only cat that will pursue its prey, and it can achieve 100km/h (63mph) in bursts – faster than any other land animal. It does this by swinging its long legs from the waist and using its non-retractile claws to give it a good grip on the ground and help it to make rapid turns. All cats have five toes on their forepaws and four on their hind paws, with pads at the base of each toe and a larger pad in the middle (see p106). These pads enable the cat to move quietly as it stalks its prey.

Many cats, large and small, live in forests and are good tree-climbers, often dropping on their prey. They therefore need a fine sense of balance, as is shown by the well-known righting reflex (see p121). All cats have highly developed 'external' senses, too, that enable them to hunt efficiently. Most important are the ears and eyes (see pp109 and 110), for they frequently seek their prey at dawn and dusk when sharp hearing and sensitive sight (aided by a reflecting layer behind the retina of the eye that increases its stimulation in dim light) give them an advantage over other animals. The sense of smell is also well developed, but is not much used in hunting; wild cats do not track their prey by its scent. However, scent is extremely important in detecting signals from other cats (see p127).

The colour and markings of wild cats' coats have evolved to camouflage them

The family feline Lions are the only wild members of the cat family to form stable sociable groups; only the domestic cat is comparable in habits. A lion pride is headed by one or rarely two dominant males, and may contain as many as 30 individuals, though most prides are smaller. It will have several mature breeding females plus immature males and females; however, the males will eventually either challenge for pride leadership or leave to form their own prides – or live on their own for a while.

Skeletal differences and, in particular, differences in the vocal apparatus distinguish the roaring great cats of the genus *Panthera* **1** from the other members of the cat family, such as the domestic cat **2**. In the latter, a paired chain of small bones called the hyoid **a** connects the voice box or larynx **b** with the skull. But in the great cats, some of the hyoid bones are replaced by cartilage **c**; this allows the mobility needed to produce the characteristic full-throated roar. Smaller cats can only make weak cries.

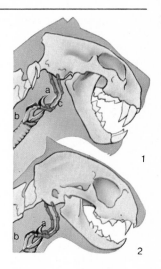

from their prey. The design therefore bears some relation to the cats' environment. Spotted cats, like the leopard and jaguar, are usually found in forests, and the tiger's stripes conceal it among tall grasses. In the dry and sandy-brown savannah of Africa lives the tawny-coloured lion. The puma is often similarly coloured, and inhabits the North American prairies. In some wild cats, such as the leopard and jaguar, a variation known as melanism occurs, producing a dark, almost black, coat. There are also white tigers that have blue eyes and white fur with light brown stripes.

Habitat and habits

Wild cats of one kind or another are to be found in all kinds of land habitats except for the treeless tundra and polar ice. Their lifestyle is generally one of inactivity punctuated by forays in search of food. They will eat as much as they can, consuming up to a third of their body weight at one sitting, and may then go without food for several days. Cats will often sleep for 18 hours a day and tend to exert themselves only when hunger dictates. The domestic cat is no different from the wild in this respect. Like domestic cats, wild cats will sometimes eat grass; this is unlikely to have any dietary function, but may help the cat to rid itself of hair swallowed when grooming – which wild cats do just as much as the domestic cat.

In the wild, most cats are solitary and keep more or less to their own territory, though a single male and several females may cohabit a given area of land while remaining apart outside the mating season. The lion is the only exception; lions usually live together, maintaining a hierarchy for purposes of breeding. Generally, a new male lion will take over the duties of reproduction about every two years, ensuring that new 'blood' occurs in every second generation. Genetic variation would otherwise disappear and the species be weakened. The continual assertion of rights over the lionesses within the pride often leads to confrontation between the pride's males. Eventually, young males leave to set up their own prides, but away from the support of other pride members they have a lower chance of survival than the females.

In other species, males and females come together only to mate. The females let the males know they are ready for mating by spraying their urine on certain landmarks within their territory. The male helps to overcome the female's natural wariness by secreting a scent that stimulates her. A period of courtship ensues, characterized by moments of tenderness alternating with ferocious quarrels, usually provoked by the female. Wild cats mate like domestic cats, the male mounting the female and gripping her by the scruff of the neck with his teeth.

The period of gestation varies from one species to another, but is generally from 9 to 16 weeks. The size of the litter also varies, some New World cats like the ocelot and margay bearing only one or two kittens while other small cats have from two to six young (as do big cats of the genus *Panthera*). The newborn cats are blind like domestic kittens, but have fur. Parental care of the young is left entirely to the female, and once they are old enough to follow their mother on hunting trips, the young cats quickly learn how to kill their prey. The young stay with their mother for at least six months before becoming independent, and some remain for more than a year.

Each species of cat hunts its prey in a slightly different way, using a sequence of actions that relates to the behaviour of the prey. The impulse to hunt is hereditary: the young cat plays with anything that moves and the movement provides the stimulus to attack. However, the techniques involved in hunting, stalking, pouncing, seizing, immobilizing and killing have to be learnt and perfected before the young leave the protection of their parent. Most smaller cats kill by severing the prey's spinal cord with their canine teeth, but lions generally jump onto their prey's haunches and break its back, while tigers go for the throat.

Interbreeding

In general, wild cats of different species cannot interbreed and produce fertile offspring. However, feral domestic cats have occasionally interbred with African and European wild cats in the wild. The offspring may be fertile, but seem to possess either domestic or wild characteristics. Though the three species are obviously closely related, they have each maintained species status. In captivity different species have been interbred to produce unusual hybrids, which in most instances have been sterile. The hybrids exhibit characteristics of both parents. Lions and tigers have been crossed: if the father is a lion, the offspring is called a liger; if a tiger, the young is a tigon. In a similar way, domestic cats have been crossed with such species as Geoffroy's cat to create handsome hybrids.

The species of cats A to Z

All the generally recognized species of living cats are detailed below, divided into the three genera *Panthera*, *Acinonyx* and *Felis*. They are listed alphabetically by their scientific names within these genera, and altenative names are given in brackets.

THE GREAT CATS

1 Lion *Panthera leo;* weight generally 135–225 kg (300–500 lb) but may reach 340 kg (750 lb). Found in Africa south of the Sahara (living in most kinds of terrain) and in the Gir Forest in India. Plain tawny-brown; male has mane.

2 Clouded leopard *Panthera (Neofelis) nebulosa;* weight 18–30 kg (40–66 lb). Inhabits dense forest and scrub in southern and south-eastern Asia. Pale brown with large blotches.

3 Jaguar *Panthera onca;* weight 40–135 kg (90–300 lb). Inhabits tropical forest and more open country from southern USA to Argentina. Yellow-brown with spots clustered in rosettes, or dark brown. The largest American wild cat. Sometimes called the panther.

4 Leopard (panther) *Panthera pardus;* weight 40–70 kg (90–150 lb). Found in all types of terrain, but prefers scrub and forest. Ranges throughout most of Africa, and from Asia Minor through southern Asia to China and Indonesia. Pale brown with spots clustered in rosettes, or very dark brown (black panther).

5 Tiger *Panthera tigris;* weight generally 110–225 kg (250–500 lb) but may reach 360 kg (800 lb). Largest living member of cat family. Found in all kinds of terrain, except desert, in southern and south-eastern Asia extending to north-eastern China and Siberia. Orange-brown with long black stripes (only truly striped wild cat). Many populations endangered.

6 Snow leopard (ounce) *Panthera uncia;* weight 45–70 kg (100–150 lb). Lives in forests and open rocky ground in the mountains of central Asia. Smoke-grey with rosettes; long-haired.

THE CHEETAH

7 Cheetah *Acinonyx jubatus;* weight 30–50 kg (65–110 lb). Inhabits all kinds of terrain but prefers open country. Ranges from Africa through the Middle East to southern Asia. Yellow-brown with dark spots; long-legged for speed (the fastest four-legged animal in short bursts).

THE SMALL CATS

8 African golden cat *Felis (Profelis) aurata;* weight 13.5–18 kg (30–40 lb). A handsome and rare cat of forest and dense scrubland in west and central Africa. Varies in colour from chestnut-brown to silver-grey.

9 Bay cat *Felis (Pardofelis) badia;* weight 2–3 kg (4½–7 lb). A rare cat found only in Borneo, where it inhabits rocky scrub. Bright reddish-brown. Sometimes called the Bornean red cat.

10 Leopard cat (Bengal cat) *Felis (Prionailurus) bengalensis;* weight 3–7 kg (7–15 lb). A common wild cat of southern and south-eastern Asia, extending from India to the Philippines, Japan, Manchuria and eastern Siberia. Lives in forest and scrubland. A small spotted cat varying considerably in basic colour.

11 Chinese desert cat *Felis bieti;* weight about 5.5 kg (12 lb). A rare cat found in the steppes and mountains of Mongolia and China. Brownish-yellow with bold markings.

12 Caracal (caracal lynx) *Felis (Caracal) caracal;* weight 16–23 kg (35–50 lb). The largest 'small' cat of Africa, extending to Arabia and northern India. Found in desert, savannah, scrub, rocky terrain and mountains. Reddish-brown, with distinctive tufted ears.

13 Domestic cat *Felis catus* (formerly *F. domestica*); weight 3–9 kg (7–20 lb). Found worldwide in human settlements, though often becoming feral. Great range of markings and colours with long or short hair.

14 Jungle cat *Felis chaus;* weight 7–13.5 kg (16–30 lb). Found in Egypt and throughout southern Asia, living in woodland, scrub, reed beds and near human settlements. Has a sandy-brown coat with some face and leg markings and a ringed tail.

15 Pampas cat *Felis (Lynchailurus) colocolo;* weight 3.5–6.5 kg (8–14 lb). A very rare cat of grassland, scrub and forest in the southern and central parts of South America. Grey-brown with brown spots.

16 Puma (mountain lion) *Felis (Puma) concolor;* weight 45–60 kg (100–130 lb). The largest of all 'small' cats and greatest jumping cat. Inhabits mountains, forests, plains and deserts through most of North, Central and South America. Varies in colour from light brown to black. Numerous other common names, including cougar, panther, etc.

17 Geoffroy's cat (Geoffroy's ocelot) *Felis (Leopardus) geoffroyi;* weight 2–3.5 kg (4½–8 lb). A cat of South American upland forests and scrub, found from Bolivia to Patagonia. Grey with small black spots.

18 Kodkod (hüina) *Felis (Oncifelis) guigna;* weight 2–3 kg (4½–7 lb). Lives in wooded Andes foothills of Chile and Argentina. Grey with dark spots and ringed tail.

19 Iriomote cat *Felis (Mayailurus) iriomotensis;* weight 5.5 kg (12 lb). A very rare cat, found only in forest and scrubland on the

island of Iriomote, east of Taiwan. Discovered in 1964, there are thought to be less than 100. A spotted cat, similar to the leopard cat, of which it may be a subspecies.

20 Mountain cat *Felis (Oreailurus) jacobita;* weight 3.5–7 kg (8–15 lb). Lives on open and forested slopes of the Andes from southern Peru to north-west Argentina. A long-haired brown-grey cat with dark spots and ringed tail.

21 African wild cat *Felis libyca* (sometimes spelt *F. lybica*); weight 4.5–8 kg (10–18 lb). Found in Africa and Asia from the Middle East to India; also on Corsica, Sardinia and Majorca. Lives in a wide range of habitats except deserts and tropical forests. Light brown with stripes, but lighter than in the European wild cat, of which it is sometimes considered a variation. Probable primary ancestor of the domestic cat.

22 Lynx (northern lynx) *Felis (Lynx) lynx;* weight 13.5–29 kg (30–64 lb). Inhabits forests and thick scrub in Europe, northern Asia and North America. A light brown, powerfully built cat with spots and tufted ears.

23 Pallas's cat (manul) *Felis (Octocolobus) manul;* weight 3–5 kg (7–11 lb). Found in steppes, rocky terrain and woods in central Asia. A handsome cat, orange-grey with black and white head markings.

24 Sand cat *Felis margarita;* weight 2–2.5 kg (4½–6 lb). Found in semi-desert regions of North Africa and the Middle East, extending to southern Russia. Plain yellow-brown to grey-brown with ringed tail; hair over the pads.

25 Marbled cat *Felis (Pardofelis) marmorata;* weight 5.5 kg (12 lb). A rare cat of the forests from Nepal to Indonesia. Light brown with striking pattern of blotches.

26 Black-footed cat *Felis nigripes;* weight 1–2 kg (2½–4½ lb). One of the smallest and lightest of all cats. An uncommon cat of desert and savannah in southern Africa. Light brown with body markings and black patches on undersides of feet.

27 Ocelot *Felis (Leopardus) pardalis;* weight 5.5–13.5 kg (12–30 lb). A handsome cat of forests and thick vegetation, ranging from the southern USA to Argentina. The body is striped and spotted, and the tail ringed.

28 Spanish lynx *Felis (Lynx) pardina;* weight 16–23 kg (35–50 lb). Restricted to remote forests and mountains in Spain and Portugal. Distinctively black-spotted; slightly smaller than the northern lynx.

29 Flat-headed cat *Felis (Ictailurus) planiceps;* weight 5.5–8 kg (12–18 lb). An uncommon cat of forests and scrub in south-eastern Asia. Plain reddish-brown with slightly flattened head.

30 Rusty-spotted cat *Felis (Prionailurus) rubiginosa;* weight 1–2 kg (2½–4½ lb). Lives in scrubland and around waterways and human settlements in southern India, and in forest and woodland in Sri Lanka. A very small cat, rust-coloured with brown blotches.

31 Bobcat *Felis (Lynx) rufus;* weight 7–16 kg (15–35 lb). Found from southern Canada to central Mexico in most kinds of terrain and vegetation. Heavily built with a short tail and a barred and spotted coat.

32 Serval *Felis (Leptailurus) serval;* weight 13.5–18 kg (30–40 lb). Found in Algeria and Africa south of the Sahara, inhabiting dense vegetation but always near water. Slenderly built with large ears, long legs and a short tail. Light brown with dark spots.

33 European wild cat *Felis silvestris;* weight 4.5–11 kg (10–24 lb). Found in all kinds of terrain and vegetation in Europe and western Asia. A black-striped tabby cat, the tail having a rounded black tip. Possible partial ancestor of the domestic cat.

34 Temminck's golden cat (Asiatic golden cat) *Felis (Profelis) temmincki;* weight 6–11 kg (14–24 lb). A rare cat of rocky terrain and forests from Tibet and south-western China south to Sumatra. A beautiful dark golden-brown with striking black face markings.

35 Tiger cat (tiger ocelot) *Felis (Leopardus) tigrina;* weight 2–3.5 kg (4½–8 lb). Found in forests and woodlands in Central America and northern South America. A light brown cat with dark stripes and blotches, otherwise somewhat similar to the margay.

36 Fishing cat *Felis (Prionailurus) viverrina;* weight 5.5–8 kg (12–18 lb). Found in marshy areas, reed beds and swamps in southern and south-eastern Asia. Thought to catch fish, having slightly webbed paws and claws not fully retractable. A light brown spotted cat.

37 Margay (tree ocelot) *Felis (Leopardus) wiedii;* weight 4–8 kg (9–18 lb). Found in forests and scrubland of Central and South America. Yellow-brown with black spots and stripes and a ringed tail.

38 Jaguarundi (jaguarondi) *Felis (Herpailurus) yagouaroundi;* weight 5.5–10 kg (12–22 lb). Lives in lowland forest and bush in Central and South America and north to Texas. Graceful and rather otter-like in appearance. Two colour phases: plain grey-brown and plain chestnut-red.

Origins of the domestic cat

The domestic cat is as docile and as used to people as any other domesticated animal, and yet it retains a streak of independence – wildness, even. Cats are somewhat solitary and can well fend for themselves. This is reflected in their domestication, which took place much later than with other animals. The dog had probably already entered into an association with people when our ancestors began to abandon a nomadic way of life and settle to agriculture 10 to 12 thousand years ago in Asia Minor. Goats, sheep, cattle and pigs were herded early on, but there is no clear evidence that cats were domesticated more than about 4,000 years ago. Although cat remains have been found among the ruins of more ancient settlements, they are probably of wild species.

Almost all the knowledge we have of the early domestication of the cat comes from Ancient Egypt; the cat may also have been domesticated elsewhere, but there is no evidence that it was. The earliest Egyptian evidence dates from about 2500 BC but is inconclusive. However, paintings and inscriptions from 2000 BC show cats under conditions that suggest primitive domestication, and thereafter there is plentiful evidence that the Egyptians kept cats.

They were certainly very interested in animal life, and kept all kinds of creatures in captivity. Most found a place in religious ceremonies, and became sacred to specific deities. The cat was no exception, and became revered and protected to an extraordinary degree (see p 238) and was interred after death in special cemeteries. In the process, it made the transition from scavenger tolerated for its usefulness in controlling vermin to household pet. It is possible that, in these conditions, selection took place favouring those animals that responded to human attention and could breed successfully even though surrounded by people. In this way, the tame character of the domestic cat may have been finally forged, to be passed on ever since.

The custom of keeping cats spread slowly throughout the Middle East, and they either reached or were separately domesticated in India and China some time later than in Egypt. Europe had to wait for the Romans to introduce the domestic cat. At a much later date, European explorers, colonizers and traders carried it to all parts of the world. In fact, the practice of carrying cats as companions and pest-destroyers aboard ships has resulted in a European influence on cat populations everywhere.

Ancestors of the domestic cat

Any pair of domestic cats today will readily interbreed, even if they should come from opposite ends of the Earth, showing that they belong to a single species (see p 12) and pointing to a common ancestor. This must be sought in the Middle East, where domestication apparently took place, and is almost certainly the African wild cat (*Felis libyca*). This cat inhabited most of Asia and North Africa at that time. It is a lithely-built animal very like the tabby domestic cat in colouring, though more sandy and less obviously striped. It has been suggested that the jungle cat (*F. chaus*) may have been involved in the origin of the domestic cat. However, the majority of skulls from Egyptian cat cemeteries resemble *F. libyca* and only a few are of *F. chaus* type. So, although the Egyptians did keep the jungle cat, it probably did not play a significant role in creating the modern domestic cat.

The tabby cat most frequently found in northern Europe is more obviously striped and darker in colour than *F. libyca*, resembling the European wild cat (*F. silvestris*) more than the African species. But this does not mean that the domestic cats of Britain and the rest of Europe are descendants of *F. silvestris* and not *F. libyca*. When domestic *libyca*-type cats from Egypt spread through Europe with the Romans, they could subsequently have adapted to their new environment in the same way as the indigenous wild cat – by changing the colour and pattern of their coat. Also, they could have interbred with the native cats and the resulting hybrids could have contributed *silvestris* tabby genes to the domestic population. It is almost impossible to assess the importance of the second factor as the first alone is enough to explain the variation. The same goes for body shape: the European domestic cat tends to be a thick-set animal reminiscent more of *F. silvestris* than *F. libyca*.

Certainly, interbreeding of the imported *libyca* cat and the wild *silvestris* cat would probably have occurred. These two wild species can interbreed and produce fertile offspring, and some authorities in fact regard the two wild populations merely as different geographical races of the same species. However, although the hybrids of domestic cats and European wild cats do take on the tabby pattern and colour of their wild parent, they also possess its wild nature and are generally quite untamable. This may not be true of all domestic/wild crosses – those with *F. libyca* and with Geoffroy's cat (*F. geoffroyi*) are said to make quite docile pets. It seems likely, therefore, that the 'domesticating' genes of the tamed *libyca*-type cat may on occasion have had a taming effect on the hybrid offspring, allowing the *silvestris* characteristics to find their way into the domestic population.

The process of domestication

Just what kind of genetic change occurred when the cat became domesticated is not understood. Nor is it for any other domestic animal, since no animal has become domesticated during the era of scientific observation, and the process has never been repeated experimentally. Some mutation (inheritable genetic change; see p 23) must have taken place, however, for a domestic cat is born tame, whereas the taming of a wild species must start afresh with each generation. Even so, any genetic

The earliest evidence of cats being domesticated is from Ancient Egypt, where they were deified as the goddess Bast, or Pasht (from which the word puss is said to come), and where thousands of cats were mummified **left** and laid in tombs. Archeologists have found that most of them were similar to the African wild cat.

Traders spread the cat in comparatively modern times **right** to every corner of the world, so that cats are today as cosmopolitan as humans. Everywhere, on land and at sea, their prowess at catching vermin made them welcome.

The cat's main ancestor was the African wild cat (*Felis libyca*) **right**, though the jungle cat (*Felis chaus*) **far right** was also probably kept in ancient Egypt, since some mummies are of this type. The African wild cat has tabby markings, but these are not so bold as in many domestic tabbies. Somewhat larger than most domestic cats, it is nevertheless more lithe in its body type than the European wild cat (below). It still exists over a wide area.

taming effect needs reinforcing by conditioning kittens to accept people from a young age; domestic cats that go feral bear kittens that grow up distrustful of humans.

Little is known about the genetic basis of any aspect of animal behaviour, but one suggestion is that the domestication mutation prevents the development of certain adult behaviour patterns – the domestic cat never quite grows up, in effect. It may be significant that adult wild cats are normally solitary except when mating, mothering or growing up in a litter, whereas feral domestic cats are much more sociable, families tending to stay together. Now, most successful domestications have been of species with highly developed social or 'herd' instincts – as with the dog. It seems that such animals accept humans as part of the herd – or, in the case of cats having early human contact, as part of the litter. Perhaps the domestic cat never develops beyond this point, to being a solitary 'normal' adult.

The genetic change could conceivably have been an abrupt one – the mutation of a single major gene – in which case domestication (or at least the potential for it) would have spread out from one particular breeding population. It seems much more likely that a gradual change in numerous minor genes resulted in a progressive domestication, encouraged by the kind of selection mentioned above. Physical as well as behavioural changes accompanied this process; the domestic cat (as with other domesticated species) has a significantly smaller brain than its wild counterpart. This may result in reduced aggressiveness – possibly another factor involved in the domestication process, since the smaller-brained, more docile cats would be more likely to breed in close proximity to people. Whatever the genetic mechanism, it is quite likely that the cat in effect domesticated itself, walking into people's lives as it were – or (in biological terms) finding a new ecological niche to exploit.

Origins of domestic breeds

The genetic and historical aspects of the various colours and breeds of domestic cats are discussed in the following chapter, but the fact that cats have been systematically bred for only about a century makes it difficult to be sure of their origins in many cases. It does seem, however, that the heavier, thickset body type found in such breeds as British Shorthairs and Persians shows the influence of the European wild cat, as already mentioned, while the foreign and oriental breeds typified by the Abyssinian and Siamese retain the lithe body of the African species. Selective breeding has emphasized these features. Long hair appears to have originated as a gene mutation in southern Russia, spreading to the cat populations of Turkey and Iran to show up in the Angora and Persian breeds.

Studies of coat colours and patterns in domestic cat populations show that some of these are very old, since they have had time to spread all over the world. Among the oldest are the black, blue and orange (ginger) colours and the white spotting (piebald) pattern. Much more recent are the Siamese and Burmese colourings, which originated in south-east Asia. Such colours have been preserved because of a human predeliction for novel features in companion animals. Some patterns spread of their own accord, however. An example is the blotched tabby, which seems to have arisen in Britain some hundreds of years ago as a mutation of the striped tabby. The blotched tabby and the black cat appear able to thrive in a high-density urban environment, with the result that they are tending to displace other colours among alley cats and non-pedigree domestic pets in some areas. Cat populations are still evolving.

The European wild cat (*Felis silvestris*) **right** may also have played a part in the domestic cat's evolution, possibly introducing the genes for the dark tabby pattern. It could well have interbred with domestic cats introduced to northern Europe by the Romans, just as it does today with domestic cats that have gone feral. Many such ferals live on the outskirts of human civilization, where they come into contact with genuinely wild populations. The cross-bred offspring **far right** are fertile, proving the genetic closeness of the two species; they are wild in temperament.

Chapter 1
THE BREEDS OF CATS

The basics of heredity 1

When two cats mate, it is no surprise that the resulting offspring are cats, and not mice, frogs or any other kind of creature. Nor is it surprising when two tabby cats give rise to tabby kittens. The fact that offspring tend to resemble their parents to a greater or lesser degree is such a commonplace occurrence that few people stop to consider why it should be so – at least until something unexpected happens.

For example, why should a particular pair of tabby cats sometimes have a black kitten? (For the answer, see page 32.) Or why should another black mated with a blue (that is, slate-grey) cat produce only black kittens – which, if mated together, may produce some blue offspring in the subsequent generation? Logically, you might expect the first generation (resulting from the cross between black and blue) to

The Mendelian ratio of three individuals showing a dominant trait (in this case black) to one the recessive (blue) is illustrated by this litter of kittens with their mother, a black cat carrying the blue trait. (The white 'spotting' is an independent trait that does not affect the inheritance of black and blue.) This is a lucky accident, in fact, for the 3:1 ratio applies to the average of many litters, not necessarily to each litter.

be more likely to include blue kittens than the second, but logic does not at first sight seem to be much use when trying to predict the outcome of breeding experiments.

Indeed, until about 1900, even biologists could not explain the quirks of heredity in terms much more sophisticated than the layman, who might think of blood being 'mixed' in successive generations, the influence of each preceding generation being felt more weakly, as if through dilution. (This idea comes up in such terms as bloodstock and pure-blooded.) The occasional unexpected result might be written off as a freak of nature or an 'ancestral throwback' – which no more explains the phenomenon than does blaming it all on destiny or divine intervention.

But the rediscovery in 1900 of the researches (carried out 40 years earlier) of an Austrian monk, Gregor Mendel, into the inheritance of characteristics by garden pea plants gave a fresh impetus to the study of heredity and founded a whole new branch of biology: genetics. Today, a knowledge of genetics not only provides reasons for why organisms (such as individual breeds of cats) have the features they do, but also enables the breeder to replace trial and error methods with scientifically designed breeding programmes.

Units of heredity

Mendel's great breakthrough was to isolate discrete characteristics – a vast number of which combine to distinguish a particular creature – whose inheritance can be studied through many generations. Such characteristics are governed by 'units of heredity', which Mendel called factors but which are now known as genes. Genes have a definite physical existence, as will be seen on page 21, and it is these that are passed on from parents to their offspring when the male sperm fertilizes the female egg (see p215). Nevertheless, they can be thought of in abstract terms as a 'set of instructions' for building an individual creature.

By controlling the growth and development of the fertilized egg into a whole organism, the genes determine that the result shall be a cat rather than a frog or any other species, that it shall be a black or a blue or some other colouring, that it shall have long or short hair, and so on. It is obvious that a huge number of genes must be needed to 'specify' the characteristics of an individual creature. However, Mendel discovered that if the effect of single genes can be isolated and studied, the way they are passed on and influence the creature's visible features is found to follow relatively simple laws. Perhaps the most remarkable thing of all is that the same laws apply to all creatures, and the results of breeding experiments in, say, mice can provide lessons for the cat breeder and can even suggest possibilities for new breeds of cats (see p98).

How genes work

The set of genes an individual inherits from its parents is called its genotype. The individual's actual physical characteristics comprise its phenotype. Mendel realized that two creatures with the same phenotype – two black cats, say – need not necessarily have the same genotype. One may have inherited a different gene that has no visible effect but may reappear in later generations.

For example, suppose a kitten receives the gene for a black coat from each of its parents (as it will if both come from a line of true-breeding blacks). There is no question

about its phenotype – the kitten will be a black. Equally, a kitten receiving the gene for a blue coat from both parents will be blue. But suppose one parent comes from a line of true-breeding blacks and the other from a line of true-breeding blues. The kitten will receive the gene for a black coat from one parent and that for blue from the other; what happens? Will the result be a kind of 'average' – perhaps blotches of black and blue, or a black with blue overtones? No. As already mentioned, it will be a perfectly normal-looking black. Although inheriting both blue and black genes, only the black has any effect. Black is said to be dominant to blue; conversely, blue is said to be recessive to black. (In fact, as will be seen in subsequent articles, both black and blue cats have black pigment [colouring matter]. The genetic difference is that the black has

---

SYMBOLIZING GENES

For convenience and brevity, genes for discrete characteristics or traits are referred to by letters of the alphabet printed in italics. A pair of alternative genes – that is, alleles – always share the same letter (usually the initial letter of the gene name), dominant genes being set in capitals and their recessive alleles in lower-case letters. For example, the dominant black (or, strictly speaking, dense) gene is called D and the recessive blue (dilute) d.

Since each individual cat has a pair of genes for each particular trait, one inherited from each parent, its genotype for each characteristic is symbolized by a pair of letters. The true-breeding black is represented by the symbol DD and the blue by dd. Both such cats are termed homozygous because they received the same gene from each parent. A black cat that carries the recessive blue gene is symbolized by Dd; it is described as heterozygous because it received different genes from its two parents.

Only breeding experiments can tell a heterozygous from a homozygous black (see p24), but the above convention means that it is quite easy to look at the symbol for a genotype and say what the expected phenotype will be. Sometimes, a genotype may be written in the form D–; this represents a black where it is unknown or immaterial whether it is homozygous or heterozygous; the dash can represent either D or d.

DD Dd dd

the gene for dense pigmentation, while the blue has dilute pigmentation, and it is dense that is dominant to dilute; but the above simplification is adequate for the present.)

The phenomenon of dominance and recessiveness normally occurs only with pairs of corresponding genes. (The gene for a black coat has no effect on that for long hair, for example, though long hair is recessive to short hair.) Such corresponding pairs are known as alleles, and it is a fundamental fact of genetics that (with an important exception explained on page 23) each individual inherits a pair of genes for each discrete characteristic – one from each parent – and will, in turn, pass on just one of this pair to its own offspring. If both members of the inherited pair of genes are identical, the creature is said to be homozygous for that characteristic – as with a

true-breeding blue or black cat, for example. But if a pair of dissimilar alleles are inherited – as with the black inheriting both blue and black genes – it is said to be heterozygous. Then the phenomenon of dominance and recessiveness comes into play, and the individual is said to 'carry' the recessive gene.

This indicates another important fact: A heterozygous individual is able to pass on the recessive gene to its offspring. If this gene then 'meets' a matching recessive gene passed on by the other parent, the two recessives will no longer be dominated and the recessive characteristic will once again assert itself and become apparent in the phenotype. In fact, a recessive trait can only be expressed in a homozygous individual. This is what occurs when two black cats carrying the blue gene mate; as mentioned

at the beginning of this article, some of their offspring are likely to be blue.

Chance plays a part in the 'meeting' of the recessive genes – essentially, it is a matter of which sperm fertilizes which egg – so the result of any particular mating cannot be predicted, only the average over a number of litters born to the same parents. Then, the proportion of kittens will in the long run always be one 'pure' (or homozygous) black to two 'impure' (or heterozygous) blacks carrying blue (one having received the blue gene from the father and one from the mother) to one blue (which, being recessive, must be 'pure', or homozygous). In terms of phenotypes, the ratio is 3:1, and it was the discovery of this proportion in features inherited by pea plants that led Mendel to discover dominance and recessiveness.   */continued*

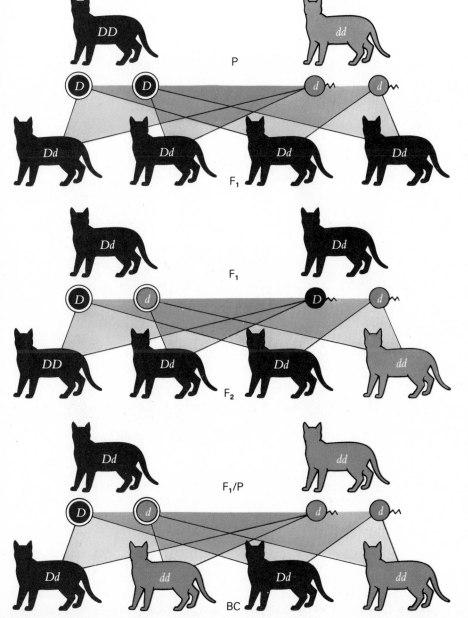

Crossing black and blue pure-breeding (homozygous) cats is bound to result entirely in black offspring. The reason is that each kitten must receive a black gene (D) via the egg or sperm from one parent – in this case, the female egg, shown as a circle – and a blue gene (d) from the other – here the male sperm, shown with a tail. Because black is dominant to blue, the result is a litter of heterozygous black kittens carrying the recessive blue gene; their genotype is symbolized Dd.
The starting point in any breeding programme is called the parental or P generation; the first-generation offspring are known as the F_1 or first filial generation.

Crossing heterozygous black cats from the F_1 generation results in far more possibilities in the F_2 or second filial generation. Each parent may pass on either the dominant black or the recessive blue gene, so that the offspring can include homozygous black kittens (DD; resulting from the meeting of an egg and sperm both carrying the black gene), heterozygous black kittens (Dd; resulting from the meeting of a 'black' sperm and a 'blue' egg, or vice-versa – it makes no difference) and blue kittens (dd; if two blue genes meet). The four possible combinations of eggs and sperm are all equally likely, and this is why, on average, there will be three black offspring to one blue.

Back-crossing a heterozygous black cat from the F_1 generation to its homozygous recessive blue parent throws up a different set of possibilities in the back-cross or BC generation. The heterozygous black cat (in this case the female) can pass on either the black or the blue gene, but the blue parent (here the male) can pass on only the recessive blue gene. Therefore the offspring can only be homozygous blue (dd) or heterozygous black (Dd), like their parents. On average, as the diagram shows, they will appear in equal numbers.
Back-crossing of this type has practical applications for breeders in determining an individual's genotype (see p 24).

The basics of heredity 2

Locating the genes

What are genes – the fundamental units of heredity – made of? As mentioned on page 20, it does not really matter as far as the basic laws of genetics are concerned, and Gregor Mendel (who first formulated those laws) himself had no idea. But knowing something of their nature does help in understanding why and how genes act as they do.

The most fundamental fact about genes is that they must exist within living cells – the minute 'building-blocks' of living matter. Since animals all begin with the fusion of an egg and sperm cell in fertilization (see p215), the egg and sperm must each contain a single set of genes which combine into a double set as already explained. And since the genes must act by directing the differentiation of the single fertilized egg cell into the billions of specialized cells of the adult organism, the double set of genes must be replicated every time a cell divides in two. When egg or sperm cells are formed, however, the genes must again be divided into two single sets.

There exist within living cells minute rod-like structures called chromosomes which behave in exactly the way described above. They occur in the dense nucleus that is found in the centre of the cell, and it is now known that the genes are carried, like beads on a string, along them. (Genes are far too small to be seen, however.) Each species has a characteristic number of chromosomes per cell – in the domestic cat it is 38 – and in normal body cells they occur in pairs which correspond to the pairing of genes; one member of each gene pair is located on each of the paired, or homologous, chromosomes.

When egg and sperm cells are formed, the number of chromosomes per cell is halved, so that in the cat there are 19 single chromosomes in each. Fertilization restores the full complement of 19 pairs, one member of each pair (with its corresponding genes) coming from each parent. Subsequent multiplication of the fertilized egg cell involves exact replication of the chromosomes and their genes.

When germ cells are formed, however, the 19 single chromosomes are not handed on as a complete, intact set exactly as they were inherited – though members of homologous pairs are separated. Instead, there is a shuffling of the chromosomes and even – through a process called crossing-over – the splitting and recombination of parts of chromosome pairs. The result is that each egg and sperm carries a random combination of genes – some derived originally from the creature's mother and some from its father – quite different from those in any previous generation. Since this occurs in every generation, features can be inherited at random from grandparents, great-grandparents and so on.

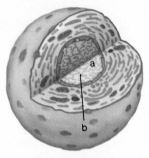

The living cell is the smallest unit of life. It has a complex structure, with many specialized parts, but the nucleus **a** is its control centre. This contains DNA, the extraordinarily complex chemical substance of which genes are made, in the chromatin network **b**. During cell division (see below), the chromatin differentiates into rod-like chromosomes. By directing the biochemical activity of all the organism's cells, genes control the features and functioning of the whole creature. Mutations consist of minute changes in the chemical structure of the DNA molecules, and in this way alter inherited features.

A karyogram displays a creature's chromosomes. A photomicrograph is taken of cells undergoing division, when the chromosomes are visible. The images of the individual chromosomes are cut out and sorted into pairs of similar size and shape – the homologous pairs – and mounted. The cat karyogram **right** is of a female, having 19 complete pairs, with two Xs.

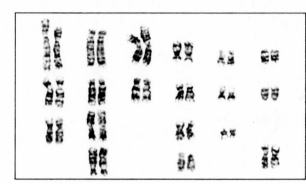

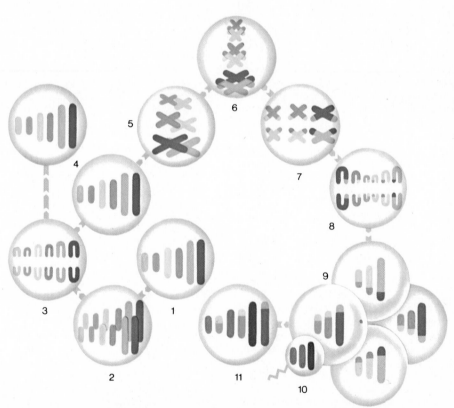

Cell division and recombination illustrate the entire life-cycle of an organism at the cellular level. A fertilized egg cell **1** has a full set of chromosomes (here, for clarity, just six are show) in pairs (here coloured distinctively). During mitosis, the chromosomes first replicate themselves **2**, **3** and the cell then divides in two to form duplicate cells, each complete with a full set of chromosomes **4**. Some cells form the sex organs – the ovaries of females and testicles of males. In these, germ cells – eggs and sperm – are formed by the process of meiosis, a special type of cell division in which the number of chromosomes is halved. During meiosis, crossing-over of parts of chromosome pairs **5**, **6** followed by replication and two stages of cell division **7**, **8** ensures that the germ cells **9** carry an assortment of genetic traits from earlier generations. Fertilization **10** results in a new-generation cell **11** containing the full set of chromosomes with genes from each parent forming new homologous pairs.

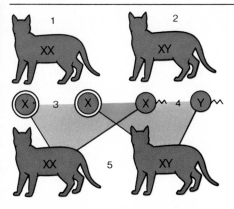

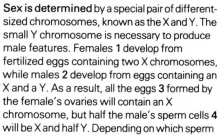

Sex is determined by a special pair of different-sized chromosomes, known as the X and Y. The small Y chromosome is necessary to produce male features. Females 1 develop from fertilized eggs containing two X chromosomes, while males 2 develop from eggs containing an X and a Y. As a result, all the eggs 3 formed by the female's ovaries will contain an X chromosome, but half the male's sperm cells 4 will be X and half Y. Depending on which sperm

fertilizes an egg – a matter of pure chance – the offspring 5 will be XX (female) or XY (male). These occur in approximately equal numbers **above** because there are equal numbers of X and Y sperm in the male's semen.
Sex-linkage of certain bodily characteristics occurs because the Y chromosome is too small to carry the partners of genes found on the X. As a result, males can have only one such gene, compares with the female's two (see p 39).

of the chromosomes that determine an animal's sex. These do not form a proper pair in the male, who has a large chromosome known as the X chromosome plus a much smaller Y chromosome in each cell, in place of the female's double X. As a result, ordinary bodily characteristics controlled by genes carried on the X chromosome may occur differently in males and females. The normal rules of dominance and recessiveness thus apply in females, but a single recessive gene can be expressed in males, since there is no second X chromosome to carry the dominant allele. An example of sex-linkage is the orange gene involved in the tortoiseshell coat (see p39).

Both sex-linkage and the ordinary kind of linkage mentioned above complicate the pattern of inheritance between parents and offspring. In fact, Mendel was very lucky not to have stumbled on a case of linkage, or he might never have obtained the clear experimental results that enabled him to show how genes are transmitted.

Linkage of genes

Generally speaking, genes for different discrete characteristics are inherited independently of each other. Thus, for example, long hair in cats is caused by a single recessive gene quite separate from the recessive gene for a blue coat (see p25). As a result, in a breeding programme starting with a cross between a homozygous long-haired black and a homozygous short-haired blue, the F_1 generation will consist entirely of short-haired blacks carrying the recessive genes for blue and long hair. In the F_2 generation, however, there will be long- and short-haired blacks and blues.

Such an occurrence indicates that the genes for blue and for long hair are carried on different chromosomes. In other cases, certain genes may be linked – that is, have a

tendency to be inherited together. This occurs because the genes are carried on the same chromosomes. Linkage is not complete, however, since crossing-over can result in linked genes being separated – but the closer the genes are, the less likely is such separation.

By studying the frequency at which genes are separated during crossing-over, geneticists have been able to 'map' chromosomes and for some creatures have located individual genes with great accuracy. Even where precise positions of genes are unknown, it has been proved that the gene for a particular trait (and any mutant allele) always occupies the same position, known as the gene's locus.

A special form of linkage is sex-linkage, which occurs when a gene is carried on one

When genes change

Another occurrence that complicates heredity is a spontaneous change in a gene. Genes duplicate during cell division with remarkable accuracy, but 'mistakes' – or mutations – do happen, and in fact are responsible for the variations found in populations of all creatures. For example, the blue cat represents a mutation of the black, and the long-haired a mutation of the short. The 'basic', unmutated creature is known as the normal or wild type because it is the form that occurred originally. (The term has nothing to do with ferocity.) By definition, the wild type is homozygous for any trait being studied, and any variation represents a mutation.

The initial occurrence of mutations in germ cells cannot be predicted, but, once they have occurred, mutant genes are passed on like any others and follow the same rules. Most, but not all, are recessive. New mutations occur very rarely – perhaps once in a million germ cells – so it is not surprising that cat breeders have adopted a mere 20 or so mutations despite the large numbers of cats bred each year.

The most important mutant genes for breeders are those producing distinctive coat colours; there are only 12 of them, but in various combinations these are responsible for a wide range of cat breeds and varieties (see pp29 to 40). Coat quality is also an essential feature of many breeds, and there are at least five coat mutants (see p43). The numerous breeds and varieties have evolved through recombinations of the mutants in various ways – by chance at first, more recently through planned breeding programmes as breeders have applied genetic principles to extend the range of colours and other characteristics.

GENES AND ENVIRONMENT

The inheritance of acquired characteristics has long caused controversy among biologists. At its most basic level, the idea has been completely discredited – for example, no professional geneticist today believes that bodily features developed during an organism's own lifetime can be passed on through its germ cells to its offspring. To take an absurd example, no matter how assiduously you might pluck your cat's whiskers, there is no way that this could affect the genes that it transmits to its offspring so that a whiskerless breed could result. Similarly, claims that the Ragdoll cat's limp habit and docile nature (see p63) might have resulted from the original Ragdoll's involvement in a motor accident can have no genetic foundation.

This is not to say, however, that environmental influences play no part in heredity. It is well known that atomic radiation, X-rays and the like increase the rate of mutations – but these are completely random and unpredictable, and are as likely to be harmful as desirable. On the other hand, the environment of a creature as it develops – especially in the early period within its mother's womb – together with sheer chance can profoundly affect how certain genes are expressed in the phenotype. An example is the way the patterning of a tortoiseshell cat develops (see p39). Similarly, the temperature of the surroundings affects the expression of the Siamese gene (see p37) and the density of the coat in all breeds. None of these effects are inherited, however.

Heredity in action 1

The inheritance of isolated bodily features governed by a single pair of genes (alleles) is relatively straightforward, as explained in the article on page 20. But when considering any particular group of creatures, such as a breed of cats, a multiplicity of traits must be taken into account.

Combinations of genes may affect an organism's phenotype in a number of ways. First there is the independent assortment of unrelated traits, as with the long- and short-haired black and blue cats mentioned on page 23. Then, in some cases, the phenotype shows the result of the combined action of several major genes that modify the effects of each other – as in the case of some of the self (solid) colours in cats (see p29). Finally, there are features such as body shape (see p41) that are governed by polygenes – large groups of genes whose individual effects are very small.

Analysing phenotypes

In the last case, the effect of any one gene cannot be analysed. In others, however, the ratios of offspring with various phenotypes occurring as a result of a particular cross, while sometimes complex, are predictable. One example has already been given: the three black to one blue resulting from crossing two heterozygous blacks carrying the blue gene (see p21). When two short-haired black cats heterozygous for both blue and long hair are crossed, the result is nine short-haired blacks to three short-haired blues to three long-haired blacks to one long-haired blue. (Within this last ratio, of course, are the ratios of three black to one blue, and three short-hairs to one long.)

Other crosses may throw up different ratios, but these are predictable so long as two fundamental rules are borne in mind: First, members of gene pairs are separated in the formation of germ cells (eggs and sperm) and, except in the case of linkage (see p23), all possible combinations of individual genes are equally likely to occur in the germ cells. Second, it is purely a matter of chance which sperm fertilizes which egg; thus, in the long run, individual genes from each parent will combine with equal frequency.

The easiest way to visualize this and to work out the genetic possibilities of any particular mating is to construct a so-called chequerboard diagram or Punnett square (named after the British geneticist who originated it). The chequerboard is constructed by setting out the various gene combinations to be found in each parent's germ cells, one set across the top and the other down the left-hand side. Corresponding rows and columns of squares are then drawn. By reading across and down, the result of each combination of germ cells can be inserted. Once this has been done for all the squares, and all the resulting phenotypes are worked out, the relative numbers of each phenotype that can be expected is easy to find by counting.

The size of the chequerboard depends on the number of different gene combinations that can occur in the particular germ cells concerned. For example, an animal with the genotype *AABB* can produce only germ cells of genotype *AB*, so a chequerboard involving this will have only one column or row. The genotype *AABb* gives rise to two possibilities – *AB* and *Ab* in equal numbers – while *AaBb* gives rise to four: *AB*, *Ab*, *aB* and *ab*. As an example, therefore, a cross between *AABB* and *AaBb* will be shown on a four-by-one chequerboard, with a total of four squares, while crossing two *AaBb* creatures needs a four-by-four chequerboard with 16 squares.

In general, the number of alternative germ cell genotypes doubles with each extra trait for which the organism is heterozygous. Thus crossing two individuals each heterozygous for five genes results in a 32-by-32 chequerboard with 1,024 squares. Since each square represents a possible offspring, this illustrates just how complex a breeding programme can become if more than a very small number of differing alleles are involved.

Testing genotypes

Apart from predicting the result of particular matings, the construction of chequerboard diagrams indicates some useful test crosses that can be employed to indicate the genotype of an individual animal. An example is the back-crossing of a black heterozygous for blue to its homozygous blue parent shown on page 21. The two-by-two chequerboard clearly shows the ratio of one black to one blue offspring, against the solely black offspring resulting if the black parent does not carry the blue gene.

Similarly, it is possible to test whether a short-haired black carries the long-hair gene and/or that for blue by crossing it with a long-haired blue. (The latter must be homozygous for both traits since both are

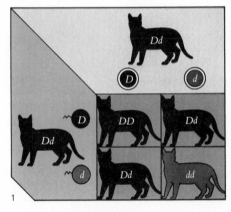

Chequerboard diagrams can be used to predict the outcome of crosses. If each parent is heterozygous for a single trait, the diagram has four squares **1**. If each is heterozygous for two traits, it has 16 squares **2**. In each case, the genotype of one parent is written at the top and below it the possible germ cell genotypes. The same is done for the other parent down the side. Then the squares are filled in by reading down and across to find the resulting combinations of genes carried by the egg and sperm; these are the offspring's genotypes. From them the resulting phenotypes can be written down (here they are pictured) and the relative numbers of each phenotype to be expected found by counting.

The first diagram shows the 3:1 ratio of black to blue kittens **below** expected when two black cats heterozygous for blue are crossed; the second shows the 9:3:3:1 ratio seen when two recessive traits are carried by each parent (here, blue and long hair). Eggs are shown as circles; sperm have 'tails'. For gene symbols, see page 28.

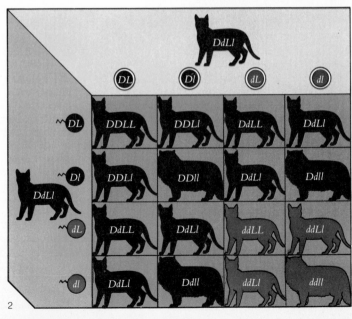

Incomplete dominance is illustrated by the Tonkinese **right**, which is the result of a cross between a pure-bred Siamese and a pure-bred Burmese. It has one Siamese gene and one Burmese; these are alleles but neither is fully dominant to the other. The chequerboard diagram **far right** shows the result of a cross between two Tonkinese: on average, two Tonkinese, one cat with Siamese colouring and one with Burmese colouring.

recessive; it is known as a double recessive.) The chequerboards for these crosses show that if the short-haired black is homozygous all the offspring will be short-haired black cats, while if it is heterozygous for either or both genes, these should show up among the offspring. Of course, the absence of blue and/or long-haired kittens from any one litter is not enough to prove that the cat being tested is homozygous; the result could be caused by chance. The occurrence of a single kitten showing the

recessive trait is enough to prove that the cat is heterozygous, however.

These examples illustrate the general principle that if a breeder wants to test whether an animal is carrying the gene for a particular recessive trait, it should be mated with one that is homozygous for that trait. Breeders normally reckon that if at least seven (and preferably ten) offspring are produced without the trait appearing, then the animal being tested very probably does not carry the gene concerned.

How genes interact

Clear-cut results of the type described above occur in many breeding experiments, but in some cases genes interact with each other or influence each other's effects. One of the commonest is incomplete dominance, in which neither of a pair of alleles is fully dominant to the other. An example is shown by the Tonkinese cat (see p 90), which represents a 'half-way' breed between the Burmese and Siamese.

Both the Burmese and the Siamese colourings result from mutant alleles of a dominant gene C, known as the full-colour gene. The Burmese allele is symbolized by c^b and the Siamese by c^s. (Small superscript letters are used for identification when there is more than one mutant allele of a gene.) Both c^b and c^s are recessive to C, hence they are written in lower-case letters, but neither is recessive to the other. In the classic colourings, they are combined with the homozygous aa for non-agouti (see p 26), which gives a solid black cat when the genotype is $aaCCDD$. A Burmese cat with the genotype aac^bc^bDD is dark sepia-brown, while a Siamese aac^sc^sDD is very pale brown except at the points (see p 36). /*continued*

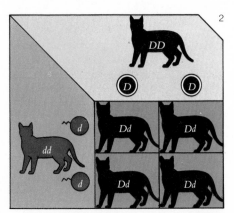

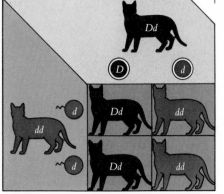

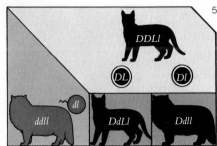

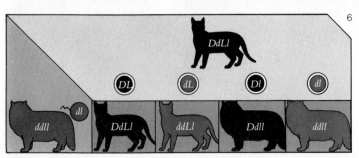

Test crosses are useful to find out if a cat is carrying a particular recessive gene, as is shown by these chequerboards. To test if a black cat is carrying blue, it should be crossed with a blue; if it is carrying the gene some of the offspring may be blue **1**, but if not they will all be black **2**. To test if the same cat is also carrying the gene for long hair, it should be crossed with a long-haired blue (a double recessive). If it is carrying neither recessive gene, all the offspring will be black short-hairs **3**. If it is carrying one recessive gene, there may be blue **4** or long-haired kittens **5** among the offspring. If both recessive genes are carried, both blue and long-haired kittens may be expected **6**.

Heredity in action 2

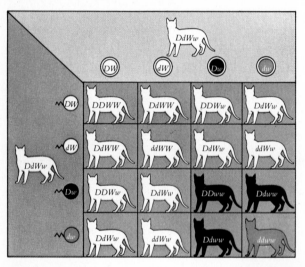

Epistasis, or masking, shows up in many aspects of cat breeding. For example, a self black kitten **above left** often shows shadowy stripes because it is genetically still a tabby; the non-agouti gene simply makes the pale agouti areas of the coat black. Another example is the red self **above**, whose tabby markings are impossible to eradicate entirely. A third example is the dominant white; the chequerboard **left** shows the result of crossing two white cats each with only one *W* gene and each carrying one gene for blue.

The result of crossing a Burmese and Siamese is aac^bc^sDD, the Tonkinese, which is intermediate in colour and considered distinctive enough to warrant a breed name. Two Tonkinese mated together will produce Burmese, Tonkinese and Siamese in the ratio 1:2:1. In fact, this is merely a modified 3:1 ratio in which the two homozygous offspring can both be distinguished from the heterozygous (see p21).

An important phenomenon that can in some cases mislead the breeder is the masking of one gene by another. Known technically as epistasis, this can make it impossible to observe the effect of one or more genes because of the swamping effect of another. An example is the effect of the dominant white gene *W* (see p31). This masks the expression of all other colour genes, producing a white cat whatever the underlying colour genotype. Mating two white cats homozygous for *W* will always result in white kittens, but mating two heterozygous whites (genotype *Ww*) can throw up all sorts of colours, depending on what other genes the cats are carrying.

The non-agouti gene *a*, which occurs in all non-tabby cats, also shows epistasis. The tabby pattern in fact arises from the combined action of the agouti gene *A* and a series of three tabby alleles responsible for the mackerel, blotched ('classic') and Abyssinian tabby patterns respectively (see p32). However, the striping effect of the tabby genes can only be seen in agouti cats, which, in the light-coloured areas between the stripes, have yellow bands across basically black hairs. In non-agouti cats (*aa*), the yellow bands disappear, making the light areas black. Genetically, the stripes or blotches are still there, however, and may be seen as a faint 'ghost' pattern in kittens.

A third example of epistasis is seen in the action of the orange gene *O* (see p30). When homozygous (*OO*), this converts all black pigment into orange. However, the non-agouti gene *a* can act only on black pigment, not on orange, so hairs containing

MIMIC GENES

Although one trait may be caused by one gene, this does not necessarily mean that another gene cannot have the same – or almost the same – effect. For example, the dominant white gene *W* is responsible for the long- and short-haired exhibition white cats with blue, copper (orange) or odd eyes. The Foreign White bred in Britain (see p92), with its deep blue eyes, has the same gene combined with the Siamese gene c^s.

Quite different cats genetically are the albino Siamese of North America, which has the c^a gene, and the European albino, which may have the c^a or *c* gene. These latter are two further genes in the albino series, to which the Burmese and Siamese genes, c^b and c^s, belong. With both c^a and *c* the fur is pure white, but c^a results in pale blue eyes while *c* is a true albino with pink eyes resulting from a complete absence of pigment. (The pink colour is due to blood vessels.)

A second example of mimicry is found in the rex cats (see p43). These have

The rare blue-eyed albino is a genetic relative of the Siamese and its colour results from a different gene from most whites.

rather similarly curly coats, but breeding experiments show that the Cornish, Devon and Oregon rexes are caused by quite different mutations.

orange pigment always have agouti banding. As a result, there is no visible difference between orange ('red') cats that carry the agouti gene and those that do not. All have some degree of tabby striping – even in the so-called self (solid) red (see p30), in which the darker red blotches cover most of the body.

How gene expression varies

The orange gene also shows two ways in which the expression of a gene – that is, the resulting phenotype – can vary from animal to animal. For example, as explained on page 39, a female cat heterozygous for the orange gene – that is, one with the genotype Oo – is a tortoiseshell, but the way in which the tortoiseshell pattern develops is due to chance accidents of growth within the

The effect of polygenes accounts for the difference in colour between the exhibition red tabby **above left** and ginger alley-cat **above**.

womb. Other variations may be due to environmental influences – such as the effect of temperature on the Siamese pattern (see p37) – or to unknown factors, as with the great variation in expression of the white spotting gene, S (see p39).

Yet other variations are genetic but not susceptible to easy manipulation because they are due to many genes, each with small effect but able, when operating as a group, to bring about appreciable modification. Such groups of genes are known as minor genes, modifiers or polygenes, and one group is responsible for the considerable colour difference between the exhibition

red tabby and most non-pedigree ginger cats (both OO). Known as the rufus polygenes, they act as a group to modify the orange phenotype, producing a rich red colouration. They have a similar action on some other pigments also, producing the rich colouring of the exhibition tabby and the warm chestnut of the Abyssinian.

Like other polygenes (but unlike major genes), the breeder cannot manipulate these individually, but their influence can be increased gradually, over many generations, by selective breeding (see p47). This involves choosing studs and queens that best show the desirable characteristics, at the same time as planning desired combinations of major genes. There are a number of groups of polygenes, among them those determining the intensity of chocolate or brown colouring in the Havana, and of the shades of blue in the Korat, Russian Blue and other blue breeds. Most important of all for the breeder of pedigree cats are the polygenes governing body conformation, or type – which includes head and body shape, carriage and other factors that go towards defining a breed of cats (see pp41 and 44).

Breeders always have to remember, however, that it is not only colour, coat, body shape and so on that are determined genetically. Heredity has a great influence over all characteristics of the individual cat from birth to death – though chance has a great effect also. As a result, once nutrition and husbandry are adequate, the only influence breeders can exercise over the quality and health of the cats they breed is in the choice of mates.

HARMFUL GENES

Just as different genes may have similar effects, so conversely a gene's expression may not be limited to its most obvious effect. The best-known side-effect of major cat genes is perhaps the deafness caused in a proportion of cats with the dominant white gene W (see p31). It results from degeneration in the inner ear, and seems to effect particularly blue-eyed whites, though orange-eyed and odd-eyed cats may also be deaf. Quite a different gene, the albino, also has a marginally harmful effect in that it de-pigments the irises of the eyes, making the cat less able to cope with very bright light. More seriously, the Siamese gene and probably also the two albino genes (blue- and pink-eyed) cause 'wrong' nerve connections between the eyes and the brain, resulting in poor binocular (three-dimensional) vision (see p111). Some cats develop a squint apparently in an effort to compensate for this.

Much more serious are genes whose side-effects are to a greater or lesser

The Siamese squint seems to arise because abnormal nerve connections between the eye and brain result in double vision. The squint represents an attempt to correct this.

degree disabling or truly lethal, sometimes causing death in the womb. A dominant gene that is lethal when heterozygous – that is, when present singly – cannot become established, of course, because no individual survives to pass it on. Other genes may be harmful but recessive, so that only homozygous individuals are affected; for example, two recessive mutant genes cause trembling in cats, one mild and the other severe.

Thirdly, one important dominant cat gene is harmful when homozygous. This is the Manx gene, which is truly lethal in homozygous kittens, causing death in the womb (see p42); Manx cats are therefore never true-breeding, since they all carry only one Manx gene. Even where heterozygous the gene is semi-lethal, since some individuals have harmful abnormalities such as spina bifida or an imperforate anus. The gene is also variable in its expression, since heterozygous Manx range from completely tailless animals to ones with a stump of variable length.

The genes of cats

The cat shows much less variation in its physical characteristics – particularly in body shape and size – than man's other common domestic pet, the dog. This implies that its genetic make-up also varies less, and the cat does seem to have an innate tendency to resist excessive genetic modification. However, in large part the difference can be put down to the fact that dogs have been selectively bred for thousands of years, whereas cats have been singled out for such attention only since the latter part of the nineteenth century. Cat breeders simply have not had the time and opportunity to isolate and develop more extreme genetic variations – nor, it should be said, have most of them been inclined to do so, since they have a high regard for the cat's structural harmony.

As a result, rather fewer mutant genes occur in cats than in dogs, and the number of breeds themselves is smaller. (As in cats, however, the same coat colours occur in many ostensibly distinct breeds of dogs.) Of course, a number of mutations may have been overlooked by unappreciative owners and failed to have come to the attention of geneticists or breeders. Another factor is that, of the many many thousands of genes of the cat, only a small proportion are concerned with the bodily features that together define a breed or variety; the great majority are simply responsible for the smooth running of the myriad aspects of the cat's physiology. Nevertheless, it can be expected that a further century of cat breeding will result in greater variations, with both 'giant' and 'miniature' breeds (reports of miniaturizing cat genes appear regularly), and also an increase in the number of breed 'types'.

The genetics of cat breeds

The important major genes of cats, with their recognized symbols and main characteristics, are set out in the chart. Most of them are concerned with coat colour and quality. As far as pure-bred cats are concerned, the only important major genes that act primarily on body structure and are relatively common are the folded-ear, Manx and polydactyly mutants, plus the gene responsible for the Japanese Bobtail if this is proved to be a distinct mutation. (A few others that cause deformities are mentioned on page 42.)

The list of genes will very likely be extended in the future, and the new discoveries will probably include both coat-colour and body-type genes. The development of coat colour is similar in all mammals (the agouti colouring is very widespread, for example) and similar mutations often occur in different species. Nearly all of the coat colours in cats may be found in other fancy-bred animals, such as rabbits and mice. If the reverse proves to be true, these indicate new colours that may be bred one day in cats (see p99).

All of the coat mutants are inherited independently of those for colour; in fact the only case of linkage definitely established in the cat is the sex-linkage of the orange gene O. This means that all colour varieties may be found with each type of coat and each body type or conformation (though not all are recognized by cat fancy registration bodies or indeed have necessarily been produced by breeders). In the articles that follow, the detailed variations of colour, coat and body conformation are examined, and these are followed by articles on individual breeds. What constitutes a breed of cats is largely a matter of definition, as is explained in the article on page 44, but in some cases at least there is a clear genetic basis for the distinction.

THE MAIN GENES OF DOMESTIC CATS

WILD TYPE			MUTANT(S)		
Symbol	Name	Characteristics	Symbol	Name	Characteristics
A	Agouti	Agouti ground-colour of tabby; hairs banded yellow/orange	a	Non-agouti	Hairs not banded; unicoloured (acts only on black/brown)
B	Black	Black pigment	b	Brown	Dark brown (chocolate or chestnut) pigment
			b^l	Light-brown	Medium brown (cinnamon) pigment
C	Full-colour	Maximum pigmentation	c^b	Burmese	Dark sepia-brown pigment
			c^s	Siamese	Light sepia-brown pigment; dark points; blue irises
			c^a	Blue-eyed albino	White coat; pale blue irises
			c	Albino	White coat; unpigmented (pink) irises
D	Dense	Dense pigmentation	d	Dilute	Dilute pigmentation (eg, black to blue)
fd	Normal ears	Normal ('pricked') ears	Fd	Folded-ear★	Folded ears; crippling when homozygous
Hr	Normal coat	Full coat of normal density	hr	Hairless	Total or almost total lack of hair on body
i	Normal pigmentation	Full development of pigmentation	I	Inhibitor★	Suppression of pigmentation from parts of hairs
L	Normal hair	Short hair	l	Long-hair	Hair longer than normal
m	Normal tail	No shortening of tail	M	Manx★	Tail shortened or missing; lethal when homozygous
o	Normal colour	Normal pigmentation (not orange)	O	Orange★	All pigment turned to yellow/orange (sex-linked)
pd	Normal toes	Normal number of toes	Pd	Polydactyly★	Extra toes, especially on front paws (variable)
R	Normal coat	Straight hairs of normal length and type	r	Cornish rex	Hair shorter than normal; curled; no guard hairs
Re	Normal coat	Straight hairs of normal length	re	Devon rex	Hair shorter than normal; curled
Ro	Normal coat	Straight hairs of normal length and type	ro	Oregon rex	Hair shorter than normal; curled; no guard hairs
s	Normal colour	No white spotting	S	Piebald★	White 'spotting' or patches (variable expression)
T	Mackerel	Striped tabby pattern	T^a	Abyssinian★	Abyssinian tabby pattern
			t^b	Blotched	Blotched ('classic') tabby pattern
w	Normal colour	Full expression of all other colour genes	W	Dominant white★	White coat; irises blue, orange or odd-coloured; masks all other colours; may cause deafness
wh	Normal coat	Straight hairs of normal quality	Wh	Wire-hair★	Hair excessively undulated and wiry to touch

★ *Mutant genes that are dominant to the wild type. The short tail of the Japanese Bobtail may also be due to a single gene. There may also be a recessive gene responsible for restricted white spotting, as in the Birman (see p39).*

The basic coat colours 1

Despite the ubiquity of both black and white self- (solid-) coloured cats, these are not the fundamental colours of the species; that distinction goes to the tabby (see p32). Nevertheless, the pigment (colouring matter) that produces the black coat – melanin – is one of the basic pigments found in cats' hairs, and almost all other self colours are due to genetic modifications either of this pigment itself or of the way in which it is laid down in the hair fibres. Furthermore, the various self colours are also found in most of the more elaborately coloured and patterned coats described in subsequent articles, so a discussion of the basic colour range of cats provides a grounding for the understanding of how other varieties come about.

A self cat – the more graphic description solid is generally used in North America – is one that is a single, solid colour throughout. There is (or should be) no patterning, shading, ticking or other variation of colour, although it is common for kittens to have slight tabby markings and scattered white hairs that disappear with maturity. In some cases, however, there is a distinction between genetically self animals and those that breeders classify as selfs for exhibition purposes. (Here, as in subsequent articles, descriptions are given in general terms; for detailed standards of excellence for shows, you should refer to the official publications of cat fancy organizations, whose addresses are listed at the end of this book.)

All cats, whatever their colouring, are genetically tabbies, possessing either the Abyssinian, mackerel or blotched (classic) tabby genes – T^a, T or t^b respectively – or a combination of two of these. The genetic difference between a tabby and a true self cat is that the latter is non-agouti (aa) in constitution. As explained on page 26, the non-agouti genes remove the yellow bands across the hairs in the light areas of the tabby pattern, so that the colour of these hairs merges with the darker 'stripes' to make a uniform colour.

Blacks, browns and blues

The black is the best-known unicoloured variety, and is seen in long- and short-haired breeds of all body types from the massive cobbiness of the black Persian (Longhair; see p54) to the sleek, glossy Foreign Black (ebony Oriental Shorthair; see p92). These all show the combined effect of three dominant genes: B for black pigment, C for full colour expression and D for dense colouration (see the chart of genotypes). In a good show cat, the colour is dense and free from any rusty tinge, white hairs or smoky undercoat.

Considering only cats with the full-colour ($C–$) genotype (genetic constitution; see p20) at first, mutations of the B and D genes have given rise to three further colours. The gene b turns black into a chocolate-brown pigment, shown at its best in the richly coloured Havana Brown and the chestnut Oriental Shorthair (known in Britain as the Havana; see pp91 and 93). A second mutation has given rise to the light-brown gene b^l, which gives a distinctly paler coat well described by the name of the as yet experimental Foreign Cinnamon breed (initially called the Pavane; see p93). It also occurs in the so-called Red Abyssinian, which is an agouti and, unlike true reds (see below), is not sex-linked. The term brown applies generically to both shades; the darker is generally termed chocolate in Britain and chestnut in North America, where the cinnamon colour is known as caramel.

Mutation of the dense gene D to the dilute d has the effect of clumping the particles of pigment in the cat's hair fibres. As a result, some parts of the hairs (individually too small to see without a microscope) reflect white light, thus 'diluting' the basic black or brown colour. The result with black melanin is the varying shades of grey described by cat fanciers as blue, and with the brown pigments a warm, soft grey shade known in North America as lavender and in Britain as lilac.

Self blue cats have occurred from time to time in most parts of the world, and their attractiveness has eventually led them to be sanctified as breeds. Examples include the sturdy blue British Shorthair and its European counterpart, the Chartreux (see p67). Among the blues of moderately foreign (oriental) body type are the Russian Blue (see p80), with its springy 'double' coat, and the Korat from Thailand (see p81). This shares with the Russian Blue a beautiful silvery sheen caused by light reflected from the bristle tips of the plentiful awn hairs – a feature that can be enhanced by selective breeding. Foreign (Oriental) blue cats (see p92) have the most extreme foreign body type of the blue breeds. All of these are examples of cats of identical colour genotype (the shade differences are minor) that are recognized as distinct breeds because of their history and exotic origin; only conformation (body shape) truly distinguishes them.

The soft colouring of the Foreign Lilac (lavender Oriental Shorthair) and other lilac breeds appeals to many cat lovers. As with the browns, there are normal and light versions (due to b and b^l respectively), but all lilac cats vary in shade more */continued*

CATS' EYE COLOURS

One of the remarkable features of the cat is the wide variation of eye colour that is inherited independently of coat colour. The term eye colour refers, of course, to the colour of the iris; the central pupil is black, except in a few cases mentioned specially.

The normal variation in iris colour is quite wide, ranging from rich orange, through shades of yellow and hazel-green to green. The brown and dilute genes b and d do influence pigmentation of the eye, but it seems that the normal variability due to polygenes and chance can swamp or over-ride the effect of these major genes. For example, the British Blue Shorthair has orange or copper eyes, while the Russian Blue's eyes are green, despite the breeds' identical colour genotypes. The b and d genes do show an effect on the eye colour of the Siamese, however.

The influence of polygenes means that, within reason, selective breeding can stabilize any desirable eye colour. In practice, it is easier to 'fix' extreme shades – such as copper or green – than intermediate ones. An exception to the above is the blue eye colour of the Siamese and various white breeds; this is definitely associated with major genes.

Cats' main eye colours : 1 orange or copper; **2** yellow; **3** hazel; **4** green; **5** blue (as with dominant white); **6** blue (as in Siamese)

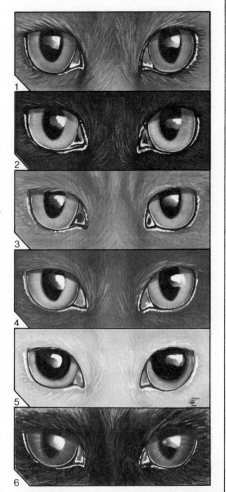

The basic coat colours 2

Self colours old and new include the black self **left** and the light brown (otherwise known as cinnamon) **right**. The former is one of the oldest mutations of the domestic cat's original tabby pattern, and is today one of the commonest among non-pedigree animals – although these may lack the richness and colour density of the good exhibition black. The light brown gene has only recently been isolated and recognized in self cats, but is also responsible for the colour of the so-called red Abyssinian.

than blues and browns, so the two can be difficult to distinguish. Such cats are double recessive for brown and dilute, so a pair of lilacs always breed true if the two shade variations are ignored. The other self colours described above carry at least one dominant gene apart from C, and for this reason they may, if heterozygous, bear offspring of a different colour. For example, two blues both carrying the brown gene (b) will have a proportion of lilac kittens.

All the self colours vary in shade to some degree, but the human eye fails to register variations of black so much as the other colours. The variations are caused largely (though not entirely) by modifying polygenes called the darkening/lightening group, whose existence means that different shades of brown, blue or lilac can be selected and stabilized by selective breeding (see p45). Breeders have used this feature principally for the blue shades, and there have been attempts to differentiate breeds by the precise shade of blue. Generally, for Persians (Longhairs) and for short-haired cats of non-foreign type, show judges prefer a medium shade of blue so long as it is uniform.

Reds and creams

The red and cream selfs – again found in both long-haired and short-haired cats – are examples of colours classified as self (solid) on the basis of the phenotype (appearance) rather than the genotype. A uniform, rich red shade or its dilute form, cream (favoured for exhibition in its pale shade, not the 'hot' fawn that used to be common at shows), are desirably but genetically impossible. As explained on page 26, this is because the non-agouti aa is ineffective on orange pigment, so there is no real difference between a red or cream self and a red or cream tabby. What breeders have done is to dissipate the tabby pattern by selective breeding, but this is an uphill task, and tabby markings often persist on the face, and sometimes the legs and tail too. Of course, in the red Persian, the long coat helps to give the appearance of uniformity, and in creams the reduced contrast between the colour bands on the hairs has the same effect.

Red and cream are caused by the orange gene O, which is carried on the X chromosome; for this reason it is sex-linked (see p23). Males can normally carry only one O gene, and this is enough for solid red

colouring. Females must have two O genes to be all red; Oo results in a tortoiseshell pattern (see p39). Cream results from the action of the dilute gene on the orange.

Burmese colours

The Burmese (see p82) is fundamentally a self cat, despite the shaded appearance of the kittens, for in the darkest variety the adult is uniformly a dark, warm sepia-brown. The North American name sable aptly describes the seal-brown colour caused by the action of the Burmese gene c^b on the non-agouti black. This gene is a member of the albino series of mutant alleles of the full-colour gene C; others include the Siamese (see p36) and two albino genes (see below).

The effect of c is to reduce the amount of pigment in the pigment granules of the hair fibres, so that the cat appears paler than the corresponding full-colour animal. The whole range of colours discussed above appear in combination with the gene, and with similar variations of shade due to the darkening/lightening polygenes. In North America, the chocolate and lilac colours are known as champagne and platinum respectively, emphasizing the lightening of the

The odd-eyed white is a curious phenomenon associated with the dominant white gene. Kittens with blue, orange and odd eyes can appear in the same litter, and these traits do not seem to be controlled by major genes; however, geneticists advise breeders who prefer one or other type to breed only from cats with the desired eye colour. Certainly, it is advisable to choose breeding stock from cats with the most intense eye tone. Similarly select against deafness, which occurs particularly (but not solely) with blue eyes.

Genotypes of self (solid) colours

Genotype	No.	Colour
$aaB\!-\!C\!-\!D\!-$	**1**	Black
$aaB\!-\!C\!-\!dd$	**2**	Blue
$aabbC\!-\!D\!-$	**3**	Chocolate (chestnut brown)
$aab^lb^lC\!-\!D\!-$	**4**	Light brown (cinnamon)
$aabbC\!-\!dd$	**5**	Lilac (lavender)
$aab^lb^lC\!-\!dd$	**6**	Light lilac (light lavender)
$C\!-\!D\!-\!O(O)$	**7**	Red★
$C\!-\!ddO(O)$	**8**	Cream★
$aaB\!-\!c^bc^bD\!-$	**9**	Brown (sable or seal) Burmese
$aaB\!-\!c^bc^bdd$	**10**	Blue Burmese
$aabbc^bc^bD\!-$	**11**	Chocolate (champagne) Burmese
$aabbc^bc^bdd$	**12**	Lilac (platinum) Burmese
$c^bc^bD\!-\!O(O)$	**13**	Red Burmese★
$c^bc^bddO(O)$	**14**	Cream Burmese★
$W\!-;\ c^ac^a;\ cc$	**15**	White

★Not true self (solid) colours since the non-agouti gene is inoperative on orange pigment.

tones; they could be described as medium chocolate-brown and dove-grey. In the red variety – not a true self for the same reason as previously explained – the fur is a golden-red colour, and there is also a cream.

Although fully recessive to C, the c^b gene shows only partial dominance to the Siamese gene c^s. As a result, c^b may be carried by a full-colour animal, but an individual carrying both c^b and c^s is midway in tone between the Burmese and Siamese; it is known as the light-phase Burmese or the Tonkinese (see pp25 and 90). A final point to note is that, although the exhibition Burmese cat in its various colour forms is bred to a particular body conformation, the latter feature has nothing to do with the Burmese gene itself. Thus cats of Burmese colouring can, in theory, be bred in any body type and coat length. In fact, some breeders have produced long-haired Burmese (sometimes known as Tiffanies; see p85), while the Himbur (a Burmese–Himalayan cross) is a long-haired cat with Tonkinese colouring.

White cats

The completely white cat, due to the dominant white gene W, is a popular breed, but behind the white exterior may lie literally any colour genotype – self, tabby, bicoloured and so on. The reason, as explained on page 26, is that the W gene masks the expression of all other colour genes. Only by carrying out test crosses with a coloured breed can the underlying genotype of an unknown white cat be discovered; then the appearance of non-white offspring may provide clues. In many cases it does not much matter, of course, since if the aim is to produce more white offspring the obvious course is to mate two whites. Even then, however, a proportion of coloured kittens will result unless at least one parent is homozygous for white – that is, carries two W genes.

Although the W gene is generally all-dominant, it does seem to vary somewhat in its masking ability. One result is an occasional slight 'breakthrough' of the underlying genotype, especially in young kittens, resulting in coloured spotting; this normally disappears when the adult coat grows. Other consequences are variations in eye colour and the variable occurrence of deafness. Most whites occur in three varieties: orange-eyed (copper-eyed), blue-eyed and odd-eyed (one of each colour), caused by variable removal of pigment from the irises. For show cats, a rich coppery-orange and/or a deep sapphire-blue are the ideal. However, except in the case of the true-breeding blue-eyed Foreign White (see below), the eye colours do not appear to breed completely true, and kittens of any variety may be bred from any combination of parental eye colour.

Deafness may affect one or both ears and, although more common in association with blue eyes, can also appear with orange. The deafness, due to degeneration of the cochlea (see p109), is irreversible and commonly begins four to six days after birth. Many deaf queens make poor mothers, because they cannot heed calls of their kittens. The best way to keep the incidence of deafness down is not to breed from deaf individuals.

Apart from the well-known long-haired and non-foreign-type short-haired whites, the dominant white gene appears in the svelte blue-eyed Foreign White (see p92). This was one of the few breeds deliberately developed on genetic principles, and resulted from combining the blue eyes of the Siamese with the white coat of the dominant white, as is described on page 47. The resulting genotype is $c^s c^s WW$, and such cats are true-breeding for blue eyes. Occasionally, however, a kitten may have eyes of different shades of blue – corresponding to the odd eye colours associated with the W gene – and breeders select against this, as with deafness.

This breed is quite different from the recessive white colouring due to the c^a and c alleles. These produce the blue-eyed albino and true albino (with pink eyes entirely devoid of pigment) respectively. The former gene is found in the American Albino Siamese – effectively a Siamese without the pigmented 'points'. The c^a gene is usually betrayed by the eye colour – a paler blue than the dominant white, and much paler than the Siamese blue of the Foreign White. Thus, although white cats manage to hide their genetic nature fairly effectively, the knowledgeable cat lover can sometimes discover clues.

Tabbies and spotted cats

Tabby cats are so universal that it is probably no great surprise to learn that they are the basic type of cat – the 'wild' type, from which all others evolved. But there are some slightly more surprising facts about the tabby. First, it is the mackerel – the tiger-striped – tabby, rather than the better-known blotched ('classic') pattern that is the true wild type, for this was derived from the domestic cat's wild ancestors (see p16). Second, apart from these two patterns, both the spotted and the Abyssinian are also genetically tabbies. Furthermore, every domestic cat in existence – even the purest white or most ethereal lilac (lavender) – is a tabby at heart; it is simply not possible to be completely rid of tabbiness, only to mask it.

How the tabby gets its stripes

The tabby is in fact a complex colour built up from two component patterns, one superimposed on the other, that are governed by two separate sets of genes. The underlying pattern is called agouti, and is a universal grey camouflaging pattern found in the great majority of mammal species, but perhaps most notably the rabbit. It is composed of hairs with a bluish base and black tip separated by yellow banding. Because of the backward slope of the hairs, this produces the freckled greyish colour between the tabby's stripes. As explained on page 26, removal of the yellow band by the non-agouti gene *a* gives rise to black and other self (solid) colours. Only with the agouti gene *A* can the true tabby pattern show up. Since this is dominant, however, a cat needs only one *A* gene to have a tabby coat. (This is why, as mentioned on page 20, two tabbies – if heterozygous – can give rise to black, non-agouti offspring.)

Agouti is an example of nondescript camouflage, helping the animal blend into its background. The tabby pattern itself, on the other hand, provides disruptive camouflage, making the individual seem to have no definite form. Among the larger cats, the disruptive pattern can be stripes (as in the tiger), spots (leopard) or rosettes (jaguar). Among the smaller cats, both striped and spotted patterns occur, and are superimposed on the agouti. Both the African and European wild cats, *Felis lybica* and *F. silvestris* (see p15), have stripes, and

these were probably passed on to the domestic mackerel tabby. Mackerel tabbies are rarely seen at shows today, but in a good show specimen there are narrow, vertical, gently curving stripes on the body and an elaborate arrangement of facial markings. Such a pattern may be found in cats of any body type, with long or short hair.

The gene responsible for the mackerel tabby is symbolized *T*. Two mutant alleles (different forms; see p21) have arisen from it, the blotched (t^b), which is recessive, and the Abyssinian (T^a), which is dominant to *T* (see p20). The blotched or classic tabby is an extremely handsome animal, especially in short-haired versions with good, dense black markings that are free of agouti flecking, contrasting with rich brown ground colouring. This is the brown tabby of cat shows, though genetically it is properly termed black (see below). The pattern is variable, and cat fancy organizations publish elaborate descriptions of the ideal towards which breeders aim; for

example, the shoulder pattern should look like a butterfly, while each flank should have a solid 'oyster' or blotch encircled by one or more unbroken rings. This can be approached only by selective breeding, using animals with the best patterns. Again, long- and short-haired cats are bred.

The fact that the Abyssinian – sanctified as a breed with a distinctive body type (see p76), but in fact a coat pattern that can clothe any feline body – is a form of tabby surprises many people. However, all Abyssinians have tabby markings on the face and sometimes faintly on the legs and tail, and many cross-bred animals have half-formed stripes low on the flanks. In good specimens, however, almost all the fur is unadorned agouti – a fact that earned the breed the name 'bunny-cat' in the early days of cat shows. Selective breeding has, however, brought a rich, warm brown colouring, while other colours of Abyssinians also exist (see below).

Some breeders have suggested that there

The striped tabby pattern gives good camouflage by confusing the cat with its background, and is found in many wild cat species, including the domestic cat's ancestors. It consists of two distinct parts: the black stripes and the ticked, or agouti, areas in between.

Genotypes of striped and spotted tabbies

Genotype		
A–B–C–D–iiT–$/t^bt^b$	**1**	Brown (black; ebony) tabby
A–B–C–$ddiiT$–$/t^bt^b$	**2**	Blue tabby
A–bbC–D–iiT–$/t^bt^b$	**3**	Chocolate (chestnut) tabby
A–b^lb^lC–D–iiT–$/t^bt^b$	**4**	Cinnamon tabby
A–bbC–$ddiiT$–$/t^bt^b$	**5**	Lilac (lavender) tabby
C–D–$iiO(O)T$–$/t^bt^b$	**6**	Red tabby
C–$ddiiO(O)T$–$/t^bt^b$	**7**	Cream tabby
A–B–C–D–I–T–$/t^bt^b$	**8**	Silver tabby
C–D–I–$O(O)T$–$/t^bt^b$	**9**	Cameo tabby

In all cases, T– animals are mackerel or spotted, while t^bt^b animals are blotched (classic) pattern. Other-coloured 'silver' tabbies are possible (see p34).

Tabby hairs in close-up right show the pattern of agouti banding. In a classic, spotted or mackerel tabby **1**, the guard hairs in the agouti areas **a** have a black tip, a yellow band – the agouti band itself – and a base shading almost to white. In the striped areas **b** and down hairs **c** there is no banding. In an Abyssinian tabby **2**, almost all the guard hairs **a** have agouti bands; down hairs **b** are again unbanded.

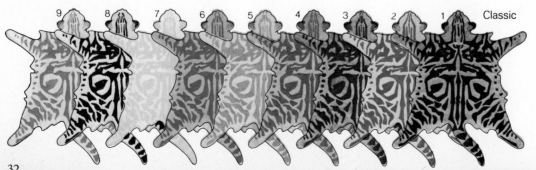

9　8　7　6　5　4　3　2　1　Classic

Mackerel

The all-agouti or ticked tabby pattern is seen in the pedigree Abyssinian, and – except in the few vestigial stripes – consists only of hairs with agouti banding (see below). This, too, is a camouflage pattern found in many species other than cats, and is best known in rabbits.

is a further mutation of the tabby gene, responsible for the spotted pattern seen in such breeds as the Egyptian Mau, spotted Oriental Shorthair and Ocicat (see pp79 and 94). The existence of spotted patterns in various wild cat species gives some support to this suggestion, but most geneticists feel that in the domestic cat the pattern is due to a breaking up of the mackerel tabby's stripes. The fact that there are many gradations, from mackerel through half-spotted to fully spotted, backs up this view. In fact, breeders of spotted tabbies must continually select for well-defined spots, or mackerel tabbies result. Barring of the chest and legs persist in any event, and it is also difficult to maintain unbroken striping in mackerel tabbies. All this suggests that polygenes are involved (see p27). Among the most striking spotted tabbies are the silvers, in which the inhibitor gene I holds back some of the lighter barring between the spots and produces a more obviously spotted cat (see below).

Colours of tabbies

As already mentioned, the basic tabby is genetically a black, having the same colour genes as the self black (see the chart of genotypes). However, breeders have selected for maximum expression of the rufus polygenes (see p27), so that the ground colour is a rich brown rather than drab grey. The same process of selection has been applied to the red tabby, to produce the rich, deep orange-on-yellow pattern that is far removed from the ginger of the alley cat; both, however, owe their basic colour to the orange gene O. As explained on page 30, all orange cats are in fact tabbies, but in the red tabby the markings are encouraged, unlike in the red self (solid red).

Although brown and red tabbies are probably the best-known varieties, tabby cats can be and are bred in any of the basic colours found in selfs – blue (resulting from the action of the dilution gene d), chocolate (from the brown gene b), cinnamon (with the light-brown gene b^l instead of b), lilac (from the combination of d with b or b^l) and cream (from d in combination with the orange gene O). These colours are most commonly exhibited with the spotted tabby pattern, and particularly in the foreign (oriental) body type. For example, virtually the full range is seen in Britain under the breed name Oriental Spotted Tabby, which was adopted in place of the earlier name Egyptian Mau to avoid confusion with the North American breed of the same name (see pp79 and 94). The Egyptian Mau of North America is also a spotted tabby bred in bronze (in fact, chocolate) and silver versions, and also as a smoke (see p35).

The silver Mau and other pure-bred silver tabbies have jet-black markings on a glistening silver-white ground colouring. As explained on page 34, these are genetically identical to the chinchillas and shaded silvers, all possessing the inhibitor gene I. Other colours of 'silver' tabby are possible, but the only well-known one is the red version, known as the cameo tabby. There is also no reason why, in theory, tabbies should not be bred in all the Burmese colours (see p30), as they have been in the Siamese to produce the tabby-point (lynx-point) varieties (see p37).

All the colour variations found in striped, spotted and blotched tabbies also occur in Abyssinians, but their different appearance causes some confusion in naming. The basic Abyssinian colour is quite reddish, for example, due to the rufus polygenes, and is known in North America as ruddy. Also well known is the 'red' Abyssinian. Unlike true red cats, this is not sex-linked, and is now known to be due to the light-brown gene b^l; for this reason, the alternative name cinnamon has been put forward (although sorrel is also used), together with fawn or beige for the dilute version previously known as cream.

The proof that these were not true reds and creams came from breeding Abyssinians with the orange gene O; the colours were much brighter than in the non-sex-linked 'red' and 'cream', with the full red or cream colour showing on the tip of the tail. Chocolate, blue and lilac Abyssinians have also been bred, together with silvers incorporating the I gene. They appear to be a long way from the basic striped tabby, but in truth are quite close relatives.

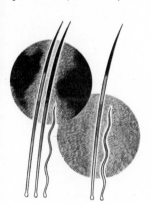

Genotypes of Abyssinian tabbies

Genotype		Description
$A–B–C–D–iiT^a–$	**1**	Usual (ruddy) Abyssinian
$A–B–C–ddiiT^a–$	**2**	Blue Abyssinian
$A–bbC–D–iiT^a–$	**3**	Chocolate (chestnut) Abyssinian
$A–bbC–ddiiT^a–$	**4**	Lilac (lavender) Abyssinian
$A–b^lb^lC–D–iiT^a–$	**5**	Non-sex-linked 'red' (cinnamon; sorrel) Abyssinian
$A–b^lb^lC–ddiiT^a–$	**6**	Non-sex-linked 'cream' (fawn; beige) Abyssinian
$C–D–iiO(O)T^a–$	**7**	Sex-linked (true) red Abyssinian
$C–ddiiO(O)T^a–$	**8**	Sex-linked (true) cream Abyssinian
$A–B–C–D–I–T^a–$	**9**	Silver usual (ruddy) Abyssinian

Other-coloured 'silver' Abyssinians are possible (see p34).

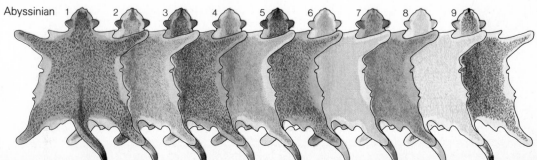

Spotted   Abyssinian   1   2   3   4   5   6   7   8   9

Shaded and tipped colours

At any cat show, among the most striking exhibits are those cats – particularly the long-hairs – that come under the general category of 'tipped'. There are golden versions of these (see below), but better known (especially outside North America) are the silver group. These range from the sparkling appearance of the chinchillas (termed silvers, in fact, by some North American cat fancy organizations) to the more dramatic smokes – apparently black in repose but displaying the brilliantly contrasting white undercoat when they move. In between are the shaded silvers, known in Britain as pewters.

All these share the common characteristic of coloured tips to the hairs (these colours include blues, reds and so on, as well as black) overlying a pale undercolour. The difference lies in the degree of tipping – greatest in the smokes, least in the chinchillas. Not surprisingly, the silver cats share a similar genetic make-up. What is perhaps more surprising is that genetically the silver tabby (confusingly, also known as the silver) is a member of this same group.

Silvers and chinchillas

The gene all the cats of the silver group possess is termed the inhibitor, symbolized *I*. (At one time a so-called chinchilla gene, related to the Siamese gene, was thought to be responsible.) The *I* gene is dominant (see p20), and its effect is to suppress the development of pigment (colouring matter), particularly in the more lightly pigmented areas of the animal's coat. In the 'wild' type cat – the tabby – these are of course the agouti areas between the dark blotches or stripes, and also the under-colour towards the roots of the hairs.

If the effect of the gene is limited, the result in a good exhibition animal is an intense black tabby pattern on an almost white ground-colour. This is the silver tabby, which can come in mackerel, spotted or blotched (classic) form, and also Abyssinian (see p32). The intense colouring is partly the result of generations of selective breeding, for the non-pedigree silver tabby often has a yellowish tinge, but is still much paler than the normal brown agouti colour. Selective breeding can also

disperse and weaken the tabby pattern, however, and magnify the expression of the inhibitor gene. The result is to drive the last remaining pigment to the tips of the hairs, so that the cat looks white to a casual glance. But it has the characteristic sparkle of the chinchilla.

Between the extremes of silver tabby and chinchilla is the shaded silver or pewter, with abundant hair tipping giving the 'pewter' colouring and the appearance of wearing a colour mantle. (The two names are synonymous except for eye colour – green for the shaded silver and copper for the pewter.) These cats are commonly produced by mating silver tabbies to chinchillas. The amount of tipping varies widely – from that of a poorly-defined silver tabby to a dark chinchilla.

The silver tabby, shaded silver, pewter and chinchilla all have an identical colour genotype (genetic make-up; see the chart), the degree of pigmentation depending on modifying polygenes (see p27). As already mentioned, they show their colouring most effectively with a long coat – in Britain the

Hairs of tipped varieties in close-up **above** show the varied tipping – least in the chinchilla **1**, but heavier in the shaded silver or pewter **2**. The silver tabby **3** has heavy pigmentation in the stripes but very little in between, while the smoke **4** and **below** is heavily pigmented all over, with white roots. The golden chinchilla **5** has black-tipped yellowish hairs.

Genotypes of tipped colours

A–B–D–I–	1	Chinchilla (silver);
	2	shaded silver;
	3	silver tabby
A–B–ddI–	4	Blue chinchilla;
	5	blue shaded silver;
	6	blue silver tabby
A–bbD–I–	7	Chocolate (chestnut) chinchilla;
	8	chocolate (chestnut) shaded silver;
	9	chocolate (chestnut) silver tabby
A–bbddI–	10	Lilac (lavender) chinchilla;
	11	lilac (lavender) shaded silver;
	12	lilac (lavender) silver tabby
aaB–D–I–	13	Smoke (black smoke)
aaB–ddI–	14	Blue smoke
aabbD–I–	15	Chocolate (chestnut) smoke
aabbddI–	16	Lilac (lavender) smoke
D–I–O(O)	17	Shell cameo (red chinchilla);
	18	shaded cameo (red shaded);
	19	cameo tabby (red silver tabby);
	20	smoke cameo (red smoke)
ddI–O(O)	21	Shell cream cameo (cream chinchilla);
	22	shaded cream cameo (cream shaded);
	23	cream cameo tabby (cream silver tabby);
	24	smoke cream cameo (cream smoke)
D–I–Oo	25	Shell tortoiseshell (tortoiseshell chinchilla);
	26	shaded tortoiseshell;
	27	smoke tortoiseshell
ddI–Oo	28	Shell dilute tortoiseshell (blue-cream chinchilla);
	29	Shaded dilute tortoiseshell (blue-cream shaded);
	30	Smoke dilute tortoiseshell (blue-cream smoke)
A–B–D–ii	31	Golden chinchilla;
	32	shaded golden
D–iiOo	33	Tortoiseshell golden chinchilla;
	34	tortoiseshell shaded golden

In all types, short-haired (*L–*) and long-haired (*ll*) versions are possible. Agouti (*A–*) varieties may be Abyssinian (*T^a–*), mackerel (*T–*) or blotched (*t^bt^b*) tabby. All varieties are normally full-colour (*C–*), though Burmese and Siamese versions are possible. Other golden colours are possible.

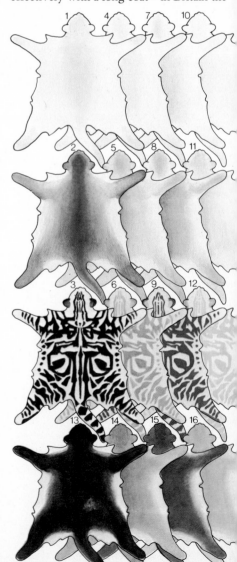

name Chinchilla applies specifically to a long-haired breed – but short-haired versions can be and are bred and shown. (In Britain they are known simply as tipped.) The best-known varieties are coloured by black pigment. However, the other major colours – blue due to the dilution gene, chocolate due to the brown gene, and lilac due to the combination of these (see pp 29–30) – are also possible. They are easy enough to identify in the shaded and silver tabby forms, but more difficult in the chinchilla. The colouring shows more clearly in baby kittens before the coat has grown too long, but in adults the best clues may come from the colour of the nose leather and eye rim.

Smokes

The above colour variations are more commonly seen in smokes, where the greater degree of pigmentation shows them up more clearly. Long- and short-haired blue smokes, for example, are well established, while the full range of colours are shown in North America in Oriental Short-

hairs (see p 92). Still the best-known smoke is the black, however, and it is due (as are all smokes) to the combined action of the inhibitor gene and the non-agouti (a).

As with other colourings, the latter allows full pigmentation of the agouti hairs, thus obscuring the tabby pattern (see p 26). The I gene produces a white undercolour, but the a gene produces extra amounts of pigment. The end result is profuse tipping, but again modifiers can increase or decrease the tipping to the extent that some smokes are almost indistinguishable from self- (solid-) coloured cats and others are very pale. The long-haired smoke with just the correct amount of undercolour and lustrous colour veiling is undoubtedly a magnificent animal.

Cameos

The cameos are the red equivalents of the chinchilla, shaded silver and smoke. They result from combining the I gene with the sex-linked orange (O). These too are beautiful cats, possessing an almost white undercolour and an overlay of rich apricot to red tipping.

There are three varieties, corresponding to the three degrees of tipping. Palest is the shell cameo (red chinchilla), with near-white undercolour and the most delicate of light red tipping. Next is the shaded cameo (red shaded), which still has a near-white undercolour, but a much redder overall appearance. Darkest is the smoke cameo (red smoke), in which the undercolour is light cream or off-white and the veiling ideally a deep, even red. As with all red cats, however, tabby markings are inherent and can be dispersed only by selective breeding. This is because the non-agouti gene is in-effective on orange pigment (see p 26), and for this reason too the smoke cameo – un-like other smokes – owes its intensity of colour only to polygenes and selective breeding, not to a non-agouti genotype. When the tabby markings are allowed to remain, the result is the cameo tabby, with red markings on an off-white ground – the red version of the silver tabby.

A very elegant series of cats are the cream cameos, produced (as with cream selfs) by introducing the dilution gene d. These are clearly of cameo form, as shown by their white undercolour, but the tipping is now cream. Again there is considerable variation

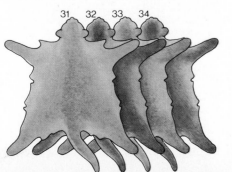

in tone, from warm cream to an exquisite pale shade, due to the action of polygenes. As with other tipped cats, both red and cream cameos may be bred with long or short coats.

Other 'silver' colours

Male cameos, like red selfs (solid reds), are generally all one colour whatever their parentage, because they can possess only one O gene (see p 30). Females, however, must have two, otherwise they become tortoiseshells (see p 39). The result is that smoke tortoiseshells – and, for that matter, shaded and shell tortoiseshells – can be bred. These again have a white under-colour, but the tipping shows the tortoise-shell pattern. Dilute (blue-cream) versions are also bred, mainly in Oriental Short-hairs, and in fact any bicolour combination could be produced as a tipped cat, if breeders considered it worthwhile.

The golden group

Golden cats show a very similar coat pattern to those described above, with dark tipping or shading. However, the under-colour is a rich, warm cream rather than white, and when combined with black tipping the 'golden' appearance results.

The different undercolour betrays a fundamental genetic difference from cats of the silver group: Goldens do not have the inhibitor gene. Instead, they seem to have a gene or group of polygenes that simply increases the amount of yellow pigment in the agouti hairs (see p 32). Without the effect of the inhibitor gene, however, colour tipping is generally heavier than in corresponding silver cats. Of course, as already mentioned, breeders of chinchillas and shaded silvers have to select for the desired degree of tipping, and the same polygenes are probably involved here. In fact, goldens occur in litters with silver off-spring if the parents are not homozygous for the inhibitor gene (see p 31).

In long-haired cats the dispersive effect of the long coat helps in creating the golden appearance, and in North America Persian-type cats are fully recognized in chinchilla golden and shaded golden colours. In Britain, the goldens are allowed for in show standards only for British Shorthair and Oriental-type cats. The basic colour has a 'black' genotype (see chart), but as with the silver group there are other colour varieties. The chocolate golden is a beautiful, richly-coloured animal with warm brown tipping on a rich golden ground. The blue golden is altogether a paler, more delicately coloured animal, and the lilac golden is also possible – as are red and cream, though it is debatable whether breeders will consider them worthwhile. Tortoiseshell goldens have also been bred in Oriental type, providing yet another range of colour forms for the cat breeder interested in new varieties.

Colours at the 'points'

The Siamese must be one of the most familiar breeds of cats, recognizable even to someone who knows nothing of cat breeding and showing. In truth, however, the Siamese is not only a breed in the strict sense, nor is it for that matter a colour. Genetically, it is a pattern – albeit most common in the cats known to fanciers and others as Siamese (including those classified in North America as Colourpoint Shorthairs; see p86), but also occurring in such breeds as Balinese (see p64), Birmans (see p62) and Himalayans (Colourpoint Longhairs; see p60).

All these have the characteristic pale-coloured hair on the body, with darker points, or extremities – nose, ears, feet and tail – and bright blue eyes. The name Himalayan is perhaps the most apt of these breed names, for the pattern of light body with dark points is well known to geneticists and breeders of other small livestock as the Himalayan pattern. In cats, however, the first breed to be developed with this colouring was the Siamese, and the name stuck. The pattern has certainly existed in the cats of Siam (now Thailand) for several hundred years, as is shown by old Thai manuscripts (see p86), but it is debatable whether it originated there.

How Siamese get their points

The Siamese pattern is caused by a gene (known as the Siamese gene and symbolized c^s) that is part of the albino series of alleles. The dominant member of this group is the full-colour gene (C), found in all of the colour varieties of cats other than the Burmese, Tonkinese, Siamese and albinos, while at the other extreme is the pink-eyed albino gene (c). As explained on page 30, the effect of the group is to progressively diminish the amount of pigment (colouring matter) in the hairs and eyes.

In the Siamese pattern, there is little pigment in the body hairs but more at the

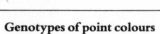

The Siamese cat's eyes are a characteristically brilliant, piercing blue quite unlike those of any other colour of cat. This colouring is unique in being directly linked with a major colour gene (see p 29). Even this can be intensified by selective breeding, however – particularly necessary with the pale point colours, such as lilac, due to the diluting effect of their genes.

Genotypes of point colours

$aaB{-}c^sc^sD{-}$	**1**	Seal point
$aaB{-}c^sc^sdd$	**2**	Blue point
$aabbc^sc^sD$	**3**	Chocolate point
$aabbc^sc^sdd$	**4**	Lilac (frost) point
$aac^sc^sD{-}O(O)$	**5**	Red point★
$aac^sc^sddO(O)$	**6**	Cream point†
$A{-}B{-}c^sc^sD{-}$	**7**	Seal tabby (lynx) point
$A{-}B{-}c^sc^sdd$	**8**	Blue tabby (lynx) point
$A{-}bbc^sc^sD{-}$	**9**	Chocolate tabby (lynx) point
$A{-}bbc^sc^sdd$	**10**	Lilac tabby (lynx) point
$A{-}c^sc^sD{-}O(O)$	**11**	Red tabby (lynx) point★
$A{-}c^sc^sddO(O)$	**12**	Cream tabby (lynx) point†
$aaB{-}c^sc^sD{-}Oo$	**13**	Seal tortie point
$aaB{-}c^sc^sddOo$	**14**	Blue tortie (blue–cream) point
$aabbc^sc^sD{-}Oo$	**15**	Chocolate tortie (chocolate–cream) point
$aabbc^sc^sddOo$	**16**	Lilac tortie (lilac–cream) point
$A{-}B{-}c^sc^sD{-}Oo$	**17**	Seal tabby tortie (patched tabby; torbie) point
$A{-}B{-}c^sc^sddOo$	**18**	Blue tabby tortie (patched tabby; torbie) point
$A{-}bbc^sc^sD{-}Oo$	**19**	Chocolate tabby tortie (patched tabby; torbie) point
$A{-}bbc^sc^sddOo$	**20**	Lilac tabby tortie (patched tabby; torbie) point

★†These are not visibly distinct. All the above can occur in long-haired versions with the addition of ll, as in Balinese and Himalayans (Colourpoint Longhairs). Birmans in addition have a white spotting gene. The agouti (A) forms may be mackerel ($T{-}$) or blotched (t^bt^b) tabby. Si-rex have the genes rr for Cornish or $rere$ for Devon. Silver (shadow) points are also possible with the addition of $I{-}$.

Genotypes of Tonkinese (light-phase Burmese)

$aaB{-}c^bc^sD{-}$	**21**	Black (seal; natural mink)
$aaB{-}c^bc^sdd$	**22**	Blue
$aabbc^bc^sD{-}$	**23**	Chocolate (chestnut; honey mink)
$aabbc^bc^sdd$	**24**	Lilac (champagne)

points. This is because the skin temperature of the points is a few degrees lower than that of the body, and the amount of pigment produced depends on temperature. The lower the temperature, the more pigment is produced. As a result, kittens reared in cool environments commonly develop darker coats than those brought up in the warm. A similar effect may be seen between kittens born at different seasons of the year, while Siamese cats of tropical regions may be lighter than those in temperate climes. Even bandaging, by retaining more body heat, can result in a light-coloured patch where the bandage was.

The effect of temperature on the Siamese coat is shown if a cat has to wear a bandage for some time. This keeps part of the coat slightly warmer than normal, inhibiting the pigmentation of newly growing hairs. Once these hairs grow out, a pale patch will appear. There is no effect on the colouring of existing hairs.

However, not all Siamese-pattern cats develop the same amount of pigment, nor do they respond equally to identical environmental changes. This is most obvious for the body colour; while some cats may have a light fawn coat, others are decidedly sepia-coloured. Body colour varies with point colour, but is influenced by modifiers, or polygenes (see p27), for breeders have selected for particular point- and body-colour combinations. But in all varieties it tends to darken with age.

Point colours
As might be expected, all the usual self (solid), tabby and tortoiseshell colours occur in the Siamese pattern, for this only represents a modification of the normal colours by the c^s allele. (Since this gene is recessive, it must be present as a homozygous pair, $c^s c^s$.) Even at the points the pigment is degraded, however, so that the 'black' members of the group have dark sepia-brown points, known to cat fanciers as seal. The seal point Siamese was the first variety to be bred. The other three basic colours, as with selfs (see pp29–30), are blue, chocolate and lilac (also known as frost) point. The requirements for body colours of show cats vary somewhat be-

tween countries and associations, but are always 'warmer' for seal and chocolate than for blue and lilac.

The above are all non-agouti in constitution (see p26). Introduction of the agouti gene (A) results in a similar series of four tabby (or lynx) point cats. (These and other variants described below are not recognized as true Siamese by many North American cat fancy organizations; cats of this type with short hair and foreign [oriental] bodies are instead classed as Colourpoint Shorthairs.) The actual tabby gene involved matters little, since the face, leg and tail markings are similar for both mackerel and blotched (classic) tabbies. However, the former is more common in Siamese. In any case, breeders' main aim is to produce regular, well-defined markings.

The red and cream points are attractive varieties, the colouring being particularly delicate in the cream. In part this is due to the lightening effect of the Siamese gene on orange pigment; breeders counteract this tendency in the red point and red tabby point by breeding selectively for rich colouring. Genetically, the difference between these last two lies in the possession of the agouti gene, but it is extremely difficult if not impossible to tell them apart visually. No one has been able to breed out the tabby markings, so the only way to discover the genotype of such a cat is by test crosses of the kind described on page 25 with a 'self' point. The occurrence of a tabby (lynx) point kitten proves that the parent is a red tabby point, not a red point. The only practical purpose of such a test, of course, is to be sure that the red point cat can be bred with other self points – for example, to produce tortie points – without unwanted tabby markings occurring.

The tortoiseshell point varieties arise from the combination of c^s and the heterozygous Oo, as with normal tortoiseshells (see p39); they are of course normally only females. The Siamese gene obscures the tortoiseshell pattern on the body except for patchy shading in some animals. On the points, the basic colour is patched or mottled with red or cream. The dilute tortie points are of course the blue-cream and lilac-cream points. By incorporating the agouti gene, it is possible to breed a corresponding series of tabby tortie points (variously known as tortie tabby points, patched tabby points or torbie points). Some people object to these, however, because the tortoiseshell pattern is often indistinct. There is the same breeding relationship between orange, tortoiseshell and non-orange Siamese-pattern cats as with others (see the chart on p39).

Eye characteristics
The eyes of Siamese-pattern cats have a clear, brilliant blue iris of quite distinctive shade that results from partial depigmenta-

tion of the eye by the c^s gene. Eye colour is variable, however, and breeders obtain the best colouring by careful choice of parents. In fact, selective breeding can almost overcome the effects of the brown (b) and dilute (d) genes, which tend to weaken the eye colour of the chocolate and blue points respectively – and particularly of the lilac (frost) point, which has both these genes. Such effects make selection for intense eye colour doubly important.

One unfortunate side-effect of the Siamese gene is to cause abnormalities in the optic nerves, resulting in faulty connections between the eyes and the brain. Most Siamese-pattern cats seem to overcome this by some kind of 'blocking' mechanism in the brain; they do, however, have much reduced binocular (three-dimensional) vision (see p111). In some, the blocking mechanism apparently does not work, so that they suffer double vision; these cats develop a squint in an attempt to compensate. Selective breeding has, however, greatly reduced the incidence of squint among pedigree Siamese.

Variations on the pattern
As already mentioned, the Siamese pattern has been incorporated in a wide range of cat breeds. Fundamental colour genotypes (genetic make-up) and breeding relationships are the same for all. Apart from the Siamese itself, there are the long-haired breeds resulting from incorporation of the long-hair gene (l). Combined with a foreign body type, this results in the Balinese, while the Himalayan (Colourpoint Longhair) has the cobby body of the Persian. The Birman is somewhat less massive, but its most noticeable feature is the white 'gloves' on all four feet – the result of incorporating a white spotting gene (see p39). Generally, the long-haired breeds show lighter body and point colours because of the insulating effect of the long coat.

The Siamese pattern can easily be combined with both the Devon and the Cornish Rex to form the Si-rex, recognized as a subdivision of the rex breeds by some North American associations. As mentioned on page 25, a cat heterozygous for the Siamese and Burmese alleles – that is, having the genotype $c^b c^s$ – has a colouring mid-way between that of a typical Siamese and a Burmese. It is the Tonkinese (see p90) – still a point-coloured breed, but with a more deeply and evenly shaded body than the Siamese and with more richly coloured points. The eyes are no longer blue, however, but green or greenish-blue, due to the influence of the Burmese gene.

But of all the breeds with coloured points, the Siamese itself is the epitome. Its lithe, sleek body has nothing genetically to do with the colouring, but nevertheless it is the total look that instantly says 'Siamese' to every cat lover.

Multiple colour patterns I

The black and white 'magpie' cat has been well loved for centuries, along with a wide range of other multi-coloured animals. A great deal of the attractiveness of these pie-bald or bicoloured cats lies in the balance and disposition of the coloured areas, and standards of excellence for show cats generally pay great attention to this point. For show purposes, tortoiseshell cats are generally considered separately from the bicolours, yet they logically belong within this same group, as does the blue-cream – which is, in fact, a form of tortoiseshell. In North America they are sometimes all grouped together as parti-colours.

Tortoiseshell patterns

The archetypal tortoiseshell is a patchwork of black and orange, usually in a random mixture and in many cases forming a fine-grained mosaic. In other cats, however, there are relatively large areas of clear black and orange. If you look closely at the orange areas, you may see that they resemble in every way the coat of a red tabby (see pp 32–33) – even to the extent of showing a clear tabby pattern. This explains the very common statement that the tortoiseshell exhibits three colours – black, yellow and orange. The yellow areas in fact correspond to the pale parts of the

red tabby's coat, while the orange ones are the stripes themselves. The colours can look quite distinct when separated by an area of black, but this is only a result of the fact, explained on page 30, that all orange (red) cats are really tabbies.

Another common fallacy is to imagine that orange and black is the only kind of tortoiseshell pattern. There are the normal range of colour variations, as in the self (solid) colours (see pp 29–30), giving rise to chocolate (chestnut), cinnamon, blue and lilac (lavender) torties – these colour names referring to the non-orange areas. The last two are dilute colours, and the dilution gene

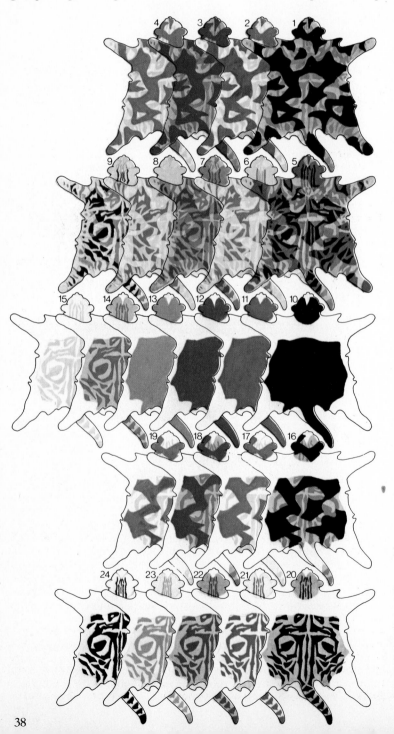

Genotypes of multiple colours

$aaB–C–D–iiOoss$	1	Tortoiseshell (normal black/orange type)
$aaB–C–ddiiOoss$	2	Blue-cream (dilute tortoiseshell)
$aabbC–D–iiOoss$	3	Chocolate (chestnut) tortoiseshell
$aabbC–ddiiOoss$	4	Lilac-cream (lavender-cream)
$A–B–C–D–iiOoss$	5	Brown tabby tortie (patched tabby; torbie)
$A–B–C–ddiiOoss$	6	Blue tabby tortie (patched tabby; torbie)
$A–bbC–D–iiOoss$	7	Chocolate (chestnut) tabby tortie (patched tabby; torbie)
$A–bbC–ddiiOoss$	8	Lilac (lavender) tabby tortie (patched tabby; torbie)
$A–B–C–D–I–Ooss$	9	Silver tabby tortie (patched tabby; torbie)
$aaB–C–D–iiS–$	10	Black and white
$aaB–C–ddiiS–$	11	Blue and white
$aabbC–D–iiS–$	12	Chocolate (chestnut) and white
$aabbCCddiiS–$	13	Lilac (lavender) and white
$C–D–iiO(O)S–$	14	Red and white; red tabby and white
$C–ddiiO(O)S–$	15	Cream and white; cream tabby and white
$aaB–C–D–iiOoS–$	16	Tortoiseshell and white; calico
$aaB–C–ddiiOoS–$	17	Blue-cream and white (dilute calico)
$aabbC–D–iiOoS–$	18	Chocolate (chestnut) tortoiseshell and white (chestnut calico)
$aabbC–ddiiOoS–$	19	Lilac-cream and white (lavender calico)
$A–B–C–D–iiS–$	20	Brown tabby and white
$A–B–C–ddiiS–$	21	Blue tabby and white
$A–bbC–D–iiS–$	22	Chocolate (chestnut) tabby and white
$A–bbC–ddiiS–$	23	Lilac (lavender) tabby and white
$A–B–C–D–I–S–$	24	Silver tabby and white

In all cases, Burmese versions are obtained by substituting $c^b c^b$ for $C–$. For shell, shaded and smoke tortoiseshells, see page 34. In all cases, short- ($L–$) and long-haired (ll) versions may be bred. The agouti (A) varieties may have blotched ($t^b t^b$), mackerel ($T–$) or Abyssinian ($T^a–$) markings.

The blue-cream is a form of tortoiseshell in which the red is changed to cream and the black to blue. The lower contrast between the agouti and non-agouti areas of cream cats means that blue-creams are more clearly bicoloured; normal torties are often mistakenly said to have three colours: red, cream and black.

(*d*) that produces them also dilutes orange to cream. The result, in fact, is the blue-cream and lilac-cream (lavender-cream) bicolours. The brown genes (*b* and *b^l*) have no effect on the orange areas, so these are identical in black, chocolate (chestnut) and cinnamon tortoiseshells.

All these colours also occur in Burmese versions, where the effect of the Burmese gene (*c^b*; see p30) is shown by a slight reduction in intensity of the various colours. Another whole range of tortoiseshells results from substituting the agouti gene (*A*) for non-agouti (see p26). Here a tabby pattern – blotched or striped – replaces the black areas. This is not a recognized exhibition variety in Britain, but is shown in North America, where it is known as the tortie tabby, patched tabby or torbie; it is also common among alley-cats. Tortoiseshell Abyssinians have also been bred.

One of the features of tortoiseshells is the tremendous variation, which may range from extensive orange to an almost black or tabby animal with so little orange that it may be overlooked. (This is particularly true of the tortie tabby.) The form of the tortoiseshell patterning is also highly variable, as is shown particularly by the different show standards for blue-creams between Britain and North America. In Britain a uniform mixing or brindling of the two colours is favoured, but American cat fanciers prefer a segregated patchwork of blue and cream. Genetically, the difference is trivial, however, for it is mainly caused by accidents of development within the womb (see illustration) and hardly affected at all by polygenes (see p27). Hence selective breeding for a balanced tortoiseshell pattern is of no avail.

Piebald spotting

Even more variable is the degree of white 'spotting' in piebald cats – from white gloves on the feet, a nose smudge or a white bib to extensive white over most of the body. It is mainly caused by a dominant gene symbolized *S*. Part of the variation is due to this gene being incompletely dominant, so that a homozygous cat with two *S* genes normally has larger areas of white than a heterozygous one having only a single *S*, but this is not consistent. Modifying genes also have an effect, and so do non-genetic variations. It is also possible that a second spotting gene – probably recessive – is at work, possibly being responsible for the minimal spotting seen on the paws of the Birman (see p62). This has not yet been fully investigated or named.

The white spotting gene or genes can be combined with any other colour genotype (set of genetic characteristics), including (as in the Birman) the Siamese pattern. Perhaps best known, however, are the various self (solid) colours and white – especially black, blue, red or cream – and the /continued

The tortoiseshell pattern occurs in female cats with one *O* (orange) and one *o* (non-orange) gene. These are on the X chromosomes, of which only the female normally has two. (In the diagram **below**, the chromosome carrying the *O* gene is coloured red.) The male has only one X plus a much smaller Y chromosome, so there is a genetic imbalance between the sexes. To compensate, one of the female's Xs becomes ineffective so that both sexes have only one 'operational' X. This inactivation does not occur immediately after fertilization, but some days later, when the embryo has grown from a single cell **1** to a cluster of cells **2** starting to differentiate into the body's tissues and organs. Thus an X has to be inactivated in a number of cells. This occurs simultaneously in all cells **3**, but it is a matter of pure chance which X chromosome is inactivated in each cell. In some, it will be the one with the *O* gene, in others that with the *o*. Once 'switched off' an X remains inactive for the rest of the cat's life, and so do all the corresponding Xs in all the cells descended from it. As a result, a patchwork of *O* and *o* cells develops as the embryo grows **4**. Ultimately, the adult cat **5** has a similar patchwork of *O* and *o* skin cells; the former grow red hairs, the latter black – a tortoiseshell.

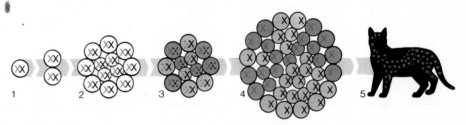

The male tortoiseshell is in theory impossible, because males have only one X and one Y chromosome, and so are genetically either entirely *O* (red) or entirely *o* (non-red). Rarely, however, an individual occurs with two X chromosomes plus a Y. The Y would produce male characteristics, but the same inactivation of one of the Xs will occur as in a female. If one of the X chromosomes carries the *O* gene and the other *o*, the result will be an XXY male of genotype *Oo* – a tortoiseshell. Such males are usually sterile, however, for the male organs may not be properly formed. Of course, an XXY male is not necessarily a tortoiseshell; if it is *OO* it will be red, if *oo* it will be non-red.

XY

XY

XXY

XXY

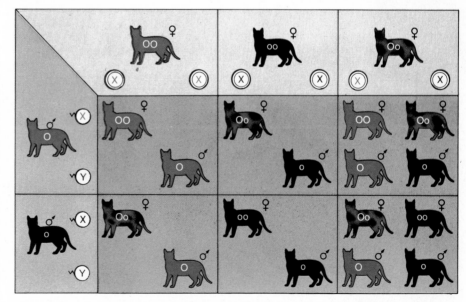

The possible offspring from various combinations of red, tortoiseshell and non-red (that is, any other colour) parents are shown in this chequerboard diagram. The dam and her eggs are shown across the top, the sire and his sperm down the side. The kittens' colour may depend on their sex as well as their parents' colours. The symbols are: male, circle with an arrow; female, circle with a cross. Phenotypes: *OO* or *O*, red; *Oo*, tortoiseshell; *oo* or *o*, non-red (the precise colour depending on other genes).

Multiple colour patterns 2

The tortoiseshell Burmese, not recognized for exhibition in North America, is popular in Europe. The tortoiseshell pattern tends to be smaller, with the colours more mingled, than is generally considered desirable in other short-haired torties, such as the British.

The patched tabby, tabby tortie or torbie is a tortoiseshell in which the non-red areas of the coat are tabby rather than black – in this case, chestnut (chocolate) tabby. Here the situation is the reverse of the Burmese, the colour being recognized in North America but not Britain.

Tortie and white, known in North America as calico, has long been a popular colour, partly because the white breaks up the red and black patches and sets them off to advantage. Here it is seen in the *mi-ke* variety of Japanese Bobtail, one of the kittens being black and white.

tortie and white. The last is commonly known as calico in North America (and blue-cream and white is called dilute calico), where show standards generally specify that the white should predominate on the lower parts. (Some associations even suggest that the cat should look as if it had been dropped in a pail of milk.) Elsewhere, standards may merely stipulate evenly balanced colour patches, and some North American associations recognize the tortie and white separately from the calico, with less stringent demands on the disposition of colours.

Bicolours should commonly have between one-third and one-half of their fur white, but there are breeds in which the expression of the *S* gene is taken to its

extreme. Examples include the Turkish Van (see p50) and, in North America, Van-pattern Persians. Both have the coloured patches confined to the extremities; the former is auburn (orange) and white, while the latter may be various colours including calico (tortie and white). The *mi-ke* variety of Japanese Bobtail (see p74) is similarly an extreme white and tortoiseshell in which the coloured patches are often separately black and orange, giving a very distinguished appearance. Separation of the black and orange areas into larger and more distinct patches than in ordinary tortoiseshells is in fact a result of interaction between the *S* and *O* genes that shows up to some extent in all tortoiseshell and white cats.

This extreme colour separation may have

a confusing side-effect. Some cats resemble an ordinary black or red bicolour, because only one of the tortoiseshell colours shows in the patches. Much to the surprise of the breeder, its offspring are what would be expected of a tortoiseshell – for example, an apparently normal black and white queen might produce a red male kitten from a mating with another black. This would immediately raise a query from a knowledgeable breeder, for it goes against the normal rules for the inheritance of the orange colouring (see the chart). Yet the result is perfectly consistent if the queen is a 'disguised' tortoiseshell. Breeders, however, may be excused for feeling that cat genetics is quite intricate enough without introducing such 'trick' complications.

White spotting is caused in the main by a dominant gene *S* with variable expression. Depending partly on whether a cat possesses one of these genes or two, the amount of white can vary from a few small patches 2, 3 to large white areas covering most of the body 8, 9. The extremes 1 and 10 represent an all-black cat (with no *S* gene) and an all-white one (usually with the dominant white gene *W*; see p31) respectively. Moderate white spotting usually affects mainly the underparts.

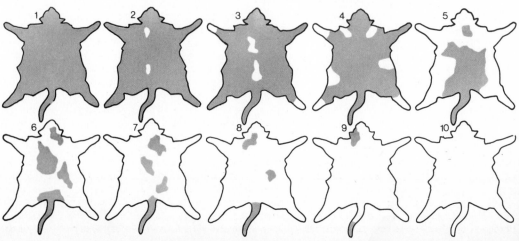

Body conformation 1

An essential attribute of most pure-bred cats is the so-called 'type' or conformation. In general terms, this encompasses every aspect of the animal's form – the size, shape and stance of the body itself, the proportions of the legs, the length and thickness of the tail, the shape of the head and the size and position of the eyes – even the form and carriage of the ears. All these are unique to a breed or a group of related breeds, yet in almost all cases they are not governed by major genes but by polygenes (see p27). In fact, any bodily change that is governed by a single major gene is very likely to turn out to be a deformity – as is the case with the Manx and, to a lesser extent, the folded-ear mutant seen in the Scottish Fold.

The polygenes determining conformation do so by modifying the growth of the underlying bone structure, muscular development and disposition of fat. All of these attributes can be affected by diet, particularly if this is deficient for any reason. The potential of a particular cat may be thwarted by poor feeding, but it is doubtful if a poor cat (in the eyes of a breeder or show judge) can be so altered by its diet as to become an outstanding exhibition animal.

The variations of body type

Geneticists usually divide genetic differences of conformation into two main categories – general, which govern overall growth, and local, which control growth of particular parts of the body, such as the head, ears, legs, trunk or tail. Examination of conformations over the span of cat breeds shows a general unity of the feline form indicating that general factors are the most important in the cat. As mentioned elsewhere, breeders' respect for this unity may be partly responsible, but it does seem that cats resist the kind of local modification shown in dogs.

Dog breeders have drastically modified the shape of the muzzle, ear size and carriage, the legs and trunk, and tail length and structure – sometimes with strange, not to say unfortunate, results. It is true that the nose of the cat has been shortened in some long-haired breeds – most extremely in the Peke-faced Persian (see p56) – with accompanying deformities of the tear ducts so that some individuals suffer from perpetually weeping eyes. But such extremes are rare among cat breeding.

As might be expected from its polygenic control, body conformation shows more or less continuous variation, but there are two principal extremes of type into one or the other of which most breeds may be categorized. At one end of the scale is the powerful, sturdily built frame found in such breeds as the British Shorthair and the Exotic Shorthair of North America (see p66) and, among long-haired breeds, in the Persian and Himalayan (known in Britain

The **cobby form** of the blue British Shorthair **left** typifies one extreme of the range of body conformations seen in domestic cats – broad, powerful, compact and short-legged. The X-ray photograph of a Persian's skull **above** shows the typical short, rounded head shape of these and related breeds. This is mostly the result of selective breeding, but may relate to the shape of the European wild cat, *Felis silvestris*.

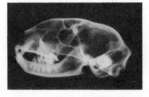

The **foreign body type** of the lilac point Siamese **left** represents the opposite end of the spectrum – lithe, lean and sinuous, with long legs and tail. The X-ray picture of a Siamese skull **above** shows the same tendency in the head – to a long, low profile; this has been carried to the extreme by some breeders. Again, these characteristics mainly result from selection, but the African wild cat, *Felis libyca*, is also relatively slim, and this may have made a contribution (see p 16).

as the Longhair and Colourpoint Longhair respectively; see pp54 and 60). The one word used to describe these cats is cobby – implying a short, compact body shape, low on the legs and deep in the chest, with broad shoulders and rump and a short tail. The head, too, is large and rounded but relatively short, and although overall size is not considered an advantage as such, these cats do tend to be bigger than the average – typically 5.5kg (12lb) or more in a fully-grown uncastrated tom.

In direct contrast are the foreign or oriental breeds typified by the Siamese (see p86). Here, the body is slim and lithe, with svelte tapering lines and fine bones. The head is narrow also, forming a wedge shape

without any nose break or 'stop' in a good exhibition animal. Everything is sinuous and more lightly built, adults rarely exceeding 4kg (9lb) in weight.

These two extremes represent the result of decades of selective breeding. Crosses between them result in an intermediate conformation, and this is one of the main reasons why many breeders strongly depreciate crosses between breeds. Nevertheless, there are considerable variations within the main categories, and many breeds are much less extreme than described above. For example, the Russian Blue (see p80) and Abyssinian (see p76) are classed as foreign, but are much less elongated than the Siamese. *continued*

Body conformation 2

Coat types

Similarly, the American Shorthair (see p68) is less cobby than the Exotic Shorthair, and the Maine Coon (see p52), although a massive cat, has a more flowing outline than the Persian. Not all of this more subtle variation is inherited – some is due to chance accidents of development – but a large enough proportion is hereditary to be standardized by selective breeding.

Monogenic bodily features
As already mentioned, a few breeds are based on bodily characteristics – arguably malformations – caused by single gene mutations. Best known is the Manx (see p72), caused by the dominant gene of the same name, symbolized M, which causes the tail to be either deformed or absent. For exhibition, complete taillessness – often with a hollow where the tail should begin – is held to be the ideal, and these cats are called rumpies. Others, with some tail remaining, are known as rumpie-risers, stumpies or longies, depending on the degree of shortening. All of these must be heterozygous for the Manx gene (see p21), having a genotype Mm, the differences arising from chance development in the womb. Homozygous (MM) animals die before birth, and even heterozygous Manx may suffer abnormalities of the lower spinal region, such as spina bifida.

There is a superficial similarity between the stumpie Manx and the Japanese Bobtail

(see p74). Genetically they are quite different, however, although the Bobtail's genes have not yet been studied fully. One report has suggested that the unusual tail is inherited as a recessive trait (see p20), but with variable expression unless stabilized by selective breeding. No other bodily abnormalities seem to be associated with it. Other tail-shortening or tail-deforming genes have occurred from time to time, most notably among Siamese, where certain strains of cats have shortened or kinked tails. This may also be due to one or more recessive genes, but the exact mode of inheritance has not been established. However, breeders select against these features, and show cats exhibiting a kink are penalized or disqualified.

The Scottish Fold breed (see p75) results from a single dominant gene called simply the folded-ear gene (Fd). This causes the tip of the ear to bend forward, the fold developing some time after birth. Abnormalities of cartilage growth around the leg joints, affecting the ability to walk, have been reported by some workers to be associated with this gene, especially in homozygous animals ($FdFd$). This, and fears – misplaced, according to veterinary opinion – that hearing and ear health may suffer, has led to the breed being discouraged in Britain (although the mutation first arose in Scotland). It is popular in North America, however, and breed surveys there suggest that the skeletal malformations may be caused by modifying genes and can be reduced or eliminated by selective breeding.

A deformity that occurs quite commonly in all breeds is polydactyly, or extra toes. This occurs most noticeably on the front feet, there occasionally being as many as seven toes, but considerable variation is seen from animal to animal and even between different feet of the same animal. The deformity seems to be caused by one or more dominant genes, the one that is definitely established being symbolized Pd. The same applies to the split-foot abnormality, caused by the gene Sp. Again, breeders select against these abnormalities and show cats in most countries are penalized for having them, although they do not seem to do the animal any harm in its everyday life.

The same cannot be said, unfortunately, for a number of other feline abnormalities caused genetically. These range from cryptorchidism (undescended testicles; see p228) and cleft palate to several severe disorders of the nervous system (see p207). When caused by recessive genes, such disorders may be widespread and very difficult, if not impossible, to eliminate. The only answer is for breeders and owners to be on the lookout for possible hereditary disorders and to seek professional advice if they suspect anything is wrong.

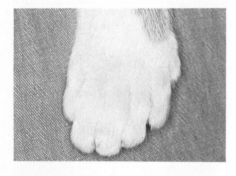

Polydactyly – the possession of extra toes – usually affects the front paws **above**, which normally each have five toes.

Split foot is an abnormal cleft in one or both front paws. The bones are deformed but, except for climbing, life is little affected.

The short-hair is the fundamental 'wild' type, but its texture varies considerably from that of the British Shorthair **above** to, say, the Russian Blue (see p80) and Burmese (see p82).

The Angora is genetically the same as the Persian, but its coat, though silky, is not so full because the down hairs are less developed.

The Cornish Rex lacks guard hairs. Its wavy coat is due to the natural curl of the awn and down hairs. The whiskers are short and curly.

The wire-hair has all the types of hairs curled abnormally in an irregular fashion, the awn hairs resembling a shepherd's crook.

The Persian has the most highly developed long coat, soft and silky, with the profuse down hairs almost as long as the guard hairs. This example is a black smoke.

The Maine Coon is another long-hair, but the coat is heavier and more shaggy, perhaps closer in type to many non-pedigree long-hairs.

The Devon Rex has all three hair types, but all are modified; the whiskers may be absent or reduced to mere stubs. Some cats are bald.

Hairlessness, as in the Sphynx, is regarded by most cat lovers as an abnormality; there is usually a thin covering of down on some parts.

Just as pure-bred cats may be divided into two major groups according to their body type, or conformation, so the long-haired and short-haired breeds form a natural and instantly recognizable classification. The basic, or wild type, cat is the short-hair, while the long-hair represents a recessive mutation (see p23). Apart from these, several other mutant coat types have occurred, the best known being the various rexes while others include the wire-hair and hairless. In all the above except for the hairless and the Cornish rex, all the basic types of hairs, as described on page 106, exist in the coat, but their proportions, length, texture, form and so on may vary.

Long and short coats

In a typical short-haired cat, the longest guard hairs average about 4.5 cm (1¾ in) in length. In contrast, in the silky, flowing coat of a good long-haired exhibition cat they may exceed 12.5 cm (5 in). The difference is due in the main to the presence of the recessive long-hair gene l as a homozygous pair. This seems to increase the period of growth in hair follicles so that the hairs reach a greater length before entering the dormant phase (see p107).

There is considerable variation – due to the influence of polygenes – in the length and texture of the long coat. The early Angora and Persian cats imported into Europe from the Middle East had a relatively short and coarse coat compared with their modern exhibition counterparts (see pp50 and 54) due to the presence of rather coarse guard hairs. Selective breeding over many generations has resulted in a longer, fuller and more silky coat in Persians, with down (wool) hairs that are both more numerous and almost as long as the guard hairs. The hair on the legs and tail is also fully developed.

Not all long-haired breeds have such a full coat, however. Breeders of Balinese and Angoras, for example, select for a long, silky, fine coat without a downy undercoat (see p64). Show standards for the Maine Coon, on the other hand, specify a heavy, shaggy coat that is shorter on the shoulders and falls smoothly but is silky in texture (see p52). Other long-haired breeds include the Somali (long-haired Abyssinian; see p78), Himalayan or Colourpoint Longhair (see p60), Birman (see p62) and Cymric (long-haired Manx; see p73).

Rex and wire-haired mutants

Various rex breeds (see p96), with short curled coats, have occurred from time to time as a result of spontaneous mutations. Cross-breeding experiments have proved that two of them – the German and Cornish – are identical, but the Devon and Oregon rexes are distinct mutants. The degree of curl varies from a marcel or ripple waved effect to an intense curl, but in each case is

caused by retarded hair growth so that none of the hairs attain normal length. All the rex genes are recessive; the Cornish is symbolized r, the Devon re and the Oregon ro.

The coat of the Cornish and German rexes (the latter name is still used in some parts of Europe, though the Cornish was discovered a year earlier, in 1950) lacks guard hairs. Although awn hairs are present, they are almost indistinguishable from down hairs; the natural waviness of these probably explains the curl of the coat. The coat of the Devon rex, on the other hand, possesses all three hair types, although the guard and awn hairs are so changed as to almost resemble down hairs; in some cats the guard hairs can be felt by a sensitive hand. The Devon's whiskers are commonly absent or reduced to mere stubs, while some cats lose the coat completely on the chest, belly and shoulders – a fault breeders strive to eliminate. The Oregon rex resembles the Cornish, but is due to an independent mutation; it may well now be extinct, in fact.

The rex genes are inherited independently of those for coat colour and length, thus it is possible to breed rexes of any colour or pattern found in the normal cat and also in long-haired versions. The latter have a rather poor coat, however, since the rex gene curbs full development of the long hairs, and as a result few have been bred. But a wide range of colours have been produced in rexes, including Siamese-pattern rex cats known as Si-rex.

The wire-hair mutation, seen in the American Wirehair breed (see p71), is quite different from the rexes. It is caused by a dominant gene symbolized Wh. The coat looks and feels wiry, being coarse, crimped and springy. The effect is due to a marked increase in the natural waviness of the hairs; even the guard hairs are wavy. The tips of the awn hairs are commonly bent over like a shepherd's crook. Some hairs are coiled or partly coiled in spirals.

Hairlessness

More or less bald cats have occurred from time to time in various parts of the world, but only in the case of the Sphinx, or Canadian Hairless, has there been a serious attempt to elevate hairlessness to the status of a breed. (This is quite distinct from the baldness that may afflict some rex cats to a greater or lesser degree.) The recessive hairless gene of the Sphinx is symbolized hr. The effect is not in fact complete, for some thin hairs may persist around the muzzle and on the legs, and a transient fine down may cover the body. Since the normal cat's fur has an important heat-retaining function, it is obviously reasonable to regard hairlessness as an abnormality. But it need not distress the cat if it is kept warm and provided with a knitted woollen substitute coat when necessary.

The 'pure' breed 1

What is a pure breed of cats, and what constitutes a pure-bred animal? These terms can have a number of meanings. One of the simplest is merely to regard as pure-bred a cat that has been properly registered with a responsible body (such as the Governing Council of the Cat Fancy [GCCF] in Britain, or the Cat Fanciers' Association [CFA] or one of the other similar associations in the United States). Such a cat will have a pedigree of similarly registered parents, grandparents and so on for a given number of generations – normally at least four. This ensures that the cat has 'respectable' parentage and is likely to be a representative specimen of the breed – though it says nothing about its quality.

However, the process of registration and the writing of pedigrees is, in a sense (and without meaning to be derogatory), merely window dressing. They simply set a seal upon a more fundamental definition of pure breeds of cats. This relates to the characteristics of the individuals constituting a recognized breed and how these may differ from those of other cats: from alley cats and from other recognized breeds. In one sense, a breed is a group of animals that sufficient people are mutually agreed to recognize as such. This is not enough in itself, however; the group must have coherent distinguishing features that set them apart from all other cats, and hence distinctive underlying genetic characteristics.

How breeds arose

For centuries, cats were kept only for utility purposes and/or as companions. It is doubtful if anyone bothered too much about how they were bred or which particular colours were produced. However, about the middle of the 19th century, a new attitude to animal breeding began to take form. People began to take pride in their pets, to regulate the breeding of them and to exhibit their efforts at competitive shows. It was a short step to the drafting of standards of excellence to embody the ideal animal. Thus the concept of breeds came into existence, and people became interested in their maintenance. Pedigrees became the vogue as a means of authenticating stock, tracing descent from outstanding animals of the past and generally safeguarding the integrity of the breed. Long before the genetics of cat breeds and varieties was discovered, breeders recognized the value of the pedigree in trying to predict the outcome of matings. Pedigree-bred became synonymous with pure-bred.

In cats, mutant colours and long hair existed from pre-pedigree days, and these were incorporated as hallmarks of breeds. A breed had to be distinctive, and what could be a better distinguishing feature than colour? More sophisticated distinctions soon developed, however. Two items gradually became of importance: a distinc-

tive conformation (head shape and body type, see p41) and exotic origin. Breeders appreciated that colour is a minor change and, at best, represents a variety within a breed. There was a precedent in that the major breeds of dogs and larger livestock are distinguished by unique conformations, colour being secondary and serving more to label a breed than to determine it.

Serious cat breeding and showing first became fashionable in Britain, and breeds based on native British cats were developing a sturdy body conformation – as befitted temperate summers and cold winters. The Persian cats had a somewhat similar conformation (as did the breeds developed much later from native American cats, such as the American Shorthair and the Maine Coon). However, the Siamese were very different. Whether by chance or for aesthetic reasons, these had a slender conformation, though less extreme than in the modern show Siamese. Possibly befitting a tropical environment, this had little to do with the Siamese gene itself (which merely governs the coat pattern; see p36), but indicates the type of cat in which the mutation occurred or the preference of the breeders who subsequently nurtured it.

The popularity of the first Siamese set the style for the foreign or exotic breeds. Henceforth, cats of domestic origin were defined by British breeders as having 'British type', while the others were 'foreign type'. When cat fancying first developed in North America, the rounder, stockier conformation was generally termed 'domestic'. (Confusingly, American breeders later developed a breed of stocky short-haired cats known as Exotic Shorthairs; see p69.)

Exotic origin – which here merely means origin in a different part of the world –

comes into the picture partly because the development of unique breeds entails breeding in isolation, and in the early days that meant geographical isolation. The second reason is that a new mutation, which could be the focal point of a breed, can occur in any part of the world. Two examples are the Siamese (based on the Siamese colour gene already mentioned) and the Angora and Persian (both based on the long-hair mutation). These cats were recognized as unusual by breeders in southeast Asia and Asia Minor, respectively, long before pedigree cat breeding came into vogue. Upon arrival in Europe they found a ready acceptance as fully-fledged breeds.

Defining cat breeds

It is impossible to give a rigid definition of a breed. Generally speaking, the term is usually applied to individuals of a definite, unique body conformation, colour pattern, hair type and/or exotic geographic origin. Many colours and patterns are regarded as varieties – that is, simply as subdivisions of a breed – but this is not always the case, particularly in Britain. North American cat fancy organizations generally define the general characteristics of a breed, and recognize various colours within that breed. In some cases, however, the situation is reversed, as with the various tabby point (lynx point) and some other colours that are recognized as varieties of Siamese in Britain, but are generally classed as Colourpoint Shorthairs in North America.

Perhaps even more difficult to justify is the recognition in recent years of 'breeds' that are scarcely more than varieties of existing breeds and, worse, are little more than someone's flight of fancy. (Examples cited by many critics are the Ragdoll, Snow-Shoe Cat, albino Foreign Shorthair and Kashmir.) Parallel to this is the production of new phenotypes – that is, cats of different appearance – by the recombination of various genes. Some of these undoubtedly deserve recognition, but the addition of unjustified exotic or fanciful 'breed' names is more dubious. (As an example, the names Balinese and Somali undoubtedly sound as attractive as the appearance of the cats bearing them – longhaired Siamese and Abyssinians respectively – but they obscure the fact that these are the creations of American breeders.)

Establishing new breeds

The number of ways by which a breed of cats may be legitimately established is limited. The first, and most fundamental, is that of mutation (see p23). A new mutation, producing an unusual phenotype, has a real claim to recognition. Many of the older breeds were founded in this fashion. More recently, this is how the American Wirehair and the Cornish and Devon rexes came into existence. It might be thought that two rex breeds would be superfluous; however, these represent mutations of different genes, and this is enough to validate recognition of both.

The second method is by recombination of mutant genes. This process usually results in colour varieties, rather than true breeds – such as the progressive development of some 10 recognized varieties of Burmese and 14 of Siamese (though not all are recognized everywhere). In the early days of the cat fancy, the development of varieties was largely a matter of chance, but recently it has been more systematic. An instance is the realization of the true sex-linked red Abyssinian (as distinct from the better-known 'red' Abyssinian which, as explained on page 33, is more properly described as cinnamon) by the mating of a normal (ruddy) Abyssinian male to a red point Siamese. The result was sex-linked

red Abyssinian male and tortoiseshell Abyssinian female kittens in perfect agreement with expectation (see p39). In many cases of new forms arising from recombination of mutant alleles, the distinction between a variety and a breed is very fine and largely a matter of opinion to be settled by debate and general agreement, or by the issue of an edict by a governing body. In others, such as the Himalayan (Colourpoint Longhair), breed status is quite clear.

The third way of establishing a new cat breed is to so mould the polygenes controlling a given characteristic that a distinctive form is created. No new mutants or recombination of existing mutants are involved, just the simple selection of the breeding stock at each generation that shows the closest approach to the desired form. This is the most difficult method and, in some respects, the least satisfactory with cats. Unlike dogs, the cat displays relatively little variation of shape and type which, by exaggeration say, can be deftly modified into something unusual. Exceptional care has to be taken not to interfere with the normal physiology of the individual. For example, selection for an extremely short nose in the Peke-faced Persian (see p56) has led to problems with breathing and running eyes. Some projects are beset with difficulties, as in the case of attempts to evolve miniature or toy cats – attempts that have failed so far without accompanying sterility or hormonal faults.

Official recognition

As already mentioned, governing bodies or associations in various countries are responsible for recognizing breeds and permitting individual cats to be registered as members of these breeds. The basis of such regulation is the desirability of excluding mutant genes that can cause serious anomalies and of not accepting breeds based on trivial differences. The decision in any particular case

may not be at all straightforward, however, and may be based on nothing more substantial than prejudice.

Modern veterinary knowledge can be valuable if it is available to and heeded by those making the decisions. For example, the Manx is a very old breed, yet if it were put up for recognition today it would very likely not be accepted. The reason is that homozygous Manx (those carrying two Manx genes; see p21) invariably die in the womb, while many Manx heterozygotes (those with only one gene) have defects of the lower spine (see p27).

Another case is the Scottish Fold (see p75). This was rejected by the GCCF in Britain because of fears about ear troubles – fears that most vets consider unfounded. Later, it appeared that some animals suffer from crippling overgrowth of cartilage at the joints – much more concrete grounds for rejection. On the other hand, the blue-eyed albino mutant (see p26) has received unjustified criticism simply because it happens to be associated with albinism. Yet the mutant is not a true albino but is in effect a Siamese without the coloured points yet retaining the blue eyes. The absence of points may be aesthetically displeasing to some people, but it has no defects that are not also shown by some Siamese.

The procedure for recognition of a breed or variety varies from one registration body to another. Some permit the registration of kittens – so that proper pedigree records may be kept – for some years before the breed is considered for recognition and show. During this period the breed is classed as experimental or preliminary, and can only be displayed at cat shows in assessment or experimental classes. This allows time for the breed to be widely observed and any unexpected disadvantages to be discovered. At the same time, a set of show standards – a description of the ideal against which individual animals will */continued*

The pedigree certificate is the heart of the system of record-keeping that is vital to planned cat breeding. This one shows the pedigree of a blue point Siamese called Shawn Blue Boy back for four generations, not only proving the cat's authenticity as a member of its breed but also giving clues to recessive colour genes that it might be carrying. The pedigree also indicates the degree of inbreeding in its ancestry and its relationship to other – possibly well-known – bloodlines. Some breeders draw attention to champions and grand champions in the pedigree by typing their names in red. (For fuller information, however, it may be necessary to delve farther back to even earlier generations.) No pedigree should have unexplained gaps, nor should it end abruptly. The form shown here is the British type, with GCCF breed numbers and colour abbreviations. These will differ with other registration bodies, but the basic information given is the same.

Breeder Miss L. Cooper,		**PEDIGREE CERTIFICATE**		Owner Mrs O. M. Penley,
Address 10 The Elms, Heddington, Lancs.				Address 101 Long Side, Heddington, Lancs.
Tel. No. Heddington 92706				Tel. No. Heddington 94820

Pedigree of: SHAWN BLUE BOY						Breed No. 24a Colour. BP	Sex. Male Regd. No. 199676 Date of Birth. 6.2.79		
Parents		**Grand-Parents**		**Great Grand-Parents**			**Great Great Grand-Parents**		
SIRE	Reg. No. 191276	Sire Shawn Favourite	Reg. No. 188199	Sire Ch. Cortex Pean	Reg. No. 179611 Breed No. 24		Sire Ch. Cortex Zulu		Br. No. 24
							Dam Cortex Pixie I		Br. No. 24
		Shawn Silver Mist	Breed No. 24 Colour. SP	Dam Cortex Cutie	Reg. No. 179521 Breed No. 24		Sire Ch. Cortex Zulu		Br. No. 24
							Dam Cortex Pixie II		Br. No. 24
		Dam Shawn Shot Silk	Reg. No. 187266	Sire Shawn The Count	Reg. No. 180182 Breed No. 24		Sire Ch. Cortex Pean		Br. No. 24
							Dam Cortex Lulu		Br. No. 24a
Breed No. 24a Colour. BP		Breed No. 24a Colour. BP		Dam Convoy Mitzie	Reg. No. 182441 Breed No. 24a		Sire Convoy Laddie		Br. No. 24a
							Dam Convoy Berr		Br. No. 24b
DAM	Reg. No. 191775	Sire Ch. Fayre Apollo	Reg. No. 187576	Sire Fayre Sonny	Reg. No. 179010 Breed No. 24		Sire Ch. Fayre Tristan		Br. No. 24
							Dam Fayre Yolanda		Br. No. 24a
		Shawn Sally	Breed No. 24 Colour. SP	Dam Fayre Funny Girl	Reg. No. 179110 Breed No. 24a		Sire Ch. Fayre Tristan		Br. No. 24
							Dam Fayre Belinda		Br. No. 24a
		Dam Shawn Sherry	Reg. No. 187651	Sire Ch. Cortex Pean	Reg. No. 179611 Breed No. 24		Sire Ch. Cortex Zulu		Br. No. 24
							Dam Cortex Pixie I		Br. No. 24
Breed No. 24 Colour. SP		Breed No. 24a Colour. BP		Dam Bushton Bluestone	Reg. No. 169702 Breed No. 24a		Sire Triton Triplex		Br. No. 24a
							Dam Dunripple Sue		Br. No. 24a

I certify that this Pedigree is correct to the best of my knowledge.
Signed. *Louise Cooper*   Date. 31/4/79

The 'pure' breed 2

be judged (see p231) – can be worked out and modified if necessary.

Some controlling bodies insist upon a set number of generations or individuals of a potential new breed or variety that must be bred before it will be considered for full recognition. This and the common requirement of a certain minimum number of breeders – in Britain the figures are 50 cats and 20 breeders – ensure adequate interest and support for the breed and are also a sensible safeguard against excessively close inbreeding (see below). When a breed does

achieve recognition, it is generally not eligible for championship or premiership classes until it has further proved itself.

Altogether, the provisions represent reasonable safeguards that are ultimately in the interest of breeders and their cats, although some potential new breeds may be lost from lack of interest while some experimental breeders fighting for recognition of their 'pet' projects may feel frustrated by what they see as bureaucracy and conservatism on the part of the governing bodies. In countries where there are several cat fancy organizations – notably the United States – the latter situation is less likely to occur, since one association may accept a breed that is not yet recognized by another; then, if the breed does prove itself, other associations will often accord it recognition.

Registration of kittens

An important aspect of pedigree cat breeding – and an important function of cat fancy governing bodies – is the registration of individual kittens, their pedigrees and their ownership. Although the details may vary, the procedure is broadly the same for all bodies in all countries. In each case, the object is to ensure that the kitten is an authentic member of the breed, and to have details of the date of birth, description, ancestry and ownership permanently recorded and available for reference whenever required. It is the responsibility of the

breeder to carry out initial registration formalities, but subsequent buyers and sellers have a responsibility to ensure that changes in ownership are registered.

General pedigree forms can be bought from cat fancy organizations or from private firms, either plain or pre-printed with the breeder's name, on which all the kitten's vital information can be written. There is normally space for four generations of parentage (although as many as seven may be required for registration in some cases), together with the breeder's

Creating breeds on scientific principles is well illustrated by the Colourpoint Longhair (Himalayan) **left** and the true-breeding blue-eyed Foreign White **opposite**.
The chequerboard diagrams on this page show the stages in creating the former. **1** A black Persian crossed with a Siamese results in black short-hairs carrying the recessive long-hair and Siamese genes. **2** Inbreeding the latter results on average in nine short- and three long-haired blacks to three short- and one long-haired Siamese-pattern cats. The body type

and owner's names and addresses. The name of the kitten is of course shown, together with its registration number, once registration is completed (see p224).

Kittens bred by a keen breeder will usually have a prefix name in front of their individual names. Such prefixes are also registered with governing bodies, thus preventing their use by any other breeder, and serve as identification of the strain to which the cat belongs. Should such a strain become famous for quality and consistency in breeding winning show animals, so will the prefix, and this will enhance the value of the pedigree. When a cat is bought by a second breeder, some cat fancy organizations permit the addition of a suffix unique to the subsequent owner. Thus a kitten whose individual name is Blue Boy might be bred by a breeder whose prefix is Shawn and sold to another breeder whose registered name is Argente. Its full registered name will be Shawn Blue Boy of Argente.

Finally, success in competition might entitle the owner to place a title such as Champion or Grand Champion in front of the name. Such titles do not become part of the permanent registered name of the cat, although they may appear in the pedigrees of its descendants.

Many countries, such as Britain, have a single governing and registration body, but others may have several, perhaps formed on regional lines or by dissidents who dis-

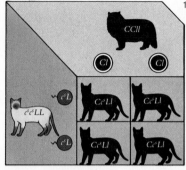

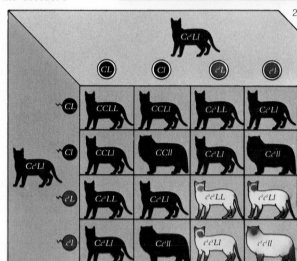

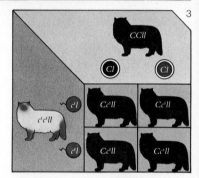

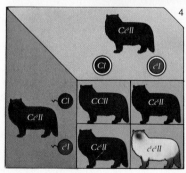

agree with the policies of a particular organization. The United States, for example, has nine associations. These vary in their aims and functions and (as already mentioned) in the breeds they recognize. Governing bodies generally lay down what breeds are permitted to appear in the pedigrees of the various breeds, and this

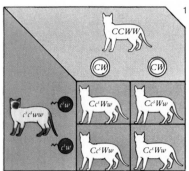

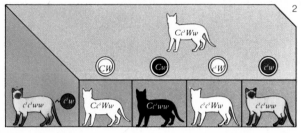

and hair quality of the last would be poor, however, being mid-way between Persian and Siamese. **3** Back-crossing to the original black Persian improves these, but further inbreeding **4** is needed to establish the Siamese pattern in a cat of Persian hair type and body conformation. The first step in producing the Foreign White this page **1** was to cross Siamese with short-haired whites, resulting in white cats with orange or blue eyes carrying the Siamese gene. **2** These were back-crossed to Siamese, resulting in whites of various

eye colours and (due to the underlying colour genotypes of the original whites) a variety of other colours (shown here as black). The whites were retained and those with blue eyes due to the Siamese (c^s) gene rather than the dominant white (W) identified by their

non-white progeny and in some cases by examination of their eyes. Further body-type improvement was made by additional back-crosses to seal point Siamese, the final outcome being a white cat of elegant type with consistently deep blue Siamese-like eyes.

crosses to the ancestral breeds are allowed in order to maintain or improve desirable features, a breed originating in the same way is termed a hybrid; examples include the Bombay, Himalayan and Tonkinese. The fourth classification is a mutation, as in the rex breeds and American Wirehair; this may be perpetuated by using the original natural breed in which the mutation arose as well as the mutant breed itself.

Principles of breeding
The establishment and/or maintenance of a breed of cats to a high degree of excellence demands careful attention to detail and great patience. Planning breeding pro-grammes on genetic principles in order to obtain desired colour varieties or other features governed by major genes (as explained in the preceding articles) is perhaps the easiest aspect. Far more diffi-cult, because it requires an appreciation of very subtle differences, is the general improvement of body type and other characteristics by selective breeding in order to reach the highest standard of show excellence. This involves assessing the quality of one's cats as objectively as possible and arranging the matings to the best advantage. (For the practical aspects of cat breeding, see chapter 5.)

If successful, however, the rewards for perseverance – in terms of satisfaction, if not financially – are considerable. In time, the quality of the breed will improve and certain individuals will emerge as outstand-ing specimens. If these are males and are placed at public stud, this will benefit the breed as a whole by handing on to future generations those combinations of genes that produced these superb specimens. There is no guarantee that their offspring will attain the quality of their sire (although they may well do so), but the important aspect is that the genes have been passed on and will benefit future generations.

One question that concerns many breeders is the degree of inbreeding – the mating of closely related cats, such as parents to offspring, brothers to sisters and cousins with each other – that is desirable. Many knowledgeable breeders – particu-larly those with above-average cats – do mate related cats with each other, and in this way the homozygosity, or *continued*

also may vary from one body to another. Where there is more than one registration body, a kitten may be registered with each provided that it complies with the various rules.

In North America, some associations, such as the CFA and the Canadian Cat Association (CCA), classify breeds into four groups for the purpose of registration. A so-called natural breed is supposedly based upon a natural population of cats, and all ancestors must be of the same breed as

the cat to be registered. Examples include the Persian, American Shorthair, Maine Coon and Siamese. Established breeds, although originating in crosses between two or more natural breeds or having differing breeds in an earlier part of the pedigree, may now be continued only by mating within the breed, crosses with the original ancestors no longer being per-mitted. Breeds in this group include the Birman, Burmese and Korat. At an earlier stage of its development, when back-

The closed stud system
1 A male is mated with a number of females to produce litters whose members are half-brothers and half-sisters to members of the others. **2** The outstanding male or males of this generation will

be the stud(s) for the next and the outstanding females the queens. These are mated, but only for strong reasons are full brothers and sisters mated, or parents mated with offspring. **3** Matings may, however, take place between a stud and

queen of different generations that are not too closely related. **4** A male may be placed at public stud, but **5** the queens are outcrossed only in order to counteract deterioration or to strengthen particular features.

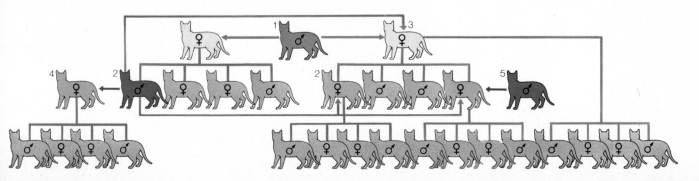

The 'pure' breed 3

'purity', of the strain is increased. In this manner, superior strains are evolved, often renowned for consistently breeding high-quality kittens. However, constant vigilance is necessary to guard against any deterioration of health or fertility.

Inbreeding is neither good nor bad in itself, but is a process that exposes both good and bad qualities in the stock. Of course, if the strain does carry a recessive mutant trait (which in the nature of things is more likely to be harmful than beneficial), then this is more likely to become quickly apparent with inbreeding – possibly a disaster in the short term, but exposure is in the long-term interests of the breed. Deleterious polygenes also tend to be recessive, and inbreeding can 'fix' these almost before the breeder is aware of it. The secret is not to inbreed too closely or too long. If inbreeding does seem to uncover more bad points than good, this is because there are so many of the former and they have been driven 'underground' by many generations of outbreeding. By inbreeding moderately and carefully selecting the better-quality offspring, a breeder can hope to fix the good points and lose the bad.

All things being equal, it is a sound policy always to mate the best to the best, even if this occasionally involves the close inbreeding of brother and sister or parent and offspring. But such matings should not be continued for too long, and cousin matings, which are less close, are generally preferable. Most half-blood relationships are harmless, in fact, but the other extreme – continual outcrossing to unrelated mates – can, unless carefully planned, merely nullify any progress that has been made in improving the strain, by breaking up a carefully built-up genetic constitution.

Many breeders consider that an ideal solution is the 'closed stud' system of mating. This centres on one or two stud males who are mated with a retinue of queens who are normally no closer than half-sisters. In each generation, the best kittens are chosen from each litter to provide breeding stock for the next generation. Except where two cats are of outstanding quality, close inbreeding is avoided, but outside matings are undertaken only to toms that are superior in quality to the stud and whose genetic background has been carefully checked.

A question of numbers

A popular breed of cats can weather ups and downs of quality and/or health and

LONG-HAIRED BREEDS

Angora (UK); Turkish Angora (US) Wedged head; body relatively slim. Tail long, bushy. Coat fine, long and silky.

Turkish (Van) Heavier build than Angora; shorter head. White, auburn head and tail markings.

Maine Coon Large, muscular cat. Medium-long head. Tail straight, long, bushy. Coat long, smooth, heavy; hair tufts on cheeks; large ruff. Norwegian Forest Cat is somewhat similar.

Persian (US); Longhair (UK) Round, short head; rounded, small ears. Body and legs short. Hair fluffy and very long. (In US, some colours are in Himalayans.)

Peke-faced Persian As Persian, but face resembles Pekingese dog, with very flat indented nose. Red or red tabby.

Colourpoint Longhair (UK); Himalayan (US) Persian-type body and coat; Siamese colouring. In US, some self (solid) colours of Persians (eg, chocolate, lilac) classed here or as Kashmir.

Birman Paws white; otherwise colouring like Himalayan/Colourpoint LH. Body slimmer and head longer. Hair straight, long and silky. Ragdoll may have similar colouring.

Balinese/Javanese Long-haired Siamese/Colorpoint SH. Wedged head; large ears. Slim; long legs. Long silky hair. Coloured points.

Cymric Long-haired Manx. Round head; full cheeks; rounded ears. Compact body; tailless; long hind legs. Medium-long coat.

Somali Long-haired Abyssinian. Medium-long body and head. Soft, dense coat. Ticked (agouti) colouring. Tail bushy.

SHORT-HAIRED BREEDS

British/European Shorthair Broad, round head; rounded ears. Compact, heavy and muscular body; broad chest; short, strong legs; relatively short, rounded tail.

Chartreux Similar to British/European Shorthair, but slightly larger. Short, dense greyish-blue coat with silvery sheen. In Europe, same as blue European Shorthair.

American/Domestic Shorthair Strong and muscular, but not so cobby or massive as British/European Shorthair. Head not so round. Somewhat longer legs and tail. Hard coat.

Exotic Shorthair 'Short-haired Persian'. Very round head with small rounded ears. Coat thick and dense, somewhat longer, softer and more plush than in other short-haired breeds.

American Wirehair As American SH, but coat coarse and wiry, like a wire-haired terrier.

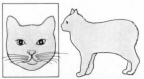

Manx Tail completely or partly absent. Short, rounded body with arched back and deep flanks; long hind legs. Head usually longer than British/European SH.

stamina, but there is a long-term danger for a breed whose population falls below a certain number. The number of widely used stud males is normally the important factor. If these are few, a large proportion of the kittens will be related to them, either directly or collaterally, and the process will be cumulative if the numbers do not rise. Just as too-close deliberate inbreeding can cause deterioration of a strain within a breed, so inbreeding due to small numbers can bring about the deterioration of a breed, the difference being that the latter is more insidious and less easy to repair. Deterioration of a strain can usually be rectified by an outcross to another strain superior in health, but this may be difficult, if not impossible, for a whole breed.

It is impossible to give a firm figure, but, as a guide, the number of active stud males

in a breed should not fall below about 12 to 14 per generation for many generations. Such a population of males gives an approximate rate of inbreeding of 1 per cent per generation. A smaller number gives a higher rate and should be regarded as dangerous. Remember that the figure is the number of actively used males; there is no safety in having 20 registered studs if more than half are scarcely utilized. Another point to watch is that, if the number of active stud cats varies from generation to generation, those with the fewest numbers will have a disproportionately large effect. A simple averaging may give a misleading optimistic picture.

What would be the consequences for a breed that had been exposed to enforced mild inbreeding for many generations? The breed would become increasingly homo-

genous – not a bad thing, one might think, especially if the quality is high. However, further improvement will become more difficult, or may cease altogether. If the breed cannot slip back, neither can it move forward. More insidious, there may be a slow fall in the average litter size, or the incidence of missed matings, or sterility, may be higher than among cats generally. The level of mortality may increase, because the breed will not have diversity of resistance to infections.

The breeding of superlative pure-bred cats is clearly beset with pitfalls for the unwary, but the modern breeder has far more information on basic cat genetics to guide him or her than any in the past. The result, perhaps, is to make the competition even keener – but the satisfaction to be gained from success even greater.

Japanese Bobtail Tail 5–8 cm (2–3 in) long, with hair fanned out like a rabbit's tail. Slender body with slim legs. Triangular face with high cheek-bones.

Scottish Fold Ears small and folded forwards and downwards, like a cap. Otherwise similar to American or British/European SH.

Abyssinian Lithe, muscular body with long head, but neither are so extreme as in Siamese. Long legs. Ticked (agouti) coat. Often some tabby markings on legs and tail. Usually warm brown or reddish. Often ear tufts.

Egyptian Mau Spotted tabby pattern (silver or bronze) with intricate face markings. Medium-size, intermediate-type body.

Ocicat Large spotted tabby. Moderately slim body; long legs. Abyssinian–Siamese cross.

Russian Blue Bright bluish-grey springy 'double' coat with silvery sheen. Unique head shape and 'look'. Green eyes.

Korat Silvery-blue coat with heavy silver sheen. Somewhat rounded, intermediate, like old-fashioned Siamese. Unique heart-shaped head; very large eyes.

Burmese Solid and muscular; moderately foreign body type but very rounded (especially in US). Round eyes and head. Coat glossy, satin-like. Often brown (sable) but other colours recognized by some associations (which in US may class them as Malayans).

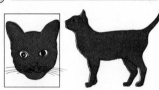

Bombay Dense black coat with sheen like patent leather. Burmese/American SH cross.

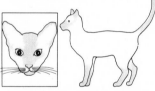

Siamese Extremely slim, elegant body with long legs and tail. Head an elongated wedge, often with no nose break at all. Large, pointed ears. Pale body with coloured points. (In US, some point colours are classified as Colorpoint Shorthairs.)

Colorpoint Shorthair Name in some American associations for Siamese with tabby (lynx), tortie or red point patterns/colours or their derivatives.

Tonkinese Intermediate in colouring and body type between Siamese and Burmese. Sometimes called light-phase Burmese.

Havana Brown Smooth brown coat. Intermediate foreign body type with unique muzzle shape. So-called Havana of UK is really brown Oriental Shorthair.

Oriental/Foreign Shorthair Same body and head shape as Siamese. Coat colours and patterns as found in British/European and American Shorthairs, etc – selfs (solids), tabbies, etc.

Cornish Rex Short, curly but soft coat. Foreign body type but not extreme. Strong hind legs. Sometimes simply called Rex.

Devon Rex Coat similar to Cornish Rex but shorter and slightly harsher. More foreign body type than Cornish, with extreme 'pixie'-like head.

Angoras and Turkish cats

The Angora is one of the most ancient breeds of cats, with its origins rooted in the history of its native Turkey. It is undoubtedly also one of the most beautiful, with its elegant body and long, silky coat. It was probably the first type of long-haired cat to reach Europe, yet until quite recently was completely overtaken both there and in North America by the much more powerfully built Persians.

The original Angoras

Although there have been suggestions that the Angora traces its descent from the manul, or Pallas's cat (*Felis manul*; see p15), most zoologists agree that fundamental differences between the two make this impossible. A more likely explanation is that the gene for long hair (see p43) mutated in – or spread to – a group of cats with the lithe body build known to cat breeders as foreign (see p41). Limited opportunities for breeding outside the group allowed the long-coat characteristic to become fixed, so that a true-breeding long-haired cat with foreign body build evolved.

When, in the 16th century, Angoras from Turkey were taken to France and England they were much admired, yet it was not until the mid-19th century that attempts were made to chronicle the differences between them and other long-coated cats coming from Persia and Russia. An English writer of 1868 described the Angora as 'a beautiful variety with silvery hair of fine texture generally longest on the neck but also on the tail'. But the breed had to compete with the Persians and Russians, and eventually the Persian became the preferred variety. Any resemblance to the Angora was frowned upon by cat fanciers. By the 20th century the breed was virtually unknown outside Turkey.

In their homeland, Angoras were (and still are) seen in many colours, each with its own descriptive name. Among these are *sarman* (red tabby), *teku* (silver tabby) and *Ankara kedi* (odd-eyed white). Other colours are brown tabby, black, red, tortie and white, and white. The whites are often deaf, as is the case with whites of most other breeds (see p31), but they are great favourites with tourists and there are some cat fanciers who claim that the white Angora is the only variety that is truly the pure native breed. It has been stated that the Ankara Zoo has a breeding programme for the recording and conservation of the pure white Angora, but this is discounted by others.

An interesting aspect of Angora history is that, while Angoras were named after the old city of Angora (now Ankara), there developed a true-breeding variety within the breed in the area of the great Lake Van. This is now known in Britain as the Turkish cat, though there and in some North American cat associations it is also called the Turkish Van. These cats are red and white (the British show standard describes the red colour as auburn), but with a coat pattern very rare in cats: The red colour is restricted to areas around the ears and on the tail. (This has come to be known as the Van pattern.) In their native region it is not only their beauty for which they are renowned but also reputedly for their habit of swimming in shallow pools and streams.

Angora and Turkish cats today

Although the Angoras of Turkey thrived in their homeland, they were extinct in the Western world until after World War II. But in the 1950s and 1960s, cats from Turkey were taken to North America, Sweden and Britain to form the foundation stock for the pedigree Turkish Angoras of North America and the European continent and Turkish cats of Britain.

The odd-eyed white Turkish Angora, known in its native country as the *Ankara kedi*, is one of the white varieties considered by some purists to be the only true Angoras. The CFA show standard for the breed states that it should give 'the impression of grace and flowing movement'.

In the United States, Turkish Angoras were recognized for full championship competition in the early 1970s, though until 1978 the largest association, the CFA, restricted competition to whites. Now, as in Europe, a wider range of colours – including black and blue solid (self) and smoke colours, tabbies and calico (tortie and white) – are recognized.

In Britain, the situation is different and somewhat confusing to outsiders. The Turkish cat is recognized for championship status only in red and white (as is the similar Turkish Van by some North American bodies). However, in 1977, a breed known as the Angora was given preliminary recognition in Britain. This is identical to the original cats of Turkey and North America, except that it is bred in the full range of colours (including chocolate and lilac) and that its voice bears a resemblance to that of the Siamese. It was in fact developed by a scientific breeding programme based on genetic principles, aiming to recreate the breed rather than rely on its reintroduction by importing cats from Turkey. The

main breeds involved in the programme were short-hairs of oriental type carrying the long-hair gene, and these cats are in fact related to many British-bred Balinese (whose body type is identical; see p64). The results were highly successful, with the result that the Angoras of Britain compare favourably with those of other countries.

The most obvious differences between Angora and Turkish cats and cats of the Persian breeds are seen in the quality of the coat, the shape of the head and the general body build. The Angora has a long, rather sinuous body, with a long pointed head and large ears. The Turkish is less foreign in build, and its head is wider and shorter, with smaller ears. But both are quite unlike the wider-headed, small-eared, sturdily built Persians, and both have the same silky long fur that (unlike the Persian's) is free from woolly undercoat and the tendency to tangle or knot.

Breeders of the recreated Angoras have been at pains to achieve the coat, conformation and other qualities of the breed known in its native Turkey, and those working with Turkish Angoras and the cats of Van have made every effort to preserve the original characteristics. The differences between the Van cats and the Angoras of other areas are probably the result of natural evolution in their homeland rather than manipulative breeding by Western cat fanciers. The Angoras and Turkish are natural breeds, and cat breeders are united in a desire to keep them so.

Personality and habits

The fact that Angoras have gentle dispositions was noted by a 19th-century writer, and is as true today as it was then. They are rather athletic in their play, and their kittens are precocious, opening their eyes earlier than those of the Persian breeds and indulging in mock fights while still in their kitten box. Females of the recreated Angora strain have proved very fertile, producing large litters, but the more normal litter size is about four. In summer they moult very heavily, so that in extreme cases they look almost like short-haired cats with fluffy tails. Yet they grow their winter coat very quickly indeed, and the lack of a fluffy undercoat makes them much easier to groom than Persians. Turkish cats are very similar to the Angoras in all these respects, and although there was once a time when they were renowned for their dislike of being handled by judges at shows, breeders have since then developed less highly strung strains. They and the Angoras both make very stylish and beautiful companions.

Buffon's plate of an Angora from his *Histoire Naturelle*, published in 1756, shows the same long, silky coat that is so admired today. The body type also is similar to that of contemporary cats. This example shows tabby markings.

Turkish Van kittens have auburn-red head and tail patches from birth, but the coat takes some time to develop the adult's luxuriant growth. This litter was raised by the breeder who introduced them from Turkey, where they are said to enjoy swimming in streams **below**.

A chocolate Angora stud male of the British breeding programme to recreate these cats is shown **right** at the age of about five years, when his coat has reached the peak of its development. The chocolate (chestnut) colour is not yet recognized in Turkish Angoras of North America.

The Maine Coon

The Maine Coon, or Maine Cat, is one of the oldest natural breeds of North America, and is generally regarded as a native of the state of Maine. There are a number of legends concerning its origin, a very popular (though biologically impossible) one being that it originated from matings between semi-wild domestic cats and racoons. This belief – bolstered by the bushy tail and the commonest colouring, a very racoon-like dark tabby – led to the adoption of the name Maine Coon. An attractive story presents an alternative theory of their origin: that Marie Antoinette, when planning to escape at the time of the French Revolution, sent her cats to be cared for in the United States until she could find an alternative home. More prosaically, most breeders today believe that the breed originated in crosses between early Angoras (probably introduced by New England seamen) and short-haired domestic cats.

Certainly Maine Coons were well established more than a century ago, and had evolved into a hardy, handsome breed of domestic cats, adept at keeping down the mouse population on New England farms. They had not only become rugged of coat and build, and tough enough to withstand even the hardest winters, but had also become one of the largest breeds physically – though it is doubtful if any ever reached the 18kg (40lb) sometimes quoted. Relatively tall and long-bodied, males commonly weigh up to 7kg (15lb), females rarely more than 5kg (11lb). The coat is long and flowing, being relatively heavy and shaggy, shorter on the shoulders and longer on the belly and tail. With their well-developed ruff offsetting the relatively long, square-muzzled head, Maine Coons are indeed handsome as well as strong cats.

First recorded in cat literature in 1861 with a mention of a black and white known as Captain Jenks of the Horse Marines, Maine Coons were popular competitors at early cat shows in Boston and New York, one winning at the 1895 Madison Square Gardens show. They declined as show cats with the arrival of the more flamboyant Persians from cat breeders in Britain, but as household pets they still reigned supreme in the north-eastern states. It is not hard to understand why these tough, agile, independent cats were thought to have wild racoon ancestry and why they were treasured as very special pets right through to the early 1950s, when cat fanciers began once more to pay attention to them, show them and record their pedigrees.

All along there had been a small core of breeders – albeit very few – who had persisted with the breed in spite of its unpopularity. Once pedigree records were established, Maine Coons once again became 'respectable', and cat lovers and breeders outside their native territory realized just how attractive they were. In 1967 a special show standard was accepted by the CCA, ACFA and ACA, but it was not until 1976 that the breed was also recognized by the CFA. A number have been sent overseas and are being bred, notably in West Germany.

Right through their history there has been no restriction, official or otherwise, on the patterns and colours acceptable in Maine Coons (with the sole exceptions of chocolate, lavender and Siamese-pattern). As a result, a wide range of colours are bred, including solids (selfs), bicolours, tortoiseshells, tabbies, tabby-torties (torbies) and shadeds. Undoubtedly, however, the brown tabby remains the most popular. Eye colours range through green, gold

The best-known Maine Coon is undoubtedly the brown classic (blotched) tabby, the pattern whose similarity to the racoon earnt the breed its name. Breeders of pedigree cats have worked hard to perfect the rich, warm brown illustrated **below**. The breed standard comments that the Maine Coon, being originally a working cat, is 'solid, rugged and can endure a harsh climate. A distinctive characersitic is its smooth, shaggy coat. With an essentially amiable disposition, it has adapted to varied environments.'

NORWEGIAN FOREST CAT

Bearing more than a passing resemblance to the Maine Coon, the Norwegian Forest Cat – or Norsk Skaukatt – is a uniquely Scandinavian breed, having evolved in the cold northern climate of Norway. Its origins are unknown, but (as with the Maine Coon) generations of living in the cold and wet gave it a heavy, weather-resistant coat. The woolly undercoat keeps the body warm, while the medium-long, glossy, hanging outer coat resists rain and snow. It has a full ruff. Necessity has also made it cautious, intelligent, quick and a good hunter. It is an extremely good climber, too, its strong claws enabling it not only to climb trees but even rocky slopes.

It was from this race of hardy outdoor cats – some semi-wild, some vermin-hunters on farms – that a group of breeders began to develop the pedigree breed as early as the 1930s. At least one was exhibited in Oslo before World War II, but the breed in fact goes back much farther than that. It is mentioned in Norse mythology, but the earliest written reference found so far by enthusiasts is in the Norwegian fairy tales that were gathered and written down between 1837 and 1852. There it is referred to as the fairy-cat, and is described as having a long, bushy tail. After the war, interest in the breed revived in the early 1970s, and it achieved championship status in FIFe in 1977. There are now more than 350 registered Forest Cats in Norway, and more abroad (especially in Sweden).

One respect in which the ideal show cat differs from the Maine Coon is that the back legs should be slightly longer than the front. Another is the double coat – which is permitted but not specified in the Maine Coon – but this is as trouble-free as its transatlantic cousin's. The only grooming needed is an occasional combing through. As with other long-hairs, however, the longest hair is shed once a year, leaving only the bushy tail to show that it is a long-haired cat. All colours are permitted. Good-natured and intelligent, Norwegian Forest Cats seem to enjoy human company. They can be extremely playful, but at the same time have a strong streak of independence.

A torbie and white Norwegian Forest Cat

Maine Coon colours virtually span the spectrum of possible shades. Shown here are a handshome red tabby and white **above**, the white emphasizing the well-developed ruff, and a shaded cameo (red shaded) kitten **above right**. The rather long head and bushy tail are characteristic of the breed.

and copper to blue; odd eyes are also permissible, and there is no restriction in the show standards on any combinations of coat and eye colour. In fact, these account for only 15 per cent of the points awarded by the judge at a show.

By far the most important features to judges are the head, body and coat. As already hinted, the Maine Coon is quite different in appearance from the Persian. The head is much longer, with high cheekbones and ears that are large, well tufted and wide at the base. The neck should be medium-long, the torso long and the chest broad. The legs are considerably longer than in a Persian, as is the tail. The closest

breed to the Maine Coon in appearance is probably the Norwegian Forest Cat (see above).

Maine Coons develop relatively slowly, and may not achieve their full size until they are about four years old. Many people consider them to be the perfect domestic pets, with their clown-like personality, amusing habits and tricks, and easily-groomed coat. Maine Coon litters are not normally very large, four kittens being the most to be expected and two or three more usual. Because of the variety of coat colours and patterns bred, many of the cats carry a variety of colour genes and every kitten in a litter may well be different.

Persian cats I

Bred in a profusion of colours, the Persians are an important part of the pedigree cat show scene, and are greatly prized by pet owners all over the world. Indeed, to many people they epitomize the pedigree cat, and in many countries fetch the highest prices of all breeds. They have a long and distinguished history in the cat fancy, appearing regularly in cat shows for over 100 years.

The long coat is produced by a recessive gene (symbolized *l*; see p43), and its most likely place of origin was Asia Minor. In a book published in 1876, long-haired cats were referred to as Asiatic cats, but they were first seen in Europe some 300 years earlier than this, probably having been first introduced into Italy and then to France. The first long-hairs seen in Britain were variously described as Angora (see p50) or French cats (the French generally being white), but gradually the tall-eared, rather rangy Angora body type went out of favour and the heavier, larger-headed but more compact body type of the French cats gained pre-eminence.

Other names given to long-hairs were Chinese, Indian and Russian, though it is impossible to say now whether these indicated true origins or were inventions intended to lend an air of mystery or exoticism to the cats. (The latter would seem to be the most likely in the case of the Chinese and Indian, at least.) However, as breeding continued towards the heavier body build and full, fine-textured long coat, they were known increasingly as Persians.

Although it is now many decades since the GCCF ruled that, in Britain, the cats be known simply as Longhairs (without a hyphen), most owners and breeders persist in referring to them as Persians. In North America, Persian is the official breed name, attractively classifying these cats separately from the long-haired cats of more foreign type, such as the Turkish Angoras, Balinese and Birmans. The only discordant note is struck by the CFA and some other North American associations refusing to recognize the chocolate and lilac solid (self) colours – which arose from Himalayan (Colourpoint Longhair; see p60) breeding programmes – as Persians; they are variously classified as solid-coloured Himalayans or as Kashmirs, but are nevertheless bred to the same standards for body type as Persians.

Another difference between British and American practice is that, in Britain, each variety of Longhair is regarded as a separate breed, with its own breed number, so that, for example, the Chinchilla has a breed status separate from that of the various self colours, tabbies, tortoiseshells and so on. In the United States, it represents just one variety within the Shaded division of Persians. In a sense, however, the British way recognizes the practical fact that body type does tend to differ slightly from one colour to another. This is not to say that the ideal varies – a massive, cobby body, low on the legs, with a broad, round head that has a short nose, full cheeks, large round eyes and small rounded ears, and a long, silky and full coat. But slight differences are noticeable on the show bench – particularly in the head shape and legs – the self blues and blacks tending to come closest to the ideals set out in the standard.

Early show Persians
When Harrison Weir first set out standards for cat varieties of the 19th century, the colours he described

in Persians were white, black, blue, grey, red and 'any other' self colour, with brown, blue, silver, and light grey and white for tabbies. Comparing these colours with those seen today, it is interesting to note that although chocolates, lilacs, creams and a wide range of tortoiseshell colours that are recognized today were not described, there no longer exist both blue and grey. It is quite probable that the blues and greys were both genetically blue (see p29), but there is the possibility that some of the early cats had genes producing a different form of blue-grey. The light grey and white tabbies were probably blue-silvers, but the most intriguing variety of all is the blue tabby, which is described by other writers of the time as having black markings on a blue ground – quite different from the blue tabbies of today.

Whatever their colours – and, with very little understanding of coat colour inheritance, the 19th-century breeders interbred their long-haired cats without much regard for colour, pattern or coat type – the breed gradually evolved to be very different from its ancestors and ideally suited to Victorian sensibilities and taste. Royal patronage was given to the breed by Queen Victoria, who owned two blues, and the Prince of Wales (who became Edward VII) is

A blue Persian queen – perhaps the most popular colour in Persians – is seen **above** with her cream male offspring, the result of a cross to a red or cream male. Most breeders mate blue to blue, breeding all blue kittens, but creams **above right** represent a triumph of selective breeding in perfecting a coat free of tabby markings. The chocolate **opposite centre** and lilac **far right** are among the newest colours, the former being particularly difficult to produce with good, dense colour that is free of shading.

An early chinchilla shows the slight tabby markings typical at the time.

recorded as having donated and presented a special prize for Persians at a popular cat show of the time.

By 1901 the colours recognized in Persians in Britain were black, white, blue, orange, cream, sable, smoke, tabby, spotted, chinchilla, tortoiseshell, bicolour and tricolour. The orange Persians were the ancestors of the red selfs and red tabbies, and the tricolours were probably tortie and whites. The sables cannot be easily identified, but were described in a 1903 book as 'a kind of brown tabby ... These cats have not the regular tabby markings, but the two colours are blended one with another, the lighter sable tone predominating' – which sound like the forerunners of today's shaded goldens (see p35). True spotted Persians were described at the same time as being rare or non-existent; almost all had some tabby lines and rings.

Persians were introduced to North America from Europe towards the end of the 19th century, and were soon being bred and shown successfully. By the turn of the century they were eclipsing the 'home-bred' Maine Coons (see p52) at shows. American breeders took the standards achieved by the British as their starting point, and went on to evolve a breed type outstanding for its compact cobby build and profuse coat. Today it is said that the British prefer a Persian with the older – that is, less stocky – type more than do Americans.

The self (solid) colours
This group today includes the whites, blacks, blues, chocolates, lilacs, reds and creams. Although the blacks are one of the oldest varieties of all (they are listed as breed number 1 in Britain) there were only 17 individuals listed when, in 1910, the GCCF came into being. Once World War I was over the Persians, including the blacks, flourished, but World War II nearly halted cat breeding altogether in Britain, and American breeders took over the premier position. They produced many fine blacks that are remembered even today. Only in more recent years have the blacks increased in numbers to any great extent in Britain, and now some very fine exhibits can be seen, with dense shining coats contrasting superbly with deep copper eyes.

Whites were among the very first   /continued

The red self Persian is probably the most difficult colour to breed to perfection, as the standards require it to be free from tabby markings – a practical impossibility due to the way in which the orange gene operates. As the painting **below** shows, a good specimen is massive and spectacular, and is highly prized by cat fanciers (see also p 231).

Persian cats 2

A red classic tabby Peke-faced Persian

THE PEKE-FACED PERSIAN

Recognized for competition as separate varieties only in the United States and Canada, these cats are amusingly but aptly named and much admired. Only bred in red and red tabby versions, the body colouring and general characteristics are the same as for the normal Persian except for the very short nose, with an indentation between the eyes. As the CFA show standard puts it, 'the head should resemble as much as possible that of the Pekingese dog from which it gets its name . . . There should be a decidedly wrinkled muzzle.' Breeders aim, by selective breeding, for very large, wide-apart, round eyes and just enough of the required facial characteristics to avoid breathing difficulties. Unfortunately, however, Peke-faced Persians are sometimes prone to running eyes due to blockages or distortions of the ducts that drain tears into the nose.

The silver tabby has always been prized among Persians for its beauty, and has reached a high standard in recent years. The extreme contrast between the black patterned areas and the silver agouti ground gives a striking effect.

long-haired cats in Europe and were renowned then, as now, for their blue eyes. In Britain they were known as French cats, but they puzzled their owners with their unresponsiveness until it was realized that many of them were deaf. Early writers suggested that the deafness was linked with albinism, but geneticists have shown that true blue-eyed albinos are not deaf and that deafness is associated with the dominant white gene (see p40); all present-day Persians are of this type. Because the Persians with the best blue eye colour were often those with the more Angora-type bodies, matings were made to cobbier cats with coloured coats. As a result, comparatively large numbers of orange-eyed and odd-eyed whites were born. Today, all three are recognized.

Due to the way the dominant white gene acts, some white Persian kittens show small clusters of coloured hair on their heads. This reveals the underlying colour genotype, giving a glimpse of what the kitten would have looked like had it not been 'whitewashed'. Many breeders believe that the presence of a head smudge indicates perfect hearing, but this is not always true. It is also believed by some that combining the Siamese gene with the dominant white (as in the Foreign White; see p47) will stop head smudging, but this too has been disproved. Very few white Persians have in fact been bred with the Siamese-blue eyes of the Foreign White; most breeders work with the standard eye colours,

selecting against deafness by judicious outcrosses to coloured Persians and neutering deaf kittens.

Among the coloured Persian varieties, the blue has always been one of the most popular (a trend set perhaps by Queen Victoria), and probably for this reason has attained the type and coat closest to the ideal. At early shows, blues, blue tabbies and blue and whites were classified together, but nowadays blue tabbies are rarely seen – even in the United States, where they have full championship status. Breeders generally prefer the lighter shades of blue in the Persian, and when combined with a deep orange or copper eye colour this makes a very attractive cat. Like other self colours, blues tend to have a scattering of white hairs, particularly in kittenhood, but breeders select against pedigrees where this is a recurring feature. Other difficulties are caused by shady coats – that is, where the tone shades to a darker colour at the ends of the hairs or ghost tabby markings are visible. This is particularly noticeable on the frill, and is heavily penalized by judges; again breeders select against it. Like most pale self or solid coated breeds, blue Persian kittens tend to show ghost tabby markings, but these normally disappear as the adult hair grows.

The rarest of all the solid Persian varieties is the red or red self for, although the show standard stipulates 'without markings', this is in practice impossible, as is explained on page 30. Nevertheless, selective

Tortoiseshell Persians are magnificent animals whether in the striking randomly patterned red and black type **above** or in the more subtle tones of the dilute version, the blue-cream **above right**. This blue-cream is an American example showing the irregularly blotched type favoured there; British cat fanciers prefer a more mingled pattern of colours.

breeding can result in cats very near to the standard, and the nature of the Persian coat helps to obscure some of the tabbiness. (Some geneticists have suggested that introducing the Abyssinian ticked tabby pattern [see p32] would help this quest.) In early cat shows, both the marked and relatively unmarked reds were shown in the same classes and were described as orange. Even before World War I, however, red or orange selfs and tabbies were placed in separate classes, and soon afterwards the name orange was dropped altogether.

The cream – a lovely buff-cream-coloured powder-puff cat – is the descendant of the 'fawn' variety of the early Angoras, but records from early cat shows indicate that they were not very popular. They only became more numerous when breeders

The dilute calico – otherwise known as the blue-cream and white – is a very attractive cat, the subdued colours suiting very well the soft, fluffy coat of a good-quality Persian.

The Persian Van bicolour – in this case a red and white example – is a recently recognized variety in North America. It combines the body and coat type of the Persian with the colour pattern seen in the Turkish Van. (see p 50).

began mating reds and tortoiseshells to blues in order to improve type. In Britain, most creams were neutered and sold as pets not for exhibition. But in the United States it was a different story, and cream Persians were much admired as a competition breed. As a result, they evolved into a variety of excellent type and sound coat long before any real progress was made in Britain. Creams are now popular on both sides of the Atlantic and – although tabby markings, a reddish-tinged coat and pale undercoat were frequent faults in many of the older cats – the winning cream Persians of today are very close to the standard laid down for judges.

The possibility of a chocolate Persian did not occur to early breeders, and it was only after the breeding programmes for Colourpoints (Himalayans; see p60) were started that cat fanciers took the idea of solid chocolate cats as a serious possibility. Genetically there was no problem producing these – they appeared alongside chocolate point long-hairs in early litters – but the coat and body were poor by Persian standards. Also, the chocolate gene is renowned for fading and bleaching, so that the pioneer breeders had a long and uphill task to produce good colour, coat and type and to gain recognition. (As already mentioned, they are classed as Himalayans or as Kashmirs by some North American associations.) Since a number of blue and blue point cats were used as outcrosses in the choco-

late breeding programme, lilac self cats were also produced. They too are now recognized for competition on the same basis.

Other colours and patterns

Tabbies have always been bred by cat lovers, and were included in the classification for the famous 1871 cat show, although silvers were much more popular than other tabby colours in the early years. In North America today both the mackerel (lined) and classic (blotched) tabby patterns are recognized in Persians, as in many other breeds. In Britain, however, only the classic type competes in shows (though it is simply termed tabby). They are bred in most of the basic colours, the oldest varieties still being shown regularly being silvers, browns (that is, genetically blacks) and reds. The blue tabby, described at the earliest cat shows, is no longer recognized in Britain, though it is included in American show standards. A more recent addition is the cameo tabby – a red silver (see p34). Tabby Persian kittens are born with relatively short coats so that the markings appear very heavy, only becoming more broken and lighter as the coat grows longer.

The tortoiseshell colouring is seen at its best in the Persian, for the pattern becomes diffused by the fall of the long coat, giving a most attractive appearance. The first torties classified were the standard black and reds, produced when red Persians were /continued

Persian cats 3

mated to blacks to improve type. As reds were also mated to blues it was not long before blue torties, or blue-creams, appeared. The tortie and whites – once named chintz cats and still known as calicoes in the United States – certainly do have that bright chintzy effect of the early 20th-century printed calicoes. The dilute (blue-cream and white) versions are also recognized, and in all types of torties judges like to see the red or cream areas free of tabby markings. For this reason, breeders generally use even-coloured red, cream or bicoloured stock, and these usually are non-agouti in genotype (see p29). Sometimes, however, an agouti (tabby) genotype crops up, and results in a patched tabby (tabby tortie or torbie) kitten, with tabby areas instead of black. These are recognized in North America but not Britain; however, a few brown patched tabbies are registered in Britain and shown as normal brown tabbies when the red areas are minimal.

Originally known as magpie cats, the bicolours were popular only in short-hairs at first, but once the tortie and white Persians were being bred bicolours were bound to appear. In Britain they were recog-

nized in all the basic colours in 1966, and recognition soon followed in the United States. In the normal type, the ideal is based upon the Dutch coat pattern well known in fancy-bred rabbits and mice – with the white areas confined to the underparts – but this is extremely difficult to achieve in practice, and some flexibility is allowed. A distinct variant – though genetically the same – is the Van pattern (see pp40 and 50), recognized only in North America for both bicolours and calico Persians.

The smoke Persian is a magnificent animal that was first granted its own breed classes in Britain in 1893. But it was always rare, and the first GCCF stud book (1912) listed only 18. By the end of World War II they were virtually non-existent in Britain, but they had always had a strong following in North America and soon recovered in Britain. Young smoke Persians look almost like solid colours except for the silver tracery – 'clown lines' – where the agouti areas would appear in a tabby. Not all kittens show these lines to any marked degree, but those that do generally develop the most striking adult coat. Some smokes – known as overlaps – never develop the silvery undercoat and only prove to be genetically smokes when bred. When smokes are judged, any tabby markings or clown lines on the head or paws are penalized; although a coat free of marks is often achieved – or nearly so – in black smokes, this is much more difficult in blues or reds.

The shaded and tipped Persian varieties developed out of the early silver tabbies and possibly the sables, the best-known member of the group being the silver chinchilla (often called simply the chinchilla). This was considered to be the ideal by the early breeders, and evolved from cats with unsound tabby coats mated to lightly tipped smokes. One of the most famous early chinchillas was called Silver Lambkin,

Smoke Persians are dramatic in effect and dominate the show scene, often being among the top winners. The full smoke effect is seen only in the adult, but 'clown lines' indicate kittens with the greatest potential. Shown here are an adult black smoke with black and blue smoke kittens, from a cross with a black smoke carrying the dilute gene.

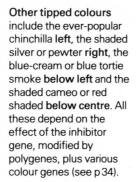

Other tipped colours include the ever-popular chinchilla **left**, the shaded silver or pewter **right**, the blue-cream or blue tortie smoke **below left** and the shaded cameo or red shaded **below centre**. All these depend on the effect of the inhibitor gene, modified by polygenes, plus various colour genes (see p 34).

and it seems possible from contemporary descriptions that he gave rise to both silver and golden kittens (see p 35). The paler silver varieties were the aim of breeders of the time, and the goldens were ignored until quite recently. Some breeders have suggested that the emergence of the golden Persians is the result of 'illegal' matings between chinchillas and solid-coloured Persians; although this could certainly result in the birth of golden kittens, the early breed records show that both types have a long history. Today, silver chinchillas are recognized only in black, red and black/red tortoiseshell versions (termed chinchilla, shell cameo and shell tortoiseshell respectively), and golden chinchillas only in black (although the American standard allows for the black to be reduced to seal-brown). Future breeding of silver and golden chinchillas in other basic colours is an obvious possibility.

Shaded silvers (termed in Britain pewters) and shaded goldens are very similar to the chinchillas, but the degree of tipping, though variable, is generally increased so that the general effect is much darker. Kittens, with their shorter coats, are sometimes so dark as to be mistakable for silver or brown tabbies. In the United States, the shaded silver is recognized under that name as a black tipped cat (with green or blue–green eyes), and in red and tortoiseshell versions (called shaded cameo and shaded tortoiseshell), but in Britain only the black versions are recognized (as pewters), with orange or copper eyes. As with the

golden chinchilla, the shaded golden Persian is recognized only in a black version, and represents one of the most recent varieties of the breed.

Breed characteristics
The Persians are renowned for their placid, gentle temperament and for their aptitude for adjusting to any new environment, making them ideal exhibition cats. They have quiet, melodious voices – at least, compared to that of a Siamese, say – and, although not usually shy, tend to be undemonstrative. Persian queens usually make good mothers, producing smaller litters than the foreign breeds; two to three kittens is the average litter size.

The kittens are born with a relatively short coat – even to the extent that cross-bred long-hairs (so-called 'three-quarter' length) may be indistinguishable at first from true long-hairs – but by the age of six weeks the glorious long coat begins to develop and gentle grooming can be started. The full adult coat often does not develop until the second annual moult, when the longest hairs are shed and the cat looks for a few weeks quite short-haired. The adult Persian requires daily grooming, whether you are preparing it for a show or not, for tangles soon develop in the fine, light hair. But this routine, far from being arduous, is enjoyed by the cat and is often instrumental in cementing the special cat/owner relationship for which the Persian breed and its owners are well known.

The shaded golden is different genetically from the other tipped colours seen in Persians (see p 35). Although it is clear from early literature that some of the early chinchillas and shaded cats were golden, the variety is regarded by cat fanciers as 'new'.

Himalayans (Colourpoint Longhairs)

This attractive man-made breed was synthesized firstly during breeding experiments to solve problems in cat genetics, and then as a deliberate programme to establish a Siamese-patterned cat of Persian coat and body type. Although British and American breeders have always agreed on this aim, there has been disagreement over name and status. In North America the breed is known as the Himalayan (a name used for this colour pattern in many other fancy-bred small livestock) and, except in one association, is classified as a separate long-haired breed. Until 1960, only Himalayan-to-Himalayan matings were permitted, but in order to improve body type back-crosses to Persians were then re-allowed. Today, most associations allow such back-crosses but continue to regard the breed as distinct from the Persian, so that solid-coloured cats derived from it (such as chocolates and lilacs) are classified as solid-coloured Himalayans rather than as Persians (see p 54). In Britain and most other countries, the breed is considered to be a colour variety of the Persian and is known as the Colourpoint Longhair. For a short time the name Khmer was used on the continent of Europe, but this name was dropped following recognition by the GCCF as the Colourpoint in 1955.

Origins and history

Crosses between Siamese and long-haired cats were first made deliberately by a Swedish geneticist in 1924, but in the 1930s two Harvard Medical School workers – one of them a scientifically-minded cat breeder – decided that more breeding, this time with cats of known pedigree, was necessary to establish the inheritance of certain characteristics. They mated Siamese with smoke, silver tabby and black Persians, producing a number of short-haired kittens. Two of these were mated to produce a long-haired black female who, when mated to her sire, gave birth to Debutante – the first pointed long-hair.

This cat was born in the United States in 1935, the same year that an experimental breeders' club was started in Britain with the intention of making similar matings. It had taken five years to achieve Debutante, but as the Harvard workers' aim had been to increase knowledge of genetics rather than to establish a new pedigree breed, they were content to conclude their work at that stage. By the standards of the British experimental breeders, Debutante was very Siamese-like in shape; they hoped to produce a truly Persian cat with Siamese colouring. During the time the Harvard research was going on, other American breeders are known to have shared their interest, and it has been suggested that the name Himalayan was proposed by them. Yet interest in them waned until 1950, when several breeders started breeding programmes towards this end.

Meanwhile, in Britain the club for experimental breeders continued and in 1947 a lady approached a well-known breeder with the request that he accept her long-haired Siamese-patterned queen to one of his Siamese studs. The breeder later wrote: 'When I saw this queen I was astonished at her beauty. Apart from her colouring she possessed practically no Siamese characteristics and was reasonably Persian in type.' The queen was of unknown pedigree, but eventually joined this breeder's cattery and inspired the whole of his breeding programmes over the next eight years. The programme of crosses and back-crosses involved in establishing the Colourpoint is outlined on page 46.

An early Colourpoint is seen **below** at the age of eight months in 1958, just three months after the breed was granted recognition in Britain. This kitten was raised by the original British breeder of Colourpoints, and several more years of selective breeding were needed to approach the ideal Persian-like body type.

Colourpoint Longhairs or Himalayans are bred in Europe and North America to exactly the same body type standards as Persians, but have Siamese-like coloured points. Shown here are a chocolate point (whose body colour should be ivory) and a tortie point (with cream body colour).

Although the early pedigrees included well-known Persians, the current GCCF rules for recognizing new breeds required three generations of like-to-like matings. This involved hundreds of cats and a great deal more inbreeding than would otherwise have been desired. So when recognition was achieved in 1955 no one knew more than the breeders themselves that outcrosses to improve type and coat were essential. Thus, after eight years of preliminary breeding to achieve varietal status, a further ten years or more were to elapse before the originators could be satisfied that their aim had been achieved – though top show success came only three years after recognition when a Colourpoint won an award for the best long-haired kitten at the 1958 Kensington Kitten and Neuter Cat Club show.

The breeding of pedigree Himalayans began in the United States in 1950, as already mentioned, but the breeders were cautious of exhibiting their cats before they considered the quality to be good enough. As a result few cat lovers knew anything about the new breed until 1957, when two cats were exhibited in San Diego. They caused a near-sensation, and a pair of kittens were presented to the president of the newly-formed ACFA – a breeder of Siamese – so that they could be shown to members of the association's council to support a request for breed status. The council saw the kittens and voted 15 to 1 in favour of recognition. The CFA followed the ACFA's lead later the same year, and by 1961 all the major American associations recognized the Himalayan.

The breed today

Some North American associations today recognize more colours in Himalayans than others. Apart from the solid chocolates and lilacs regarded as Himalayans in some, the generally accepted colours are seal point, blue point, chocolate point, lilac point, flame (or red) point, all colours of tortie point (including blue-cream point) and all colours of tabby (lynx) point. In Britain, all the solid point colours mentioned above are recognized, plus cream point and all colours of tortie point. Breeders are working hard to perfect tabby points, and once the genetics of shaded silver and golden cats becomes better understood by breeders a wealth of other colour varieties are likely.

Although it is only one of several Siamese-patterned long-haired breeds, the Colourpoint/Himalayan is instantly recognizable with its wide head, small ears, short legs and tail, short nose and soft silky coat. Dense points and pale body colour are regarded as essential by judges, but the long coat prevents them ever developing quite the same density of point colour as found in Siamese. This is because the Siamese effect is temperature-dependent and even the short hair on the mask of a Colourpoint/Himalayan is longer and traps more warm air than the flat-lying short hair of the Siamese. Although this weakens the point colour, it does make a pale body colour easier to achieve than in Siamese.

Most breeders agree that it is desirable to breed cats with really deep blue eyes, but that this is very hard to achieve. It has been suggested that the deep blue eye colour of the Siamese is controlled by genes which are incompletely linked with those determining the long, straight nose. But this theory has not found favour with geneticists, who usually recommend improvement by selective breeding.

Breed characteristics

In temperament, cats of this breed vary just as much as do those of any other, but the general behaviour pattern can be described as combining the qualities of the Siamese and the Persian. One very well-known breeder has been extensively quoted as saying that Colourpoints/Himalayans are much more enterprising than the solid-coloured Persians and that they provide a rest cure for owners who have previously endured the domineering ways and the boisterous and violent affections of the Siamese.

Females may call as early as eight months – somewhat earlier than with most Persians, and betraying something of their Siamese ancestry – and have been known successfully to rear litters that young; but breeders normally prefer to delay the first litter until the queen is at least a year old. There are, however, exceptions, and some queens – later to become very good 'broods' – have delayed their first call until nearly two years of age. Males are not normally ready to sire until they are about 18 months old, and in general are slow to mature.

As with Persians, litters are much smaller than those of the Siamese and related breeds, with two or three being usual and four being considered ideal. At birth the kittens have fluffy but not long hair, and are uniformly creamy-white in colour. The point colour begins to appear in a few days, being first visible as a thin line at the edge of the ears and then on the nose leather, paw pads and tail. Although some kittens have fluffier coats than others, none look really long-haired and the age at which the adult coat first starts to grow is variable. At maturity the ideal cat has a coat some 12 cm (5 in) long.

Recognized colours of Colourpoints/Himalayans span virtually all those allowed in Siamese (including most of those classed in North America in Colorpoint Shorthairs). Shown here are two of the oldest colours – seal point **top left** (showing excellent eye colour and contrast between points and body) and the much more subtly toned blue point **top right** – plus two newer ones: red (flame) point **above right** and seal tabby (lynx) point **above**.

The Birman

Also known as the Sacred Cat of Burma, the Birman is truly a cat of mystery, for more than 50 years after its first acceptance as a pedigree breed (in France in 1925) there remains uncertainty about its real origin. Some say that it truly originated in south-east Asia, others that it is a concoction of French breeders, but what cannot be doubted is that it is a strikingly majestic and unusual breed.

Despite the similarity of names, the Birman has no connection with the Burmese (see p82). With its pale-coloured body, dark points (mask, ears, tail and legs) and long coat, it bears a superficial resemblance to the Himalayan (Colourpoint Longhair; see p60). But one feature sets it firmly apart: the white 'gloves' on its paws, possibly due to a recessive white spotting gene (see p39). Its coat is less fluffy than a Himalayan's – it is silky, and more like that of a Turkish

those of the goddess. Its legs turned brown, except where the feet rested on its master, there they remained white. The transformation inspired the other priests to drive the raiders off, but seven days later Sinh also died, carrying with it into paradise the soul of Mun-Ha. The next morning all the other white cats of the temple had undergone the same transformation as Sinh. From then on the priests guarded their sacred golden cats, believing them to have custody of the souls of the priests.

The original Birmans of France are said to have been a gift from the priests of a new temple of Lao-Tsun in the mountains of Tibet. Two cats were reputedly sent to France, one – a male – dying in transit. The female, already pregnant, is said to have survived and become the founder of the pedigree Birman breed of Europe. It is intriguing that when,

Angora in length and texture – and the cat does not have the cobby, Persian-type body. It is low on the legs, but longer in both body and head, with a longer nose and larger ears. The eyes – a beautiful sapphire-blue – are generally deeper in colour than those achieved in Himalayans. The tail is bushy.

The attractive and unusual colouring of the Birman is the subject of an equally attractive legend set in Burma. The story goes that, before the time of Buddha, the Khmer people built beautiful temples to honour their gods – principally the god Song-Hyo and the goddess Tsun-Kyan-Kse. One of these temples was the Temple of Lao-Tsun, where a golden figure of the goddess, with sapphire eyes, was kept – and also 100 pure white cats. One of these was Sinh, the companion of an old priest, Mun-Ha, whose golden beard was said to have been braided by Song-Hyo himself.

One night, Thai raiders attacked the temple, killing Mun-Ha as he knelt before the figure of the goddess. Immediately the cat Sinh jumped on the body of its master and faced the goddess. The priest's soul entered the cat, and as it did so the white hair of its body became golden – like the goddess, or like the old priest's beard, according to different versions of the story – and its eyes became sapphire-blue like

in 1960, a pair of 'Tibetan temple' kittens were given to a North American cat lover, they had colouring identical to the Birman and were accompanied by the same legend – even down to the 100 temple cats. Yet there are breeders who maintain that the whole story, while fascinating, is a fabrication, the breed being produced in France itself by matings between Siamese and long-haired black and white cats. Certainly, cats looking like Birmans have occurred as the result of accidental matings.

Whatever its true origin, the Birman is a fascinating variety which became very successful in France until World War II decimated the feline population. After the war the breed was again reduced to two individuals, and it was a long time before it could recover fully. Birmans were first taken to England from France in the early 1960s, and were accepted for Championship competition in 1966. The CFA recognized them in North America in 1967. The GCCF in Britain recognizes only seal and blue point colourings, but the CFA also allows chocolate and lilac point (see p36). Breeders are also raising cats with the other point colourings, however, including red (flame), tortoiseshell and various tabby points. Nevertheless, some purists claim that only blue and seal are the true Birman colours.

A blue point Birman, one of the original two colours (with seal point) introduced by French breeders in the 1920s, and still the only colours universally recognized. FIFe on the European continent also recognizes chocolate, and the CFA and other American bodies both chocolate and lilac. All standards specify white 'gloves' on all four paws. On the hind paws these should extend up the back of the hock to a point known in North America as the 'laces'.

The Birman's body is large and low on the legs, but longer than that of a Persian or Himalayan (Colourpoint Longhair). This is another blue point, bred in the United States, where the body colour is required to be a colder, bluish-white tone, rather than the more golden shade preferred in Europe. The coat is silkier and less full than a Persian's; the neck ruff is a characteristic of the breed in North America.

Seal point kittens show their coloured points and gloves clearly at a young age, though the adult coat and the full depth of eye colour take much longer to develop.

Birmans are moderate in temperament: less placid than Persians but less highly strung than Siamese. They are precocious cats, often being ready to mate as early as seven months. Litters normally contain three to five kittens, which are born almost white. Within a few days the coloured points become discernible, however, as a hint of colour at the edge of the ears and on the tail. When they first open the eyes are baby-blue, but they develop gradually into the deeper adult colour. Birmans remain relatively uncommon, but they have a widespread and increasing circle of admirers.

In the United States, some breeders have produced short-haired Birman-pattern cats known as Snow-Shoe Cats or Silver Laces. They are recognized by one or two of the smaller associations, but they have never become really popular.

THE RAGDOLL

Supposedly originating with a white Persian queen who had been injured in a road accident, the Ragdoll is sometimes mistakenly confused with the Birman. It does have coloured points – which may be seal, blue, chocolate or lilac – and may have white on the head, body and legs (when it is known as bicolour), white on the abdomen and feet (mitted) or no white at all (colourpoint). The body build, however, is heavier than that of a Birman.

Ragdolls' alleged inability to feel pain or fear, or to fight other animals, is claimed to be a direct result of the original queen's accident. Other breeders and geneticists dispute this, as it goes against all genetic principles (see p23), and state that the docile temperament could be purely the result of selective breeding among highly domesticated animals. They also point out that all the varieties known as Ragdolls could be produced by a white queen if her mate carried the Siamese and long-hair genes and if either of them also carried the white spotting (piebald) gene (see p39). (White spotting could be present, undetected, in a white Persian.)

There remains a great deal of controversy over this breed, both its origin and validity being questioned. The few cats that exist are mainly in California, and much work will be necessary

A lilac and white bicolour Ragdoll

The Snow-Shoe Cat is a rarity even in North America and non-existent elsewhere. This example shows the seal point colouring and white gloves well, but the head is longer than would be considered desirable in a Birman – probably due to the influence of the short-haired breeds that must have helped create it.

before most breeders and cat fanciers will regard it as fully established. By the late 1970s only a few of the cat registration bodies in North America had given it recognition.

The Balinese

The Balinese got its name because its svelte lines and grace of movement – emphasized by the flow of its silky long coat – reminded one of its pioneer breeders of Balinese dancers. The choice of name was also a happy one in that it evokes echoes of the Siamese, whose colour pattern and body type it shares, but in fact the breed has nothing to do with the island of Bali. Rather more prosaically, it was developed by breeders in the United States.

For many years, long-haired kittens had appeared from time to time in litters of particular Siamese bloodlines. They had been generally regarded by cat fanciers as 'faulty', since the long hair disqualified them from show as Siamese, but in the 1940s two breeders in California and New York began to work towards gaining recognition for these cats as a separate breed. Because the gene producing long hair (l; see p43) is inherited in a recessive manner, any 'long-haired Siamese' must be homozygous (true-breeding) for long hair. This means that it must carry two of the long-hair genes, and the progeny from matings between two such cats will all be long-haired. As the numbers of the variety grew, so did their admirers, but it was not until 1970 that the CFA, the largest North American cat association, recognized the Balinese for championship competition, and then only in the four main Siamese coat colours. (Others have been allowed to compete since 1980 as Javanese; see below.) The Balinese is now recognized by all North American associations, but at the end of the 1970s British breeders were still striving to gain full recognition from the GCCF.

The ideal Balinese resembles the Siamese in every way except for the long coat. Judges look for a fine-boned, sleek body, with a long wedge-shaped head and deep blue eyes. The coat is quite different from the thick, fluffy coat of the Persian and related breeds; it has no woolly undercoat, and the hairs lie more or less flat along the body. The long tail has a plumed appearance. (As with Siamese, any squint or kink in the tail is disallowed.) Although the Siamese-pattern colouring is similar to that of the Himalayan (Colourpoint Longhair; see p60), the latter is a quite different cat, with the body type, coat and temperament of the Persian. A closer comparison would be with the Birman (see p62), but this is not so lithe and elegant, and also has white paws that would be heavily penalized by a judge if seen in a Balinese.

The early Siamese from which the Balinese were developed were those of a type popular in the earlier days of cat shows, with a heavier body structure and shorter head than is favoured today. As a result, some Balinese bred today still include the features of their ancestors. In order to 'correct' these, and also sometimes to introduce new colours, breeders outcross some Balinese to Siamese and then intermate the progeny. A Balinese mated to a Siamese normally produces short-haired Siamese-pattern kittens, but these have a slightly fuller 'plush' coat, and cannot be

A lilac point Balinese – one of the four varieties fully recognized in North America. The CFA standard notes that 'the ideal Balinese is a svelte, dainty cat with long tapering lines, very lithe but strong and muscular... Because of the longer fur the Balinese appears to have softer lines and less extreme type than other breeds of cats with similar type.' As with other long-haired pointed cats, there is less contrast between body and point colour than is normally seen in Siamese (see p37).

registered in the United States as Siamese. (Siamese may have only other Siamese in their pedigree.) The plush-coated cats, sometimes called Balinese variants, are in fact 'short-haired Balinese' – hybrids that carry one gene for long hair – and if mated to similar cats or to pure Balinese their litters will include some pure Balinese kittens.

Such matings between Siamese and Balinese are the only ones permitted in most North American associations, although there has been some opposition from Siamese breeders afraid of 'contamination' of their bloodlines by the plush-coated variants. Connected with this is the claim by many Balinese breeders that the long hair represents a spontaneous mutation occurring in the Siamese. Whether this is true, or whether it resulted from chance matings between Siamese and long-haired cats, possibly before the days of pedigree breeding, can never be proved. Certainly, the long-hair gene in the Balinese is the same as in the Persian (the difference in coat quality is due to polygenes; see p27), but the spontaneous recurrence of a gene mutation has been known to happen.

Whatever the truth of this, the restriction that only Balinese and Siamese may appear in the pedigree means that the CFA recognizes the Balinese only in the four 'basic' Siamese point colours – seal, blue, chocolate and lilac. Breeders in other associations have however produced red, tortie and lynx (tabby) point Balinese – colours recognized only in Colorpoint Shorthairs, not Siamese, by many North American associations. The long-haired versions of these are now recognized by the CFA under the breed name Javanese. In Britain, all the above colours are also being developed, along with cream and blue cream point. The British version of the breed is not yet fully established, however, and some breeders prefer not to outcross to Siamese; instead, they keep their cats pure for long hair and improve type by matings to Angoras, which in Britain are bred to the same standards for body type as Balinese.

As might be expected, Balinese share many characteristics as pets with Siamese. They are acrobatic, liking to run, jump, climb curtains and ride on the shoulders of their owners. They are very affectionate and demand affection in return, and yet at the same time retain an indefinable air of aloofness that characterizes the Siamese. They become sexually mature younger than most other long-haired breeds, and make wonderful parents, rearing their litters with great care and enjoying sessions of play that would tire other cats. Litters normally comprise three or four young, but may be smaller or larger. One characteristic is not to some people's liking – the voice, which is very like that of the Siamese. But they do have a great advantage over Persians and similar cats in that the long coat is much easier to keep groomed and tangle-free. And they are undoubtedly among the most striking and elegant of all breeds.

Other popular colours of Balinese include the seal point **left** and the blue point **above left**, the latter example being a cat owned by a British cat fancier but from American stock. In Britain, imported Balinese have been crossed to Siamese and the progeny then mated back to Balinese to produce cats with the fine Siamese head shape shown **above**. In this case a tabby point Siamese was used, resulting in a blue tabby point cat. In the CFA this would be classed as a lynx point Javanese.

Shorthairs, European and American 1

The cream British Shorthair – known on the continent of Europe as the European Shorthair – is one of the most difficult varieties of the breed in which to achieve the ideal coat colour, a pale cream shade free from any tabby markings. Often the colour is too 'hot', and there is usually some residual barring on the tail and markings on the face. For all colours, the show standard comments, 'The British cat is compact, well balanced and powerful . . . The head is round with good width between the ears . . .'

The brown tabby British Shorthair **below** lived in the early years of this century; the body type has changed little since then. These cats are basically selectively bred versions of the native European non-pedigree short-hairs.

Somewhat looked down upon by a few cat lovers, probably because they are not considered distinctive enough, are the heavily built short-haired breeds typified by the British Shorthair, its Continental counterpart the European Shorthair, and the American Shorthair. It is true that these do not have the appeal of originating in some faraway part of the world, nor do they have the luxuriant coat of the Persian or the feline slinkiness of the foreign and oriental breeds. In fact, their stockiness betrays their humble origins, for they were developed mainly from the non-pedigree pet and working cats of Europe and North America – although the closely related Exotic Shorthair is a hybrid breed created by North American breeders.

But, in truth, the best of these 'occidental' (for want of a better word to signify the opposite of oriental) short-haired cats are poles apart from the alley cats to which they are distantly related. You only have to look at (and preferably handle) a superb champion specimen of a British or European Shorthair, with its massive round head, deep-chested cobby body, dense fur and superb rich colouring, to realize that. The pure-bred American Shorthair is closer in body type to its non-pedigree counterpart than is the more massive British Shorthair, but again in body, coat and colouring it represents the peak of quality. In each case, the difference between the pure-bred and non-pedigree animal is the result of generations of selective breeding.

Whatever their aesthetic qualities, the native short-haired breeds of Europe and North America have considerable advantages as domestic companions over many of the more exotic cats. They have a hardiness and stamina born of countless generations of life in all kinds of weather, and they are easy to raise and look after. Temperamentally, too, they are well suited to family life, being less excitable than cats of the foreign breeds, while the short coat causes far fewer problems than the long hair of the Persian and related breeds.

British and European Shorthairs

The Romans are said to have introduced the domestic cat to northern Europe – no doubt mainly to hunt vermin – nearly 2,000 years ago, so it is no surprise that when cat breeding and exhibiting first became popular in the second half of the last century, many British breeders concentrated their attention on these native cats. When the first really comprehensive book on cats was published in Britain in 1889, the British Shorthair was the most important breed, and it was certainly given pride of place in the earliest cat shows held at the Crystal Palace in London. Long-haired cats were rapidly becoming popular, however, and a few Siamese had also been imported, and by the end of the century the situation had changed considerably, with Persians outnumbering British Shorthairs four-to-one at shows. The numbers are no more evenly balanced today, and British Shorthair kittens never fetch the price of a Persian (Longhair) of equivalent quality. A keen group of breeders have remained dedicated to them, however – and, of course, among non-pedigree cats the short-hairs remain far more numerous.

In the earlier days (and still to some extent today), the self (solid) colours were the favourites, probably because they were less commonly seen in non-pedigree pets. Of the various self colours (see p29) the most highly prized was the blue (which is in fact bluish-grey). It has remained popular throughout the years, and largely as a result of this the blue British Shorthair (sometimes given solitary breed status as the British Blue) is regarded by cat fanciers as the epitome of the breed.

In the cat clubs of the European continent, the epithet British may be regarded as chauvinistic, for the same short-haired cats and their locally bred equivalents are known there as European Shorthairs. In point of fact, British cat lovers were the first to standardize and judge their cats, so they have some precedence, and many European Shorthairs were imported from Britain or have British ancestors. In any event, the attributes of a prizewinner are now expected to be the same, whatever the nomenclature: It should be compact and powerful, with a deep body and full chest, short strong legs with rounded paws, a short and thick tail with a rounded tip, and a massive round head with full cheeks, a firm chin and a short straight nose. The eyes are expected to be large and round, the ears small, rounded and set well apart. The coat should be short, firm and dense, without woolliness.

All European cat breeds suffered during World War II, but perhaps the British Shorthairs worst of all. In the immediate post-war period there were very few pedigree stud males left, and as a result some breeders mated their cats to short-hairs of foreign body type. In doing so, the heavily built conformation was almost lost. During the 1950s, efforts were made to reverse the trend by mating out to massively built blue Persians. This restored many of the breed's qualities, but it did tend to produce kittens with longer, softer coats (the result not of the recessive long-hair gene, but of the polygenes for a full, luxuriant coat encouraged by Persian breeders) and a more Persian head shape. The show standard for British and European Shorthairs specifies a straight nose – difficult to achieve with Persian ancestry, even though the Persians of Europe are not so short-nosed as those of North America. Some */continued*

THE CHARTREUX

Referred to as long ago as 1558 and supposedly bred by the Carthusian monks, the blue short-haired Chartreux is a native French breed. The naturalists Linnaeus and Buffon recognized it as a distinct variety, and one French vet of the 1930s even bestowed a scientific name upon it: *Felis catus cartusianorum*. Massive in body, but with not such a round head as the British Blue, the coat colour is slightly more silvery.

Today, however, few truly 'pure' Chartreux remain in France. Most have some Persian or British blood – or both – and since 1973 the British and French versions have been officially judged by the same standard. Indeed, over the years the differences between the two have virtually disappeared. However, Chartreux are still classed separately in some North American associations, and are judged at shows by their own standard of points, some of which specify silver highlights in the fur. Colette once wrote of her own cat, 'The sun played on her Chartreux coat, mauve and blue like a woodpigeon's neck.'

A pedigree red tabby can be a magnificent animal, far removed in richness of colour from the popular ginger household pet. This example of a British Shorthair has a fine, broad head and excellent blotched tabby markings.

THE EUROPEAN ALBINO

In some European countries there is a variety of short-haired white called the European Albino. It is similar in build to the European Shorthair, and has the latter in its ancestry. Unlike most other white cats, however, its colour is due to the recessive blue-eyed albino gene (c^a) rather than the dominant white gene (W; see p31). The eyes are a paler blue than those of other blue-eyed white Shorthairs and the pupils have a pinkish reflection. One great advantage is that these cats are not troubled by deafness. In Britain, European Albinos are eligible for registration but not for competition at shows.

The British Tipped Shorthair is in fact a short-haired chinchilla. This cat is genetically black, so that the hairs have black tipping, the majority of the coat being pale silver. Blue, chocolate, lilac, red and cream versions are also recognized.

Shorthairs, European and American 2

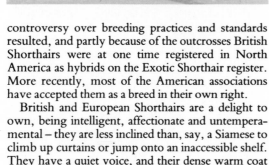

American Shorthairs
The black smoke **above**, the blue-cream **above right** and the blue tabby **above far right** all clearly show the somewhat less massive build that is characteristic of this breed. There are other interesting comparisons with the British and European Shorthairs: The blue-cream has much more distinct colour patches than are required in Europe, while the blue tabby – although still rare in North America – does have its own classes at cat shows there, unlike its equivalents in Europe.

controversy over breeding practices and standards resulted, and partly because of the outcrosses British Shorthairs were at one time registered in North America as hybrids on the Exotic Shorthair register. More recently, most of the American associations have accepted them as a breed in their own right.

British and European Shorthairs are a delight to own, being intelligent, affectionate and untemperamental – they are less inclined than, say, a Siamese to climb up curtains or jump onto an inaccessible shelf. They have a quiet voice, and their dense warm coat makes them exceptionally hardy and resistant to cold. Kittens are usually born without much trouble to either the mother or the owner, the usual litter size being about four – though more than this, or as few as one, may be born. At about four weeks the kittens

are walking firmly on four legs and ready to climb out of their box. They learn to eat solid food quickly and with the minimum of trouble, and generally grow into strong, healthy adults.

The American Shorthair
It may be that the first domestic cat reached North America aboard the *Mayflower*, and certainly the non-pedigree cats of North America – like their European cousins – earned their keep as hunters of vermin for 2½ centuries before anyone took much interest in systematically breeding and showing them. Moreover, the early cat shows held in the north-eastern States late in the last century were dominated by the long-haired Maine Coon (see p 52). However, the tough conditions under which

The best-known American Shorthairs are the silver tabbies **right**. Here a classic (blotched) tabby adult is shown with classic and mackerel tabby kittens; in the kittens the markings are less clearly defined at first. The CFA breed standard describes the American Shorthair as 'lithe enough to stalk its prey but powerful enough to make the kill easily . . . Its legs are long enough to cope with any terrain and heavy and muscular enough for high leaps . . . The face is long enough to permit easy grasping by the teeth . . . No part of the anatomy is so exaggerated as to foster weakness . . . The general effect is of the trained athlete.'

Van pattern kittens – an attractive variation of the bicolours only quite recently standardized for American Shorthairs – have the colour restricted largely to the head, tail and legs, with one or two small patches on the body also permissible. The name derives from the Turkish Van (see p 50). Apart from these and other bicolours, tortie and white and blue-cream and white versions are bred.

both these and the short-haired working cats lived – particularly in the northern half of the country, with its harsh winters – resulted in equally tough cats. As a result, today's American Shorthair is exceptionally strong and hardy, able to go out in most weathers if its owner allows. And although its breeding lines were strengthened in the early days by pedigree British Shorthairs, it has evolved into a distinctive type of cat.

The history of the American Shorthair can be said to date from 1900 or 1901, when a pedigree red tabby was sent from England to an American cat lover. It was a male, although blessed with the distinctly female name Belle, and was the first short-haired cat to be registered as a pedigree animal by the CFA. Thus the first registered American Shorthair was actually a British Shorthair. Others followed, including a male silver tabby called Pretty Correct, but breeders of the time also registered cats from their own firesides. The first 'home-grown' member of the breed to be registered was Buster Brown, a male smoke 'born supposedly 15 January 1904'.

Originally the breed was known simply as the Shorthair, but it soon came to be called the Domestic Shorthair – a name by which it is still often known today. It was bred in a variety of colours, but development as a show breed was slow at first. It really began to make progress only in the late 1930s and early 1940s. By the late 1950s, the CFA stud book listed 50 Domestic Shorthairs – whites, blues, smokes, shaded silvers, and red, silver and brown tabbies. More and more breeders began to take an interest in these cats and, renamed the American Shorthair in 1966, it has graduated from being merely tolerated at cat shows to taking some of the top

awards. To retain its roots as a natural American breed, registration associations decided to allow the registration of non-pedigree cats and kittens, and in 1971 one such cat was declared best American Shorthair of the year by the CFA.

A medium to large cat, with a muscular body and a very hard, short coat, the American Shorthair is less square in shape than the British/European Shorthair. It has an oblong rather than round head, larger ears and longer legs. At shows, judges penalize exhibits with soft fluffy coats or deep breaks in nose profile. Apart from their renowned hardiness, American Shorthairs are noted for their good temperament, intelligence and hunting ability. They are easy to feed and rear, the average litter size being four. The kittens normally open their eyes at nine to ten days.

The Exotic Shorthair

For many years, a number of breeders in North America outcrossed American (or, at that time, Domestic) Shorthairs to Persians – just as they did in Britain with the British Shorthair. But the end result, many cat lovers felt, was that most of the truly American short-hairs at cat shows were to be found in the non-pedigree household pet classes. In the mid-1960s, it was decided that a new breed name be created for cats of mixed Persian and Domestic Shorthair parentage. This was the Exotic Shorthair, and its creation left the newly renamed American Shorthair breed free of cats with mixed ancestry.

The Exotic Shorthair could be described as a short-haired Persian, though it is not as short-coated as other short-haired breeds. It is undoubtedly one of the most beautiful cat breeds to those who prefer the cobby type of body. It is chunky, with */continued*

An Exotic Shorthair has a much rounder head and a shorter nose – with a distinct 'break' – than the other Shorthairs. This is a fine example of a dilute calico (blue-cream and white), showing clearly defined patches of the three colours.

Shorthairs, European and American 3

short firm legs and a strong head. Its nose is shorter than that of a British Shorthair, and although the early show standard specified a straight nose, this was changed to the Persian type, with a distinct break.

An even coat is considered essential, and judges fault any suggestion of feathery hair on the ears or tail, or any tufting between the toes. The Persian has, as a result of selective breeding, evolved a full coat with down hairs much longer than in non-pedigree long-hairs; this, together with differences in texture and length of the guard hairs, is a prime characteristic of the exhibition Persian (see p43). In the Exotic Shorthair, the fullness of the coat – which is due to polygenes (see p27) – has been retained while its overall length – due to a single major gene – has been shortened. The result is an intermediate-length coat with a fluffy texture.

Initially, several of the better-known Exotic Shorthairs were from mixed Persian and Burmese parentage, because the North American Burmese (see p82) has a rounded head, broad chest and compact body – all desirable attributes for the new breed. However, cat fancy organizations felt that it was undesirable to introduce the Burmese gene (c^b; see p30) to the Exotic colour range. For this reason, it was decided to restrict the breed to cats derived from Exotic Shorthairs, American Shorthairs and Persians. At this time, British Shorthairs were registered by some organizations as Exotics, for not only are they closer in appearance to these than to American Shorthairs, but they also commonly had Persian blood. More recently, the British Shorthair has been given recognition as a separate breed in North America (see above).

In temperament, the Exotic Shorthair resembles its Persian ancestors, being a delightful companion. Breeders find very few problems in its rearing, all that is needed being common sense. As with the other Shorthairs, the average litter size is four. The kittens are usually born darker than their parents and reach full beauty of coat only at maturity.

Colours in Shorthairs

In theory, it is of course possible to breed any of the short-haired cats covered by this article in any of the colours described on pages 29 to 40. However, show standards restrict the number of recognized colour varieties, the British/European having fewer colours than the American and Exotic Shorthairs. However, recognition is not the same thing as popularity, and certain breeds are known for exceptional quality in particular colours.

The British Blue has been already mentioned as epitomizing the breed. The equivalent for the American Shorthair is the silver tabby; throughout the breed's history, outstanding examples have been produced. On the other hand, the red self (solid red) is not a recognized colour in the British Shorthair, and although recognized is very rare in the American. In fact, it is almost impossible to breed such cats free of tabby markings (see p30). However, the slightly longer coat of the Exotic Shorthair more effectively masks the markings, and some superb examples of this variety have been bred. Other self colours – especially white, cream and black – have also been popular varieties.

Although the brown tabby was probably the original short-haired cat, and in a good show specimen looks superb, it is something of a rarity today. Red tabbies are also bred, but silvers are the most popular on both sides of the Atlantic. A feature of the British show standards is a greater range of colours for spotted tabbies than for the classic

The shell cameo Exotic Shorthair – in effect, a short-haired version of the red chinchilla Persian – has the same colour genotype as the red British Tipped Shorthair (see p67), but varies slightly in type and coat quality. The wording of the CFA breed standard is identical to that for the Persian except in regard to the coat. This should be 'dense, plush, soft in texture, full of life. Stands out from the body due to density, not flat or close-lying. Medium in length, slightly longer than other shorthairs but not long enough to flow.'

(blotched) and mackerel (known on the Continent as tiger) tabby patterns. As a result, such colours as cream, blue and lilac are exhibited in the spotted pattern. So far, none of the short-haired breeds described here has been bred with the ticked (Abyssinian) tabby pattern, but this is perfectly feasible in theory.

Good examples of pedigree tortoiseshell short-hairs of all breeds look magnificent, and their dilute form, the blue-cream, although rare, is also extremely attractive whether in the mingled colour pattern favoured in Europe or the clearly defined blotches exhibited in North America. Bicolours are also recognized in a range of colours, but are not very popular, probably because of their ubiquity among non-pedigree cats. Finally there are the various shaded and tipped colours described on page 34. Smokes do not show their coats so strikingly in short-haired breeds as in the long-hairs, but various colours are bred in the other shaded and tipped varieties. In 1978, the GCCF recognized the British Shorthair Tipped (once known as the Shorthair Chinchilla) for competition in a number of colours, extending further the range of pedigree varieties available to those who prefer the native type of cat to more foreign breeds.

THE AMERICAN WIREHAIR

In 1966, a litter of kittens were born to a pair of farm cats called Bootsie and Fluffy near Vernon, in upper New York state. One of them had a sparse, very wiry coat. The owner contacted a cat breeder, who bought the kitten and one of its normal short-haired littermates, a female. With the help of a colleague, the breeder started out on a programme of matings designed to establish the genetic nature of the oddity and, if possible, to establish it as a new breed.

Coat samples were sent to Britain for study by geneticists, and this confirmed it as a different coat type from all others previously studied in the cat: It represented a spontaneous mutation (see p23). Each of the longer hairs was bent into a hook at the end, and the hairs themselves were all crimped and wiry – more so even than those of a Wire-haired Terrier. (In contrast, the other curly-coated cats, the rexes, are quite soft to the touch; see p43). It was agreed to call the new coat variety and its mutant gene the wire-hair, and the new breed the American Wirehair. It is one of the very few cat breeds truly native to the United States.

The original wire-haired farm kitten, Adam, was a red and white male. When mature, it was mated with its normal littermate – reputedly a brown tabby and white, but more probably a brown tabby tortie (patched tabby, or torbie) and white – and their first litter was born on 7 July 1967. There were four kittens, two of which were wire-haired red and whites like their father. Both were females and one died young, but the other (named Amy) later gave birth to a number of other wire-haired kittens. Among them was Barberry Ellen, the first homozygous (true-breeding; see p21) American Wirehair, which was sired by Adam and born in 1969. Adam was also mated to an unrelated short-haired white cat, and their litter included three more wire-haired kittens, thus establishing that the wire-hair gene is inherited in a dominant manner (see p20).

All American Wirehairs trace their ancestry back to the original mutant, Adam. This was born to non-pedigree pet cats, which can in the United States be registered as American Shorthairs so long as they conform to the required standard. For this reason, breeders felt that the new wire-haired breed, once elevated to exhibition status, should conform to a similar standard – except, of course, for the coat description. Both Adam and Amy were rather too long and slim, with longer legs and tail and taller ears than the ideal. Therefore the breeders began a breeding programme aimed at 'improving' body conformation and at the same time producing a thicker, more protective coat, while retaining its wiriness. As the wire-hair gene is dominant, it was possible to outcross for such improvements without losing the wiriness.

Considerable variations are still found among the coats of Wirehairs, but breeders have avoided crosses with cats having Persian blood, so as to standardize on short, wiry hair. They have been bred in a variety of colours – almost all colours permitted by cat fancy organizations for American Shorthairs are also permissible for the Wirehair – and in 1977 were given championship status by the CFA, the largest of the American associations.

Wirehair owners describe their cats as sinewy, muscular, bright-eyed and independent. They are said to rule their homes and other cats with 'iron paws', but at the same time make devoted and dependable parents. The breed is too young to assess average litter sizes, but litters of one to four kittens occurred among the first eight litters bred. American Wirehair kittens are easy to identify from the moment of birth, for they have whiskers and hairs on the face and ears that are crimped and project at wild angles, as well as a coat that is obviously different from those of normal short-haired kittens. Longer-coated kittens are born with real ringlets of curls, but those with shorter hair have an irregularly coarse coat all over the body.

Within less than 10 years of the original mutation, examples of the breed were to be found in Canada and Europe (notably Germany). They seem set to have a great future, for not only are they remarkably unusual but they also have a unique attractiveness.

A silver mackerel tabby American Wirehair

Manx cats

The tailless Manx has the dubious distinction of being a very ancient breed of cats that might very well be refused recognition if introduced to the cat fancy today, for some people would consider its chief feature to be a deformity rather than a positive attribute. Be that as it may, throughout its history the breed has had a band of cat fanciers fanatically devoted to its interests.

Nor is there any lack of legends concerning its origin. The Isle of Man, midway between England and Ireland, is generally agreed to be its homeland, but there are many stories of how it came to be there, minus its tail. Some say that Irish invaders stole the cats' tails for helmet plumes, others that the mother cats bit the tails from their offspring to prevent that very fate. Manx are said to have been transported from Japan to the British Isles by Phoenician traders in ancient times. A rival legend states that the Manx swam ashore from a ship of the Spanish Armada, while one old ballad recounts how the cat lost its tail – bitten off by a dog – while sailing in the Ark with Noah at the time of the Great Flood. (A slight variation says that the cat was the last aboard the Ark, and Noah slammed the door on its tail.)

At a rather more mundane level, modern science blames the Manx's taillessness on a mutant dominant gene (see p23). The original mutation must have occurred long ago, however, for the Manx breed was well established and popular before the earliest days of the cat fancy. A Manx Club was formed in Britain in 1901, and it is said that King Edward VII owned several Manx cats as pets. The breed also figures early in North American pedigree cat registers. It declined somewhat in popularity in Britain in the 1930s and

suffered during the war years, but on both sides of the Atlantic its popularity grew in the post-war period. For many years, owners and breeders had obtained much of their stock from the Isle of Man, but the demand – particularly from North America – was such that the supply dwindled, and more and more stock was bred in Britain and North America.

A major reason for the scarcity is that Manx litters are small – generally only two, three or four kittens – and this is a direct result of the Manx gene. As explained on page 42, homozygous Manx – those inheriting the Manx gene from both parents – die in the womb at an early stage of development, and these amount to an average of a quarter of the kittens conceived from Manx-to-Manx matings. The Manx known to cat lovers is the heterozygote – that is, it has one gene for Manx taillessness and one gene for a normal tail. Even these show a higher proportion of still-births and early deaths than in most other breeds, mainly because the Manx gene can cause malformations in various other parts of the body apart from the tail. Spina bifida, in particular, is relatively common, and there are often fusions of bones in the lower spine.

Any breed that is forced to be a heterozygote can never breed true, and a number of normal-tailed kittens are liable to occur in any Manx litter, due to the inheritance of two genes for a normal tail. Even the Manx kittens show great variability, and for ease of classification have been divided into four groups: rumpies, the true exhibition Manx, which are completely tailless and often have a dimple at the base of the spine; rumpy-risers, which have a small number of tail vertebrae forming a small knob; stumpies or

The Manx can be exhibited in all patterns and colour combinations in Europe and almost all in North America; this is a blue-cream of the intermingled type preferred in Britain. The most important features are the body and head, and this example shows well the rounded rump and deep flanks desired by breeders and judges. All show standards express this requirement, though in different words. The CFA sums it up: 'The overall impression of the Manx cat is that of roundness.'

A rumpy Manx, such as this red classic tabby kitten, is the ideal exhibition animal, the only type permitted in most shows and always the preferred. Ideally, there is a dimple where the tail would normally be.

A stumpy Manx, such as this red mackerel tabby and white, has a short tail stump. Genetically the same as a rumpy, it can be used to breed rumpies but is barred from shows in Britain and most other countries.

A brown tabby Cymric

THE CYMRIC

A number of breeders working with Manx in North America were delighted when, in the late 1960s, long-haired kittens began to appear in some litters. This meant that the recessive gene for long hair (see p43) had been inherited from tailed short-hairs used as outcrosses in the past. Rather than neuter their kittens, as had occurred with some other breeds 'throwing' long-hairs, the breeders decided to breed more like them and to develop the variety as a separate breed. Although many of the people of the Isle of Man are Celts, like the Welsh, the links between them are somewhat tenuous; nevertheless, it was agreed to name the new breed Cymric (pronounced kumric) from *Cymru,* the Welsh name for Wales.

The Cymric only began to gain recognition in the late 1970s – by when it had been given preliminary status by the CCA and some other cat fancy organizations but was not yet recognized by the CFA. It had still to appear in Europe. However, a small but growing band of enthusiasts were becoming devoted to its unique look, with its tufted ears and jowls, and smooth medium-long coat.

stubbies, the Manx with a definite tail stump that is usually movable but often curved or kinked; and longies, which have an almost normal, though shortened, tail. It is sometimes difficult to distinguish between longie Manx and normal-tailed cats (which make up about half the offspring of a Manx-to-normal mating and one-third from Manx-to-Manx). Among the Manx from such matings, all or any of the variations mentioned above can occur; they may all be registered as Manx, but for exhibition purposes Manx should be rumpies. In a few associations, rumpy-risers without any visible stump are permitted, but true rumpies are always preferred.

Breeders of Manx, when outcrossing, normally mate Manx with Manx-bred normal-tailed cats of the type described above rather than with British or American Shorthairs. This is because, although similar, there are differences in the ideal body and head type between the Manx and the Shorthairs. The breeders' aim is for a totally rounded look – not only in the rump but in the head and whole body. The back is short and the cheeks full. The combination of short back with long hind legs – and, some say, skeletal abnormalities – results in the characteristic bobbing, rabbit-like gait known as the 'Manx hop'. It is quite unlike the sinuous movement of the normal-tailed cat, but many breeders regard it as a fault and believe that their cats should be able to walk normally. Certainly, any deformity bad enough to prevent a cat walking or standing properly would result in disqualification in a show.

Another desired attribute is a distinct double coat – with a well-defined difference between the soft underhair and the glossier, coarser top coat – but the achievement of this together with all the other features set out in the standard of points is often elusive. In Britain, the GCCF recognizes the Manx in any colour or pattern, and the colours and markings are taken into account only if all other points between two cats are equal. In North America the situation is somewhat different, the CFA excluding varieties displaying the effects of the chocolate-brown or Siamese genes – including the lilac (lavender) colouring – and judges awarding up to five points (out of 100) for colour and pattern.

Although there is undoubtedly an element of curiosity value that attracts owners to the Manx, they have a reputation for intelligence and ease of training. In spite of the handicap of lacking a tail to help them balance, they are good hunters and, given a chance, tree-climbers. They are certainly affectionate and unique companions.

The Japanese Bobtail

It seems certain that the domestic cat first arrived in Japan from China or Korea, but historians differ as to the actual date. It must have been at least 1,000 years ago, for the first written record of cats in Japan is that old, appearing in a manuscript written by a tutor-governess to the Empress. However, it would seem that, even if the unusual tail structure of the cat now called the Japanese Bobtail was then known, it was not considered remarkable enough for mention; all the description is concerned with the beautiful markings and colours.

Nevertheless, the bob-tailed breed has certainly existed in Japan for many centuries; it features in

The traditional colour of the Japanese Bobtail is the *mi-ke* or tricolour, corresponding to the tortie and white or calico of the Western cat fancy. Bobtails have flourished in Japan for hundreds of years and appear in many works of art. Typical is the woodcut **below right** by Hiroshige. Dating from 1858, it is called *Festival of the Cock* and is one of the series *One Hundred Views of Edo.*

ancient prints and paintings, and is shown on the facade of the Gotokuji Temple in Tokyo with paw upraised to symbolize good fortune. It also established itself as the family cat. The favourite good luck colour is known as the *mi-ke* (pronounced mee-kay), and corresponds to the calico, or tortoiseshell and white, of other breeds. (As a tortoiseshell, this is almost invariably female; see p39.) It is said that the first cats to step on Japanese soil were black, and that they were followed by whites and then orange cats – and thus the *mi-ke* (which means three-fur, referring to the red, black and white pattern) was born.

It was only after World War II, however, that Western breeders became interested in it. An American cat lover arriving with the occupying forces was enchanted by the gentle soft-coated cats with bobbed tails. She took in large numbers, attempting to breed in particular the *mi-ke,* but the

Japanese themselves showed little interest even though they were at that time establishing a pedigree cat fancy. Japanese interest grew only after the first visit of American judges to a Japanese cat show in 1963, when they much admired the indigenous pets.

In 1968, the original American breeder in Japan sent the first three Bobtails to the United States, and later took 38 of the cats with her when she returned home. The breed became popular there, and is now recognized for championship competition by all the North American cat fancy organizations, though it has yet to reach Europe. Any colour except Siamese-pattern or Abyssinian-type agouti is permitted, but the preferred colours are the *mi-ke* and those colours that can be used to create it: white, black, red, black and white, red and white, and tortoiseshell. Vividly contrasting colours and bold markings are preferred in the bicolours and tortoiseshells.

The Japanese Bobtail is a medium-sized cat with a well-muscled, rather slender, foreign-type build and a medium-length, soft silky coat. It has particularly high cheek bones and these, combined with the large oval eyes, which are set at a pronounced slant, give its face a distinctive Japanese appearance that is quite different from that of other foreign breeds. The tail is somewhat like that of a stumpie Manx (see p72), and is variable in length. For exhibition it should be 10 to 12 cm (4 to 5 in) long when straightened out, but only half this length when allowed to curve; it is normally carried erect. However, the bushy tail hair forms a pompon or rabbit's-tail appearance that disguises the underlying structure. Although the breed has not yet been investigated scientifically to discover its genetics, breeders say that, unlike the Manx, it is due to a recessive gene and breeds true.

It is certainly an endearing cat, quiet of voice and forming close family groups. It is an ideal family pet.

The Scottish Fold

One day in 1961, a Scottish shepherd noticed a kitten with 'lop' ears at the farm where he worked; instead of being upright and pricked as in a normal kitten, they folded and bent forward, like those of a puppy. This was the first Scottish Fold, a breed whose wide-eyed look of surprise and, perhaps, sadness has since captivated many a cat lover, particularly in North America, and caused indignation in others.

The shepherd, William Ross, realized the uniqueness of the abnormality. When, two years later, the original Fold (whose name was Susie) bore two more folded-ear kittens, he acquired one of them – a white female – named it Snooks and registered it. A breeding programme was begun and, in collaboration with breeders and geneticists, test matings were undertaken to discover the genetics of the variety. It was discovered that ear folding is due to a single dominant gene, so that all Scottish Folds must have at least one folded-ear parent (see p 20). In this respect it is like the Manx, but the gene is not lethal when homozygous (inherited from both parents; see p 42).

The breeding tests showed that there is great variability in the degree of ear folding. This does not seem to be related to the genotype (genetic make-up), since some homozygous Folds have more loosely folded ears than some heterozygotes (those with only one folded-ear gene). It was also noticed that some Folds have thicker, shorter tails with a rounded tip. At first, breeders favoured this feature as contributing to the overall look of the breed, but it later transpired that some of these cats have thickened limbs. Such cats are inconvenienced, although viable, so it is considered an undesirable abnormality. (In North America, such thickening or other tail abnormality brings disqualification in a show.)

The cause of the thickening remains something of a mystery, since it affects only a proportion of cats, including both homozygous and heterozygous ones. In fact, breeders have kept its incidence very low by not breeding from Folds with thickened tails and by outcrossing to British Shorthairs or, in North America, to American Shorthairs. However, in the early 1970s, the GCCF in Britain decided to stop registering Scottish Folds, in effect banning them from all shows. The official reason was a fear that the breed would be prone to ear mites (see p 202) and deafness – both denied by breeders, who pointed out that only normal hygiene is needed to keep the ears free from mites, as with any breed, and that a number of the early Folds were whites, which are always prone to deafness.

As a result of this decision, British breeders were forced to register their cats with overseas associations or to part with them as unregistered pets. Although a fairly large population has remained and been bred in Britain, the main centre of activity with the breed switched to North America. There, it has rapidly gained in popularity, and gained full championship status with the largest American cat fancy organization, the CFA, in 1978. It is recognized in most of the colours allowed for the American Shorthair – that is, in most colours except chocolate (chestnut), lilac and Siamese-pattern.

Scottish Folds make loving, placid and companionable pets, getting on well with both humans and other pets. They are good parents, bearing an average of three or four in each litter. At birth, the prick-eared and folded-eared kittens are identical, but any with shortened, thick tails can soon be differentiated. By the time the kittens are climbing out of their box, at about four weeks, the ears of the true Folds can be seen to bend forwards. The effect increases gradually up to adulthood.

Perhaps because of their Scottish ancestry, the Folds are strong and particularly resistant to disease. In their native land, they roam free even in the wildest weather, seemingly impervious to cold. American experience, too, suggests that, so long as they are selectively bred for health, they are as robust as many much longer-established breeds. The sad look is, apparently, no indicator of their inner feelings.

The folded ears and resulting sad expression are the hallmarks of the Scottish Fold, an increasingly popular breed in North America, though officially banned in its native country. The CFA show standard expresses a preference for small, tightly folded ears over larger, more loosely folded ones. It states: 'The ears should be set in a caplike fashion to expose a rounded cranium.'

Scottish Fold colours are almost unlimited. The painting **left** is of a red mackerel tabby, a particularly attractive variety. Another popular colour is the black **below**. The blue-cream **below left** is a long-haired folded-ear kitten. A number of the original Scottish Folds had long hair, but this version of the breed has never been standardized.

Abyssinians and Somalis 1

Striking, attractive and totally different from any other short-haired cat, the Abyssinian is one of the oldest breeds. It is also, after many ups and downs, one of the most popular breeds today, particularly in North America. More fundamentally, it and its much more recent long-haired version, the Somali, are unique in the pedigree cat world in being based on a single mutant coat pattern gene that is not found in any other pure breed; no other breed is so exclusive in terms of colour genetics.

The gene concerned is known as the Abyssinian (symbolized T^a) and is one of the tabby series of alleles (see p32). It gives the Abyssinian and Somali their unique ticked coat, in which each hair has two or more dark bands – as many as a dozen in the case of the Somali – together with the residual tabby markings found on the head and sometimes the tail and legs. Although it is unrelated to the tabby pattern gene, these cats also have a unique body shape: long, lean but powerful – definitely foreign in type, but far less extreme than the Siamese.

The Abyssinian

Like many old breeds, the Abyssinian's origins are obscure. There are those who would trace it directly back to the Nile valley, and it certainly bears a striking resemblance in body type to the cats worshipped, painted and sculpted by the Ancient Egyptians. It does seem that a cat called Zula was

The silver Abyssinian probably existed in the early days of the cat fancy, and has returned in recent years thanks to the work of a few British breeders. It has not yet achieved official recognition, however.

taken from Abyssinia (now Ethiopia) to Britain in the 1860s, at the end of the Abyssinian War, and this and possibly other imports were bred with similarly marked cats of partly unknown origin.

Of course, this was a period of great interest in everything to do with this part of Africa, but these distinctive cats were initially known by an assortment of names as well as Abyssinian, including Hare cat, Rabbit cat and Bunny cat. Certainly their coat is very similar to that of the wild hare or rabbit (and today the normal Abyssinian colouring is known in France as *lièvre*, or hare). In considering the breed for

Abyssinians have a very alert, lively appearance that must account in no small measure for their great popularity as pets. Medium in size and moderately foreign in type, they do not have the extremes of physical or psychological traits for which many other foreign

breeds are known. At shows, judges look for an absence of barring on the legs, chest and tail, but – in Britain, at least – like to see dark colouring up the back of the hind legs, on the tip of the tail and around the eyes. Ear tufts are considered to be a desirable attribute.

The so-called 'red' Abyssinian has been offically renamed sorrel in Britain and Canada, acknowledging the fact that it is not the same genetically as other red cats. The tone is a rich, brownish coppery-red.

its first show standard, a pioneer cat fancier wrote in 1889: 'It is mostly of a deep brown, ticked with black, somewhat resembling the back of a wild (only not so grey) rabbit.' Then, as now, white spots were considered faults, but arguments raged as to how important these were as compared with a sooty coat. Some of the early cats were probably silvers, a colour that became almost extinct in Abyssinians until quite recently (see below).

Food shortages and other problems almost wiped out the breed in Britain during World War I, and again (after a remarkable recovery in the inter-war period) during World War II. But already in 1917 the first Abyssinian was registered with the CFA in North America, and several top-quality cats were exported from Britain to the United States in the late 1930s, forming the foundations of the breed's present-day American popularity. It was also established on the European continent, being recognized in France in 1929. When, in the 1960s and 1970s, feline leukaemia virus (FeLV; see p205) decimated British Abyssinians, some breeders reimported stock from other European countries where the virus had not gained a hold.

Although very similar, Abyssinians are judged in shows to slightly different standards in Europe and North America. Both specify a moderately foreign head shape, far less elongated than in the Siamese, but American cats tend to have a slightly shorter, more rounded profile than the European. The ears are large and pointed, often with characteristic tufts, and set so as to appear pricked, so that the cat seems to be listening attentively. In fact, the whole animal gives the impression of being alert and athletic, and is a great tree climber if given the chance.

Gentle and affectionate to humans (though not always keen to live in large cat groups), Abyssinians make ideal companions – no doubt a major reason for their popularity. Their voice is quiet, even when they are on heat. Litters average about four – smaller than many foreign breeds. The kittens are born with a fluffy coat that has dark markings, but these normally disappear with maturity. They develop somewhat more slowly than most other breeds (though not so slowly as the Somali).

The standard colouring for the Abyssinian is simply called usual or normal in Britain, but is termed ruddy in North America. It is a rich golden-brown ticked with black, adult hairs showing two or preferably three bands of ticking. Genetically, it is black, the ruddiness being due to rufus polygenes (see

p27). However, other colours have frequently occurred in the history of the breed, the so-called red Abyssinian being mentioned as early as 1887. Here the coat is coppery-red ticked with a light chocolate-brown, the undercoat being a warm apricot.

As explained on page 33, the genetics of this variety have been elucidated only quite recently, and it is now known to be due to the light-brown (b^l) gene and is not a true 'red' at all. As a result, the alternative names cinnamon, russet and sorrel have been proposed. (The last is already used by some North American associations, including */continued*

The Somali should look exactly like an Abyssinian except for its coat, which is not exceptionally long but long enough to show many bands of ticking. Both the Abyssinians and the Somali painted on these pages are the normal colouring, known in North America as ruddy.

Abyssinians and Somalis 2

Newer colours of Abyssinians include the blue far left, recognized in Britain but still very rare; the agouti banding is beige rather than warm brown, and the ticking is blue.
The Abyssinian kittens left are all from a single litter raised by a progressive breeder in Britain; they are (from left to right) 'red' or sorrel, lilac, usual (ruddy) and blue.

Newer colours of Abyssinians include the blue far left, recognized in Britain but still very rare; the agouti banding is beige rather than warm brown, and the ticking is blue. The Abyssinian kittens left are all from a single litter raised by a progressive breeder in Britain; they are (from left to right) 'red' or sorrel, lilac, usual (ruddy) and blue.

the CCA in Canada, and has recently been adopted in Britain too.) The description red could then be reserved for the true sex-linked red, which has now been bred, along with the true sex-linked cream, the chocolate, lilac and other colours. Blue Abyssinians have had a show standard in Britain for some years, but are not eligible for championships. Some breeders, as already mentioned, are reintroducing silver varieties, but these (like the other new colours apart from blue) are not yet recognized. Even the blue is unrecognized by the CFA in North America, and its classification of the Abyssinian as a natural breed means that outcrosses to other breeds in order to introduce other new colours are forbidden.

Ruddy Somali kittens are born quite dark. The show standard acknowledges that it takes a long time for the full beauty of their ticked coat to develop.

The Somali

The same problem hampered breeders trying to get recognition for the first Somalis in North America, since some Abyssinian breeders claimed that out-crosses to long-haired breeds must have taken place. In fact, however, certain breeding lines of Abyssinians are now known to have carried the recessive long-hair gene (*l*) for many generations – probably dating back to the registration of some non-pedigree Abyssinians in Britain in the 1930s or earlier. Although many breeders preferred to ignore the fact and hurriedly neutered any unwanted long-haired kittens, others found the cats extremely attractive.

In the late 1960s, they set out to develop a long-haired Abyssinian breed under the name Somali, and it now has championship status in all North American associations. The first 'official' Somalis in Europe were imported from the United States by a German breeder in 1977, but in fact in both Europe and Australasia some long-haired Abyssinians were already being bred. In particular, a group of Australian and New Zealand breeders were independently trying to establish the breed, using Abyssinian stock imported from Britain that later turned out to have been distantly related to many early American Somalis. A Somali was in fact exhibited in Australia as early as 1965.

The Somali has the same ticked coat as the Abyssinian, but it is silkier, softer and very much longer. Instead of two or three bands of ticking on each hair, there are 10, 11 or even 12, and the colouring – which may be normal (ruddy) or 'red' (sorrel) – is deeper and altogether richer. Some Somali strains produce much longer coats than others, due to the influence of polygenes alongside the major long-hair gene (see p 43). In general, however, the coat is full without being woolly, and is easy to groom. It takes a long time to develop fully, kittens being born very dark

The 'red' Somali has a beautiful, richly coloured coat when adult – fine, dense and very soft to the touch, the warm, glowing red colour ticked with chocolate-brown.

and only achieving the fully ticked, ruddy brown or red colouring at about 18 months.

Since long hair is a recessive trait, Somalis always breed true for long hair. Crossed with an Abyssinian, however, a Somali will have short-haired kittens carrying the gene for long hair. These have a plushier coat than most normal Abyssinians. Mated together, they will result in long-haired and short-haired offspring in the ratio of 1:3 (see p 24). All such short-haired Somali offspring must be registered as Somalis in North America, even though they are identical genetically to many Abyssinians, which may also carry the long-hair gene.

With its somewhat shaggy coat, its exaggerated ear tufts and full tail like a fox's brush, the Somali is a wild-looking cat. Yet it is gentle in nature, like the Abyssinian: soft-voiced and companionable, yet vigorous and athletic. The only snag is that litters tend to be small – averaging three to four kittens – so that breeders may have difficulty meeting demand.

The Egyptian Mau and Ocicat

The Egyptian Mau

The spotted tabby pattern (see p33) is found in a number of breeds of cats, but only one has any serious claim to be a natural spotted breed, rather than the deliberate creation of modern-day breeders. This is the Egyptian Mau, whose ancestors, it is claimed, go back to the time of the pharoahs. (The name Mau simply means cat.) Certainly, many of the Ancient Egyptian depictions of cats that do indicate colour or coat pattern generally show a spotted tabby. For example, there is a wall painting from a temple at Thebes (dating from about 1400 BC) showing a spotted cat on a duck-hunting trip (see p238) and a papyrus of about 1100 BC showing the sun-god Ra in the form of a spotted cat.

Introduced to the United States from Egypt (via Rome) in the early 1950s, the Mau should not be confused with the breed that was for a time called by the same name in Britain. The latter, first bred in the late 1960s, is now known as the Oriental Spotted Tabby (see p94), and has a far more extreme foreign body type than the Egyptian Mau. Although the first pair of Maus – Gepa and Ludol – reached North America in 1953, it was 15 years before the first cat association, the CFF, gave it official recognition. All the North American associations now recognize it as a championship breed, though the GCCF in Britain does not. However, in 1978 the first true Mau in Britain was imported direct from Egypt.

A svelte cat, the Mau is similar in build to the Abyssinian (which has also been compared to the Ancient Egyptian cats; see p76). Its head is a slightly rounded wedge shape, and its hair of medium length, with one or two bands of ticking in the agouti areas. Judges prefer the spots to be round and evenly distributed, but they tend to be rather random and sometimes run together to form broken stripes. The tail and legs are in any case banded, and the head marked intricately with a pattern sometimes likened to a scarab beetle. The recognized colours are silver (black spots on a silver agouti background), bronze (chocolate spots on bronze agouti) and smoke (black spots on grey, with a silver undercoat). This last is unusual in showing clearly defined tabby markings in spite of being a smoke (see p35). In all colours, eyes of a pale 'gooseberry'-green are preferred.

Maus are friendly cats, though said to be somewhat aloof with strangers. They have a quiet, melodious voice. Both sexes make good parents, caring for and playing with the kittens, which develop rather slowly.

The Ocicat

Although having a similar coat pattern to the Mau, the Ocicat is a hybrid developed in the United States by crossing a chocolate point Siamese with a hybrid queen from an Abyssinian pointed Siamese breeding programme. The first kitten, Tonga, reminded its breeder of a baby ocelot – hence the name Ocicat. It has also been likened to the Ancient Egyptian fishing cats. A number of generations have been bred, but by the late 1970s the breed had not yet gained full recog-

nition. It is classed for registration as a hybrid. Apart from the Ocicat itself, breeds allowed in the pedigree are the Abyssinian, American Shorthair and Siamese.

A rather large breed, averaging 5.5 to 7 kg (12 to 15 lb) when fully grown, the Ocicat has a well-knit, muscular body and a short, shiny coat. It is remarkable for its rich jungle-like coat colouring: originally either chestnut-brown spots on a cream background or light chocolate on cream, both with golden-yellow eyes. These are due to the presence of the brown gene (b) and light-brown gene (b^l) respectively (see p29). More recently, a few breeders have been developing silver and bronze Ocicats, as in the Mau.

The Ocicat is characteristically a large, long-legged cat with a strikingly spotted coat. It has not yet been accepted for competition. This is a silver.

The Egyptian Mau of North America is similar in body type to the Abyssinian. The breed standard pays great attention to the pattern, and this accounts for 25 per cent of the points given in judging. It states that the forehead is 'barred with "M" and frown marks . . . The cheeks are barred with "mascara" lines . . . The shoulder markings are a transition between stripes and spots . . . Markings on the body are to be randomly spotted . . .' The cat illustrated here is a bronze.

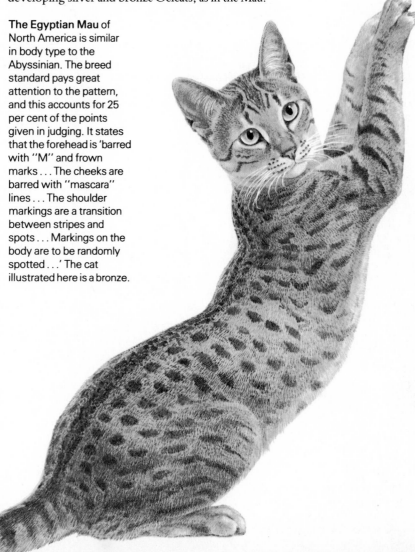

The Russian Blue and Korat

Exotic origin has always been a great asset to any breed of cats. Moreover, blue has always been one of the most coveted of the self (solid) colours. So it is not surprising that two of the most subtly distinctive breeds should be blues identified with specific geographical localities – albeit many thousands of miles apart. The Russian Blue and the Korat are both blue breeds with a silver sheen and brilliant green eyes. Both are broadly foreign in type, but there the similarity ends – except that both encountered some difficulty in getting established against other short-haired blue breeds.

The Russian Blue

Believed to have originated at the White Sea port of Archangel – from where sailors are said to have taken them to western Europe in the 1860s – the Russian Blue was known in the early years of the cat fancy under a variety of names. Among these were Spanish Blue, Archangel and Maltese. At cat shows in Britain

around the turn of the century, all the short-haired blue cats competed in one class, whatever their body type. The British type – cobby and round-headed (see p66) – invariably won, and interest in the finer-boned, narrower-skulled Russian breed waned. It was only in 1912 that separate classes were established for British and Russian (though at this time generally termed Foreign) blues, and the latter flourished in the years up to World War II, though they almost became extinct during the war.

In the late 1940s and 50s, Scandinavian breeders also began developing the breed, crossing a blue cat from Finland with Siamese carrying the dilution (*d*) gene (which is responsible for blue colouring; see p29). At about the same time Russian Blue breeders in Britain decided to outcross to a blue point Siamese and produced cats of much more extreme foreign body type. This process went so far that the official Russian Blue show standard was rewritten accordingly, and it was only in 1965 that a group of British breeders began a co-ordinated attempt to return to the prewar characteristics of the breed: a head in the shape of a short wedge, with prominent whisker pads and upright ears. In 1966, the show standard was changed once again, stating specifically that 'Siamese type is undesirable'. But the most distinctive feature of a Russian Blue has always been its double coat: short, soft, silky and upstanding – like the coat of a seal or beaver – and of a medium blue colour, so that the silver tipping of the guard hairs reflects light, giving the cat a silver sheen.

Russian Blues existed in North America as long ago as 1900 (though often called Maltese) but it was not until 1947 that they were bred systematically and

Two contrasting blue breeds, both of moderately foreign type but each highly distinctive, are the Russian Blue (reclining in the foreground), showing the characteristic tall ears and medium blue beaver-like coat, and the Korat (shown sitting upright), with its heart-shaped face, large green eyes and silvery tipped coat.

for a further 20 years few appeared at cat shows. The main reason was probably that they were so variable in type and not different enough from the already established blue American Shorthairs and others to interest many people as a viable breed. Gradually, however, descendants of newer imports from Sweden and Britain became the foundation of more stable Russian Blue breeding lines and greatly strengthened the breed. They have also become established in Australasia, where a Russian White is also recognized as a pedigree breed.

Very affectionate towards each other and their owners, Russian Blues make good parents, rearing litters of around four kittens with apparent ease. They tend to be quiet-voiced, sometimes making it difficult for an inexperienced breeder to tell when a female comes into heat. Because of their dense, thick coat – which insulates them against extreme weather conditions – they are very hardy. In young kittens, faint tabby markings can often be seen in the coat, as

in other breeds, but these should disappear with the moult of the kitten coat.

In one respect, Russian Blues that are to be exhibited at cat shows may need special treatment: when grooming. Because of the upstanding coat, care must be taken not to polish and flatten it, though the coat of a top-quality Russian Blue should spring up regardless of which way it is brushed. Grooming powder, if used, should be of a coarse texture, and the coat should first be brushed firmly against the lie of the hair and then gently finished by brushing lightly back in the natural direction.

The Korat

Known for hundreds of years in its native Thailand (Siam) as the Si-Sawat, the Korat has a hard, muscular, curved body, not fully foreign in type but built like that of an old-fashioned Siamese (see p86), and a silver-blue coat described in an old Thai poem as having 'roots like clouds and tips like silver'. Even in Thailand Korats are rare and are prized for their beauty and reputed power to bring good luck. Believed to have originated in the Korat province, they were also well known in other parts of the country – as is shown by manuscript books created by artists and poets of the old capital, Ayudha, between 1350 and 1767.

These books show that the Korat of today not only has the semi-cobby body build of the ancient breeds of Thailand but also retains the coat texture and other qualities so attractive to its owners centuries ago. In this respect it is probably unique, for other native Thai breeds – shown in paintings to be of the same build as the Korat – have today been developed by Western breeders into cats totally unlike their ancestors. (Among these other breeds were the Supalak or Thong Daeng – brown cats now considered to be ancestors of the Burmese and possibly also the Havana Brown, some of them now being imported into North America and bred into Burmese lines – and the Seal Pointed, undoubtedly the ancestor of our Siamese.)

The Korat was probably first seen in a cat show in 1896, when a blue cat was entered in the Siamese class at a National Cat Club show in England. It was disqualified by the judge and was described as 'blue instead of biscuit-colour'. Its owner claimed that not only had it come from Siam but that there were many others there just like it. This cat is claimed by some to have been a blue point Siamese, but there is also a record of an early breeder of Russian Blues acquiring an all-blue cat of Siamese type – claimed by its owner to be Siamese – in 1889. Although the all-blue cats of Siam were often referred to in subsequent cat fancy literature, there is no record of Korats being registered until 1959, when a pair named Nara and Darra were obtained from a Bangkok breeder and taken to the United States. They were later joined by others and in 1965 a breed club was formed to promote them. The first associations to recognize Korats were the ACA, CFA and UCF in 1966, but by 1969 all the other North American bodies plus those in Australia and South Africa had given them recognition.

The first Korats to reach Europe were taken from the United States to Britain in 1972. There was opposition at first from cat lovers who felt that they were not different enough from other recognized blue short-hairs, but much of this melted away once they had appeared at a number of shows. They were recognized, though at first without championship status, in 1975.

Certainly they are quite unique, with a heart-shaped face, very large and alert-looking green eyes, big, tall ears, and rounded tail. The coat – glossy, short to medium in length and close-lying, of a silver-blue colour apparently tipped with silver – is quite unlike that of any other breed. The tipping, producing an effect like a halo, results from light reflected from the fine, tapering hairs. Cat fancy organizations in New Zealand, Japan, the European continent and Scandinavia have now adopted the Korat as a breed, and it continues to thrive in North America. One requirement insisted upon by all Korat clubs is that it should be maintained as a natural breed, outcrossing to other breeds being forbidden, and that all Korats should have ancestry tracing back to the original cats of Thailand.

Korats make intelligent and loving pets, and have pretty, rather quiet voices. They seem somewhat prone to respiratory virus infections (cat flu), so vaccination is vital. Females have proved to make ideal mothers, rearing litters of three to four (in some cases up to nine) and retaining their youthful playfulness even when they become grandmothers. However, the kittens, although they grow quickly, go through an 'ugly duckling' stage and do not reach their full perfection of coat and eye colour until they are two to four years old – so bear this in mind if you wish to acquire one of these unusual cats.

Burmese cats I

Distinctive and appealing, with its alert, wide-eyed look and sleek, richly-coloured coat, the Burmese has never been a common breed but is one of the most sought-after. It was the first pedigree breed to be developed completely in the United States and one of the first to be subjected to a thorough genetic study. But it is also perhaps the most striking example of British and American breed standards differing. Recognized colours differ sharply; the CFA in the United States for many years recognized only the original sable (brown) as true Burmese, now classifying some of the newer colours under the breed name Malayan, while some of the smaller American associations permit these to compete as Burmese and the British GCCF recognizes a wider range still. Also, breeders' and judges' ideas of the ideal body and particularly head shape are quite different.

Over several generations, three types of kitten were found among Wong Mau's descendants: cats with the typical Siamese colouring of dark brown 'points' and a pale body, those (like Wong Mau herself) with a very much darker brown body but still a discernible further darkening at the points, and cats that were dark brown all over – the first true Burmese. These and further breeding experiments established the existence of the Burmese gene (c^b; see

The sable or brown Burmese is the original colour and still the one that typifies the breed. The cat illustrated **above** is of American type, considerably more rounded and less foreign in head shape than those in Europe and elsewhere. The breed standard states that the head should be 'pleasingly rounded, without flat planes whether viewed from front or side'. It comments that Burmese are surprisingly heavy for their size.

Early history
Virtually all modern pedigree Burmese can trace their ancestry back to a single walnut-brown female cat called Wong Mau, which was taken from Rangoon to the United States in 1930. At that time, no similar cats were known, although historians of the Siamese breed have described all-over chocolate-brown cats at 19th-century cat shows which, by their breeding performance, could well have been early Burmese or Burmese-Siamese hybrids; similar cats are also described and illustrated in ancient Thai manuscripts (see p81). Wong Mau's owner – US Navy psychiatrist Dr Joseph Thompson – was attracted by her unique colouring, but at first most other cat fanciers were not impressed, regarding Wong Mau and her offspring as rather poor-coloured Siamese. With a few other breeders and geneticists, however, Dr Thompson began a controlled breeding programme in an attempt to investigate the genotype (genetic make-up) of Wong Mau and establish a new breed. Since there were no other similar cats available with which to mate Wong Mau, crosses with the closest available breed – Siamese – were carried out, followed by crosses between the offspring and back to Wong Mau herself.

p30); all Burmese cats are homozygous for this (see p20). Cats like Wong Mau, with intermediate colouring, have one Burmese gene and one Siamese (c^s), which are closely related; these hybrids are now being deliberately bred in some countries as Tonkinese (see p90).

During the 1930s and early 40s, Dr Thompson and other American breeders developed the Burmese as a pedigree breed (it was first officially recognized by the CFA in 1936) and increased its numbers. A few more cats were imported from Burma so that the degree of inbreeding could be reduced, but with so few Burmese available some outcrosses to Siamese had to be made. One result of this was that the CFA suspended registration between 1947 and 1953, though Burmese remained registered with other North American associations. It was at about this time that the first kittens were exported to Europe, brown Burmese being recognized by the GCCF in Britain in 1952 and blue in 1960. They have since become well established on the European continent – particularly in Germany, Holland and Scandinavia – and are thriving in Australia and New Zealand (where Burmese are especially noted for their rich golden eye colour).

The coppery-brown cats of Siam, such as that in the centre of the group illustrated **right** in the *Cat-Book Poems*, were known as the Supalak or Thong Daeng. They may have included ancestors of today's Havana Browns (see p91), but almost certainly were also early examples of Burmese.

Other Burmese colours – classed as Malayans by the CFA – include the blue **right**, with its smooth-lying steel-grey coat, and the chocolate (champagne) **far right**. The latter is difficult to breed as there is great colour variation between different strains. Some pointing shows even in adult chocolates.

which should be shiny and fine in texture – is a marked feature. Every cat fancy organization agrees that brown (known in North America as sable) is the primary colour of the breed. As explained on page 30, it is genetically black modified by the c^b gene. Although born much paler (and sometimes with faint tabby markings), the mature cat is a rich, warm seal- or sable-brown, shading to a slightly paler colour on the belly. In blue Burmese – recognized by most cat fancy organizations around the world except the CFA (which classifies it as the blue Malayan) and the largest American Burmese breed club – the coat is a soft silver-grey, again shading slightly to the belly and with a distinctive silver sheen on the rounded parts. The tone is decidedly less blue than in other 'blues', such as the Russian and British. The colour is due to the dilution gene (d), and first appeared in a

Standards and colours

The show standards for Burmese in North America and Britain (and in Europe, Australia and New Zealand, which have generally followed the British standard) have never coincided to the point of complete agreement on what a Burmese cat should look like. Perhaps because Wong Mau herself – and the Siamese of the time which were used in early breeding – while foreign in general type, were much more round-headed than modern show Siamese, the American standards have always emphasized this roundness. In Britain and some other countries, on the other hand, a moderately wedge-shaped head is regarded as the ideal – certainly not as narrow as in the Siamese, but a good deal more foreign-looking than in North America. In all areas, breeders strive for medium-sized, widely-set ears with rounded points, but while American show standards call for round eyes, British judges prefer a more oval shape. The differences may seem small to the uninitiated, but while both types of Burmese have a singular appearance – and both are very solidly built, feeling heavier than they appear – they look quite distinct if placed side by side.

In all Burmese, the short, dense and glossy coat –

litter born in Britain to a second-generation Burmese import from the United States. The gene, which is recessive (see p20), was probably transmitted to the Burmese breeding lines from Siamese used in early breeding programmes – or just possibly from early imported cats from Burma.

Other colours in Burmese were developed in two main groups. The chocolate – known in North America, whether in the Burmese or Malayan, as champagne – and later its dilute form lilac – called platinum in North America – were first bred in the United States in the late 1960s and early 70s. The former is a pale milk-chocolate colour, with a slightly darker head, the latter a pale dove-grey with slight pinkish shading and again a slightly darker mask. The kittens of both these colours – the lilacs particularly – are almost white when born, and it is some-times difficult to tell lilac from chocolate until they are a few weeks old. As the adult cats grow older, the chocolate Burmese's colour tends to become dis-appointing, those retaining their evenness of tone generally becoming too dark, in most breeders' opinion, while those that remain pale develop too much of a contrast between mask and body tone. Due to their relatively recent importa- */continued*

Burmese cats 2

Newer colours include the lilac **above** and the cream **above right**. The former should ideally be a pale pinkish tone, but many are faulted by show judges for being too blue or too fawn. The cream Burmese, like the blue, is much paler than in other breeds.

tion from North America, many lilac and chocolate Burmese in Britain and elsewhere retain traces of the typical American stockiness of body type.

The second new group of Burmese colours, based on the orange gene (O; see p30), includes reds, creams and tortoiseshells, and these were developed mainly in Britain. The red in Burmese came from three sources: a short-haired ginger tabby, a red point Siamese and a tortie and white farm cat. From these three lines a breeding programme was evolved, and by the mid-1970s clear coats – as free from tabby markings and bars as is possible in a red or cream cat – had been achieved. The reds are a light tangerine-red colour (paler than other reds, due to the influence of the c^b gene), with somewhat darker ears and pink nose and pad leather; the creams a rich cream with only very slightly darker ears. Tortoiseshells are, of course, almost invariably females (see p39); the equivalent of the normal tortoiseshell of other breeds is the brown tortie, in which the red patches can be so light as to appear cream, while blue torties are a mixture of blue and cream. In both cases, blotched, patched or intermingled patterns of the two colours are allowed in the show standards, but Burmese generally tend to have a smaller colour pattern than other tortoiseshells.

By the mid-1970s, British breeders of both the new colour groups felt that interbreeding between them would help to improve the body type of both groups as well as extending further the range of colours. As a result, chocolate torties and lilac torties (lilac-creams) have been bred, making Burmese among the most varied in colour of all pedigree cat breeds in Britain, the European continent, Australia and New Zealand. As yet, however, none of the North American bodies recognize all of these colours, even as Malayans, and even in Britain there is opposition from some breeders, who still regard the brown (and possibly the blue) as the only 'real' Burmese.

Breed characteristics

Even if there is disagreement about colours and standards, owners and breeders of Burmese throughout the world agree as to their temperament. Athletic, brave and humorous, with extraordinary ingenuity, they are unusually adaptable, being equally at home in a city apartment as in good

Tortoiseshell varieties are the most recent to achieve official recognition in Britain. The blue tortie (blue-cream) **above** shows well the mottled, small-scale, evenly balanced colour pattern that breeders like. The lilac tortie (lilac-cream) kitten **above right** has the full adult colouring as yet undefined; this characteristic makes the early assessment of a kitten's colour potential very difficult.

LONG-HAIRED BURMESE

Attractively named Tiffanies by some of the breeders in North America who raise these cats, they are unusual for combining silky long hair with the shaded brown tones of the Burmese. Born a pale *café au lait* colour, the sable colouring and long coat together develop gradually – though the colour is usually lighter than in Burmese of similar age. Like all kittens, they are born with blue eyes, these changing through grey to the adult golden colour.

THE BOMBAY

Sometimes referred to as mini-panthers, the Bombay has been described as a 'patent-leather kid with new-penny eyes'. The name was chosen because of their supposed similarity – though in miniature – to the black leopard of India, and with their shining black coat and glowing copper eyes they are eye-catching and attractive on the show bench and in the home.

Although similar in body type to the Burmese, Bombays are not simply black Burmese. So far bred only in North America, they were first produced by a mating between a black American Shorthair (see p68) and a sable (brown) Burmese in 1958. The resulting offspring, having only one Burmese (c^b) gene, were black but had the fine, silky, sleek short coat of the Burmese. The breed was slow to become established, but by 1976 was accepted by the CFA for championship status. Breeders prefer the eye colour to be copper – the greater the depth and intensity of colour the better.

Because of their mixed ancestry, Bombay kittens show characteristics of both Burmese and American Shorthairs. They are usually born in litters of four or five, and develop very rapidly. They have voracious appetites and grow into quite large yet graceful adults. Playful without being garrulous, they are middle-of-the-road in temperament, too.

A Burmese family group – a red mother with her chocolate tortie female and cream male kittens, resulting from a mating with a chocolate male carrying the dilute gene – shows further variations on the Burmese theme. These cats are of the somewhat narrower-headed British type, more wedge-shaped than American breeders prefer.

hunting country. They can catch and eat quite large rodents – two Burmese living in southern England once shepherded (but did not eat!) a large duck into their owners' home – but happily they will play for hours retrieving rolled-up pieces of foil. Boisterous without the nervous temperament some Siamese are noted for, some are extrovert and some retiring, but all are affectionate and beguiling.

They are quite precocious, females first coming into heat at about seven months and, when allowed to mate, bearing on average about five kittens. Some breeding lines have produced a relatively high proportion of congenital (inborn) skeletal abnormalities, possibly due to inbreeding during the years when the breed was under development. However, very many Burmese live for 16 to 18 years, or even more, and are sadly missed by their owners, who regard them as cats for the connoisseur.

Siamese cats I

To many people, the Siamese represents the ultimate in feline beauty. Of all breeds, it is the most instantly recognizable, with its coloured mask, ears, stockings and tail – the 'points' – combined with a paler body and brilliant, piercing-blue eyes, and its long, elegant, yet muscular body. Its history is documented in the ancient literature and art of Siam (now Thailand), so it can also boast of an authentic exotic origin, and ever since its introduction to the Western world over 100 years ago it has become ever more popular – even fashionable – as a pet and show cat.

Today it is one of the most popular – perhaps *the* most popular – of pedigree breeds. Like many others, however, it has been the centre of disagreement and controversy among breeders and cat fancy organizations. Firstly, opinions on what makes the 'ideal' show Siamese differ considerably on the two sides of the Atlantic, Americans favouring an extremely foreign body and a very narrow wedge-shaped head with a very straight profile like a Roman nose, whereas Europeans are more moderate in their demands. Secondly, many of the cats shown in Britain and elsewhere as Siamese – those with red, tabby (lynx) and many other point colours – are denied this name by the CFA and some of the other American associations, but have to be registered and shown as Colorpoint Shorthairs. As a result, breeding between the two colour groupings is restricted for breeders registering with the CFA.

Origins and myths

Although there have been many theories about the origin of the Siamese – including even suggestions that it is related to Egyptian and Manx cats – it is now quite certain that it was a well-loved variety in the ancient Siamese city of Ayudha. Ayudha was founded in 1350 and was Siam's capital until it was burnt down by invading Burmese in 1767. In the Thai National Library, in the present-day capital Bangkok, are manuscripts saved from Ayudha that provide a record of the native cats, dogs and birds of the time. The manuscripts – the best-known is called the *Cat-Book Poems* (see p 240) – depict beautiful pale-coated seal point Siamese and include verses describing them as having black tails, feet and ears, with white hair and reddish eyes. (The latter may possibly refer to the characteristic reddish eye shine of the Siamese; see p 111.)

The people of Siam did not regard the pointed cats as their only native variety, but there is evidence to suggest that they were particularly valued and kept by royalty in their palaces. Other native cats recorded include the Si-Sawat (self blue; see p 81) and Supalak (copper-brown). The pointed cats recorded by the artists of Ayudha had a very pale coat and their pointing is minimal, with the leg colouring little more than 'socks' and the mask merely a smudge of colour on the nose and whisker pads. This may, of course, have represented an idealized cat; certainly the next recorded mention of the Siamese pattern – many thousands of miles away in central Russia in 1793 – was of a much darker colouring.

This was an account by naturalist Simon Pallas, who described three cats having a light chestnut-brown body colour, blacker on the back and paler on the sides and belly. They had a black streak running along the nose, around the eyes and up to the forehead, while the ears, paws and tail were quite black.

The difference in climate between Russia and southeast Asia would account for the darker colouring, for the formation of pigment in the Siamese depends on temperature – the cooler the surroundings, the darker the colour. But no one knows whether these cats were descended from imported Siamese or whether the Siamese gene mutation (see p 36) occurred spontaneously in this area. It may be significant, however, that Pallas describes the cats' heads as being longer towards the nose than in 'the common cat' – as with those in Siam – though the illustration accompanying his report shows them to have been quite rounded by modern standards.

The same is true, however, of the first Siamese to reach Europe from Siam, which were the subject of much speculation and comment. They were accompanied by (or soon supplied with) many stories, among them accounts of the supposed origins of the squinting eyes and kinked tails that were a common feature of the breed. It was said, for example, that the

An ancient Siamese is illustrated in the *Cat-Book Poems* **below** with colour restricted to the extreme points, possibly in part an idealization but also showing the effect of a hot climate.

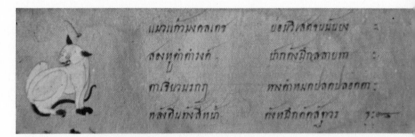

sacred Siamese temple cats were left in charge of a very valuable vase and that, in order to guard it properly, they curled their tails around it and stared at it so hard that their eyes became crossed. Another explanation of the kink has it that the royal princesses of Siam relied on their cats to look after their rings; these were kept on the cats' tails and the kinks developed to stop them falling off. Modern explanations are more mundane, for both features seem to have a genetic basis. The squint in particular seems to be directly linked with the Siamese gene (see p 37); the heredity of the kink is unclear, but it is quite common in south-east Asia. Breeders are reducing the incidence of both defects by selective breeding.

Siamese in the cat fancy

It is unclear when the first Siamese cats appeared in the Western world. There is a well-authenticated account that the British consul general in Bangkok acquired a pair of seal points in 1884 which his sister

Siamese in Europe were first exhibited at the 1871 Crystal Palace cat show and illustrated in the engraving **above**. The photograph shows early 20th-century kittens, less fine-boned than today's. One has white paws – a bad fault today.

exhibited in London the following year. However, there were certainly Siamese in Britain at least 14 years earlier than this, for they appeared at the first modern-style cat show, in 1871; they were described as 'an unnatural, nightmare kind of cat'. Despite this early reaction, they were a rapid success, and others were obtained by a number of cat fanciers – although they were notoriously difficult to obtain and rear. It was very soon realized that they were susceptible to enteritis and respiratory problems (see p 192 and 197), but by the end of the 19th century the breed was well established in Britain. One writer noted, however, that the Siamese 'is never likely to be common, as the cats are delicate in this country'. Siamese first reached the United States around 1890 – supposedly given by the king of Siam to an American friend – and were seen in shows there in the first years of this century.

The first standard of points was devised in Britain in 1892 and was rewritten some ten years later. Then the Siamese was described as 'a somewhat curious and striking cat of medium size, if weighty not showing bulk as this would detract from the admired svelte appearance. In type, in every particular the reverse of the ideal short-haired domestic cat and with properly preserved contrasts in colour, a very handsome animal, often distinguished by a kink in the tail.' The kink, in fact, was regarded equivocally, and it was many years before it came to be seen as a fault; the first-ever Siamese champion in Britain – a cat called Wankee born in Hong Kong in 1895 – had a kinked tail. In another respect, too, this description reads strangely – at least in comparison with contemporary photographs of Siamese – for these cats were very round-headed compared with even the more moderately foreign modern Siamese of Europe, let alone the extreme type produced by some American breeders today.

Most of the early writers on the breed stated that there were two kinds of Siamese among the early imports, though it was the pale-bodied /continued

Seal point Siamese The group **below** shows the development of point colour from the very young kitten, where pointing is pale and minimal in extent, through older kittens, where the points become more dense and the coat may show transient darker shading, to the young adult, where the points are a dense seal-brown and the body a pale, even cream to fawn. At the same time, the body – and particularly the head – develops its full, elegant adult length.

Siamese cats 2

The main colours of Siamese, apart from the seal point **overleaf**, are the blue point **right**, which for exhibition should have a 'cold', glacial white body, the chocolate point **above** with ivory body colour, and – most recent of all – the lilac point **below right**, which in Europe is required to have an off-white body, whereas a glacial white tone is preferred by judges in North America.

Colour variations recognized as true Siamese in Europe but only as Colorpoint Shorthairs in most North American associations include tortie points **below** and tabby (lynx) points **below right**; both of these examples are the chocolate versions.

pointed kind – generally referred to then as the royal Siamese or the royal cat of Siam – that was most highly regarded. Others were described as chocolate – still with dark points, but with the body colour a rich dark brown all over – and with hindsight it would seem likely that these were Siamese-Burmese hybrids (which today would be called Tonkinese; see p 90) and that probably there were pure brown Burmese among them too. Reports from early shows also indicate the existence of chocolate point (see below) as well as the darker seal point Siamese, but there is some confusion here. It was not until the late 1920s that the Siamese Cat Club in Britain decided to promote only the blue-eyed pointed Siamese.

It is also not clear when the first blue point Siamese appeared. In a book published in 1912, it was reported that a Mr Spearman, just home from Siam, exhibited a blue point at a show in 1896 and that it was disqualified by the judge (cat lover and artist Louis Wain). Other reports, however, suggest that this was a self blue like the Korat (see p 81). Although the ancient Siamese manuscripts show only the seal point, not blue point, blue selfs lived there (and are illustrated, as already mentioned) and interbreeding between the two types would certainly have resulted in blue points. Perhaps they were not highly regarded. In any case, at least one blue point Siamese was registered before 1900 and a good many more in the early years of this century. They appeared in North American shows in the 1920s and received full recognition by the CFA as early as 1932, but the GCCF in Britain did not recognize them until 1936.

Chocolate point Siamese were undoubtedly bred soon after the first cats left Siam, but the use of the word chocolate to denote solid brown cats makes it difficult to establish which cats were truly chocolate points. The first undoubted Siamese of this colour to be registered in Britain was born in 1931 but (like blue points) they were not favoured by most breeders, who regarded them as poor-quality seals. A few persevered, however, and they were officially recognized as a separate variety in Britain in 1950 and in the United States a year later. Early cats varied in colour, but by the late 1950s some fine examples, with rich, warm milk-chocolate point colouring, were being bred. Since then, the colour quality has declined again until today a cat with truly milk-chocolate points is a rarity; most are nearer the 'poor seal' colouring remarked in the early years.

Lilac point Siamese are produced when the blue dilution and chocolate brown genes are combined (see p 29). In view of the fact that both these genes were present in the native Siamese population long before cats were taken to the West it is surprising that they were not officially recognized until the mid-1950s in the United States (where the name frost point was, and by some associations still is, used) and 1960 in Britain. Many of the first British-bred lilac points had Russian Blues among their ancestors, and their breeders had to contend not only with the antipathy of other breeders but also with the fact that very few female lilac point kittens were born.

Red, tabby (lynx) and related colours

The four colours described above are the only varieties regarded by many American cat associations (and many traditionalist breeders elsewhere) as the true Siamese. (Some people indeed still draw the line at the seal point.) But whether classed as Siamese or Colorpoint Shorthairs, many more colours have been bred in the years since World War II. The first of these new colours to be established were the red and tortie points, and in fact two red point cats were shown at a Siamese Cat Club show in England in 1934 (when they were known as orange points). But present-day red points are derived from breeding programmes begun in the United States in 1947 and in Britain in 1948.

In order to introduce the orange gene, outcrosses to non-Siamese had to be made (to a long-haired red tabby in the United States and to a half-Siamese tortoiseshell in Britain), and the pioneer breeders were long hampered by poor (for a show Siamese, that is) body type. With hindsight, it is easy to see that they would have been better off backcrossing their earliest red points to seal points in order to establish the desired Siamese body type and then to have allowed more generations to stabilize the red colour. As it was, the cobbiness of the early red points increased other breeders' prejudice against them. In Britain the GCCF at first offered to recognize them as Pointed Foreign Shorthairs, but their breeders refused to accept this. Recognition as Siamese – but under a different breed number from the original four colours – came in 1966. In the United States, the CFA voted against their recognition as Siamese in 1963, but in the following year they were fully recognized as Colorpoint Shorthairs. At the same time or shortly afterwards, in both countries, other related colours were recognized: tortie points – now bred in blue, chocolate and lilac versions as well as seal – and cream points, together with tabby (lynx) points.

A Siamese tabby was mentioned as early as 1902, and in 1924 a Swedish geneticist published the results of breeding experiments in which he produced tabby points. A few more were bred in Scotland in 1940, but it was only in the 1960s that cat fanciers became interested in them once more. In 1960 a seal point Siamese belonging to a British breeder mated with a local tom, which must have been a tabby. A tabby kitten from that litter was mated with another seal point and bore a litter of six Siamese, four of which had tabby-striped seal-coloured points. They were first shown publicly in 1961, to great acclaim, and were officially recognized five years later. At the first cat show after recognition, a tabby point was voted supreme Siamese in the show. There was some debate on naming before recognition, some breeders feeling that the term lynx point was more appropriate to their attractiveness. In Britain the name tabby point was finally chosen, but they are still called lynx points in North America, where they were first recognized in the mid-1960s.

Most, if not all, of the early tabby points were seal coloured, and for a long time breeders believed that the variety would be restricted to seal, blue, chocolate and lilac. The fact that red points and red tabby points, though genetically different, look identical (see p37) caused breeding problems until it was agreed to register them both as red tabby points unless proved otherwise by their pedigree or offspring. (The difference only matters to breeders who want to be able to predict whether tabby point and/or self point offspring are likely to appear in a litter.) For a similar reason it was decided to register tabby tortie points under the tabby group rather than the tortie.

One variety not considered possible was the silver

tabby point, though it is now known that the first lilac tabby point Siamese were, in fact, lilac silver tabby points. This was because, until 1970, geneticists and breeders thought that the silver colouring was produced by the so-called chinchilla gene, one of the albino series of genes of which the Siamese gene is also a member (see p30). This would mean that a cat could be either silver or Siamese, but not both. But the discovery of the inhibitor gene (I; see p34), responsible for the silver colouring in cats, meant that this combination was possible. The first of the group deliberately bred, although registered as a /continued

The red point Siamese (recognized in North America as a Colorpoint Shorthair) shows the brilliant red point colouring and pale cream body characteristic of the variety; red points invariably show some tabby markings even though they are not genetically tabby cats. Like all good show Siamese, this cat has the long tapering lines well described in the British show standard: 'The Siamese cat should be a beautifully balanced animal with head, ears and neck carried on a long svelte body, supported on fine legs and feet with a tail in proportion. The head and profile should be wedge shaped, neither round nor pointed.' The only disagreement with American breeders is on how far this aim of an elongated appearance should be taken. The CFA standard specifies that the head should be a 'long tapering wedge . . . In profile, a long straight line is seen from the top of the head to the tip of the nose.' The body is described as tubular.

Siamese cats 3

blue tabby point, was a blue silver tabby point raised in Britain. Other silver tabby points have been raised, including seal, chocolate, red and cream, but no action has yet been taken to obtain official recognition except in New Zealand; they are simply registered as ordinary tabby points or as experimental.

Other new colours

Another direct result of the genetic investigation of the silver was the establishment of the smoke pointed varieties – now known to British breeders as shadow points. As with non-Siamese smokes (see p35), these have heavy tipping on the coloured areas – that is, the points – and are genetically non-tabbies. In the late 1960s a British breeder raised two such kittens, but believing them to be poor seal points sold them as neutered pets. With new understanding of the genetic mechanism of the smoke, an explanation for these kittens was available, and when breeders kept them until their adult coat characteristics developed it was apparent that they had an unusual attractiveness of their own.

The name shadow point was adopted because the points show a shadowy tabby pattern, like taffeta or watered silk. They are now bred in all colours, but do not show their true beauty until they are adults; kittens are heavily shaded on the body and can easily be mistaken for dark-coated self point Siamese. Bred only in small numbers so far, no attempt has yet been made to obtain official recognition for them in Britain. In a similar situation are the chinchilla or shaded silver equivalents, known variously as tipped Siamese or pastel pointed Siamese, which are, however, more likely to achieve recognition (at least in Britain) among the Oriental Shorthairs than as Siamese (see p92). As with silver tabby points, New Zealand was the first country to recognize the shadow and pastel points.

Three other Siamese colours are known, but these too are unrecognized in both Britain and North America. They are the cinnamon point, a truly milk-chocolate pointed cat produced by the light brown gene (see p29); the lavender point, a pale pinkish variety similar to the lilac point but produced by a combination of the light brown and blue dilute genes; and the caramel point. This last has points of a *café au lait* colour, and is produced by the action of an as yet unnamed dominant gene upon a blue ground.

Finally, there is the albino Siamese – a cat of Siamese type carrying the blue-eyed albino gene rather than the Siamese gene, so that it is not truly a Siamese at all. It has become established in small numbers in both Europe and North America, but in Britain is known as the Recessive White and in most American associations as an Oriental Shorthair.

Characteristics

Whatever the colour of their points, Siamese all demonstrate the capacity to be extra-affectionate, extra-noisy, extra-demonstrative, extra-angry, extra-active, extra-sexy, extra-fertile, in fact extra in every way. They have been credited with great intelligence and are ideal pets for those who are prepared to give and receive a lifetime of devotion. As one turn-of-the-century breeder noted: 'They are dog-like in their nature, and can be easily taught to turn back somersaults, and to retrieve, and in the country take long walks like a terrier.' Few owners nowadays choose to treat them this way, but they do seem more amenable to exercising on a leash than most other breeds. To some people, however, they are just too spooky.

Siamese litters are often larger than those of other breeds, and the kittens develop rapidly, sometimes opening their eyes when only a few days old and leaving their box at three to four weeks. They are born nearly white, the first hint of colour appearing in a thin line at the edge of the ears and gradually becoming evident on the pads, nose leather and tail. Through kittenhood the pigmentation gradually develops, the full colouring appearing only when the cat is nearly adult. The full glory of their eye colour develops as the 'baby blue' of kittenhood changes, generally at about eight weeks. Their precocity extends to sexual behaviour, females often calling as young as five months. In most cases, however, a show Siamese's career is over by the age of three years, for the body colour often gradually darkens.

A silver tabby point Siamese, still relatively rare, has a paler body than normal and is silver between the tabby stripes.

A natural mink Tonkinese

THE TONKINESE

Probably genetically similar to the all-brown 'chocolate Siamese' of 80 years ago, this hybrid of the Siamese and Burmese was the first pedigree breed to originate in Canada, and the CCA was the first association to give it full recognition. Several others in North America, Europe and Australia have since accepted it.

The Tonkinese carries one Siamese (c^s) and one Burmese (c^b) gene (see p25), and its physical features represent a blend of its two parent breeds. A Siamese/Burmese cross produces all Tonkinese, whereas mating two Tonks produces, on average, two Tonkinese kittens to one each with Burmese and Siamese colouring. The Tonkinese has dark points, but these merge gently into the body colour, which is intermediate between Burmese and Siamese colouring. The commonest colour is termed natural mink, which corresponds to seal and brown (sable), but three other colours are bred: honey mink, champagne and blue (blue-grey), corresponding to the Siamese colours chocolate, lilac and blue respectively. The body shape is also intermediate, the head being described in the show standard as a modified wedge with a squarish muzzle. The eyes are blue-green in colour. Described as outgoing and affectionate, it is said to be both a beautiful show cat and an ideal household pet.

The Havana Brown

Reputed by the poets of ancient Siam to be of great beauty, protecting their owners from all evil, the all-brown cats were treasured in that country and were among the early Siamese to arrive in the West. It now seems likely that there were several distinct genetic types among them, including representatives of what would now be termed Burmese and Tonkinese (see pp 82 and 90) as well as self (solid) chocolates – though it is virtually impossible to tell, from mere descriptions, which cats were which. In 1888 such a cat won a first prize at a British show, and 40 years later one won a special prize at a Siamese Cat Club show for having 'the best chocolate body'. Soon after, this club ruled that it would encourage the breeding of the blue-eyed cats only, and the few browns of the day sank into obscurity until the arrival from the United States of the first Burmese.

In the early 1950s, two breeders in Britain (at first independently, later working together) set about producing solid brown cats with the chocolate colouring of the Siamese rather than the sable of the newly-imported Burmese. At that time the only recognized foreign breeds other than Siamese were the Russian Blue and Abyssinian. The first kitten of the new colour was born in 1952 from a cross between a seal point Siamese carrying the chocolate brown gene and a short-haired black (itself produced by crossing a seal point with a black cat). It was first exhibited in 1953, and became the foundation of the new breed, to be known as the Havana after the rabbit breed of the same colour. In 1956, the breeders reported their breed ready for recognition, but it was to be two years before this came. In those two years arguments raged over the desired body type and registration status, and many people criticized it for its similarity to the Burmese.

At about this time, a pair of Havanas were taken to the United States to found the breed there. The problem of mistaken identity with the Burmese was not so acute in its new home since the Burmese was much better established. Official breed recognition was granted in 1959, with the word Brown added to the name. The standard for judging Havana Browns at shows followed that for the Russian Blue except that the colour was described as a warm, rich, mahogany-brown. But in Britain the emphasis of breeders and show judges moved with increasing momentum towards a Siamese-type body, whereas Americans stayed with the earlier moderately foreign type. When, in 1958, the GCCF in Britain gave official recognition, it was under the name Chestnut Brown Foreign; this has since been changed to Havana, but it is quite a different cat that really belongs in the Oriental Shorthair group (see p 92).

The Havana Brown has now developed as a uniquely North American breed, with a head slightly longer than it is wide and a distinct 'stop' on the nose between the eyes. The oval eyes are chartreuse to green in colour. In temperament, it resembles the Russian Blue, and is highly intelligent, showing a great desire for human companionship and attention. It is slightly less vocal than the Siamese and Orientals, but tends to talk constantly to its kittens. These are born slightly paler than the adults and often show shadowy tabby markings which later disappear.

Closely related to the Havana Brown was the Lavender Foreign Shorthair (not to be confused with the American lavender Oriental Shorthair or the

British Foreign Lilac, which are both Siamese in type). It evolved naturally from Havana Brown lines, tracing ancestry back also to the Russian Blue. The latter introduced the blue dilution gene (d; see p 29) which produced the delicate lavender colour. It was recognized by the ACFA, but not the other North American associations, and was at one time popular. However, after the emergence of the lavender Oriental Shorthair its numbers declined.

Havana Browns developed from early British-bred cats of moderate type **left** sent to the United States in the 1950s. In Britain they evolved into Siamese-type cats, but the true Havana Brown **below** is unique, as its breed standard points out: 'Due to its distinctive muzzle shape, colour and large forward-tilted ears, it is comparable to no other breed.' The colour – a rich, warm chocolate-brown – is, in fact, no longer quite so unique with the development of brown Oriental Shorthairs.

Oriental Shorthairs 1

In their ancestral home, Siamese were not defined solely as cats with colour restricted to the points, and it was only by chance – and their distinctiveness – that the first cats from Siam (now Thailand) to attract the attention of the Western world were pointed. In the old manuscripts of Siam were described and depicted the ancestors of some modern brown (see p83) and blue (see p81) breeds, and also such cats as whites and shaded silvers. All-black cats must also have been known, for matings between the two known varieties of browns produce black. Certainly a black and white bicolour was recorded; it was called the Singhasep. A recent survey of Thai domestic cats showed that today in the Bangkok area only 20 per cent are pointed, while over 50 per cent are self (solid) coloured or selfs with white.

The original 'Siamese' of the Western cat fancy included some cats that were coloured all over, as is explained in the preceding articles. It was not until the end of the 1920s that the Siamese Cat Club of Britain issued a definitive statement on the Siamese: 'The club much regrets it is unable to encourage the breeding of any but blue-eyed Siamese.' From that time on the self (solid) coloured cats with yellow or green eyes were excluded from the Siamese classes at shows. Although in the short term this spelt their decline, it also marks the beginning of the history of a separate breed of cats, now known to breeders world-wide as Oriental Shorthairs.

This group encompasses all the cats with a Siamese body shape that are not pointed – that is, those with an all-over solid colour or pattern, including bicolours, tortoiseshells, tabbies, tipped colours and so on. Technically they are all members of one breed – like the Siamese itself they have an elegant, lithe and sinuous body, long tail and narrow wedge-shaped head, and are far removed from their original, relatively cobby forebears in south-east Asia. But, just as in the Siamese section of the cat fancy, differences of policy and opinion have produced a situation where in some associations – mainly those of North America – all these cats are known officially as Oriental Shorthairs, while in Britain the names Havana, Foreign and Oriental are all applied to the same breed type. The name Havana was retained for historical reasons (as explained on page 91, it is not now the same as the American Havana Brown, which is much less Siamese-like), and for reasons never fully understood by the breeders of the cats the GCCF decreed that the self coloured Siamese-type cats should be known as Foreign, only the patterned varieties being given the name Oriental.

The self colours

From the date of their exclusion by the Siamese Cat Club, all-over coloured foreign-type cats began to disappear into anonymity as far as Western cat fanciers were concerned, although all-black and all-blue cats of similar body shape were described by a German professor writing just before the outbreak of World War II. He expressly stated that they were 'beautiful strains with good capability of inheritance', but there is no further record of them. Breeding probably stopped with wartime restrictions and economies. It was only after the war that a breeding programme was planned in Britain for the production of all-brown coated cats with a foreign body shape (see p91). Once this new breed was under way they became the trailblazers for the Siamese-shaped whites soon to appear. A few tabbies and torties of foreign type were produced during the creation of the early red, tortie and tabby (lynx) point Siamese (see p88). But real progress towards the Orientals of today did not start until 1962.

In that year, a British breeder and geneticist began a ten-year programme to create a breed of true-breeding blue-eyed white cats. (The stages involved are explained and illustrated on page 47.) Two other breeders in fact started similar programmes at the same time, and all three joined forces in 1964. As early as 1965 the manager of a cat show held at York reported: 'The BBC Television paid us a visit and viewers were able to see us all in action. There was special interest in Miss Turner's experimental "white Siamese".' In fact, these blue-eyed whites – with none of the deafness problems and totally different in appearance and character from the other white breeds

Two Oriental selfs of great beauty are the black or ebony **below** – the green eyes looking superb against the glossy jet-black coat – and the much more subtly toned lilac or lavender **below right**. Wherever they are bred, Orientals are expected to conform to the same body standards as Siamese.

Other varieties of Foreign or Oriental selfs include the popular white **below** – in this case an American cat, in which green eyes are permitted as well as blue – the British-type Havana or Chestnut Brown Foreign **right**, which is fully Siamese-like in body shape, and the blue self **far right**.

– proved equally attractive to lovers of the pointed Siamese and became the talk of the cat fancy. To follow the precedent of the Havana, recognized only on condition that it was renamed Chestnut Brown Foreign, the new breed was put forward for recognition as the White Foreign or Foreign White. Full recognition with championship status (under the second name) came in 1977, by which time they were reliably true-breeding for blue eyes as brilliant as those of any Siamese and the best cats were very close to the top winning Siamese in body type. The breed had its first grand champion in 1979.

Because the white coat of the breed is dominant and masks any underlying colour genes (see p26), and because back-crosses to pointed Siamese were necessary to 'fix' the blue eyes and to produce a truly Siamese body shape, some of the kittens bred in the early Foreign White litters were non-white. And since the original white cats used in the programme were not from Siamese ancestry, non-Siamese genes were also present. As a result, some of the kittens did not simply have coloured points but were coloured all over. Some of the first of these were spotted tabbies, solid reds and solid blacks. A few were exhibited, but interest centred mainly on the whites and most were not bred further. But one such kitten had the rich chestnut colouring desired by breeders of the Chestnut Brown Foreign. Not only did it have markedly Siamese body shape but, being sired by a lilac point Siamese, had the potential to breed both its own colour and lilac. This cat went on to found a dynasty of Siamese-type Chestnut Browns and was instrumental in the move towards a Siamese body shape for this breed (see p91), whose show standard was eventually amended accordingly in 1974.

The repeated use of lilac point Siamese as mates in the Chestnut Brown breeding programme resulted in the birth of a number of Siamese-type solid lilacs, and the Foreign Lilac breed gained full recognition at the same time as the Foreign White. Other self colours have been bred over the years, but with the exception of the Foreign Black (which was given provisional status in 1978) none have yet achieved recognition in Britain. In most of the colours other than the Foreign White, green eyes are specified.

Newest of all the colours to appear in Oriental Shorthairs are two pale browns, seen in their self versions in the Foreign Cinnamon and Foreign Caramel. The former – a warm light brown colour reminiscent of milk chocolate – is genetically related to the Havana (Chestnut Brown), the only difference being the possession of the light-brown gene (symbolized b^l; see p29) in place of the /continued

Oriental Shorthairs 2

normal brown (*b*). The former is recessive to the latter, and many Havanas in Britain carry the gene. It also occurs in the non-sex-linked 'red' (sorrel) Abyssinian, known since the 1880s. But it was only during the 1970s that outcrosses to Siamese – carried out in order to elucidate the genetics of the red Abyssinian – produced the first deliberately bred light brown cats. At first the colour was known as milk chocolate; under the name Cinnamon they are now bred in several countries. Type has been improved through back-crosses to Siamese and Chestnut Browns.

The genetics of the caramel – a *café au lait* shade – has not yet been fully investigated, but it seems to be produced by the dilution of blue and lilac by the action of a dominant non-sex-linked gene. In Britain and Holland, both Siamese (see p90) and Oriental Shorthair versions (including torties, silvers and tabbies) have been bred, but the aim of the main

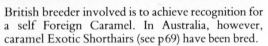

British breeder involved is to achieve recognition for a self Foreign Caramel. In Australia, however, caramel Exotic Shorthairs (see p69) have been bred.

Tabbies, silvers and other colours
During the period when the Foreign Lilacs and Foreign Whites were still being developed in Britain, a few breeders became interested in tabby cats with Siamese shape, and a number were shown and won prizes. But the real impetus came when a British breeder became intrigued by the spotted cats shown in ancient Egyptian frescoes. Quite independently of the American breeders of the Egyptian Mau (see p79), she determined to recreate the breed with British stock, and started her breeding programme with a Siamese-type tabby produced during the development of the tabby point Siamese. She later crossed two Chestnut Browns with tabby points and produced some beautifully marked spotted tabbies of Siamese type. In their earlier years as an unrecognized variety these were known as the Egyptian Mau, but the name eventually requested for breed recognition (which was given in 1978) was Oriental Tabby. This name acknowledges the fact that they are much more

foreign in type than the original American-bred Egyptian Maus. So far only spotted versions are recognized in Britain – in all the basic self colours – but ticked (Abyssinian-type), mackerel and classic tabbies have also been bred.

A new direction in Oriental breeding in Britain began in 1970 when an accidental mating between a chinchilla Persian and a chocolate point Siamese resulted in the birth of two foreign-type shaded silver kittens. Their owner contacted the same breeder who was developing the blue-eyed Foreign White. She acquired the kittens, their mother and an aunt. Thus began the breeding programme that not only established – in just one generation – that the inhibitor gene (*I*; see p34) responsible for silver, shaded and smoke colourings is dominant and independent of the Siamese gene, but also resulted in a variety of new coat colours attractive to cat fanciers. These are the various degrees of tipped Siamese and Orientals, which, even though some of them are pointed, seem more likely to gain recognition (in Britain at least) as Orientals than as Siamese. The tipped silver Siamese seem the likeliest candidates for official recognition. They have an almost silver-white coat, tipped with

Patterned Orientals include tabbies in a wide range of colours and often bred in the spotted pattern. Illustrated here are a lilac (lavender) tabby **opposite top**, a blue tabby **left** and – most recently introduced of all – a cinnamon tabby **far left**. Other new varieties include shaded and tipped cats, such as the shaded silver **above** (one of the early cats in the pioneer British breeding programme, with too rounded a head to satisfy today's judges) and tortoiseshells **right**. A number of these varieties have yet to achieve full championship status in some countries.

only a trace of seal-brown at the points and with deep blue eyes encircled by almost black lines. In New Zealand these cats are known as pastel point Siamese, but in the United States neither the tipped Orientals nor the tipped Siamese are yet bred.

All cats of this breeding programme so far trace their ancestry back to one of the original shaded silver kittens born in 1970. The other kitten never bred, and progeny from subsequent matings between the two chinchillas and Siamese did not survive. But not only did this programme introduce the smoke, silver, shaded and tipped varieties to the Oriental Shorthair, but it also contributed to development of the Oriental Spotted Tabbies. Today the most brilliantly marked of these are in fact silver tabbies whose ancestry combines cats of the original Oriental Tabbies with those in the silver group.

Orientals around the world

American cat fanciers visiting British shows and catteries in the early 1970s realized immediately that, while in North America the Havana Browns (and Lavenders) had continued to be bred to standards differing only slightly from the original standards

drawn up in Britain a decade earlier, in Britain itself the varieties had evolved into much more svelte creatures of Siamese type. They subsequently pioneered the North American Oriental Shorthairs by founding an international breed club which was joined by many Siamese breeders. The name Oriental Shorthair was approved and provisional recognition given by the CFA – the largest association – in 1976. The breed reached championship status only a year later, and within one season had seven grand champions and a number of 'best in show' awards, and also featured among the CFA's all-American top twenty cats.

Competition was allowed by the CFA in five groups: solids, shaded, smokes, tabbies (of all patterns) and particolours. Not all possible colours were allowed in every group, but the system is much more straightforward than in Britain, where each self colour has to qualify for separate breed status and have its own breed classes and breed number. Thus, in North America, ebonies (blacks), blues, chestnuts, lavenders, reds, creams and whites may all compete for championship honours. In Britain, the blues, reds and creams may not at present compete at all, the Foreign Blacks may compete but without championship status and the Havanas, Foreign Lilacs and Foreign Whites may compete for championships. There is similar disparity and confusion among the shades, smokes, tabbies and tortoiseshells.

Oriental Shorthairs are now well established worldwide, even if their status is in some confusion, and the standards used to judge them in cat shows vary very little. One minor, though significant, difference is that whites in North America may have blue or green eyes – and amber is not penalized heavily – while in Britain only the blue is permitted. American breeders do not make a point of breeding the consistently blue-eyed white type. A minor problem that occurs everywhere is that of Siamese-pointed kittens occurring occasionally in the litters of Oriental parents. This is only to be expected since many Orientals carry one Siamese colour gene. In some associations these kittens have to be registered (if at all) as 'any other variety' Orientals rather than as Siamese.

Breed characteristics

The personality of the Oriental Shorthair is identical to that of the Siamese (see p 90) for, in truth, the only difference between the two breeds is in one or two colour genes. Like Siamese, the individual cats develop varying personalities but all tend to demand a lot of attention from their owners and to engender and give total devotion.

Females may be keen to mate early, but most breeders delay this until they are over nine months old. Litters are often large, those in the silver breeding programme begun in 1970 being particularly large. (One shaded silver tortoiseshell gave birth to six kittens in her first litter and never less than eight in subsequent litters, her largest being of 13 kittens.) Orientals make devoted mothers, and their kittens are extremely active – even to the point of exhausting their owners. They are great climbers, practising first on the furniture and curtains of their own home and then, if allowed to have freedom outdoors, scaling even tall trees. They are not the cats to acquire if you want a peaceful life.

Rex cats

The curly-coated Cornish and Devon Rex cats – two distinct breeds despite their superficial similarity and close origins – have been appearing at cat shows in Europe since the 1950s and North America soon after, yet they are still unusual enough to provoke curiosity and debate among many cat lovers. The Cornish Rex, developed from a mutation (see p23) occurring in Cornwall, England, in 1950, has a curly, plush coat and has been bred with a moderately foreign body type and a rather 'Roman' nose. The Devon Rex originated with a different mutation occurring a few years later in neighbouring Devon and has a very short wavy coat; show cats have a very pronounced foreign-type body with a unique pixie-like head shape and often curious tufts of longer hair at the back of the ears.

The genetic mutations involved in these breeds, and the resulting hair types, are discussed on page 43. Since the mutations are distinct, mating Cornish and Devon Rexes together results in kittens with straight coats – albeit of a slightly different texture from those of normal short-hairs. Because of this, breeders made a deliberate decision in the early 1960s to breed them selectively along different lines to make them more easily distinguishable, and not to interbreed them. In a sense, however, the body differences are superficial; the bases of the breeds lie in the gene mutations and coats.

Similar mutations have also occurred elsewhere, but with the exception of the German Rex – since proved to be genetically identical to the Cornish – none have been established as viable breeds. The Ohio and Oregon Rexes, both originally occurring in the United States, seem to have died out. Long-haired rexes have also been bred, but are not generally considered to be attractive, their coats appearing lank and sparse; overall they present a rather ragged appearance.

History

The first known rex cat was the German Rex, observed in the form of a feral hospital cat in East Berlin as early as 1946 but not 'adopted' by breeders until 1951, a year after the first Cornish Rex was born to a farm cat. This kitten was named Kallibunker, and his owner contacted a well-known cat breeder and a rabbit fancier with an interest in genetics. By back-crossing, more rex kittens were produced, and the mutation was proved to be recessive (see p20); it was named after the similar mutation in the rabbit. In 1957, two descendants of Kallibunker were sent

The Cornish Rex has a foreign-type head and body, the former **above** showing straight lines from ears to chin, a rather long nose and oriental eyes. The American-bred blue Cornish Rex **left** demonstrates well the long legs, whippy tail, straight nose and dense wavy coat that are the primary characteristics of the breed.

The Devon Rex has been bred with a quite unmistakable head shape **above** that is unique in pedigree cats. Its nose is quite short, the whisker pads prominent and the ears huge. The example **left** is a blue tortie (blue-cream), showing the short curly coat that in some cats may be rather sparse. The whiskers are characteristically curly.

The Si-Rex is an unofficial name for rex cats with Siamese colouring. This example is a seal point Cornish Rex bred in the United States, where they are not recognized by the CFA but are popular with many cat lovers for their unusual and attractive appearance.

to the United States to found the Rex breed there.

Meanwhile, a curly-coated feral cat was observed in 1960 to be living near a disused tin mine near Buckfastleigh, Devon. A young tortie and white stray cared for by a nearby resident mated with this cat – in retrospect they were probably related – and gave birth to a curly-coated kitten, which was adopted and called Kirlee. The publicity given to the Cornish Rex enabled Kirlee's owner to contact the breeder involved in the Cornish Rex programme. She was persuaded to part with Kirlee so that it could be bred into the Cornish Rex line. To the breeders' surprise, no curly kittens resulted from several matings, and it was only then realized that the two lines represented unrelated mutations that would have to be established by separate breeding pro- grammes. By this time, several litters of cross-bred kittens had been born, so test matings had to be carried out to discover which rex genes each carried. It was also decided at this point to selectively breed towards two different body types, the unique head shape of the Devon being based on that of Kirlee.

In 1960, a German Rex was sent to the United States, soon to be followed by two more. They were said to resemble the Devon Rex in body build, but two separate litters born in the United States in 1970 from German-Cornish crosses were of curly kittens, proving that the mutations are the same. In Britain, both the Cornish and Devon Rexes were recognized as separate breeds for championship competition in 1967. In North America, they were officially recog- nized by the CFA as separate breeds in 1979; until then it (unlike the ACFA) had not distinguished between them. In FIFe, on the European continent, the breeds have the same status as in Britain, though most of the early breeding, not unnaturally, was with the German line, and the name German Rex is still sometimes used.

Both Cornish and Devon Rexes are bred in a wide range of colours. In Britain, the show standard simply states that the former can be of any colour, the latter any colour except bicolours. The American standard is a little more restrictive, allowing all colours except lavender, chocolate and Siamese- pattern. The last is, however, quite widely bred under the unofficial name Si-Rex.

Characteristics and care

Rexes of both varieties make intelligent, extrovert and affectionate pets. They are very easy to groom as they do not constantly shed hair, unlike the Persians and some short-haired breeds. Normally all that is needed is hand-grooming – that is, firm stroking from neck to tail – but it may be an advantage to use a comb once a week. Because the rex has a finer coat than other short-hairs – completely lacking in guard hairs in the Cornish – it is not so well protected against changes in temperature and should not be allowed out in extremes of weather. (Some, indeed, are born almost hairless.) Breeders have found it an advantage to counteract the increased loss of body heat by boosting the intake of calorie-rich fats; many use shredded suet, giving about a dessertspoonful a day to adults, a teaspoonful a day to kittens. They use only cats with good coats for breeding.

Rexes normally make ideal mothers. Average litter size is much the same as for other foreign breeds (except the Oriental Shorthairs), averaging three to six. The kittens are normally active at a very early age, and once they begin to climb out of their box soon begin to exhibit a great inquisitiveness that remains a characteristic of the breeds.

The shaded silver Cornish Rex is a variety that breeders are still striving to perfect, the colouring being ideal to show off the waviness of the coat. An agile cat, the CFA show standard comments: 'Its arched back and muscular hind legs develop the flexibility for high jumps, quick starts and amazing speed. At ease its relaxed appearance is contradictory to its capacity for sudden and fast movements. When handled it feels firm and, because of its short coat, warm to the touch.'

Cats of the future?

It may seem preposterous – even, to some cat lovers, distasteful – to imagine a cat with a pitch-black back, haunches, flanks, head and tail, combined with a brilliant tan-coloured belly; or one whose coat has the sheen of satin; or a long-haired cat with a fringe falling forward over the eyes. Yet these are, some geneticists believe, only three of many possibilities that await cat breeders in the future. The reason is that they all occur in other small livestock, such as rabbits, cavies, hamsters and mice, and that the genetics of coat colours and types seems to cross species boundaries. (For example, the Siamese or Himalayan coat pattern is seen in cavies, gerbils, hamsters, mice, rabbits and rats as well as cats.) Indeed, there have been reports – as yet unconfirmed, and certainly not yet developed to the status of breeds – that some of the gene mutations (see p23) causing these unusual effects have already been observed in cats. So if you want a foretaste of the future of cat breeding, take a look at some breeds of other fancy-bred livestock.

Most mutant genes produce only their minimal effect when first noticed. By selective breeding, fanciers can try to produce a brighter colour, or better marking, or clearer pattern, as desired, by manipulating polygenes (see p27). This means that any cat appearing significantly different from other cats in coat type, coat colour, eye colour or even body structure has the potential to make feline history. It should be investigated and, so long as the variation is not harmful to the wellbeing of cats in general, preservation of the difference and the development of a new pedigree variety is worth considering. The steps necessary can rarely be taken by an individual, and the help of geneticists and other breeders, and perhaps also of existing cat clubs, is advisable. In many – perhaps most – cases the alarm will prove false, but this is how the really distinctive cat breeds of the future will be discovered.

New coat types

Up to now, the most unusual coat types to appear in cats – apart from hairlessness, as in the Sphynx – are the rex and wire-haired mutations (see p43). Among the most interesting future possibilities are those produced by the so-called rough (symbolized R) and star (St) genes in the cavy. (The gene symbols given in this article are those used in other livestock; if identified in cats different symbols might be used.) Both these cavy genes produce a rosetting effect, with the hair growing outwards from central points at various parts of the body. (Similar, though much less spectacular, changes of hair growth direction can be seen on a short-haired cat's bib or at the back of its

Gene mutations to look out for in the domestic cat include those responsible for the coats of other small fancy-bred animals illustrated **above**.
The Peruvian cavy on the **left** is a long-haired rosetted animal showing the effect of the rough gene; there have already been reports of this being observed in cats in Britain. The fawn satin mouse **centre** has a beautiful and spectacular light-reflecting coat in which the basic fawn colour is highlighted and given an almost metallic gleam by the modified hair structure. The black and tan rabbit on the **right** is a variety produced by a gene at the agouti locus; this gene locus is an important one in the domestic cat, but the tan mutation has not yet been identified.

THE SPHYNX

Bred by a few breeders in North America, the Sphynx is regarded by many others as the negation of almost all they admire in the cat. It originated with the birth of a hairless kitten in Ontario in 1966. This grew up to develop a very short transient downy coat on the body, and thin short hair on the ears, muzzle, tail, feet and testicles. The Sphynx is today recognized as a pedigree breed only by a few of the smaller North American cat associations. Coat colours and patterns are discernible in the vestigial coat and the underlying skin. Partially hairless cats have also cropped up in some rex breeding programmes, but have never been developed as a breed, being regarded as serious faults.

HYBRIDS WITH WILD CATS

Another approach to developing a new cat breed is that of mating domestic cats with wild cat species. In most cases, the offspring are wild in temperament (see p16), but some American breeders have claimed that crosses with Geoffroy's cat (*Felis geoffroyi*; see p14) are both tame and fertile. Certainly, they are beautiful creatures, with the exotic spotted coat of their wild ancestors. Indeed, this introduces a coat pattern not so far seen in domestic cats – the ocelot-like rosette, or ring-shaped, spots. These cats are known as Feral Domestic Hybrids – a misnomer, in fact, since the term feral is properly applied to a domestic cat that has reverted to the wild – or Safari Cats.

legs.) The effect of the *R* gene is modified by others to produce the exhibition Abyssinian cavy – a beautiful animal with rosettes distributed evenly over the body and ridges of normal hair in between. The effect is heightened by the cavy's coat, which is very smooth and stiff. In cats, it would probably show to best effect on a coat like that of the British Shorthair. There have already, in fact, been reports of rosetted kittens, but there is no question of using the name Abyssinian for them, as in the cavy, since it is already used for the well-known breed of cats.

Long hair in cats, if combined with rosetting, would result in a forward fringe of hair over the eyes and a coat flowing out in all directions instead of, as in existing long-hairs, falling naturally from head to tail. Long-haired rosetted cavies are also bred; they are known as Peruvians. Another form of rosetting, produced in cavies by the *St* gene, is seen in the Crested cavy. This has only one small rosette on the forehead, and a crested breed is a distinct possibility for cat breeders of the future.

Another coat type, already eagerly awaited by breeders familiar with it in mice, hamsters and rabbits, is the satin. The satin gene (*Sa*) changes the structure of the hairs so that they have a greater light-reflecting surface, and the name exactly describes the effect produced. This most beautiful coat would, many breeders feel, be a real asset if established in cats, not only changing the quality of the coat but, by an optical effect, deepening the colour so that white becomes platinum, cream becomes gold and so on. Because satin hair is softer it lies rather limply and is not always attractive when long. But on a foreign-type short-hair (such as an Oriental Shorthair; see p92) the addition of the satin gene would produce a dramatic effect: a glistening coat and sparkling eyes showing the lithe, muscular body to advantage. To date, however, there have been no verified reports of satin-coated cats.

New coat colours

Although the fact that there may eventually be new breeds with as yet unknown coat types is well understood by many cat breeders, the possibilities for new coat colours are much less widely appreciated. It is often stated that, with such proliferation of colours already recognized, there are few new possibilities and those will be the result of new colour combinations rather than new colour genes – as with the golden Persians (see p59) and the tipped Orientals (see p94). This is not the case, and there are many interesting colour varieties yet to be reported and/or developed in the cat. Two of these, well known in other animals, are the tan and the pink-eyed dilute.

The tan gene (*aᵗ*) is an allele of the agouti (*A*; see p26) – that is, tan pattern is a genetic alternative to agouti and non-agouti, and bears the same relation to these as the Siamese gene does to the full-colour and albino genes. So, although it is only known in dogs, mice and rabbits, it is quite possible for the required mutation to occur in cats. The exhibition tan mouse or rabbit is a magnificent animal, with a brilliant, rich tan belly, and the flanks, haunches and back black or chocolate. Or, in the dilute form, the back parts may be blue or lilac, when the belly is a warm fawn colour. In all of these, the demarcation between the two colours is a straight horizontal line like a tide-mark. So far, no reports of tan cats have been verified, but the first will probably be similar in pattern to cross-bred tan rabbits, with a pale agouti belly (like the hairs between a tabby cat's stripes) and a back that is not as solid-coloured as in the exhibition animal. It would take many generations of selective breeding to produce tan cats with the intensity of colouring seen in other fancy-bred species, but the final result would be dramatic indeed.

Another whole range of colour varieties could be produced by the pink-eyed dilute gene (*p*), provisionally reported but not so far verified in cats. In other species, there are in fact several different genes at the pink-eyed dilute locus (see p23), some but not all affecting eye colour as well as coat colour. The best-known pink-eyed dilutes are those produced by mouse breeders, some of whose colour varieties are fawn, argente (a golden agouti, the reddish-fawn colour being overlaid with silvery-grey ticking), dove (a pretty dove-grey), champagne (pale fawn) and silver (grey-platinum). All these have a red eye colouring, but this would not necessarily be so in cats. Because the *p* gene has very little effect on the richness of the belly colour in tan mice, only affecting the back colouring, the dove tan is a popular variety. A dove tan cat – with a dove-grey back, a brilliant tan belly, and probably blue or pale green eyes – is certainly a possibility at cat shows of the future.

A cat of the future or a breeder's nightmare? If geneticists' understanding of how similar mutations can occur in different small animal species is correct, this dove tan Oriental Shorthair could be seen on the show bench one day in the future.

Chapter 2
UNDERSTANDING YOUR CAT

The cat's body 1

Like humans, dogs, elephants, horses, mice and many other creatures, the domestic cat is a mammal and its body shows typical mammalian features. Like all mammals, it has a bony internal skeleton, maintains a constant body temperature (38.6°C or 101.5°F), has hair (rather than feathers or scales) growing from its skin, and bears live young that develop to a relatively advanced stage in their mother's womb, nourished via a placenta, and are then suckled on milk and cared for until they are able to cope on their own.

At a more fundamental level, it shares features with more lowly creatures. The body consists of cells which are grouped to form a variety of tissues and organs. Some of these carry out related tasks, forming organ systems. Some complex organs, such as the liver and pancreas, do different jobs in different systems.

Bones, joints and muscles form the musculo-skeletal system, which gives the animal its size, shape, speed and strength. The digestive, circulatory, excretory and respiratory systems maintain the body's internal environment, ensuring that all tissues and organs are able to perform their functions efficiently. Controlling and integrating all the activities of the body systems are the nervous and endocrine (hormone) systems; between them they regulate the body's internal economy and receive, interpret and initiate reactions to information from the outside world. Finally, the reproductive system ensures perpetuation of the species after the individual animal's death.

But the cat is more than just a mammal. A member of the Felidae – the cat family (see p 12) – it is a highly successful member of the group known as carnivores, and from the standard mammalian basis has evolved a variety of adaptations to suit a hunting, meat-eating way of life. Modifications to the skeletal and muscular systems give it a strong, flexible, fast-moving hunter's body. The jaw is short and has only 30 teeth – fewer than any other carnivore – but they are all built to cut meat, and give the cat a lethal bite.

Structural systems

The overall shape of the cat's body is determined by its skeleton, a jointed framework of light, strong bones which enables the animal to move about. Like the standard mammalian skeleton, it is built around a central flexible girder – the backbone or spine – attached to which are the skull, rib cage and (via the pelvic and pectoral girdles) the limbs. Individual bones are linked by joints of various kinds – some (as in the dome of the skull) immovable, some (as in the limbs) highly mobile. Closely linked to the skeleton is the system of voluntary muscles controlled by the conscious brain. As befits a hunter, these muscles are highly

The muscular body of the cat enables it to move in a fascinating variety of ways, from sinuous stretching **left** to the rapid, powerful and superbly controlled actions of the hunt (see pp 118–123). The cat has more than 500 separate skeletal muscles **right** (compared with some 650 in the far larger human body), the largest driving the powerful hind limbs. The strength of those in the neck and forelimbs is equally important in the capture of prey. In addition to these muscles, which are under the voluntary (conscious) control of the brain, numerous 'smooth' muscles operate in many of the internal organs. The cat may be aware of their contractions, but cannot consciously control them since they respond only to nerve signals from the unconscious part of the brain.

CELLS AND TISSUES

The cat's body contains more than four million million cells, almost all of them too small to be seen individually without a microscope. (A single drop of blood, for example, contains several million blood cells.)

The cells all share certain features: They are each surrounded by an outer 'skin', the cell membrane, and all except for red blood cells have a dense central nucleus that contains the chromosomes and their genes (the hereditary material; see p 22). Around the nucleus is the cytoplasm, a watery fluid containing numerous minute structures that carry out specialized functions in the life of the cell – for the cell is a self-contained unit of living matter as well as contributing to the functioning of the whole body.

Although having these basic similarities, there are several hundred different types of cell in the cat's body, each with a specialized function, and the basic plan is modified in consequence. Fat cells are large and distended with stored fat globules; some white blood cells are able to engulf bacteria and digest them; cells in the pancreas secrete digestive juices; brain and nerve cells can transmit nerve signals; and so on.

Groups of cells of varying types combine to form tissues having specific bodily functions. Some tissues – such as nervous tissue and muscular tissue – are specialized in function, while others are found in many parts of the body: Epithelial tissue, for instance, forms the lining of both the inside and the outside of the body, while connective tissue binds together and supports the body's various parts. Individual organs may be built from various types of tissue; for example, the heart contains muscular, connective, epithelial, nervous, vascular (blood) and other tissues.

developed in the cat and are under very precise control. See the article on movement and balance (p 118).

The degree of bone and muscle development in cats is remarkably uniform, and most adult cats fall within a quite restricted size range. Adult entire (uncastrated) males usually weigh between 3.5 and 7 kg (8 and 15 lb), females and neuters castrated when young between 2.5 and 4.5 kg (5½ and 10 lb). The heaviest recorded cat weighed 19.5 kg (43 lb), but most of the excess was fat, not muscle. Breeds do, of course, vary

between the chunkiness of British and European Shorthairs and the slimness of Siamese, but the extremes of body size and shape seen in dog breeds are unknown in cats. See the article on body conformation (p 41).

Also largely structural in function – though it performs many other tasks as well – is the skin, which qualifies as the largest single organ. See the articles on skin and coat (p 106) and touch (p 108). As with general body conformation, there are of course striking breed differences in coat quality and colour (see pp 29–43).

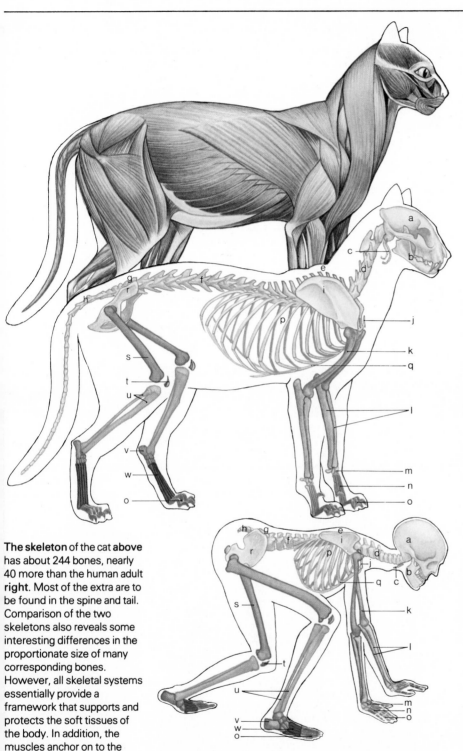

The skeleton of the cat **above** has about 244 bones, nearly 40 more than the human adult **right**. Most of the extra are to be found in the spine and tail. Comparison of the two skeletons also reveals some interesting differences in the proportionate size of many corresponding bones. However, all skeletal systems essentially provide a framework that supports and protects the soft tissues of the body. In addition, the muscles anchor on to the bones to make a system of levers employed in all bodily movements (see p 119). The principal bones include the following: **a** cranium (brain box), a composite of many individual bones, **b** lower jaw or mandible, **c** hyoid – all the above comprising the skull – the many bones of the vertebral (spinal) column or backbone – **d** cervical (neck) vertebrae, **e** thoracic (chest)

vertebrae, **f** lumbar (back) vertebrae, **g** sacral vertebrae and **h** caudal (tail) vertebrae – **i** scapula (shoulder blade), **j** clavical (collar bone, these together forming the pectoral girdle), **k** humerus, **l** radius (shorter) and ulna (longer), which articulate with the humerus to form the elbow joint, **m** carpals (wrist bones), **n** metacarpals (hand or forepaw bones), **o** phalanges

(finger and toe bones), **p** ribs, **q** sternum (breastbone), **r** pelvis or pelvic girdle, **s** femur (thigh bone), which forms the hip joint with the pelvis and the stifle or knee joint (protected by the patella or knee cap **t**) with the lower leg bones **u** – the tibia (thicker) and fibula (thinner) – **v** tarsals (ankle or hock bones) and **w** metatarsals (foot or hind paw bones).

Maintenance systems

All parts of the body need oxygen and food to function, and produce wastes that must be removed or they will poison the body. The circulatory system provides transport for all these, also carrying chemical messengers (hormones; see below) and warmth, and having vital defensive functions against disease. At the centre of the system is a pump: the heart. The cat's heart is relatively small and not so sharply pointed as the human version, but conforms to the standard four-chamber design. It beats – contracting to squeeze the blood along – about 110 to 140 times per minute, or up to twice the normal human rate.

Blood is mostly plasma, a straw-coloured solution of glucose, fats, amino acids (protein derivatives), proteins themselves, salts and other substances in water (which makes up 90 per cent of the total plasma volume). Suspended in the plasma are red and white blood cells. The latter are responsible for protecting the body from invading bacteria (see below), while red cells are the oxygen carriers. They are made in the bone marrow and contain the red pigment haemoglobin, which has a great affinity for oxygen and for the waste gas carbon dioxide. Red cells have a lifespan of between two and six weeks – about half the human norm – and when damaged are destroyed in the liver and spleen. The spleen also acts as a store for red blood cells 'in reserve' until they are needed.

Blood picks up oxygen and dumps carbon dioxide in the lungs, a pair of spongy sacs that form the link between the blood and the outside air. Expansion of the rib cage by muscular action draws air in through the nasal cavity, trachea (windpipe) and bronchi to the lungs, where it eventually reaches tiny thin-walled air sacs called alveoli. These are enmeshed by equally thin-walled blood vessels – capillaries – so that oxygen and carbon dioxide can easily pass through. When the blood reaches the rest of the body the reverse takes place, providing cells with oxygen.

Cats at rest take about 30 to 50 breaths (in and out) per minute – about four times as many as a resting human. Like dogs, cats use breathing as a cooling mechanism, panting to evaporate moisture from the mouth and lungs in very hot weather.

The blood is also the means for conveying food to the body's cells and waste materials formed from the breakdown of foods away again. Food is collected from the digestive system – the stomach and intestines, with their ancillary glands, including the liver and pancreas – where the meat and other materials eaten by the cat are broken down into a form that the body can use. This consists of relatively simple chemical substances such as amino acids, fatty acids and sugars; see the article on feeding your cat (p 148). Practi- /continued

The cat's body 2

The blood circulation of an average cat contains about 250 ml (½ pint) of blood. It passes once around the body in an average of 11 seconds. Oxygen-rich blood (red) from the lungs pours into the left side of the heart **a** and is pumped out through the big artery called the aorta **b** to the head and forelimbs **c** and the trunk and hind limbs **d**. Flowing through progressively narrower tubes called arterioles it reaches tiny capillaries **e** in all the tissues; there it gives up oxygen and nutrients and collects wastes. Deoxygenated blood returns to the right side of the heart through veins, the biggest of which is the vena cava **f**. It then passes to the lungs for reoxygenation. The liver **h** and kidneys **i** have special blood supplies. Another branch picks up food from the intestine **j** and takes it directly to the liver via the portal vein **k** for further processing.

The cat's skull, apart from having huge eye sockets, is most notable for its killer's jaw **above**. This has well developed anchorage points for muscles and, in the adult **right**, 30 teeth (4 more than kittens but 2 fewer than humans) – 16 in the upper jaw, 14 in the lower. The tiny incisors (red), which do some ripping and scraping, are flanked by paired dagger-like canines (purple) for holding and killing prey and tearing flesh. Cats cannot chew, so it is the job of the cusped premolars (blue) and solitary molars (green) to cut meat into ingestible pieces. In particular, the lower molars and last upper premolars act together like shears; they are known as the carnassials.

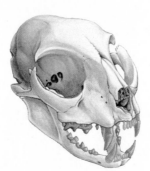

Digestion of food starts in the mouth **a**, where food is sliced, mixed with saliva and swallowed. On reaching the stomach **b**, powerful digestive juices start their work, as the food is churned to a pulp. The mixture is passed a little at a time into the small intestine **c**, where further digestive juices from the pancreas **d** and the gut lining complete the process, aided by bile made by the liver **e** and stored in the gall bladder **f**. The resultant dissolved nutrients are then absorbed into the bloodstream through the gut wall. Finally, in the large intestine **g**, most of the water in the remaining waste material is absorbed, leaving the semi-solid faeces to be passed through the anus **h**.

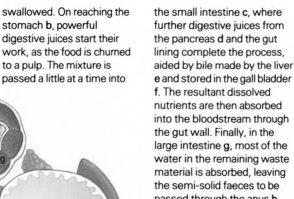

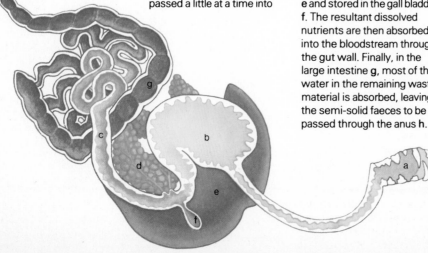

cally the whole of the abdominal cavity is given over to the digestive system.

The principal waste-disposal organs are the kidneys, which filter off from the blood unwanted materials and excess water to form urine, which is stored in the bladder until it can be conveniently voided. In this way, the kidneys perform the vital task of maintaining the body's water balance – that is, the concentration or dilution of the blood and the fluid bathing the tissues. If hot weather or lack of water to drink makes this concentration rise, the urine becomes very concentrated as the kidneys cut down water excretion. Although not related in function, the reproductive organs are closely linked with the urinary system; see the article on reproduction (p213).

The passage of faeces from the anus is not excretion, since the contents of the bowel are never really part of the body but are only 'passing through'. (The faeces consist of solid waste matter left over after the useful materials have been removed.) In fact, they do contain a small amount of truly excreted matter passed into the intestine by the liver, one of whose functions is to detoxify (neutralize) and get rid of poisons (including drugs).

Protective systems
Apart from the skin, which forms a very effective barrier to harmful organisms and substances, the main defensive systems of the cat's body are the lymphatic and circulatory systems. Running parallel to the circulatory system of the blood, the

lymphatic system forms a one-way network of vessels draining the tissues and eventually leading to one large vessel – the thoracic duct – which empties into the jugular vein. The fluid in the system is lymph, which is very similar to the intercellular fluid that bathes the tissues, and is basically blood plasma containing some white (but not red) blood cells.

At various points the lymph vessels pass through lymph nodes or 'glands', where bacteria (germs) and other 'foreign' particles are filtered out. The lymph nodes contain large numbers of lymphocytes (a type of white cell), while others circulate in the bloodstream. They produce antibodies, which act in two ways, by neutralizing bacterial poisons and by causing bacteria to clump together so that the second type of white blood cells – granular leucocytes – can engulf and destroy them. Most lymphocytes are manufactured in the spleen, but in the young kitten the thymus gland (which later shrivels) also produces them. The granular leucocytes are produced in the bone marrow.

Control systems

The job of co-ordinating the various body systems, so that they function in harmony, is performed on two levels, by the nervous system and the endocrine system. The nervous system is direct, precise and fast. Its sensory receptors detect events in the outside world and within the cat's body, the brain and spinal cord process this information, and nerve messages are sent out to initiate and control the body's responses. The brain also acts at the subconscious level to control many bodily processes, such as breathing. See the articles on the brain, senses and movement (pp 108–121).

The endocrine system consists of glands which produce chemical messengers called hormones. These travel through the bloodstream and cause reactions in other parts of the body. Thus the endocrine system is slower, more diffuse and longer-acting than the nervous system. For example, thyroid hormone influences growth and the rate of chemical processes in body cells; the sex hormones produced by the male's testicles and female's ovaries produce secondary sexual characteristics and other changes (see p 213); the adrenal glands produce hormones that regulate kidney action, mobilize the body's resources when the cat is frightened or angry, and help it to cope with stress and injury.

The 'master' gland of the body is the pituitary; one of its hormones helps to regulate blood pressure, but most of the others act on other glands, causing them to produce their secretions. The pituitary itself is under the control of the adjacent part of the brain, the hypothalamus, which thus rates as perhaps the most important control centre of the whole cat's body.

Naming the parts The major bodily systems of the cat are shown **right**. The nervous system **1** consists of the brain **a**, spinal cord **b**, 12 pairs of cranial nerves connecting directly to the brain stem and paired sets of peripheral nerves **c** extending from the spinal cord to every part of the body. The endocrine system **2** consists of glands that secrete hormones into the bloodstream. The 'master' gland is the pituitary **a**, which controls many others; others include the thyroid **b**, adrenals **c**, pancreas **d**, small glands in wall of the gut **e**, part of the kidneys **f** and the gonads – the male testicles **g** and female ovaries **h**.
The circulatory system **3** has a muscular pump, the heart **a**, and a network of arteries **b** and veins **c**; the spleen **d** is an emergency blood reservoir.
The respiratory system **4** comprises the nose **a**, larynx (voice-box) **b**, trachea (windpipe) **c** and bronchi leading to the paired lungs **d**, the latter enclosed in the thoracic (chest) cavity by the diaphragm **e** and rib cage.
The lymphatic system **5** is a one-way system of lymph vessels **a**; it has no pump but empties into the bloodstream. Lymph nodes **b** filter bacteria from lymph and may become swollen in disease; those in the neck **c** and hind legs **d** are easiest to feel.
The digestive system **6** comprises the mouth and teeth **a**, oesophagus (gullet) **b**, stomach **c**, small intestine **d**, large intestine **e**, liver **f**, pancreas **g** and rectum **h**.
The urinogenital system **7, 8** is really two separate systems with some shared parts (see also p 213). The urinary or excretory system in both sexes consists of the paired kidneys **a**, ureters **b**, bladder **c** and urethra **d**. In the male **7** the latter opens at the tip of the penis **e**; in the female **8** it opens in the vulva **f**. The main male reproductive organs are the testicles **g** and sperm ducts **h**. In the female they are the ovaries **i**, fallopian tubes (oviducts) **j**, uterus (womb) **k** and the vagina **l**.

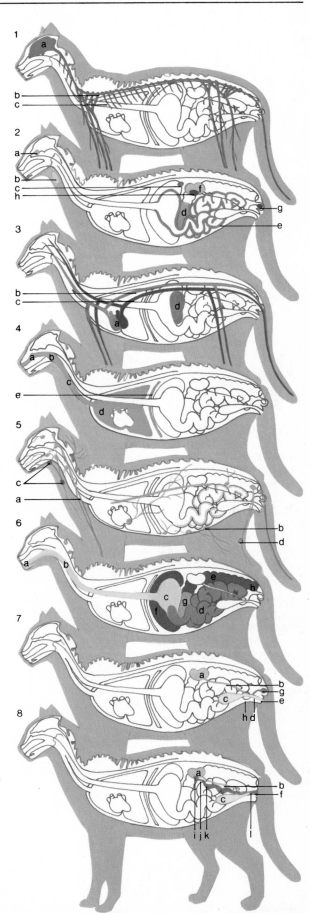

The skin and coat

One of the most striking features of any cat is its beautiful coat. Yet, from the cat's point of view, the important thing about the coat and the skin beneath it is not their appearance but their role in protecting the cat and in helping to maintain its bodily equilibrium. They form a barrier between the outside world and the rest of the cat's body, preventing excessive water loss from the tissues and providing protection against physical injuries, heat and cold, harmful chemicals and excessive sunlight, as well as the invasion of germs.

The skin actively regulates heat loss from the body. Its looseness ensures that most wounds sustained in fights are merely superficial – and also probably aids escape. It contains numerous glands and sensory receptors (see p108), while on the toes skin tissues are modified to form the claws. Even the mammary glands, which supply the newborn kitten with milk (see p225), are specialized skin structures.

Clearly, in order to carry out its varied functions, the skin must have a complex structure. It is made up of two main tissue layers – the inner dermis and the outer epidermis. The former contains the important specialized organs and other structures, while the latter is mainly protective. It consists of several layers of cells (see p102); those next to the dermis actively multiply to form new cells, which move gradually outwards to replace dead cells shed from the surface. As they move outwards, they become flattened and horny, forming a tough waterproof barrier. Overall, however, the cat's skin is remarkably thin, varying from 0.4mm ($1/64$ in) on the belly to 2mm ($1/12$ in) on the neck.

The coat

Hairs are the most obvious of the skin's structures. Growing from tiny pits, called follicles, in the dermis, there may be as many as 200 hairs per mm² (130,000 per sq in) on the cat's belly, thinning to half this number on the back. There are two types of hair follicles, and biologists classify the hairs accordingly. The primary or guard hairs, forming the coarse top coat, grow from individual follicles. The finer secondary hairs, forming the soft underfur, grow in groups from single openings. Secondary hairs themselves vary widely in appearance, however, the so-called awn hairs having thickened, bristle-like tips, while the wool or down hairs are fine and crinkled.

In addition to all the above, there are the highly sensitive whiskers, or vibrissae, found on the face; they grow from a special type of follicle. Related to these are the eyelashes, while groups of whiskers called carpal hairs may be found on the backs of the forelegs; they too are especially sensitive to touch, and are a characteristic feature of carnivores that use their forelegs for grasping prey.

Hair types in the cat's coat **below 1** are long guard hairs **a**, awn hairs **b** and down or wool hairs **e**. Some biologists recognize intermediate awned down hairs **c**, **d**, while others divide them all into primary (guard) and secondary types. Enlarged, the former **2** shows its scaly outer cuticle and solid, pigmented inner medulla, while a down hair **3** is ladder-like, with air spaces that make it soft.

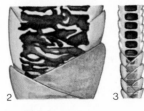

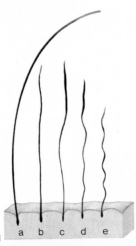

Hairless skin of the nose pad **right** and foot pads **far right** is protected by epidermis **a** up to 75 times thicker than on other parts of the body. Pigment granules **b** colour it, and sensory nerve fibres and receptors **c** respond to pressure and temperature. These are in the dermis **d**, as are the eccrine sweat glands **e**, found only in the foot pads. A fat layer **f** acts as a cushion. The nose pad **1** is ridged in a pattern as unique to each cat as a human finger-print. The hind paw **2** has four toe pads **a**, four claws and a large metatarsal pad **b**. The forepaw **3** has five toe pads **a** and five claws, plus a metacarpal pad **b** and a carpal pad **c**. The fifth claw, which corresponds to our thumb-nail, is much used in climbing and for holding prey.

Hairy skin that covers most of the cat's body **below** has millions of hairs growing in follicles **a** in the lower skin layer, the dermis **b**. Single guard hairs **c** are surrounded by clusters of awn **d** and down **e** hairs. Each awn and down hair follicle has several hairs emerging from each opening in the epidermis **f**. In the base of the follicle **g** clumps of dividing cells form the bulb **h** and shaft of the hair, which is coloured by pigment. Each follicle has blood **i** and nerve **j** supplies, and the hair is 'oiled' by a sebaceous gland **k** and moved by an arrector muscle **l**. Apocrine sweat glands **m**, involved in social signalling, are associated with hair follicles. Throughout the skin there are receptors **n** that sense touch, pressure, heat, cold and pain. Deep in the dermis are subcutaneous fat deposits **o**.

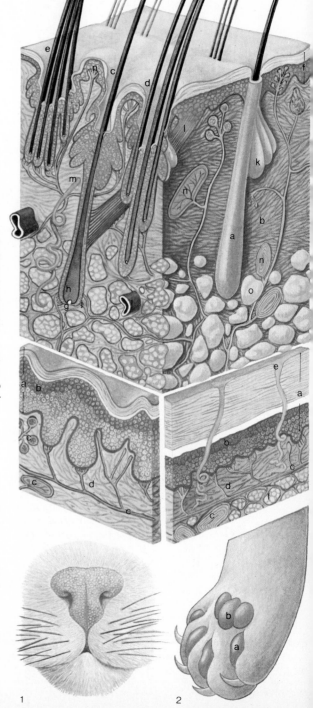

Normal body hairs occur in clusters, with about 25 secondary hairs to every guard hair on the belly, but only half this proportion on the back. The overall length and proportion of the types vary from breed to breed of cat (see p43), and in some the guard hairs are completely absent. Colour and coat pattern also vary with breed (see pp29 to 40), and depend on the presence, proportions and location of pigments (colouring matter).

Apart from protecting the skin from small cuts and abrasions, the coat provides both extra waterproofing (see below) and insulation. Tiny muscles connect with the roots of the guard hairs, and when these contract the coat fluffs out. In cold weather, this traps a thick layer of warm air next to the skin, providing insulation. When the cat is angry or frightened, the same reaction increases the cat's apparent size, making it seem a more fearsome adversary.

The thick winter coat and the thinner summer coat allow seasonal regulation of body temperature. Cats' hair grows at about the same rate as human hair – approximately 2mm (1/12in) each week. Growth occurs from the root, and each follicle has a period of growth, followed by a slowing and finally a resting phase. In the last phase, the mature hair remains in the follicle but has become detached at the base. When the follicle becomes active again, most notably in spring, a new hair pushes out the old, causing moulting.

Skin glands

Associated with hair follicles over most of the cat's body are the sebaceous glands. Their oily secretion, sebum, forms a waterproof film on the hairs and gives the healthy coat its shine. It also contains the fatty substance cholesterol, which sunlight converts to vitamin D. The cat takes in this vital nutrient when licking its coat. Some uncastrated tom cats develop a greasy matting of the fur at the base of the back due to over-active sebaceous glands; this is known as stud tail (see p189).

Also found all over the body except on the nose are sweat glands. There are two kinds. Apocrine sweat glands, some of which open into hair follicles, produce a milky fluid whose scent may be involved in sexual attraction. In certain areas, such as the chin, temples, and base of the tail, groups of special apocrine and sebaceous glands produce a scent that is important in many aspects of feline social behaviour, such as territorial marking. By rubbing these parts of its body on objects in the environment, the cat leaves traces of scent as a signal to others (see p124).

Unlike the human body, the cat has eccrine (merocrine) sweat glands, which produce watery sweat, only on the foot pads. They secrete when the cat is hot or frightened, causing damp footprints. Apocrine sweat produced elsewhere has little cooling effect because of the furry coat. Alternative ways of losing body heat are by panting and by the evaporation of saliva from grooming the fur.

Hairless skin

Hairless areas of the cat's body – such as the nose, lips, anal and genital areas, nipples and foot pads – have a distinctive skin structure. For example, the thick yet sensitive skin of the nose has no sweat or sebaceous glands; the damp nose of a healthy cat is due to the mucous secretions of the nostrils. The thick, rough skin over the foot pads – generally about 1.2mm (1/20in) thick – provides a tough surface for protection when walking and a firm grip on slippery surfaces, yet creates a noiseless tread when stalking prey.

But this skin is highly sensitive to touch and temperature, enabling the cat to use its forepaws to test objects as well as to swat, stun and hold prey and to scoop up food. The nose, also, is particularly sensitive (see p108), and thus the skin truly acts as both a link and a barrier between the cat and its environment.

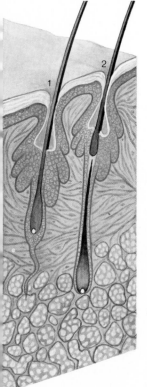
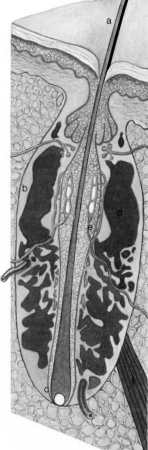

Moulting The diagram **above** shows that after a period of active growth and dormancy **1**, a new hair starts to grow in the same follicle **2**, pushing out the old hair.

Whiskers The long sensory whiskers or vibrissae **left a** are more than twice as thick as guard hairs and extend three times deeper into the dermis. They are strengthened further by a fibrous capsule **b** around the follicle **c**. Richly supplied with blood vessels lying in cavities **d** and a dense network of nerves **e**, the slightest whisker movement stimulates the nerve endings and provides information on the cat's immediate surroundings. They may even detect deflected air currents, and with arrector muscles **f** to move them, they can be put 'on the alert' when required. **below** Cats generally have about a dozen whiskers in rows on each upper lip, a few on each cheek, tufts over the eyes and bristles on the chin.

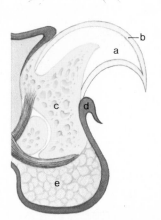

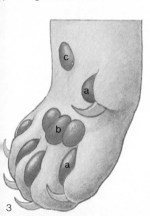

Anatomy of a claw Made of keratin, the horny protein that forms the outer layer of the epidermis, claws **right** are part of the skin, not the skeleton. Each claw has a dermis or quick **a** covered by hard cuticle **b**, and is anchored to the terminal bone **c** of the toe. It can be retracted under a skin fold **d** lying over the foot pad **e**. Worn down with use, claws grow continuously from just below the upper skin fold (see p157).

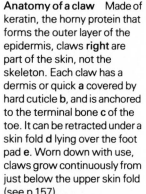

The senses of touch

Touch seems to be one of the less important senses to the cat, in spite of the pleasurable response and purring evoked by stroking in the 'right' place – or the instant shudder or even flaying paw evinced if this is 'wrong'. Yet touch – which in fact conveys the five separate sensations of gentle and heavy pressure, warmth, cold and pain, and is subdivided even further by some biologists – provides the cat with a vital awareness of its immediate surroundings and, of course, warning of injury. Specialized nerve endings, or receptors, that respond to the various sensations are found throughout the skin (see p 106). When stimulated, they send rapid messages through connecting nerves via the spinal cord to the sensory areas of the brain (see p 114).

The sensitive pads

The hairless skin of the nose and paw pads is particularly sensitive. The cat's nose and mask respond markedly to touch, warmth and cold – as when the cat gauges the temperature as well as the smell of food. Touch receptors on the tongue then assist the senses of taste and smell when it decides on the palatability of the food (see p 112).

The paws are also highly tactile, and are used to investigate the texture, size, shape and distance of an unfamiliar object. Cats will often extend one paw and gently tap the object, then touch it more firmly, and finally use their nose for closer inspection. The relatively large area of the brain dealing with messages from the forepaws shows their tactile importance.

The pads also relay information that helps maintain the cat's posture, feeding back sensations as it moves. These are sensed by large receptors called Pacinian corpuscles in the dermis and fatty layer of the foot pads, which respond to firm pressure. They are also common in the tongue, nose pad and many other parts of the body. In the full bladder they signal the need to urinate. The pads may even detect vibrations, and thus enable the cat to 'hear' through its feet. Almost certainly, their extreme sensitivity is the reason many cats seem to hate having their pads stroked.

Sensation through the hairs

The hairless skin is by no means the only type that is sensitive to touch, however. The hair follicles – especially those of guard hairs (see p 106) – are richly supplied with several types of touch receptors. These are responsive to the slightest movement and so provide a close-range detection system without the need for skin contact. As with most carnivores, this system is most developed in the stiff, coarse whiskers, or vibrissae (see p 107), which are found on the face and 'elbows'.

The vibrissae are stiff enough not to collapse on contacting hard surfaces, and are probably important in sensing and

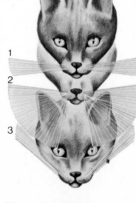

The 'felunculus', or feline form of homunculus, **left** is distorted to illustrate the relative touch sensitivity of different parts of the body. It is based on the numbers of sensory nerves that relay touch sensations from the various parts. It is meant only as a rough impression, but clearly shows that the head (especially the tongue and nose) and the paws are the most sensitive. Pawing and nosing **below left** are often used for close investigation.

The cat's whiskers are long, stiff, highly touch-sensitive hairs. **1** An inquisitive cat may fan them forwards **2** when investigating something, but a cat on the defensive holds them back against its face **3**.

investigating close objects. Cats with poor vision tend to walk very cautiously and move their heads from side to side when negotiating gaps. Perhaps, too, normal cats rely heavily on their whiskers in dim light, when the fully dilated pupil would make focusing on very close objects rather difficult (see p 110).

The vibrissae may also be sensitive to air currents deflected by objects, and thus enable the cat to feel its way in the dark without actually making contact. Certainly, loss of the whiskers can hamper a cat's skilled movements. Finally, the facial whiskers act as additional eyelashes, for any potentially dangerous object touches the whiskers before the eyes and immediately stimulates the protective eyeblink.

Apart from the hair roots, the skin between the hairs is well supplied with tactile pads. They form small bumps in the skin – from 7 to 25 per cm² (45 to 160 per sq in) – and are stimulated by the lightest pressure; this is enough to set the cat's whole skin quivering.

Temperature and pain

The skin also contains warmth and cold receptors that inform the cat of the temperature of its surroundings. It will seek the warmest sleeping spot and responds to cold by curling up. But, except for the face, the cat's body is relatively insensitive to temperature. Cats will sit on stoves too hot for human touch, and often burn their fur. They show no signs of pain until their skin temperature reaches about 52°C (126°F); humans, on the other hand, feel discomfort at only 44°C (112°F).

Of the various touch sensations, pain is the most important for cats' survival; through experiencing it they learn to avoid harm. The puzzle of pain is that some injured cats are miserable, depressed and aggressive if the injured area is handled, while others with very serious wounds remain alert and friendly, and may purr in seeming unconcern. The tolerance to pain varies, it seems, even though it is in the forefront of the senses that guard the body's barrier to the world.

The ears and hearing

For a hunter, super-sensitive hearing is a valuable bonus to keen eyesight, and the cat's auditory world is very different from the one in which we live. Not only is it filled with noises too faint for human ears to hear, but cats are tuned in to a multitude of ultrasonic sounds far higher in pitch than we can detect.

A cat on the prowl is able to locate with amazing accuracy the squeaks and rustlings of small rodents hidden entirely from view. The cat's ears are also constantly on the alert for sounds signalling danger. And sensitive hearing enables cats to use a whole range of vocalizations as a means of communication (see pp 127–128).

but an arrangement of small muscles attached to them can dampen down vibrations caused by loud noises, thus helping to prevent ear damage.

The structure of the feline cochlea enables it to respond to sounds as high as 65kHz (65 kilohertz, or 65,000 cycles/second) and possibly higher. This is at least 1½ octaves above the limit of human hearing, which is about 20kHz, and even exceeds the better-known ability of the dog to hear high-pitched sounds. Human and feline hearing are not very different at low frequencies, the cat's lower limit being about 30Hz (30 hertz, or 30 cycles/second), but the cat's greater sensitivity to high notes is shown by

Sound location and communication

Apart from having wide-ranging and sensitive hearing, normal cats can locate the source of a sound very efficiently. They can discriminate between two sound sources only 5° apart – about 8cm at a distance of 1m (3in at 3ft). This is not accurate enough to hunt in total darkness, but it is a great help in locating prey. Two main mechanisms perform this discrimination. Sounds reaching one ear may be slightly louder than those reaching the other, but more important is the slight time delay as sounds coming from one side take a minute fraction of a second longer to reach the second ear. The brain cannot directly

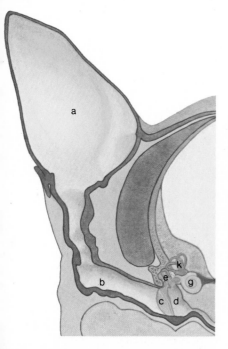

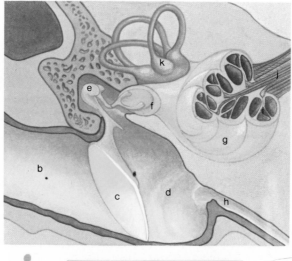

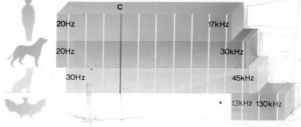

The cat's ear is mostly hidden within the skull bones.
left The pinna **a**, or ear flap, merely funnels sound waves down the external auditory canal **b** to the ear-drum **c**.
below In the concealed middle ear **d**, the ear ossicles **e** – the hammer, anvil and stirrup – act like a system of

levers, converting relatively large but weak vibrations of the ear-drum into smaller but stronger vibrations of the oval window **f** of the cochlea **g**. The eustachian tube **h** leading to the throat equalizes air pressure on either side of the ear-drum to let it vibrate freely. The snail-like cochlea, part of the inner ear, is fluid-filled and contains the sound-sensing organ of Corti **i**, which extends along the spiral. Different-pitched sounds cause maximum vibrations in different parts of the organ, and the louder the sound the larger the vibrations. These cause nerve signals to be sent along the auditory nerve **j** to the brain.
The semi-circular canals **k** are balance organs (see p 121).
The range of hearing of humans, dogs, cats and bats differs considerably. The bars **left** represent the absolute range of frequencies sensed, the figures the points at which sensitivity tails off. The divisions represent octaves (each a doubling or halving of frequency) above and below middle C.

How cats hear

All sounds consist of vibrations, and reach the ear as pressure waves in the air. The pitch of a sound depends on the frequency of the waves – the number of vibrations per second – and its loudness on their amplitude, or size. In order to be heard, the vibrations must trigger nerve signals to the cat's brain that differentiate between sounds of various frequencies and amplitudes. The part of the ear that does this, the cochlea, is deep within the bones of the skull; apart from the section concerned with balance (see p 121), the rest of the ear – including the visible ear flap, or pinna – collects and transmits the vibrations to the cochlea.

Cone-shaped and equipped with more than a dozen muscles that enable it to be moved through 180° and 'pricked' towards the source of a sound, the pinna collects the lightest sound vibrations. It funnels them down the auditory canal to the ear-drum. The latter's vibrations are transmitted to the cochlea by three tiny bones called the ear ossicles. These strengthen the vibrations,

its greater responsiveness to high-pitched human voices and to the squeaks of kittens and mice.

Some white cats, notably blue-eyed whites (see p31), have degenerative changes of one or both cochleas that cause deafness from the age of about five days. Cats also tend to be deaf in old age (see p 164) as the ear ossicles become less mobile and nerves in the inner ear degenerate. Ear infections (see p202) can also affect hearing. Deaf cats probably compensate by a sharpening of vision and smell, and by becoming extra-sensitive to vibrations (possibly 'hearing' through their feet).

measure the delay, but can detect the difference between the two nerve signals. Directing the ear flaps towards sounds does not appreciably help direction-finding, but it does enable faint sounds to be detected.

Ear movements are also very expressive of cats' moods (see p128), and hearing itself plays an important part in their social life – especially courting behaviour. Cats learn to respond to danger signals; when catnapping they are immediately alert to strange noises. They also learn to react to certain familiar sounds, such as their owner's footsteps, the sound of a particular car, a whistle or even the call of their name.

The eyes and perception

Cats' eyes are, perhaps, their most distinctive feature – a clear indication that sight is a highly developed sense in the cat. True to the lifestyle of a hunter, they are set well forward on the head, pointing forward for three-dimensional vision and betraying negligible concern for predators that might creep up from behind. They can function in almost total darkness and yet work equally well in bright daylight.

How the cat's eyes see

Although they have some special features, cats' eyes are basically similar to those of other mammals, and show parallels with a camera. The curved cornea (the clear part of the eyeball in front of the pupil) and the lens just behind the iris together transmit light from the field of view and focus it to form an image on the light-sensitive retina at the back of the eye (as on a camera's film).

Light stimulates a chemical reaction in millions of special cells in the retina, triggering nerve impulses in the optic nerve fibres. The pattern of these electrical signals represents the image on the retina; they are transmitted to the visual area of the brain, where they reach the cat's consciousness so that it actually perceives or 'sees' the scene before it.

Adjusting to changes

The lens performs fine adjustments to the focusing of retinal images. It is surrounded by an arrangement of ligaments and muscles, and when these contract the lens bulges and brings nearby objects into focus. Relaxing them allows the lens to flatten somewhat, focusing things farther away. In humans, this focusing ability (known as accommodation) is very well developed, but the cat has a relatively large lens controlled by rather weak muscles. As a result it cannot focus very well on nearby objects and sees best at about 2 to 6m (7 to 20ft).

The cat's eyes are designed to collect the maximum amount of light, the cornea and lens being large in relation to the other dimensions of the eyeball. (In photographers' parlance, they have a wide aperture, or *f* number.) They are also highly curved and the lens set farther back in the eyeball compared to the human eye. The effect of all these factors is to give the cat's eyes a relatively short focal length and thus wide angle of view, and also to project an image on the retina as much as five times brighter than in the human eye. This, combined with the greater sensitivity of the cat's retina enables the cat to see in light at least six times dimmer than humans.

In dim light, the pupil may open to a diameter of as much as 12mm (½in) to allow the maximum amount of light to pass. (Anger or excitement may also cause dilation.) Yet in bright light it can be narrowed to a mere slit or even closed completely in the central portion, allowing

The cat's eye is set in a bony socket in the skull **a**, cushioned by pads of fat. Muscles **b** connecting the eyeball to its socket allow the cat to move its eyes in various directions. Two eyelids **c** – almost camouflaged by hair – close to protect the eye if anything touches the eyelashes, whiskers or the eye itself. Lacrimal (tear) glands **d** provide lubrication and an antiseptic eyewash. Tears drain into the nose.

The third eyelid, also known as the nictitating membrane or haw, is a thin fold of skin that flicks diagonally across the eye under the eyelid. It helps to lubricate the cornea

by spreading tears and also has a protective function. It is controlled by a muscle behind the eyeball, but why it should appear in illness is not fully understood (see p 200).

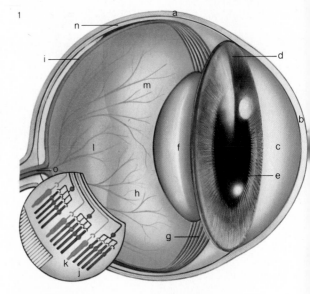

Eye structure   Somewhat egg-shaped and 18-22mm (¾–⅞ in) in diameter, a cat's eye **1** is surrounded by the tough white sclera **a**, which is replaced at the front by the transparent cornea **b**. On the outside is the thin conjunctiva. Behind the cornea are the aqueous humour **c**, the iris **d** around the pupil **e**, and the lens **f** suspended by muscles and ligaments **g**. The jelly-like vitreous humour **h** fills the chamber behind the lens. At the back is the retina **i** with its blood vessels and light-sensitive rods **j** and cones **k**. Backing part of this is the reflective tapetum lucidum **l**, the rest the dark tapetum nigrum **m** (both part of the choroid **n**). The optic nerve **o** transmits signals to the brain. The short focal length – due to the curvature of the cornea and lens plus the shortness of the eyeball – gives it a wide angle of view **2** compared with that of the human eye **3**.

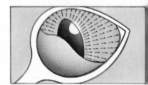

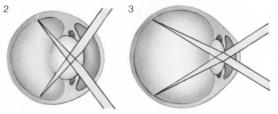

light to pass only through two tiny openings at the top and bottom. The variation is caused by muscles in the iris – the coloured part of the eye. Its colour can vary widely (see p29) – commonly yellow in non-pedigree cats, but also shades of green, blue, lavender or orange (copper) – though all kittens are born with blue eyes.

Seeing in the 'dark'

Cats' eyes, as every motorist knows, shine when caught in a beam of light at night. This is due to the tapetum lucidum, a mirror-like structure that lines most of the

back of the retina. Present in all cats (and also in most other nocturnal animals), this reflects any light not absorbed on its first passage through the retina. As a result, the retina's light-sensitive cells receive a second stimulation, increasing the eye's sensitivity to dim light.

Like ours, cats' eyes have two distinct types of light-sensitive cells in the retina – rods and cones – and in dim light the more sensitive and more numerous rods come into operation. There are about 25 of them to each cone (human eyes have four to one), and their nerve connections are arranged in uch a way that stimuli to a large number of ods reinforce each other to trigger a signal n one nerve fibre. As a result, the response of many rods to very dim light is pooled, so that (when combined with the wide pupil aperture and the effect of the tapetum) far less light is needed for the cat to perceive objects than for humans. It is a fallacy to say that cats can see in the dark, however – it may seem dark to us, but some glimmer of light must be there for the cat to see.

There is a penalty for such sensitive sight. Because large numbers of rods (spread over a relatively large area of the retina) contribute to a single nerve signal, cats' dim-light vision is somewhat fuzzy – they cannot distinguish fine detail and small objects. (The same effect occurs to a lesser extent in human perception.) In daylight, the rods become inoperative and the eye depends on cone vision. Each cone is connected by a single nerve fibre to the brain, and so cones convey a much sharper image. The greatest concentration of cones is found in the macula in the centre of the field of view, so this area corresponds to the sharpest area of vision. However, the relatively small number of cones in the cat's eyes probably means that they can never resolve such fine detail as ours.

Do cats see colours?

In the human eye, three different types of cones absorb red, green and blue light and enable us to see colours. For many years, scientists believed that cats could see only in monochrome, because they found it impossible to teach them to distinguish between different colours (for example, to gain a reward of food). However, cats that are trained for long enough are able to distinguish some colours, and green and blue-sensitive cones have now been found, though not yet red-sensitive ones.

It seems that colours as such play little part in cats' everyday life, for they take a long time to learn that the 'point' of an experiment is to distinguish between two colours. Given time, however, they can distinguish red and blue from each other and from white, though green, yellow and white probably look much alike, and red appears as a dark grey.

Perception in depth

As nerve signals pass along the optic nerves and into the brain, they are processed to give the cat information about what it sees. For example, as might be expected of a predator, the cat is particularly responsive to movement. (Any cat owner will have found that moving their pet's food dish around quickly attracts its attention.) Scientists have found specific nerve cells in the cat's brain that respond to movement.

In general, most of the rods and cones stimulated by light coming from the right-hand side of the field of view send signals to the left-hand side of the brain, and vice versa. This applies to both eyes. As a result, each side of the brain receives two sets of signals, one from each eye. The separation of the eyes means that the signals differ slightly, corresponding to the slightly different viewpoints. Comparison of the two images enables the cat to perceive the distance and depth of objects – to see in three dimensions. Its ability in this respect is somewhat less than ours, however – though it equals or exceeds that of any other mammal. In Siamese and albinos, the optic nerves do not feed some of the visual signals to the correct side of the brain, so that some parts of the brain 'see' two completely different images; some cats develop a squint in an effort to compensate (see p 27).

Learning to see

All cats are born blind, a kitten's eyes remaining closed for seven to ten days after birth. The retina is at first incompletely developed and vision very poor. The kitten has to learn to interpret the images falling on its retinas and its brain to process the signals it receives, and it is not able to see as well as an adult cat for about three months. From then on, vision becomes an extremely important – perhaps the most important – of the cat's senses.

The pupil, almost round **1** in darkness, becomes oval **2** in brighter light and narrows to a slit **3** in bright sunlight, due to the figure-of-eight plan of the iris muscles.

Nocturnal eyeshine occurs when light is reflected from the mirror-like tapetum lucidum. Visible at night because the pupils are wide open, the colour can vary.

Greenish light is often seen in yellow- or orange-eyed cats. 'Siamese'-blue eyes reflect a reddish glow – blood-colour – probably due to absence of the tapetum nigrum.

Binocular vision Fusion of the slightly different images from each eye in the visual area of the brain (shown red) enables cats to see in three dimensions and judge distance, depth and size. This ability depends on an overlap (tinted red) of the visual fields of the eyes – covering an angle of about 98° when the cat looks straight ahead – and crossing over of some optic nerve fibres. (Fewer crossing fibres may mean that Siamese have poor binocular vision.)

Peripheral vision (mauve) extends another 44° each side, giving a total field of view of 186°. Only by moving its head can the cat see all around; in contrast, hunted animals see almost all round but have poor binocular vision.

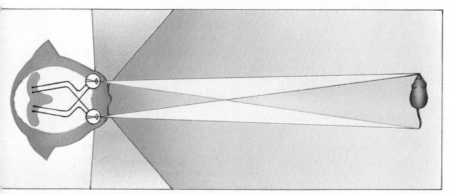

Smell and taste

The visual landmarks and subtleties of colour that dominate the human perception of the world are probably substituted by smells in the feline world picture. Any cat-watcher will realize the importance of smell for individual recognition from the way in which any new object, person or cat is thoroughly sniffed before being tolerated. Similarly, food is first identified by the sense of smell, and only if acceptable will it be tasted and eaten. Smell and taste stimuli also dominate the sexual and aggressive displays of cats (see pp 124 to 131).

Taste and smell in fact form important parts of a wider sensory system in all mammals known as the chemical senses. These enable the animals to monitor chemical events occurring both inside and outside their bodies. Almost all moist surfaces of the body, such as lips, respiratory tract, cornea of the eye and the whole digestive tract, as well as the tongue and nose, carry receptors that initiate nerve signals when stimulated by chemical substances. However, only special receptors in the mouth and nose actually convey information to the brain related to the chemical nature of the stimulating substance, enabling it to be identified.

Cats, like all other mammals, require two distinctively different types of chemoreceptors which are typified by the organs of smell and taste. Smell receptors in the lining of the nose are sensitive to volatile airborne substances. Taste receptors on the tongue allow cats to detect and recognize substances which dissolve in water or saliva during licking and eating food. Smell and taste are very closely allied, as the nasal passages open directly into the mouth.

Cats also have a third chemical sense,

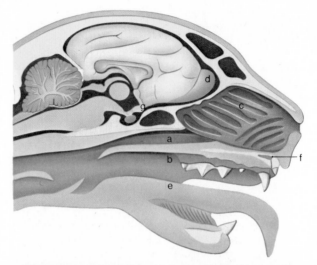

Smell and taste organs are closely linked, since the nasal passage **a** opens into the mouth **b**. Receptors in the olfactory mucosa **c** monitor airborne substances and send signals to the olfactory lobe **d** of the brain. Taste receptors on the tongue **e** respond to substances in food; their signals also go to the olfactory lobe. A duct leads from the roof of the mouth to the Jacobson's organ **f**. This is lined with olfactory cells that are connected to centres in the hypothalamus **g** of the brain concerned with sexual behaviour and appetite.

The flehmen reaction A cat 'flehming' may look to its owner either profoundly stupid or utterly disgusted. It stretches its neck, opens its mouth and curls back its upper lip in a snarl. Actually, it is trapping airborne molecules or an intriguing smell on its tongue, for the taste buds to process, and then flicking the tongue back to press on the opening of the Jacobson's or vomeronasal organ. This relays chemical information to the hypothalamus of the brain, which in turn dictates the cat's response. Entire toms – particularly when they are on the trail of an oestrous queen – are champion flehmers.

THE CATNIP 'TRIP'

The smell of certain plants can arouse intense interest in cats. The response that cat owners through the centuries have most marvelled at is that to catnip or catmint (*Nepeta cataria*). This grows as a weed throughout the temperate zones of Europe and North America, and can easily be grown in gardens or as a houseplant. If it is in your garden, you are sure to find it partly trampled and chewed by cats. The essence of the plant that affects cats, nepetalactone, has been extracted and chemically characterized, and is now commercially available in aerosol cans or impregnated upon toys such as catnip mice. Valerian (*Valeriana officinalis*) has a similar effect.

The catnip response has been observed in a wide variety of wild cats, including lions, pumas and leopards, as well as domestic cats. The characteristic behaviour sequence is to sniff, chew, rub, roll and miaow. This varies in intensity from

cat to cat, and tom cats tend to get more excited than females. Not all cats respond to catnip, however, as the capacity to detect it is inherited, but the 50 per cent or more that do respond seem to enter a trance of intense pleasure lasting for 5 to 15 minutes.

Whatever the sex of the cat, some of the postures adopted are like those shown by females in oestrus, such as treading, rolling and the flehmen reaction. However, it is probably unrelated to sexual behaviour, because males and spayed females show the catnip response as readily as intact females. Rather, it seems that a true psychedelic state is induced by molecules of nepetalactone reaching the brain. Cats have been observed sitting and staring at infinity, or seen chasing phantom mice. The same biochemical pathways are affected by the smell of catnip as by marijuana or LSD, though fortunately the effect is short-lived, non-addictive and quite harmless.

The cat's tongue is long, muscular and highly mobile. In lapping below it is spoon-shaped and flicks in and out rapidly. The cat swallows after every four or five laps. The centre of the tongue is covered with hooked filiform papillae, making it abrasive for grooming. At the tip, sides and base are the taste buds, buried in the surface of the fungiform and vallate papillae. The taste cells cluster like segments of an orange around tiny openings.

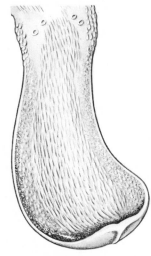

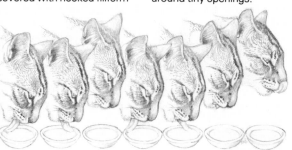

which is almost a hybrid between taste and smell. This has its own receptor in the mouth. Called the vomeronasal organ or Jacobson's organ, after its discoverer, it is a tiny cigar-shaped sac with a narrow passage leading from the roof of the mouth. It has also been found in several other species such as deer and horses, but is absent in man.

The Jacobson's organ is stimulated by odorous chemicals which are 'captured' by the tongue from the atmosphere and transferred to the opening of the organ when the cat presses its tongue against the roof of the mouth. Cats make a quite distinctive facial gesture called the flehmen reaction (from a German word for which there is no translation) when the Jacobson's organ is stimulated. It is normally seen in tom cats responding to the 'sexy' smells produced by the urine from females on heat, but can be observed in animals of either sex (including neuters) when they are confronted with catnip.

The organs of smell

Most of the organ responsible for detecting odours is hidden from view; you see only the nostrils. Behind the cat's nose lies a maze of bones and cavities. As it breathes, air passes across these and is warmed and moistened. Part of the air is channelled across a special area of nasal lining known as the olfactory mucosa. In the cat this covers a relatively large area of 20 to 40 cm² (3 to 6 sq in) – nearly twice the size of the olfactory mucosa of either rabbits or humans. This is an indication of the importance of smell to the cat.

Microscopic examination of the olfactory mucosa reveals a very complex arrangement of cells, but the type which holds the key to detecting smells is the olfactory cell. There are some 200 million of these, and they have a combined function of both making the first signal in response to an odour and then transmitting that signal through connecting nerves to the olfactory bulb of the brain (see p 114).

The organs of taste

The cat's tongue has several functions associated with eating and grooming, and its surface carries a great variety of sensory receptors such as special detectors for temperature as well as taste.

Everyone will at some time have wondered why an affectionate lick from a cat is so much like being stroked by emery paper. That abrasive quality is due to numerous knobs called papillae. There are several kinds of papillae, but those in the centre (the filiform papillae) form backward-facing hooks which help to hold food or struggling prey and to lick bones clean. They do not carry taste receptors. Other mushroom-shaped (or fungiform) papillae along the front and side edges of the tongue carry taste buds, as also do four or six large vallate (cup-shaped) papillae at the back of the tongue.

The responsiveness of taste cells to different stimuli has been extensively mapped in cats. There are generally four basic dimensions to taste in mammals – sweet, salt, bitter and acid. Cats are unusual

if not unique amongst the animal kingdom because they exhibit no significant response to sweet things. To complicate issues still further, cats have a remarkable sensitivity to the taste of water, and this active 'water taste' may be connected with their lack of response towards sweet substances. It appears that the water taste receptors dominate the few sweet taste buds the cat has; if the water taste in a liquid is suppressed by adding small amounts of salt, cats take to sugary drinks.

All this is particularly mysterious because cats do not tolerate sugars in their diet very well, and one would have thought that a sensitivity towards sugar would enable them to avoid eating it. Instead, some cats (especially Siamese) develop diarrhoea in response to the lactose (milk-sugar) content of cow's milk, and most cats can tolerate only low levels of glucose (fruit-sugar) and sucrose (cane-sugar) in their diet.

Flavour recognition

Of course, in nature cats eat meat, which provides a diet high in protein and animal fats. Scientists have discovered that many chemical compounds that contain nitrogen and sulphur (such as some of the amino acids from which proteins are built) particularly stimulate cats' taste receptors. (It is not clear whether other animals have the same responsiveness to protein-derived chemicals.) The fats in meat are probably not 'tasted' by cats but rather stimulate their sense of smell. One meat smells quite different from another – rabbit has a different smell from beef, and liver smells differently from kidneys – and cats are very sensitive indeed to different smells. This probably explains how they form quite definite food likes and dislikes (see p 151).

Taste recognition comes very early in cats; kittens one day old can differentiate between salted and non-salted liquids. But as the cat ages the acuity of its senses of taste and smell almost certainly deteriorates, just as it does in man. Certain respiratory virus infections, or 'cat flu', particularly FVR (see p 197) can cause the temporary and sometimes permanent loss of the sense of smell through congestion of the nasal passages with mucus. At such times, cats may lose their appetite for normal foods, and can be tempted to eat only by particularly pungent delicacies such as smoked herring or grilled liver.

This relationship between smell and appetite illustrates the importance of odour to a cat. There are other cases where the normal behaviour of cats is significantly affected by the loss of smell, notably sexual courtship, toilet habits, scent marking and success at hunting. All in all, our somewhat poorly developed senses of taste and, in particular, smell leave us ill equipped to appreciate the subtleties of a cat's social and gastronomic experiences.

Brain and behaviour

If one bodily feature distinguishes a creature's abilities and position on the evolutionary scale from all others, it is the brain – command centre of all bodily processes, site of instincts, memory and intelligence, and core of the entire nervous system (see p 105). It receives sensory messages from the creature's environment, decides on the actions to be taken and then controls those actions – that much is common to all advanced animals. But the complexity and sophistication with which these processes are carried out varies strikingly across the animal kingdom.

One measure of a species' evolutionary development and behavioural potential is the ratio of brain weight to body weight. In the cat this is greater than in most mammals other than apes and humans. More importantly, the cat has the large and highly convoluted cerebral hemispheres typical of other relatively intelligent creatures.

Brain development

The physical development of a kitten's brain is most rapid during the first few days of its life, and is more or less complete by the age of five months. This directly parallels its behavioural development (see p 135). Poor nutrition can, however, retard the achievement of full behavioural potential and may even lead to permanent brain damage. Normal brain development also depends on a kitten receiving adequate levels of physical and sensory stimulation. This is one function of the vigorous licking mother cats normally give their kittens, but it can be supplemented or substituted by handling by the owner for a short period each day (see p 134).

Apart from such general stimulation, the brain areas associated with the various senses have to be 'exercised' from an early age if they are to function normally in the adult cat. For instance, the nerve mechanisms governing the visual system will not register meaningful information to cats that are raised in the dark or are not exposed to varied visual stimuli. In practical terms, the supercats of this world are those that were born to a conscientious queen, were well fed as kittens and were raised by people who handled and played with them regularly, thereby providing an interesting and changing environment.

Instincts and learning

Many of the behaviour patterns exhibited by kittens and cats seem to be inborn, and develop with little evidence of practice or learning. Inborn behaviour ranges from simple reflexes during suckling and movement to more complicated and integrated sequences such as maternal care and mating. The suckling reflex (see p 132) is a good example of the value of such inborn behaviour – kittens must take milk soon after birth, otherwise they will die. There

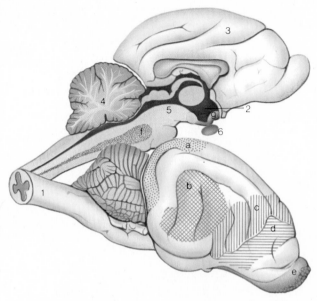

The feline brain, like that of other mammals, consists of a series of swellings at the top of a sealed hollow tube that runs from head to tail – the spinal cord **1**. The brain itself weighs 20 to 30g (⅔ to 1 oz), and is shown here about 1½ times life-size. It is also hollow, having central fluid-filled cavities – the ventricles **2** – while a series of fluid-buffered shock-absorbing membranes and the skull surround and protect it.

The most important part of the brain is the cerebrum, made up of two cerebral hemispheres **3**. These – particularly their highly convoluted outer cortex – preside over all aspects of conscious behaviour. Various areas are devoted to the senses of sight **a**, hearing **b**, and touch **c**, and to the control of bodily movements **d**. The olfactory bulbs **e** – relatively large in the cat – deal with the important sense of smell.

Generally speaking, the left-hand hemisphere is concerned with the right-hand half of the cat's body, and vice-versa. It is also in the cerebral hemispheres that memories are stored. Behind the cerebral hemispheres lies the cerebellum **4**. This co-ordinates balance and movement, and is exceptionally large and well developed in the cat.
The central core of the brain is the brain stem **5**, which forms a continuation of the spinal cord. Among its most important parts are the reticular formation **f**, which is concerned with keeping the brain awake and alert – it 'switches off' during sleep – and the hypothalamus **g**, which controls such basic instincts as hunger, fear, aggression and sexual and maternal behaviour. Very close by, linked to and under the control of the hypothalamus, is the pituitary gland **6**, the 'master gland' of the body's hormonal system (see p 105). By controlling the release of pituitary hormones the hypothalamus controls many aspects of the cat's behaviour.

Chasing birds is a favourite pastime of most cats. An alert cat will fix upon almost any small moving object and, if the opportunity arises, chase and swat it. This reaction is one of an inborn hunter; a kitten taught by a diligent mother will develop these instincts into skilled hunting behaviour, along with the many other skills it needs for survival.

re many other inborn skills that cats need for individual or species survival – for instance, righting themselves after a fall, so that they land on 'all fours', and displaying the right sexual reactions at the right time.

Any behaviour that is typical of cats as a species must be inborn in the sense that the potential for its expression has been inherited. However, there is obviously more to feline behaviour than a series of stereotyped reflex actions, which is what pure instinctive behaviour amounts to. Cats are both highly idiosyncratic and adaptable to changing circumstances because they can learn and remember, and use their acquired skills and knowledge in novel situations.

It is difficult to differentiate completely between instinctive and learnt behaviour, because cats constantly supplement, modify or alter their behaviour as they observe and learn. Hunting is a prime example of learnt behaviour. Most cats spend their formative weeks under intense maternal tutelage. If the mother is a hunter, she will teach her kittens how to combine their frenetic repertoire of pounces, swipes and leaps into a coherent, efficient method of killing. The kittens of non-hunting mothers will not learn to kill, however expertly they stalk and swoop. Similarly, toilet training is an amalgam of reflex and learning. The urge to bury faeces is instinctive; it protects small animals from predators who may follow their trail. As a result, the tiniest kitten will scrabble among the deodorized granules in a litter tray, but it may have to watch its mother actually using the tray properly before it grasps the connection.

Largely because they are less responsive to simple vocal commands such as 'Sit', 'Heel' and so on, cats are often dismissed as being less intelligent than dogs. Yet they are generally more adept at fending for themselves in the wild, and are quite amenable to training if their natural habits and responses are respected and positive rewards such as titbits and petting are used at the appropriate moments. For example, they can be taught to retrieve objects, to open doors and cat flaps, and to perform numerous tricks – such as 'sitting' for food, or 'shaking hands'. The knack is to use the right rewards (see p152); physical dominance or punishment is not recommended for training cats because they usually react by trying to escape and become fearful of their trainer.

Cats learn other interesting idiosyncracies without formal training; witness how some rouse their owners by tapping on windows, scoop pellets of dry cat foods from part-opened packs or, worse, acquire the knack of 'accidentally' knocking over milk jugs when there are no witnesses about. They have observed, deduced and acted on received information.

Do cats think?
There is as yet no IQ test for cats. Claims are made for the intellectual superiority of certain breeds, such as Siamese, but there is no scientific evidence to back them up. The only measures of feline intelligence are observation and a few psychological tests, but two unusual characteristics stand out. Firstly, cats are extraordinarily good at solving problems, and then adapting this solution to a later different problem. This is the feline equivalent of insight, and is seen in such situations as opening a door latch or retrieving an inaccessible object. Secondly, they are profoundly unmoved by the work ethic. Rats, mice, pigeons and even monkeys will press levers endlessly to get a food reward; cats are more likely to fall asleep and only work as a last resort.

Obviously there are bright cats and dim cats. For every one that can 'knock over' the cream jug there is another that will get its head stuck inside, but as a species their intelligence cannot be denied. They are curious; proverbially so. They will explore a situation not immediately related to their survival – surely a sign of intelligence far beyond the level of mere existence.

Cat magic
Cats have a very good sense of time, and learn to anticipate the movements of their owners if food and warmth are payoffs. They also display remarkable homing abilities when the need arises. There are many reliable accounts of cats negotiating great distances across natural obstacles such as rivers and cities in order to return to a familiar territory. It is thought that they navigate across unknown terrain by responding to a combination of the sun and the earth's magnetic field, but when close to home they probably reconnoitre using familiar sights, sounds and smells.

In fact, the majority of the 'unearthly' behaviour so long attributed to cats is due entirely to their excellently developed senses. They may or may not have a 'sixth' sense, but the five they undoubtedly do have respond much more quickly and efficiently to outside stimuli than the human equivalents can. People puzzle over cats' anticipation of natural events such as storms or earthquakes, or how cats know that their owners are going on holiday. There is no need to resurrect medieval notions of feline magic to explain these things. Cats are basically hunters, even if some of them never exploit their potential, and their bodies and senses are finely attuned to outside events: They can sense a pressure drop, feel miniscule earth tremors, smell far-off rain, observe the break in routine and make provision for their future comfort.

Some ailurophiles have even suggested that cats possess extra-sensory powers and can follow their owners to previously unvisited places. (This is called 'psi-trailing'.) While there is no proof that cats are not in touch with the universe at a different level, it is more likely that they just 'smell out' their owners. This explanation may sound more prosaic, but in truth it pays a greater tribute to the cat's abilities than to invest it with magic powers.

Drinking water from a tap is one of the many tricks that a cat masters easily. An adept technician and possessing an inquisitive character, a cat given the right incentive will do almost anything a dog will do, from opening doors to retrieving objects and shaking hands. However, apparently selfish at heart, felines perform best for their own gain.

Sleeping and dreaming

Feline insomnia is unknown. Cats sleep away about two-thirds of their lives, yet why they spend twice as much time asleep as most other mammals is not understood. The daily sleep ration varies greatly with the weather, degree of hunger, sexual arousal and age of the cat. Kittens and old cats sleep more than healthy adults, but a combination of warmth, security and a full stomach can provoke sleep in any cat at almost any time of day.

The natural pattern of sleeping consists of numerous, short 'catnaps' throughout the day, unlike the typical human pattern of a single, eight-hour session. However, some cats with working owners will spend most of the day asleep, reserving their wakeful periods for socializing in the morning and evening. Similarly, bored cats or those confined in catteries may use sleep to while away the time.

The nature of sleep

Because cats are such expert sleepers, they have been extensively used in sleep studies and have thereby helped to provide much of the present knowledge about the function and mechanisms of sleep. Sleep is not a passive state, as was once thought, but an active process which increases activity in certain brain areas. Such activity produces tiny electrical impulses that provide a reliable basis for monitoring and classifying the various stages of sleep. Electrical activity of the brain can be recorded in an electroencephalogram (or EEG) trace by placing small, painless electrodes upon the skin of the forehead and amplifying and displaying the impulses discharged by the underlying brain.

The EEG of a wakeful cat has a low amplitude and no regular pattern, because it fluctuates continuously in response to body activity and external stimuli. As the cat becomes drowsy and falls into light sleep the EEG changes towards a pattern of slow, irregular, high-amplitude waves. The cat may lie down, but not necessarily, and the neck and trunk muscles retain their tone. At

this stage it is easy to awaken – by the distant sound of a can-opener, for example. This light sleep may continue for 10 to 30 minutes, after which a second change in the EEG pattern and the body position occurs as periods of deep, or active, sleep alternate with periods of slow-wave light sleep.

The most characteristic physical indication of deep sleep is a sudden burst of eye movements – between 8 and 30 movements at each burst – under the closed or semi-closed eyelids. Deep sleep is therefore known as rapid eye movement or REM sleep. The whole body becomes slack and the cat tends to roll over onto its side. At the same time, individual muscles twitch in an uncoordinated sequence: there may be a flexing of the paws and quivering of the ears, whiskers and tail, while the rest of the body remains relaxed. The cat may mutter.

Owners may like to think that the cat is dreaming. Of course, the content of cat dreams will remain forever unknown, but cats probably do have semi-conscious experiences analagous to our own. REM sleep is known to serve an important biological function because humans deprived of it become thought-disordered and irritable, and REM-sleep-deprived cats 'catch up' on the missed sessions as soon as possible.

The paradox of deep sleep – also known

as paradoxical sleep – is that although the sleeper is at the lowest level of consciousness and is difficult to awaken, the EEG patterns suggest that the brain is as active as it is in the waking state. And it may still respond to previously established danger signals. After six to seven minutes of deep sleep the cat returns to a 20- to 30-minute period of slow-wave light sleep.

Once into the cycle, the cat will sleep through alternating periods of deep and slow-wave sleep until it awakens once more. Fit adult cats spend about 15 per cent of their lives in deep sleep, 50 per cent in light or slow-wave sleep and 35 per cent awake. Kittens experience only deep sleep for the first four weeks of their lives, and spend about 50 per cent of their time in this state. Thereafter the typical adult pattern develops.

Sleep and warmth

Warmth is the all-important factor for sleep, and cats will move their sleeping spot with the sun to help counteract the slight fall in their body temperature. This desire or need for warmth presents a potential danger, since a cat attracted to the warmth of a baby could unwittingly suffocate it. Cats living outdoors should have access to a draught-free shed and dry bedding; hay or straw is ideal.

Every cat has its favourite sleeping spot – a chair, bed or window-sill perhaps. On hygiene grounds, it should be discouraged from sleeping on the owner's bed; otherwise, a sleeping cat is best left alone. After all, what could be a more powerful symbol of secure homeliness than a cat asleep on a rug by the fireside?

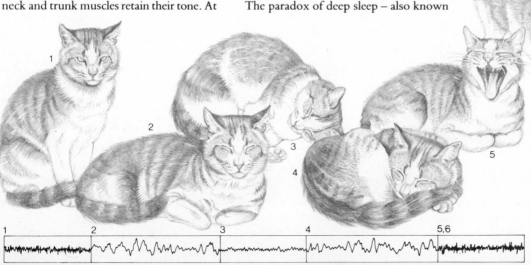

Stages of sleep An alert cat 1 has irregular brain waves **below**, which slow and become larger as it falls into light sleep 2. In deep sleep 3 the cat relaxes completely and probably dreams, but its brain waves are like those of consciousness. Deep and light sleep alternate 4 before it reawakens 5 and stretches 6 to restore circulation.

Self-grooming

One of the reasons cats are so pleasant to have as pets is that they usually keep themselves fastidiously clean. Only the long-haired breeds need much assistance from humans to groom their coats. A well-groomed coat is a useful indication of a cat's good health, just as a deterioration in normal grooming and toilet behaviour often occurs as a result of illness.

The barbed tongue (see p113) and the forepaws are the main instruments of grooming, together with the occasional use of teeth and claws to remove debris trapped in the coat. The sequence in which parts of the body are groomed is highly idiosyncratic, although individual cats tend to be predictable in their grooming pattern. Some groom a lot, others only rarely; some repeatedly wipe paws over the ears, whereas others neglect the head altogether. Similarly, the time devoted to grooming varies from nothing to one-third or more of the waking hours.

Why cats groom

Grooming is not just a matter of feline personal hygiene. Licking stimulates skin glands which keep the coat waterproof, and at the same time the cat ingests small quantities of vitamin D, an essential nutrient. Grooming is also a necessary part of temperature regulation in cats, because evaporation of sweat is ineffective due to the fur (see p107). Saliva substitutes for the cooling function of sweat.

This explains why cats groom more in warm weather than when it is cold and why bouts of grooming often follow strenuous activities such as hunting, play and feeding, or sleeping in a warm spot. In hot climates,

Grooming each other, cats solve the tricky problem of cleaning behind the ears. Probably more important, however, is the social role of mutual grooming in reinforcing the relationship between cats that share a common territory. This is often extended to human owners.

prodigious quantities of moisture may be lost from the body via this cooling mechanism, which must be replaced by drinking. Thirsty cats attempt to conserve their body water by not grooming and by producing reduced quantities of more concentrated urine.

The other practical functions served by grooming are to remove loose hair, debris and parasites from the fur. Broken and detached hairs probably irritate the underlying skin, and grooming stimulates new growth from replacement hair follicles. Skin parasites such as fleas and lice are particularly likely to lodge around the head because it is the one place that the cat cannot lick. Cats that rarely groom and long-haired cats which cannot groom efficiently are more likely to suffer infestations all over the body. Dust, dirt and plant burrs in the fur usually provoke intense grooming by cats, just as a little butter smeared on the coat is a safe and easy way of encouraging a lazy cat to groom itself.

Cats often groom themselves in response to fright or indecision about how to cope with a puzzling situation. Psychologists call this displacement activity – a piece of inappropriate behaviour that in some way helps the animal to cope with conflict. However, it is possible that fear or embarrassment provokes a rise in body temperature as muscles prepare for action, and extra heat has to be disposed of by grooming. Under the same circumstances, human beings blush and sweat in order to lose heat.

Excessive self-grooming, often induced by emotional upset (see p136), can sometimes lead to medical problems such as skin inflammation, hair loss or, worse, the development of an obstruction in the intestine by a hairball. It is quite normal for cats to ingest their own fur and to bring up hairballs without assistance, but long-haired breeds are particularly liable to form obstructive hairballs (see p194). Such cases need urgent veterinary attention, but you can prevent it altogether by regular combing and brushing (see p154).

Mutual grooming

Grooming is one of the first activities kittens learn. They begin at about three weeks, and by six weeks are efficiently grooming themselves and each other. Until then it is the mother's responsibility to groom the litter, an activity which is vital for ensuring the proper development of kittens (see pp132 to 134). The social bond between mother and kitten is reinforced during grooming sessions because it seems to be a pleasurable activity accompanied by much purring. As the kittens grow, they begin to lick their mother.

Mutual grooming between pairs of cats may persist well after kittenhood; indeed, it may continue throughout adult life. Grooming then becomes one of the many sociable activities that bind cats together. One cat licking another behind the ears is both a practical solution to an anatomical problem and a means of communicating intimate feline feelings.

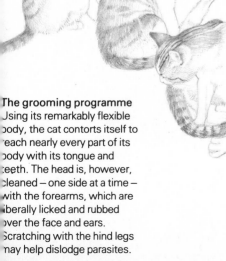

The grooming programme Using its remarkably flexible body, the cat contorts itself to reach nearly every part of its body with its tongue and teeth. The head is, however, cleaned – one side at a time – with the forearms, which are liberally licked and rubbed over the face and ears. Scratching with the hind legs may help dislodge parasites.

Movement and balance 1

Designed as hunters, cats are strong, quick and agile. An extremely well-muscled body gives strength; a skeleton modified in various ways from the mammalian norm gives exceptional flexibility; and a highly developed area of the brain, the cerebellum, is devoted to the co-ordination of sense organs and muscles, producing the superbly controlled movements essential to a predator. That cats are enviably graceful is a bonus for their owners. A unique feline asset is their retractile claws. These are normally kept sheathed for sharpness, but can be quickly extended in order to make sharp 'crampons' for climbing or weapons for hunting and fighting.

The specialized skeleton

Like dogs, cats walk on their toes; the foot and hock (ankle) bones are arranged so that only the part in front of what is the ball of our feet touches the ground. This is called digitigrade posture, as opposed to the flat-footed plantigrade posture of humans. Digitigrade movement is the most efficient for a hunter, as it combines speed with stability. In effect, it lengthens the limbs and so lengthens the stride; it accelerates movement, as only a small area of the foot touches the ground, so the limb can move on quickly.

Another adaptation for speed and flexibility is the reduced collar bone, or clavicle; it is just a sliver in cats, and may be absent entirely. This liberates the shoulder blade, allowing it to move freely with the rest of each forelimb. The reduced collar bone and narrow chest enable cats to keep their forelimbs close together to negotiate a narrow fence top successfully, or to pick their way through a crowded mantelpiece. At the hind end of the skeleton, modifications are not so noticeable. This is the centre of power and is designed to carry the muscles rather than for flexibility. Many of the muscles that move the hind limbs attach to the pelvic girdle, which is fused in the midline to make one large, strong bone.

Joints and muscles

Efficient joints are essential to the smooth and easy movement of the limbs. The ends of the limb bones are rounded or flattened and covered with a layer of cartilage so that the two bone surfaces can slide smoothly over one another. The whole joint is surrounded by a protective capsule that

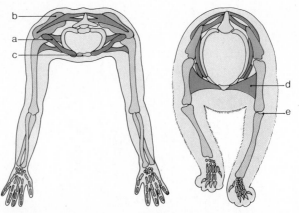

The forelimbs of humans and cats have significant structural differences. In humans above left the collar bones a are rigid struts between the shoulder blades b and breast bone c. In cats above right they are vestigial (and sometimes absent) so that the limbs are connected to the chest only

by muscles d. The 'liberated' shoulder blades of the cat are able to move the limbs up and down, back and forth and, to some extent, sideways. They are free to move with the swing of the legs and, coupled with the fact that they lie against a narrower and deeper chest than in humans, this increases the length of the cat's stride.

The elbow joint e is designed to hinge backwards. Normally the elbow is slightly flexed, but when a strong support is needed the joint is extended and the elbow is 'locked' by the surrounding muscles and ligaments to keep the whole limb rigid.

Twisting and squeezing to negotiate narrow gaps and awkward places is easy with a

skeleton as flexible as the cat's, so that the two halves can twist in opposite ways.

A walking cat first moves its right hind leg, then its right foreleg, left hind leg, left foreleg and so on. The feet are placed neatly in front of each other, so that feline tracks make virtually a straight line. Breaking into a trot, the hind legs' speed increases so that they catch up with the diagonally opposite forelegs; now the right foreleg and left hind leg are moving at the same time, and vice versa.

When the cat gallops, however, the trot changes into a series of long, low half-bounds, the spine alternately flexing and stretching. The cat thrusts itself forward from both back feet at once, lands on one front foot and then immediately transfers its weight onto the other; the latter is set down a stride farther on. The cat's back feet then land on the ground and it pushes itself off once again.

The hind limbs have sacrificed power for mobility; the stifle (knee) **a**, hock (ankle) **b** and foot cannot move sideways. The pelvis **c** provides a large area for muscle attachment. It articulates at the hip joint **d** with the thigh bone **e**. Each muscle is attached to bones at each end by tendons. When individual muscle fibres contract, the whole muscle gets shorter and thicker, and the bones are pulled towards each other. Some muscles, called extensors (shown green) – like the quadriceps **f** and the gastrocnemius **g** – cause joints to extend (straighten). Others – flexors

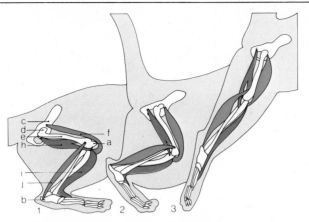

(red) like the hamstring **h** and tibialis **i** – flex (bend) joints. When jumping, the cat leans back **1** and the extensor muscles produce a powerful extension of the knee and ankle joints **2, 3**. The reaction to the downward thrust pushes the pelvis (and the rest of the body) up.

'Walking the plank' is helped by having a narrow chest and a tail for a balancing pole.

secretes a viscous liquid, the synovial fluid, which lubricates the joint.

Many of the cat's joints are modified to allow considerable freedom of movement. In the forelimbs, the shoulder joint consists of a shallow cavity at the end of the shoulder blade (scapula) in which the head of the upper arm bone (humerus) rotates. The humerus is also able to glide forwards and backwards during movement of the limb. The elbow joint is more restrictive, but provides stability when moving at speed; it acts as a hinge, most movement being in the vertical plane.

The hind limbs join the pelvis at the hip joint in a ball and socket arrangement similar to that in the human body. This type of joint provides considerable freedom of movement of the limb, but there are also very firm attachments for the muscles. The knee joint, or stifle, bends in the opposite direction to the elbow. On looking at a cat's skeleton (see p 103), it seems to form a fairly loose connection between the leg bones (femur and tibia); in the living animal, however, there are specially-shaped cartilages within the joint and extremely strong ligaments around it. These produce an extremely stable joint, which moves mostly in the vertical plane, an arrangement well adapted to transmit the strong thrust from the big thigh muscles.

Cats owe most of their flexibility to their extremely mobile backbone. As in humans, a small fibrous disc, which acts as a shock-absorber, separates each spinal bone (vertebra) from the next. The degree of movement between individual vertebrae is small, but as they are connected to each other less tightly than in many other animals, overall flexibility is great. Cats can bend and stretch their bodies into a wide variety of postures: they can arch their back into an inverted U shape, sleep in a circle,

bend themselves in half, and rotate the front half of the spine through 180° relative to the back half.

At the top of the vertebral column – in the neck or cervical region – the first two vertebrae (atlas and axis) are specially shaped to enable the head to make a wide range of movements. This freedom of movement is increased by the other cervical vertebrae, whose joints are also relatively mobile. In contrast, the chest or thoracic region of the column allows only a moderate degree of movement, and the vertebrae have large, prominent spines for the attachment of the powerful muscles that move each scapula and anchor the fore-limbs to the rest of the body. The lower back (lumbar) region also allows only limited movement between the vertebrae, which again have prominent spines for the attachment of the major back muscles. There may be 19 to 28 small vertebrae in the tail – except of course in the Manx and the Japanese Bobtail – which twists and stiffens to help the cat balance.

Cats in motion

The actual process of feline movement is easy to observe but difficult to interpret. The strong back legs propel them forward while the front legs play a more supportive role. Cats generally proceed at a leisurely, investigative pace, but are capable of the extremely slow, controlled movements necessary for hunting by stealth. The high degree of muscle control means they can stop in mid-stalk and hold the pose for a period that would be agonizing for humans. They can also move at a business-like trot, a purposeful and speedy version of the walk, legs all a blur.

At speed, they are less efficient. The feline gallop is really a series of half-bounds, and the amount of ground they cover depends on the length of the leaps and how far they can push themselves forward by flexing and stretching their backbone. Rarely do they go fast enough for the front and back legs to cross in mid-stride, the mark of a true runner such as the cheetah (see p 12). Like cheetahs, however, cats are sprinters, and cannot sustain a great speed for long. The great power of the hind-quarters gives explosive acceleration from a standing start, but the muscles tire very quickly. To escape or to catch prey, cats prefer jumping to running. /continued

Movement and balance 2

Jumping

Cats can clear up to five times their own height. Most have a considerable jumping repertoire: the vertical jump, calculated and rehearsed; the impromptu jump taken when being pursued; the hunting pounce, often seen as a play pounce in domestic cats (see pp 122 and 134); and the surprise jump, which is usually backwards and lifts the cat up in the air, all four feet leaving the ground at once. A cat jumping up onto an accustomed ledge or wall does so from a walk. Ascent onto an unknown surface or a great height is usually carefully estimated first. A good jump thrusts the cat well above the objective, whether it is a table-top or a mouse, with its front legs thrust out ready to grab its prey or to balance itself. A bad jump ends in flurried scrabbling with front and back legs.

Although going up is easy, coming down presents problems. Cats have excellent depth perception and often dither on the brink of a height they have ascended with Olympian nonchalance. They shorten the jump to the ground by edging the front of the body down as far as possible first. If coming down from a very great height, they will try to make an intermediate jump, giving their back legs a chance to push away from the wall and convert the jump into a horizontal leap, which is much less hard on the front legs. Cats who land heavily will shake their paws vigorously or lick their paw pads.

Climbing

Climbing presents the same problems as jumping. Most cats seem to enjoy climbing, and will often go up trees or poles for a short distance, apparently for fun. The climb usually starts with a powerful leap; then the cat rapidly moves upwards using the strong muscles of the back and hind-limbs, and extending its front and rear claws to grip.

However successful at climbing, cats tend to become stuck in trees, on roofs or up telegraph poles. This is unusual if the climb is purely recreational, but if the cat ascends intent on hunting, or in great haste when being pursued by a dog, it can happen depressingly often. When the cat finally becomes aware of its surroundings, it is alarmed at its height and will often remain immobile until rescued or until it drops down in exhaustion.

Even if the cat attempts to climb down head first, it is not well equipped for the task. The claws, which point backwards, do not provide the grip required and the powerful hind limbs can give no support, so the result is an undignified slide. Some cats will descend backwards and jump down the last few feet. Climbing should not be discouraged as it is good exercise, but rescuing a tree- or roof-bound cat can be a tedious business (see p 180).

Balance and co-ordination

A hunter's body is no good if bones, muscles and senses are uncoordinated. The cat has a highly efficient co-ordinating centre in the cerebellum (see p 114), where visual and other information is swiftly correlated with the signals from the cerebral hemispheres that instigate movement and with data fed back from the muscles and joints. In the cat all these nerve messages are very fast, enabling it to respond exceptionally quickly.

Unfortunately, the almost supernatural powers of balance and agility that are attributed to the cat have invested it with an inflated reputation for indestructability. Cats can miscalculate, often fall off things (especially if carrying something in the mouth) and occasionally land on their head. You should not expect skilful landings if there is no time to execute the necessary manoeuvres before hitting the ground. Similarly, a cat falling from a very great height may land on all four feet, but its legs will probably be broken. Obviously cats differ in their ability to survive great

heights; a lot depends on their weight and age. An average-size cat reaches its maximum falling speed within 20m (65ft). Theoretically, therefore, if the animal survives a fall of 20m it will survive anything greater; few owners would care to experiment, however.

The cat's brain receives information on its orientation and movements both from its eyes and from a specialized sense organ known as the vestibular apparatus. which forms part of the inner ear. This detects the direction and acceleration of any head movement as well as sending nerve impulses to the brain to tell the cat which way up it is. When combined with signals from the muscles and joints that give the cat an 'internal' sense of its body's orientation, the brain has a complete perception of the animal's position and movement in space.

This information is vital for balance. It is transmitted to several areas of the brain and is used to produce the posture required. Any sudden change in the animal's orientation results in a reflex response aimed at correcting the change; for example, if a cat

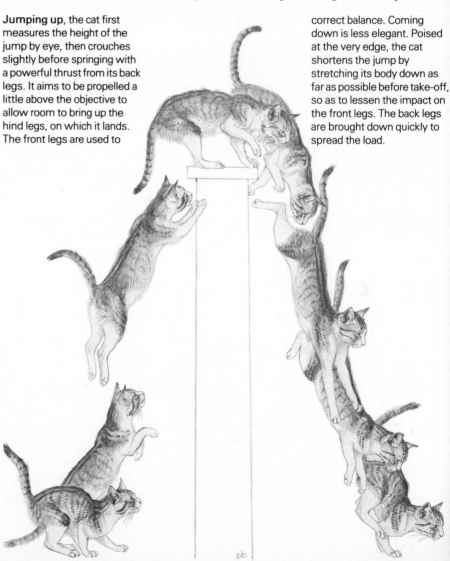

Jumping up, the cat first measures the height of the jump by eye, then crouches slightly before springing with a powerful thrust from its back legs. It aims to be propelled a little above the objective to allow room to bring up the hind legs, on which it lands. The front legs are used to correct balance. Coming down is less elegant. Poised at the very edge, the cat shortens the jump by stretching its body down as far as possible before take-off, so as to lessen the impact on the front legs. The back legs are brought down quickly to spread the load.

s pushed to the left, its left legs will extend almost instantaneously, preventing the animal overbalancing.

The righting reflex

Possibly the most famous feline attribute, the ability to land on all fours is really two reflex actions combined. The information reaching the brain from the eyes and vestibular apparatus enables the neck muscles to turn the falling cat's head so that it is horizontal and upright. The rest of the body is then repositioned to suit the head as a result of a reflex action involving nerves along the spinal column. Therefore when a cat twists to fall on its feet it always starts at the head.

The control of movement and balance is a skill that must be learnt by young kittens. At birth, a kitten is blind and unable to walk efficiently, but it does have a righting reflex and can orientate itself. Once the eyes have opened and the kitten begins to walk, then it rapidly develops a well co-ordinated gait, although it takes several weeks before this approaches the sensitivity and efficiency of the adult cat's.

The vestibular apparatus in the inner ear (see p 109) is the balance and orientation monitor, telling the cat which way up it is. It comprises several fluid-filled chambers lined with millions of tiny hairs. Sensory nerve endings send signals to the brain whenever the hairs move. In the larger chambers – the utricle **a** and saccule **b** – tiny crystals of calcium carbonate (chalk) rest on the hairs. They press down on whichever hairs are at the bottom, and

Unsheathing the claws

Each claw is attached firmly to the end toe bone, which is in turn linked to the next by elastic ligaments **a**. These bones connect to muscles in the leg via tough tendons **b**. **1** In the padded paw, the claws are retracted within a

thus signal mainly information on up/down orientation. In the semi-circular canals **c** the hairs project into flaps of tissue, which are moved whenever the fluid in the canals moves. This happens – like the sloshing of water in a glass – whenever the head moves. The three canals are arranged at right-angles to each other, and thus signal the direction and acceleration of movement in any direction. The cochlea **d** is the organ of hearing.

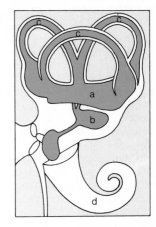

sheath of skin by the ligaments. To use the claws **2** the muscles contract, pulling on the tendons. One of these rotates the end bone forward and automatically pushes the claw out; the other straightens the toe for maximum extension.

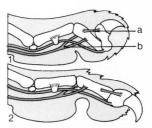

Climbing A cat climbs a tree **left** by jumping the first stage and then extending its claws to make crampons. It adjusts the position of its front legs to suit the curve if necessary, and scrambles up powered by its hind legs.

The descent is less assured. The animal can either come down backwards, which often results in undignified slithering, or turn round to come down face first. In this position, the backward-curving claws give no grip and the power of the back legs is for once no advantage. The cat will jump outwards to the ground as soon as it can.

Falling on its feet Cats have evolved an automatic sequence of moves **right** to guarantee a safe landing. A falling cat rights itself by first levelling its head. With front legs close to its face and hind legs pointing straight up, it jack-knifes its body and rotates the front half through 180° to face the ground. It brings down the front legs, stretches the back legs sideways and turns the rear half of the body last. The tail may be used to counteract any overbalance, and the cat lands neatly on all four feet, its back arched to help cushion the impact.

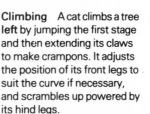

The hunting instinct

Cats may look attractive and make good companions, but it was as hunters of vermin that they were originally domesticated. Selective breeding over many generations has produced cats with a great variety of appearances, yet their natural hunting tendencies remain largely unaffected. Owners often have ambivalent feelings about this aspect of feline behaviour, being unhappy about the number and variety of wildlife killed by a cat with access to outdoors, but making an exception when rats or mice are caught. There are individual differences in hunting abilities because, although cats' predatory disposition is largely inherited, it is modified by early experience. Cat owners can therefore encourage or discourage hunting by taking this into account.

Under natural conditions, a queen supports her kittens by carrying whole or parts of prey to the litter. All kittens stalk and pounce on each other, on pieces of paper and on their own tails, but it is the early introduction to prey that is probably the most important determinant of whether or not kittens will grow up to be hunters. Bits and pieces of carcass may figure in early play, but the mother may eventually encourage her kittens to practise on live prey. Later, their education is completed by accompanying her on hunting trips.

First, the prey must be located. Cats may invest much time and energy in exploring the locality in search of suitable victims. Areas where prey is abundant or easy to catch are obviously favoured, and the territory or home range of feral cats may be largely centred upon a rabbit warren, hedgerow or barn (see p 124). Planning, careful observation and surprise are the key elements of a successful attack upon mice and other small ground-living mammals. Cats are the most patient of hunters, and will remain immobile for long periods until

Choreography of the hunt begins with location of the prey. The cat then usually stalks furtively and its belly drops to the ground for an undercover approach. Satisfied that distance and timing are perfect, it lunges, keeping its hind legs firmly on the ground. It grabs the prey with its front paws and (often after spending some time playing with the catch) finally deals the fatal neck bite. Some cats even then continue to toy with the corpse.

Stealth and cunning are the hallmarks of the hunter in wait for unsuspecting prey. Prime hunters are undoubtedly farm cats with both opportunity and terrain for good hunting.

After capture, the thrill of the hunt is prolonged by patting the prey playfully between the paws before it is dispatched. Many captured creatures are never eaten.

the prey can be pounced upon. The final leap must be from the right position, because prey not properly grabbed the first time is very likely to escape. Birds and fast-moving mammals such as rabbits are more likely to be stalked and rushed as and when opportunity presents, though some cats learn to hide and wait in ambush for birds.

The hunting sequence

All cats, wild or domestic, go through the same sequence of motions when hunting. The prey is located, by sight or smell or both. The cat creeps as near as possible, as quickly as possible, running silently along with its stomach nearly on the ground. It may take one or two sorties to get near enough for the pounce. The cat freezes, concentrating totally on the prey, ears pointing forward, eyes all pupil.

As the excitement mounts, the cat begins to quiver. The hind legs tread soundlessly and the rump sways from side to side. The head moves from side to side, helping the cat to judge its distance precisely. Then the cat lunges forward, forepaws extended, to grab its prey. Cats very rarely leap in the air

and pounce. They like to keep their powerful back legs firmly on the ground to give them stability if the prey is awkward to hold down or the fighting gets rough.

Cats generally kill with a bite on the nape of the neck, responding to the visual cue of the indentation between head and neck. Their long, sword-like canine teeth slip in between two of the neck bones and sever the spinal cord. Death is instantaneous. When thoroughly proficient at hunting, cats are able to position this bite with deadly accuracy, 'feeling' their way with touch receptors at the base of their teeth and with their whiskers. Cats with mutilated whiskers are less able to dispatch their prey.

In spite of the accuracy of this death bite, cats may fail to kill outright at the first attempt. Wily prey may hunch up and make the target area of the nape disappear. Or prey may be just too large, and the cat must knock it down first and subsequently miss the spot. In this case, the cat may throw its victim violently to one side to disorientate it, then pounce again.

If it is a fairly large animal, such as a rat, the cat may change tactics altogether. With

It is tempting to presume that cats' selection of different food or prey is guided by nutritional needs. For instance, liver and nervous tissues such as the brain are eaten eagerly, and these organs are rich sources of vitamin D and essential fatty acids respectively. However, there are many unanswered questions about the nutritional requirements of cats (see p148), and it would be rash to interpret their likes and dislikes in terms of nutritional wisdom.

Bringing back the bacon
Although cats are generally solitary hunters, the spoils may be carried back to the home area to be shared with other cats or as a gift to the owner. (Prey is always carried or dragged by the neck.) This habit reveals the truly social, almost altruistic side of feline character which tends to be underrated. Cats often present hunting trophies with a great show of affection, although these emotions may not be reciprocated by owners! Cats whose owners acquire another pet may step up their production of headless mice until certain that they are not rejected.

It is never pleasant to find one's cat hunting songbirds and other valued forms of wildlife, although the long-term ecological impact of such predation by domestic cats may not be serious. (American observations indicate that songbirds constitute less than a quarter of the average feline catch.) Many owners would rather their cat did not hunt, but once the predatory habit is formed it becomes self-reinforcing and very difficult to eradicate by normal training procedures (see p153).

The most effective preventive measure, unless you keep your cat indoors, is to select a kitten weaned at about six weeks from a mother who is not a hunter. For similar reasons, those who want a good mouser would do well to select a kitten from a mother showing the same characteristics. Ideally, such kittens should not be removed before they have been introduced to the desired prey by the mother up to the age of eight to ten weeks. Further practice will permanently establish the hunting habit, but it does need to be reinforced from an early age. Despite having all the optimum early experiences, some cats never become good hunters, however, and the converse is equally true.

its hind legs firmly braced, head up and ears back, it will try to beat the prey into submission with blows from its front paws. Even so, cats are not invincible killers; observation of farm cats shows that the chances of escape are quite favourable. Over 90 per cent of birds evade capture, and fewer than 25 per cent of mouse hunts are successful.

Small prey are often not killed immediately, but may be repeatedly released, stalked, pounced upon and shaken. Many playful elements are incorporated into this ritual, in which bites are generally inhibited and claws retracted, so the luckless victim may not suffer further injury until the final coup. Movements by the prey are crucial for maintaining the interest and excitement of the cat, and there may be much patting and prodding to keep the game alive. Even dead prey is sometimes used as a grisly plaything. The cat will clasp it, roll about with it and wrestle with it as if it were a fellow feline.

Some scientists argue that these predatory games occur because brain centres controlling hunting go through a fixed time–activity sequence. Others have suggested that this behaviour has evolved for the same reasons as play itself (see p134), and enables the cat to perfect its hunting techniques.

Finding refuge, a lucky mouse is safe for a time – though the cat may well wait for a long period for it to attempt to escape. In fact, very many hunts are unsuccessful.

Hunting and nutrition
Hunting, fighting and feeding behaviour occur quite independently of one another and are influenced by different brain areas. Well-fed cats may be keen hunters, just as dominant toms are no more or less likely to hunt effectively than neutered males and females. Cats often do not eat their prey, and such surplus killing is characteristic of many other carnivorous species.

It is well known that cats are fussy feeders, and some species of prey are apparently less attractive than others; for instance, voles are usually rejected. The gall bladder, small intestine and fur may be spurned by some cats; others will eat everything. Small prey are usually eaten head first, going with the 'grain' of the fur. If the skin is swallowed it is usually regurgitated as a furry mass some time later. Most cats regard birds as choice food, and only a few feathers may remain after a meal; some make token attempts at plucking birds before they eat them, but usually give up very quickly.

Feline territories

Cats are territorial animals. Most pet cats live alone with their owners in personal territories that are bounded by brick, wood and glass. Intrusions by other cats are rare. If they do occur, they are resented, giving the mistaken impression that cats are asocial. All they are doing is defending their territory.

But the social behaviour of domestic cats has been so much modified by their association with people that it is necessary to look at the way wild or feral (semi-wild) cats organize their lives for a more informative account of 'natural' cat behaviour. Unfortunately, very little is known about the domestic cat's closest wild relatives (*Felis libyca* and *F. silvestris*; see p16), except that the latter (the European wild cat) is relatively sociable and seeks the company both of its own species and of domestic cats. To fill this gap, there has recently been a spate of research into the habits and social organization of domestic cats living more or less independently of people in free-roaming feral communities on farms and in cities.

Clearly, such research is more relevant to cats that are allowed outdoors than to those confined to a home, but it does relate also to indoor cats, particularly if more than one share a home. In the main, however, this article and the one that follows concentrate on the behaviour of cats with access to the outdoors. These, recent research shows, do maintain individual territories, but their social repertoire is flexible enough to allow the peaceful sharing or even amalgamation of territories and the formation of integrated communities. The result is a complex net of relationships of which the average owner is at best only dimly aware.

Identifying territories
Every cat has its own personal home base, sometimes no more than a favourite sleeping place. Surrounding the home base is the home range, an area encompassing a number of favoured places regularly used for sleeping, dozing, playing, sunbathing, keeping watch and so forth. The shape and the extent of the home range depend on the amount of cover it offers, the number of cats in the neighbourhood and, most important, the abundance and reliability of the food supply. Literally hundreds of cats may

contentedly inhabit a physically confined area where food is plentiful and regularly supplied, such as a garbage dump or dockyard. Where food and shelter are scarce, lone cats may exist on individual ranges extending over as much as 40 hectares (100 acres), or even more.

The dimensions of the home range also depend on the sex, age and, to some extent, temperament of the resident. Females and neutered cats usually occupy small, well-defined areas, but they generally defend these vigorously, even though they may not win every fight. Established tom cats may command an area ten times the size of the female range; however, the boundaries are less rigidly defined, and tom cats may be more tolerant of temporary intrusion than females. Beyond the home ranges lie the hunting ranges; these are linked to the home range by paths, which often follow long and circuitous routes around territories defended by other cats. Areas between paths are therefore very rarely used.

Like feral or wild cats, house cats possess the territorial urge, though it may not be obvious to their owners, especially in a one-cat household. The only manifestation of territorial behaviour may be the spirited defence of a favourite sleeping spot – usually the best armchair – against all comers. The home range is 'defended' by the cat's owner and there is no need to compete or even forage for food.

In multi-cat households, territorial behaviour may be more apparent as each cat establishes its home base. The home range becomes a shared responsibility and may be slightly larger than a single-cat range, although few urban cats can hope to command anything much bigger than the garden or yard around the house. Few pet cats need a hunting range. As with semi-wild cat communities there are neutral areas, used by the neighbourhood cats for their meeting rituals. Cats also seem to visit the areas beyond their individual territories from time to time, but why they do so and what for are unknown.

Establishing a territory
In the wild or feral state, cats choose and regulate their territories according to the local cat population and food supply. In

contrast, most domestic cats have their territories thrust upon them by owners who have little or no knowledge of existing feline land rights. A newcomer to the district has to fight its way in, and in some cases does not succeed.

The garden of the newcomer's home may have been incorporated into adjacent territories, and any attempt at annexation will be strongly resisted. However, the proximity of familiar humans confers an important psychological advantage on the newcomer, and it usually takes its cue from its owner's movements when marking the limits of its intended claim. Confrontation is inevitable, but whether there is fierce fighting or not depends on the age, strength and sex of the newcomer and the existing territory-holders. Again like feral and wild cats, females and neuters are fierce, though not necessarily successful, in defending their small, well-defined territories. Toms hold a larger, more diffuse territory, but do not necessarily defend it so single-mindedly; they are, however, generally more successful in the fights they pick. In most cases, the results of these skirmishes are final, and the new status quo is accepted without further fighting.

Marking the boundaries
Once the territory has been claimed, cats use scent marks and visual signals produced by scratching to indicate territorial limits. Tom cats spray bushes and boundaries with the pungent urine that not even humans can miss. Females and neuters also spray, but the results are not so noticeable to humans or other cats. More subtle marks are left by rubbing against upright features in the territory (including people's legs) with the chin, forehead and tail, where scent glands are concentrated.

Scent-marking is probably intended to be informative rather than deterrent. Cats investigating new scent marks do not recoil in fear and loathing but move closer, 'flehming' to pick up as much olfactory information as possible (see p112). If the mark was made by head or chin rubbing, a subsequent cat may even superimpose its own scent. Scent marks indicate who has passed and when, so that other cats can adjust their movements accordingly.

Marking informs cats of the status, sex and route of others. The strongest scent-marking is the result of urine spraying **1**; even humans can detect it. Head and cheek rubbing **2** and tail entwining **3** both deposit scent from the sebaceous glands (see p106). Scratching **4** leaves visible boundary marks and deposits scent from sweat glands on the paw pads.

Adjacent territories form a patchwork (stippled and hatched areas) that are often three-dimensional 1, so that roofs, fences or trees may not necessarily 'belong' to the cat whose territory is beneath. Most home ranges are limited to the owner's garden or yard, and may support several cats from the same household. The territory of a female or neuter 2 may be small but is vigorously defended, particularly by a female with kittens 3. A tom 4, however, may command an extensive area. This may incorporate part of the garden of a no-cat household 5, which has been carved up by neighbouring cats. A newcomer 6 must confront these existing claimants in trying to stake its home range. Cats sharing territorial boundaries or particular areas 7 within a multi-cat household avoid conflict by establishing rights of way at different times of day. For the same reasons there are communal highways 8 for access through closely juxtaposed home ranges. Chance meetings 9 are often resolved by a staring match. Areas not annexed by any cat may include the territory of a dog 10 and communal areas 11, sometimes only reached by crossing the home range of another cat 12.

Defending the territory

All cats defend, and may try to increase, their territories by psychological warfare. Vocal and visual threats, bluffs and appeasement rituals keep actual fighting to the minimum (see p128). If the rituals do backfire, the ensuing fight is nasty, brutish but usually short. Cat fights rarely last long if the loser is able to escape.

There is one instance of defensive behaviour that always results in real fighting: Female cats defending their young dispense with ritual posturings and attack immediately, tackling cats, dogs and even foxes with startling ferocity. However, in domestic cat communities the urge to minimize or deflect territorial violence is great. With the cat population density as high as it generally is, the animals simply cannot afford the time and energy needed to pursue every confrontation to a conclusion. On average, 70 per cent of any pet cat community is neutered before reaching maturity, and this may diminish aggressive tendencies. At the same time, domestic cats are more tolerant of each other than wild cats. Regular nocturnal meetings on 'neutral' ground (see p126) enable cats allowed outdoors to get to know each other, and this may help prevent fighting.

It is not merely a question of avoiding bloodshed on the doorstep. Domestic home territories are often crowded together and even share boundaries. There has to be a network of individual paths and shared thoroughfares to meeting grounds and the areas beyond home ranges that is much more complex in a conglomerate of domestic cat territories than in the wild. Fighting at every junction is just not feasible, so the community usually evolves a kind of highway code based on mutual avoidance. A cat about to set off usually checks the paths ahead, waiting for a clear route. On communal pathways the cat on the path seems to have right of way, regardless of its social status (see p126).

Another avoidance technique is time scheduling. Cats have an excellent time sense which they use to increase the size of their territories. For example, cats who share territory boundaries may establish a routine whereby one has right of way in the morning and the other in the evening. In multi-cat households, time sharing within the home range can also be observed. One cat will have an uncontestable right over a sunbathing spot in the morning which will revert, equally uncontestably, to a second cat in the afternoon.

If confrontation is not deflected, it may be resolved with a mild threat, such as a staring routine. For example, two cats approaching a crossroads will both stop and perhaps endeavour to stare each other down for the right of way. One may win, or they may both retreat. Occasionally, neither budges and a full-scale threat ritual may result. Very rarely, it will end in fighting. More usually, one will flee, the victor chasing. However, these skirmishes do not confer permanent status on the winner; the next time the cats meet, the other may win. Social status, a cat's place in its society, is not just a territorial matter.

Cats' social life 1

Thanks to Kipling, cats are often assumed to walk by themselves, pursuing lives of enigmatic and aloof solitude. Actually they are highly social animals. Possibly the misconception arose because cats generally hunt by themselves. At home, so long as food and shelter are freely available, most cats – with the exception of some toms – lead very sociable lives, supporting each other in small groups and efficiently controlling larger communities by forming social hierarchies.

Group living

Feral and wild cats live in groups based on the mother-kitten unit, some mature males assuming a paternal role while others become solitary nomads. Cats living with people are usually more tolerant of each other, and several cats from completely different litters may cohabit amicably in a multi-cat household if they are introduced together as kittens. A lone pet will generally direct its social urges towards its owner.

Within any cat group, individual members greet each other affectionately with nose kisses, body-rubbing and sniffing at anal regions. They may sleep in companionable heaps, groom each other, play and defend their home range (see p 124) together. Females may share babysitting and guard duties, and may even bring food to nest-bound nursing mothers. Queens who give birth at the same time often amalgamate their litters and pool feeding and cleaning duties. There are even instances of experienced mothers, not giving birth themselves, acting as midwives to the inexperienced, severing umbilical cords and licking new kittens clean.

Outside the immediate family circle the urge for group socialization persists. Neighbouring cats that are allowed outdoors by their owners soon become members of a kind of feline social club that meets on 'neutral' ground at night. Membership of the club and regular attendance at the meetings presumably help to reduce conflict between neighbours, but their precise function is not understood.

Social hierarchies

Wild and semi-wild cats develop a complex social organization with a distinct hierarchy from submissive up to dominant animals. However, this varies according to the time, place and context of meetings. A cat that is clearly dominant over all other cats within its home range may be deferential a short distance away. A pair of cats might sleep and groom together quite amicably, but be intolerant of each other when active.

The female hierarchy, which is very loose-knit, is based on motherhood; with each litter a female goes up the social scale a little. But at the time when she actually has the kittens, whichever litter it is, her dominant status increases dramatically.

Getting to know each other, cats use a complex body language. Acquaintances may greet each other by rubbing noses **top,** and a similar contact response may be solicited on meeting a human friend **above left.** Conflicting claims to a favoured spot **above** are often resolved by visual confrontation, the social inferior moving peacefully away. The friendly 'tails up' posture **left** expresses the close mother–kitten bond.

Females neutered after they have borne litters drop down the hierarchy very quickly; if they are neutered before they ever come into heat they never even establish themselves.

The tom cat hierarchy is rather different. It is devoted to the meticulous ranking of every tom in the neighbourhood according to his 'machismo quotient'. Dominant toms command the largest territory but do not necessarily mate with the greatest number of females. No entire (unneutered) tom escapes initiation. Whether a newcomer to the district or an adolescent reaching maturity, he is visited by estab-

lished males. He must usually fight several other males before his rank is established. These fights may take place over several nights, but once established a tom should not need to fight again unless he is challenging for a higher rank, is himself challenged or takes part in 'blooding' a newcomer.

The toms confront each other with a great deal of spitting and snarling, but usually aim their blows at the relatively armoured region around the head and neck. Most torn ears and missing eyes are the result of unscheduled clashes, poor defence techniques or a tom fighting out of his class. Toms do however fight for a chance to

On the tiles During the day a solitary cat may sun itself on its exclusive roof-top territory **above**. But at night local cats 'club' together, as depicted in the engraving **right**, usually outside any one cat's home range. They groom one another, purr and chirrup, and generally engage in friendly activities, usually without sexual contact or hierarchical posturings. Before dawn clubbers drift back to their home territories.

A real top cat Cats crowded together become neurotic and aggressive, and the normally flexible social hierarchy breaks down. Removal of a cat's 'personal space' – its ultimate territory, stretching about 50 cm (18 in) around its body – necessitates the evolution of a new social system. There emerges an autocrat – the 'king' of the colony – a middle group of equal ranking and, at the very bottom, one or two totally subordinate 'outsiders'.

mate, assembling outside the female's home or wherever she may be to take each other on in ear-splitting succession. One puzzling aspect is the fact that the female is not obliged to succumb to the winner and may choose 'losers' unopposed by superior toms. It may therefore be that the fighting is stimulated by a territorial rather than a sexual urge, as the toms are necessarily trespassing on alien ground. Proximity may also provoke fighting.

The hierarchy of the brotherhood is very rigid. The leader may be toppled occasionally by the next in line, or an incoming tom may prove stronger than all the ranks.

Toms that have been socially graded when entire and are then neutered gradually slip down the hierarchy, their descent paralleling the drop in male sex hormone levels. Cats neutered before initiation have no place in the hierarchy.

When large numbers of cats are forcibly housed together in a small space, a very rigid status or dominance order develops as a means of avoiding social breakdown. A single despot usually emerges, a dominant cat that has absolute priority over all the others for sleeping spots, feeding and so on. At the other end of the scale, one or two pariahs represent the safety valve and scape-goats of the community and are uniformly abused by the rest of the colony, all of whom share equal middle rank.

Cat communication

The civilized social life most cats enjoy is supported and reinforced by their ability to communicate with each other through smell, body language and vocalizations. Cats seem to recognize each other mostly by body smell. Acquainted cats always greet each other by touching noses and then sniffing the head and anal regions; glandular secretions in these areas identify individual cats by their unique scent. Very friendly cats will rub each other's bodies, scent-marking their companion for future recognition. Pet cats rub their owners for the same reason. Scent-marking objects and territorial boundaries by scratching, spraying and rubbing (see p 124) is communication at a distance. Apart from helping to define the limits of a cat's territory, it leaves a record for other cats to estimate how recently the owner has passed by.

Cats' bodily postures are more easily understood by human onlookers as a form of communication than scent-marking. Body language is composed of many elements – posture, tail position, angle of head, facial expression and so on – which can be likened to a vocabulary. Subtle arrangements of this vocabulary occur as moods swing from fear to aggression, for instance, or from noncommital encounter to recognition to friendship. However, some 'phrases' may be significant only in particular context; for example, some postures seen in the threat and appeasement sequence also occur, without the same meanings, in play and hunting.

There are a range of facial expressions that register a cat's mood and react from outrage to ecstasy (see the illustration on page 128). Tails can be just as expressive. Kittens following or running towards their mother hold their tails up high, and in doing so expose their ano–genital region for inspection and cleaning. Adult cats use their tails as a greeting gesture to both friendly humans and other cats. A brief vertical tail, on the other hand, is slightly threatening. A flailing tail is an offensive threat and an arched bristling tail a defensive threat. The posture of the cat itself may range from the crouching submissive pose to the well-known arched back signifying a defensive threat.

Talking cats

Cats possess a rich vocal language, though individuals differ in the type and variety of sounds they produce. I have distinguished at least 16 basic vocalizations; cats may well differ many more. Some individuals and breeds, notably the Siamese and their relatives, are more vocal than others.

Cats' social life 2

Cat language consists of three general sound categories: murmurs, vowels and strained high-intensity sounds. Murmuring includes purring and the soft sounds used for greeting, calling attention, acknowledgement and approval. Most of these sounds are made with the mouth shut. Purring is the sound most appreciated by cat lovers because it signals contentment. It is also remarkable for its continuity; cats can purr for hours with hardly a change in rhythm or intensity, breathing in and out.

The vowel sounds are used in quite specific contexts. The several variations of miaow – 'mee-ow', 'mew', 'mew'wow' and so on – are used to demand, beg and express bewilderment and complaint. They form distinct words in that the cat terminates each sound by closing its mouth, and they are the sounds that are used for 'talking' with owners. Most cats have a small but impressive vocabulary covering such concepts as 'out', 'in', 'please', 'thank you', 'help', 'food', 'come here' and 'no'. The way cats pronounce their vowel sounds gives them their individual, often recognizable voices.

High-intensity strained sounds are generally reserved for inter-cat communication. The mouth is kept open and tensed, but changes shape. Cats may growl or give an angry wail, snarl or utter the 'spit' used in fighting and the hiss of threat-cum-warning when another cat is sensed to be invading territory, the shriek when in pain and the high-pitched mating cry produced by the female (see p131). There is also the curious tooth-rattling stutter of frustration produced whenever an inaccessible bird is seen through a window.

Kittens do not share the full vocal repertoire of adult cats, but they can purr, spit, growl and make noises to signal greeting, distress, bafflement and anger. The distress call, which even newborn kittens can make, is particularly important because it elicits a search and comforting reaction from the mother. By the 12th week most of the other adult sounds can be produced, and thereafter cat language develops in virtuosity according to social circumstances.

Making faces is a fundamental mode of feline communication. A happy cat **1** has perky ears, pupils normal for the prevailing light level and relaxed whiskers. An angry cat **2** keeps its ears erect but furled back; its pupils constrict to slits and its whiskers 'bristle' forwards. A frightened cat **3** is 'wide-eyed' and lays its ears and whiskers flat. A cat playing or hunting **4** wears a face between those of anger and fear; the pupils are open but the ears are pricked and, like the whiskers, thrust forward. The pleasure of being petted shows in the half-closed eyes of the face of ecstasy **5**.

The vocal apparatus of cats **right** is different from that of humans. Cats can vocalize when breathing in as well as when breathing out, and the tongue's position is not nearly so critical as in human speech. Variations in the phonetic quality of sounds are mainly achieved by changes in the tension of muscles in the throat **a** and mouth, and by changes in the speed of air moving over the vocal cords **b**, which are stretched across the larynx or voice-box **c**. The false voice cords **d** may be involved in purring.

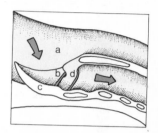

Feline encounters When any two cats meet **below 1**, they investigate each other first by sniffing at scent glands on the face. Their expressions are normal, with alert ears and relaxed bodies.
The signal for confrontation is generally a baleful stare.
2 One cat takes the initiative, investigating the base of the other's tail and growling an offensive threat; it expresses its aggression with erect ears, constricted pupils and tail swishing in a low arc close to the body. The second cat is forced onto the defensive; its ears begin to flatten and its pupils become larger.
3 The aggressor pursues its advantage and gives the other a full-frontal stare, its body poised to strike; its ears are up and its tail scything. The defensive cat retreats to a cringing position, crouched down with averted eyes half closed, ears flat and tail tip thumping the ground.
4 As the aggressor **a** advances, the defendant **b** may back off, its expression showing indecision whether to flee or make a stand.
5 The aggressor may then feel that it has won the fight and walk haughtily away **a**, leaving the defendant **b** to slink quietly out of range.
6 If the defendant cannot, or chooses not to, back down it may try the defensive threat. As the aggressor strains forward to attack, growling once more, its adversary's tail bristles and bends into an inverted U shape. The now assertive defendant turns its body sideways and arches its back to look large and impressive; its ears are flat and its pupils dilated.
7 The aggressor, unappeased, keeps on coming. The second cat increases its defensive display by pressing its ears even flatter to its head and opening its pupils to their utmost; its tail is held to one side, its teeth are bared and it is hissing.
8 The aggressor finally presses home its attack. The other crumbles, falling on its back so that it can take the attack with all four paws and kick with its powerful hind legs, claws fully extended. The skirmish continues until the subordinate cat spots a chance to escape with dignity.

In multi-cat households, brief 'conversations' are conducted between members, while solitary cats may similarly converse with human companions. Probably the most sustained vocal exchange between adult cats occurs during the mating season. Tom cats caterwaul, females 'call' loudly, both sexes croon throatily and at the point of consummation the female lets out the mating yowl of indignation. However, it is the conversations between a mother and her kittens that are the most enlightening to observe. Mother cats communicate incessantly with their offspring, purring during nursing, greeting each kitten, later calling them for food, warning them of danger, admonishing them – with a different noise

Contact between species is the natural substitute for a feline deprived of normal interaction with other cats. Most commonly, a human owner acts as the surrogate **left**, but a breeding queen's maternal instincts may even extend to other small animal species **right**.

in each case. And there is evidence that individual kittens' distress calls represent individual 'call signs', allowing the mother to account for each one.

Cats, people and other animals

The characteristic patterns of social interaction and communication displayed by cats have their origins in the wild where there was little possibility of forming sustained relationships with other species. So it is all the more remarkable that two-way communication occurs as often and as easily as it does between cats and unrelated species such as dogs, horses and humans. Having evolved along completely different lines, they must learn each other's language from first principles.

After an initial wariness, cats and dogs generally get along very well with one another, and many become inseparable companions. For any very intimate relationship to blossom, however, cats should be introduced to dogs when they are kittens. Adult dogs will often tolerate kittens and cats, but an adult cat may not countenance sharing its home with a puppy or adult dog if it has not had any previous canine contact.

Many elements of normal feline body language are used by cats whose social life revolves exclusively around humans and dogs. The greeting approach is invariably characterized by a cheerfully vertical tail (with the tip bent slightly forward) exactly as two friendly cats meet. Rubbing the legs and body of the owner is a modification of the manner in which cats investigate and exchange one another's body odours for future recognition. The hiss that cats emit during threatening encounters with each other will also be used if the owner teases too much or the dog oversteps the mark. Cats will also groom dogs and owners.

However, pet cats acquire some behavioural displays that are reserved solely for dealings with their owners. These idiosyncrasies differ from one cat to another; everyone's cat has its own way of soliciting food or petting, getting the window open and so on. Predatory attacks may be made upon their owners' legs, ankles or hands – sometimes simply in play, at other times in anger or frustration. The multiplicity of such individual quirks may be seen as an expression of individual cats' personality or, more dispassionately, as an illustration of how adaptable cats can be in modifying their behaviour to suit the environment of the moment.

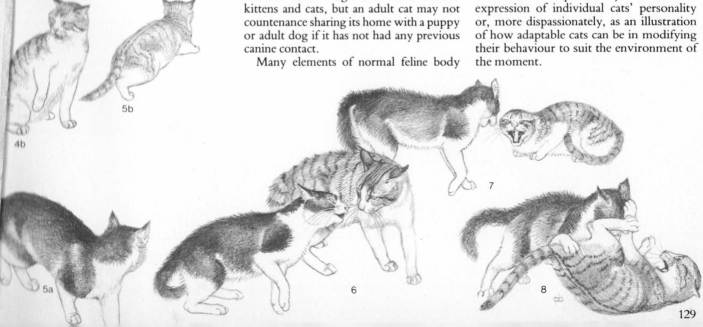

4b

5b

5a

6

7

8

Sexual behaviour

Most people are familiar with the sexual exploits of cats if only by reputation or through being wakened at night by the noisy and often bloody fights of vying toms and the raucous cries of courtship. Cat owners are perhaps more aware of the restless activity of females, the distress caused by roaming toms and the inconvenience of intensified spraying. For cats, as for any other species, success in reproduction is the key to survival, which is why so much of their behaviour is related to sex.

It begins at puberty, when the female's ovaries and male's testicles begin active production of germ cells (eggs or sperm) and sex hormones (see p214). The age of puberty in cats can vary between 3 and 18 months, depending on the breed (somewhat earlier in Burmese and Siamese, for instance), the time of year and nutrition. Females generally mature at 3 to 9 months, males at 7 to 12 months, but feral or free-ranging cats may not mature until they are 15 to 18 months old.

The mating season

Female cats, or queens, normally experience several cycles of sexual receptiveness for part of each year, usually in late winter to early spring and late spring to early summer. Each cycle spans, on average, about three weeks and consists of two phases. In the receptive phase (or oestrus) of up to ten days (four to six days if the cat is mated and ovulates), oestrogens (female sex hormones) are produced by the ovaries and the queen is sexually attractive to tom

Sexual activity plays a very important part in the life of entire (un-neutered) cats. If owned and allowed out, these will roam in search of a mate; males will fight and females inevitably present their owners with unwanted kittens. If uncontrolled, a feline population explosion results. Neutered cats are much less likely to stray and make more devoted pets.

cats. During the quiescent phase (or anoestrus) – the infertile phase of the reproductive cycle – the body prepares for the next cycle. In warmer countries the first season may be earlier in the year, and can be followed by three further series of breeding cycles instead of one. However, increased daylight can regulate the breeding condition of cats. Cats housed indoors in artificial light can be sexually active at any time of year. A day-length of 12 to 14 hours seems optimal for bringing queens into season.

Tom cats go through a period of springtime 'rut' which declines to a low in sexual activity during the autumn. However, it is not known whether male cats have an annual sexual cycle controlled by daylength, because their sex life may simply be turned off and on by the availability and sexual condition of females in the vicinity.

The normally reserved behaviour of a female cat undergoes a dramatic change when she is in oestrus, or 'heat'. It varies from cat to cat, but the queen generally shows signs of restlessness and decreased appetite, and urinates more frequently than usual. A repeated monotone 'call' is made, sometimes for hours on end, and especially loudly by Siamese – the nymphomaniacs of the cat world – who are prone to prolonged oestrus. Confined cats will sit at the window and howl.

aroused. **2** She rolls provocatively, treads with her front paws and calls, while the male circles and then runs forward. **3** He grasps her by the scruff and mounts her, front legs first. **4** He arches his back to position his penis, and the female twitches her tail aside to present her vagina. After one or two pelvic thrusts he achieves penetration and quickly ejaculates. **5** The queen pulls forward, crying out. **6** She turns on the male, who **7** retreats to safety to wash paws and penis. **8** The female rolls over voluptuously and washes. **9** After some minutes she may pat the male and they start again.

The mating game may be prolonged, though the sex act itself is very brief. **1** The wise tom approaches a female from behind and only when she is obviously sexually

Body postures are particularly characteristic: the queen becomes affectionate, rubbing against objects and people, rolling on the ground and mewling repeatedly. Any touch to the back of the tail is likely to stimulate a crouch position, and stroking at the base of the tail further exaggerates this receptive posture. Oestrous queens often engage in rhythmic 'treading' of the paws, the rump is lifted and tail deflected to one side. This is called lordosis.

Females behaving like this are almost certain to attract a congregation of neighbourhood tom cats by a combination of their urine odours, vaginal secretions and vocal calls. Amorous toms emit courtship cries in return for those of the queen, and their presence, scent marks and urine sprays further excite her condition.

Cats are not naturally monogamous, and if several eligible toms are available more

A queen in heat displays the characteristic lordosis position. The cat crouches, presenting her hindquarters for mating, treads with her front paws and croons. This pre-copulatory position can be elicited by scratching at the base of the back; the cat will twitch her tail to one side and thrust up her buttocks. She may show a face like that of fear or anger (see p 128).

than one may be selected by the female. Some considerable caterwauling and fighting may take place between rival males at this time, but the winner or most dominant tom is not necessarily accepted by the queen. Mating of a queen during one period of oestrus may occur on many occasions, at up to ten times an hour, and usually until exhaustion of the male. He may then be replaced by a successor or successors.

Courtship and copulation

Courtship between a pair of unacquainted cats on strange territory may last for several hours before copulation begins, although it may be brief with a frequently used stud cat

by the male. At the moment of ejaculation the female releases a loud piercing cry, followed by an almost explosive separation as she turns upon the male. Such a dramatic change in mood while mating has no parallel in other domestic animals.

The reaction is thought to be due to the special shape and function of the male's penis. The penis bears numerous spines at its tip which induce an intense and possibly painful stimulation of the female's vagina. This event is of great importance because the stress invoked stimulates a chain of nervous and hormonal reactions, culminating in ovulation (release of an egg cell) some 24 hours after mating, and with that

breeders, as a simple means of terminating unwanted and persistent oestrus. Frequent oestrous cycles of long duration occur in some queens, especially Siamese, and the resulting nymphomania can be a problem if the cat cannot be spayed or mated. Artificial induction of ovulation is a cheaper and probably safer treatment than injection of synthetic hormones of the type used in the 'pill' (see p 217).

The effects of neutering

An indication of the control that hormones from the testicles and ovaries have on the behaviour of male and female cats is shown by what happens when these organs are removed (see p 156). Although the primary reason for neutering is usually to render the cat infertile, many owners request the operation simply to eliminate what they regard as undesirable sex-related behaviour, such as urine spraying by toms and 'calling' by female cats.

Castrated toms do fight less, roam less, spray less and make less pungent urine, but are more affectionate and may become fatter and lazier. The age of castration greatly affects the behavioural outcome; in general the younger the cat, the greater is the suppression of sex-related behaviour. Thus, a fully adult, sexually experienced tom cat may continue to mate females (but not fertilize them), mark territory and fight with other males for months after castration, whereas a young male castrated at puberty or before will never develop this male potential. Spaying of females induces

or between a pair of cats who know each other well. The tom cat's reading of the queen's receptivity is quite important during the courtship phase because a premature attempt to mount is liable to provoke a vigorous attack from her. (Junior toms often get beaten up.)

During the prelude to copulation, the male sniffs the female's genitals and shows the flehmen reaction (see p 112). Eventually, he grasps the queen by the skin over the nape of the neck to immobilize her while he mounts. Genital contact lasts only ten seconds at the most, and involves a few deep pelvic thrusts and ejaculation of sperm

the possibility of conception (see p 215). After mating, the queen usually exhibits the so-called after-reaction of rolling on the ground and purring, but occasionally she may take an aggressive swipe at the seemingly bemused male, who sits nearby, awaiting the next session.

Whether or not pregnancy does ensue, the duration of oestrus is considerably reduced compared to that in queens that are prevented from mating. Ovulation can be stimulated artificially by gently probing the vagina with a smooth, blunt instrument, and this procedure may be recommended by veterinarians to trained people such as

few immediately noticeable changes in behaviour, and indeed spayed cats usually behave like intact females in anoestrus.

Sexual activity plays a very important part in the life of entire (un-neutered) cats. For the cat owner who does not intend to breed it is a constant and unnecessary problem best eliminated by neutering. All in all, castrated male cats are probably more amenable, affectionate and home-loving pets than their intact counterparts. Similarly, spayed females do not attract toms, and provide very pleasant company without imposing the worry of numerous pregnancies and innumerable kittens.

Maternal behaviour

Among wild and feral cats, the care and training of kittens in preparation for adult life is usually the unaided responsibility of the queen. The bond between male and female is weak or non-existent after mating, and in any case queens are generally promiscuous. Cat society does not rally round to support its mothers-to-be; they are on their own. If a queen is a good mother the kittens may survive; if she is a poor mother they will certainly die.

Under wild conditions, therefore, the pressure of natural selection is strongly in favour of cats that show good mothering ability. For our domestic pets we have partially eased that pressure by providing food, water and shelter to pregnant queens, even fostering rejected kittens and the offspring of queens with a poor milk supply. In a sense, therefore, owners' actions allow or even encourage the evolution of queens that do not care fully for their offspring, but there is a code of maternal behaviour that most female cats will follow.

Establishing the nursery
All sorts of unlikely sites may be chosen by a pregnant queen in which to fashion a nest for the future family. Cats will sometimes look for days, and frequently change sites. Dark, quiet and easily guarded sites are the most popular, and of course these may be almost inaccessible to interested observers, such as the cat's owner. On the other hand, some confident queens choose a familiar and favoured sleeping spot like the owner's bed, and remain quite relaxed and apparently even pleased to receive attention from a known and trusted person. You should always provide a warm, dry, draught-proof nesting box with plenty of newspaper bedding for your pregnant cat (see p221), but do not be disappointed if she rejects it in favour of the sock drawer.

At the onset of labour, the queen will

The bond between a mother and her kittens, originating in the dependent relationship of the early weeks, survives into adulthood only if there is no interruption through separation.

retreat to her nest. If you own more than one female cat, you may find the others assuming the role of midwife. As each kitten is born, the mother licks it clean (this also stimulates breathing in the kitten), nipping through the umbilical cord with her teeth. She eats the birth sac and after-birth. Between births, she cleans herself. When the last member of the litter is delivered, the mother gives herself a final wash and settles her body in a warm, secure crescent around the brood. Mothers usually purr loudly throughout the entire experience, but why they do this is not known.

Nursing and cleaning
For the next two days, a good mother will devote almost her entire attention to the litter. She will leave the kittens only for brief periods in order to stretch, to use the

litter tray and to take food and water, and in any case will not go far. She sleeps much less than normal, taking 'catnaps' between spells of suckling. To survive, the kittens must take milk during the first 24 hours. Their mother will encourage them to feed a few minutes after birth, lying on her side and guiding them to the nipples with gentle nuzzling and licking. Like all mammals, kittens are born with a rooting reflex and usually manage to find the source of their food. Meanwhile, hormonal changes in the queen establish a tranquil mood and prepare her for the reflexive release of milk when suckled.

Until the kittens are about three weeks old, the queen looks after them totally, grooming them daily and regularly licking their hindquarters in order to stimulate the release of urine and faeces. Failure to do so would rapidly lead to their death. The wastes are either eaten by the queen or deposited away from the nest area. She continues to initiate feeding, waking the kittens by licking and nuzzling, and curling around them to present her nipples. At this stage, the queen spends about 70 per cent of her time nursing. Of course, this is not continuous feeding, since kittens do not all feed simultaneously and often fall asleep at their post.

The mother now leaves the kittens for short periods – never more than an hour – to feed herself and use the litter tray. But she is still alert to the kittens' every move. She responds more to the sound than the sight of them. Touch, warmth and smell are the critical senses to kittens, and disturbance or removal from the original nest provokes intense, repeated crying. The queen will always respond to these signals and use them to find any of her kittens who have strayed. She will retrieve the errant kitten by grasping and carrying it by the scruff of the neck. This maternal grip by the teeth

Maternal devotion For the first three weeks after birth the queen is totally committed to her offspring. **1** She licks them clean as they are born and **2** encircles them to encourage suckling; each kitten usually adopts a particular nipple. She grooms them regularly, licking their hindquarters **3** to stimulate urination and defecation. After about three weeks she is able to leave the nest for longer periods, often dragging along a suckling kitten **4**. If marooned, it may follow a scent trail home; otherwise, its cries soon bring the queen to retrieve it **5**.

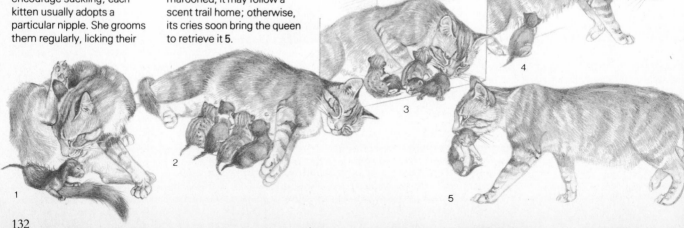

rarely damages either the skin or the neck muscles of kittens, despite a worrying similarity to the death-bite used by cats when killing prey.

Caring for the 'toddlers'

Once the kittens have learnt to use their eyes (by about the end of their second week at the latest), they have their full complement of senses. They begin to demonstrate some independence, and their changed behaviour modifies the mother's responses. During the third and fourth week, the kittens will try to totter after their mother when she leaves the nest, which she now does more frequently and for longer periods. When she returns, she sits near the kittens rather than with them. They will also initiate feeding, responding to their own feelings of hunger and going to her to start suckling. A fair-sized litter of determined kittens will often ambush their mother for food. She responds by gradually withdrawing herself, eventually spending only 20 per cent of her time nursing. The kittens are being gradually weaned, and owners should stand by to provide solid food for the kittens (see p225).

As the kittens become more mobile, the mother cannot keep them all in one place. Mothers of large litters often retreat to a high vantage point – the mantelpiece or a shelf, for instance – where they can oversee the actions of their offspring. They chirrup and call to the bolder litter members who stray out of sight, and will come down from their perch to retrieve them. It may seem to observant owners that each kitten has its own 'call-sign' – and there is certainly some evidence that mother cats can distinguish kittens by their cries – but not enough scientific research has been done on communication between mothers and kittens to establish any hard facts.

After three to four weeks, the queen may look for a new nest site, because the litter has outgrown the old nest or she perceives dangers. Most queens can carry their kittens over considerable obstacles and distances holding them by their scruff; there is rarely a mishap or a lost kitten. In the wild state, queens start to introduce kittens to solid food from the time they are about two weeks old. Choice of a second or subsequent nest site is therefore critically influenced by the availability of prey. Domestic cats will still move the litter, although there is no need to follow the food source. Queens may carry meat and other solid food to the litter, but never regurgitate food for their young as bitches do.

Teaching and learning

Cat mothers are good teachers. Among the many lessons that have to be learnt by kittens, hunting is perhaps the most critical for survival in the wild. The queen may initially offer the kittens only shreds of meat, but if she is a good hunter the whole carcass of prey may later be presented as a plaything for the litter. Domestic or pet cats will do the same if prey is available. By six to eight weeks, live prey such as mice may be presented, but may well escape from the badly co-ordinated mauls of the kittens.

A number of scientific studies have demonstrated that kittens can master quite complex tasks, such as negotiating a physical obstacle or opening a door latch, when first given a 'demonstration' by their mother, whereas they remain poor at accomplishing the same task unaided. An unrelated adult cat is not as good a demonstrator as the mother. It is clear from such experiments that something akin to schooling is given to kittens by the queen. If you provide a litter tray for the kittens, the queen will always teach them to use it by example. You should never have to house-train (housebreak) well-brought-up kittens.

Separation

If the kittens are removed when they are six or eight weeks old, separation does not usually seem to upset the queen for more than a day or so, though the kittens may emit occasional distress calls for several days afterwards. These calls are likely to have a powerful effect upon a queen who still has, or has recently had, kittens of her own. Even a strange kitten can elicit the retrieval response in such a queen, though if older than three or four weeks of age the kitten is unlikely to be effectively fostered. Even the most devoted mother will often fail to recognize – and may even attack – her offspring if they are taken away and then brought back some months later. However, mothers who keep their kittens will continue to demonstrate maternal behaviour towards them – bringing food scraps, calling to them and so forth – well into the kittens' middle age.

Good mothering behaviour in cats is not simply a matter of their expressing inborn instincts, but rather it is the culmination of a whole range of complex learnt skills that the queen has acquired both before and after giving birth. The problem of mis-mothering is probably exacerbated in domestic cats by a combination of early weaning and misguided genetic selection. Many pure-bred cats are thereby denied the genes and social experience that are required to support the future role of being a mother. There is no feline equivalent of an ante-natal clinic, but experience tells, and most queens do eventually become competent mothers after lessons learnt from their first litter.

Gaining independence

After three to four weeks, the maternal bond starts to weaken. The mother plays with her kittens 6 but will cuff or move away from any that annoy her 7. She is also less 'available' for suckling; the kittens are now capable of taking some solid food.

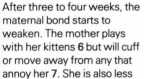

Teaching by example is the final role of motherhood. By six weeks, kittens should be using the litter tray 8. From an elevated post the queen can supervise mischievous pupils 9 and find peace. She may present prey 10 to teach the rudiments of hunting.

Learning to be a cat

Kittens are fun to own, and it must surely be great fun to be a kitten. Their waking hours seem to be almost entirely occupied – except when they are feeding – by play. Yet play has a serious purpose, for it is through play that skills, intelligence and other adult behaviour traits develop. At the same time, kittens undergo important physical changes during the first few months of life (see p 225), as their bodies develop in parallel to their behaviour.

Senses and skills

The newborn kitten is highly dependent on its nose. Suckling soon begins, and while littermates compete at first for their mother's nipples, a definite preference soon develops. The kitten then finds its way to the preferred nipple by smell, as the area around each nipple is marked by the odour of the kitten in possession. Other nipples, if vacant, may be used, but are readily relinquished when the 'owner' turns up.

Territorial marking by smell also begins early. Kittens recognize the boundaries of the nest by smell and, if removed from the nest area, try to find their way home by sniffing out a familiar odour trail. By about two weeks, however, their eyes begin to function, and as kittens' visual skills improve, their bodies co-ordinate better. By their third or fourth week in the world they are tottering about actively.

Handling and stimulation

Kittens' individuality is also developing throughout the first two or three weeks of life. They have the inborn potential to develop a repertoire of traits, but the expression of this potential is moulded by

Elements of play seen in a single session by a six- to eight-week-old may span the whole repertoire, from solitary tail-chasing **1**, the mouse pounce on an imaginary object **2** and the rearing that solicits interaction with a littermate **3** to mock fights **4**. The fact that sparring partners rapidly swap roles **5** shows that fights are not serious. Similarly, mutual swatting **6**, grappling with neck-biting **7** and general wrestling **8** are carefully controlled. Among postures 'practised' is the fluffed-out equivalent to the adult defensive threat **9**. Sessions often end in a helter-skelter chase **10**.

early experiences. The mother normally provides a general stimulation that promotes development, but human handling can be an effective supplement or substitute. This has been shown by experiments in which young Siamese kittens were handled for 10 minutes a day for the first 30 days of their lives; their development – including opening of the eyes, exploratory behaviour and even development of the adult coat pattern – was faster than in non-handled kittens, particularly if the latter were also deprived of their mother and littermates.

One explanation is that handling and general stimulation affect the functioning of the parts of the brain, pituitary gland and adrenals (see p 105) that are involved with reactions to stress. As a result, handled kittens are less emotional, more exploratory, more playful and better at learning. Orphaned kittens who have no contact with their littermates and are not handled by people grow up to be over-fearful or aggressive in their dealings with other cats, people and indeed any novel stimulus. (On the other hand, kittens that are over-handled may form unnaturally strong attachments to people; see p 137.)

Such social skills and attitudes are largely learnt within the first four to five months of life. Ideally, the people, dogs, cars, loud noises and other features of everyday life should be experienced, so that appropriate reactions develop, within that period. Behavioural skills missing in the adolescent

cat will probably be lost forever. Most importantly, perhaps, kittens must have the opportunity to learn how to react to other cats. This they do through play.

Playing and learning

Play is common to the young of most mammals. Some birds play, but it is rare in cold-blooded vertebrates such as fish, amphibians and reptiles. Why some play and others do not is not understood, but the most playful species – such as crows, dolphins, apes and monkeys, and most carnivores – are also among the most intelligent and sociable. Play may seem something of a puzzle: not only is it apparently unproductive, but it also places the participants at risk of being surprised by predators. However, nature is never frivolous, and there must be a good reason for play.

Play is one of the most endearing characteristics of cats young and old. Whether it is with a human companion, with a pet of a different species, with littermates or on their own, kittens play at every opportunity. Hiding, chasing and 'hunting' games are particularly popular, and even though they play less after about five months, even middle-aged and elderly cats will indulge if given the right encouragement or chance.

insect, or even spots of dust in a beam of sunlight. The fish scoop manoeuvre is incorporated into most sequences of kittens' play; feathers or paper balls are enthusiastically patted and scooped, and litters of kittens can work up a vigorous game of soccer.

Kittens appear at their funniest when play involves no physical or social stimuli, when they stalk, chase and fall over imaginary monsters. Their play can sometimes be very repetitive, but at other times behavioural elements are combined in novel and rapidly changing sequences of, for example, self-grooming, stalk-chase and roll-over-scuffle. The participants have to recognize these patterns as being playful, even though the same signals in adult life may have a serious meaning. For instance, a hissing, arch-backed kitten is unlikely to be taken as a serious threat to another, and bites and scratches during a playful scuffle are delivered with just a little less vigour than in a real fight. Such signalling of intent is called meta-communication, and is equivalent to 'let's pretend' in children's play.

Growing out of play

The frequency, duration and vigour of play by cats generally declines from the age of about five months, but no one knows why. Possibly it is because in the natural state kittens may be left to their own devices as early as 4½ months; everything they learnt in play now must be done in earnest. Or perhaps they have simply come to the end of the learning programme.

However, play can be elicited in cats of any age if it is encouraged by the presence of a like-minded companion. A well-matched pair of cats will keep one another fit and lively, and will be generally more fun to own than a single cat. Three or four cats in a household will often interact socially in a manner remarkably similar to kitten behaviour – only more dignified, of course. It could be regression, but it could also be an efficient method of dealing with social pressures. Certainly, some people equate the domestication of the cat with the retention of juvenile behaviour (see p17). But if there is only one cat in a household, the responsibility rests with the owner to keep it playful.

The most widely held scientific explanation is that play provides a framework within which the social repertoire of the species can be explored and learnt, together with such subsidiary benefits as physical exercise and the learning of survival skills such as hunting. Kittens that grow up in social isolation become both social misfits and poor hunters, largely through being deprived of play opportunities.

Kittens start playing when they are about three weeks old. Early play consists mostly of mock-aggressive rushes and rough-and-tumble with the mother and littermates, clearly foreshadowing the territorial and dominance behaviour of adult life (see pp 124–127). More elaborate play patterns develop as the kittens grow older. At four weeks they can wrestle, clasping with the front paws and kicking furiously with the

hind legs. The stiff-legged sideways leap and the pounce may be perfected by the fifth week. By the sixth they can chase and leap on each other with reasonable accuracy, and will also play-groom themselves and each other.

The programme of play motifs is constantly expanding, but three that relate to adult hunting manoeuvres – the 'mouse pounce', the 'bird swat' and the 'fish scoop' – constantly recur from about the sixth week. The trailing end of a piece of string or the twitching tip of the mother's tail will reliably elicit stalking behaviour, the kitten squirming stealthily forward, tail twitching, followed by the mouse pounce. The bird swat sequence is easily stimulated by a dangling piece of string, a butterfly or other

7   8   9   10

Abnormal feline behaviour

The conditions under which cats evolved for life in the wild are very different from those experienced by contemporary pet cats. For instance, wild cats choose their own company, withdraw from situations in which conflicts arise and develop their own cycle of daily activity. The urban domestic cat has had to forego most of these freedoms, and yet its basic physiology and behaviour is still broadly similar to that of its wild ancestors and relatives. It is small wonder that some cats respond to these stresses by developing illnesses and behavioural aberrations analagous to psychiatric conditions in people.

Causes and symptoms

Animal psychiatry is a relatively new branch of veterinary science, so the diagnosis and treatment of psychological disorders in cats is still at a relatively early stage of development. Yet experiments conducted over 50 years ago showed that cats exposed to irreconcilable conflicts develop severe behavioural abnormalities – commonly known as neuroses – and become physically ill with so-called psychosomatic disorders that have no physical cause. Some of the situations employed in these early experiments have their parallels in the home. For example, a cat teased near its food bowl will develop stress symptoms. So will a cat whose normal responses are rewarded on some occasions but punished on others; this can occur when human members of the household have different opinions about where the cat should or should not eat, sleep and so on.

Change in the physical or social environment often causes a psychosomatic reaction. A large-scale upset in the routine of an adult cat – such as a spell in a veterinary hospital or boarding establishment, or moving to a new home – obviously causes stress, but there may be more subtle forces at work that are more difficult for owners to recognize. For instance, new neighbours may have brought an unfriendly dog with them, builders may be knocking the house about, visitors unsympathetic to the cat may come to stay, the cat's owner may have got married or a new baby may have arrived. Cats may react to such situations by exhibiting psychosomatic (but nonethe-

Signs of stress: 1 anxiety and depression; **2** inappropriate defecation; **3** compulsive grooming; **4** coprophagia; **5** overaggression.

less real) wheezing, diarrhoea, facial tics or eye infections. Of course, one's life cannot reasonably be ordered with the cat as sole consideration, but a little planning and understanding can greatly ease the impact of change.

Some cats develop behavioural aberrations that are not apparently related to any external cause or stress. Sucking wool and coprophagia (eating faeces) are examples. Siamese in particular commonly suck and chew wool, and may even eat socks and other woollen items. In some it may be a passing phase; in others it becomes an ingrained habit and a serious problem for both cat and wardrobe. It seems to be an inherited condition and rarely occurs in non-pedigree cats. Explanations for its cause range from the urge to satisfy nutritional deficiencies to the stimulation caused by the lanolin content of wool. In any case, it should be discouraged; apart from the damage to clothes, swallowed wool can block the cat's stomach. Eating of faeces may be caused by a biochemical disturbance in the cat's body or may have a psychological basis. Although the cause of these specific problems is unknown, the possibility that they may indicate a neurological or metabolic disorder means that a full veterinary examination is needed.

Naughty, neurotic or normal?

It can be very difficult to decide precisely what is normal and what is abnormal cat behaviour, because this distinction depends on the owner's expectations. For example, scratching furniture and chasing birds are clearly normal feline traits, although they may be irritating or repugnant to people. Such behaviour should be regarded as undesirable or misdirected rather than as abnormal, and the cat can be trained to suppress the behaviour or direct it elsewhere. It is also quite normal for cats to mark their territory by urine spraying, but spraying indoors may be regarded by owners as undesirable and therefore treated as a psychological problem. It is true that sudden spraying from neutered males or females, or from normally well-behaved cats, may be a distress response to a change in the cat's routine. However, like scratching, it can normally be eradicated by retraining as described in the article on page 152. Much the same applies to defecating in inappropriate places.

Some behaviour that is quite normal may

seem bizarre or neurotic, especially to new owners. Anyone who has not seen a female cat in heat may be startled when their neat little pet starts to roll about in abandon, drooling, purring and calling in a completely strange voice, exhibiting all the classic symptoms of oestrus (see p130). Anxious and inexperienced owners have even hastened to the vet, fearing an outburst of insanity.

Another classic but misconstrued example of bizarre behaviour is the periodic 'seeing Martians' programme that most cats go through from time to time: A normally sedate, maybe quite elderly, cat will suddenly stare into the air, fixated on an object invisible to the owner, which it then pursues loudly around the house, up and down stairs and all over the furniture. A variation involves a helter-skelter chase backwards and forwards through the length of the home as if chasing an imaginary rabbit. In either case, when it comes to an end the cat goes back to sleep or grooming as if nothing has happened.

There are few convincing explanations for this behaviour, but it certainly does not indicate an abnormality. One theory – by no means universally accepted by animal behaviourists – suggests that it is a behavioural residue from the hunting programme, never fully discharged in a well-fed pet cat. After the few dilatory or frustrated hunts to which urban cats are normally restricted the cat's brain is still geared up and needs to resolve the 'chase and destroy' behaviour pattern. Such behaviour is mistimed rather than neurotic, and is harmful only to the decor.

There is little doubt that certain behaviours are abnormal and undesirable under any circumstances, however, and these are generally termed neuroses. Neurotic behaviour is not a single clinical entity, but rather a convenient way of describing behavioural abnormalities that are learnt and are specific to certain stimuli, or triggers. The tendency to react neurotically to normal circumstances may be inherited, as are many facets of behaviour. It is therefore sensible to compare the behaviour and misbehaviour of your own cat with that of its littermates, parents and ancestors. Some breeding lines produce a high proportion of nervous or unreasonably aggressive cats, and should be discontinued.

Examples of neurotic symptoms include depression, loss of appetite, overeating,

repeated outbursts of unprovoked and inappropriate behaviour such as attacking the owner, self-mutilation, hysteria, phobias and numerous other disabling eccentricities. It is essential that a vet examine such a cat because only then can the possibility of a complicating physical ailment be ruled out. For example, one of the commonest reasons for overeating is an infestation of intestinal worms. Nymphomania or continued sexual behaviour long after a female cat's normal season may be stimulated by ovarian cysts. Apparently hysterical symptoms – such as sudden shuddering accompanied by yowling – may indicate epilepsy or some other brain disorder (see p207). 'Neurotic' pacing in circles or compulsive head-shaking may mean a bad case of ear mites.

Treatment for a neurosis with no apparent physical cause may take many forms. In some cases, it may be sufficient to treat the symptoms without fully understanding the cause – such as dosing a cat that will not eat with vitamin B, or giving tranquillizers to combat anxiety. However, a more pragmatic and long-term stratagem is to identify the incident or environment that first provoked the problem, make a comprehensive behavioural analysis and institute a programme of reorientation.

Common behavioural disorders

The antisocial cat All cats can be forgiven for avoiding some people some of the time, but some cats are fearful of all people all of the time. In all probability, such animals were not given sustained human contact in their early months of life, and are best avoided when you are selecting a pet (see p142). However, if a fear of human beings and the world in general develops in a hitherto amiable adult cat, you should try to find out why. The cause may be obvious; a cat taken to the vet and left for a long period may think it has been abandoned to pain and loneliness by its owner. A neuter may have been severely mauled by a neighbourhood tom. Not so obviously, a cat may have been teased or even tortured by other people, or traumatized by a car or dog. General nervousness and withdrawal often follow such an incident, particularly if it recurs or threatens to do so.

A depressed and anxious cat may crouch in immobility, its pupils constantly dilated. It may refuse to eat or groom itself, and may urinate where it sits because it is too anxious to move. Patience and tender loving care are often sufficient to re-establish relationships with the owner, though it may take some considerable time before affection is shown spontaneously.

The oversocialized cat While the most sensible strategy for raising kittens is to give them as much handling and social contact as possible, some cats become too dependent on human company in general or one person in particular. In a particular case, a hand-raised orphaned kitten developed acute behavioural disturbances whenever it was left alone in the home, becoming extremely agitated whenever the owner dressed to go out and hiding until her return, even if this was more than a week later. At the same time it lost its appetite, and its toilet habits deteriorated. Most proprietors of cat boarding establishments are very familiar with the problems of dealing with over-dependent cats; some become so severely anorexic that they need force-feeding until their owner's return.

There are two practical measures which may help to reduce the likelihood of problems from the oversocialized, hyper-dependent cat. The first is to accustom the cat to being left alone, initially for brief periods that are gradually extended. It is often helpful to feed the cat just before you go out, rather than immediately after your return, and always leave a selection of toys – a cork on a string, some paper bags, a catnip mouse – for a newly-acquired kitten. The second strategy is to provide company for the cat. A dog makes a good companion so long as you introduce it when the cat is a kitten, or a young kitten may be able to wean an excessively humanized cat back to more feline ways. If you cannot provide another animal companion, a softly playing radio or a tape recording of the owner's voice may ease the effects of loneliness.

Similar symptoms to those just described may be shown by bored cats – commonly urban pets constantly confined to the home. They may express themselves by overeating or anorexia, or even by chewing on their own bodies. Compulsive grooming can wear away the fur, and badly afflicted animals sometimes bite their own tails into bleeding. Otherwise, the cat may turn to behaviour the owner construes as vandalism, such as pulling over and biting into houseplants, tearing curtains and loose covers, chewing the furniture or 'stealing' jewellery and small objects to play with. Combat such behaviour by providing company or stimulation, and make sure that the cat can get plenty of exercise. If it does eat houseplants, check that none of them are poisonous (see p158).

The aggressive cat It is normal for cats to exhibit occasional aggression towards other cats and dogs in defence of their home range, but it is not normal or acceptable for this to be a habitual response or for them to attack people. Of course, tail-pulling, violent teasing and abuse will provoke defensive action from any self-respecting cat; in this case the problem is with the humans rather than the cat. There is little point in intervening when one cat attacks another, even if this seems to be unprovoked. They usually have a reason (see p126), and it is best to let cat society operate by feline law. However, attacks upon dogs should be punished for the sake of both species. Once a cat learns that most dogs make easy prey, they can inflict serious injury, especially to the eyes. While castration is a reliable means of reducing aggression between cats, it does little to reduce the likelihood of attacks upon other species.

Spontaneous attacks by the cat upon humans are generally restricted to the owner and family within the confines of the home. Meal times are the period of greatest risk, and all too often the behaviour is reinforced by the owner then feeding the cat, forming a stimulus–response–reward sequence (see p153). This behavioural pattern can have innocent beginnings in the first playful pat by a hungry kitten, but it can assume very nasty proportions when an adult cat applies its teeth and claws to one's ankles – or to the hands of children who approach to give a friendly stroke.

Treatment should begin at the earliest possible age. Firmly discourage nips and scratches during play with the kitten by a firm 'no' command combined with a gentle flick on the nose. An older cat with a long history of combat is conveniently discouraged by pouring a glass of water over it, again with a firm 'no'. Never feed the cat after an attack, but wait for an hour or until the cat is placid and accepts being petted.

Any inexplicable explosion of violence in a well-adjusted, happy cat should be referred to a vet. Unprovoked, viciously aggressive behaviour accompanied by a threatening body posture, spitting and snarling may indicate a tumour or lesion in that part of the brain which controls aggression. An electroencephalogram (EEG) will usually disclose the site and extent of any brain damage or tumour. Unfortunately, no effective treatment for this condition has yet been developed – though it may eventually be possible to use some form of brain surgery – and brain damaged cats must normally be put down.

Anticipating problems

A catalogue of feline abnormalities should not discourage potential owners. You can eliminate as many problems as possible by choosing the right animal in the first place. A kitten raised and trained by a sociable mother in a family context is much more likely to grow into a well-adjusted cat than a stray or orphan, however appealing. Once you have the cat, use your common sense, respect its feelings within reason when you order your life, and anticipate a period of adjustment after any major upheaval. Make allowances for age or sickness, and try to discover the cause of any unprecedented 'misbehaviour' before taking correction measures. When things go wrong, do not delay or 'put up' with it; seek professional advice.

Chapter 3
KEEPING A CAT

Acquiring a cat 1

Cats have been kept as domestic animals for thousands of years, originally as controllers of rats and mice, or as objects of worship, but increasingly in recent centuries as companions. In the second half of the 20th century they have begun to challenge the dog as the most popular domestic pet in many countries – in some areas even outnumbering dogs – including some places where cats were once (save in a few religious communities) widely regarded as vermin.

There are undoubtedly many reasons for the cat's popularity. Many cat lovers like to attribute it to the cat's personality and beauty – and certainly the cat offers amusement, fidelity and love while retaining a satisfying independence. Others point to the cat's self-sufficiency or its general social acceptability, while for some people – particularly the elderly – a major reason is economic. Even a pedigree cat is generally much cheaper to obtain than a pedigree dog (and a non-pedigree cat can easily be acquired for little or nothing), and the costs of upkeep are also significantly lower.

Why choose a cat?

Apart from financial considerations, cats have many advantages when it comes to choosing a household pet. They are scrupulously clean – generally needing little or no house-training (housebreaking) – and where necessary are useful for killing and discouraging mice and other vermin. They require less care and attention than many other pets, while providing excellent companionship, love and loyalty. But a cat's love has to be earned; unlike many dogs, it will not give devotion to a domineering owner. Once given, however, the love is life-long, and will survive even prolonged absence due to travel or illness.

A cat has particular advantages over a dog in an urban environment (while being equally happy in the suburbs or country). There are arguments for and against the desirability of allowing a cat – whether in the city or country – the freedom to go outdoors (see p158), but it is certainly possible to keep it happily confined to a high-rise apartment. A dog, on the other hand, needs to be exercised on a leash at least twice a day. (Many medical authorities would consider this a point in the dog's favour, in fact, since it encourages the owner to have regular exercise.) To many people, the strongest point in the cat's favour is its fastidiousness in burying its excrement; others, however, point out that it is dog owners, rather than dogs themselves, that should be blamed for their fouling public places.

Children and old people can both benefit from having a cat as a pet, though in both cases careful thought should first be given to the practicalities and future implications. With proper parental instruction on how to treat it – particularly how to pick up and

hold it – a child can learn valuable lessons of responsibility from cat ownership, and may be able to witness the birth and rearing of kittens. 'Contact comfort' is important to children, and cats convey a feeling of security by being around to be petted. It is not wise, however, to acquire a young kitten until a child is old enough to appreciate how it should be treated, and for a minority of both children and adults an allergy to cats, resulting in asthma or eczema, may rule them out as pets.

For the elderly and handicapped, and for anyone living alone, a cat provides affection without too many demands. People in retirement may appreciate the routine and purpose imposed by cat ownership, but friends or relatives should be aware of possible problems connected with infirmity or forgetfulness. Of course, people living in institutions or other special accommodation may not be permitted to own cats, but some hospitals for the mentally ill today recognize the therapeutic value of cat ownership for some patients.

Cat ownership spans every age group and every part of the world. Cats' relative self-sufficiency plays a large part in their popularity as pets; symbols of homeliness, they can become a part of the family without unduly intruding upon the owner's time. Kittens provide ideal amusement for equally energetic children. Elderly owners can enjoy the need to care for a 'dependent' that is relatively undemanding and inexpensive to keep. All owners will find, however, that love and affection are totally reciprocated.

The cat owner's responsibilities

The prospective owner must, however, be aware of certain responsibilities involved in owning a cat. Too many young cats are abandoned or destroyed when the first novelty of ownership has worn off and the kitten has outgrown the playfulness of its youth. A cat has a life expectancy of at least 14 years, and like all pets is bound to impose to some extent on its owner's lifestyle. It must be provided with regular meals and clean litter, groomed and played with, and if necessary let in and out of the home.

Moreover, cats become attached to their home territory and most dislike travel; they become very unsettled if their owner has to move frequently for business or other reasons. And for those who go away from home regularly for any reason there is the problem of arranging care for the cat during this time. Although cats are relatively inexpensive pets, all owners must reckon with the cost of food, litter material, veterinary bills and possibly boarding fees.

The sexual proclivities of cats put off

many potential owners. An uncastrated tom will spray its pungent urine and a queen is liable to produce unwanted kittens – possibly resulting in unnecessary suffering if these are abandoned or destroyed. Neutering (castrating or spaying; see p156), however, is a routine, safe and humane procedure that should be always carried out unless the owner specifically intends a cat to breed. The result will be a happy, healthy pet, and in most cases a more affectionate one.

Kitten or adult?

For the busy family, or for an elderly person, it may be best to acquire an adult cat, which is more sober in its ways than a kitten. It is also arguable that any undesirable traits – physical or psychological – will be more apparent in an adult. Sources of such cats include animal humane organizations, who almost always have homeless cats to offer, or a breeder who may have a 'retired' stud or breeding queen – or a queen that has failed to breed – that would make a good pet once neutered.

Before buying or accepting as a gift an adult cat, however, always try to find out why it is available; few people wish to part with an animal that has been a faithful companion for years, and it may have a physical or psychological problem. Be particularly aware of possible disease when acquiring a cat from a shelter for abandoned or stray cats, since any cat kept alongside many others is likely to harbour fleas, ear mites, or other parasites or diseases. An early veterinary examination is particularly necessary for such pets. The same precautions apply if a stray should 'adopt' you.

With any adult cat, you should also remember that some time may be needed for it to become attached to its new owner and home; if allowed out it may wander or try to return to its old home. Several months may pass before it can be considered emotionally secure. A kitten, on the other hand, will soon get over its initial feeling of loss for its mother or litter-mates, and will rapidly integrate with your family. Apart from providing guaranteed entertainment with its mischievous and playful antics, a kitten is fun to watch growing up and is much more easily trained to fit in with the ways of the household. The more attention and training a kitten is given, the more fun it will be as an adult and the closer its relationship will be with its owner.

Male or female?

If you do not intend to breed your cat, and if you follow universal veterinary advice and have it neutered, it makes very little difference whether you decide on a male or female cat. They make equally intelligent, affectionate and playful pets. (The supposed laziness of neutered cats results mainly from owners' failure to play with

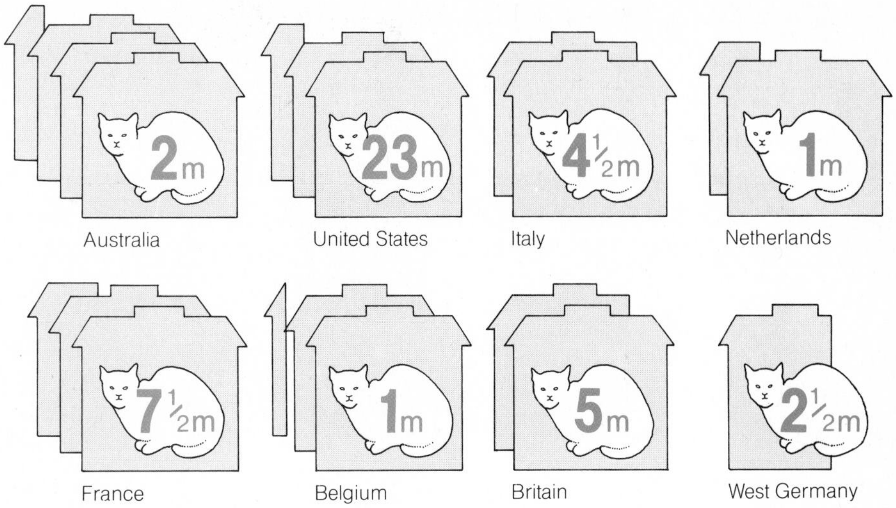

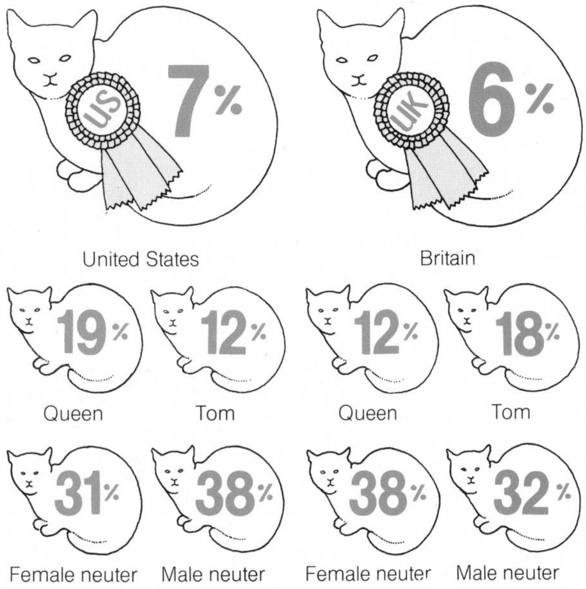

Australia 2m · United States 23m · Italy 4½m · Netherlands 1m

France 7½m · Belgium 1m · Britain 5m · West Germany 2½m

United States 7% · Britain 6%

Queen 19% · Tom 12% · Queen 12% · Tom 18%

Female neuter 31% · Male neuter 38% · Female neuter 38% · Male neuter 32%

Cat populations are shown above in millions compared with the percentages of households owning a cat. (Each 'house' represents 10 per cent of households.) In Europe, France leads in both cat numbers and percentage ownership, West Germany (which favours dogs) trailing well behind with fewer than 10 per cent of families owning a cat. Most pet cats are non-pedigree, as shown by the (very similar) percentages of pedigree cats in Britain and the United States left above. The proportions of neutered and entire males and females left below show marked differences, however.

them.) Males will generally grow a little larger and may be slightly more aggressive than females, but these traits are really significant only in uncastrated toms.

If you insist on not having your cat neutered, a male kitten will reach sexual maturity at about six to eight months. If allowed out, it will start wandering about the neighbourhood, marking its territory (see p124) and looking for a mate. It will probably start spraying indoors whether or not it is let out – and the strong smell of tom cat spray is very unpleasant. (For this reason, stud toms are generally kept in special quarters; see p216.)

Female kittens generally become daintier cats, but may start to 'call' (see p130) from as early as five months, and will then come on heat as often as every three weeks during the breeding season. This can be suppressed with drugs or shortened by induced ovulation (see p217), but there is always the danger of unwanted litters if the female cat has access to a tom. Generally speaking, however, an unspayed queen is easier to

keep as a household pet than an uncastrated tom, and if you wish a pedigree queen to breed it can be sent away to stud (see p217).

Pedigree or non-pedigree?

A far smaller proportion of cats than dogs are pedigree animals, and thus recognized members of specific breeds (see p44). This is largely because the breeding of pedigree cats is a relatively recent phenomenon, and the individual breeds of cats are less distinctive than are the breeds of dogs. There are, however, both physical and temperamental differences between the various breeds, as you will see by reading the articles in chapter 1. If these are important to you – and particularly if you are attracted by the body form, coat or colouring of a particular breed, then a carefully chosen pedigree animal will probably best satisfy you.

In theory at least, an animal of known pedigree should have a more predictable character and be more free of hereditary defects than a non-pedigree animal of mongrel (mixed) ancestry, */continued*

Acquiring a cat 2

though this may not be true in practice. However, there is good and bad in every breed, and each cat should be judged individually (see below). Certainly, there are differences in health and longevity between breeds, but there is no truth in the commonly held belief that pedigree cats in general are less healthy than non-pedigree.

The former are certainly far more expensive to acquire, and therefore possibly at greater risk of being stolen if allowed out of the home. However, it is fair to expect to pay something even for an unwanted non-pedigree kitten, if only to meet some of the cost of feeding mother and kittens and of vaccinations. (Do not be taken in by glib sales-talk that 'only pedigree kittens catch diseases'; all are susceptible.)

One possible compromise if you are attracted to the characteristics of a particular breed but are not interested in breeding and showing, and do not want to pay too much, is to buy a cat or kitten that is 'faulty' in some way. Such an animal may not have the correct colouring for exhibition, or it may diverge from the show standards in some other way, but it could make a beautiful and delightful household pet. Such a cat may be graded by a breeder as 'pet' quality (as opposed to 'show' and 'breeder' grades) and sold quite cheaply, possibly without a pedigree certificate.

It may have been neutered or the new owner may have to agree in writing to have it neutered to prevent the 'faults' being passed on. Alternatively, you may be able to acquire a kitten cheaply (or at no cost) from a breeder under 'breeding terms' that give the breeder the right to direct the mating of the kitten with a particular stud or studs and then to choose one or more of the resulting offspring. Before entering into any such conditional purchase, however, remember that the agreement constitutes a legal contract and could lead to a dispute – and even legal action – if you were to break the terms (see also p 168).

Which breed?
If you do decide to acquire a pedigree cat, there are many breeds to choose from (see pp 50 to 99). As far as personalities are concerned, Persians and most related breeds are probably the most placid as adults, while the foreign and oriental breeds – particularly Siamese and their relatives – are the most highly strung and least suitable for a nervous owner. The latter also demand the most affection (and give similarly) and are more sexually active when not neutered. Rex cats are extroverts, but for busy working people or families with children a British or American Shorthair is ideal – hardy, resilient, affectionate and playful.

These short-haired breeds are also easier to keep clean and well groomed than long-hairs. Persians and similar cats in particular need frequent grooming to keep their hair free from tangles. Long-haired cats with a less full coat, such as Angoras and Balinese, are easier in this respect. One factor to bear in mind when choosing a breed, particularly if you intend to let your cat go outdoors, is the climate of your locality. Unless your home is centrally heated and/or air conditioned, it may be preferable not to keep a Persian in a hot climate or a Siamese or similar breed in a very cold one. Non-foreign short-hairs such as the British and American are hardier, however.

Where to buy your cat
Whatever type of cat you decide to acquire, it is a good idea to consult a local vet specializing in small animals, who will probably know local breeders and other suppliers. The vet may well advise against buying from a pet store, as all too frequently the kittens sold there are incubating or suffering from one of the many feline illnesses. Since these spread rapidly in the confines of a pet store, it is vital that certificates of vaccination against feline enteritis and preferably also respiratory virus infections (cat flu) be supplied – together with a rabies vaccination certificate where this disease occurs. An added precaution is a written guarantee of good health, though you may well have adequate legal protection even without this (see p 168).

Advertisements in local newspapers or, as already mentioned, vets or animal welfare organizations are good sources of non-pedigree kittens, but for a pedigree animal it is far better to go to a specialist breeder. Cat fancy organizations and/or cat breed clubs will provide names and addresses, and in most countries there are weekly, monthly or annual publications in which breeders advertise (see the bibliography). It is also a good idea to visit big cat shows, where some of the cats and kittens on display may be for sale and it is possible to meet and talk to breeders and owners. If you eventually want to show your cat, such visits will also help you to understand the qualities demanded of show cats.

Choosing an individual kitten
If at all possible, when choosing a pedigree or non-pedigree kitten, arrange to see the whole litter with their mother in their home surroundings. It may be impossible to 'meet' the sire of pedigree kittens, as many breeders send their queens elsewhere to stud, but you can deduce a lot from the conditions in which they are kept. The first essential is warm, clean and uncrowded surroundings, since cold, dirt and overcrowding are conducive to disease. Provided the kittens are old enough – four weeks or more – they should be kept some-

where that allows plenty of human contact, so that they can become accustomed to handling and grow up to be good family pets (see p 226).

When viewing the kittens, carefully note whether they are alert and playful, and if they are clean and of reasonable weight in relation to age (see p 225). (The tiny runt of the litter may be very appealing, but may not be really fit.) It is best to choose a lively kitten, and one that responds to being stroked and does not shy away. The best age to acquire a kitten is when it is 10 to 12 weeks old; it should then be eating a varied solid diet, so if possible ask to see it being fed. (The breeder should supply a diet sheet if and when you finally buy the kitten.)

Carefully look for any signs of ill-health, and in particular check the kitten's coat, eyes, ears, nose, mouth, abdomen and anus (see the illustration). If possible, check whether the litter tray shows any signs of diarrhoea. Inquire whether and how often the kitten has been wormed, and ask to see its vaccination certificate.

Should a kitten obtained from a breeder become sick, or fail to settle in with its new owner, the breeder will usually agree to take it back within a week, but it is as well to discuss the possibility before purchase. Consumer protection laws may give you redress should a kitten turn out to be carrying disease, have congenital disorders or not be of the claimed show or breeding quality, but this of course varies from country to country. In any case, it is safer to make your purchase conditional upon a veterinary examination.

If you are acquiring a pedigree kitten for show or breeding, especially if you are not already very familiar with the particular breed, it is wise to take a more experienced friend with you to see the intended acquisition. An experienced eye can see 'faults' in a kitten that a novice would not appreciate. In any case, bear in mind that the full adult coat and colouring will not develop for some months.

Unless the kitten is being sold as a 'pet' without papers (in which case the price should reflect the fact), ask to see the pedigree certificate and make sure that this is complete and that the kitten has been registered with the appropriate cat fancy organization. On completing the purchase, make sure that a transfer certificate (showing change of ownership) or other appropriate registration document is completed and registered, for without such formalities you will be unable to show your new pet in the pedigree classes of a cat show and will not be able to register its offspring.

Having made a final choice and attended to the business details of the purchase, it only remains to make sure that your home is ready for the new resident and that you have all the equipment you need, and to make arrangements for collection.

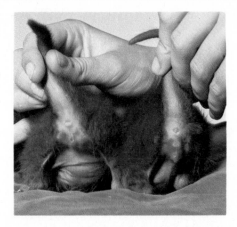

Sexing a kitten can be more difficult than an adult, since the sexual characteristics are smaller. **above** Hold the kitten facing away from you, and lift the tail. In both the female **left** and male **right** there are two openings – that closest to the tail being the anus – but they are much closer together in the female than the male. In the female kitten **1**, the vulva is a vertical slit, almost joined to the anus like a small letter i. In the adult **2**, the space between them is about 1 cm (½ in); neuters and entire queens look alike. In a male kitten **3**, the tip of the penis is hidden in a small round opening about 1 cm (½ in) below the anus, and the two are entirely separated by the scrotal sacs, which appear as raised darkish areas. The testicles are not usually obvious until the kitten is about six weeks old, and are of course clearly visible in the entire adult tom **4**. The two openings are now more than 2.5 cm (1 in) apart in neuters and entire toms alike.

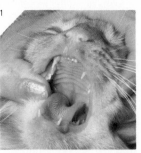

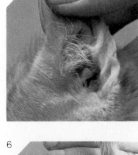
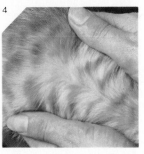

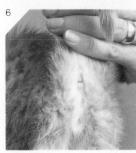

A preliminary examination should give the prospective owner a good idea of a cat's general condition and betray any signs of ill-health.
1 Look inside the mouth for signs of inflammation or abnormal redness; healthy gums are pale pink. The teeth should be white, although those of an adult cat may be slightly yellowed by tartar.
2 The eyes and nose should be clean and free of any discharge. A healthy nose is cool and slightly damp. Sneezing or redness of the eyes may indicate a respiratory virus infection (cat flu). Protrusion of the third eyelids ('haws') may also indicate an ailment.
3 Examine the ears for infection or excessive wax, which may indicate ear mites.
4 The coat is a good indicator of condition; it should be glossy and free of mats, with no trace of fleas or other parasites. Check for skin sores, dandruff or round bare patches (a sign of ringworm).
5 The abdomen should be full but not pot-bellied – a sign of roundworms. Feel for any lump that might be an umbilical hernia, and check the tail for kinks and the legs for any deformities. Watch the cat walk for signs of lameness or stumbling.
6 The anus (and vulva of a female) should be clean. Look for signs of a discharge, diarrhoea or worms.

First steps with a new cat 1

If a stray cat simply walks into your life, there is very little you can or need do by way of settling it in (presuming you decide to keep it) beyond obtaining a few items of equipment and arranging for a thorough veterinary examination (see p 165). If such a cat is an experienced adult, it will generally make itself at home quite quickly – though it is also quite likely (particularly in the first week or two) to walk out on you once again.

But if you acquire a cat more deliberately – whether a pedigree animal bought from a breeder or a non-pedigree pet from a friend or pet store (see p 142) – you should plan ahead to ensure that you have everything ready to make the new member of the family feel at home. Not only is the settling-in period a potentially traumatic one for the newcomer, which can be greatly eased by sensible and sensitive handling, but (especially in the case of a kitten) training

given in the first days and weeks (see p 152) establishes the 'house rules' and habits that the cat will follow for the rest of its time in your company.

Getting the home ready

Apart from a carrier of some kind with which to bring the cat home, you will need to obtain a few items of equipment for the new pet. The main ones are a sleeping basket or box with some bedding material, feeding bowls and a supply of fresh or preserved cat food (see p 148), and a litter tray and some cat litter. A few other items, such as a scratching post and toys, may be obtained later, but it is essential to have the basics before the newcomer arrives.

The cat or kitten will probably be bewildered at first by its new surroundings, so it is important to keep its own special 'furniture' in one place. In this way, the newcomer will soon establish a routine.

Position its bed in a quiet, dimly-lit, warm and draught-free corner. Take particular care if you acquire a kitten in the winter and your home is not well heated. If you allow the cat to sleep on a chair or other item of furniture, it is advisable to provide a washable cover for cleanliness and hygiene; cats are creatures of habit, and will usually be quick to adopt one or more favourite sleeping spots.

Wherever the cat sleeps, it must be within easy reach of the litter tray. Ideally, this should be positioned to give the cat privacy and should then always remain in the same place. The feeding place, too, should remain constant. Choose a position that allows the cat to eat its meals undisturbed, and if there is more than one cat (or other pet) in the household, provide separate feeding bowls for each. These can be placed in the same feeding area, however. If your cat is not allowed outdoors (see below), it is

---

Beds and bedding Cats spend much of their lives asleep, and while they will tend to please themselves where they sleep, you can discourage the use of chairs and your own bed by providing bedding of their own. Cleanliness, comfort and warmth are the basic requirements, with protection from draughts if necessary. The bed should be big enough for the cat to stretch out when fully grown, and enclosed on three sides for cosiness and a sense of security.

Wicker baskets **1** are available from pet and department stores, but those made of plastic or glass-fibre **2** are less draughty and easier to clean. However, a lined cardboard box **3** is perfectly adequate if it is high enough to prevent draughts while allowing entry (a 'stile' can be cut in the side for kittens), and so long as it is replaced when worn or soiled. Any of these types of bed can be lined with several layers of newspaper for warmth, topped by an old towel, sheet or blanket; old babies' blankets are ideal. Change all bedding regularly to ensure that it is kept clean and dry. For kittens or for ill or nursing cats in cold or draughty situations, you can provide a hot-water bottle or an electrically heated pad or plate **4**, which acts like an electric underblanket. (Some glass-fibre beds have built-in

electrical heating.) Several layers of bedding are advisable over the heater to prevent burns – this is particularly important with an immobile sick cat – and if the heater is placed at one end of the bed the cat can move if the heat becomes too intense. A popular alternative to a basket or box with bedding is the 'bean-bag' or 'sack' bed **5** filled with polystyrene foam granules. Not only can the cat work it into an ideal 'nest' shape, but it is very warm.

A cat carrier is the easiest way to transport your new pet home, but the type you should choose depends on how much you expect to travel with your cat – remembering that even journeys to the vet will be easier with a container. A folding cardboard carrying box **6** is cheap and, provided it has enough ventilation holes, is adequate for the occasional journey; however, it cannot be cleaned properly and must be destroyed when soiled or infected. Plastic boxes of similar design are more durable. For more frequent journeys it is better in the long run to choose a longer-lasting carrier – such as a wicker basket **7** or one of the other designs shown on pages 160 and 161. These can be scrubbed out and disinfected (see p 178) when necessary.

Food and water bowls may be made of any easily cleaned and reasonably heavy material, such as stainless steel **8**, glazed pottery **9**, enamelled metal or heavy plastic **10**, shown here in both single and twin varieties. A rim about 5 cm (2 in) high is ideal, as this helps to avoid spilt food; nor is the cat able easily to turn the whole bowl over. Even so, some spillage is inevitable, and a tray, rubber mat or newspaper underneath will help to keep the feeding area clean. Each cat should have its own food bowl. As with litter trays, disposable food bowls **11** are convenient at times, and in an emergency you can always use old dishes **12**. To avoid any risk of cross-infection it is wise to wash your cat's bowls separately from family dishes.

a good idea to provide a tray or pot of long grass, such as oats or cock's-foot grass, for it to munch (see p 158).

Some items of equipment are useful but optional. A scratching post, for example, may be especially beneficial if the cat is permanently confined indoors. Even cats allowed the freedom to go outdoors where they can claw trees may occasionally try to sharpen their claws on furniture or carpets if no scratching post is provided. With an indoor cat it may be worthwhile to have more than one post – one being kept near its sleeping place for use on waking.

The settling–in period
Aim to collect the new cat or kitten when it can be given as much attention as possible, such as on a weekend or during a holiday. Try to avoid a long journey in hot weather, since for the sake of both safety and comfort the cat should be transported in a carrier,

which can become stuffy. Make sure that it is not fed before the journey, and if travelling on a train or bus do not take it out of the carrier before reaching home. If undertaking a long journey by car, the cat can be offered the use of a litter tray provided that you keep all the car's doors and windows closed so that it cannot escape.

When you reach home, shut all windows and doors and generally ensure that the home is safe (see p 158) before lifting the cat from its carrier. Offer a bowl of water (or milk if you know that it will drink this), and introduce it to the litter tray. During the first few hours, the cat or kitten will want to explore every corner, savouring each new scent with interest – although sometimes with apprehension – so set aside as many hours as possible to spend with it. Be ready to amuse it with suitable toys, but allow it to sleep whenever necessary.

Kittens are best confined to one room

until they have gained confidence. Avoid the presence of too many people and distracting noise, but at the same time give plenty of attention. Make sure that children are quiet and gentle with the new cat, and in due course show them the correct way to pick it up. Toddlers too young to understand how to treat a cat are best kept out of the way until the cat has settled in.

After the first excitement of exploration is over, show the cat its bed. In all probability a kitten will still want to play, but knowing where its bed is will be reassuring. One common sign that the kitten or cat is settling in is when it starts to groom itself. Now may be a good time to offer some food. The breeder or previous owner should have provided information on feeding routines and food likes and dislikes. With a kitten it is particularly important to keep closely to the diet sheet and timetable, in order to reduce the chance */continued*

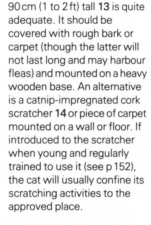

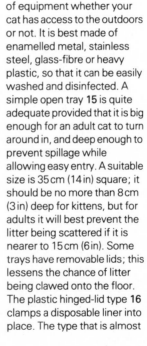

A scratching post provides an alternative to your furnishings for the cat to sharpen its claws. Some owners erect a veritable climbing frame of logs, ladders and platforms – which will give the cat plenty of exercise – but simply for a place to scratch a straightforward post 60 to 90 cm (1 to 2 ft) tall **13** is quite adequate. It should be covered with rough bark or carpet (though the latter will not last long and may harbour fleas) and mounted on a heavy wooden base. An alternative is a catnip-impregnated cork scratcher **14** or piece of carpet mounted on a wall or floor. If introduced to the scratcher when young and regularly trained to use it (see p 152), the cat will usually confine its scratching activities to the approved place.

The litter tray is a vital piece of equipment whether your cat has access to the outdoors or not. It is best made of enamelled metal, stainless steel, glass-fibre or heavy plastic, so that it can be easily washed and disinfected. A simple open tray **15** is quite adequate provided that it is big enough for an adult cat to turn around in, and deep enough to prevent spillage while allowing easy entry. A suitable size is 35 cm (14 in) square; it should be no more than 8 cm (3 in) deep for kittens, but for adults it will best prevent the litter being scattered if it is nearer to 15 cm (6 in). Some trays have removable lids; this lessens the chance of litter being clawed onto the floor. The plastic hinged-lid type **16** clamps a disposable liner into place. The type that is almost

fully enclosed **17** isolates waste from children and other pets, but by containing smells may make you forget to change the litter regularly. Disposable trays **18** are useful for travelling or sick cats, at cat shows or in catteries as a guard against cross-infection. Various absorbent materials can be used in the tray. Sand, peat (peat moss), soil or commercial litter can all be used for short-haired cats, but avoid peat for long-hairs as it tends to form mats in their coat. Soil is messy and may harbour disease organisms, while torn-up newspaper is cheap but may lead the cat to regard any newspaper as a potential toilet. Wood shavings can be used but are not very absorbent; sawdust may be eaten by a kitten. Although relatively expensive, commercial cat litter – usually made of fuller's earth, a type of clay – is highly absorbent and deodorant. It need not all be thrown away after use if the soiled parts are removed with a special scoop **19** available from pet stores. You can also economize by lining the tray with newspaper (which also aids disposal). Deodorants are available to add to other types of litter. Whatever you use, thoroughly wash and disinfect the tray at least once a week. Always remove soiled litter promptly; you cannot expect a cat to use a dirty litter tray.

First steps with a new cat 2

of stomach upsets. As it grows, the amount and type of food and the frequency of meals will have to be adapted (see p 150).

After feeding, the cat should once more be shown its litter tray. A kitten should have been house-trained (housebroken) by its mother (see p 133), but may still need encouragement to use the tray. It is also important to begin other aspects of general training as soon as possible (see p 152); for example, this is the time to start teaching the kitten – with a gentle but firm reprimand – not to climb the curtains, jump on tables, and so on.

Meeting other pets
If another pet, such as a dog or another cat, is already in residence, extra care is needed in the introduction of the new cat cr kitten, for an unplanned meeting could result in permanent enmity. Ideally, the first pet should be shut in one room while the new cat roams around and becomes accustomed to the other's scent. After an hour, gently pick up the cat, release the other pet to detect the newcomer's scent, and remain with the latter in a quiet room. The first introductions can be made at feeding time, when you should give each animal a separate dish in the usual feeding area. If all goes well, they will enjoy their meal before looking up to see their neighbour, but you must stand nearby at this time as injuries could be inflicted – though the only signs of aggression may well be a few bouts of spitting. It is wise to have a blanket handy to throw over them should a fight start.

Introducing a kitten onto the territory of a neutered female cat is probably the easiest, while attempting to introduce two adult uncastrated males is almost guaranteed to result in bloody fights, and is inadvisable. Take particular care when introducing a kitten to a 'resident' adult dog, as a jealous dog can easily behead a small kitten with one snap of its jaws. If there are any problems with introductions, it is a good idea to confine the new cat in a wire playpen at first, so that it can be investigated by established pets without danger. The pen will also be useful if you ever need to keep a kitten out of harm's way for a while. Even if two animals do establish a speedy friendship, they should always be fed in separate dishes, as sudden jealousies can be aroused.

Pet birds and fish should be adequately protected before the new cat makes its tour of inspection. Commonsense measures include fitting wire mesh over fish bowls and aquariums and placing bird cages out of reach. Cats pose no real threat to babies, but nets for prams (buggies) and cots (cribs) are available as a precaution.

The great outdoors
A basic question that faces all cat owners is whether to allow their pet or pets to go outdoors. It is a question that arises quite

Making introductions to existing pets – particularly cats and dogs – is an important part of settling a cat or kitten into its new home. It is easiest if both are young.

early on, because once a kitten has been allowed the freedom to go out it cannot fairly (or easily) be confined once again. The various arguments for and against allowing a cat this freedom are discussed on page 158, together with advice on providing amenities and a safe environment for a cat that is housebound.

If the new cat is to be given the freedom to roam, it should not be allowed out for at least a few days. A kitten should not in any case be taken outdoors in extremely cold weather, and this is a good reason not to acquire a new kitten born late in the season if you live in a region with harsh winters (see p 142). But, whatever the season, you should let the newcomer become completely familiar with its new home before taking it out. This is particularly important with an adult cat, which may try to return to its previous home, however far away, if it has not fully settled in.

The first outings should always be made in the company of the owner, for any unexpected noise may cause a kitten to bolt in fright, with possibly tragic results, and an adult cat may wander in unfamiliar territory. The first one or two times, you can carry a kitten or adult cat out into the garden, but after that it should walk (accompanied), so that it gets to know the way in and out and begins to mark the route with its own scent. As a kitten matures, it can be allowed to play alone in a safe enclosed garden, but remember that before long it will want to explore farther afield, and will easily scale most garden fences. It is important to fit a collar or harness with an identification tag before this stage, to improve its chances of return if the cat does wander and get lost.

Of course, the owner of a pedigree cat destined for show may feel that marking of the neck caused by even the softest of collars could lose a few vital points on show day, and this is one factor to be considered in deciding whether to let the cat outdoors.

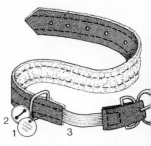

Picking up a cat, place one hand under the chest behind the front legs and the other beneath the hindquarters to take the weight **1**. The cat can then be positioned in the crook of your arm for carrying. Never leave the back legs unsupported, and avoid holding the cat towards you or it will claw to gain a hold. If the

cat struggles, use the same method but simply grip both front legs with your hand. Kittens may be lifted by the scruff of the neck **2**, provided again that the hindquarters are supported, but use this method for an adult cat only in certain emergencies (see p 180) or if the cat is struggling violently (see p 179).

Collars can be used to carry an identification tag or tube **1** bearing that cat's address and its owner's telephone number. A bell **2** may help in locating the cat and to warn birds. Any collar must fit properly; too loose and it may catch in the cat's mouth, too tight and it may choke or rub. If not made of elastic it should have an elastic section **3** so that the cat can escape if the collar catches in some hazard. For exercise on a leash, a harness is better (see p 159). For flea collars, see page 187.

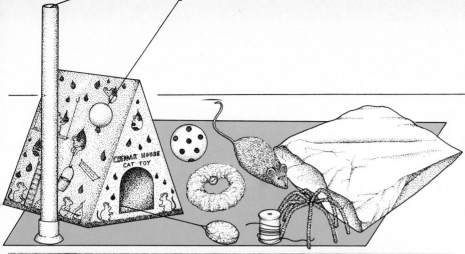

Toys give cats much enjoyment and exercise that is particularly valuable if they are housebound. They need not be expensive. A table-tennis ball, empty cotton reel, paper bag or a 'spider' made from entwined pipe-cleaners are all simple yet fun. Fur rings and catnip-impregnated mice are great favourites, but eyes and so on must be securely fixed. The spring-mounted 'mouse in a house' or a ball on a string stimulate hunting games. Avoid balls of wool and soft rubber or sponge toys that may be eaten, causing choking or stomach troubles.

There is also the danger, from the age of as little as five months, of unwanted pregnancies. Unless you want your cat to breed – in which case it is not advisable, particularly if it is a pedigree animal and you want to produce pedigree kittens, to allow it to roam freely – the best course is to have it neutered (castrated or spayed; see p 156).

Most vets in Britain feel that this is best done at the age of four to five months; their American colleagues suggest six months for a female, seven to eight months for a male. At whatever age, it is then quite safe to give the kitten full freedom within a few days, or when the sutures (stitches) are removed in the case of a female.

Many owners of cats that are allowed out fit a cat door or flap so that their pets can come and go as they wish. You can easily train a cat to use such a door (see illustration). It is particularly important, however, to train an outdoor cat to come when it is called, for it is desirable to lock it safely indoors at night.

A cat door is a great convenience to both cat and owner if the former is allowed outdoors. Fit it at the right height for the cat to step, not jump, through. Various types are available, with wooden, plastic or rubber flaps. Most operate two ways **1**, and have a light spring or magnet to close them after use and prevent draughts. Another type swings only outwards **2**; the cat must be let in again or taught how to lift it with its paw (see below). A third alternative has flexible plastic triangles **3**, but, unlike more traditional designs, which can be blanked off or locked when necessary, it is open at all times. The main snag with most cat doors, in fact, is that they also allow in strange cats. An excellent, but expensive, answer to this problem is a door fitted with a battery-operated lock that is triggered

by a small magnet worn by the resident cat on its collar. Training your cat to use a flap requires the same 'little at a time' technique (see p 152) used for other tasks. Attempt training at mealtime and reward success with a titbit of food. Begin by propping the flap open, to overcome the cat's fear of it closing on its head or tail, and tempt it through with a titbit. Do this in both directions, or the cat may learn to use the flap only one way. Then prop the flap only partly open so that it must push with its paw to go through. It should soon be pushing the closed door. With the one-way type, hold the flap partially open, so that the cat must use its head to open it the rest of the way. If you gradually diminish the opening, the cat should learn to use its paw to lift the flap and its head to gain entry.

Your cat's diet I

The most important thing to remember about feline nutrition is that cats are not dogs. Despite several thousand years of domestication, the cat remains (like its wild relatives) a strictly adapted carnivore, unable to survive without eating animal products. The dog, like ourselves, is a meat-loving omnivore, prepared to eat anything, plant or animal. It has kept its metabolic options open and will do quite well largely on household scraps – or even on a sensible vegetarian diet. The cat, on the other hand, is like a miniature lion with mouth and teeth made for killing and eating whole animals, which provide a rich and balanced diet.

The muscle of the prey supplies large quantities of protein, the bones and offal valuable vitamins and minerals. In addition, most of the cat's fluid intake comes from its prey, which is 70 per cent water. Because the cat has evolved on such a diet it has become metabolically 'lazy'; its own metabolism cannot create certain chemicals that are essential for life, so it relies on other animals' bodies to supply them. As a result, its nutritional demands are unique among domestic pets and its need for animal products means that commercial cat food tends to be more expensive than dog food.

The cat's special requirements

The feline body needs and uses nutrients in a broadly similar way to other animals (see the box opposite), but differs significantly in its detailed requirements. Cats have a particularly great need for protein – they require a diet twice as rich in protein as do dogs – and only animal products such as meat, offal, fish, eggs and milk can provide a high enough concentration of the right kind of protein, containing certain essential amino acids. For example, the amino acid derivative taurine is vital for the cat's eyesight, but cats cannot (unlike other animals) make this from other materials, so they need a preformed source. Overall, some 30 to 40 per cent of the diet should consist of animal-type protein.

Fat, which should ideally provide 25 to 30 per cent of the cat's calorie intake, or about 10 per cent of its food by weight, is also vital as it supplies the so-called essential fatty acids. Most animals can convert the fatty acid linoleic acid (found in both vegetable and animal fats) into the arachidonic and linolenic acids their bodies need. Cats cannot, so they have to have a supply of animal fat – from meat, fish or milk – which is the only source of these essential nutrients. Cats enjoy fat in their diet, and can digest much more of it than we can. Since most flavours and aromas are fat-soluble it also helps to make food more attractive and palatable.

Animal fat is also a good source of vitamins A, D and E. The first of these is particularly important because, unlike

Water is an essential part of the diet; if cats' food is not moist enough they must drink fluid. Many prefer water from puddles, ponds, aquariums or even toilets rather than the fresh, probably chlorinated water in a bowl.

Grass is often eaten by cats, but the reason is obscure. It may add roughage to the diet or represent a deliberate attempt to get rid of hairballs. If your cat is housebound, it is a good idea to provide grass in a pot (see p158).

herbivores and omnivores, cats cannot make it from the carotene found in plants. Liver and fish liver oils are good sources, and liver also supplies the B vitamin niacin (nicotinic acid); again the cat is at a disadvantage compared with most other animals, which can manufacture niacin from tryptophan, found in other foods. Animal products are also the best way of supplying the cat's need for finely balanced amounts of the minerals calcium and phosphorus – which in the wild come from the prey's bones.

The cat's metabolic dependence on its prey is not limited to foods. Cats have only a poor ability to detoxify and excrete poisonous substances from their body, as if assuming that their prey has already done the work for them. Consequently, relatively harmless drugs such as aspirin are extremely toxic to cats (see p184). So is benzoic acid, a widely used food preservative – another argument, besides that of nutritional inadequacy, for not feeding your cat a human diet.

Giving fresh food

Although most domestic pet cats today live – and thrive – on commercial cat food, some owners prefer to give fresh food, and this can be cheaper if you have several cats. A balanced diet is more difficult to achieve, however.

The cardinal rule is variety. Feeding steak, chicken, boned fish and other muscle meats on their own will inevitably lead to bone disease, stunted growth in kittens, poor eyesight and other problems, because these foods lack calcium and vitamin A. Too much liver, however, will cause vitamin A poisoning since, unlike the other vitamins, this is stored in the body and cannot be excreted. It is no good relying on the cat's natural instincts to choose what is good. It is biologically sensible for a wild cat to have a taste for liver as a source of the B vitamins, but if presented with nothing else cats will over-indulge. Meat and liver given in a five-to-one ratio will be nutritionally acceptable, however, provided extra calcium is supplied.

Protein
Fat
Carbohydrate
Vitamins and minerals
Salt

The constitution of commercial cat food is shown here for **1** an all-meat canned food, **2** a 'balanced' canned food with cereal, **3** a semi-moist food and **4** a dry food. The foreground shapes show the percentage of water (dotted areas) and of solid food (hatched). The coloured areas in the background show the percentage composition of the dry matter in the foods.

Milk is a good source of calcium – 200 ml (7 fl oz) of milk will provide the adult daily requirement – but is not tolerated by many adult cats. They cannot properly digest the milk sugar lactose, which passes into the large intestine and ferments, causing gas and diarrhoea. The surest way of providing enough calcium is to add to the meat the correct amount of a sterilized bone-flour supplement (not gardeners' grade bone-meal), calcium phosphate, calcium lactate or calcium carbonate – or a proprietary supplement such as 'Stress'.

Giving too much of certain fish can be nutritionally dangerous, as oily fish (particularly tuna) is rich in polyunsaturated fats, which through oxidation destroy vitamin E and lead to a deficiency disease called steatitis or yellow fat disease. Too much horsemeat may have the same effect. Commercial cat foods containing fish have a vitamin E supplement to compensate.

It is usually best to cook fresh food, as raw foods can contain harmful substances. Raw fish, for example, contains an enzyme that causes vitamin B_1 deficiency. Raw meat and fish can also carry germs that cause diarrhoea or other infections such as toxoplasmosis (see p 191); however, cats can safely enjoy an occasional treat of raw minced beef (or other raw meat or offal apart from pork) provided it is fresh and suitable for human consumption. Raw egg white contains a substance that destroys the B vitamin biotin, but egg yolk and cooked egg white provide valuable protein, fat and vitamins. Meat should in any case be only lightly cooked to avoid destroying vitamin B_1. Yeast tablets will provide extra B vitamins in a home-made diet, and there is no risk of over-dosing in this case.

Feeds containing bones should be minced after cooking to prevent bones lodging in the cat's throat or intestines. Remove fish bones altogether and give a calcium supplement instead. You can give cooked cereals and vegetables – given raw they are not digested properly – separately or mixed in with the food up to a proportion of one-fifth of the total. A fresh diet generally contains enough moisture for the cat, but always provide extra, in the form of milk (if tolerated), water or gravy.

Giving canned food
The safest and probably the easiest way to feed your cat a diet that mimics its natural food is to use one of the formulated proprietary cat foods. Of these, canned food is the most popular and, having been available for about 25 years, has been thoroughly tested on generations of cats. Good canned cat food contains carefully balanced amounts of protein and fat, some carbohydrate and fibre, and adequate vitamin and mineral supplements to compensate for their losses in processing.

The canned cat foods produced by reputable manufacturers are adequate for all cats, or give instructions on supplementary feeding for kittens and pregnant or lactating females. However, be sure to read labels carefully. Since 1969 in the United States all cat food labelled 'scientific', 'complete' or 'balanced' has had, by law, to   /continued

---

FOOD COMPONENTS
Cats need food to provide body-building materials, for fuel to keep body processes going and to replace worn-out parts.

Protein and energy
The energy content of food describes its value as a fuel, and is commonly measured in calories (strictly speaking, in kilocalories or 'big' Calories – abbreviated kcal – each equalling 1,000 'small' calories). Sometimes the metric equivalent, the kilojoule (kJ), is used; 1 kcal equals 4.2 kJ. Since all bodily activities consume energy, calorie requirements represent a basic measure of food needs. These vary with a cat's age and body size and the amount of exercise it takes (see the table on p 150). All cats use most of their energy intake simply to keep their body systems (such as the heart and circulation) working and to keep themselves warm. Only a small amount is used for muscular activity and growth.

The three major components of food – protein, carbohydrate and fat – can all provide energy. Fat gives about 9 kcal per gram (250 kcal per ounce), pure protein and carbohydrate each 4 kcal per gram (110 kcal per ounce). Protein is also the main structural material of the body; a growing (or pregnant or lactating) cat therefore needs a liberal supply for building new tissues, while every cat needs protein to replace losses from wear and tear. As mentioned in the main article, the chemical make-up of the protein – its amino acid content – is important; good sources are meat, fish, eggs, milk and cheese.

Carbohydrates and fats
Fats – including butter, lard and animal and vegetable oils, as well as the fat on meat – are not only a concentrated energy source, but also make up a vital part of all cell membranes (see p 102). Again, the type of fat consumed is important.

Carbohydrates, such as starch and sugar, are not essential but add energy and bulk to the cat's diet. Cereals and potato contain starch, which must be pre-cooked (to start the breakdown into its component sugars) before being fed to the cat.

Vitamins and minerals
These can be considered as bodily 'spare parts', although some minerals are important in body structures such as bones. Vitamins also help to regulate bodily processes, and any shortage causes deficiency disease (see p 195).

Cats need the correct amount of vitamin A for good vision, growth and a healthy skin; liver, egg yolk and butter are good sources. Vitamin B_1 (thiamine) is also needed in quite large amounts for growth and for general body functions; cereals, liver, eggs and milk are rich sources, but this vitamin is destroyed by high cooking temperatures and lost in boiling. Liver and yeast tablets are also rich sources of other B vitamins.

Ascorbic acid (vitamin C) is important for a healthy skin, coat and gums, but is not needed in the cat's diet (unlike that of humans) as it can be manufactured in the body. Cats need only small amounts of vitamin D for healthy bones and for absorbing and regulating the blood level of calcium and phosphorus; good sources are fish liver oils and some animal fats, but it is also made by the action of sunlight on skin oils and consumed by the cat when it grooms itself. Vitamin E is needed for growth and maintenance of the skeleton and muscles; it is found in most foods, particularly liver and cereals, but is destroyed by some fish oils.

Two of the most important dietary minerals are calcium and phosphorus, which the cat needs in approximately equal amounts for a correct balance in the body. Calcium is essential for building bones and teeth (which together contain 99 per cent of the body's calcium). It is also involved in the action of the muscles and in the clotting of the blood. Rich sources of calcium and phosphorus are the bones of other animals and animal products such as milk.

Other necessary minerals include sodium and chlorine (the constituent elements of common salt), iron, magnesium and iodine, but these are found in almost all foods and there will be enough of them all in a varied diet.

Water
This can be considered a nutrient as it is important in almost every body function and makes about 70 per cent of the cat's body. Cats normally take in 50 to 70 ml of water per kilogram body weight per day (about 1 fl oz per pound). On a canned food diet most of this comes from the food. Compared to a person, the cat has a remarkable ability to concentrate its urine and retain water if its intake is restricted. Fresh water should, however, always be available.

Your cat's diet 2

THE FOOD NEEDS OF CATS

Age/type of cat	Normal weight range	Energy needs (kcal/day)	Daily total food allowances (complete foods)*		
			Dry food	Semi-moist food	Canned/fresh food†
KITTENS					
30 weeks	1.5kg (3lb 5oz)	150	42g (1½oz)	48g (1¾oz)	120g (4¼oz)
	2.7kg (5lb 15oz)	270	76g (2¾oz)	86g (3oz)	216g (7¾oz)
40 weeks	2.2kg (4lb 13oz)	175	48g (1¾oz)	57g (2oz)	141g (5oz)
	3.8kg (8lb 6oz)	300	84g (3oz)	99g (3½oz)	243g (8¾oz)
ADULTS					
Inactive	2.2kg (4lb 13oz)	155	44g (1½oz)	48g (1¾oz)	123g (4½oz)
	4.5kg (9lb 15oz)	315	90g (3¼oz)	99g (3½oz)	252g (9oz)
Active	2.2kg (4lb 13oz)	185	53g (2oz)	59g (2oz)	150g (5¼oz)
	4.5kg (9lb 15oz)	380	108g (3¾oz)	122g (4¼oz)	306g (11oz)
Pregnant	2.5kg (5lb 8oz)	250	70g (2½oz)	80g (2¾oz)	200g (7oz)
	4.0kg (8lb 13oz)	400	112g (4oz)	128g (4½oz)	320g (11½oz)
Lactating	2.2kg (4lb 13oz)	550	154g (5½oz)	176g (6¼oz)	440g (15¾oz)
	4.0kg (8lb 13oz)	1,000	280g (10oz)	320g (11½oz)	800g (28½oz)

*Note that figures given are total daily allowances; if you give, say, one dry meal and one canned, halve the quantities for each meal. †Fresh food is approximately equivalent to canned if it comprises about three parts protein food (red meat, fish, eggs, cheese, etc) to one part cereals or vegetables, plus dietary supplements and milk. For allowances up to 30 weeks, see page 226.
Figures adapted from Nutrient Requirements of Cats (National Academy of Sciences, Washington, DC; 1978).

The size of meals depends on the type of food as well as the cat. These are equivalent meals – each half a day's ration for an active adult of average weight – of (from left to right) dry, semi- moist, canned and fresh food. Clearly, judging by bulk and weight alone, without taking the type of food into account, can lead to over-feeding with the dry or semi-moist types.

be nutritionally sufficient for all cats from weaning onwards, including those that are pregnant or lactating. In Britain, 'complete' foods may often recommend feeding milk as well; if your cat does not like milk avoid these foods, and where appropriate check that the food is labelled as being sufficient for growing kittens or a pregnant or lactating queen.

Cans boasting '100 per cent beef' contain nothing else and are nutritionally in- complete. In the United States, those labelled 'beef', 'beef dinner' or 'beef and gravy' have from 25 to 95 per cent beef and may be balanced, provided the necessary vitamins and minerals have been added. 'Beef flavour' is literally only flavoured and may or may not be balanced. Whereas the ingredients in commercial canned cat foods vary with availability and cost, those in 'science diets' are strictly formulated and these diets are adequate for all cats. 'Speciality' or 'gourmet' rations, on the other hand, are usually nutritionally in- complete and should only be given as occa- sional tasty treats.

Canned foods generally contain more animal protein than other commercial rations and have a higher fat content, which makes them more palatable. They are usually about 75 per cent moisture, and cats may therefore not drink much on a canned food diet, although fresh water should still be available.

Beware the temptation to give your cat canned dog foods. These may contain con- siderable amounts of cereals and vegetables and as a result not enough animal protein for cats. When fed to cats over long periods they have been known to cause blindness since they lack the taurine cats need – though the deficiency may take a year or so to appear. Dog foods may also not provide enough vitamins A and B_1 or the essential fatty acids found only in animal fats. Dual- purpose cat/dog foods are really cat foods acceptable to dogs, and should be nutrition- ally adequate.

Semi-moist and dry foods

The semi-moist and dry foods have become increasingly popular since they were first introduced in the 1960s, partly because they are less expensive. Although based on animal products, many contain some texturized vegetable protein supplemented with nutrients to make them the equivalent of canned cat foods at less cost.

The semi-moist types also contain a special chemical called a humectant, which prevents them drying out or going mouldy. As a result, they keep well in the bowl and, if necessary, the cat's food for the day can be put out all at once. They contain less than half as much water as canned foods and more protein and fat than dry foods, which makes them more palatable. They may not, however, be nutritionally complete, especi- ally for growing kittens, so alternate them with canned or fresh food, or ensure that the cat drinks milk as a general nutritional supplement.

Dry foods contain only about 10 per cent water, and cats on this diet must have fluid with each meal and must drink at least 200ml (7floz, or a large cupful) a day. This can be in the form of water, milk or gravy alone or mixed with the food. If your cat consistently fails to drink on a dry diet or is prone to bladder problems, stop the diet. Insufficient fluid can cause the urine to become too concentrated and the various salts it contains to settle out, forming stones. The resulting disease (called feline urological syndrome, or FUS; see p203) prevents normal urination and is fatal unless treated promptly. The high magnesium (and possibly phosphorus) content of some dry foods coupled with low water intake may be involved, but factors other than diet may also predispose to this disease. Some manufacturers have increased the salt level in dry foods to about 3½ per cent to make the cat thirsty, and magnesium levels are generally kept below 0.15 per cent.

The particular advantage of dry foods is that they provide exercise for the cat's teeth and gums, and may help to prevent the build-up of tartar (see p 196). The dry diet is so different in texture from all other cat foods, in fact, that your cat may need two to three weeks to get used to it. Even if dry foods are accepted, you should alternate them with others.

(calorie) content. Like people, big cats need more calories than small ones, so recommended daily calorie requirements are given per kilogram or pound body weight (see the chart). For a given weight, however, a growing, pregnant or lactating cat needs more calories, and an active free-ranging cat more than a sedentary housebound one. Extremes of environmental temperature, illness and general stress also increase the calorie requirement. Elderly cats tend to need fewer calories and obese cats most certainly do.

Individual food needs are so variable that the only real guide is to feed the amount that maintains the cat's normal weight. An excess causes obesity – which, although not

the wrong type of feeding dishes can all put the cat off its food – though competition from another cat may encourage a poor eater. And, because the cat's sense of taste and smell is so acute (see p 112), food that is only slightly stale may be refused. Cats will also soon lose interest in very bulky foods with a low concentration of protein.

The temperature of the food is another important factor. Most cats prefer food at a temperature between about 25° and 40°C (77° and 104°F), so do not serve fresh or canned food straight from the refrigerator. Let it warm to room temperature first, or add warm water; if the cat still refuses to eat, try heating it a little.

Lack of appetite is probably more dis-

Fresh foods for cats should be varied, a 'staple' of muscle meat being mixed with cooked cereal or vegetables and supplemented

with occasional liver, fish, fats, dairy products and tasty extras like bacon rind. If milk is not taken, adults need 2 to 5 g (½ to 1 teasp)

of sterilized bone-flour a day or the prescribed amount of a proprietary calcium supplement. Up to 1 teasp per week of cod liver oil may be

given if the cat eats no liver, and yeast tablets to provide vitamin B. Your vet may recommend a general vitamin supplement.

How much and how often?

One of the frequent worries of cat owners is how often and how much a cat should be fed. In the wild, cats will gorge enough food at one 'sitting' to last for many hours. If an adult cat is left enough semi-moist or dry food for the day it will choose its own mealtimes, and will seldom overeat unless it is constantly presented with very large quantities.

Canned food will probably keep 12 hours in the bowl if it is in a cool place and flies are kept away. It is best to feed it in two separate meals, but take care not to give the whole day's ration each time. You can train your cat to eat its meals promptly by removing the food after about half an hour. Growing kittens and pregnant and lactating queens must have several meals a day. A kitten's stomach is smaller than its head, and it is incapable of eating its daily requirement in one or even two meals. A cat recovering from an operation or illness needs to be tempted with tasty snacks, little and often (see p 178).

The amount of food that each cat needs depends on its age, weight, breed, condition and individual differences. The weight of food to give is determined by its energy

nearly the problem that it is in dogs, affects about one pet cat in every ten. It is particularly common in neuters, though whether they have a slower metabolism, exercise less or eat more through boredom is not known. However, part of the fault probably lies with the owner providing too much food, possibly to a very bored animal. It is difficult to state ideal weights for cats because these vary so much between individuals and breeds but if you cannot feel the ribs, then your cat is probably overweight.

Likes and dislikes

Whether feeding dry, semi-moist, canned or fresh foods, it is essential to accustom your cat to a variety of flavours and textures from a very early age. This will not only ensure a balanced diet but will prevent the cat becoming addicted to a particular food. Past experience plays an important part in the cat's likes and dislikes, and if at some time it needs a special diet – perhaps when it is old or ill – it may starve rather than eat a new food.

A cat's appetite can be greatly affected by how its food is prepared and presented. Noise, the presence of strange people and

tressing to the owner than overeating. Apart from the factors already mentioned, appetite may also be affected by a move or by boarding, but should return to normal with encouragement and attention. Sexual activity may also divert the cat's interest from food. If the cat is allowed free range, it may of course refuse food if it is also being fed tasty titbits by a neighbour!

However, if the cat seems generally unwell, or if the loss of appetite persists for more than a day or two, you should seek veterinary advice. The diet may simply be deficient in vitamins, but it may indicate something more serious, from a mouth or tooth disorder or a hairball in the stomach (see p 194) to a wide range of general diseases. Then the vet may prescribe a special diet. For certain disorders such diets are available commercially. If the cat has kidney disease, for example, it may require a low-protein diet, FUS one that has a high moisture content, and diabetes a diet low in sugar. However, if the cat is so ill that it cannot be tempted to eat, remember that it is essential to get it to drink plenty of fluids – by force if necessary – since dehydration will be a more immediate problem than hunger.

Training your cat

Cat behaviour is not pre-ordained from birth; many individual habits and personality traits are conditioned by experience. To a pet cat, the most important influence should be its owner, who can encourage desirable behaviour and discourage unwanted habits. Contrary to popular belief, cats are very quick learners so long as certain basic principles of training are well understood and followed consistently.

In general, training should be viewed as a positive contribution to the well-being of the cat and the harmony of the household. Not only is it a practical necessity to suppress or redirect such undesirable behaviour as furniture scratching, but cats can also be taught such skills as the operation of a doorbell and other tricks that are useful and/or fun for all concerned.

Principles of training

Before planning any training strategy, make a mental list of those activities and stimuli that the cat enjoys and those that it dislikes, so that you can capitalize on them. It is essential to incorporate the natural response tendencies of cats into a training programme from the start. For instance, most cats like food, warmth and company, and dislike water, loud noises and cold weather, but other individual likes and dislikes can be usefully exploited.

The relationship between a cat and its owner is always a delicate one and can be easily undermined by using inappropriate punishment techniques to mould behaviour. Whereas dog owners can capitalize upon their own dominance or 'pack-leader' position to compel compliance, cat owners find that it is more effective to 'buy' favours by reward and persuasion. Obviously, there are occasions when it is appropriate and necessary to punish a cat, but such 'negative reinforcements' should be contrived so that they seem to have nothing to do with the owner. For instance, a well-aimed ball of paper or a squirt from a water pistol can descend upon an errant cat without it blaming and consequently mistrusting the owner. A further advantage of such a system of impersonal punishment is that the cat learns a new strategy for all occasions and not just a style of 'best behaviour' when in the presence of its owner.

Although continuous and consistent reward will quite rapidly establish desired habits, you may have a problem with intermittently rewarded behaviour. Rewarding a particular action only occasionally may mean the lesson takes longer to learn, but it does ensure that it is less likely to be forgotten once the teaching period is over. This sort of behaviour is often something the cat teaches itself; for example, begging at the table, scratching at the window to be let into the house or hunting for mice or birds are all likely to give positive results only occasionally. But the corollary is that,

if you want to suppress a habit originally established this way, passive techniques of non-reward (for example, simply refusing to give food at the table) are useless; you will have to resort to punishment so that a new response is learnt in place of the old.

Another general rule is to approach the task of training a little at a time – a method psychologists call successive approximation. Whether you want to teach a cat a new and relatively complex task, such as opening a cat flap, or to modify an existing habit, it is best to tackle the problem by breaking down the desired behaviour pattern into simple linked steps and training the cat to perform these one at a time in a logical sequence. If there is any indication that an earlier step in the sequence has not been learnt, you should go back and start again at a point where the animal will definitely succeed. This technique needs skill in monitoring progress and a lot of patience, but is very successful.

Discouraging spraying

Urine spraying is a quite normal part of feline social behaviour (see p124), and should not be mistaken for a lapse in toilet

manners. The frequency with which it occurs varies from cat to cat, depending on such factors as hormone levels, sexual state and social standing. Since spraying is increased by male hormones, tom cats not required for breeding should be castrated.

The social context within which spraying occurs is the best guide to preventative measures. An isolated outburst of spraying, especially in neutered cats, is usually the result of stress. A major upheaval in routine unsettles the cat's territorial sense. Several cats living in the same home often spray because there is insufficient scope for them to form individual territories; the only 'cure' may then be to reduce numbers.

There are several training measures that owners can use to discourage spraying or at least to redirect it from indoors to outside. Hitting the cat and rubbing its nose in the sprayed area are futile. More subtle approaches to training such as dissociated punishment by water pistol may be successful if the cat can be regularly 'caught in the act'. You can also discourage the spraying of particular pieces of furniture or walls by feeding the cat close to the target, since cats naturally tend to spray (and urinate) away

How cats learn Cats learn many basic habits by copying. In more formal teaching situations, such as learning to come when called **above**, success often depends on repetition of a sequence of stimulus, response and reinforcement. Here, the stimulus is the call **1**, the response that of coming indoors **2** and the reinforcement some food **3**. Reinforcement is anything that induces the cat to learn the correct response, and must be closely associated with it. It may be positive (a reward) or negative (a punishment). To be effective a reward must fulfil a need or desire, such as hunger or a liking for warmth or being petted. Learning to open a door **left** may be taught like this or be learnt gratuitously.

from feeding areas. Alternatively, crinkly strips of aluminium foil hanging and laid around the spraying point sometimes work as a deterrent.

Saving the furniture

Cats scratch objects for two distinct reasons: to sharpen their front claws by removing loose scales and fragments of skin, and to leave a visible mark which will be noted by other cats. Some surfaces tend to be repeatedly scratched, and smell signals from the footpads provide semi-permanent marks of possession. The longer an object or piece of furniture has been used as a scratching post the more difficult it becomes to provide a substitute. Kittens should therefore be trained to use an acceptable scratching post as soon as they are weaned (see p 145). Hold the animal near the post, positioning the claws appropriately; it will soon learn what to do, and will probably then use the same post wherever you put it in the house or garden.

Owners who want to redirect their cat's scratching of furniture or draperies should first offer an alternative material close to the existing scratching area. Soft, raw pinewood is often a favourite, but some cats prefer a cloth-covered piece of wood. When you introduce the post, cover or remove the items that have been inappropriately scratched. If that is not possible, cat repellent or a strongly scented polish on the scratched area may avert the cat.

Toilet training

Cats are usually easier to toilet train than dogs because they naturally cover their urine and faeces. Moreover, well-reared kittens will be expertly trained by their mothers. If you do have a kitten that does not know what the tray is for, show it what to do. Stand the animal in the tray, hold its front paws and show it how to scratch in the litter material; most kittens get the idea very quickly. Always be ready to place it in the tray whenever it seems about to defecate.

A breakdown in good toilet manners is unusual. It is rarely mere 'naughtiness'; cats usually choose an inappropriate area of the house for a toilet because the alternatives are not attractive. Litter trays may not have been regularly cleaned out, the litter may have a strong scent that the cat does not like, or the tray may be of an awkward design (see p 145). The tray may also be spurned because it is in an exposed position, perhaps where the cat has previously been frightened by dogs or children.

If none of the above reasons apply, you may have to try a retraining programme. First, make the place unacceptable as a toilet spot by feeding the cat nearby and by swabbing the area with vinegar. At the same time, place two or three clean and suitably designed litter trays around the home, leaving one of them close to the spot

that is being inappropriately used. If the litter tray is now used, let the habit form for a week or so and then begin a gradual movement of the tray to an acceptable permanent location.

Good or desired toilet habits should be reinforced by praise, petting and titbits. If the cat persists in using unacceptable places, discourage it by mild punishment, such as a shouted 'no' command or a squirt of water, but only if the animal is caught in the act. Never resort to rubbing the cat's nose in past mistakes; nothing is learnt this way except a healthy distrust of people.

The sudden onset of inappropriate urination in a cat that is normally house-trained (housebroken) may indicate a blockage of the urinary tract, and veterinary advice should be sought immediately (see p 203). Old cats may be forgiven occasional lapses in sphincter control, but repeated incidents warrant a thorough examination of the urinary system by your vet.

Discouraging bird hunting

It is normal for cats to hunt, but cat lovers are often also bird lovers and would rather see the two coexist. If you cannot bear the blood and feathers and want to allow your cat to roam outdoors, choose a kitten whose mother was not a hunter (see p 123). Otherwise try re-educating your pet. There is no point in punishing a cat after it has caught a bird. The only hope of modifying its predatory behaviour is to concentrate training into the moments just before and during attacks upon birds, and this demands considerable patience. The best training aid is a well-aimed water pistol or garden sprayer. It also helps not to mind appearing somewhat ridiculous.

Find a suitable hiding place for yourself. Take a small stuffed or toy bird and dangle it by a piece of string in an established bird-hunting area; a victim of a previous bird hunt will serve even better as a decoy. When the cat approaches, jerk the string so that the decoy 'flutters' convincingly. Wait until the cat is just about to attack, then squirt the water. It is most important that your presence is not associated with this punishment, otherwise the cat will not relate water to birds in general and will continue to hunt when on its own. The training procedure may have to be repeated many times before the cat develops a consistent aversion for birds.

Training to come when called

Cats can be trained to perform many tricks, but the most useful is surely to come on command. The starting-point of this task must be a secure and loving relationship between cat and owner, because it is impossible to teach it to come by fear or punishment. A young kitten is an easier subject to train than a mature cat, and you should exploit every mealtime and petting session

to reinforce an awareness of its name. Single-syllable names are obviously learnt faster than compound sounds, but whatever the name it should be repeated constantly during play.

Once the name has acquired arousal properties to the kitten, it can be used as a forerunner to the word 'come'. Mealtime is the best occasion to train it; just say the word after the kitten's name when food is being presented. When it has learnt to respond to its name and the 'come' command at mealtimes, you can start calling at other times of day, always rewarding the correct response by titbits and petting. To ensure that it responds to the words rather than a particular tone of voice, various members of the household should participate in the training programme.

This positive approach to training works well if the cat is hungry for food or affection, but the response is likely to be less than electric if it is well fed and comfortable away from the owner. Since the 'come' command can be of lifesaving importance when a cat is lost, compliance can be enforced during training by arousing the animal with a well-aimed light object thrown nearby. Or it can be surprised with a light spray of water, so long as the surprise seems to come from heaven and not from the owner. As soon as it is aroused, call the cat's name and 'come', reassuring and rewarding it in the appropriate way.

Training for tricks

One can train cats to sit, beg, eat with their paws, walk to heel on a lead, jump through a hoop or even play tunes on a piano. However, most owners accept that the more extreme examples represent an unnecessary and unacceptable infringement upon natural feline behaviour patterns. Training should not be used to change or suppress a cat's basic personality, rather to make some minor adjustments to its behaviour.

The basic training method is the same for all tricks: a firm but quiet verbal command followed by instant reward with a favourite titbit. Be patient – you will need to repeat the trick at least 20 times per session – and accompany the action with the same word each time: 'up' for begging, 'shake' for shaking paws, 'fetch' for retrieving and so on. Rewards must be prompt, but you may be able to commute titbits into petting as learning progresses

Whether a cat learns any tricks beyond those necessary to ensure a comfortable life for itself depends on its intelligence and its willingness to indulge its owner. If your cat refuses to perform, it may mean that it has not understood what you want or simply does not want to oblige. If you then try to force it – or if you punish it one day for doing something (such as jumping on a table) that was rewarded before – the only result is likely to be a neurotic pet.

Grooming and routine care

A sleek and glossy coat is an excellent reflection of a cat's health and general well-being. Taught by their mothers, most cats do an expert job of keeping themselves clean, and this often becomes a mutual activity if more than one cat lives in a home (see p 117). But by supplementing a cat's self-grooming habits the owner plays an important part in keeping the cat free from parasites and, in the case of long-haired breeds, the coat free from tangles. Long-haired cats invariably need more thorough and frequent grooming than short-hairs, but with all cats regular attention removes dandruff (dead skin particles) and loose hairs, and keeps ears and eyes clean. And by examining the cat closely during grooming sessions the owner receives early warning of many possible problems.

Grooming the coat

From the time of weaning, it is a good idea for a kitten to become accustomed to a gentle daily grooming. In addition to keeping the kitten in immaculate condition, the grooming period can become an enjoyable play-time, and is particularly useful training for kittens that are destined to appear in cat shows, where they will be handled by many people. Long-haired kittens in particular should be carefully groomed from the earliest days. Special attention needs to be paid to the back of their thighs and between the toes after they have used the litter tray.

The grooming routine should include a careful inspection of the skin as well as the coat, to keep watch for such parasites as fleas and lice (see p 186) and other skin disorders such as ringworm (see p 189). This is particularly important after a visit to anywhere that might involve direct or indirect contact with a number of other cats – such as a boarding cattery, a cat show or a stud.

A sure way of finding live fleas on a kitten or short-haired cat is to comb through the coat from ears to tail with a fine-toothed metal comb. (You will have to move quickly, however, for fleas are remarkably agile.) Such a comb is an important piece of grooming equipment, together with a wide-toothed version (especially for long-hairs) and a brush. The last is best made of natural bristle, as this causes less static electricity and broken hairs than the nylon type. For a short-haired cat, a rubber brush is excellent for removing dead hairs, while the coat of an exhibition short-hair can be given a final polish with a soft chamois leather or a piece of silk or nylon stocking. A very short-bristled soft brush is needed for rex cats, which are sometimes prone to baldness if groomed too vigorously.

The grooming of a kitten or short-haired cat is very simple, but a long-hair needs considerably more care (see the illustrations). If the latter is groomed daily, its hair should remain free of mats. However, you

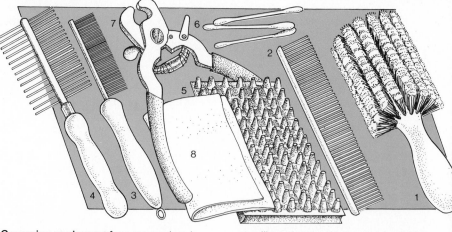

Grooming equipment for a cat needs to be neither extensive nor expensive. Basic requirements include a brush **1**, preferably of natural bristle, a wide-toothed metal comb **2** and a fine-toothed flea comb **3** (or, alternatively, a combination comb **4**). For short-haired cats a rubber brush **5** is very useful, while for all cats

you will need cotton buds or swabs **6**. Nail or claw clippers **7** are an optional extra, while for long-haired cats to be exhibited at cat shows talcum powder or cornflour (corn starch) will be needed. Short-haired show cats benefit from a final polish with a soft, clean chamois leather **8** or a silk or nylon pad.

can gently loosen the occasional tangle with your fingers and then slowly tease it out with a wide-toothed comb or the blunt end of a knitting-needle. Unfortunately, the only way to deal with bad tangles is to carefully cut them off.

In spring and to a lesser extent in autumn, all cats (except for the curly-coated rex) undergo a period of moult or shedding (see p 107), when the old coat seems to come out in handfuls. Careful grooming at these times is doubly important, as the cat will lick itself and swallow great quantities of loose hair, causing a 'hairball', which may need veterinary attention (see p 194).

A long-haired cat whose coat appears greasy can be treated with talcum powder, which is then brushed out, though some people prefer cornflour (corn starch). Some cats, mainly males, develop an excess of oil

at the base of the tail, causing discolouration and even hair loss. Known as stud tail, treatment of this consists of washing the tail twice weekly, then rinsing and drying well.

A light-coloured cat may need an occasional warm bath – more regularly if it is a show cat. For this reason, it is a good idea to accustom a light-coloured kitten to being bathed from the age of about four months. Since any cat can become nervous and even unmanageable in the bathtub, it is a good idea for one person to hold and calm the cat while another bathes it. A shampoo made for human babies is suitable, though special cat shampoos are available.

If the cat's coat or paws become contaminated with tar, paint, grease or other difficult-to-remove substances, the hair should be cleaned with household detergent if possible. An alternative is to soak the

Bathing a cat can be traumatic unless it has been accustomed to this from an early age. If possible get a helper to hold and calm the cat while you wash it. Place a rubber mat in the bottom of the basin or bowl to give the

cat a good footing, and fill it to a depth of about 10 cm (4 in) with warm water. (Test with an elbow, as for a baby.) Holding the cat gently but firmly, wet the head first, then the rest of the body. Then, using a safe cat or baby shampoo, work up a lather, being extremely careful not to get soap in the eyes or ears. (Some experts suggest plugging the ears with cotton wool [absorbent cotton] but this may alarm the cat.) Thoroughly rinse the cat, using a spray if possible, then wrap it in a towel. Dry it very carefully with this, or with a hair-dryer set to 'warm' and held at a safe distance. Avoid draughts until the cat is dry.

Cleaning ears is best done with cotton buds moistened with baby oil or surgical spirit (rubbing alcohol). Use at least two buds for each ear to remove dirt and excess wax from inside the flap. Never probe down into the ear canal.

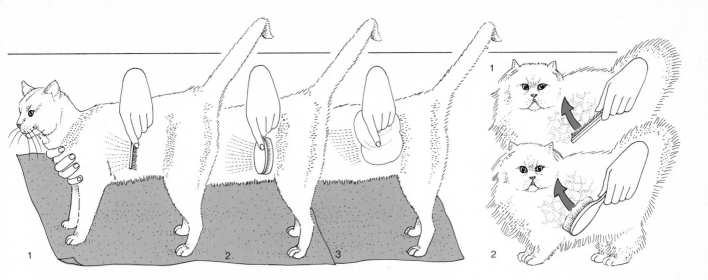

Grooming a cat, stand it on newspaper (which should later be disposed of) to catch any fleas or debris. With a short-hair **above**, **1** draw a fine-toothed comb from the head towards the tail, not forgetting the chest and underparts. **2** Then brush in the same direction with a bristle or rubber brush. (For rex cats use a very soft baby's brush.) Finally **3** rub down with a chamois leather or a silk or nylon pad to give the coat a gleam. Every time you use it, comb out, wash and rinse the brush.

With a long-hair **above right**, use a wide-toothed metal comb to groom the legs free of tangles, then comb the belly, flanks, back, chest, neck and tail – all in an upward direction **1** so that the hairs stand out in a fluffy cloud. Use a fine-toothed comb or a toothbrush for the shorter hair on the face. Brushing the coat – also the 'wrong' way **2** – completes the routine. Brush the ruff up and out to frame the face. (See also the illustrations on page 234.)

affected areas in cooking oil to loosen the contaminant before bathing the cat. With heavy contamination, it may be necessary to cut off the affected hair. If you think the cat may have licked the area and swallowed the contaminant, consult a vet, as the substance may be poisonous (see p 185).

Eyes, ears and mouth
During the regular grooming it is wise to note if the eyes are bright and clear. Any discharge is a sign that all is not well and you should consult the vet. White cats, particularly Persians, may show some tear staining around the eyes. This is quite normal and can be removed by careful bathing with warm water. Owners of show cats may, once the area is dry, press in a little talcum powder, but none must be allowed to get into the eyes.

Once a week, it is advisable to clean the outer part of the cat's ears with cotton buds or swabs, as debris easily collects in them. Although owners are sometimes advised to clean the ear canal, which leads from the flap to the ear drum, this should never be done without veterinary instruction, since probing too deep is dangerous and can be very painful. Do, however, use a bright light to examine the ear canal. Normally, it will contain a little honey-coloured wax; dark-coloured and offensive-smelling wax may be the first sign of ear-mite infestation, which will require immediate veterinary attention (see p 202).

Examination of the cat's gums and teeth is a part of grooming that many owners forget, but it is very important to ensure that the teeth are clean and gums free of any soreness. Cats of any age may develop a layer of tartar on the teeth, which can become bad enough to cause loss of appetite. Once again, the vet should be consulted; it may be advisable to remove the tartar under a light anaesthetic (see p 196). The 'milk' teeth are normally shed quite easily, but if the kitten appears disturbed veterinary help may be necessary.

Attending to the claws
All cats and kittens need to clean and sharpen their claws on a rough surface, and for this reason a scratching-post (see p 145) should be provided if the cat is not allowed access to a garden with trees. In any case, a cat will sometimes ignore its owner's commands and use its claws on furniture or carpets. Some owners, particularly in North America, resort to declawing in this situation (see p 157), but the damage can be lessened if not eliminated much less drastically by occasionally clipping the tips of the claws.

Usually two people are needed, as it is something most cats resent at first. Scissors should never be used, as they tear the nail. Instead, use nail clippers – either special ones from a pet store or the type used for manicuring human nails. It is essential to take care not to cut the quick, which can clearly be seen as a pinkish area about 1 mm ($^{1}/_{25}$ in) inside the claw (see also p 107).

Even simple trimming of the claws should be performed only where necessary, however, and not as a routine. In all aspects of grooming, in fact, it is as well to remember that cats are by nature extremely fastidious. You should encourage them to groom themselves – perhaps with a little butter on the coat, if parental training is inadequate (see p 117) – and supplement rather than replace their efforts at grooming with your own.

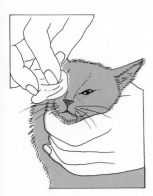

Cleaning eyes, ideally done before grooming, should be performed with cotton wool (absorbent cotton), not buds (whose sticks can be dangerous). Use a separate swab for each eye, soaked in warm (not hot) clean water.

Examining the mouth should be part of the grooming routine, for it will reveal sore gums, tartar (a hard brownish deposit on the teeth), broken teeth, bad breath and any other disorders. Most of these require veterinary attention.

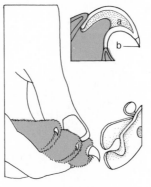

Clipping claws, be sure to avoid the sensitive pink quick **a** and to remove only the very tip **b.** By squeezing the toe between your forefinger and thumb, the claw can be easily extended and trimmed with special clippers.

Neutering

One of the most important early decisions the new cat owner may have to face (unless, of course, the cat has been acquired for breeding) is whether to have it neutered. The terms used to describe the operation vary widely – from the euphemistic 'dressing', 'doctoring', 'fixing' and 'altering' to the more straightforward de-sexing, castration (of a male) and spaying (of a female). Whatever the name, neutering is a routine operation performed by the vet to remove the cat's sex organs. This makes the cat sterile (incapable of reproducing) and also stops the production of hormones responsible for the cat's secondary sexual characteristics, including sexual behaviour. Such behaviour includes spraying by an un-castrated male (commonly termed a tom) and regular periods of heat in an unspayed female (or queen). An un-neutered cat is also referred to as entire, intact or whole.

The pros and cons of neutering

An entire female cat can produce three or even four litters a year – a dozen or more kittens that must be found homes, abandoned or destroyed. There is no knowing how many kittens an unconfined tom may sire, but given access to enough mates it could run into hundreds, cats being promiscuous creatures. Neutering is the surest way of preventing such unwanted pregnancies and the resulting over-population.

For many owners, however, a more immediate problem is the behaviour of entire cats (see p 130). When in season, a queen is restless and noisy, and if confined will become frustrated and possibly bad-tempered, and may spray. Artificial induction of ovulation or, where permitted, the use of birth-control drugs suppresses these signs (see p 217), but spaying prevents a queen from coming into season at all. A castrated tom is much less likely to spray – with the accompanying unpleasant smell of

tom cat urine – or to wander and become involved in fights or street accidents. In fact, statistics show that neutered cats – particularly males – live considerably longer than entire ones (see p 164).

Neutered cats make more gentle, affectionate and tranquil pets. They are more people-orientated and, given a chance, more playful. Their basic personality does not change, however. They make just as good mousers, if that is their purpose – possibly better, since they stay nearer home. Males castrated young may not develop such big bones or heavy muscles as whole toms, but it is a fallacy that all neutered cats are fat and lazy. They do need slightly fewer calories (see p 149), but with all cats – neutered or entire – excess weight

is due to a combination of over-feeding and lack of adequate exercise.

In a few cases, neutering is a veterinary-medical necessity – particularly in some hormonal disorders or diseases of the reproductive system (see p 228). Apart from a variety of female conditions, these include cryptorchidism (undescended testicles) in males. Also, a breeding queen or stud is best neutered once its breeding days are over.

When to neuter

It is a myth that female cats should be allowed one litter before spaying; this is neither physically nor psychologically beneficial. Most vets consider that both sexes should be neutered as early as possible, and preferably before reaching sexual maturity.

The plague of cats seen in this 19th century engraving, merrily ransacking their owner's parlour, is a fanciful reminder of the irresponsibility of allowing cats to breed unrestrained. Yet it is not so very far from the truth. Every year, hundreds of thousands – possibly millions – of unwanted cats are born, only to fill the ranks of the pathetic strays that roam every city of the world. Their rural cousins are more fortunate in having a natural food supply, but urban strays put a great strain on the services responsible for catching, looking after and eventually destroying them. Some voluntary organizations carry out mass neutering (see p 165), but every owner can help by neutering all cats not intended for breeding.

Castration (orchidectomy) **right** involves the surgical removal of the male sex organs, the testicles. In the entire male **1** the reproductive system comprises the testicles **a** within the scrotal sac **b**, the spermatic cord (vas deferens) **c**, the accessory glands **d** and the penis **e**. The castrated male **2** has had part of the spermatic cord and both testicles removed. The operation involves making a tiny incision in the base of the scrotal sac. After tying and cutting the spermatic cord, with its blood vessels, the testicles are removed. In most cases sutures (stitches) are unnecessary; eventually the scrotal sacs will recede.

Spaying (ovario-hysterectomy) **left** involves removing most of the female's sex organs. In an entire female **1** these are the ovaries **a**, fallopian tubes **b**, uterus **c** and vagina **d**. In the spayed female **2** the ovaries, fallopian tubes and uterus are removed. The operation may be performed in the midline of the abdomen (see p 177) or in the flank **below**.

Declawing

Very young kittens are not physically strong enough for the operation, however, so four to five months is generally considered the best age by vets in Britain; American vets generally leave it a month or two later. Castrating an immature cat has the advantage of preventing sexual behaviour before it starts; this decreases only gradually when an adult tom is neutered.

It has been suggested that males neutered when immature are more prone to urinary disorders as a result of their small, immature urethra (see p 203); most vets now discount this. Owners of some pedigree show males may also delay castration so that the head and bone structure can fully develop. If, for one of these reasons, you do decide to delay neutering, the operation is almost as simple and straightforward as for a younger cat. However, an adult female should never, unless it is vital, be spayed when in season, as her reproductive organs are enlarged and active, and there is a greater chance of complications.

The neutering operation
Although usually straightforward, neutering is done under a general anaesthetic, and an advance appointment should be made with the vet. You will be told to starve the cat of food for about 12 hours and of fluids for 6 hours before the operation. The operation itself takes only a few minutes for castration, 10 to 20 minutes for spaying. The cat regains consciousness after about 5 to 10 minutes with a gaseous anaesthetic, but an hour or more following an injection.

Males and many females are generally allowed home later the same day, but females (and some males) may be kept overnight. In any case, the patient should be confined to the home and kept quiet and under the owner's observation for at least the next 48 hours. (For further general information on operations and postoperative care, see page 177.)

Alternatives to neutering
Apart from the use of drugs or induced ovulation already mentioned, the only alternatives to neutering or confinement if you do not want your cat to breed is tubal ligation for females or vasectomy for males. These consist of cutting and/or tying the female's fallopian tubes (which lead from ovaries to womb) or the male's vas deferens (sperm duct) – as with humans.

These operations are somewhat more complicated and expensive than neutering, and most vets advise against them. They cause sterility by preventing the release of eggs and sperm, but sex hormones are still produced and therefore sexual behaviour continues – including periods of heat in females and territorial spraying and aggressive behaviour in males. More important, females are still prone to various gynaecological problems.

Although many people consider the operation to be cruel, it is possible in some countries for an owner who objects to a cat clawing and damaging furniture to have the cat declawed. Not to be confused with the simple and straightforward procedure of clipping the claws or nails, which any owner can perform if necessary (see p 155), declawing is a surgical procedure performed by the vet in which the claws are completely removed. In most cases, it is only the front feet that are declawed, since these are the most damaging.

The whole matter is extremely controversial, however, and there is considerable disagreement between vets as well as owners about the advantages and disadvantages of the operation. But it is significant that the GCCF in Britain, the CFA and most other cat fancy associations in the United States, and similar organizations in most other countries ban declawed cats from shows – generally in both pedigree and household pet classes.

The pros and cons of declawing
Many people – including the great majority of the veterinary profession in Britain – feel that, although declawing is convenient for the owner, it is cruel and unnatural for the cat. The opposing view, held by most American vets, is that – so long as it is done properly – it is not a cruel procedure. Correctly performed, declawing is permanent. It inevitably affects, to a greater or lesser degree, the cat's ability to climb and defend itself. (If the hind claws are left, these to some extent form a substitute.) For these reasons, vets are virtually unanimous in advising against declawing cats that are allowed out of the home (see p 158).

Apart from possible psychological effects, physical complications can follow the operation. If the whole of the claws, including the germinal cells from which

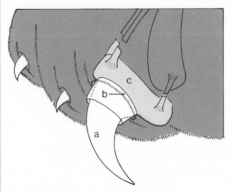

Declawing (onychectomy) involves the surgical removal of the claw **a**, including the germinal cells **b** responsible for its growth, and part or all of the terminal bone **c** of the toe. The vet extends the toe and uses sterile nail trimmers to sever the bone and ligaments at or just after the last joint. Wrongly positioned, the cut may involve the pad or regrowth may occur.

A scratching post may be a more acceptable alternative to declawing. Properly trained (see p 153) a cat will use it instead of furniture.

they grow, are not completely removed, misshapen claws may regrow. Postoperative infection can occur, but those in favour say that, performed by a competent vet, there is no more risk or discomfort than with neutering. The cat's feet may be tender at first, but full recovery takes only five to seven days. They also argue that declawing does no harm to the cat's personality or lifestyle – provided it is an indoor animal – but the owner does have to ensure that, if it subsequently has to go to another home, the new owner will similarly keep it indoors.

Whatever you feel about declawing, you should only consider it after all attempts at training the cat to use a scratching post (see p 145) have failed and regular trimming of the claws proves insufficient.

The declawing operation
Cats can be declawed at any age, but most vets recommend it to be done at between three and four months. The younger the cat is, the more likely it is to adapt quickly to coping without claws. As with neutering, the cat is given a general anaesthetic. A tourniquet is used to stop blood flow to the foot while sterile nail trimmers are used to cut through the last joint of each toe being declawed. In some cases, the vet cuts through the bone near the joint. The toes may need to be sutured (stitched), but in many cases it is only necessary to firmly bandage the feet. The bandages are usually removed the next day, and the cat allowed home 48 hours after the operation.

Exercise and the housebound cat

Although the cat is by nature a prowling hunter, many cat owners – whether deliberately or by default – keep their pets confined to the home. People living in a high-rise apartment may have a housebound cat simply because they find it inconvenient to let it in and out. But, in North America particularly, many cats are kept indoors for safety. This is particularly true in cities, where free-roaming cats are inevitably exposed to a high risk of street accidents. Kittens and elderly or deaf cats are, of course, particularly at risk, but few cats acquire enough traffic sense to deal with large numbers of vehicles. Suburban and country cats may be in less danger, but any cat – particularly an uncastrated tom – may wander and become a stray, or may fall victim to cat thieves.

This last risk is obviously greatest in the case of valuable pedigree cats, and cat breeders everywhere commonly keep their queens and toms in restricted quarters if not totally indoors. Whether pedigree or not, tom cats free to roam are liable to suffer wounds in fights, and entire (intact) females may constantly present their owners with unplanned litters. Outdoor cats are more likely to pick up infectious diseases and parasites and if let out indiscriminately in localities with extremes of temperature may suffer from heat stroke or exposure. All in all, there are potent reasons for restricting your cat to the home, and they are endorsed by many vets – particularly in North America.

Against all this is the undisputed fact that the cat is a lithe and athletic creature that enjoys exercise. Very many owners would consider it cruel and unnatural to deny their pet the opportunity of running in the wind, chasing birds and mice, and climbing trees. The cat should be allowed its natural instincts, these owners feel, and claim that free-roaming cats suffer fewer behavioural problems. In any case, the risks of an outdoor life vary considerably from one locality to another.

Whatever the balance of arguments, only the owner can make the final decision. Certainly, a housebound cat can live a perfectly healthy and contented life, provided that it has never had full freedom. The decision to confine it must be made when it is a kitten, for it is undoubtedly cruel to arbitrarily confine a cat that is used to going out. And, unless it is to be used for breeding, the housebound cat should be neutered (see p156), for the behaviour of a confined tom or queen can present many problems (see p130).

General care and safety

There is no difference in principle between looking after a housebound cat and one that is allowed out, but even more attention must be paid to providing its needs. A regularly cleaned and emptied litter tray is a must, and should always be kept in the same place. Be sure to provide regular, balanced meals; a succession of titbits is particularly likely to lead to obesity in a cat that has little exercise.

If you go out to work all day, regular feeding is particularly difficult. Morning and evening meals may be sufficient for an adult cat, but kittens need more frequent feeding. If fresh food is left out it may be contaminated by insects or go bad in hot weather. Semi-moist and dry cat foods (see

Grass in pots provides indoor cats with the greenery they seem to need (see p148). Pre-sown trays of cock's-foot or lawn grass **left** may be bought from pet stores, or you can

sow the seeds of these or cereal grasses such as wheat or oats **centre** in potting mixture. Keep moist, warm and dark until germination, then place in a well-lit spot.

For a continuous supply of succulent leaves, sow a pot or tray every few weeks. If your cat enjoys catnip (see p112), you can also grow this in a pot **right** on a sunny window-sill.

Household safety with a cat is mainly a matter of forethought and common sense in locating danger points (asterisked). Cats are naturally curious, so take care not to shut one accidentally in a refrigerator, oven, washing machine or dryer. Never allow a cat to jump onto a stove; one day it may do so when the stove is hot, or it may overturn a pan of boiling water or fat or be scalded by a jet of steam. Jumping onto shelves may cause injuries from falling utensils. All open fires should be guarded even when not lit, as cats are intrigued by chimneys. Never leave clothes airing by an open fire where a playful cat may pull them over. Kittens are invariably tempted to play with electric cables and may be electrocuted if they bite through the insulation, so disconnect all unattended appliances and teach kittens that cables are taboo. Rubber bands, buttons, needles and pins, and other small objects can be lethal if swallowed and painful if stuck in paws. Plastic bags can suffocate. Many household substances (see p184) are toxic to cats, which are most commonly poisoned when licking contaminants from the coat. Some houseplants and cut flowers and foliage (fresh or dried) are also poisonous – notably

philodendrons, dumb cane (*Dieffenbachia*), true ivies (*Hedera*), caladiums, poinsettias, winter cherry (*Solanun capsicastrum*), oleander, rhododendrons and azaleas, common or cherry laurel (*Prunus laurocerasus*) and mistletoe.

An outdoor pen is ideal for providing a housebound cat with exercise and fresh air – at least in moderate weather. It should be built of strong wire mesh on a sturdy wooden or steel frame. The roof must be closely fitting to prevent escape. The pen should be sheltered from cold winds and

partially shaded from hot sun. If possible, it should be partly grassed and partly concreted for use in the wet. Direct access from the house via a cat flap is ideal. Provide shelves for exercise and sunning, and a branched tree-trunk, special climbing tree or even a cat tree-house.

p 150) are convenient because they do not spoil, but you must introduce your cat to a dry diet gradually and be sure to provide plenty of water with each meal. Cats with working owners are also likely to become lonely and bored; probably the best solu-tion here is to provide the companionship of another cat or a dog.

If a housebound cat is to be left alone for long periods, it is particularly important to ensure that your home is safe and neither too draughty nor too stuffy for the cat. You can fit windows with a hinged frame onto which plastic-covered 5 cm (2in) mesh is nailed. Then you can open the window for fresh air without the risk of the cat escaping or falling. (In areas where mosquito screens are the norm, these will of course double for the cat so long as they are strong enough.) Balconies, at whatever level, must be similarly 'cat-proofed' and roofed with wire mesh. It is also possible to build a sunporch out from a window, or fit an observation perch to the inside sill.

To many owners, the safety of the home's contents is as important as that of the cat. Soft furnishings and carpets are inevitably at risk from a bored feline's claws. Early training to use a scratching post (see p 145) should prevent this prob-lem, but adult cats may not be easily deterred from using valuable furniture in preference. Clipping the cat's claws (see p 155) is possible, but is only a temporary solution, and some owners go to the extent of completely removing the claws (see p 157). If, like very many owners and vets, you abhor this measure, the only solution other than finding the cat a new home is to confine it, when you are out, to a part of the home where it can do little damage.

A fairly common problem concerns houseplants. A cat kept indoors is more likely to nibble its owner's plants than one free to eat vegetation outdoors – and some houseplants are poisonous. Growing the cat its own greenery may provide a solution, but otherwise plants will have to be placed high out of reach or in positions that make nibbling awkward. Some cats may also use a plant pot as a litter tray. Kittens can easily be taught not to do so, and adult cats also usually respond to the right training measures (see p 153). You may, however, have to use a special repellant spray or cover the potting mixture with a layer of pebbles to prevent the cat pawing it.

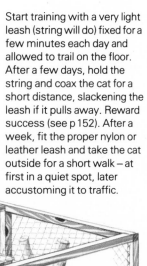

Walking on a leash allows even urban cats to exercise outdoors safely. Fit a collar (see p 146) or preferably a harness before training starts. The harness, of soft leather, nylon or elastic, should be designed not to choke the cat if it strains and not to let it back out. Non-elastic types must be slightly loose.

Start training with a very light leash (string will do) fixed for a few minutes each day and allowed to trail on the floor. After a few days, hold the string and coax the cat for a short distance, slackening the leash if it pulls away. Reward success (see p 152). After a week, fit the proper nylon or leather leash and take the cat outside for a short walk – at first in a quiet spot, later accustoming it to traffic.

Exercise

Many of the confined cat's destructive habits may be due to boredom, and pro-viding plenty of entertainment and exercise may be the answer. A collection of large, strong cardboard boxes with holes cut in the sides, or a few wide-bore cardboard tubes, will give endless fun as the cat rushes in and out of the tunnels. A climbing tree will be much appreciated, and you should build up a collection of toys (see p 147).

Owners with gardens may be able to construct or buy an outside pen, which can be fitted with shelves for jumping and trees – artificial or natural – to climb. If this is not possible, it is perfectly feasible to train the housebound cat to go for walks on a lead. Provided that it also has regular balanced meals, plenty of companionship and a safe home, it will be just as contented as its free-roaming counterpart – and may well have a longer and healthier life.

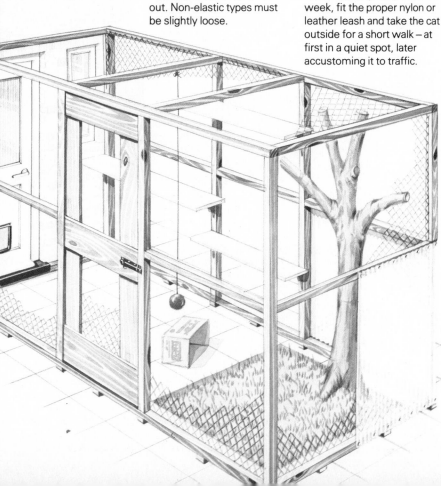

The travelling cat

Some cats are easy travellers, especially if accustomed to travel when young, but many do not take kindly to it. There are times, however, when it is essential: At the very least, your pet may have to be taken to the vet or to a local cat show, or you may have to move to another home, send your cat to stud or transfer it to a new owner. On other occasions there is a wider element of choice, and it is wise to take into account the age and temperament of the cat, and the length and type of journey, before deciding to subject it to an experience that may be at best uncomfortable and at worst extremely traumatic.

For example, many owners take their pets with them on holidays really for their own convenience and companionship, without fully considering the animal. In many cases, it would be safer and less disrupting for a cat to stay at home and be cared for by relatives or neighbours, or to go to friends or to a boarding establishment (see p162). If you move to a new home, consider whether you can do the same thing for a temporary period while you get the new home ready and can then spare time to settle the cat in properly (see p145). In any case, whenever you take your cat on anything more than a local journey, be sure to make proper preparations and, if public transport or hotel accommodation is to be used, check well in advance that your cat will be accepted and what regulations, if any, will be imposed. This is vital if you go to another country with a cat.

Travelling by road and rail

Even for short car journeys, a suitable carrier is essential, and it is wise for the cat's name and address to be attached to a collar or harness in case of escape (see p146). A reliably placid cat may be allowed to sit on a passenger's lap, but the carrier should be available in case the cat becomes agitated; never allow a cat to roam around a moving car, for safety reasons. If the cat is on a leash, use a specially designed harness, not a collar, to reduce the risk of choking if it moves suddenly. If the cat is not leashed, keep the car windows closed.

When using the carrier, position it so that sudden braking or cornering does not throw it to the floor. Ensure that ample air reaches it. Never put a cat – in or out of a carrier – in the boot (trunk) of a car, and do not leave it unattended; on a hot day it can quickly be overcome by heat exhaustion, and in very cold conditions may be chilled. There is also the risk of escape or theft. If a cat is ill and will accept its carrier without fuss, all well and good; otherwise it may be warmly wrapped in a blanket and held by a passenger. An injured cat must be moved as little as possible; it is best to lay it flat on a blanket or towel in a cardboard box and steadied throughout the journey.

On a long journey exceeding about six

Carrying containers for cats should be roomy enough to let the cat stand up, turn around and lie down, well ventilated (preferably on two sides) and securely fastening. The inside should be smooth. Layers of newspaper and a blanket at the bottom provide warmth and absorbency, or use disposable nappies (diapers). Glass-fibre containers are light and easy to clean; the type fitted with a grille or mesh front 1 is best. A holdall-type carrier 2 is cheaper, but the zip top may not easily close to prevent escape, and poor ventilation may cause condensation. A plastic-coated wire basket 3 is airy –

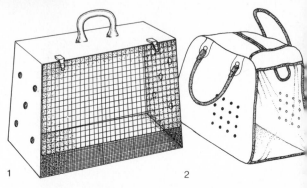

perhaps too much so for cold areas – and easy to clean. Like the traditional wicker basket shown on page 144 it must be lined with newspaper to absorb urine. (The cardboard type also shown on page 144

hours, a cat must be provided with water and if possible occasional access to a litter tray. It is best to withhold food immediately before travelling, as cats may suffer from travel (motion) sickness. Little can be done about this except to be prepared with plenty of newspaper and tissues. An extremely nervous cat may, however, be prescribed a tranquillizer by the vet. On arrival at the destination, keep the cat quiet, preferably in a darkened room, with access to milk and water and a litter tray. Luckily, recovery from travel sickness is generally quite swift provided the cat is left in peace.

Bus and rail operators may only accept cats in approved secure containers, if at all, while some permit passengers to take a cat

is suitable only as a temporary measure or for short journeys.)
Long-distance carriers must be approved by the airline or shipping company concerned, and must be strong, leak-

Putting a cat in a carrier is easiest if you stand the basket with the open door at the top. Grasp the cat by the scruff and support its weight with a hand under the rump. Lower it hind-first into the container; keep holding the scruff while closing the door.

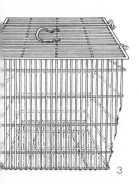

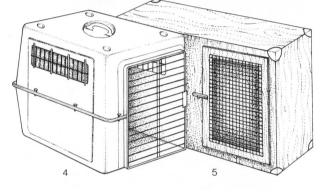

proof and very well ventilated. Label the carrier with your name and address, full travel details and if necessary instructions for collection on arrival; mark it 'live animal' and indicate the right way up.

Lock it if possible and fix the key to the outside.
A carrier made of plastic **4** may weigh only 3.5 kg (8 lb) and is ideal for air travel. The type shown separates to form two cat beds. Smaller types are

available that fit under aircraft seats, but they are very cramped. A more substantial wooden carrier **5** is suitable for long sea journeys but is heavy and difficult to clean thoroughly.

on a leash – though this is inadvisable because of the risk of escape. On a train, a cat may have to travel – in a carrier – in the luggage compartment; in this case, you should visit it as often as possible and provide water. Where regulations allow the cat to travel unaccompanied, make sure that adequate arrangements are made for collection at the destination, and check that water and (if the journey is longer than about 24 hours) food are provided.

Travelling by air and sea
As with bus and rail travel, each airline and shipping company has its own rules about the transport of animals, and these are often backed up by national or international regulations. Charges may vary from one airline to another, too. Cats may only be carried on aircraft in approved carriers (which can often be purchased from the airline). Some airlines allow cats to travel with their owners in the passenger cabin, in which case the carrier should fit under the seat. Otherwise, whether accompanied or not, it will travel in a special pressurized and heated section of the cargo hold. Advance arrangements are essential.

If the cat is to travel unaccompanied, it should be delivered to the airport cargo centre about four hours before take-off. A shipping agent may be employed to deliver the cat to the airline, but it is better if the owner stays with the cat until departure. The airline will normally handle any transfer to an interconnecting flight and should check the condition of the animal at each stop. (There is no access to the cargo hold during a flight.) If the cat is in transit for more than 24 hours (or a kitten for more than 12 hours), the owner will be required to provide food, together with written feeding instructions; the dry or semi-moist type of cat food is most convenient (see p 150). It is essential to make clear and careful arrangements for the cat to be met at its destination by a private individual or shipping agent. Few airports have boarding facilities for animals in transit.

Most cats travel very well by air, but it is both unkind and unwise to send a pregnant queen on such a journey. Most airlines will also not carry very young kittens. A cat must only be given mild tranquillizers under veterinary supervision and never a drug that makes it insensible.

Sea travel is much less important these days, and its slowness for long journeys makes it less desirable for a travelling cat. On some ships, the accommodation provided for animals may also be inadequate. However, if accompanied, the cat can be visited regularly by the owner and exercised on deck, with a leash and harness. If the cat becomes ill, the ship's doctor may be able to help, but remember that (just as with people) seasickness is a common problem and it is wise to seek veterinary advice before departure. On short-distance ferry journeys, cats may generally be transported in portable carriers, but again you should check regulations well in advance.

Health and other regulations
Before travelling to another country or state, it is essential to take great care to find out exactly what documentation and vaccinations are required. Many countries demand that an imported cat has a certificate of health issued by an approved vet within a certain number of days of the start of the journey. In the United States, such a certificate may be needed even when travelling between states or when taking any trip by air. Export documents and rabies vaccination certificates may be specified, and many countries have a quarantine law applicable to animals whether or not they have been vaccinated. The period of quarantine varies from one to six months or even more. Australia, Britain, New Zealand and Hawaii have some of the strictest quarantine requirements because they are among the few places free of rabies (see p 206). Regulations can and do change, however, and you should always check with the embassy or consulate concerned.

If the cat is travelling to a country where quarantine is imposed, the owner or recipient must generally make an advance booking with an officially-run or approved quarantine cattery or kennels (see p 163). It may be necessary for a licensed agent to transfer the animal to the quarantine quarters. In Britain, cats must be vaccinated twice against rabies (at the owner's expense) while in quarantine (which is, of course, also at the owner's expense), and visits to the animal may be strictly regulated. Cats owned by temporary visitors to quarantine countries have only to be quarantined for the duration of their stay if this is less than the normal period.

Apart from such health regulations, the normal laws governing the carriage of goods apply to cats, so that anyone 'in charge' of the animal is normally responsible for its care and well-being. It may be difficult to define who is responsible at any particular time, however, so owners (particularly of valuable pedigree cats) are well advised to insure their pets for the duration of the journey, making sure that an appropriate valuation is agreed upon.

Boarding your cat

At one time or another, almost all cat owners face the problem of what to do with their pet while they are away from home. If you cannot make satisfactory arrangements for the cat to be looked after in its own home – which is usually to be preferred if possible – the best solution is to book it into a reliable boarding establishment. There, regular care and human companionship are assured.

In some places, such as the United States, these places are commonly called boarding kennels and may accommodate both cats and dogs. Boarding catteries, which are usually reserved for cats, are to be preferred, but the advice given here will apply equally to mixed establishments. For convenience, the term cattery is generally used in this article but this should not be confused with a breeding cattery (also often called simply a cattery) where cats are raised for show and sale. (There are some dual-purpose establishments but for health reasons the two sides should be separate.)

Choosing a boarding cattery

Arrangements for boarding your cat must be made well in advance, ideally when you are finalizing your own travel plans. Good catteries are very heavily booked, particularly in summer. Unfortunately, bad ones outnumber the good, and many owners return to find their cat in poor condition, obviously having been inadequately fed and cared for. In Britain all boarding catteries have to be licensed by the relevant local government authority. But in some countries there are no restrictions and standards are set by individual proprietors.

It is not enough to telephone the nearest cattery and make a reservation. A friend or the local vet may recommend a good one, and your local animal humane organization or cat club may provide lists of reputable establishments. Many vets feel that (although there are exceptions) the risk of disease spread is less in country catteries than in urban ones, which may be more crowded. Ideally, however, no cat should be booked into any cattery that has not been thoroughly inspected by the owner. Most good catteries have a brochure that states clearly their conditions and terms and hours of business, and will welcome a visit and questions from the owner.

You should find out whether the cats are fed regularly twice a day, whether they are groomed, and whether the present boarders look well cared-for and contented. When inspecting the premises, bear in mind that there exist catteries with 'show-piece' chalets and less desirable quarters tucked away in the background. There should always be an isolation unit on the premises, some distance from the main cattery. Here sick cats – or those suspected of carrying an infection – can be confined to avoid the spread of disease. If special isolation filter cages are not used, the cages must be as far apart as possible. Cats in isolation units should be barrier-nursed (see p178).

Some boarding catteries will take pregnant or nursing queens and kittens, and many have facilities for several adults belonging to the same owner to be accommodated together (cats from different households should never be allowed to share the same accommodation). Many have larger long-stay quarters for cats that have to be boarded for months or even years (for example, if the owner is ill or abroad). Not all catteries are willing to take entire (unneutered) males, however,

Points to look for in all boarding catteries are basically the same whether they are in the city or the country, indoors or outdoors. If weather conditions permit, however, catteries with outdoor runs and separate chalets **right** are ideal, as there is much less chance of infection spreading.
In such a cattery, each cat or family of cats must have its own hut or chalet **a** and outside run **b**. Ideally, the chalet should be about 1.2 m (4 ft) square for a single cat and high enough to allow a shelf **c** and jumping space. It should be light **d** and airy, odourless and spotlessly clean. A lining of non-porous material, such as a lead-free gloss paint **e** and a vinyl floor covering **f** extending a little way up the walls, provides easily washed and disinfected surfaces. The walls and roof should be insulated **g** and the hut equipped with a safe heater, such as an infra-red dull emitter **h**. The cat must have a bed **i**, litter tray **j** and feeding bowls **k** that are easily sterilized or are disposable. A cat flap **l** gives free access to the run during the day, but should be lockable at night. The run, ideally about 1.2 m (4 ft) by 2 m (6 ft) long, must be made of strong wire mesh and should be concrete based for easy cleaning. A scratching post **m** may be provided, and possibly a climbing post, though such furnishings are limited as they must be sterilized for new boarders. There should be a space of at least 60 cm (2 ft) between adjoining runs or some form of solid barrier to prevent direct contact between neighbouring cats. The door to the run **n** needs to be bolted and labelled with the cat's and owner's names. A double door prevents escape; otherwise there should be some form of safety passage **o**. A corrugated plastic roof **p** over the run and safety passage gives protection against the weather and sun.

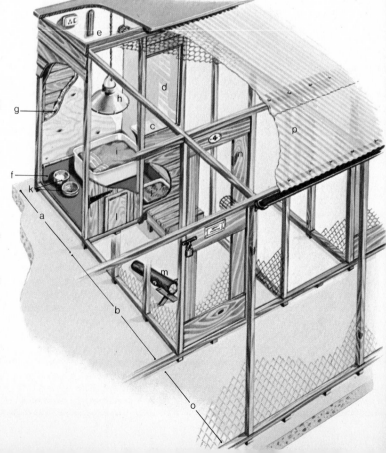

because of the accompanying problems of their sexual behaviour (see p 130).

Boarding fees vary considerably and may depend on the facilities provided; heating costs and special dietary requirements, for example, will be important factors. Fees will have to be paid at regular intervals if the cat is a long-term boarder. Otherwise, they may be payable when the cat is collected, or in some cases on arrival.

The boarding arrangements

Having chosen the cattery, make a firm reservation. It should not be necessary for the cat to have a health check from a vet before booking unless you suspect that the cat is not well or could be a source of infection. The cattery proprietor will check the cat's condition when it arrives and has the right to refuse admission if there is any suspicion of a contagious disease, such as ringworm (see p 189). Most will, however, be willing to treat minor conditions, such as fleas. You will have to produce a current certificate of vaccination against feline infectious enteritis (FIE; see p 192); check in advance that this is up-to-date and a booster is not due. Some proprietors also insist on vaccination against respiratory virus infections (cat flu; see p 197).

If the cat has its own bed, most catteries will welcome this. Otherwise, a familiar woollen jumper or rug will comfort the cat in strange surroundings. Beds, litter trays and feeding dishes are provided. The cat carrier can usually be stored at the cattery during the stay.

On arrival the proprietor should record the owner's permanent address and if possible a temporary one in case of emergency. Written particulars of the cat should include details of its normal diet, and any foods to be avoided or drugs to which the cat is allergic. The owner should be asked to sign an agreement that if the cat becomes ill a vet will be called to give treatment at the owner's expense. The proprietor will probably be insured against the death of animals by accident or sickness, or their loss by theft or escape. The owner may, however, wish to take out a private insurance. Some cat breed clubs automatically provide insurance against accidents, but you should check that this still applies if the cat is boarded.

Before leaving the cattery, see that the cat is safely installed in its accommodation. No one breed of cat accepts boarding more readily than another; all cats are individuals with varying temperaments. Although adult cats may take a day or two to settle, most cats will happily accept their stay.

Quarantine catteries

Cats must be boarded for a certain period if they are imported into a country with quarantine restrictions (see p 161). Quarantine catteries are specially designed to completely isolate each animal until it is certain that it is not incubating rabies. (Cats belonging to the same owner and arriving in quarantine at the same time may, however, be allowed to share quarters.) The premises are normally privately owned but under government control and have to maintain strict standards of security, hygiene and husbandry. In Britain the premises are licensed and periodically inspected by the Ministry of Agriculture; a further inspection must be made by a designated cat vet every day. Stringent requirements are essential to prevent escape or contact with other cats.

If you have to take your cat to a quarantine country, you should apply to local veterinary health authorities or the relevant embassy for details of regulations and the addresses of approved quarantine catteries. Some of these are owned with boarding catteries, but are run completely separately within their own perimeter wall. Many quarantine dogs as well as cats. On writing to a quarantine cattery in Britain, owners will usually be sent details of accommodation fees, charges for collection from the port of entry by a licensed carrying agent (see p 161) and an import licence application to be completed and returned to the cattery to ensure a booking. The government then issues boarding papers, which authorize air or shipping lines to accept the cat.

Most cats soon settle down to their stay in a quarantine cattery and owners may make visits, although appointments are usually necessary and strict safety rules have to be observed.

An indoor cattery can be as safe and comfortable for cat boarders as an outdoor one provided that high standards of hygiene are supplemented by adequate air circulation to carry away airborne germs. The ideal is a separate air supply for each cage. Otherwise, windows or screen doors with vents, together with extractor fans, should be arranged for maximum cross-ventilation – 10 to 15 air changes per hour if possible. Heaters can if necessary warm incoming air to maintain a temperature of 18 to 21°C (64 to 70°F), but in hot areas air conditioning is desirable, to control humidity as well as temperature. The cattery should be well lit by both natural and artificial lighting; ultra-violet lights help to kill airborne germs. Cages should be at least 1.2 m (4 ft) square, if possible with access to an outside run in suitable weather. Solid side partitions are essential; ones made of clear plastic give neighbours visual interest. Facing rows of cages must be at least 2.5 m (8 ft) apart. Tiered cages are undesirable, but in any case must be arranged so that food, water and excrement cannot reach the cages below. All surfaces inside and outside the cages must be easy to clean and disinfect. (This is easier if the floors of the cages are raised above the general floor level.) General safety measures should be similar to those of an outdoor cattery.

A quarantine cattery has to meet even more stringent requirements, for it must completely isolate each cat until it is proved to be free of rabies. The compartments must be escape-proof and prevent any contact, direct or indirect, between cats. Each cat must have its own sleeping quarters and exercise area – in Britain totalling at least 1.5 m² (15 sq ft) per cat. The walls of the sleeping area must extend from floor to roof and a separate exercise run must have solid side partitions and a nose- and paw-proof roof. Other fittings are similar to those for a boarding cattery. Access must be via a safety passage or double doors forming an escape-proof trap. For added security, there may be an area into which visitors are locked before entering a cat's quarters, while the entire quarantine premises are surrounded by a high perimeter fence (clearly seen **left**). Any corridor between the perimeter fence and the quarantine building must be roofed.
Hygiene is as important as security, and equipment such as food bowls and bedding must be reserved for individual cats and be burnt or thoroughly washed and disinfected after use. Staff should wear protective clothing which they change before leaving the premises.

The elderly cat

Popular belief has it that a year of a cat's life equals seven of ours. In fact, kittens mature more quickly than this and cats slow down in their later years, so that one feline year then equals about four human. In any case a cat is well into middle age by the time it is eight. As with people, the threshold from middle into old age is indefinite – much depends on care and diet – but the fact that very many domestic pet cats easily outlive the 'normal' lifespan of about 14 years indicates that much of their life is spent in what is technically old age.

This is not true of their uncared-for cousins; solitary urban strays have an average lifespan of only two years, while cats in feral colonies are very lucky to survive more than ten. The oldest cats are generally neuters; roaming entire toms are the least likely to make old age. There is little concrete evidence on the comparative longevity of different breeds, but any closely inbred breed – as may occur if the number of active breeding cats falls too low (see p 48) – tends to have a shorter life.

Signs of old age

Old age is probably most noticeable in breeding cats, especially queens. Although still coming into heat and mating if not already spayed, their litters gradually become smaller from the age of eight until, usually at 11 or 12, they fail to produce kittens even after a successful mating. Most breeders have their queens spayed some years before this, however, and such neutered queens can perform a valuable service 'babysitting' the litters of younger cats. Stud males retain their potency into comparatively old age, often siring kittens at 15. However, since their life is of necessity a lonely one, many owners prefer to castrate toms at about 12 years, allowing them to 'retire' to the fireside (though they may continue to spray).

Generally speaking, a pet cat's pace of living slows down gradually as it ages. It seeks warm spots and sleeps more. Its coat may thin and there may be some greying around the muzzle. Some lazy, overfed cats become obese, but most lose weight as they age, the skin hanging more loosely so that the spine is more prominent. As in humans, sight and hearing may become less acute, and the cat may become less fussy about personal cleanliness.

General care

Cats have a remarkable ability to adapt their lifestyle to cope with any incapacity arising from old age, but the owner must contribute common sense and a keen eye for any sign of trouble that may need veterinary attention. (For a discussion of the common disorders of old age, see page 208.)

A warm bed away from draughts is a basic need, and the cat, even if allowed out freely when younger, must never be left

Old age rests gracefully on feline shoulders. Cats can enjoy life well into their teens, usually remaining alert and playful.

outside for long in cold weather. In hot, humid climates air conditioning eases the cat's decreased heat tolerance. Older cats often become fussy eaters, and it may help to offer small, frequent meals (as in kittenhood). High-quality food is particularly important (see p 148). Mouth and teeth problems are common (see p 196), so check these if even strong-tasting food fails to tempt. Ample fluid is another necessity since kidney function declines, but excessive thirst may indicate kidney disease or diabetes. Constipation – sometimes due to drinking too little – is a common problem, but occasional occurrences can be cured with a 5 ml teaspoonful of medicinal liquid paraffin (mineral oil).

Treat any lapse of toilet habits firmly but sympathetically (see p 153), and always ensure that a clean litter tray is available even if the cat normally goes outdoors. If necessary provide trays in several rooms. All elderly cats, but particularly long-hairs,

need help with grooming to prevent hair matting and the development of hairballs (see p 194), which older cats have more trouble regurgitating. If necessary, clean the cat's face and anal region regularly with warm water, and pat dry. It will help longhairs to trim the hair around the hindquarters. Claw-trimming (see p 155) is also important, since less exercise means that the claws may grow too long.

Coping with special problems

Deafness and failing sight are problems that can be counteracted, if not overcome, by the caring owner. If only the eyesight is affected, your voice and the cat's sense of smell will be enough to guide it through its daily routine. If it is also deaf, then life becomes more difficult, but a partially deaf cat can be called or warned by sharp handclaps and its sense of smell will still tell it when you are near. It is obviously vital to make your home as accident-proof as possible (see p 158), and vulnerability to street accidents means that outdoor access, if any, must be restricted in urban areas. Old cats may be more prone to bone-fractures, in fact, because they are less nimble. Changes of routine and environment and separation from the owner are all particularly traumatic, so take special care over arrangements for looking after the cat if you go away from home.

Despite every care and all the advances in feline medicine, there may come a time when it is obvious that life has become an intolerable burden for the cat. This is something you must come to terms with yourself. The vet will advise on whether euthanasia (see p 209) is the kindest solution, but it is the owner's responsibility to decide what is best for the cat.

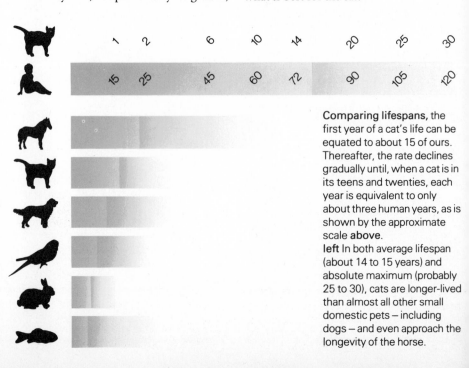

	1	2	6	10	14	20	25	30
	15	25	45	60	72	90	105	120

Comparing lifespans, the first year of a cat's life can be equated to about 15 of ours. Thereafter, the rate declines gradually until, when a cat is in its teens and twenties, each year is equivalent to only about three human years, as is shown by the approximate scale **above.**
left In both average lifespan (about 14 to 15 years) and absolute maximum (probably 25 to 30), cats are longer-lived than almost all other small domestic pets – including dogs – and even approach the longevity of the horse.

Working and stray cats

No one knows how many stray cats there are, though one estimate suggests that there is at least one stray for every two pet cats – which means that there could be three million strays in Britain and a huge twelve million in the United States.

Cats stray for many reasons. They are frequently – and irresponsibly – abandoned by owners moving away. Unwanted kittens may be dumped far from home. They may simply get lost. A stray cat has three alternatives: it can struggle on alone for a while, probably soon to die; it can join a feral colony; or it can find itself a new home. Feral cats are domestic cats who have learnt to handle life in the wild. Colonies of feral cats roam specific territories (see p124) chosen for the food and shelter they can offer. Dockyards, waste land at the edges of cities and rubbish dumps are all favourite locations. However, left to themselves, feral cats reproduce at a spectacular rate. This means that the surplus animals either starve, if the food supply is inadequate, or are forced to form breakaway colonies.

Mid-way in status between these 'wild' animals and the thoroughly domesticated lap-cats are the numerous working cats – nowadays by far the greatest proportion of them found on farms – all over the world. The cat originally entered human society as a rat and mouse catcher (see p238) and even in the age of effective rat poisons this role continues to benefit mankind.

Managing feral colonies

Ever since the last century, animal humane societies around the world have taken in stray cats (and dogs), particularly in cities where the problem has for long assumed almost plague proportions. In the vast majority of cases, the animals' fate has been a short stay in confined quarters followed by extermination by more or less humane means. Only a lucky few were (and are) adopted by families.

In recent years, voluntary organizations in many countries have been tackling the problem in a different way, by neutering or contraception. Whole colonies are rounded up, neutered and returned to their territory. Alternatively, food containing contraceptive drugs – similar to those used in the contraceptive pill – may be given to the cats weekly. Either method is highly successful in cutting the birth-rate, and thus the size of feral colonies, without the necessity of culling, but the second clearly involves much more work and, in the long term, expense.

Adopting a stray

A stray – particularly if young and home-reared or very used to human company – may approach a human for a home. If approached, first try to make sure – by inquiries to vets, neighbours and so on –

Lucky strays may find refuge in the home of an animal lover **left**, but millions more lead a short life fending for themselves. Other cats work for their living. From 1950 until his death in 1964, Tibs **above** was chief rat catcher at the Post Office headquarters in London. On a salary of 2s 6d (12½p, then about 35 cents) per week, this imposing 10.5kg (23lb) white collar worker was a well-known and respected member of the Post Office staff.

that it really is unowned. Then consider the responsibilities and expense of taking it in. A thorough veterinary examination is essential; it is bound to have fleas and probably ear-mites and intestinal worms; it will certainly need to be vaccinated; you will need to find out if it is neutered (not easy with a female) and if necessary have the operation done; if female it may well already be pregnant.

All this will cost money for possibly no reward. You have no notion of the animal's toilet habits or personality. It is likely to be psychologically disturbed for some time, may be aggressive and will almost certainly cause jealousy if you already own a cat. It may even run away again. If you decide against keeping it, do not encourage it by feeding it, but hand it over to your local animal humane society. But if you do decide to adopt, follow the advice on settling in given in the article on page 144.

Working cats

From the granaries of ancient Egypt to modern public buildings, ships and farms all over the world, cats have an honourable history of working for humans as catchers of vermin. Their great advantage is that they enjoy their work. The apparently unchallenged champion mouser of all time was a Lancashire warehouse cat called Mickey; he is claimed to have killed a thousand mice a year throughout his 23-year career.

Farm cats continue to thrive, and studies have shown their effectiveness decisively; one group of Californian farm cats eliminated nearly 90 per cent of the mice in a 35-acre area. But the worldwide spread of rabies and the replacement of wooden ships with steel, making rats a rarity on ships, have doomed the ship's cat to steady decline. A similar decline has occurred in the cats on the payroll of public buildings, many of whom used to receive an official stipend for their duties. One group of studies have in recent years answered a question that has long been argued: whether feeding working cats reduces their efficiency as hunters. The answer is no. In fact, cats that are fed are more dependable because they remain where they are rather than wandering off.

Of course, there is one group of working cats whose skills are very different. These are the acting cats, whose earnings in films and particularly in advertising – mainly selling cat-food to other cats, or rather their owners – can be enormous. A top cat can earn £75 (over $150) a day, plus its keep. One enterprising American trainer keeps 100 cats, every one a star, on his 'farm'. Alley cats often make the best actors, it seems; highly bred animals may be too nervous. Of course, their less fortunate cousins 'work' in medical laboratories or may even be shot into space, but most working cats achieve fame or at least warm appreciation for simply doing what comes naturally – whether it is performing (when they choose) or catching mice.

Keeping an exotic cat

Exotic cats are wild species that can be kept as 'pets'; they are, at most, tamed rather than domesticated. Among the most popular are ocelots and margays, though many others have shown some adaptability to being kept as companion animals, including pumas, jaguars, leopards, bobcats, jungle cats, lynxes, jaguarondis and servals (see pp 12–15). The cheetah – which, like the dog, can be trained as a hunter to run down game – has been kept by people in some parts of the world since ancient times. Other lesser-known species, such as the sand cat of North Africa and Arabia, have become relatively tame through centuries of contact with local peoples.

The ethics of ownership
The beauty of these felines is undeniable, but the ethics of keeping such cats is more open to discussion. Although it is true that many wild cats become very tame and remain affectionate for all their lives, some will revert to wildness as they get older, becoming unpredictable and unsafe as household pets. Then the alternatives are to send them to a zoo, to have them destroyed or to let them live the rest of their lives in restrictive captivity, being neither totally tame nor wild.

Because of their natural instincts and inbred wildness it can be argued that we have no right to keep such animals merely for the sake of owning an unusual or different pet. And if, as is often the case, the capture of young wild cats involves the slaughter of their mother, such ownership can exacerbate the rarity of endangered species. On the other hand, the very fact that many exotic cats are in danger of extinction can be seen as justification for keeping them in captivity, so long as they are in breeding pairs, to help conservation of the species.

It is, however, less easy to justify enforcing domestication of such cats by making them more adaptable to the human way of life through surgical alteration. Declawing (see p 157) may be carried out because the cats are often too destructive in the home and use their claws a great deal even in play. The canine teeth may be removed for similar reasons; this is a particularly unpleasant operation because the teeth are firmly rooted and there is a danger of breaking the jaw-bone. Neutering (see p 156) is usually undertaken as the most practicable way of reducing the smell of exotic cats – which can be particularly overpowering in the male – but completely nullifies the conservation argument.

Acquiring an exotic cat
With many exotic cats now listed as endangered, it is becoming increasingly difficult and expensive to obtain and keep them as pets. In many countries there are laws restricting the importation of certain species, and the prospective owner is likely to need an official licence to import and keep the animal, entailing strict health and safety regulations. It is essential to find out what such regulations entail before trying to acquire an exotic cat. Apart from official sources, there are specialist clubs in some countries who can give advice, while someone with a serious purpose may find co-operation at a local zoo.

For both practical and ethical reasons, it is most satisfactory, though difficult, to buy a zoo–bred or privately–bred cat; having been reared in captivity, this is more likely to be suitable as a pet than one captured in the wild. A local exotic cat club may be able to help with acquisition. Otherwise, in some countries certain species can be ordered and purchased through reputable animal dealers. Costs are often very high – typically tens or even hundreds of times the cost of a good–quality pedigree domestic cat –

Hand-rearing an exotic cat such as the six-week-old mountain lion cub **above** is a difficult task sometimes made necessary by the method of capture, which may involve slaughter of the mother. It should be attempted only by an experienced person. As with domestic cats, an alternative is to find a foster mother. The serval kitten **left** has been adopted by a blue Burmese queen. Care must be taken, however, as exotic cats are never to be completely trusted.

Play is vital for captive exotic cats to obtain adequate exercise. Toys must, above all, be indestructible. Those made of hard wood, nylon or tough rubber **left** are particularly suitable. If the animal spends much of its life in a cage, the owner should make a point of playing with it as often as possible.

and because of the many procedures and transactions involved in bringing the cat from the wild to its eventual home it may take months to arrive. Imported cats may then have to undergo a period of quarantine as an insurance against the spread of rabies and other diseases (see p 161).

In choosing a cat, find out as much as possible about your intended species in advance, since temperaments, habits and needs do differ. One sex really has little advantage over the other, although male cats are sometimes said to favour a female owner and vice-versa. Males are likely to spray, and although neutering may reduce

the strong odour it may well not eliminate the habit completely.

A reliable dealer or breeder should agree to a veterinary examination as a condition of sale; the exotic cat is prone to many illnesses and parasites in its natural environment, and to more still when out of it. It is particularly important to ensure that it has been vaccinated against feline infectious enteritis (see p 192), since this attacks exotic cats just as much as domestic ones. Depending on local laws, rabies and certain other vaccinations may also be required, and the vet may recommend immunization against respiratory virus infections (cat flu).

The owner's special responsibilities

Exotic felines require specialized veterinary care; they are not ordinary cats. One of the most important considerations in buying an exotic cat, therefore, is that there should be, within easy reach, a vet who is experienced in and equipped to deal with its ailments and injuries. Again, a local zoo or club may be able to help.

Another important point to remember is that – for its own safety and that of the general public (see p169) – an exotic cat is likely to have to be confined for much of its life to quarters that are properly designed and sturdily constructed. Even within the home it is unlikely that the cat can be given a free run because of its destructive instincts. At the same time it will need a considerable amount of exercise.

Walking on a leash does not really exercise and develop the cat's muscles sufficiently and is likely to pose problems in public places. The confined cat, however, derives a great deal of exercise through play. But toys must be selected very carefully; most are ultimately destructive, and as a result small pieces of wire, rubber, plastic and wood may be swallowed, with very serious consequences. Balls made of smooth hardwood or hard rubber can be used, so long as they are too large to be swallowed. Old tyres make much appreciated swings but must be removed if the cat starts tearing them apart. Above all, design the quarters to allow ample opportunity for climbing and jumping.

Like its domestic counterpart, the exotic cat will need food and water dishes, a high-sided litter tray and a bed or nesting box, but only those made of chew-proof material are suitable. A strong carrying box or cage is essential when taking the cat anywhere. One made of heavy-gauge wire with a thick wooden base is suitable for the larger cats, whilst fibre-glass carriers like those for domestic cats are strong enough for smaller species. Transparent sides or tops are not recommended, as a nervous cat may easily be upset by curious passers-by. An additional and indispensible item of equipment is the squeeze box or restraint cage, for this is the most satisfactory way of handling an uncooperative and otherwise uncontrollable exotic cat.

Keeping an exotic cat as a pet is time-consuming and costly – a 14kg (30lb) ocelot, for example, needs up to 1kg (2lb) of meat per day – and requires a great deal of patience. The domestic cat adapted through centuries of selective breeding to true domestication, and although exotic felines can be tamed they may, because of their inherent wildness and unpredictability, never be completely trustworthy as household pets. On the other hand, the patient, skilled and lucky owner may be able to establish a rewarding relationship based on mutual respect.

An outdoor cage makes the best quarters in a mild climate. It must be securely enclosed and roofed – like an outdoor cattery (see p162) but with materials in proportion to the cat's strength. A concrete floor is easiest to clean and protects against soil-borne parasites, but an area of grass provides a more natural environment. Tree stumps, branches and ladders make climbing apparatus for arboreal species such as ocelots and margays. Some cats, including the ocelot, love to play in water, but this must be changed often as many cats will urinate into it. If the cat's sleeping quarters are also outdoors, they must shelter it from wind and rain. Provide cold-weather heating by an infra-red dull emitter. The sleeping box should be raised off the ground and insulated.

An indoor cage should be spacious and high enough for climbing and jumping. It must be easy to clean and totally escape-proof. There should be a secluded sleeping area, particularly for nocturnal species. As exotic cats tend to spray when urinating, a litter tray with three sides 60cm (2ft) high will help to keep the cage clean. Indoors or out, the structure and fittings must be unchewable.

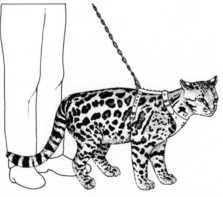

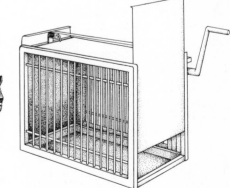

A harness and leash are used to control rather than exercise an exotic cat. A twin-loop harness (see p159) can be used, but a martingale type **above** is preferable because it is escape-proof. Made of strong leather, it consists of a neck loop and a belly loop. These are linked by both a back strap and a martingale strap (with buckle fastening) running under the belly between the forelegs. The leash clip is positioned where the back strap and belly loop meet; it must be self-closing and escape-proof. A chain leash of suitable weight should be used – not one of leather or plastic, which can be chewed through – ideally fitted with a leather wrist strap.

A restraint cage or squeeze box **above right** allows a vet to examine a frightened and unmanageable exotic cat with the minimum of delay and distress to the animal. The cage can also serve as a carrier. Made of aluminium and stainless steel, there are solid or barred doors at both ends. One side is adjustable and can be pushed towards the other side on a ratchet to restrict the cat's movement. The bars can be slid up and removed one by one, giving access to any part of the body. Some cages also have an adjustable top, which can be pushed towards the floor, allowing two-way restraint.

Cats and the law

Few people, in the first joy of acquiring a cat, give any thought to the remarkable bundle of legal rights and duties that come with it. Yet an amazing amount of law – much of it not specifically designed for cats, but nevertheless encompassing them – applies to cats and their owners. In many cases, this extends to the keeper of a cat – the person who looks after it – whether or not this is the legal owner. Another whole body of law governs how cats should be treated by people in general, by the veterinary profession and by officialdom.

Most of these laws apply to all domesticated cats, whether they have homes or are strays. Exotic cats kept in captivity are in a different position in some respects and are governed by special laws, whereas feral cats (see p 165) are regarded equivocally. For example, in Scotland they are legally vermin and may be treated as such – to the extent of being poisoned – whereas American laws against cruelty forbid poisoning.

This illustrates the fact that law is far from universal; it varies from country to country, from state to state, even in some cases from one community to the next. This article is based mainly on English and American law, but attempts as far as possible to discuss the law relating to cats in general terms, using examples where appropriate. Therefore, even though broadly similar laws often exist in different places, if you have a specific legal problem you should turn to specialized literature or to the actual legislation applying where you live. Of course, in a serious situation there is no substitute for professional legal advice.

Buying and selling
Cats can be bought and sold in the same way as any other goods, and the transaction – whether verbal or written – will carry the same rights and obligations in law. This law is, however, often complex, and you should seek advice from a lawyer or a consumer advisory organization if you feel aggrieved.

Depending on the consumer protection laws that apply, there may be certain implied warranties and legal protection if you buy from a breeder or pet shop. But there is usually very little protection if the seller is a private individual selling just the occasional litter. The key is whether or not the person who sells the cat is in the business of selling or breeding cats. Of course, there is often scope for argument as to whether the seller is 'in business' or whether breeding is merely incidental to keeping a cat or two, but in the latter case, unless there is a clear agreement, you must generally take the cat as you find it. Any cat sold by a breeder, however, should normally comply with the breeder's description of it – for example, as to age, sex, pedigree and so on – and if it does not you may be able to cancel the transaction, or claim compensa-

tion, or both. (A misleading statement made in the course of business may also be a criminal offence.)

Similarly, there is usually an implied warranty that the cat is in a fit state to be sold – in American law, the phrase is 'of merchantable quality' – and this normally encompasses its health and freedom from physical defects unless the cat was obviously ill or deformed at the time of purchase and you accepted it anyway. This means that illness developing soon after purchase – so soon that the disease must have been present when you bought the cat – is also usually grounds for compensation or cancellation. In some places, including the United States, such rights cannot be taken away, even if you agree in writing to waive them, unless it can be shown that consent to waive these rights was 'knowing and informed'. But elsewhere you may find that a written 'guarantee' provided by an unscrupulous breeder may take away some of your legal rights.

In spite of this, and provided you clearly understand the meaning of any written document, it is important, in order to minimize potential disputes, to put in writing any transaction involving a valuable cat, special requirements or complicated terms. This is particularly true of the sale of a cat on so-called 'breeding terms'. Here the price is not money, but the right of the seller to choose one or more kittens borne by the cat sold. Such agreements probably lead to more legal disputes over cats than any other, and you should be quite sure that you fully understand the terms before agreeing to them. Such conditions as the choice of stud, the number of kittens to be taken and the responsibility for the cat's health and safety should be set down clearly, preferably by a lawyer, and the many pitfalls (including perhaps death, escape or failure to breed within a given time) foreseen and provided for.

Similar arguments can arise when a kitten is sold on condition that it is neutered (in some cases with a 'pet quality' kitten, a breeder may refuse to hand over the pedigree certificate until proof of neutering is supplied) or with restrictions on breeding outside the specific breed to which the cat belongs. Many vets and lawyers advise owners not to enter into conditional purchases of this kind, but if you do so you should be aware that the agreement constitutes a legal contract that the breeder can normally enforce in the courts.

Rights of ownership
Since a cat can be owned, so interference with the rights of ownership – such as theft or injury – will often amount to a criminal offence. If the offender is caught and convicted – and this, it must be admitted, is rare – the court may be able to order the return of the cat or compensation to be paid.

Otherwise, the owner can sue in the civil courts for its return and/or compensation. If the thief should sell the cat, the true owner can still recover it within a certain time (this limit varies from state to state).

The liability for compensation may also exist if a cat is killed or injured in a street accident. This is in spite of the fact that, in some states, cats are treated differently from dogs when it comes to such accidents. Drivers are often obliged to report any accident involving a dog, but may not need to do so in the case of a cat. Traditionally, if an animal has no market value, its owner cannot sue for harm done to it. But a few states now recognize that a cat's value to its owner can have nothing to do with dollars and cents. Deliberate injury may also be a crime (see below).

If a cat is injured in an accident, the owner should be found, if possible, to authorize veterinary treatment. Failing this, emergency first aid may be given or, if necessary, the cat destroyed, since failure to prevent suffering could be construed as cruelty. It would be difficult for the cat's owner to sustain a claim for damages for unauthorized interference with the cat in such a situation, so long as the treatment was reasonable and all due care was taken.

Stray cats usually continue to belong, in law, to their owner even if they appear lost or abandoned. If you find a stray, you should make all reasonable inquiries for its owner before adopting it; otherwise you could be guilty of theft. In spite of this precaution someone who can prove ownership can reclaim the cat (again within a limited period). The law also gives prior claim to the person on whose land the cat was found over the actual finder. If you do not want a stray cat, you can use reasonable means, short of harming it, to remove it from your property, but as already mentioned it usually cannot be treated as vermin. Of course, there may be local provisions for disposing of strays through animal pounds and so on, but again you may be risking accusations of theft if the owner turns up to claim his or her animal.

From time to time, cats make headlines on receiving bequests from doting owners. Under most legal systems, a cat cannot itself own property or receive a gift in its own right. But a gift can be made – either during the donor's lifetime or in a will – for the benefit of a cat during its lifetime. To be sure of satisfying legal technicalities, such a bequest or trust should be drawn up by a lawyer. Of course, it is always possible to give or bequeath money or property to a cat charity or to found a new such charity – for example, to set up a home for stray cats – but again it is best to obtain legal advice.

Responsibilities of ownership
The owner or keeper of a cat – or of any other animal, for that matter – has certain duties in civil and criminal law. The

question of cruelty and the special responsibilities of keeping an exotic cat are discussed separately below, and in other respects controls over keeping cats are often much less strict – and less strictly enforced – than in the case of dogs. For example, although dog licensing is very common, not many places require cats to be licensed – and in those that do, very many people fail to comply. (This is not to say that licensing might not be a good way of financing animal pounds to deal with strays, which are a serious problem in many places.)

In the United States, a landlord has the legal right to refuse to rent on any but his or her own terms regarding pets. In some cases a standard 'no pet' clause in a lease may be legally ineffective, but apartment renters would do well to negotiate these clauses with the landlord before signing a lease.

Controls on cats' freedom to roam outdoors are regarded rather more equivocally. In many North American cities and in France, among other places, the law requires owners to keep cats indoors or allow them out only on a leash. This, many people feel, has a sound basis in public health (France, for example, has an increasing rabies problem), but just as many others vehemently defend cats' rights to a natural lifestyle – and certainly such restrictions are widely ignored. Rather less rational are local laws that try to put a curfew on cats, or stop them caterwauling or killing birds (in the last case by sometimes requiring cats to wear a bell around their neck). In many places, 'poop' laws against the fouling of public places by dogs also apply to cats, but here cats' natural fastidiousness tends to keep them (and their owners) out of trouble.

Most people – cat lovers and others – would agree that the most important laws controlling cats and their owners are those concerned with vaccination against rabies (where applicable; see p206), health checks and quarantine of cats crossing frontiers (see p161) and other public health matters, including the control of strays and feral cats (see p165). Although there is international liaison on some of these matters, regulations vary widely, and they can affect re-entry into the United States as well as travel abroad. For detailed information on those that apply in your area consult a lawyer, vet or public health official.

In civil law, the obligations of a cat owner or keeper can be enforced by a court action claiming compensation (damages) for harm done or an order (injunction) to prevent recurrence of the infringement, in just the same way as a cat owner can seek redress for infringements of the rights of ownership. These duties deal mainly with responsibility for death, injury or damage caused by a cat. It is widely known, for example, that under most legal systems a cat owner is not responsible if the cat strays onto someone else's property without permission; but liability for damage caused by the cat during its trespassing is a more complicated issue, governed by varying local laws.

In any case, this does not exonerate the owner for actions that are covered by laws other than those of trespass. For example, if injury or damage occurs through the owner's negligence – for example, if the cat causes an accident that the owner should have foreseen yet took no steps to prevent – then there will be a liability. In places where the criminal law restricts the rights of cats to wander outdoors, this may also restrict owners' rights to wash their hands of their cats' actions. In English law there is a provision that a person who 'accumulates' cats on his or her property is responsible for any harm they may do if they escape, even if not liable under trespass or negligence. And an owner can also be liable for a 'nuisance' – for example, excessive noise or smell – that interferes substantially with the lives of neighbours.

Domestic cats (but not exotic ones) are generally in the same position as dogs if they attack and bite or scratch someone: they are normally 'allowed their first bite', the owner being liable only if the cat is already known to attack people – or at least has done so on a previous occasion. A notice saying 'Beware of vicious cat' or some such is little or no protection, and certainly applies only within the property to which it is attached. But if a cat is normally good-natured the owner is not liable if it suddenly attacks someone; nor is there liability if the attack was provoked.

Cat health and welfare
Most countries and states have laws that forbid cruelty to cats and other animals, and regulate how and by whom they may be given veterinary treatment. However, the exact provisions of these laws vary widely, and the enforcement of cruelty laws is largely left to voluntary animal welfare organizations.

At one extreme are laws, like England's, that forbid both the outright infliction of injury and also the failure to give a cat proper care or doing anything to cause it unnecessary suffering; among specific provisions are prohibitions on poisoning, trapping, abandoning or, without a licence, performing experiments on cats. At the other extreme, several American states prohibit only 'willful' or 'unnecessary' cruelty, and in some it is not a crime to abandon an animal. Laws often control the training and display of performing animals, including cats, but in some places there is no legal obligation even to feed, water and provide shelter for a pet. In others, however, a third party may intervene to provide food and water for a neglected animal.

In most advanced countries today the only people permitted to give veterinary treatment – including diagnosis, surgery and giving advice based on diagnosis – are, in general, qualified veterinarians or veterinary surgeons, or other licensed practitioners. The licensing authority – usually a state board in the United States – has legal disciplinary powers, but vets and others are also controlled by specific laws. Examples are laws concerning the dispensing and use of medicines, those requiring that all but certain minor operations be carried out under anaesthesia, and those giving powers to the authorities in the case of an outbreak of a disease transmissible to humans (such as rabies and certain forms of food poisoning).

There are a few exceptions to laws forbidding unqualified or unlicensed people – however knowledgeable – to treat a cat. For example, it is generally permissible for anyone to give first aid treatment in an emergency, and in Britain and some other countries a cat owner is allowed to treat his or her own cat.

Cats as business
Running a breeding or boarding cattery may entail special legal controls as well as the normal business problems of tax, employment and similar laws. Building permits may be needed for constructing or adapting buildings, and licences obtained for premises where cats are to be boarded, quarantined or sold. The proprietor must ensure that the cattery is reasonably safe and that the cats are properly cared for. A visitor who suffers injury, or an owner whose cat is killed, injured, lost or stolen as a result of the proprietor's negligence, can generally sue for damages. The cattery's conditions of trade may exclude or purport to exclude such liability, but in many places (including the United States) such exclusions are invalid unless it is clear that consent to the exclusions was knowing and informed. If a cat owner fails to collect a cat boarded at a cattery, the proprietor ultimately may have the right, subject to certain legal conditions, to sell or dispose of it.

Exotic cats
Any cat other than a domestic cat – for example, an ocelot, margay, lynx or true wild cat (see pp14 and 166) – is treated in law like many other species of dangerous wild animal, sometimes requiring a special licence if you want to keep it, and in some cases subject to special import and export controls for the protection of endangered species. The owner or keeper of an exotic cat is generally responsible for any harm it does – whether or not there is any prior indication that it may cause such harm – and is also liable for any trespass it may commit, unlike in the case of a domestic cat. If you want to keep such a wild cat, you would be well advised to go thoroughly into the legal problems first.

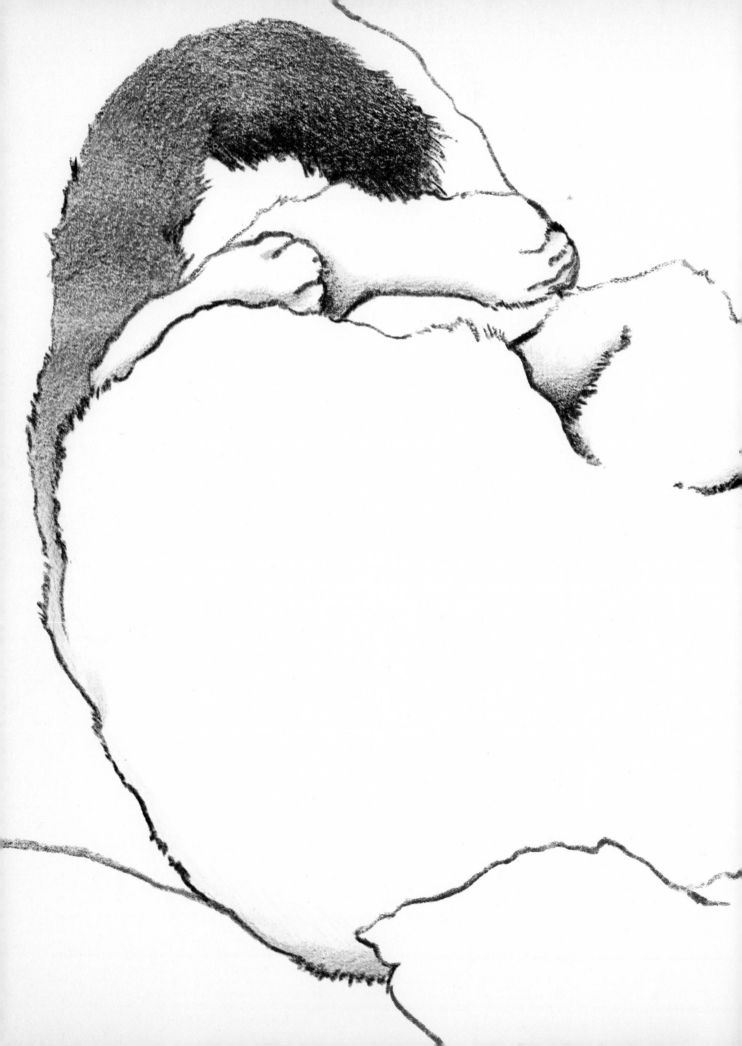

Chapter 4
YOUR CAT'S
HEALTH

Keeping your cat healthy

Although cats are generally regarded as tough, resilient and more resistant to illness than many other animals, they are under constant challenge from disease organisms of all kinds that abound even in 'clean' surroundings. Like other animals, they are also liable to sustain physical harm through fighting, falls, poisoning and other accidents. And when under stress – which can have a wide range of causes, from cold, travel and the administration of certain drugs to being in 'heat' and kittening – cats are less resistant to infection.

However, there is a great deal the owner can do to lessen the chance of a pet succumbing to illness or accident by taking some commonsense precautions. A cat's different habits and needs have to be taken into account, of course, but there is no difference in principle between cats and people in this respect. If you extend and adapt the normal measures you would take for keeping yourself and your family healthy to your cat, it should live a happy, healthy life. However, always be alert to the signs of possible trouble – the articles later in this chapter will help you recognize them – and be ready to seek prompt veterinary advice whenever necessary.

Everyday care

A sensible, well balanced diet (see p 148) is a fundamental need that will prevent many ailments, and is particularly vital in the growing kitten and the lactating queen. A second basic precaution that many people, particularly in North America, advocate is to keep your cat indoors, or at least to allow it out only under close supervision. This, the proponents claim, drastically cuts the risk of accidents and disease and is particularly necessary for city cats. Few British cat lovers may accept the necessity for this, however, except in the case of valuable pedigree breeding stock, suggesting that cats are much more robust creatures than they are given credit for. The question is discussed more fully on page 158, but there is general agreement that a cat should be kept indoors when it appears ill, to ensure a constant environmental temperature.

Cleanliness of the cat and its surroundings and equipment is an elementary precaution. For human as well as feline health, the litter tray should be cleaned daily or whenever soiled (see p 145) and food dishes should never be left for long, full or empty, where flies or other insects can reach and contaminate them. Regular grooming (see p 154) not only keeps the cat's coat clean, healthy and attractive but also enables you to look for any signs of parasites or skin disease. You should at the same time check ears, eyes, mouth and claws, together with the anal/genital area.

Remember that a visit to a cat show or boarding establishment, where there are many other cats, inevitably exposes a cat to

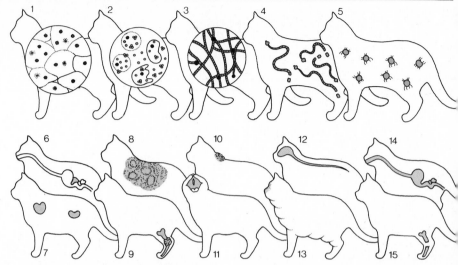

Causes of ill-health in cats are basically the same as in people even though the precise diseases may differ. There are two fundamental types of disease: infectious and non-infectious. Infectious diseases **top** (which may or may not also be contagious, or 'catching') are often caused by micro-organisms (germs) such as viruses **1** (as in many of the most serious feline diseases), bacteria **2** (as in an abscess, an example of a non-contagious infection) and microscopic fungi **3** (as in ringworm). Other transmissible disease organisms include internal animal parasites **4** such as worms, and external parasites **5** such as mites.

Non-infectious diseases **above** (which are also non-contagious) may be caused by hormonal disorders such as diabetes **6**, malfunction of an organ such as the heart or kidneys **7**, an allergy – especially of the skin **8** – improper nutrition (as in vitamin deficiency or its opposite, hypervitaminosis **9**), certain tumours **10** (though other forms of cancer in cats can be caused by viruses), congenital (inborn) defects such as a cleft palate **11**, psychological disorders **12**, and degeneration due to old age **13**. Although not usually regarded as diseases, poisoning **14** and accidents **15** come into the non-infectious category.

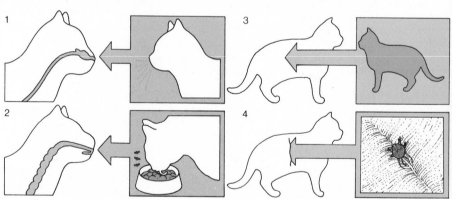

Disease transmission takes various routes.
1 Viruses in particular spread through sneezes, airborne droplets entering the lungs. **2** Food, drink or utensils contaminated – directly or via insects – with a diseased animal's faeces, urine, vomit, saliva or pus can infect via the stomach; cats may also eat disease-carrying insects or prey. **3** Direct contact without ingestion or inhalation spreads some diseases. **4** Insect or other bites are another route.

a higher than normal risk of contracting all kinds of disorders – and breeding cats are similarly exposed. Even with an apparently healthy cat it is wise to have a general veterinary check-up once a year; at the same time it can be given its booster vaccinations.

Vaccinations

The most important and valuable preventive medication for any cat is vaccination. Vaccines are available for several of the most dangerous infectious cat diseases – notably feline infectious enteritis (also called panleukopaenia or FIE), respiratory virus infections (commonly known, particularly in Britain, as cat flu) and rabies – and pharmaceutical laboratories are working to produce others, such as a feline leukaemia virus (FeLV) vaccine. Your cat should be vaccinated against all possible diseases with which it may come into contact – certainly rabies in those countries where it occurs (although routine rabies vaccination may be forbidden elsewhere), and FIE and

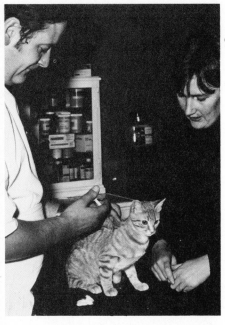

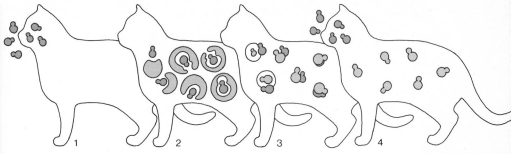

How immunity works When disease organisms such as bacteria or viruses enter the cat's body **1**, two types of white blood cell move into action. **2** Phagocytes attack and ingest the invading organisms, while **3** lymphocytes produce antibodies that make the organisms harmless. This latter process takes some time because the lymphocytes have to 'learn' how to make the specific antibodies needed. If the same disease organisms later attack the cat again **4**, some antibodies may remain in the bloodstream to neutralize them, while the lymphocytes 'remember' how to quickly produce more. This is why some diseases confer immunity from future attack. A kitten has some short-term immunity because it receives antibodies from its mother's colostrum (first milk; see p225), while injecting a serum containing antibodies has the same effect. However, vaccination **left** gives much longer-term immunity. This is because vaccines contain dead or weakened disease organisms which stimulate the lymphocytes to 'learn' how to produce antibodies without causing illness.

(when available) FeLV everywhere. Most vets also recommend cat flu vaccinations, especially for cats that will mix with others in a breeding or boarding cattery.

Generally, the risk and cost of vaccination are small compared with the health risk and cost of treatment if your cat becomes ill, so you should regard it as an insurance policy. Generally, kittens ought to be first vaccinated at the age of about two months (before then some immunity is acquired from the mother), and then receive regular boosters. Their frequency depends on the type and brand of vaccine, and your vet will advise you; it is commonly once a year.

Preventing the spread of disease
Any cat suffering from an infectious disease will obviously pose a threat to other cats it may encounter, and the vet will often advise isolation of the patient until it returns to normal health. Isolation is rarely possible or even useful in a household with several cats, because the disease will probably already have been transmitted to one or more feline contacts by the time the diagnosis is made. However, it is wise to restrict normally outdoor cats to the home, if only to prevent spread of the disease to neighbouring cats outside. This is particularly important with cat flu. But an understanding of how diseases are transmitted enables any owner to take commonsense precautions to limit the spread of disease – including the frequent cleaning and disinfection of litter trays and other equipment. (For suitable disinfectants for cats see page 178.)

All sizeable breeding and boarding establishments should have isolation facilities away from the main areas. Then any animal showing (or suspected of showing) signs of illness can be quickly removed and 'barrier-nursed' in an attempt to minimize the spread (see p178). In a few cases – notably rabies – any infected cat must be strictly quarantined for observation (as must any feline or canine contacts), and all human contacts vaccinated (see p206). Some vets and breeders have also advocated destroying cats suffering from (or shown to be carrying) feline leukaemia, since they pose a threat to any contacts. Others, however, feel that preventing carriers coming into prolonged contact with healthy cats – especially breeding stock – is sufficient precaution. Certainly, many vets advocate routine testing for the leukaemia virus, especially in breeding cats (see p204).

Preventing accidents
Although the indoor cat undoubtedly runs some risks (see p158), traumatic injuries are more frequent in cats allowed out. There is little the owner can do to lessen the natural inquisitiveness that attracts cats onto window ledges and up trees in pursuit of anything from birds and squirrels to flies – often resulting in quite nasty falls. Although the cat has a legendary ability to fall safely (see p121), first aid and veterinary attention (see p181) are commonly needed.

Street accidents are also frequent feline emergencies, and one great advantage of neutering (see p156) is the effect of minimizing straying, particularly by males in search of queens. Also, most street accidents involving cats seem to occur at night, so it is wise not to allow your cat out after dark – or at least to supervise it during its late-night toilet outing. Cats are also subject to attack by a number of predators – notably dogs, foxes and, in North America, racoons – but such cases are quite rare, probably because cats can find safety by climbing high: another life-saving aspect of their great agility and natural suppleness.

CATS AND HUMAN HEALTH
Feline health is not merely a problem for cats. People can and do catch diseases from their pets, though this is rare and cats are – probably with some justice – blamed less in this respect than dogs. Such diseases transmitted from animals to people are called zoonoses (pronounced zoo-o-no-seas), and where they pose a particular threat, warnings are given in the individual articles later in this chapter.

However, the most important cat zoonoses include rabies where it occurs (see p206), the fungal skin disease ringworm (p189), septic wounds resulting from bites (p183), and certain parasites, especially fleas (p186). Cat bites or scratches may also transmit a virus or similar organism that causes fever and swollen lymph nodes ('glands'); known as cat-scratch fever, this is normally mild, but all wounds inflicted by cats should be cleaned very thoroughly.

Some people have been worried by reports of cats transmitting toxoplasmosis (a disease caused by a tiny single-celled animal; see p191) to humans, resulting in miscarriage by pregnant women or abnormalities in their babies. While this may happen, the risk is low and it is important to realize that very many other animals can also transmit the disease, including pig and lamb meat. Nevertheless, pregnant women should probably not clean the cat's litter tray, since faeces may be a source of infection. Of course, covering children's sand pits against contamination is a sensible general precaution.

Diagnosing feline ailments

Any departure from good health is normally accompanied by one or more observable changes in a cat's bodily activities or responses. Such changes are known as signs and symptoms; being highly variable, it requires training and expertise to detect many of them, and even more to interpret them and diagnose their cause. This is the job of the vet. However, the observant owner is a great asset in the early detection of illness in a pet cat and can provide many clues that help the vet make a quick diagnosis.

Knowing the cat well, the owner is ideally placed to observe any departure from normal behaviour. But it should always be remembered that diagnosis is often difficult to reach because of the range of combinations of symptoms – which may vary dramatically from one patient to another. For this reason, the chart accompanying this article is emphatically not intended as a do-it-yourself diagnostic aid, except possibly as a last resort if you have no access to veterinary help. It is rather intended to help you to understand the kind of symptoms the vet will look for – and thus indicates the changes you may yourself observe and report to the vet.

General signs of illness

Symptoms of illness in the cat vary according to the temperament of the patient, the type of disease and the stage this has reached, but generally speaking an ailing cat is easily spotted. Often it loses – either partially or totally – its appetite, and will lie around listlessly or sit hunched up, very commonly with a dull look to the eyes and a fluffing up or 'spiking' of the coat. Such cats may well resent handling and will not be tempted to play. They may hide themselves away in a dark place; outdoors, they may occasionally excavate a hole in the soil in which they will lie. (These actions are the origin of the well-known idea that cats hide themselves away when about to die.)

The cat may drink more or less than usual, and in some cases will be seen to crouch over a water bowl or sink, making no attempt to drink but appearing absolutely miserable and dejected. The cat may show an abnormal preference for water as opposed to milk, or vice-versa; the significant thing is the change in habits. There is commonly an accompanying foul smell on the breath, and additional symptoms may be easily detectable – for example, sneezing, vomiting, diarrhoea, a discharge from the eyes and nose, partial covering of the eyes by the third eyelids, or 'haws' (see p110), and so on.

Specific health checks

Certain more detailed observations can be helpful to the vet. Breathing should first be observed from a distance. More important than the specific rate of breathing is whether the cat has any apparent difficulty in drawing its breaths – in which case the breathing will usually be rapid and shallow. The pulse rate also increases in many illnesses, while infections commonly cause a fever – often as high as 41°C (106°F). However, some conditions depress the body temperature well below the normal 38.6°C (101.5°F).

Bowel habits are also a matter of simple observation, though this may prove a problem if your cat prefers to find a hidden spot outdoors when emptying its bowels or bladder. However, simply placing a litter box indoors and confining the cat for 24 hours will usually allow you to observe whether faeces are passed and, if so, to check whether the cat has diarrhoea or the faeces contain signs of worm infestation (see p190). (However, some cats will voluntarily not defecate for some time if suddenly confined.) Also try to observe whether urine is passed easily or with difficulty, and whether it is the normal straw-colour or is blood-stained.

You should note carefully any signs of swelling of the abdomen or any other part of the body, and also any signs of pain. Depending on where the pain is, this may be accompanied by various symptoms – for

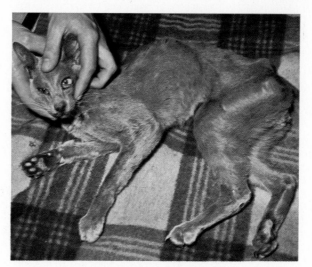

A sick cat may present a pathetic picture, lying or crouching listlessly and taking no interest in events around it. A common symptom in many conditions is protrusion of the third eyelids left; but it is conspicuously absent in others, and there is disagreement among vets as to its significance. It certainly occurs, but no one knows for sure why. In general, however, the owner can help the vet to come to a speedy and accurate diagnosis by noting and reporting any changes in appearance and behaviour.

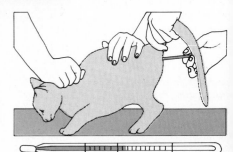

Measuring the pulse rate can be difficult. You may be able to observe the heart-beat by watching or feeling the chest. Otherwise use light fingertip pressure on the femoral artery, high on the inside of either hind leg above. The breathing rate can be found by observing the rise and fall of the chest (one rise plus one fall equals one breath). In both cases, take the measurement while the cat is lying quietly at rest. Count for 30 seconds and double the figure. The normal resting pulse rate is 110 to 140 beats per minute and the breathing rate 30 to 50.

Taking the cat's temperature is carried out rectally – via the anus. If possible, an assistant should restrain and comfort the resting cat while you take the temperature above right; otherwise, hold the standing or lying cat against your body with your elbow and forearm, the cat's head to the rear, and hold its tail.
Preferably use a rectal thermometer, which has a small round bulb; if this is not available, use a small-bulbed normal clinical thermometer. Shake it down and lubricate it with petroleum jelly, medicinal liquid paraffin

(mineral oil) or vegetable (cooking) oil. Insert it gently but firmly into the anus, pushing straight towards the animal's head and slightly rotating the thermometer if necessary to overcome the resistance of the sphincter muscle. About one-third of the thermometer should be inserted, then gently held to one side so that the bulb rests against the wall of the rectum. Leave the thermometer in place for at least a minute. Then remove it, wipe it and read it. The cat's 'normal' temperature is about 38.6°C (101.5°F), but 39.2°C (102.5°F) is not unusual.

example, the cat may be lame on one leg and may limp or even carry the leg, which may be sore to the touch. Similarly, it is possible to pinpoint pain along the back or the abdomen by watching carefully and by feeling with a light touch. (Be very gentle if you suspect pain, as the cat may react violently to a clumsy touch.)

Specialized tests and false signs
When first examining a patient, the vet will carry out observations of this type, and possibly more. In some cases the particular combination of symptoms and the history of the case recounted by the owner will point to a clear cause. In others, just as in human medicine, further ancillary tests may be needed – such as X-rays, blood tests, urine or faecal analyses, microscopic examination of blood or other tissues, and so on – before treatment can begin.

However, for every symptom there is not necessarily a specific disease, and one of the commonest problems – diarrhoea – is often encountered in otherwise perfectly healthy cats; this may be caused purely by an allergic or idiosyncratic reaction to one item in the diet – commonly milk. Again, refusal to eat may be simply a psychological reaction to a change of routine or environ-ment. As with humans, completely healthy cats may sneeze if they breathe in dust, so do not jump to the conclusion that every snuffle is a sign of respiratory virus in-fection (cat flu).

It is a well-known failing of books on human medicine that they prompt the reader to believe that some serious ailment is present when there may well be a simple and non-pathological answer. The same is true of veterinary medicine, so treat the descriptions of symptoms here and else-where in this chapter with caution. Be aware of possible problems that can afflict your cat, but try to be objective.

Making sense of symptoms represents a major part of veterinary training, so the layman should use this chart of symptoms often seen in major feline disorders with extreme caution. It inevitably represents a great simplification – the vet considers the overall clinical picture presented by a patient – and it can list only the most common conditions and symptoms. In the case of the former, many of those listed are general categories rather than specific diseases. Among the symptoms, note the qualifications such as 'apparent', 'sudden' and 'excessive'. The symptoms are 'rated' as follows:
Red: Major symptom that almost always occurs with this particular condition, and is highly significant.
Orange: Common symptom that usually occurs but is not decisive on its own.
Green: Variable symptom that may occur in some patients but not in others.
Grey: Not significant in this condition.
Page numbers are given where further information can be found, but remember that if you are in any doubt you should consult your vet.

CONDITION: Feline infectious enteritis (panleukopaenia; FIE) · Gastroenteritis (food poisoning) · Hairball · Rabies · Respiratory virus infection (cat flu; FCV, FVR, etc) · Feline infectious anaemia (FIA) · Feline leukaemia virus (FeLV) · Feline infectious peritonitis (FIP); pyothorax · Urolithiasis (cystitis, FUS) · Kidney disease · Heart disease · Heat stroke · Tumour (cancer) · Hernia · Dietary disorder · Roundworms · Tapeworms · Toxoplasmosis · Dental/mouth disorder · Conjunctivitis · Ear disorder · Fleas, other external parasites; fungal infection; etc · Abscess; bite wound · Haematoma · Trauma; fracture; dislocation; street accident; etc · Poisoning · Snakebite · Queen in heat ('calling') · Pregnancy · Gynaecological problem

SYMPTOM: Vomiting · Diarrhoea · Apparent constipation · Abnormal urination · Lack of appetite · Excessive thirst · Salivation and/or sneezing · Coughing and/or sneezing · Third eyelid showing · Eye discharge · Ear discharge · Nose discharge · Anal discharge · Genital discharge · Wound discharge · Dehydration · Wasting · Pallor of gums · Breathing difficulty · Unconsciousness · Paralysis · 'Sudden death' · Depressed temperature · Fever · Swollen abdomen · Swelling under skin · Skin irritation · Apparent pain · Lameness · Hair loss; skin lesions · Abnormal behaviour · No apparent symptoms · Shock · Page number to other cats · Danger to other cats · Danger to humans

192 193 194 206 197 204 204 193 203 203 204 184 208 194 195 190 191 191 196 201 202 186 182 183 180 185 183 131 220 228

175

Choosing and using a vet

For the new cat owner, or for one moving to a new home, selecting a veterinary adviser is one of the most basic and important decisions to be made. The vet – known properly in Britain as a veterinary surgeon, in North America as a veterinarian – may well be looking after the feline patient for 15 years or more. There are good vets and bad, and the right initial choice, followed by regular contact so that patient and vet get to know each other, will ensure a happy relationship and the best treatment, routine or emergency, whenever needed.

How to choose

You may learn of local vets by personal recommendation from friends, breeders or cat clubs, or by perusing lists maintained by animal welfare organizations, professional veterinary bodies or the police – or even by looking up a classified telephone directory. In most advanced countries today, vets must receive a university or similar training before being licensed to practise, but qualifications (and hence the letters after the name) vary. Veterinary training has progressed rapidly since World War II, and the experience of an older vet must be weighed against the more modern knowledge and techniques acquired by the recent graduate. There is a trend towards specialized study of particular types of animals. If not too far away, a cat specialist – or, second-best, a small-animal vet – is preferable over a general practitioner, although the latter should always be ready to refer any difficult cases to a second opinion.

Probably the prime requirement is that you should feel confidence in your vet, who should answer your questions clearly and explain matters in non-technical language to your satisfaction. Ancillary staff too should be helpful, and confident in their handling of both clients and patients. Most practices looking after small animals have extensive behind-the-scenes facilities, like a miniature human hospital, with an animal ward for resident cases, a small laboratory, a pharmacy, an operating room equipped with an anaesthetic machine, and also X-ray equipment, a sterilizer and so on. Such departments must of course be kept scrupulously clean, so entry is usually closed to all but the staff; the vet may allow you to see them by appointment, however. Reception and waiting areas should also be clean, and some practices have separate waiting rooms for cats where dogs are not allowed. If a vet does not have the facilities mentioned above, ask what alternative arrangements there are for hospital cases.

Of course, equipment must be paid for, so you may find that a vet with modern and extensive facilities charges more than one without. (Equally, do not be blinded by technology; it is the quality of treatment that matters.) In any case, it is wise and perfectly reasonable to inquire in advance as

IN AN EMERGENCY

Keep calm. Do not move the cat unless it is in further danger. Telephone your vet, explain as coherently as possible what is wrong, and follow his or her advice. If it is night-time or a weekend, and the phone is answered by a referral or answering service, you may be told to call another number. Remain calm and call the referred number.

If all this fails, try your local humane society, such as the RSPCA in Britain or the ASPCA in the United States, or the police. There is no point in putting your cat in the car and dashing off to the vet's premises or a clinic without checking first that they are manned and without asking for preliminary advice.

As a precaution, always keep a note of your vet's emergency number.

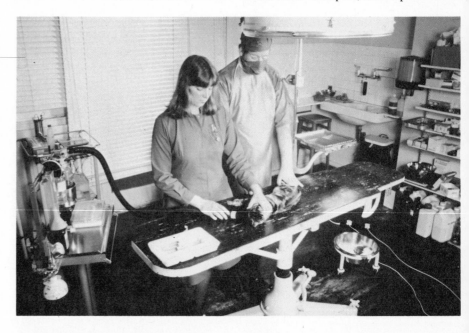

A modern veterinary practice may be equipped like a miniature hospital, with full facilities for investigating ailments, performing surgery and accommodating long-stay patients. If these are not all available on the premises, the vet should have arrangements for referral.

to the scale of fees charged. In many countries it is possible to insure against at least a proportion of veterinary fees, and most vets will be able to give you details. For those genuinely in need, an animal welfare organization may be prepared to pay for all or part of treatment. There are also charitable animal clinics in some places where a low fee or voluntary donation is requested, but you will inevitably not have the continuing relationship of a private vet. One vital final point to check is the system for dealing with emergencies; in Britain all

vets must provide a satisfactory 24-hour service, either direct or through a locum, but this is not true everywhere.

How to use

It is courteous and wise, though not usually essential, to register your cat with the chosen vet at or before the first visit (which will often consist of a general check-up and first vaccination of a kitten). If the vet uses an appointment system, be sure to make and keep appointments, to avoid wasting the vet's time and delaying other patients, but in any case keep a note of consultation hours. In almost every case, it is better to take the cat to the vet's premises, where specialized facilities for tests and treatment are available, than to ask for a house call, but if in doubt ask for advice by telephone.

A prime rule is to seek veterinary advice as soon as you notice that something is wrong. Have a good cat carrier (see p160) available for transport, and keep the cat in it until you are in the examining room. A good vet should not expect you to hand the cat over to ancillary staff except in such cases as routine neutering. Be ready – with written notes if necessary – to give the vet full information about the case.

On a rare occasion, you may be dissatisfied with your vet's treatment or advice; it is then perfectly reasonable to ask for a second opinion, and the vet will normally agree willingly. If necessary, you are within your rights to seek such an opinion yourself, though you should give the second vet the fullest details of the first consultation and you would of course normally be expected to pay the first vet's fees for the treatment to date. Happily, such conflicts are very unusual and most cat owners build up a constructive and trusting relationship with their veterinary adviser.

Surgery and postoperative care

As with a human patient, a cat may on occasion need surgery. The commonest surgical operations are neutering (see p 156) and the repair of wounds, but in some cases broken bones may have to be set, tumours, bladder stones or decayed teeth removed, or more extensive internal surgery performed. Because a cat, even if tranquil by nature, is liable to struggle during the operation, local anaesthetics are used for only the most minor operations such as suturing (stitching) a small wound. All others involve a general anaesthetic.

Preparation and anaesthesia

The vet's preliminary examination will show not only what surgery is needed, but also whether the cat is strong enough to undergo the operation. Except in an emergency, it will have to be starved of all food for at least 12 hours before surgery, to reduce the risk of vomiting during the operation. Before anaesthesia, a pre-

A surgical operation on a cat, here a routine spaying, begins with the administration of a general anaesthetic by injection **top left** or gas **opposite**, followed by expression of urine from the bladder and clipping of hair from the surgical site. Then the site is sterilized with antiseptic

medicant injection is commonly given to calm and sedate the cat, to dry up saliva and bronchial (lung) secretions, and to reduce the amount of anaesthetic needed.

The type of anaesthetic and the method by which it is given depend on the type of operation, the age and health of the patient and the vet's personal preferences. Commonly, an anaesthetic is injected into a leg vein or muscle; in a few seconds this produces unconsciousness which is maintained with gaseous anaesthetic. In other cases, a gas such as halothane mixed with oxygen is

given through a face mask from the start. For chest surgery and in some other cases, a tube may be inserted into the cat's trachea (windpipe), through which anaesthetic gas and oxygen are passed – if necessary, breathing being maintained artificially by machine or hand. Whatever the method, the patient's heart rate and breathing are constantly monitored.

The operation

The principle of veterinary surgery is the same as in human medicine; it is called aseptic surgery. The operating room and all its fittings are kept scrupulously clean, and all gowns, instruments, swabs and so on sterilized before use. This stops the transfer of germs into the animal's body. In most cases, the surgeon's first step is to clip hair from the operation site, and then clean the skin with a suitable antiseptic, thus removing another source of infection. Veterinary surgical techniques are also very

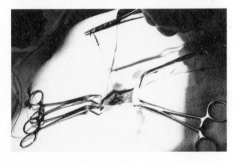

top right before an incision is made in the abdomen and both ovaries and the uterus are removed **lower left**. Finally, the incision is sutured (stitched) **lower right**, just as in human surgery, before the cat is taken to the recovery ward to regain consciousness.

like those of the human surgeon; bleeding must be kept to a minimum and incisions repaired with sutures (stitches). The length of an operation may vary from a few minutes to as much as five hours in the case of major internal surgery. An antibiotic injection is often finally given to reduce the risk of postoperative infection.

Postoperative care

Cats vary considerably in how long they take to regain full consciousness, even with the same anaesthetic, ranging from a few

minutes after gas to several hours after an injection. When partially conscious the cat may try to move but stumble as if drunk; it may also have spells of excitability, and strike at any approaching hand. For these reasons, the patient will normally be kept by the veterinary staff in a container or cage, lying on a blanket, until fully conscious. Only then, when the vet is confident that no dire consequences will arise, will it be allowed home. This may be later on the same day as a minor operation, or a day or more later in more serious cases.

If a cat remains unconscious for a longer period, the veterinary nurses will turn it every two hours or so to prevent the development of bedsores or a form of pneumonia due to fluid collecting in the lower lung. Another possible complication is surgical shock resulting from loss of body fluids or extensive tissue removal during the operation. This resembles the shock experienced by animals in street accidents and other severe traumas, and results in a weak fast pulse, shallow fast breathing, dilation of the pupils, and weakness or collapse. It may need to be controlled by the vet setting up a drip under the skin or directly into a vein.

When returning the patient to its owner's care, the veterinary staff should give advice on feeding and after-care (which will vary from case to case). Generally, the cat should be kept warm and quiet, and under observation, for at least 48 hours. It is best to allow it to use its own familiar sleeping place – whether box, basket or other place – but if it seems restless and struggling, it is wiser to restrain it in an enclosed container such as a carrier, with a soft towel for bedding and a luke-warm hot water bottle underneath. In any case, even a cat that is normally allowed out should be kept indoors. After major surgery, some restriction is needed for up to four weeks. Do not allow children to handle the cat, and try to keep it in a room where there are no tempting shelves or furniture for it to jump on to and tear its stitches.

It is perfectly normal for a cat to gently lick and clean an operation scar, but if necessary you should fit an Elizabethan collar (see p179) to prevent stitches being removed. If these are of the absorbable type, they will dissolve after 7 to 14 days; if not, a return visit to the vet for their removal will be necessary. This is in any case advisable for a check-up after all but the most trivial operation. But you should anyway keep a close watch on your pet and consult the vet if you notice any abnormal symptom – including a gaping or discharging incision, swelling in this area, fever or listlessness, refusal to eat, or a significant change in behaviour. Most feline surgical cases make a quick and complete recovery, but sharp observation will reduce the danger of any complications.

Nursing a sick cat

Cats make rather uncooperative patients. Their habit of fastidiously removing any 'foreign' material from their skin leads them to interfere with wounds and dressings. Their independent nature results in strenuous objections – using their supple bodies, loose skin, and sharp claws and teeth – to force-feeding or medication. And because of their instinct to hide when ill they must be confined where they can be observed. All this means that any seriously injured or ill cat – including one that is incontinent – is better nursed by professionals in an animal hospital. But for lesser ailments and during convalescence the owner can, under veterinary supervision, do all that is needed.

General care

The greatest problems arise when a cat that lives in a group or in contact with others has a contagious ('catching') disease. In principle, such a cat should be isolated and 'barrier-nursed'; this involves all handlers changing their outer clothing and washing their hands thoroughly after dealing with the patient and before handling other cats. It is advisable to use rubber gloves. In addition, with any cat suffering from a contagious disease, all bedding, food and water bowls and litter trays should be disinfected, using a non-toxic antiseptic (see below). All cat litter, excrement, soiled dressings and other waste should be burnt, sealed in plastic bags for garbage collection, or buried deeply in soil – preferably covered with garden lime or quicklime.

Never allow a sick cat outdoors unobserved, for it may hide away, but keep it in a warm and airy (but draught-free) room. Reasonable peace and quiet are needed, but do not shut it away from the

THE FELINE MEDICAL CHEST

The items suggested below are best reserved for the sole use of your cat or cats:
Antiseptic suitable for cats (see below)
Cotton bandages, 2.5 and 5 cm (1 and 2 in) wide
Crepe (elastic) bandage, 5 cm (2 in) wide
Elastic adhesive tape
Cotton wool (absorbent cotton)
Sterile pads or dressings
Curved, blunt-ended scissors
Blunt tweezers
Rectal (small-bulbed) clinical thermometer
Petroleum jelly
Medicinal liquid paraffin (mineral oil)
Hydrogen peroxide
Light kaolin or other anti-diarrhoeal (not chlorodyne or any other preparation containing morphine)
Antihistamine cream
Eye-dropper
Elizabethan collar

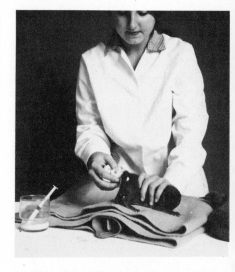

Looking after an ill cat mainly involves keeping it clean, warm and nourished; medical treatment should be under the vet's guidance.

people it knows. Soft bedding such as towelling, which can be easily laundered, will help make it comfortable. Placing the bedding in a tall-sided box will give protection from draughts and prevent a weak cat straying from warmth or injuring itself in some way. Except in hot weather, keep the cat warm with a safely positioned infra-red heater, fan heater or radiator, or by placing a luke-warm hot-water bottle or electric heating pad under the bedding. To avoid harmful temperature fluctuations, make sure that central heating is not programmed to switch off at night.

Grooming a sick cat is much the same as for any other (see p 154), but pay particular attention to eyes, ears, nose, mouth and the hair around the anal and urinary passages.

Wash these gently, using warm water or a very dilute safe antiseptic.

Many sick cats will not eat, and while going without solid food for a day or two does little harm, it is vital to prevent dehydration. You can give almost any fluid – small amounts of water, milk with added sugar, beef broth or milky baby cereal, for example. If the cat is very weak, you may need to give it fluids by dropper or syringe; however, cats do not take to force-feeding at all well, and it may be necessary in extreme cases for the vet to administer fluids by 'drip', via a hypodermic needle into a vein or under the skin. A cat that is not too weak can be given small quantities of solid food like a pill (see opposite).

Generally speaking, feed the invalid cat

DISINFECTANTS FOR CATS

Many items of cat equipment – but particularly litter trays, carrying containers and permanent quarters in catteries – need to be disinfected from time to time, especially if used by a cat that is ill.

Since the purpose of disinfectants is to kill viruses, bacteria and fungi, they are all to a greater or lesser extent toxic to living cells; a balance must be struck between their effectiveness against micro-organisms and their danger to people and pets. Unfortunately, many common disinfectants are extremely poisonous to cats, and should never be used on their equipment. Foremost among these dangerous disinfectants are those containing or derived from coal-tar or wood-tar (including pine oil) and the chemicals found in these, such as phenol (carbolic acid; also found in 'TCP' and other disinfectants), cresols (found in 'Jeyes Fluid', 'Lysol' and so on) and

chloroxylenols (found in 'Dettol'). Others to avoid include hexachlorophene, iodine and iodophors.

Commercial disinfectants are often not labelled with their ingredients, so for safety use only a preparation known to be harmless. In some circumstances, such as disinfecting the living quarters of cats infected with ringworm, formaldehyde (formalin) may be used in a concentration of 2 to 5% – that is, 25 to 60 ml of commercial formalin (containing 40% formaldehyde) to 5 litres of hot water (about 1 fl oz to 1 gallon).

Formaldehyde is a rather unpleasant disinfectant for general use, however, and a much better one is sodium hypochlorite, which is commonly used in dairies, as a bleach and for sterilizing baby-bottles. (It is found in such products as 'Milton', 'Clorox', 'Linco', 'Domestos', 'Chloros' and 'Chlorsan'.) For disinfecting floors, walls and equipment, dilute 150 ml of commercial dairy hypochlorite or bleach in

5 litres of hot water (¼ pint to 1 gallon). At half this strength it can be used to disinfect bedding, but bear in mind that it has a strong bleaching action. Other disinfectants safe for cats include quaternary ammonium compounds (in such products as 'Shield' and 'Roccal' and including cetrimide ['Savlon']) and dodecine ('Tego').

When using any disinfectant, remember that it works properly only when the surface to be disinfected is free from dirt and grease. Many disinfectants are also incompatible with soap or detergent, so thoroughly wash the surface or piece of equipment with soap or detergent and water, and rinse well with clean water, before applying the disinfectant. If possible, allow the disinfectant to work for about 15 minutes before wiping dry. Always make up a fresh solution, as disinfectant solutions deteriorate when left, and wear rubber gloves.

Force-feeding is a last resort, as cats are not co-operative patients, but if necessary liquid food can be given with a syringe.

whatever it will eat. After certain illnesses, such as respiratory virus infections (cat flu), its sense of smell may be impaired, and it may be tempted only by strong-smelling foods such as sardines, pilchards, tuna or liver. However, avoid rich meat, such as heart or liver, in any case involving vomiting or diarrhoea. In general, light foods such as fish (canned or fresh), eggs (hard-boiled or scrambled), white meats (such as veal, rabbit, chicken or tripe) and meaty baby foods are all acceptable. Fresh fish should be boiled or steamed, meat either raw and minced (so long as it is very fresh) or cooked and chopped, to taste.

Special treatment

The vet will give instructions and advice on any special measures that need to be taken. It is unlikely that you will need to change dressings since this gives the vet or nurse a chance to check progress. If you do have to apply bandages, however, be sure not to make them too loose (so that they fall off) or too tight (restricting circulation and causing swelling). Any medication needing an injection will be administered by the vet, but you may have to give medicine in liquid or tablet form. Be sure to follow the dosage instructions carefully, and seek advice if the cat vomits soon after taking a medication. If you are unsure of how to administer the medicine, even after referring to the illustrations here, ask for a demonstration.

The length of convalescence is highly variable. It may be as little as 24 to 48 hours for uncomplicated conditions such as an abscess, but with severe illnesses like respiratory virus infections (cat flu) the cat may take as long as a month to recover. Whatever the illness, however, warm, airy, sunny surroundings, nourishing foods – plus, of course, the right medication – all help to speed convalescence.

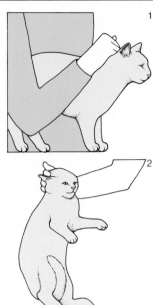

Restraining a cat is best accomplished with the least necessary force, but you must act confidently. Calm the cat first by stroking it. **top** In some cases you will need only to hold the cat's head with one hand while your forearm holds its body against your side. Or grip it by the scruff of the neck and use the other hand if necessary to restrain its legs. With a violently struggling cat, you can wrap its whole body and legs in a towel or blanket; alternatively, lifting it by the scruff **above** will normally immobilize it safely.

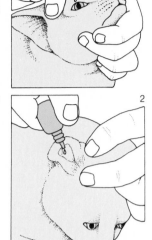

Eye and ear medications
With the cat firmly held, approach from behind and **top** open the eyelid with the thumb and forefinger of one hand. Apply the ointment directly to the cornea, making sure that only the ointment, not the tube, touches the front of the eye. Apply eye drops in a similar way. If necessary, clean the eyes first with moistened cotton wool.
above Administer drops into the ear while the cat is restrained and its head turned to one side; gently massage behind the ear to spread them.

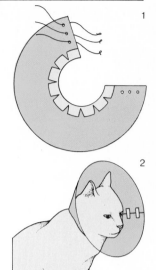

An Elizabethan collar can be uncomfortable and cruel but is sometimes advised to prevent a cat irritating a wound or dressing. **top** You can make one from heavy flexible cardboard cut into a circle 30 cm (12 in) across, with a 10 cm (4 in) hole cut from the centre. Also remove a one-quarter to one-third segment from the ring of cardboard and pad the inner edge. **above** Fit the collar by lacing or taping together the straight edges or by lacing it onto a normal collar. Make sure it is comfortable.

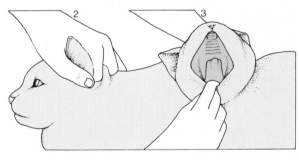

Giving a pill, restraint by an assistant is usually essential.
1 Grip the cat's head with one hand, your thumb and forefinger at the angle of the jaw. Tilt the head well back and press on the corners of the mouth to ease it open. Then, with the other hand, press down on the lower jaw and place or drop the pill as far back as the tongue as possible. Close the mouth and

hold it closed; stroke the cat's throat until it swallows, keeping its head tilted up. If you release the cat too soon it will spit out the pill.
An alternative method can be used by one person alone. Sit the cat on a table facing you and hold its head in one hand, gripping the ear with your thumb and the skin at the back of the head with your fingers. **3** Turn the head on its

axis – without raising it – until the nose points upwards. It is then easy to open the mouth with your other hand and drop in the pill. Again, keep the cat's mouth closed until it swallows the pill.
Coating the pill with butter may help to ensure swallowing, while those afraid of bites while placing a pill at the back of the cat's tongue can use a 'pill gun' **4**.

Accidents and first aid 1

Curiosity has killed or injured many a cat, and most owners will at some time or another have to deal with an accident or emergency -- and will come up against the problems involved. One of these is that, when in pain or frightened, a cat is not at all a co-operative patient, so that it is even more useful to have two people present when giving first aid than for more routine veterinary care. Also, the cat's habit of hiding itself away from all human contact when sick or injured means that it may be difficult to find; as a result, any first aid measures may be applied rather late.

For these reasons, the useful measures you can take are somewhat limited. Do not go in for heroics. Get the animal to a vet as quickly as possible, following the advice on page 176. Unless you are a long way from veterinary care, only undertake such first aid measures as are vital to save life – such as stopping severe bleeding, treating shock and, in certain cases, applying artificial respiration and/or cardiac massage – and do not attempt these at the expense of delay in obtaining professional help.

Prevention is, of course, far better than cure. Accidents to cats most commonly occur in the home, so – whether your cat is kept always indoors or not – study the advice on page 158 and make your home as safe as possible. The second most common place for feline accidents in most countries is on the road, so if you believe in allowing cats outdoor freedom, make sure that kittens at least are confined to the home and an enclosed garden. And remember that even adult cats seldom acquire enough road sense to deal with modern traffic volumes.

Dealing with an injured cat

Detailed advice on dealing with common cat accidents is given on subsequent pages, but there are some general points that apply to many cases. The first rule is to approach the injured cat gently and cautiously, so that it remains relatively calm. Have a towel or small blanket – or even a shirt or coat – ready to wrap around it to restrain it if necessary before or while you are lifting it. Talk to the cat to soothe it. Remember to call your vet by telephone before leaving.

Shock can occur in a wide variety of accidents, particularly falls and road accidents, electrocution, and any injuries causing bleeding, external or internal. It represents collapse of the circulatory system, and results in lowered blood pressure and, if severe and untreated, death. The main symptoms are collapse, rapid shallow breathing, a fast feeble pulse (see p174), cold extremities and dilated pupils. Immediate first aid must be given.

Among vets, the argument continues as to whether warmth or cold shock treatment is best. For the non-professional, however, it is best to keep the cat warm and comfortable while getting it quickly to the vet.

The rescue of a cat from a tree is seldom justified unless the animal is injured. Most cats will eventually climb down unaided.

Lowering the head helps to maintain blood flow to the brain. Forcibly giving fluids by mouth can be dangerous, but the vet may administer these by hypodermic or intravenous drip. Sometimes stimulant drugs are given. Secondary shock can follow four to six hours after an accident, and is often

> **WARNING**
> Some first-aid measures – especially artificial respiration and cardiac massage – can be dangerous. Do not attempt them unless you are out of reach of prompt veterinary help and/ or it is a matter of life and death. Never delay reaching a vet while you try to apply first aid.

due to internal bleeding. Veterinary treatment is vital at this stage.

In certain conditions – notably drowning, suffocation, electric shock and poisoning (including an overdose of certain drugs) – breathing and/or heartbeat may stop altogether. These must be restarted within a few minutes if the cat is to survive, but due to the fragility of the cat's rib cage, internal injury is commonly caused by amateurs' attempts at artificial respiration. For this reason, you should leave it to a vet if you can reach one quickly. In any case, be sure that breathing and/or heartbeat really have stopped (see p174) before you attempt such measures.

General accidents

Street accidents These are commonest in urban areas, particularly in regions where cats are not commonly kept indoors at all times. Even if no one saw the accident, it is almost always possible to identify the cause – unlike in other domestic animals – because cats usually extend their claws to grip the road surface at the instant of impact. As a result, the claws will be fragmented, showing the vet that a vehicle was involved and thus the likely extent of injuries.

Any feline street accident victim, unless killed outright, should be taken to a vet as quickly as possible. Lift the cat gently and transport it in a suitable container. Try to stop any severe bleeding (see p182), and keep broken or dislocated limbs in as natural a position as possible; do not attempt to apply splints. Shock is always present to some degree (see above), so cover the patient to keep it warm and also to prevent escape and further injury. Concussion is less common in such accidents than in falls, but it may cause partial or complete unconsciousness – in which case the treatment is the same as for shock. Persistent

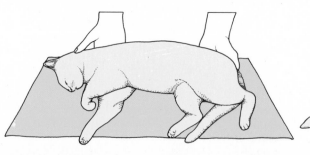

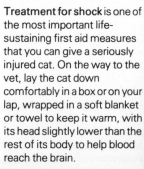

Lifting an injured cat If you think that the cat may have internal injuries or fractures (as from a car accident), pick it up gently by the scruff of the neck from behind (so that it cannot claw you) and give light support to the rump, as shown on page 146. This spreads the weight over the skin and lessens pressure on internal injuries.

Alternatively, if the cat is lying on its side and is calm, lift it gently on two outspread hands – one under the chest, the other under the hips **above**. Avoid twisting or bending the body. Lay the cat down on a towel or newspapers in a carrying container or cardboard box. If it struggles, cover it with a cloth before picking it up.

Treatment for shock is one of the most important life-sustaining first aid measures that you can give a seriously injured cat. On the way to the vet, lay the cat down comfortably in a box or on your lap, wrapped in a soft blanket or towel to keep it warm, with its head slightly lower than the rest of its body to help blood reach the brain.

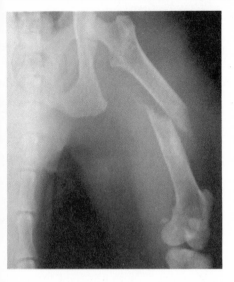

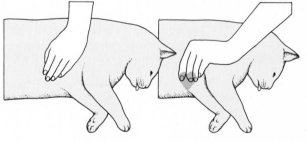

Setting fractures – aligning the broken ends of bones and fixing or holding them so that they can grow together – is usually carried out under a general anaesthetic. An X-ray **left** is normally needed to determine the exact nature of the fracture. With minor limb fractures, an external splint **1** or a plaster cast **2** may be sufficient. In other cases, however, it may be necessary to operate and fix the bone internally with a pin in the central cavity **3** or a plate attached to the side **4**, or to use an external rod splint pinned to the bone **5**. A broken pelvis is a special case; sometimes internal fixation is needed, but in other cases the cat may need only enforced cage rest. Dislocations of joints are treated similarly, being manipulated into position under anaesthetic and then held with a plaster cast, pin or splint until tissues heal.

laboured breathing after shock has passed may be caused by a ruptured diaphragm (the sheet of muscle separating the chest cavity from the abdomen); this can only be certainly diagnosed by X-ray examination.

Once shock has been dealt with, the vet can attend to any broken bones – in street accidents, most commonly the long bones of the limbs, the pelvis and/or the spine, or (if the cat has run into the street and collided head–on with a vehicle's hub-cap) injuries to the nose and hard palate. The outward appearance of the cat may suggest fractures but these can only be diagnosed properly (and differentiated from dislocations) with X-rays. In many cases, this means giving the cat a general anaesthetic (so that it remains stationary) after primary shock has passed – frequently some 24 hours after the accident. The method of treatment depends on precisely which bones are broken, and where. Fractures and dislocations of the spine all too frequently involve severe damage to the spinal cord – the main nerve leading to the brain – resulting in total paralysis of the hind legs; in such a case, the only humane solution is euthanasia.

Falls The main victims of serious falls are young cats living in high-rise apartments with unguarded open windows. There are no doubt many causes, but the fact that many occur on summer evenings suggests that the cat is often attempting to catch a moth or other insect shown up in the light. Generally little harm results from falling, even onto concrete, from heights up to 6 m (20 ft), thanks to the cat's flexibility and its well-known ability to right itself during its fall (see p 121). Above this height, injuries are likely, especially if railings or other objects are struck en route, although cats have survived falls of 18 floors or more.

Because cats tend to land with their head down, the injuries are often worse at the front than the hind end. Facial injuries are common, including a split hard palate (roof of the mouth) which can easily be seen by opening the mouth. If mild, this will heal spontaneously, but more severe cases need surgical repair. Also common is a fracture and/or dislocation of the lower jaw – often in the middle but also on either side. A fracture can usually be seen and felt, but in dislocations the cat cannot close its jaw normally even though no break can be felt.

In nearly all cases surgical repair under general anaesthetic is needed – as it is with broken forelimbs, another common result of falls. Concussion and shock also occur, as with road accidents, and with falls from considerable heights there may be serious internal injuries (particularly to the chest) and bleeding.

The trapped cat In spite of its news value, this is not very common and seldom results in actual injury. Cats that appear to be trapped in tall trees, for example, will generally find their own way down. Leave strongly flavoured food (such as canned fish) at the base of the tree and then leave well alone for several hours; do not stay and watch, as this only makes the cat unwilling to move. Many cats will come down safely even after 24 hours.

If you attempt rescue after that, do not do so in the dark. Apart from the obvious danger to yourself, there is a very real danger to the cat; if frightened and unable to make good its escape, it may well launch itself into space, with disastrous results. In most cases you will need a ladder to reach the cat, and so long as it can see what is happening it will usually be quiet and amenable to handling. Much the same advice applies to a cat trapped on the roof of a building unless there are adjoining roofs to which the cat can escape and become lost; then it is best to attempt an earlier rescue.

Drainage and ventilation ducts present a rather different problem, since cats can (and often do) become physically *\/continued*

Artificial respiration can cause injury if performed incorrectly, but if breathing stops for more than about four minutes brain damage makes death inevitable. In a case of drowning, or if the airways are blocked with vomit, blood or mucus, swing the cat by its hind legs as shown on page 184. This is also worth trying in other cases since it stimulates breathing as well as clearing the lungs. If the cat is still not breathing, lay it on its side, open the mouth and pull out the tongue. Make sure that the airway is clear. Press down on the chest with the palm of your hand quite firmly and sharply – enough to see the chest move noticeably – to expel air. Then immediately release the pressure to allow air to re-enter the lungs. Repeat about 20 times per minute. Note that the action is more jerky than the rhythmic resuscitation of a human patient. Another alternative is 'mouth-to-mouth' resuscitation, covering the cat's mouth and nose with your mouth; blow hard enough to see the chest rise.

Cardiac massage may be tried if the heartbeat has stopped. Compress the part of the chest just behind the cat's elbow between the fingers and thumb about 120 times a minute – twice a second – but stop as soon as the heartbeat is felt again. Artificial respiration will usually be needed at the same time; alternate the two.

Accidents and first aid 2

unable to move. As a result, the cat will generally become panic-stricken and therefore difficult to handle. It may be necessary for a vet to give it a tranquillizer injection before it can be extricated.

Wounds

Bites by other animals Wounds in general represent the most common situation where home first aid is of real value, and the most important category is probably the bite wound from another animal (venomous bites and stings are covered separately on the opposite page). A dog bite is usually a lacerated (torn) wound, and can be extensive, deep and dangerous – even if there is no rabies risk, as there is in many countries (see p 206). The first priority is to stop or slow down bleeding if this is severe. Direct finger pressure on the site of the wound may be enough if it is quite small. Otherwise, bleeding from a limb is best countered by a pressure bandage applied to the bleeding point. (Do not waste time cleaning the wound first.) Take the cat to your vet as soon as possible, as further surgical repair will be needed.

Clean more minor lacerations with a weak solution of either common table salt, sodium bicarbonate (baking soda) or hydrogen peroxide. It is best not to use any other antiseptic, since this may lessen or even nullify the effect of any antibiotic treatment later prescribed by your vet, and may also inflame the tissues and retard healing. If veterinary treatment is available within 12 to 24 hours, then it is probably better to leave such a wound uncovered.

A cat or rodent bite is usually a very different matter. It is commonly a puncture wound, and is seldom visible when it happens. In many cases, an abscess forms three to four days later, showing as a swelling accompanied by local inflammation, pain and general malaise. In some cases, the first the owner knows about it is when the abscess bursts, releasing pus; sometimes a whole patch of dead skin and fur comes away. If caught earlier, however, the vet will lance and drain the abscess, leaving it open to heal slowly. In either case, antibiotic treatment together with regular cleaning of the wound is needed if the abscess is not simply to re-form in a week or two. In fact, if you do know that your cat has been bitten by another it is worthwhile taking it to the vet immediately for an antibiotic injection, as this will often prevent an abscess forming.

Gunshot wounds If these are caused by bullets or more than a very few shotgun pellets, the result will probably be rapidly fatal, but air-rifle pellets and stray pellets from shotguns can cause treatable wounds. As with other wounds the first priority is to arrest bleeding, if any, and then to obtain veterinary help. In many cases, the damage

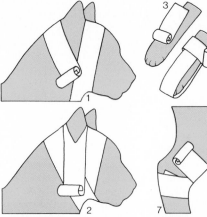
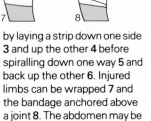

Bandaging a cat can be very difficult unless one person holds the cat while another bandages. The head is bandaged in a figure-of-eight **1**, with a hole for each ear **2**. A paw or tail may be bandaged

by laying a strip down one side **3** and up the other **4** before spiralling down one way **5** and back up the other **6**. Injured limbs can be wrapped **7** and the bandage anchored above a joint **8**. The abdomen may be

bandaged and anchored to the tail **9** or a many-tailed bandage **10** can be used. Proprietary tubular gauze bandages are also useful for cats. Do not fix bandages with pins, but tie off or stick down the ends firmly.

is not confined to what can be seen. The cat may have broken bones and internal injuries, and the pellets may still be lodged in the body. For this reason, an X-ray examination will often be needed to assess the extent of the damage and to decide what repair measures are necessary.

Fish hooks and traps These are obviously mainly a problem on river and canal banks and beside lakes and reservoirs, where they may be left by careless fishermen. The barb on the hook of course makes it impossible to withdraw it backwards along its course of entry. It usually has to be removed in two parts, the cat being sedated or even anaesthetized to prevent further injury or tissue damage. In some parts of the world, porcupine quills pose a similar hazard, and may have to be removed from a

cat's muzzle or head while it is under general anaesthetic.

One of the cruellest accidents that can befall a cat is to have its foot caught in a spring trap or a snare. Even if the victim is found quickly, the injury from the trap can often be so severe as to require amputation of all or part of the injured limb. A wire snare may have the same result if constriction of the blood supply leads to gangrene. Shock is probable in all cases. Fortunately, such injuries are rare and mainly confined to rural areas; amputees generally adapt well to life on three legs, however.

Other cuts and lacerations There are many causes of these, but the commonest are broken glass, barbed wire and nails. These injuries should be given first aid along the lines suggested for dog bites. In

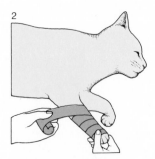
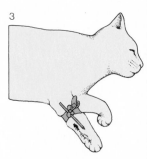

Stopping bleeding First make sure that the cause of the injury (such as a piece of glass) is not still embedded in the wound. Then **1** in minor cases press directly on the wound with your fingers. (If available, it is worthwhile for cleanliness to cover it first with clean gauze or a

handkerchief.) **2** With more extensive leg wounds, apply a pressure bandage: Cover the wound with a piece of lint or gauze, cover this with cotton wool (absorbent cotton) and bandage as tightly as possible up from the foot to cover the wound. **3** In very severe cases (such as a crushed or severed

foot or tail, or in some snakebite wounds), apply a tourniquet between the wound and the body. A tightly knotted handkerchief will do, twisted tight with a pencil, but it must be loosened every 15 minutes to allow blood to reach the tissues, or gangrene is liable to occur.

some areas, tetanus ('lockjaw') bacteria are prevalent in the soil, and your vet may advise giving a tetanus injection in all cases of wounding. In some cases, generally following a blow, the skin may not be broken but there is bleeding below the surface, leading to swelling. This is like a severe blood blister, and is known as a haematoma. It is commonest on the ear flap. Cold compresses may be enough to reduce it, but in other cases the vet needs to drain it, like an abscess.

Foreign bodies

In the eye and ear These are almost as variable as with humans. In most animals, increased tear secretion safely washes away the vast majority of small particles in the eye. The most usual persistent problem is caused by seeds of grasses that have backward-pointing barbs. They often become lodged under the nictitating membrane (third eyelid, or 'haws'; see p110); the vet has to remove them under general anaesthetic. The same applies to grass seeds in the ear.

In the mouth and throat Fish and meat bones commonly become lodged on or between the teeth or trapped in the larynx (voice box). While they cause marked distress, with the cat pawing its mouth and possibly seeming to choke, suffocation is rare. (The cat is unique among domestic pets in suffering a spasm of the larynx following any mild trauma there; this causes asthma-like symptoms that may distress the owner more than the cat.) Unless you can easily remove the obstruction with tweezers, it is best to leave this to the vet. If you fail to remove it cleanly and completely, the object may go down farther and cause greater damage.

A sewing needle is the other most common foreign body found in the throat. In some cases, this will still have the thread

attached; safe removal then may not be too difficult so long as the needle can be clearly seen. At the other extreme, the needle may become totally buried and only visible with X-rays. Here, and if any foreign body passes farther down the alimentary canal (gut), surgery will probably be needed. If a thread is seen to be passing from the cat's anus, do not cut or pull the thread but obtain veterinary assistance, as there may be a needle still attached within the gut.

In the feet Again, the offender is often a grass seed that becomes embedded in the soft skin between the toes. From there it can migrate some distance, eventually causing an abscess in quite a different part of the leg. Again, surgery under anaesthetic is needed, since not only must the abscess be drained but the sinus (cavity) opened and the seed removed, followed by antibiotic treatment.

Tin cans and plastic bags As with fish-hooks, prevention is the best measure; do not leave such containers around for your cat to investigate, and it will not get its head trapped. If this does happen, the cat will very likely panic and may need to be

sedated before the object can be removed. Removal is usually easy if the patient will allow it, but with cans the canine teeth may penetrate the edge and act as a very efficient locking device. As with children, plastic bags can cause suffocation.

Venomous bites and stings

Snakes Some regions, of course, have no venomous snakes, others (like Britain) have very few, while in others (such as parts of Australia and North America) they can be a very real and everyday problem for any cat that is allowed outdoors. Apart from possible vomiting and signs of shock, a snakebitten cat will probably have a large swelling at the site of the bite – usually on the face, neck or foreleg. If you are to save the cat's life, it must be treated immediately – within an hour or two. Meanwhile, try to keep the cat calm so that the venom does not spread.

If a leg has been bitten, apply a firm tourniquet (see opposite) above the wound to restrict blood-flow and prevent spread of venom. Some vets suggest lancing the swollen area and squeezing out venom, but it is doubtful if this does much good in a cat. It is more important to get it quickly to a vet (or a hospital or clinic) who has supplies of antitoxin (antiserum) to counteract the venom of snakes commonly found in the area. A useful first-aid measure en route is to apply ice-packs to the area of the bite.

Insects and spiders These again constitute a very variable hazard. In many temperate zones, wasp and bee stings may be the only likely problem, and the cat seems remarkable resistant to these. Occasionally a cat may swallow a stinging insect, and in many cases the mouth area is stung. Elsewhere, the coat may prevent exact location of the sting, so if any treatment is needed it will consist of an /continued

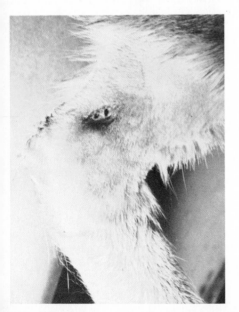

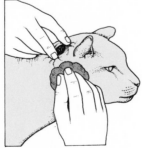

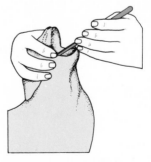

Abscesses often result from a cat bite **left**. 'Draw out' the pus with cotton wool (absorbent cotton) soaked in hot water, and apply gentle pressure. Continue bathing after it bursts, with hydrogen peroxide added as an antiseptic. Antibiotics are very often needed.

Removing a fish bone or other foreign body caught in the mouth should be attempted only if you can see and reach it easily. The cat will need to be firmly restrained while its mouth is held open as described on page 179 for giving a pill. Use tweezers to remove the object.

Objects in the paw can also be removed with tweezers. With a fish-hook, the cat should be under restraint, sedation or even anaesthesia. Pass the hook forward until the barbed tip emerges. Cut this off with wire cutters and withdraw the shank backwards. Clean the wound.

Accidents and first aid 3

COMMON FELINE POISONS

Substance	Symptoms*	First aid*	Veterinary treatment; comments
RAT, MOUSE AND SIMILAR POISONS			
Alphachloralose	Convulsions; coma; depressed body temperature	E within 30 minutes; keep warm	No sedatives to be given; used as pigeon killer
Alpha-naphthyl-thiourea (ANTU)	R; coma; death	E immediately	Rapidly fatal; no antidote
Phosphorus	V; collapse	D (not olive oil); ST; no E	Copper sulphate orally
Red squill	V; paralysis	E; ST	No specific treatment; treat symptoms; uncommon because unpalatable to cats
Reserpine	V; D; collapse	D; ST	No sedatives to be given
Sodium fluoroacetate	Crying; convulsions; death	Probably useless	No antidote; odourless and tasteless; can be absorbed through skin; now banned in many countries
Strychnine	Twitching; convulsions; hypersensitivity to noise	E; strong tea	Sedation; stomach pump; no longer allowed as rodenticide in many countries, but may be used illegally or to kill moles
Thallium	V, D, R if acute; hair loss if chronic; convulsions	E	Dithizone is antidote; a slow-acting poison; little used in Britain
Zinc phosphide	Convulsions; V; D	E, but probably useless	No antidote; usually fatal
OTHER PESTICIDES			
Arsenic	V; D; staggering; convulsions; collapse	E quickly	No safe antidote; found in some slug baits and weedkillers
Chlorinated hydrocarbons	Drooling; convulsions; R	ST; wash from skin	Sedation; used as insecticides; include benzene hexachloride (BHC; lindane), which may be wrongly used on cats for fleas, etc
Metaldehyde	V; D; convulsions; coma	E; D; ST	No antidote; used as slug bait

injection of antihistamine or corticosteroid. In tropical and subtropical zones, of course, spiders and scorpions are a real threat. In Australia, for example, an inquisitive cat may encounter a funnel-web spider under logs or in piles of rubbish. The bite of any venomous spider or scorpion needs the same treatment as snakebite.

Burns
Heat burns Scalds, especially from hot water or cooking fats, are much more common than dry burns in cats, because they seem to have an inbuilt distrust of such objects as domestic irons. But cats' affinity for warmth can lead to their being burnt accidentally by stoves and fires. It is vital to appreciate that any extensive burn will cause shock (see p 180), and early treatment of this is vital. First aid treatment of the burnt area is very secondary to this, though dousing the area with cold water within seconds will reduce tissue damage. And in any case, as soon as possible apply a cold compress to the injury and smear it liberally with antihistamine cream. Get professional shock treatment immediately.

Electrical burns These are a particular problem with young cats, which are tempted to play with and eventually bite through any electric wire. This results in extensive burning of the mouth and tongue, with accompanying shock and in some cases cardiac arrest. Make absolutely sure that the current is switched off before

you attempt to help. Artificial respiration and/or cardiac massage may be needed unless you can reach veterinary help within five minutes. The latter is in any case needed to treat the shock and injury.

Sometimes pulmonary oedema (fluid collecting in the lungs) develops an hour or more after the accident, causing foaming at the mouth and difficulty with breathing; prompt veterinary treatment can alleviate this. Electrical burns usually damage deep

Treating burns, whatever their cause, is primarily a matter of treating for shock (see p 180) and getting the animal to the vet as quickly as possible. If you can act promptly enough, however, dousing the burnt area with cold water will minimize injury, and the same method should be used to remove caustic chemicals.

tissues and are slow to heal. Also, mouth injuries will make the cat reluctant to eat or drink, and it may have to be fed with a drip.

Chemical burns Caused principally by caustic acids and alkalis, these may take from a few hours to several days to cause visible injury. In all cases, use copious cold water to remove any chemical residues and again apply antihistamine cream. If tissue damage is extensive, see your vet.

Swinging a drowned cat drains water from its lungs and is such a safe and good way to stimulate breathing that many vets advise its use as a routine method of artificial respiration. Hold the hind legs of the cat – one leg in each hand – above and around the hock (ankle), with the cat's belly facing towards you. Stand with your legs apart. Swing the cat forward and then, with a slight jerk at the end of the upward swing, bring the cat down and between your straddled legs. Swing it back to the front of you again, ending each swing with the cat horizontal. Repeat about six times before trying other methods. It is surprising how much space is needed to 'swing a cat'!

Substance	Symptoms*	First aid*	Veterinary treatment; comments
Organophosphorus compounds	V; D; convulsions; R	ST; wash from skin	Sedation; some have specific antidotes; commonly used as insecticides
PETROCHEMICALS AND RELATED SUBSTANCES			
Benzoic acid	Rage; convulsions	E	Sedation; used as food preservative (safe in correct amounts)
Carbolic acid (phenol); cresol	Burnt mouth if concentrated; convulsions; R; coma	D if swallowed; remove from skin; ST; no E	Used as disinfectants; can be absorbed through skin; never use on cat
Creosote	Convulsions; R; coma	D if swallowed; remove from skin; ST; no E	Can be absorbed through skin; do not use as wood preservative on cat's quarters
Ethylene glycol	V; staggering; paralysis; coma	E; ST; remove from skin	Used as antifreeze; sweet taste attractive to cats
Other petrochemicals, tar, turpentine, paint, etc	V, D from licking from coat; convulsions; coma if acute	D; ST; remove from skin; no E	Some can be absorbed through skin; cat may persist in licking despite nasty taste
MISCELLANEOUS DOMESTIC HAZARDS			
Aspirin	Severe V, D; staggering	E; D; ST	Reaction varies from cat to cat; never administer to cats
Biological toxins	V; D; sometimes convulsions, coma	E; D; ST	From eating various house and garden plants, or poisonous toads in some countries
Boric (boracic) acid	V, D with blood	E; D; ST	Used as antiseptic and as powder on some white show cats – must be brushed out
Carbon monoxide; methane	Coma; death	Fresh air; artificial respiration; ST	From car exhaust fumes, boiler (furnace) fumes; coal gas, natural gas
Smoke	R	Fresh air; ST	Includes burning fat

Abbreviations: Symptoms: D = diarrhoea; R = respiratory distress, choking, etc; V = vomiting.
First aid: D = demulcent; E = emetic; ST = shock treatment (see p 180).

Heat; cold; drowning

Heat-stroke and exposure are both probably less common in cats than dogs. Cats seem able to withstand greater extremes of temperature, and indeed seem to revel in heat that would severely distress a dog. However, in hot weather a cat can quickly succumb to heat-stroke if in a confined space such as a parked car. The symptoms including panting, vomiting and the signs of general shock. Its body temperature may rise to 41°C (106°F) or more. Act quickly to reduce this. Douse the cat with cold water, or wrap it in cold wet towels and apply an ice pack to its head; fan it. Then quickly get it to a vet for shock treatment.

Cats generally adapt to cold conditions well, but in very extreme climates may suffer from frostbite if outdoors for a long time. The feet, tail and ears are mainly affected. Again, veterinary treatment is advisable, but the frozen parts should meanwhile be thawed out slowly and gently. The cat may, of course, be suffering from exposure and shock.

Few cats enjoy water, but they can swim well if need be, and are only likely to drown if the water is rough or they are unable to climb out and tire. If you do pull a drowned cat from water and believe that it has only recently succumbed (within a few minutes), hold it suspended by the hind legs and swing it quite vigorously to and fro. This will effectively remove excess water from the lungs and also acts as an efficient stimulant to breathing. In some cases, how-ever, artificial respiration and/or cardiac massage will be needed unless a vet can be reached very quickly (see p 181).

Poisoning

Although the cat's natural caution may prevent it consuming most poisonous substances, its habit of licking any contamination from its paws and hair puts it in danger. Some poisons can be absorbed through the skin, while its poor ability to neutralize and excrete poisons makes even relatively harmless substances like aspirin toxic.

Probably the greatest hazards are rat and mouse killers, which can not only poison a cat directly but also if a poisoned rodent is eaten. Also, as mentioned on page 178, the cat has a peculiar sensitivity to certain organic chemicals – particularly petrochemicals, coal-tar products and related substances. Anything of this nature should be quickly removed from the hair or paws, using a household detergent, and rinsed off with plenty of water. With paint or tar, butter or vegetable oil can be used to soften the contamination before washing.

Poisoning is always an emergency that requires veterinary assistance, but, unless the cat is seen to consume the poison, diagnosis is often difficult. Not only are the common symptoms of poisoning (such as vomiting and diarrhoea) similar to those of many other conditions, but various poisons cause very similar symptoms. If possible, take some of the poison or its container with you to the vet; any identification of the precise poison makes treatment more sure, but in many cases there is no specific antidote, and the vet can only treat the symptoms such as vomiting, diarrhoea and shock. With some poisons a sedative may be needed, but others are themselves depressant in effect and no sedative must be used.

The scope for first aid is limited unless you know for sure the nature of the poison (see the table). Emetics (to induce vomiting) can help reduce the absorption of poison by the stomach, but must be given within 30 minutes to be of any use. They must never be given to an unconscious cat, in cases of phosphorus poisoning or where corrosive substances or certain volatile materials (such as petrochemicals) are consumed – so if in doubt leave well alone. Where they can be used, suitable emetics include a pea-sized piece of washing soda, a teaspoonful of hydrogen peroxide (straight from the bottle, not diluted), mustard and water or strong salty water. Administer one of these as you would a medicine (see p 179).

With irritant poisons, a demulcent (soothing mixture) can be given – for example, milk and egg-white, or olive oil. Where the cat is overcome by a gaseous poison such as smoke or fumes, fresh air is the most important requirement; some cases may need artificial respiration if there is to be any chance of survival. Remember too that most, if not all, poisons cause shock which must be treated as advised on page 180 while you get the patient to a vet as quickly as possible.

External parasites 1

External parasites are small, often microscopic, organisms that feed on the cat's skin. Their movements and secretions irritate and can cause allergies. By damaging the skin they open the way for further infection, and some themselves carry and transmit other diseases. Those that suck blood may cause anaemia, and some produce toxins that make the cat ill. Insects that bite or sting rather than parasitize cats are dealt with on page 183.

The external parasites that affect the cat include fleas, flies and lice, which are all insects, with six legs, and mites and ticks, both eight-legged relatives of the spiders. Some are worldwide in spread; others are restricted to particular zones or localities. Cats anywhere can pick up parasites, but many types are rare in cats restricted to the home. In all cats regular grooming helps to give early warning of infestation, but if you do find evidence of parasites it is often worth seeking veterinary advice since different parasites, needing different treatments, may produce very similar outward signs. Be sure, when giving treatment, that you use only approved pesticides; some can be fatal to cats.

Fleas

Fleas are probably the most ubiquitous of the cat's external parasites and under favourable conditions – such as in the modern dry, centrally-heated home – can quickly multiply. The adults are pinhead-sized, dark brown wingless insects, which feed on the cat's blood. Fleas are not limited to a particular host, so that although the cat has its own species, dog fleas, rabbit fleas, human fleas and even bird fleas will infest cats. Conversely, cat fleas frequently infest dogs and bite humans. Fleas travel from animal to animal in prodigious leaps, but because they survive for long periods off the host, premises and bedding long vacated by cats may still carry fleas ready to infest a new occupant.

Flea bites produce small reddish patches, which the cat scratches vigorously. This is a nuisance rather than a major problem because the fleas can be eradicated (see below). But with repeated bites the cat may develop an allergy to flea saliva. Flea allergy dermatitis, also called miliary dermatitis or miliary eczema, is one of the most common skin diseases in cats, particularly in warmer areas. The cat develops numerous small pimples with hard, dry, crumbly crusts, usually on the hind part of the back and along the spine, where fleas are most commonly found. In severe cases the entire body, except for the head and the lower parts of the limbs, is affected. Almost continuous licking, scratching and biting produces patches of raw, almost hairless skin and, unable to rest, the cat soon loses condition. As a result of this 'licker's skin', ulcers may appear on the abdomen and

inside the thighs, and because they irritate they tend to persist long after the fleas have been destroyed.

Fleas can also infect the cat with the common tapeworm (see p191). This uses the flea as an intermediary host, and its larvae are swallowed with the carrier fleas when the cat grooms itself.

Treatment In controlling fleas, not only the cat but its immediate surroundings and anywhere else it frequents must be treated. The cat itself is easily treated with a suitable insecticide spray or powder. Your vet will advise on which are most effective, as fleas can become resistant to certain preparations. When applying the insecticide, some cats will only need to be held gently, while kittens and nervous cats may need the maximum of restraint (see p179). Some cats become frightened by the sound of an aerosol, so powders are preferable in such

Life cycle of the cat flea
(*Ctenocephalides felis*) **right** can be completed in a few weeks. The adult female **1** lays up to 500 tiny white eggs **2** in floor and wall crevices, bedding and upholstery. Any laid on a cat usually drop off. In about a week they hatch into whitish-yellow larvae **3**; these spin cocoons, inside which the pupae **4** develop over the next three to four weeks into adults. The pupae can, however, remain dormant for many months, waiting for vibrations from a prospective host or for the temperature to rise above 10°C (50°F).

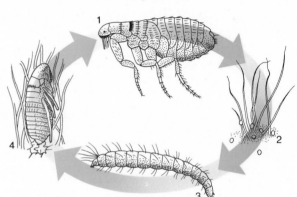

cases. The treatment needs to be repeated at least once after an interval of seven to ten days so that larvae hatching from any remaining eggs are destroyed. Flea collars (see opposite), insecticidal shampoos and flea dips, which are applied to the coat as a liquid and allowed to dry, are also useful methods of control.

Any other cats (or dogs) on the premises must, of course, be treated. Ideally, you should burn the cat's bedding, and the sleeping and habitual resting areas should be treated with insecticide and vacuumed regularly. You can wash floors and walls

with a suitable disinfectant (see p178) supplemented with washing soda, which kills flea eggs. Dichlorvos (DDVP) fly strips suspended above the cat's bed will kill fleas on the cat as well as those in its immediate surroundings, but can be dangerous if the cat is already wearing a flea collar (see opposite). Flea allergy must be tackled by the vet, who may use a steroid ointment or other medication to counter the irritation and allow the skin to heal.

Mange mites

Mites are minute round or oval parasites with eight legs. They provoke a range of skin conditions, from simple dandruff to bald crusty patches, that are collectively called mange. This is generally highly contagious, being transmitted either by direct contact or through infested bedding and grooming equipment. Some mites live in the coat, others on or in the skin itself.

Other cat parasites include **below 1** the fur mite (*Cheyletiella*), **2** harvest mite larva (*Trombicula*), **3** head mange mite (*Notoedres*), **4** demodectic mite (*Demodex*), **5** sheep tick (*Ixodes*) and **6** biting louse (*Felicola*).

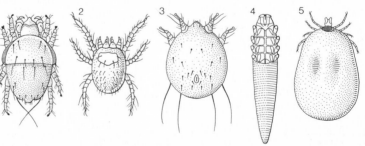

Fur mites Also known as the body mite or 'walking dandruff' mite, the fur mite is commonly found on dogs and rabbits as well as cats. Although there is some cross-infestation, each domestic pet has its own species. The eggs are glued to the cat's hairs and the life cycle of four to five weeks is completed on the cat. The mite may cause itching, but the usual sign is profuse dandruff (skin scales), particularly on the back and sides. Although this is not one of the serious cat manges, people can contract it – more readily in fact than from any other pet. In humans it usually appears as itchy wheals and blisters progressing to dry scaling on the hands and forearms and sometimes the chest. Infestations in the cat are often symptomless, so if you develop an itchy skin, it is worthwhile checking combings from your cat's coat with a magnifying glass for the presence of moving mites.

Fur mite mange usually responds well to bathing with a selenium sulphide shampoo, followed by thorough rinsing, once a week for three weeks. Even weekly soap-and-water baths will soon kill the mites. You should treat all cats within a household, wash their bedding and treat soft furnishings with a safe insecticide. In catteries, hanging dichlorvos (DDVP) fly strips has proved a useful control measure.

Other superficial mites Some superficial mites, notably the harvest mite (also called the red bug, heel bug or, in North America, chigger), live in decaying vegeta-

tion as adults and are only parasitic in their young stages. Larval harvest mites appear as orange, yellow or red specks, clumped in thin-skinned areas such as the ears, mouth and the webs between the toes, where they feed for about three days. They feed by injecting saliva and then sucking back the predigested 'soup'. This results in severe irritation and the formation of oozing sores with hard scabs or patches of raw skin.

A mild infestation may be treated with a safe dusting powder or medicated bath, but preventing reinfestation is difficult unless the cat is confined indoors. (The harvest-mite season may extend over several summer months.) However, a safe insecticide dusted into the roots of the hair in vulnerable areas is of temporary value when mites are especially troublesome.

Skin mites The most ubiquitous of these is the ear mange mite, which is discussed

with other ear problems on page 202. One of the least common is the microscopic head mite, but paradoxically this causes the most important skin mange, notoedric mange (sometimes called feline scabies). It most often affects whole litters of kittens and their mother, and also older male cats. It is highly contagious and spreads by direct contact, the mites being unable to live for more than a few days off the cat. There have also been reports of rare cases of transient human infestation.

The female mites burrow into the horny layer of the skin, making tunnels in which to lay their eggs. The skin becomes inflamed and itchy, and, with persistent rubbing and scratching, wounds develop, first on the ears and then on the rest of the head. Very severe cases affect the whole body and kittens left untreated may die. Patches of hair fall out and the skin becomes scabby, thickened and wrinkled. /continued

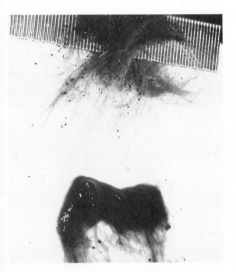

Evidence of fleas is shown clearly by their small brown or black comma-shaped droppings. **left** Stand your cat on a white surface and brush it briskly. The droppings will fall as a shower of 'black pepper'. To distinguish them from ordinary dust, wipe the surface with a moist cloth. If the specks are flea droppings they will leave a blood-coloured smudge. The adult fleas are harder to find, though they may be caught in a fine-toothed comb (see p 154). Concentrate on the back, from head to tail, where most fleas congregate.

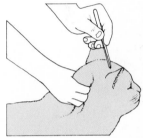

Getting rid of fleas is best done with a pesticide spray **1** or powder, used as directed and aimed or worked well in against the lie of the coat. Flea collars **2** or tags **3** may deter some fleas but often cause a skin reaction.

Removing a tick, apply ether or alcohol with a cotton bud to make it relax its grip. Then you can pick it off with tweezers or your fingernails without it leaving its barbed mouthparts in the skin – which could result in an abscess.

SAFE EXTERNAL PESTICIDES

Insecticides are toxic products and must be chosen and applied with care. Never use those sold for other pets or for garden use. Those containing DDT, dieldrin, benzyl benzoate, benzene hexachloride at a greater concentration than 1 per cent, phenols and tars (see p178) are lethal to cats. Others are safe only if used correctly, particularly with the constant risk of their ingestion during grooming. They should not be used on very young kittens, or on sick, pregnant or nursing cats. Some can be cumulative if the cat is exposed to different sources.

Parasiticides in the table are recommended as effective and safe when used correctly, but it is wise to seek the advice of your vet on which to use. Most products are sold under trade names, but the active ingredient should be listed on the label. Read this carefully and observe any precautions.

Active ingredient	Type(s) of product	Parasites affected
Benzene hexachloride* (BHC; gamma-BHC; HCH; lindane)	Shampoo; ear drops; dusting powder; flea collar*	Mange mites; ticks; fleas; lice; ear mites
Bromocyclen	Spray; dusting powder	Fleas; lice; mange mites (except *Demodex*)
Carbaryl	Dusting powder; ear drops	Fleas; lice; ticks; ear mites
Dichlorvos† (DDVP)	Spray; wettable or dusting powder; plastic fumigant strip; flea collar	Fleas; lice; ticks; mange mites
Fenitrothion†	Spray; wettable or dusting powder	Fleas; lice; ticks; mange mites
Lime sulphur	Wettable or dusting powder; shampoo	Fleas; lice; ticks; mange mites
Malathion†	Dusting powder; shampoo	Fleas; lice
Piperonyl butoxide	Dusting powder; lotion	Fleas; lice; ticks; mange mites
Pyrethrins (pyrethrum; pybuthrin)	Dusting powder; lotion	Fleas; lice; ticks; mange mites
Rotenone (derris)‡	Wettable or dusting powder	Fleas; lice; ticks; mange mites (especially *Demodex*)
Selenium sulphide	Shampoo	All external parasites; some skin diseases (see p 189)

Note: Safe for cats only at a concentration below 1 per cent (flea collars not recommended);
†*organophosphorus compounds – may have cumulative effects;* ‡*also rather toxic to cats, especially kittens.*

External parasites 2

The corrugated facial skin makes the cat appear old. Wounds may become infected by bacteria and the cat die from blood-poisoning. Because the mites burrow and are so small, they can only be identified by microscopic examination of skin scrapings, but the sites of damage give a strong indication of the cause of the condition.

Treatment, under veterinary supervision, initially involves bathing in warm, soapy water to remove the hard crusts, followed by medicated baths at ten-day intervals to kill the mites. With localized damage, however, you may only need to apply a safe insecticide. All cats on the premises must be treated, all bedding destroyed and equipment thoroughly disinfected. Secondary bacterial infections need antibiotic treatment by a vet, and an Elizabethan collar (see p179) will prevent further scratching of head wounds.

Among other skin mites, the one that causes sarcoptic mange, or true scabies, is common enough in dogs and man but is hardly ever seen in cats. Its effect and treatment are similar to that of notoedric mange. One of the most persistent manges is demodectic mange, and fortunately it is rare in cats. It is caused by a barely-visible, cigar-shaped creature with stumpy legs which lives deep in the skin in the hair follicles (see p106) and probably is spread by direct contact. Usually the mange is mild, with a rash and loss of hair around the eyes and on the eyelids. In exceptional cases it may spread to the neck and forelegs and there may be pustules and a reddening of the skin. Because the mites are difficult to reach this is a relatively obstinate condition. But by persevering with suitable ointments or lotions (see table) massaged regularly into the skin, and by supplementing the diet with vitamins, it can eventually be controlled and seldom recurs.

Ticks

Ticks are relatively large eight-legged parasites with six-legged larvae. They are not often found on cats because of thorough self-grooming, but they can be picked up by cats allowed outdoors, particularly in areas with long grass and low bushes. They may not be easy to detect, as they do not seem to cause much irritation, but because they feed on blood a heavy infestation can cause anaemia. And in warmer countries, particularly Australia, a toxin secreted by the salivary glands of some species of tick produces so-called tick paralysis. Usually the hind limbs are first affected, but eventually the whole body is paralysed; however, recovery is rapid once the parasites are removed.

Ticks are most likely to be found on the cat's ears and neck and between the toes, where they appear as brown or bluish-grey lumps. They vary in size because they parasitize the cat at various stages in their

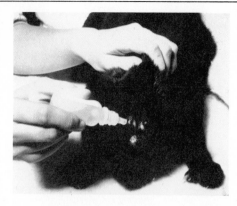

Treating head mange, if localized, may require only the application of a suitable insecticide lotion prescribed by the vet.

life cycle and swell up when feeding. An unfed larval tick is no bigger than a pinhead, whereas a fully engorged adult female can be 1 cm (½ in) long. The common European species, which also attacks sheep and cattle, is easily recognized because it looks like a castor bean when fully fed. There are numerous tick species in North America, mostly confined to specific regions and only a few affecting cats; your vet will know if they are prevalent in your area. It is difficult to prevent reinfestation in roaming cats in tick areas, but weekly dusting with a powder containing pyrethrum and piperonyl butoxide will act as a deterrent.

Lice

A healthy and well-cared-for cat is unlikely to be troubled by lice. Large numbers of these wingless insects are usually present only as a symptom of some other disorder. Malnutrition, for example, can lead to severe lousiness simply because the cat is listless and weak and stops grooming.

Lice are highly host-specific, so that only cat lice infest cats and there is no possibility of their infesting humans. The whole life cycle is spent on the cat, so lice are spread only by direct contact or through bedding or grooming equipment recently in contact with affected cats. The biting cat louse feeds on hair and skin debris, while the sucking louse feeds on tissue fluid and blood. The cat is restless, scratches a great deal and neither feeds nor sleeps well. With a heavy infestation it may injure itself by scratching, and will lose hair and develop scaly skin. Young cats are more severely affected. In addition, sucking lice are a cause of anaemia, and biting lice, like fleas, spread the common tapeworm.

Lice can be found anywhere on the cat's body, but particularly on the head, as slow-moving, yellowish-white, pear-shaped objects about the size of a pinhead. Their numerous whitish eggs – known as nits – are glued firmly to the cat's hairs and resemble a scattering of flour. In a heavy infestation of the parasite the coat is dirty,

matted and unkempt, and has a 'mousy' smell when damp.

In very bad cases it may be necessary to clip off the thick mats of fur, and this will also remove hundreds of lice and their eggs. The cat is usually highly irritable, but you should make an attempt to bathe it with a safe insecticide. Failing this, scatter a suitable insecticide powder liberally over the back and shoulders, and massage it from there into the rest of the coat. Repeat the treatment in 10 to 14 days to kill any lice that may have hatched from eggs in the coat. Severely anaemic and debilitated cats with heavy infestations can go into shock (see p180) with too vigorous a treatment. Start by reducing the numbers of lice with a dusting powder. Feeding a high-protein diet will help to improve the cat's general condition, and when it is stronger it can cope with more thorough treatment.

Maggots

Occasionally cats suffer from myiasis, in which the larvae (maggots or grubs) of a fly develop in or on the cat's skin. The most serious of these afflictions is caused by a type of botfly, a bee-like insect occurring in the warmer areas of the world. In the United States it has a wide distribution, with its highest concentration in the West, but it is absent from most of Europe, including Britain. The infestation almost always occurs in summer, when egg-laying is at its maximum.

If a cat should lie on the ground on which the fly has laid its eggs, the larvae will hatch out and migrate into the skin. As a result there are prominent swellings, usually on the neck, back, sides and belly, and occasionally around the nostrils, eyelids and jaw. Unless the grubs are very numerous or large there is usually no disturbance to the cat, but since the grub breathes through an opening in the skin, bacteria may enter here; if the grub dies there may be serious suppuration (pus formation). Very rarely a grub may migrate into the cat's brain and cause symptoms which can simulate rabies.

The grub can be removed by squeezing, or gently pulling it out with forceps (tweezers), through its breathing hole. After flushing out the cavity with antiseptic, as when treating an abscess (see p183), the wound will quickly heal.

If a cat has an open wound that has not been treated, or has a badly soiled damp coat, certain flies of the group to which the bluebottles belong (the calliphorines) will be attracted and lay their eggs. The larvae that hatch out will eventually grow into large maggots and will invade the skin, enlarging the original wound or making a new one under the soiled fur. The area should be bathed repeatedly in warm water to remove the maggots and, after applying a suitable antiseptic ointment, should be left open to the air to heal.

Skin diseases

Cats are relatively free from non-parasitic skin problems, and most that do occur are non-contagious and easily cleared. Ringworm, however, is one of the more serious cat diseases and is readily transmitted to humans and other cats.

Ringworm

Despite its name, ringworm is caused by a parasitic fungus, not a worm. It spreads by direct contact or via objects in contact with infected animals. The commonest form of this in cats is also the usual cause of ringworm in dogs and can infect humans (especially children). The spores can live for years and, once established in a group of cats (such as in a breeding cattery), ringworm can be difficult to eradicate. In general it is a disease of young cats – often unweaned kittens – and may then clear up spontaneously as resistance to reinfection develops. Such cats may be symptomless carriers of the disease.

The fungus grows only in the surface layers of the skin and in the hairs, but toxins (poisons) released into the skin cause inflammation and itching. Affected hairs fracture. Symptoms appear two to four weeks after infection and vary considerably. There may be only a few broken hairs on the face and ears, but usually small round or oval hairless patches appear. They are most common on the head and ears, forepaws and back. There may be mild irritation but usually little effect on the cat's general health. As other disorders can produce the same symptoms, a Wood's lamp should be used to detect the fungus. This produces ultra-violet light which is filtered through cobalt glass; the ringworm organism usually fluoresces with a characteristic greenish-yellow colour, betraying an infection. However, lack of fluorescence does not rule out ringworm, since in up to 40 per cent of cases the Wood's light test gives a false negative. For positive diagnosis, a scraping must be taken for culture.

The only effective treatment is the antibiotic griseofulvin given, usually in tablet form, for four to six weeks or until tests for the fungus are negative. This drug has few side-effects, but must not be given to a pregnant queen or it may cause deformities in her young. It is effective only against the fungus in the skin, not on or in the hairs, or against the spores, so you should clip off all dead or broken hairs from time to time or the infection will persist.

Disinfection during and after an outbreak is essential. Burn all contaminated bedding and sterilize metal and wooden utensils, baskets and cages by soaking them in a hot formalin solution (see p 178). If you breed and/or show cats, discontinue sales, matings, visits to shows and so on until the infection has been eradicated. It is a wise precaution for all cats arriving at a boarding cattery or a stud to be screened with a

Ringworm (*Microsporum canis*) appears as rounded patches of scaly skin, up to 5 cm (2 in) in diameter. They have a stubble of broken hairs and a raised, inflamed outer edge. Often disclosed by a Wood's lamp, a cell culture is needed for positive diagnosis.

Stud tail, like feline acne, is caused by over-secretion of the large sebaceous glands at the base of the tail or (in acne) on the chin. If infected, these may become pustulate. Commonest in entire toms, it can also occur in females and neuters of either sex.

Balding, or alopecia, is often due to hormonal imbalance, but may also rarely be hereditary. Congenitally affected cats have a sparsely growing coat and, as they get older, progressively lose their hair until the skin is partly or totally bare.

Wood's lamp. Fungicidal shampoos are available for treating cats suspected of being exposed to infection.

There are other forms of ringworm that cats occasionally pick up from rodents. In mouse favus, for example, the hairless patches are in cup-shaped depressions. Such infections do not show up under the Wood's lamp, but are treated in the same way. They tend to be short-lived and are not transmitted to other cats.

Dermatitis and ulcers

Dermatitis is a term for a number of inflammatory skin diseases (commonly called eczema), which are generally itchy and can be dry and scaly, or weeping and pustulate, or both. Allergic dermatitis results from sensitivity to certain foods (see p 195) and to the substances injected by skin parasites (see p 186). Contact dermatitis is an itchy rash caused by such irritants as detergents (such as in shampoos) and insecticides (as in flea collars). In all cases you must find and remove the irritant and gently bathe the affected area; if necessary your vet will supply a cream containing a steroid drug to reduce the inflammation. Dermatitis can also have nervous origins, particularly in highly-strung foreign breeds.

Solar dermatitis may affect the ears of white cats (or coloured cats with white ears). As with sunburn, the skin is inflamed, often itchy and very sensitive; patches of hair fall out. You can control the disorder by keeping the cat indoors; otherwise a daily application of a suntan cream or lotion suitable for babies may help. Without treatment, it worsens each summer and eventually ulcers (open sores) appear and may bleed. You should swab these with a safe feline antiseptic (see p 178), but if they do not begin to heal in a few days the vet may

have to scrape away the dead tissues, leaving a clean wound to heal. In long-neglected cases a skin tumour may develop, necessitating surgery; it may even spread to the face. Fortunately skin tumours are rare in cats, but if they do occur they are often cancerous and untreatable.

Chronic skin ulcers on the feet, ears and elsewhere may also rarely be caused by the rhinotracheitis virus (FVR; see p 197), one of the group of respiratory virus infections known in Britain as cat flu. And sometimes skin ulcers are associated with 'rodent ulcer' in the mouth (see p 196).

Other skin problems

Apart from wounds and abscesses (see p 182), one of the other commonest feline skin complaints is stud tail, an excessive secretion of oil from the sebaceous glands at the base of the tail (see p 106) that occurs mainly in uncastrated males. This does not usually bother the cat unless secondary bacterial infection causes irritation, but the greasy patches of hair are unsightly, particularly on pale-coloured cats. Feline acne, on the chin and edges of the lips, is caused by an accumulation of oil in similar glands, which blocks their openings and hardens to form blackheads. Bacterial infection may form small abscesses, or pimples. In both stud tail and acne, regularly washing the area with a cat shampoo or rubbing it with an antiseptic preparation such as chlorhexidine usually helps, but antibiotic treatment is sometimes needed.

Balding, or alopecia, is occasionally seen in cats, especially neuters. Hair falls out on the hindquarters and abdomen, but there is no itchiness or change in the skin. The cause may be hormonal, and there have been apparent cures in some cases through the use of synthetic sex hormones (see p 213).

Internal parasites

Internal parasites – small creatures that live inside the body – are a common problem in cats. Although few of the several hundred parasitic candidates cause serious diseases, heavy infestations are invariably detrimental to the cat's general condition and can even be a human health hazard. They are easily prevented, however, with some understanding of the life cycles of the parasites and simple methods of control.

Apart from a few microscopic single-celled animals, all the cat's internal parasites are worms. Most are long and round (roundworms), some are flat and ribbon-like (tapeworms) and a few are small and leaf-like (flukes). Many spend the young stages of their life cycle in another animal (the intermediate host) and can only infect the cat and develop into adults when the cat preys on and eats this other animal. Cats allowed to hunt are therefore more liable to be parasitized than those confined indoors.

Infestations are also picked up in several other ways – for example, via external parasites such as fleas or via soil contaminated with an infected cat's faeces – and not all cats are exposed to the same infestations. Age, for example, affects the cat's susceptibility to different parasites, and a problem parasite in one locality may never occur in another.

Internal parasites need never be a problem, however, if simple rules are followed. Observe strict hygiene about the disposal of faeces and the cleanliness of runs and pens. Keep surfaces dry, as most worms cannot stand desiccation. Control external parasites that may be intermediate hosts. Try to prevent your cat eating prey, and avoid raw fish in areas with fish-borne parasites. Have your cat regularly checked for internal parasites – especially breeding animals and kittens, which can be severely weakened by heavy infestations. Finally, remember that a healthy, well-cared-for cat is less likely to succumb to an internal parasite infestation.

Worms can parasitize many parts of the cat's body, but those discussed in this article, which live in the cat's digestive system, form the majority. Lungworms (see p198), heartworms (see p204) and eye-worms (see p201) are covered with other ailments relating to that part of the body.

Ascarid roundworms

Ascarids are the most widespread and familiar of the roundworms. *Toxocara* and *Toxascaris* species (like many parasites, they have no specific English common names) are the thick, white worms, up to 10cm (4in) long, that are commonly seen in the cat's faeces and vomit. In most parts of the world about one cat in five is infected with *Toxocara cati*. Adult worms feed on digested food in the cat's intestine and lay eggs that are passed on via the faeces – either direct or through mice, rats and beetles that

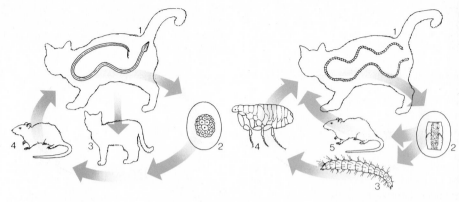

Ascarid roundworms grow to a length of 10cm (4in) in the cat's intestine **1** and shed eggs **2** via its faeces. These remain viable for years and if swallowed by a cat the larvae hatch in the intestine. Those of *Toxocara cati* migrate in the blood to the liver and lungs and may be transmitted to

kittens **3** via the milk. After two to three weeks the larvae return to the intestine to become adult worms. Larvae of *Toxascaris leonina* do not leave the intestine. Any eggs eaten by a mouse **4** or other abnormal host encyst in its tissues and infect a cat that eats the host.

Tapeworms grow up to 1m (3½ ft) long **1** and consist of egg-filled segments **2** passed in faeces. *Dipylidium caninum* eggs are eaten by lice or flea larvae **3** and infect the cat via the adult parasite **4**. Eggs of *Taenia taeniaeformis* eaten by a rodent **5** infect a cat that preys on the rodent.

Tapeworm (two-thirds life-size)

Ascarid roundworm (half life-size)

Hookworm (twice life-size)

Whipworm (1⅓ times life-size)

accidentally take in eggs. It is now known that infective larval stages may be found in the milk of nursing queens, having migrated there from the mother's tissues at the start of lactation. This means that kittens can be infected as soon as they are born and start to suckle.

This is disturbing because, whereas ascarids rarely cause more than restlessness in adults, kittens can be seriously affected. Larval worms migrating through the lungs to the intestine can invoke a cough and even pneumonia. More commonly the kitten weakens, appears malnourished despite an excessive appetite and has a dull dry coat and a swollen or pot belly. It usually has diarrhoea and sickness, often vomiting worms or passing them in its faeces.

Adult roundworms can be easily destroyed (see box). If necessary, kittens infected at birth can be treated under veterinary supervision when they are two or three weeks old. Control measures to prevent reinfestation (see above) are essential and are especially successful in kittens, which can quite easily be prevented

from hunting infected prey. There are as yet no drugs that will eliminate the infective larvae in the queen, however, and the only guarantee of raising worm-free kittens is to hand-rear them from birth. As long as the reservoir of infection in the queen remains, *Toxocara* can never be fully eliminated.

Hookworms

Hookworms are generally a problem only in hot humid areas, such as parts of Australia and the southern United States, where the conditions are right for their rapid development and spread. The name comes from the hook-shaped head end, which has spines for attachment to the host's gut.

The most important are species of *Ancylostoma*. These small blood-sucking roundworms are so highly evolved that they select their blood not from veins but from the rich small arteries of the intestinal wall. Under favourable conditions the eggs passed out in the faeces develop through three larval stages, outside the host, within a week. The larvae can then infect the cat either by being swallowed or by penetrating its skin. As a result they are likely to be picked up by cats lying on damp, dirty bedding. The worms mature within about three weeks of entering the body.

Adult hookworms living in the intestine can cause weakness, severe anaemia (see p 204) and diarrhoea, with characteristically dark faeces occasionally flecked with blood. Cats may even die through severe blood loss. When the larvae penetrate the skin, they often induce a skin reaction, which after several infections may develop into an obstinate moist dermatitis (see p 189). Hookworm infestations can be effectively treated with drugs given under veterinary supervision. In hookworm infested areas, the only way to prevent reinfection is to keep the cat indoors, change its litter regularly and provide clean, dry bedding.

Whipworms and threadworms

The whipworm (*Trichuris*) and the threadworm (*Strongyloides*) are rare in cats but in certain areas – notably parts of the United States and Australia – whipworm infestations are increasingly being discovered. The eggs and larvae, which have no intermediate host, can be ingested, and threadworms may be transmissible through the mother's milk. The tiny, slender worms live in the large intestine and can cause anaemia, weight loss and diarrhoea. However, the infestation is usually symptomless and in whipworm- and threadworm-prone areas routine veterinary check-ups should include examination of the cat's faeces for their eggs. The worms are easily destroyed.

Tapeworms and flukes

Tapeworms and flukes are both flatworms that spend their larval stages in other animals, which must be eaten by the cat before it can be infected.

The most common cat tapeworms are *Dipylidium caninum*, picked up by the ingestion of infected lice and fleas during grooming, and *Taenia taeniaeformis*, transmitted by infected prey, such as mice and rats. Tapeworms are common intestinal parasites, and although they rob the cat of food that it has eaten, they are seldom harmful. Heavily infested cats may lose condition, become restless and have a digestive upset, but usually the only sign of infestation is the appearance in the faeces of whitish tapeworm segments. When dry, these resemble grains of rice. Those of *Dipylidium* can initially move like caterpillars, and the irritation they cause shows in the cat's preoccupation with its anal region. In rare cases children have become infected with *Dipylidium* by accidentally swallowing a flea, but cat tapeworms are not a serious human health hazard.

Drugs to eliminate tapeworms must be strong enough to make the parasite let go of the gut wall. It is best to consult your vet about which to use as some over-the-counter drugs are so toxic as to cause unpleasant side-effects. Adult tapeworms can be effectively eliminated but deworming must be combined with control of fleas and lice to prevent reinfection in the case of *Dipylidium*, and with restriction of hunting and careful cooking of meat and fish to avoid the recurrence of other tapeworms.

Flukes are seldom found in cats and the rare infestations of the intestines, liver and lungs (see p 198) are usually the result of eating infected raw fish. Signs of fluke infestation vary and need veterinary diagnosis. Drug treatment is not always successful, so in areas of risk (which include parts of North America and the tropics) cats should be prevented from hunting and given potential carrier fish only if cooked.

Single-celled parasites

A few relatively minor intestinal parasites are microscopic, single-celled animals called protozoa. *Isospora* (a coccidian) is carried by many cats without any ill-effects; the numbers of parasites are rarely enough to cause disease, called coccidiosis. But kittens infected via other cats' faeces – usually in unhygienic premises – can develop enteritis (see p 192), often with anaemia. The infection responds well to sulpha drugs combined with treatment to combat dehydration, but is debilitating enough for recovery to take some time.

The most significant protozoan parasite of cats – and the most dangerous of the group to humans – is *Toxoplasma*. As in the case of other mammals, the cat is often a symptomless carrier of the infection (toxoplasmosis), although after maturing in the intestine the parasites can infect any tissues in the body, producing symptoms that are confusingly similar to other diseases. Blood and faecal samples are needed to confirm diagnosis, and the infection has responded to certain drugs.

Toxoplasma can occur in any animal, but only the cat spreads the parasites via infective cysts shed in its faeces. As a result, it is one of the few diseases that can be directly passed from cats to humans (see also p 173). Although it usually goes unnoticed, there is a risk that, if transmitted by a pregnant woman to her unborn child, it may cause congenital abnormalities. Cat *Toxoplasma* is undoubtedly a significant health hazard, but handling and eating raw or undercooked meat is an equally important source of infection – in both cats and people – and it can also pass directly between humans.

Fortunately, *Toxoplasma* infection is easily prevented. To reduce the chance of feline toxoplasmosis, feed only heat-processed commercial cat foods or well-cooked fresh meat. If possible, prevent the cat eating wild prey. Pregnant women should take especially stringent precautions against infection. If the cat has possible symptoms, your vet can test its faeces; if infective cysts are found it can be isolated for a few weeks until shedding stops. However, since the cysts take up to five days to become infective, changing the litter each day and regularly disinfecting the litter tray are adequate protection. Rubber gloves can be worn, but even with this added precaution pregnant women should avoid the duty. Always wash your hands after handling raw meat, and cook all meat thoroughly. Gardening gloves prevent contact with *Toxoplasma*-infested soil, and sand pits should have lids to avoid contamination by cat faeces.

DEWORMING

In general, you should never attempt to deworm a cat without consulting your vet, although some vets consider that preparations containing piperazine are safe enough for routine use against ascarid roundworms if the directions are followed carefully. However, worm medications can be fatal in excess, or if given to very young or sickly cats, or for an illness wrongly diagnosed as worms.

After veterinary examination of a faecal sample, the drug prescribed, its dosage and the number of treatments will depend on the type of worm and on the cat's age, weight and state of health. The vet may perform the deworming if, for example, the medication is relatively dangerous. Otherwise instructions will include distinguishing between possible natural side-effects, such as diarrhoea and vomiting, and a toxic reaction.

Tablets, such as those of piperazine for roundworms, can be crushed up in food or milk. For tapeworms, tablets of salicylamide or niclosamide are given orally (see p 179) after a 12-hour fast; a coating on some tablets prevents their absorption until in the gut, so these must be swallowed whole without chewing. Occasionally, such as in fluke infestations, the vet will give the drug by injection.

The worms are expelled in the faeces from a few hours to several days after dosing. For the following day or so the cat needs a bland diet. Worming is usually repeated at least once during the next two to three weeks in the case of ascarid roundworms, or after one to three months for hookworms, whipworms and tapeworms. This kills any roundworms that have matured from larvae in the cat's tissues or tapeworms that have developed from scolexes (heads) left behind in the gut wall. If worms appear after the second deworming, the cat has probably become reinfected.

Digestive and abdominal diseases 1

The most significant signs of problems of the digestive system (gut) and associated organs are vomiting, diarrhoea and constipation. Each symptom, however, has numerous possible causes, so that the more details you can provide the easier it is for your vet to make a diagnosis.

Do not confuse vomiting with retching, in which the cat stretches out its neck and dramatic contractions of the abdomen may bring up mucus but not vomit, or either of these with coughing. There is also a distinction between regurgitation, which returns food that has pooled in the oesophagus (gullet), indicating a problem in the first part of the digestive tube, and true vomiting, in which food is ejected from the stomach. Food regurgitated after feeding may have a characteristic sausage shape and may be eaten again, even by other cats – unlike vomit, which has been made distastefully acidic by stomach secretions.

The difference between diarrhoea and constipation, which are both associated with diseases of the intestine, is self-evident. However, signs of constipation can be confused with a urinary problem (see p 203), for a cat that repeatedly squats and strains is more likely to be straining to pass urine than attempting to defecate. It is helpful to note the appearance of the faeces and when and how the faecal output changes, but these are unlikely to be noticed in cats allowed to roam outdoors. In some cases, the vet will need a sample of the faeces for laboratory analysis before a positive diagnosis can be made.

These symptoms are not always a cause for concern, because occasional vomiting is normal in healthy cats – following grass-eating (see p 148) and when getting rid of hairballs, for example, or after overeating or a minor change in diet – and short-lived bouts of diarrhoea are a common reaction to stress, such as moving to a new home. In such cases it is sensible to offer smaller meals more frequently and to feed bland, easily digested foods such as finely minced or pureed white meat or fish. Mild constipation can easily be relieved by giving a small (5 ml) spoonful of medicinal liquid paraffin (mineral oil).

But if the symptoms persist for more than a day or two, or if there is blood in the faeces or vomit, or the cat has a fever, is weak or shows signs of abdominal pain by appearing hunched up and crying out if handled, you must seek immediate veterinary help. The condition may be chronic (persistent) and need specialized long-term treatment, or acute (critical), as in poisoning (see p 185) and feline infectious enteritis, when any delay may prove fatal.

Feline infectious enteritis

This disease – also commonly known by its initials FIE, or as feline panleukopaenia (FPL), and sometimes wrongly called feline

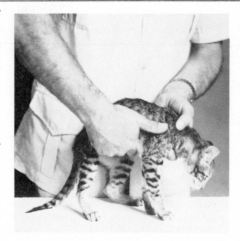

Examining the cat with abdominal trouble, the vet carefully palpates (feels) the abdomen for signs of swelling or tenderness.

A kitten suffering from diarrhoea looks extremely thin and dejected. Unless quickly treated it can die from dehydration.

distemper – is one of the most serious cat diseases caused by viruses (see p 172). It is common throughout the world, highly contagious and potentially fatal. The virus is capable of surviving in the environment for up to a year and is resistant to most disinfectants. Like all viral feline diseases, FIE primarily affects young cats and can develop so rapidly that death occurs before symptoms appear. Its effect at any age, however, largely depends on the cat's degree of immunity to the disease. The virus is transmitted by direct or indirect contact, and it takes two to ten days after contact for symptoms to develop (the incubation period).

The virus attacks any rapidly dividing cells (see p 22), especially those lining the gut – hence the resulting diarrhoea – and also the white blood cells, or leucocytes. (The name panleukopaenia comes from the characteristic drop in the number of these.) The damage to the gut lining may never be completely repaired and cats that recover from FIE may always be prone to diarrhoea. The virus also attacks the rapidly dividing cells in the cerebellum (part of the

Typical symptoms of FIE include loss of appetite, depression and fever **1**, followed by vomiting **2** (usually frothy and stained yellow by bile) and diarrhoea **3**. As a result of the diarrhoea the cat becomes dehydrated and may crouch over its water bowl **4**, though unable to drink. It crouches in a characteristic posture of pain **5** and eventually collapses **6**.

brain; see p 114) of the foetus during the last few weeks of pregnancy or the first few weeks of life, and an affected kitten is born with (or soon develops) a wobbly gait, known as ataxia (see p 207).

Early diagnosis means that the cat can be isolated to prevent the virus spreading and that treatment has more chance of success. Careful nursing is essential. Warm fluids to combat dehydration are most effectively given intravenously by the vet, who will also prescribe antibiotics against secondary infection. A vaccine virus may also usefully compete with the virulent virus in the early stages, or a serum may be given to provide antibodies (see p 173).

Vaccination is, however, far more valuable in preventing the disease. Kittens are usually first vaccinated between 8 and 12 weeks of age, when the protection of maternal antibodies – obtained during suckling – is declining. Two sorts of vaccine are available, one containing dead FIE viruses, the other live but weakened viruses. Some vaccines are combined with that for respiratory virus disease (cat flu). A second dose may be necessary two to four weeks after the first. A kitten particularly at risk can be vaccinated as early as six weeks old, but several subsequent doses are then necessary, the last one being given at 12 to 16 weeks. (Before this the level of maternal antibodies may interfere with the development of active immunity.)

A booster given at one to two years of age is probably sufficient in cats allowed to

mix with others, as they will boost their immunity naturally. However, many vets recommend annual boosters; an additional dose is certainly a sensible precaution before boarding a cat, and some establishments require a recent vaccination certificate. Pregnant queens must receive only dead vaccine, which will not affect the developing kittens. Vaccination with such a vaccine prior to or after mating is ideal, however, for it boosts the level of antibodies in the colostrum, or first milk (see p 225), and as a result increases the protection of kittens during the first weeks of life.

Despite the success of vaccination, control measures are also necessary, particularly when cats are kept in groups. Recovered cats may act as carriers for the virus, and even fleas may transmit it. All objects contacted by an infected cat should be either destroyed or disinfected by

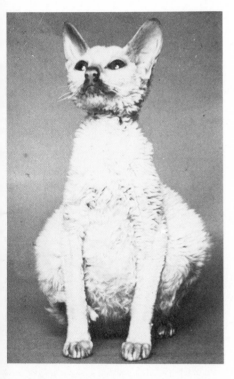

A cat with advanced FIP may have a grossly distended abdomen due to the accumulation of fluid resulting from inflammation of the peritoneum – the abdominal lining. Once the disease reaches this stage the cat inevitably dies. In spite of its name, however, FIP does not always involve peritonitis and can cause a confusingly wide range of other symptoms.

soaking them in formalin (see p 178) – one of the few disinfectants to which the virus is susceptible. If possible, wait at least three to six months before acquiring another cat and have it vaccinated before it arrives. Isolate all newcomers from other cats for at least the incubation period of the disease.

Other forms of enteritis
There are causes other than FIE of enteritis (inflammation of the lining of the intestine) and gastroenteritis (where gastritis – inflammation of the stomach lining – is also involved). All require veterinary treatment, which may involve measures to counteract dehydration, instructions on providing a bland diet until the inflammation subsides, and giving coating agents such as kaolin to soothe the inflammation and possibly antibiotics to fight infection.

Cats occasionally consume irritants and poisons, especially via grooming a contaminated coat. The resulting gastroenteritis produces severe vomiting and diarrhoea, and needs emergency veterinary treatment (see p 185). Very rarely, a cat may eat spoilt, contaminated or improperly cooked food carrying 'food-poisoning' bacteria. *Salmonella* is the most important, as humans can be easily infected and cats may remain carriers for some time. A stomach upset can cause vomiting, abdominal pain and excessive drinking to replace lost fluid. An infection in the intestine results in diarrhoea and, in kittens, can be fatal.

If the kidneys are not functioning efficiently, the waste products that they normally excrete may accumulate in the bloodstream and irritate the lining of the stomach and intestines, producing vomiting, sometimes diarrhoea and usually excessive thirst and halitosis (bad breath). Chronic kidney failure is a common condition of old cats (see p 203). Other causes of vomiting and diarrhoea include heavy infestations of intestinal parasites (see p 190) and food allergies (see p 195).

Colitis (inflammation of the colon, the lower part of the intestine) is less common than gastroenteritis. Attacks are characterized by diarrhoea, containing mucus and fresh blood because the condition is usually chronic and the intestinal lining forms ulcers and bleeds. Because the precise cause is often unknown, treatment is generally aimed at soothing the damaged intestinal lining with coating agents and steroid drugs, often combined with antibiotics.

Diseases of the liver and pancreas
Hepatitis (inflammation of the liver) is not common in cats but can result from damage by ingested poisons or be secondary to other major diseases. Symptoms include depression, loss of appetite and weight, and diarrhoea or constipation, but most distinctively the whites of the eyes and the inside of the mouth become bright yellow or orange. This discoloration, known as jaundice, is well known in human liver patients; it affects the whole skin and is caused by bile pigments from the damaged liver accumulating in the bloodstream.

In chronic hepatitis, normal liver cells may be replaced by fibrous tissue – cirrhosis of the liver – and congestion of the veins coming from the liver increases the pressure in nearby capillaries and causes fluid to leak out and accumulate in the abdomen, giving the cat a pot belly. This condition – called ascites – is also a symptom of other diseases. Jaundice and ascites, as well as intermittent vomiting, can be caused by liver cancer.

Pancreatitis (inflammation of the pancreas, a gland producing digestive enzymes and also hormones, such as insulin) is rare in cats and of little importance. Chronic cases may however lead to diabetes – the disorder of carbohydrate metabolism due to insufficient insulin that is well known in human patients and is seen mainly in old cats.

Peritonitis
Peritonitis – inflammation of the peritoneum, the membrane lining the abdomen and covering the organs within it – is always a serious condition. It can result from bacteria and toxins spread from wounds and diseased or ruptured organs elsewhere in the body or, more significantly, from an infectious virus responsible for feline infectious peritonitis (FIP). FIP, like FIE (see above) is one of the four major viral cat diseases. The virus, one of the corona group, attacks many parts of the body, but peritonitis is a common (and extremely important) result.

Fortunately, most cats develop a natural immunity to FIP. The virus cannot live long away from its host and is easily killed by careful disinfection, but where many cats are in close contact – as in multi-cat households and catteries – it spreads rapidly from infected cats and possibly from 'carrier' animals. Cats under three years old are most susceptible, and the symptoms (which may not appear for several weeks or months after contact) are typically loss of appetite, fever, weight loss and a swollen abdomen, or ascites (due to the accumulation of tacky yellow fluid). Sometimes there is vomiting, diarrhoea, jaundice and anaemia. However, FIP is not an abdominal disease alone, and it may affect areas such as the liver, kidneys, central nervous system and eyes, producing signs that /continued

Digestive and abdominal diseases 2

mimic other diseases, as does toxoplasmosis (see p 194). Some cats have an accumulation of fluid in the chest or, rarely, in the sac surrounding the heart. Diseased cats are sometimes also infected by feline leukaemia virus (see p 204), which may lower their resistance to FIP.

Once cats develop signs of the disease they almost invariably die, usually within a few weeks. Measures to combat dehydration, inflammation and loss of appetite make the cat more comfortable, but there is no effective treatment and as yet no method of immunization. The only way of preventing the disease spreading is to isolate and/or destroy the infected cat.

Symptoms of non-viral peritonitis – which is not common and usually follows abdominal surgery – appear more rapidly after infection than with FIP, and the cat soon looks unwell due to fever and abdominal pain. However, with antibiotics, intravenous fluids and good nursing, cats with bacterial peritonitis at least have some chance of recovery.

Obstructions of the gut

Constrictions These are often caused by congenital abnormalities. A kitten may, for example, be born with a constriction of the pylorus, the ring of muscle that controls the outlet of food from the stomach into the intestine. Siamese cats seem particularly prone, and the incidence in members of the same family suggests that the condition is hereditary. As fluids may pass through normally, the defect (known as pyloric stenosis) is often noticed only during weaning, when solid food accumulates in the stomach and eventually is forcefully vomited, often some distance from the kitten. In time the kitten loses condition and its growth is stunted.

Your vet can make an accurate diagnosis by giving a barium meal and monitoring its progress through the gut by a series of X-ray pictures. In this case, the barium (which blocks X-rays and shows up as a shadow on the film) will be released only slowly, if at all, into the intestine. The cure involves an operation in which slits are cut into the pylorus to dilate the muscles. Unfortunately, the constriction may return as scar tissue forms over the slits when they heal.

Sometimes the defect is in the oesophagus (gullet), which leads from the throat to the stomach. This may lack the muscle tension needed to pass food down into the stomach, so that the kitten constantly regurgitates its meals. By feeding it in an upright position, standing it on its hind legs with front legs lifted up, gravity may pull food into the stomach. By doing this repeatedly the muscles of the gullet may 'learn' to function normally; unfortunately, it is rarely successful, and euthanasia is usually necessary.

Another congenital defect narrows the

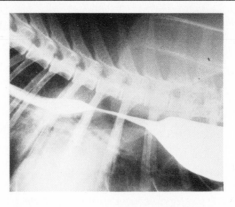

Pyloric stenosis is a congenital problem of the lower, 'outlet' valve of the stomach. This X-ray, taken after a barium meal, shows the stomach to the right and the constricted intestine running to the left.

gullet by compression, a defect in the blood vessels of the chest 'strangling' the gullet and blocking the passage of food. A non-congenital constriction of the gullet – seen mainly in young cats – is the result of compression by a malignant tumour of the thymus gland in the neck. This is generally caused by the feline leukaemia virus (see p 204), and is fatal.

Stricture of the gullet is also a rare complication following surgery. During anaesthesia digestive stomach acids may sometimes flow into the gullet and later ulcers develop. As they heal, scar tissue contracts, narrowing the tube. The vet can usually use mechanical devices to progressively expand the constriction. On the other hand, in middle-aged, usually nervous cats the gullet may malfunction for 'psychological' reasons, causing regurgitation. Smaller and more frequent, easily digested meals, together with kaolin and pectate, may help. The vet may also prescribe atropine drops or tablets which are given a few minutes before feeding to dilate the muscles at the base of the gullet.

UMBILICAL HERNIA
Occasionally a kitten shows a lump on its abdomen, particularly when standing, in the region of where the umbilical cord was attached. This is due to a weakness in the abdominal wall allowing part of the intestine to protrude. It may be due to an accident at birth or to malformation during development in the womb, and is possibly hereditary.

Blockages Cats are careful feeders, but bones can get stuck in the mouth and 'toys' such as thread with needles attached, string, and pieces of plastic may be inadvertently swallowed. For emergency treatment in such cases, see page 183.

A more everyday problem is a hairball in the stomach, from hair swallowed during grooming. A cat usually vomits this without any problem, but if not it can accumulate in the stomach or intestine, causing loss of appetite and possibly vomiting and/or constipation. It may need to be surgically removed, but usually a mild laxative, such as medicinal liquid paraffin (mineral oil), will clear the hairball through vomiting or via the faeces. Cats with a tendency to this problem, especially long-haired varieties, should be regularly groomed (see p 154) and given an occasional preventative dose of liquid paraffin.

Serious blockage due to constipation is mainly a problem in old cats, when the muscles of the large intestine lose their tension. Occasionally, blockage is caused by a tumour of the gut wall. Growths in the gullet and stomach may form ulcers so that regurgitated and vomited food is streaked with blood. They are usually cancerous and are discovered too late to be removed. Tumours of the intestine, also usually fatal, cause progressive weight loss and intermittent diarrhoea, and are the most common tumours of old cats (see p 208).

Complications following diarrhoea
Occasionally, a bout of diarrhoea (or the measures taken to treat it) may lead to more severe complications. For example, the gut of a healthy cat contains a number of different bacteria – the intestinal flora – which are essential for normal digestion. There is a natural balance between them and they do no harm, but over-treatment of initially trivial cases of diarrhoea with antibiotics may upset this balance. The drug suppresses one type of bacteria and allows rampant growth of another type, leading to chronic diarrhoea. It may take some time, with careful attention to diet, before the flora return to normal.

Intussusception is a complication that may follow chronic diarrhoea, especially in young kittens. One part of the intestine folds, or telescopes, back onto the adjoining section, and may cut off its blood supply, killing the incarcerated tissue. Toxins released into the blood cause vomiting, loss of appetite and a generally severe illness. A vet must usually operate immediately to remove the diseased section of gut. Severe diarrhoea, especially in kittens, may somewhat similarly cause the rectum – the final section of the gut – to prolapse (slip down) and protrude from the anus. The vet will replace the prolapse, using surgery, if necessary, and then treat the underlying cause of diarrhoea.

Dietary problems

Considering the unique nutritional needs of cats, dietary problems are relatively uncommon. Most of those described below are seen at all frequently only in laboratory animals fed deliberately unbalanced diets. With a few exceptions, such as food allergies and giving a cat dog food (which may lack taurine and eventually cause blindness; see p 148), most of those that do occur in domestic animals can be blamed on owners providing too much appetizing food. The usual result is obesity and nutrient 'poisoning', but overindulgence in certain foods can cause deficiency diseases. Some specific remedies, to be given under veterinary guidance, are mentioned below, but in virtually every case the long-term answer is to provide the correct amounts of a balanced diet (see p 148).

Too much muscle meat

Cats may be quite content on a sole diet of best steak or chicken, but muscle meats lack vitamin A, and signs of deficiency are likely to appear within a few months. They are clearly apparent in kittens, where growth is stunted and some bones 'over-grow'; those of the skull press on the spinal cord, paralysing both hind legs and forcing the head back into a position vividly described as 'stargazing syndrome'. Other symptoms include night blindness and eventually total blindness and increased susceptibility to infections. Severe lack of vitamin A in pregnant queens can induce spontaneous abortions, foetal malformations, stillbirths and ultimately sterility. Most symptoms can be put right by adding two to three drops of cod liver oil – no more – to the daily diet.

An additional (and more common) risk of an all-muscle-meat diet is lack of calcium. Meat does contain some calcium, but because it also lacks vitamin D and is relatively rich in phosphorus, this is not absorbed properly from the intestines. To compensate, the mineral is drawn out of the cat's bones; as these soften the limbs may become bowed (as in rickets in other animals) and are more liable to greenstick fractures (which produce sudden lameness and pain, without bone distortions).

The cats most prone to this disorder, which is sometimes called paper bone disease, are lactating queens (which are supplying prodigious amounts of calcium in their milk) and growing kittens. Such queens may show an acute form of calcium deficiency known as eclampsia (see p 229). Kittens often remain outwardly healthy but become less active, suddenly weak or painfully lame and reluctant to move. Short-term treatment involves giving dietary calcium supplements or milk, if acceptable, plus foods rich in vitamin D, such as liver, to increase calcium absorption.

Too much liver and fatty fish

Vitamins A and D are as dangerous in excess as when deficient, and cats unfortunately have a natural greed for foods rich in them, such as liver and fatty fish. Cats consuming abnormally high levels of vitamin D absorb too much calcium and deposit it as chalk in their soft tissues. More spectacular are the signs of vitamin A poisoning, which is not uncommon since a cat allowed to indulge its appetite on a diet solely of liver would get 50 times as much of this vitamin as it needs.

The earliest sign of vitamin A overdose is usually swollen, painful joints, leading to lameness. Confusingly, other signs are similar to those of vitamin A deficiency; for example, queens may produce congenitally deformed offspring. In mild cases the cat regains the mobility of its joints once its diet is corrected, but if poisoning is severe it will be permanently lame.

Fatty fish is also rich in unsaturated oils, which oxidize and destroy vitamin E. As a result, a diet based on such fish – particularly unsupplemented tuna – can cause a deficiency of this vitamin. Also known as steatitis (or pansteatitis) because of the

A fat cat, like a fat person, is usually the result of over-feeding combined with lack of exercise. Most correctly fed cats maintain a weight of between 3.5 and 7 kg (8 and 15 lb), depending on sex and breed.

resulting inflammation of body fat, or yellow fat disease (which describes the discoloration that occurs), this is relatively common. The affected cat has a fever, is generally 'off colour' and may lose its appetite. It is reluctant to move and unwilling to be handled as this causes pain. The disorder is rapidly corrected with a daily dose of vitamin E.

Lack of B vitamins

Fatty or not, fish can also be blamed for another deficiency disease, because, when fed raw, some fish (such as carp and herring) contain an enzyme that destroys vitamin B_1 (thiamine). The vitamin can also be eradicated by the high temperature used in processing commercial cat foods, but extra thiamine is normally added to these. Cats lacking thiamine become anorexic, suffer convulsions and may die within a few days, but if given doses of the vitamin early enough they recover within hours. Deficiencies of other B vitamins are usually caused by body disorders which, for example, increase their excretion or decrease their absorption from the gut. Treatment is generally by giving tablets or injections of multi-B vitamins.

Food allergies

Although some foods provoke vomiting, food allergies usually cause profuse diarrhoea. An intensely itchy skin may also develop, with loss of hair and oozing sores from constant scratching. Once the cat is diagnosed as having such an allergy, it is usually possible – though time-consuming – to isolate and eliminate the allergenic foods by placing the cat on a stable diet and introducing the suspect foods one by one.

CATS AND MILK

Cats' love of milk is usually taken for granted – after all, they were suckled on it – and many enjoy their daily drink of cow's milk unaware of its value as a source of protein, vitamin A and especially calcium. Some cats, however, simply dislike it; others – especially foreign breeds, such as Siamese – cannot tolerate milk and develop diarrhoea if given it. This may indicate an allergy, but is often due to a lack of lactase, the enzyme needed to digest lactose (milk sugar). Some cats lack the enzyme right from weaning; others develop a deficiency of it with age, while sometimes cats have a temporary lack due to an intestinal illness.

Feeding watered-down milk may help with partially deficient cats, possibly gradually increasing its strength in the case of intolerance after digestive upsets. If the problem persists, it may be due to the cat's hypersensitivity to specific milk proteins, and other types of milk (such as goat's or evaporated milk) may be successfully given as an alternative. Similarly, evaporated or skimmed milk may be tolerated by cats that are not able to digest milk fat.

Cats unable to tolerate milk must receive a balanced diet of other foods, and you should seek veterinary advice on giving calcium supplements (see p 149). This is particularly vital for pregnant or lactating queens and kittens.

Mouth and teeth problems

Cats rarely suffer from the dental decay that afflicts humans, but teeth and other mouth problems are nevertheless among the most common feline ailments. They are often difficult to treat, because the cause may be hard to pinpoint or because they have been overlooked too long. Indeed, they may turn out to be only secondary symptoms of a more generalized disorder, such as kidney disease, or the sole manifestation of a respiratory virus infection (cat flu). These are good reasons for regularly checking your cat's mouth for signs of trouble and being able to recognize the early symptoms.

The most significant type of oral disease is inflammation of the mouth lining, known as stomatitis. The commonest form of this is gingivitis, or inflammation of the gums, while sometimes ulcers may form on the gums or elsewhere. Severe gingivitis may lead to a condition called gingival hyperplasia in which there is uncontrolled growth of gum tissue in an attempt to heal the inflamed, ulcerated areas. The excess tissue encroaches on the teeth and becomes damaged during feeding, leading to further trouble. Severe gum infections may lead to pyorrhoea, with a discharge of pus from the tooth sockets.

Acute stomatitis
Among the causes of acute (suddenly developing) mouth troubles, with the cat showing considerable distress, are fish bones lodged between the teeth, ingestion of irritant chemicals (especially from the coat during grooming) and accidents. All may need first aid (see p 180) and immediate veterinary help. Not quite so abrupt in producing symptoms, but more common and potentially more serious, is the calci-virus (FCV; see p 197) responsible for one form of upper respiratory tract disease (cat flu). This may result in ulcers, particularly on the tongue, and/or gingivitis. With some strains of the virus, mouth troubles may be the only symptoms.

Chronic stomatitis
More gradually developing inflammation may or may not be associated with dental problems. In mild cases, there is often only reddening where the gums and teeth meet, while in severe cases the whole gums may be red, swollen or bleeding. The cat will often show difficulty in eating (especially hard foods) and perhaps drooling, but no loss of appetite. There may be halitosis (bad breath), symptomatic of bacterial infection, but this can also be caused by such conditions as kidney disease and stomach upsets.

On examining the mouth (which is often painful to open), ulcers may be seen, especially around the angle of the jaw, near the hindmost teeth. Although, as mentioned above, ulcers may indicate a virus infection, there are other causes which are unknown. Very commonly, especially in

middle-aged or elderly cats, the teeth will be coated with tartar, a hard deposit – sometimes much larger that the teeth themselves – that stains them brownish-yellow. This may be the primary cause of the trouble, which in severe cases can lead to pyorrhoea; some teeth may even fall out.

Treatment depends on whether or not the teeth are involved, or only the gums. In the earlier stages of tartar build-up, this can be removed by a vet, usually under general anaesthetic. Antibiotics may be prescribed if there is serious gingivitis, with or without periodontitis (inflammation of the tooth sockets). In very bad cases, teeth may have to be removed – a skilled job, because feline

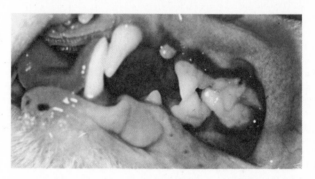

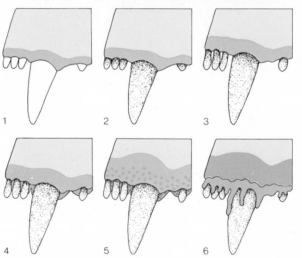

teeth are brittle and it is vital that no broken roots are left in their sockets. Treatment of persistent inflammation is often not very successful. Steroid drugs may help, but often only temporarily. Multivitamins can stimulate new cell growth, while it may be necessary to surgically cauterize (burn out) ulcers so that new tissues can grow. With extensive ulceration and hyperplasia, the removal of apparently healthy associated teeth may be the only way of easing the condition.

In the longer term, providing some hard foods in the diet may help to clean the teeth, though some vets dispute their effectiveness. Antiseptic mouthwashes aid oral hygiene, but may not be tolerated by the cat. A few cats will allow a toothbrush to be

used to remove the mushy white plaque that precedes tartar. Failing this, cats prone to tartar should be regularly examined and have their teeth descaled by a vet before serious trouble develops.

Other mouth problems
Cleft palate may be the result of an accident (see p 181) or be a congenital (inborn) and sometimes hereditary defect of the roof of the mouth. Because the cleft allows the mouth and nasal passages to communicate, kittens cannot suckle, as milk passes back through the nose. Unless the cleft can be surgically repaired when the kitten is very young, euthanasia is normally necessary.

Gingivitis, or inflammation of the gums, often first shows where the teeth and gums meet. Its causes may include injury, foreign bodies between the teeth, a build-up of a hard coating of tartar on the teeth or kidney failure. Apart from treating the basic cause, antibiotics, cleaning or even removal of teeth and saline washes are needed.

How gingivitis develops
Whether due to primary inflammation where the teeth enter the gums **1** or a build-up of tartar on the teeth **2**, the gums recess or are pushed back **3**, showing the base of the teeth and creating pockets **4** where food can collect. This makes an ideal environment for bacteria to grow, causing secondary infection **5** so that the gums appear red and swollen. The tooth sockets may become involved, leading to severe inflammation of the gums with purulent (pus-type) discharge **6**. This gum disease is known as pyorrhoea.

The commonly (but wrongly) termed rodent ulcer which may be seen on the top lip or elsewhere is not, unlike the human disorder of the same name, cancerous. The proper name for the condition is eosinophilic granuloma. It responds well to steroid drugs and to cryosurgery (in which the ulcer-like growth is destroyed by freezing). True cancerous mouth tumours are, unfortunately, quite common in cats, occurring mainly on the gums, tongue, tonsils, lips and nose. They cause swelling, difficulty in eating and bleeding from the mouth. Although they tend not to metastasize (spread to other sites in the body), they usually recur soon after removal. In fact, removal is often not possible and the cat eventually has to be put down.

Respiratory ailments I

Cats commonly suffer from the feline equivalent of human influenza and other respiratory ailments. They are particularly susceptible to viral and other infections of the nose and throat – collectively termed upper respiratory infections, but commonly known in Britain and some other countries as cat flu – and these are among the most frequent conditions with which vets have to deal. Diseases affecting the lower part of the respiratory tract, in the chest, are less common, but are extremely serious and often life-threatening.

The signs of respiratory problems are very characteristic. In upper respiratory disease there may be sneezing, noisy breathing ('snuffles'), a nasal discharge and coughing. Often there are also eye and mouth signs such as conjunctivitis and ulcers. Laboured breathing (the veterinary term for which is dyspnoea) is the cardinal sign of diseases affecting the lungs and thorax (chest). There are many possible causes of this, however, and distinguishing them often depends on extensive tests using X-rays, blood samples and so on.

Unfortunately, no direct treatment is available to combat the viruses that cause the commonest feline respiratory diseases, although antibiotics may help to prevent secondary damage by bacteria. However, early diagnosis gives a much greater chance of survival, for careful nursing is absolutely vital in such cases and can make all the difference between the cat recovering or succumbing to the disease. (It has been said that, almost uniquely among feline ailments, the cat's chances of recovery from this disease depend more on the owner than on the vet, once diagnosis has been made.) Early isolation of affected cats is also very important in reducing the chances of the disease spreading.

A special feature of nursing feline respiratory patients is the need for extreme care when handling a cat with dyspnoea. Unlike people and dogs, cats are very reluctant to breathe through the , mouth, so that breathing difficulties may result when only the nose is blocked, let alone the deeper respiratory passages or lungs. But irrespective of the site of the problem, if you do not handle such a cat very gently, the dyspnoea may worsen, with fatal consequences.

Respiratory virus infections

Causes and effects Although various micro-organisms can infect the cat's nose and throat, viruses are by far the most significant. A number of different viruses may be involved, and the symptoms they produce differ somewhat. The most important are the feline viral rhinotracheitis (FVR) virus – a herpes virus like that which causes cold sore in humans – and the feline calcivirus (FCV). In the United States, other organisms have been implicated, in particular the feline pneumonitis agent,

Chlamydia psittaci – an organism known as a rickettsia that is part-way between a virus and a bacterium in characteristics, and is therefore susceptible to certain antibiotics – and feline reoviruses, which generally produce only mild symptoms such as running eyes. Usually a cat with upper respiratory disease is attacked by only one of these organisms at a time, but in groups of cats, where the disease is relatively common, combined infections may occur.

Unlike some other feline viruses, FVR and FCV are relatively short-lived outside cats' bodies – about 24 hours and three days respectively – so that transmission from cat to cat is mainly by direct contact or airborne

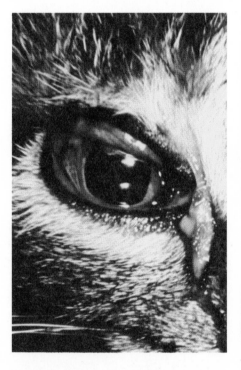

A cat with FVR shows the typical discharge of purulent mucus from the eyes and nose. The cat will be extremely ill for some weeks, and ulceration of the eyes can follow – sometimes leading to partial or even total blindness.

droplets (from sneezes and coughs). As a result, the danger areas are boarding and breeding establishments, veterinary hospitals and cat shows, where large numbers of cats come close together. Stress from strange surroundings, poor health, insufficient immunity in kittens or reduced resistance in old cats all increase the cat's susceptibility to infection.

Stress also plays a part in the spread of FVR because carriers of the virus – and that includes the majority of cats that have recovered from the disease – may be stimulated by stress to shed the virus, sometimes without themselves showing any symptoms. Carriers of FCV – again, about half of all survivors of the disease – on the other hand shed this virus continuously. Carrier

cats can harbour the virus for several years, but tests are available to identify them. It may even be possible for vaccinated cats to become carriers if exposed to a virulent strain of the virus.

FVR usually causes the most serious form of upper respiratory disease, symptoms appearing within two to ten days of contact. The main direct effect of the virus is to damage the linings of the nasal passages and sometimes the windpipe (rhinotracheitis means inflammation of the nose and trachea) and also the conjunctivas of the eyes (see p110). The damaged tissues react by producing the copious discharge that is characteristic of FVR. The cat slowly de-

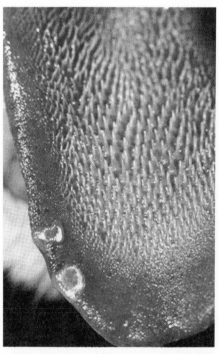

A cat with FCV may show few nasal symptoms but typically has ulcers on the tongue and elsewhere in the mouth. These can be painful, so that the cat refuses to eat, but FCV is in general a less severe disease than FVR.

velops a fever (reaching a peak about the fifth day), is listless and loses its appetite. Later it has fits of sneezing, develops conjunctivitis (see p201), and the eye and nose discharge may become purulent as secondary bacterial infections develop. Ulcers may occasionally be seen in the mouth. Other secondary effects of FVR may include pneumonia (see below) and, in pregnant queens, possibly abortion.

FCV exists in many different strains, of varying virulence, and symptoms of infection vary from those that are almost indistinguishable from FVR to cases so mild as to go unnoticed. The most common and characteristic signs are, however, ulcers on the tongue and elsewhere in the mouth. Nasal and eye discharges are */continued*

Respiratory ailments 2

usually absent, but the cat often has a fever and its reluctance to eat (due to the ulceration) results in a loss of weight. The disease usually lasts only about ten days, and most cats recover. However, some strains cause pneumonia, and this can be serious in cats with a secondary bacterial infection and fatal in kittens. As already mentioned, pneumonitis and reovirus infections are both usually mild and are rarely fatal, the former being treatable with tetracycline antibiotics.

Treatment and control   A cat with FVR or the more serious form of FCV needs careful nursing (see p178) and – if it is not too young, too old or too much out of condition – will usually start to recover within about a week of developing symptoms. The main needs are warmth, rest, plenty of fluids (if necessary by intravenous drip) and nutritious foods – best liquidized if the cat's mouth is inflamed, and highly flavoured to tempt a dulled palate. Regularly clean any discharge from the face, and apply a little petroleum jelly to damaged skin around the eyes and nose. Your vet will usually prescribe antibiotics (given by injection or mouth) to combat secondary infections. Multivitamins may also be advised and in some cases steroid drugs. It may be tempting to relieve nasal congestion with an inhalant, but many of these are toxic to cats and should be used only if advised by your vet.

The cats most likely to die from upper respiratory infections are the old or debilitated and kittens, about a quarter of which succumb within two weeks of first showing symptoms of FVR. Kittens are easily dehydrated and weakened by fever and loss of appetite, and their symptoms are always more pronounced. In bad cases that survive, the eyes may become matted with pus and may ulcerate (see p201), causing partial or total blindness.

The control of FVR and FCV has improved considerably with the development of effective vaccines (though these are not yet quite 100 per cent effective). Vaccines containing live but weakened viruses can be injected or given as nose or eye drops, in which case immunity starts to develop within 48 hours rather than the seven days needed for injected vaccine. Vaccines containing inactivated ('dead') FVR viruses are also available, as are vaccines combining protection against feline infectious enteritis (FIE or panleukopaenia; see p192) with respiratory disease.

In general, breeding queens should be vaccinated before mating, as live vaccine may damage the unborn young. If necessary, however, inactivated FVR vaccine can be given to a pregnant queen. Only healthy cats should be vaccinated, and vets recommend that kittens be first immunized at the age of about 10 to 12 weeks. If, however, there is a high risk of their contracting the disease earlier – from a carrier queen, say, or from other inmates of the cattery (although this should not happen if kittens are reared in isolation; see p226) – then a dose of vaccine may be given as early as three to four weeks. Annual boosters are recommended, or revaccination at least four weeks before entering a boarding cattery or cat show.

Additional control measures include the isolation of newcomers to a group for up to two weeks to check for signs of infection. If respiratory virus is prevalent, it is best to keep cats in small groups and to isolate carriers, especially of FCV. Ensure adequate ventilation of indoor quarters (at least 10 to 15 air changes per hour, with cross-ventilation, are recommended where a number of cats are housed in an indoor cattery or hospital ward with a shared air supply; see p163) and use disinfectants such as hypochlorite or cetrimide (see p178) to kill viruses in the environment.

Other upper respiratory problems
Chronic rhinitis (commonly known as the 'chronic snuffles') is an infection of the nasal cavities, usually seen as a sequel to FVR infections. Viruses are involved in the build-up of the condition, but there is then a serious secondary bacterial infection. Affected cats will sneeze, snuffle and have a runny nose from time to time – in some cases the nasal discharge becoming purulent – but they otherwise seem well and do not show the more generalized signs (such as poor appetite and depression) seen in FVR or serious FCV cases. The noisy breathing occurs because of cats' reluctance to breathe through the mouth. There may also be conjunctivitis and – if inflammation spreads up into the sinus cavities of the face – sinusitis with swelling between the eyes.

Unfortunately, the secondary bacterial infection is usually very severe, and responds poorly to treatment. The cat may improve with antibiotic treatment, but as soon as this is stopped the symptoms tend to recur. Surgical treatment – drilling a hole into the frontal sinus and irrigating the cavities with antibiotics – may be tried but is often unsuccessful.

Rhinitis may also develop if a foreign body lodges in the nasal cavities. The same initial symptoms in older cats may result from a cancer inside the nose, but this will generally spread in time, often causing swelling of the face; if the the diagnosis is confirmed by a biopsy (tissue sampling), euthanasia is advised as soon as the cat's health deteriorates. Rarely, rhinitis may be caused by a yeast-like fungal infection; this can be transmitted to humans. It is treatable with an antifungal agent, but this is rather toxic and treatment is unlikely to be successful.

Pharyngitis ('sore throat') may be provoked by a foreign object or irritant chemical, or may be the by-product of an upper respiratory infection. Laryngitis

LUNG PARASITES

Lungworms are not a major cause of feline respiratory disease, but may be implicated – especially in chronic cases – because they are common in most countries and are estimated to affect 10 to 20 per cent of the cat population, especially in rural areas.

The commonest species, occurring worldwide, uses snails and slugs as intermediate hosts (see illustration). The slender, hair-like adults, which are up to 10mm (³⁄₈in) long, develop within the deep tissues of the cat's lungs after it has consumed the intermediate host or another animal that has eaten this host. Most cats show no signs of infection, but if they do the most common symptom is a persistent cough. Positive diagnosis

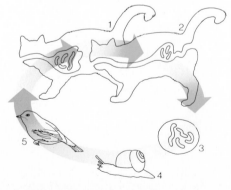

Lungworms lay eggs **1** which hatch into larvae that are coughed up and swallowed **2**. They pass out in faeces **3** and enter a snail **4**. This is eaten by a cat or by another animal **5** that is eaten. They reach the lungs via the blood.

often depends on finding the characteristic comma-shaped or coiled microscopic larvae in the cat's faeces. Most cases are best left alone and will usually clear up within a few months, but severe infestations can be treated by a vet.

There are several other lungworms, but none are so widespread as *Aelurostrongylus*. *Capillaria aerophilia* is also hair-like but produces only an occasional wheeze and cough. It has been recorded mainly in Australia, while *Mammomonogamus ieri* is restricted to the West Indies; it parasitizes the upper air passages. A fluke, *Paragonimus kellicotti*, has been found very occasionally to cause a wheezing cough in North American cats, but it can be caught only by eating larva-carrying crayfish or crabs.

(inflammation of the voice box) can result from a mild attack of FVR or FCV, or may mark the early stages of a more severe attack. The result may be a loss of or change in the voice, but this will return to normal when the cat recovers.

Chest infections

Bronchitis can occur in cats of all ages, and the most noticeable feature is coughing caused by the inflammation of the air tubes (the bronchi and bronchioles) in the lungs. It often follows upper respiratory disease, but may also be caused by bacterial infections and such things as chemicals, dust and smoke, which cause irritation or an allergic reaction. Bronchitis is usually mild in cats, but the inflammation may rarely spread to nearby lung tissues, causing pneumonia (see below). Unless it is clear that an allergen is involved, treatment generally involves the use of antibiotics given until about a week after all symptoms have disappeared. If, however, the cough persists the vet may need to anaesthetize the cat and take a swab from the airways in order to identify the micro-organisms responsible and the best drug to use.

Pneumonia – inflammation of the lung tissue itself – is not common, but may occur as a secondary bacterial infection following a bout of FVR or as a direct result of certain FCV infections. In these cases it mainly affects young kittens or debilitated adults. It may occasionally be caused by a direct bacterial or fungal infection – that is, without FVR or FCV involvement – or invasion by certain parasites. Inhalation pneumonia – caused by small amounts of food or fluid passing down into the lungs – can result if the cat has difficulty in swallowing, has a cleft palate (see p 196), or is subjected to unskilled attempts at force-feeding or medication.

Cats with pneumonia may show a variety of signs, including fever, loss of appetite, depression, dehydration, coughing and breathing difficulty. They need urgent veterinary attention, with broad-spectrum antibiotics to fight the infection, good nursing and in some cases oxygen. Given such attention, the chances of recovery are usually good, except in cases of fungal infection.

Asthma – due to acute oedema (sudden collection of fluid) in the lungs – sometimes occurs in cats, and is characterized by episodes of dyspnoea with wheezing, gasping, coughing and cyanosis (a bluish tinge to the gums). In bad attacks, a cat may lie on its chest, its mouth hanging open, showing the bluish colour. The exact cause of asthma is unknown, but as in people an allergic reaction is probably responsible. Also as with human patients, drugs can provide relief by dilating the airways, but to prevent further attacks the allergenic factor must be found and removed.

Tuberculosis can infect cats, just as it can humans and other animals, although this is now very uncommon in most countries. Cats are most susceptible to the bovine strain of the disease, and this is rarer now that it is effectively controlled in cattle, but it can be caught from infected milk. Human tuberculosis can also be transmitted from owners to their pets. The disease may infect various body systems of the cat, with varied symptoms, but the respiratory form causes sneezing, a nasal discharge, wheezy coughing and dyspnoea. Treatment is possible, but any affected animal should be destroyed because of the risk of spreading the disease to other animals and people.

Other respiratory troubles

There are many possible causes of laboured breathing apart from disorders within the respiratory system itself. In general, these result in a decrease in the space available for the lungs to occupy in the chest. As a result, they cannot expand to their full extent, so that the cat cannot breathe in as much air as normal. This can occur abruptly, but in many cases the underlying cause has been present and progressing for some time. At first the cat adapts by adjusting its lifestyle to a slower pace, and the condition may become noticeable only when eventually the cat has to breathe faster to compensate for the lost volume.

One of the commonest causes of dyspnoea is a rupture of the diaphragm, which usually results from a street accident. As a result, some of the contents of the abdomen (belly) – most of whose organs are held rather loosely in place – can pass into the chest cavity. Which organs are involved depends on the exact site of the tear, but in severe cases so many of the abdominal organs pass through the diaphragm that the cat's belly suddenly seems much thinner. The reduced lung volume obviously makes anaesthesia

dangerous, and the fact that the abdomen and chest are now connected means that the lungs may collapse, but in most cases surgical repair is successful.

Dyspnoea can also be caused by a tumour (growth) in the chest, the most common being lymphosarcoma of the thymus gland, which is a result of feline leukaemia virus infection (FeLV; see p 204). Such a growth, as well as encroaching on the lungs' space, tends to cause fluid to collect in the pleural cavity between the lungs and the actual chest wall, and this can make the dyspnoea worse. Such fluid can be caused to collect by various other conditions, including accidents that rupture blood or lymph vessels (see p 105), feline infectious peritonitis (FIP; see p 193), a form of pleurisy, tumours of the lung itself and heart disease (see p 205).

Removing fluid from the chest of a dyspnoeic cat not only aids breathing but helps the vet diagnose the cause, for laboratory analysis of the fluid may reveal clues. For example, exudative pleurisy, which is a quite common cause of dyspnoea in cats, results from pus forming. It may be caused by a penetrating wound, but in most cases the underlying problem is unclear. Treatment entails drainage of the pus to enable the lungs to expand fully and antibiotics to control the infection. Many cats will respond well, although it may be necessary to continue treatment for some time to prevent recurrence.

One final condition that results in dyspnoea is pneumothorax, in which air collects in the chest (but outside the lungs, of course). This can result from penetrating wounds, but sometimes a street accident may cause a tear in the lung without visible external damage. In either case, the affected lung collapses and this may allow a tear to heal. Once this or the external injury is repaired, the remaining air is re-absorbed and lung function returns to normal.

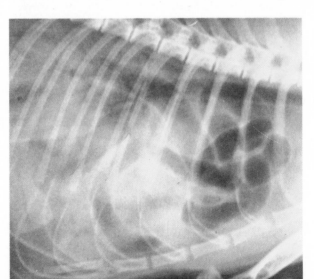

A ruptured diaphragm – the sheet of muscle separating the abdomen and thorax (chest cavity) – is a common result of a street accident. This X-ray shows clearly the resulting protrusion of organs from the abdomen into the chest, which severly reduces the space available for the lungs and causes dyspnoea (breathing difficulty).

Eye disorders

Cats' eyes are usually remarkably trouble-free – certainly in comparison with dogs'. The most common eye conditions in cats are those affecting the eyelids and conjunctivas (the membrane on the outside of the eyeballs and lining the eyelids), together with injuries resulting from street accidents and fights. The fact that the eyes are well protected in their bony orbits (sockets) and by the eye-blink and other reflexes means that other injuries are rarer.

When eye problems do occur, many can be treated by a vet in general practice, but some types of surgery are a matter for the specialist. Infections can usually be countered by using antibiotic drops or ointment (see p 179) plus cleansing with tepid salty water, but many other conditions require surgery. This can be very simple; there have been cases where a foreign body such as a thorn penetrating quite deeply into the eye has been successfully withdrawn and no further repair needed. In other cases, the vet may be able to repair a wound surgically, but in serious injuries removal of the eye may be necessary. The same is true in some progressive conditions such as a malignant tumour (cancerous growth) of the iris, but if there is no danger to the cat's general health and the condition affects only one eye it may be better to avoid the trauma of surgery. Cats with only one good eye – whether through blindness or surgical removal of the other – are handicapped in some ways, but generally seem to cope very well.

For general information on the eye, including an illustration of its anatomy, see page 110. For first aid treatment of certain eye accidents, see page 183.

Eyelid problems

Congenital (inborn) abnormalities of the eyelids are rare, apart from entropion (in which the edge of the lid is turned inwards) and ablepharon (in which all or part of the lid is missing). Severe cases of the latter may require euthanasia. Entropion is more common in Persians and related breeds, but may also follow certain eyelid injuries, conditions in which the eyeball sinks into its socket, or where there is a spasm of the eyelid due to discomfort. The inturning of the lid means that its hair comes in contact with the cornea (the clear front of the eye), causing discomfort, watering and possibly conjunctivitis and keratitis (see below). In most cases, the vet must perform surgery to correct the deformity. Inflammation of the edge of the eyelid – blepharitis – is fairly common, and may be associated with conjunctivitis; treatment is as for the latter.

Wounds of the true eyelids are uncommon, but cats involved in fights may sustain lacerations (tears) of the nictitating membrane, or 'third eyelid'. Foreign bodies – especially the awns (bristled flowers) of grasses – may also become lodged behind it

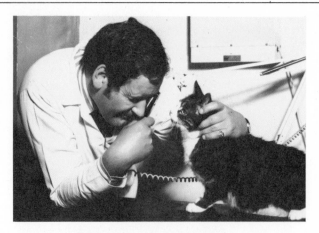

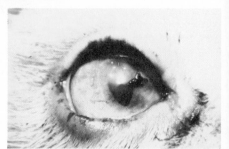

Examining the cat's eye, the vet employs the same techniques as the human ophthalmologist, using an ophthalmoscope **left**. Many conditions, including mummification of the cornea **below**, may need correction by surgery. For this – and even for less serious operations, such as removal of a foreign body **below left** – the cat is given a general anaesthetic by injection. (The mask used for gaseous anaesthesia would interfere with surgery.)

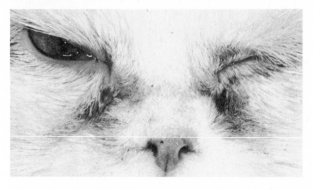

Weeping eyes often result from something blocking the ducts that drain tears from the inner corner of each eye into the nasal cavity. This may be due to inflammation – most commonly associated with a respiratory virus infection (cat flu), particularly FVR (see p 197). In some cats, selective breeding for a very short muzzle results in the ducts being malformed from birth.

(see p 183), producing excessive watering, conjunctivitis, swelling of the conjunctiva and spasm of the eyelid. The cornea (the transparent 'window') may be damaged. Surgery is sometimes needed to repair the membrane or remove the foreign body, followed by treatment for the inflammation.

There is some controversy among vets as to the circumstances in which the third eyelids may become prominent – 'the haws up' – due to a condition in quite another part of the cat's body. There is a pad of fat behind each eyeball that to some extent controls the position and movement of the membrane. Any irritable eye condition that causes the eye to contract in its socket and put pressure on this pad will make the membrane protrude. So will respiratory virus infections (cat flu) and, many vets believe, many debilitating conditions that diminish the amount of fat behind the eyeball – notably a heavy tapeworm infestation. Others point out that many debilitated cats do not show their haws.

Whatever the cause, some cats certainly

do have protruding third eyelids when nothing is wrong with the eyes themselves. Many owners seeing this think that their cat is going blind or that the eyeballs have rotated; indeed, in some cases the membranes extend so far across the eyes as to render the cat temporarily blind. Treatment depends on finding and curing any underlying cause there may be – such as the tapeworm infestation – and possibly giving general tonics and a nutritious diet to restore the body fat. In some persistent cases, surgical correction is needed.

Wet eyes

Excessive tear production or a blockage of the canals that normally drain tears into the nasal cavity may cause tears to overflow at the inner corners of one or both eyes. This is of course a handicap in a show cat, but otherwise it is little problem in itself – only as a sign of some other trouble. For example, it may result from irritation, as in entropion (see above), or inflammation of the conjunctiva, especially where there are adhesions between the conjunctiva and nictitating membrane. Infections may also block the tear canal, but this can result from congenital defects, especially in cats with a very foreshortened face (such as the Peke-faced Persian; see p56).

Conjunctivitis
This has many causes, and the precise symptoms seen vary with each; usually, however, you will first notice watering, the discharge later becoming thicker. The conjunctiva becomes red and may swell, especially when the cause is an allergy, and the cat often shows signs of discomfort. In the later stages the cornea may be affected, producing keratitis (see below).

Apart from allergies, causes of conjunctivitis include irritation by foreign bodies, wounds, entropion (see above) and such chemicals as soap, detergents, fumes and aerosol insecticides used against parasites. It can be caused by eye parasites, notably the eyeworm *Thelazia californiensis* in the United States. Various micro-organisms have been found in cases of conjunctivitis, and it is common in viral respiratory diseases (cat flu; see p197). In some cases of virus infections the eye reaction may be quite mild, but with feline viral rhinotracheitis (FVR) there is usually swelling, a discharge and considerable discomfort.

Conjunctivitis is never something to be taken lightly because of the possibility of virus infection and because it may spread to involve other parts of the eye. You should seek veterinary advice; treatment usually includes saline eyewashes, antibiotic drops and possibly other medications. In young kittens that recover from virus infections, chronic conditions may develop in which there are adhesions between the conjunctiva and eyeball or between different parts of the conjunctiva; these are sometimes very difficult to treat.

Disorders of the cornea and iris
The only important congenital defect of the transparent cornea – and this is rare – is a dermoid. This is a mass of normal skin tissue, often coloured and usually with hairs protruding from its surface. It normally has to be removed surgically. Injuries to the cornea are common, usually from fights. Simple wounds normally heal quickly, but penetrating claw wounds may cause some of the inner parts of the eye (such as the iris) to protrude, requiring surgical repair. Even without such complications keratitis (inflammation of the cornea) and iritis (inflammation of the iris) may result.

In keratitis, the cornea becomes cloudy, pus may collect behind it and later there is reddening as new blood vessels grow into it; in iritis, the pupil (the central opening) may be abnormally small. Both conditions can be serious, and may need treatment with antibiotics and, in the case of iritis,

steroids and other drugs to dilate the pupil. Occasionally the whole depth of the cornea may become inflamed and opaque, in which case treatment may or may not be successful. One of the commonest and most important internal eye conditions is uveitis, in which the iris, the ciliary muscles that control it and the layer of the eyeball known as the choroid (see p110) all become inflamed. This is often associated with feline infectious peritonitis (FIP; see p193) or feline leukaemia virus (FeLV; see p204).

Ulcers can develop on the cornea following injuries, but this is not common; when ulceration does occur it is usually in Persians and related breeds with rather prominent eyes. A special form of ulcer is associated with FVR infections (see above) in young kittens, usually between two weeks and six months old. It can also occur in older cats, and usually is very slow to heal. A condition unique to cats, so-called mummification of the cornea, shows as a black area, usually in the centre of the cornea. It consists of dead, dried, 'mummified' cells that move gradually towards the surface. The cause is not known, but it seems most common in long-haired breeds, particularly Colourpoint Longhairs (Himalayans) and Persians. In most cases there is watering and some discomfort, and the black mass may be mistaken for a foreign body. In many cases, surgery is needed to remove it.

Disorders inside the eye
A serious condition that can follow iritis or several other disorders, including a tumour or bleeding inside the eye, is glaucoma. In this there is increased fluid pressure in the chambers of the eye, due to interference with the drainage mechanism or other causes. As a result, the cornea becomes cloudy and the eyeball enlarges. It may be very painful, and any apparent enlargement should receive prompt veterinary examination. If not corrected, the eyeball may eventually require removal, but prompt treatment can save it.

As with people, cats' vision may be affected by the lens becoming opaque; this is known as a cataract. It is not common, but when it does occur is usually due to injury. It can also be congenital or be associated with diabetes or certain eye inflammations. The only treatment is surgical, but unless both eyes are affected this is not usually justifiable. Hardening of the lens, which is a normal ageing process, is sometimes mistaken for cataract, but does not interfere with vision. Dislocation (slipping) of the lens, so that it becomes loose within the eye is not common, but may eventually lead to glaucoma.

Disorders of the retina
Degenerations of the retina – the light-sensitive part at the back of the eye – are not

uncommon in cats, and many different causes have been discovered, ranging from inherited conditions (often betrayed by abnormally large pupils) to nutritional deficiency. The latter occurs especially if the cat is fed on a diet lacking the amino acid taurine (see p148) – for example, by feeding certain canned dog food for a long period. If the degeneration reaches the stage of blindness it cannot be reversed, but feeding the correct food earlier leads to recovery.

Other causes of retinal degeneration include some forms of anaemia (see p204), toxoplasmosis (see p191), tuberculosis (see p199), and feline infectious peritonitis (FIP; see p193). In one type, known as generalized retinal atrophy, the cause is not known but the ultimate result is blindness – although there is not usually anything obviously wrong with the cat until the disorder is quite far advanced. In another form, central retinal degeneration, which occurs in middle-aged or old cats, vision is not much affected.

A final problem that occasionally affects the retina is its detachment from the back of the eyeball. Again, the cause is often not known – though it may be associated with an inflammation, tumour or accident – and many cases are not discovered unless both eyes are seriously affected, impairing vision. A widely dilated pupil on one side may, however, lead to the discovery of detachment in one eye.

Disorders of the whole eyeball
Inborn abnormalities of the eyeball are not common, but occasionally a kitten may be born with an abnormally small or large eye. Injuries involving the whole eyeball are also uncommon, but in street accidents the eye may be forced out of its socket, requiring immediate veterinary help. There may, of course, be other injuries to attend to (see p180), but do not attempt to replace the eye in the socket; simply keep it moist with salty water, medicinal liquid paraffin (mineral oil) or even plain water until help arrives. The vet will replace the eye surgically unless there is extensive damage.

A squint may be caused by a foreign body or an ulcer on the eye or by damage to the muscles or nerves that control eye movements, when treatment clearly depends on correcting the basic cause. As is well known, Siamese are prone to a hereditary squint (see p27); alternatively, the eyes may rhythmically oscillate (a condition called nystagmus), the rapid movements stopping when the animal fixes its vision on some object. Neither condition seems to have much effect on the cat's ability to see, and the occurrence of both has been reduced by selective breeding. Nystagmus may also occur in certain brain or middle ear disorders (see p202) or in a cat with cataracts, when once again treatment depends on curing the basic cause.

Ear disorders

The cat's ear is an extremely sensitive and complex piece of apparatus, responsible for both hearing and balance (for anatomy, see p100), and any disorder is likely to cause considerable distress. This agitation may take various forms, but the signs to watch for include obvious pain when the ears are touched, persistent scratching of the ears, persistent ear-twitching and head-shaking, any discharge, bleeding or unpleasant smell from the ears, loss of balance or a tendency to walk in circles with head tilted, and of course deafness (which is difficult to assess in cats).

In general, disturbances of hearing or balance are likely to indicate a problem in the inner part of the ear, deafness being most commonly a congenital (inborn) defect associated with a white coat colour (see p31). Signs of irritation (including a discharge) usually indicate a problem in the outer ear, including the auditory canal; this is, in fact, among the commonest feline disorders encountered by vets.

Apart from disease conditions as such, the exposed position of the pinnae (ear flaps) makes them very prone to injury in fights and so on; for information on first aid, see page 180. Such injury may be self-inflicted through scratching, often taking the form of a large but painless haematoma (blood blister) that must be drained and repaired by the vet. White cats are prone to ear damage from solar dermatitis in summer (see p189) and in extreme cold all cats may suffer frostbitten ears (see p185).

Outer ear disorders

Inflammation of the ear canal – termed *otitis externa* – is a whole complex of conditions that can form a vicious circle, making the condition worse (see diagram). Successful treatment hinges on identifying and removing the basic cause, or 'trigger factor'. Among possible causes are foreign bodies such as grass seeds in the ear canal, a tumour (growth) or, less often, a direct infection by fungi or bacteria. (More usually, these follow rather than cause the initial condition.) Or, in by far the majority of cases, there is an infestation of ear mange mites (*Otodectes cynotis*).

Up to two out of every three cats – including many of the best-cared-for pedigree and house cats – harbour these tiny eight-legged grey mites, often without showing any symptoms. This means that there is always a 'reservoir' from which the mites can be passed on to young cats. They live mainly on the surface of the ear canal, and do not burrow into the skin, but their legs and body spines can cause irritation. This troubles the cat little unless they multiply. Then the skin inside the ear reacts, producing a dark brown wax that is usually the first sign of infestation.

Later, dry crusty material accumulates and the canal may be blocked; if bacterial

Ear mange may be suspected whenever a cat persistently scratches its ears or shakes its head. You should be particularly suspicious if there are signs of dark brown ear wax. The vet will examine the lower part of the ear canal with an illuminated magnifier **right** and may be able to see the tiny eight-legged mites **far right** – which are less than half a millimetre long.

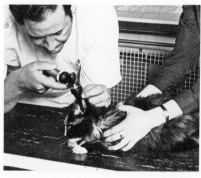
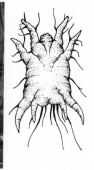

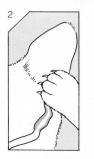
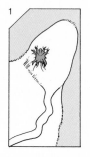
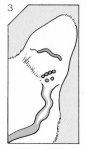
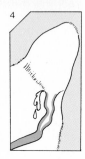

The otitis cycle is a cause-and-effect sequence that perpetuates and worsens any disorder of the outer ear. **1** Trigger factors, such as mites, foreign bodies, tumours or a primary infection, cause irritation and discomfort. **2** As a result, the cat scratches its ear and shakes it head, possibly causing injury and certainly inflammation, with wax production, swelling and ulceration. These create ideal conditions for secondary infections **3**, producing an ear discharge **4**. As a result, there is further inflammation **5**, worsening the irritation and possibly leading to chronic changes in the ear lining.

infection follows, pus may form, usually causing pain. In severe cases, ulcers may form on the ear lining, or the infection may spread to the inner ear's hearing and balance centres, causing behavioural symptoms such as walking in circles or even spasmodic 'fits'. Scratching in response to the irritation worsens the condition.

Otitis does not just 'go away' if untreated; it gets worse. So it is important to check your cat's ears regularly for signs of mite infestation or other inflammation (see p155). Do not poke into the ear canal, however. To positively identify ear mites, the vet will have to use an auriscope, or otoscope (illuminated magnifier), or examine a swab taken carefully from the ear canal under a microscope or magnifying glass. It is important to follow veterinary advice when treating mites, to ensure using a preparation non-toxic to cats. Most proprietary drops for otitis are oil-based, so that they help soften and break up ear wax, making pre-cleaning of the ears usually unnecessary. (For how to give ear drops, see page 179.) It is often advisable also to treat the paws and tip of the tail (which usually rests near the head during sleep) to prevent re-infestation, and to use an Elizabethan collar (see p179) to prevent scratching.

If there is a bacterial infection, drops containing antibiotics may be prescribed, thus helping to break the vicious circle. Rarely, surgery may be needed to remove a tumour or to repair self-inflicted damage. And, of course, removal of foreign bodies such as grass seeds or awns, although quite simple, often needs a general anaesthetic because the animal is so distressed.

Middle and inner ear disorders

The signs of middle ear infection are similar to those of *otitis externa*, but apart from head-shaking, scratching and occasionally a discharge, the cat may transiently tilt its head towards the affected side. This is an important distinction from inner ear diseases, which result in a persistent head tilt coupled with loss of balance, incoordination, circling and deafness. Infections may reach the middle ear from the external ear canal or from the throat via the eustachian tube, and may then pass to the inner ear. Once it is established, permanent damage to the delicate structures may result. Both types of infection are treated with antibiotics, cortisone also being used in the early stages of inner ear treatment. However, some drugs – notably streptomycin – are actually responsible for balance problems by affecting the inner ear nerve.

True tumours of the middle and inner ears are rare and generally untreatable. Occasionally, polyps (sac-like growths) may develop in the inner ear and extend on a stalk all the way down the eustachian tube to the throat, causing breathing difficulties. These can be removed surgically.

Urinary problems

Diseases of the urinary tract – the kidneys, bladder and passages connecting these and passing to the outside – are not uncommon in cats and can be very serious. This is because they affect the major route by which waste products – many of them toxic – are cleared from the body. The most commonly seen conditions fall into two main categories: those affecting the upper part of the urinary system (the kidneys) and those involving the lower part (the bladder and urethra; see p 105). Kidney failure is mainly seen in older cats, but bladder problems affect all ages (though neutered males seem more prone than other cats). Although laboratory tests may be needed to positively diagnose urinary problems, the signs shown by the cat often give a clear indication of the site of the disease.

Kidney disease

In most forms of kidney disease, the cat's ability to eliminate wastes is reduced progressively; since the kidneys have considerable reserve capacity, signs of illness may appear only when damage is well advanced. However, as the disease progresses, the kidneys try to compensate by producing more dilute (weaker) urine, and the first recognizable sign is often an increased thirst. As more kidney is damaged, however, the build-up of unexcreted wastes – the most commonly measured being urea in the blood – becomes more serious. The cat loses its appetite, becomes lethargic and loses weight. In the later stages it may develop a characteristic uraemic (urine-like) smell. Chronic mouth infections (gingivitis; see p 196) and anaemia (see p 204) are also commonly seen in kidney failure. If untreated, the cat eventually dies from uraemia – the build-up of toxic waste products in the body.

There are a number of causes of chronic kidney damage of this type. The most common is chronic interstitial nephritis, a disease of unknown prime cause in which the kidneys become small and scarred. Bacterial infection of the kidneys – pyelonephritis – is less common, as is a condition called amyloidosis, in which abnormal substances are laid down in the kidneys and elsewhere. In addition, the kidneys may be involved in such generalized diseases as certain tumours (growths) and a form of feline infectious peritonitis (FIP; see p 193); in both these cases no treatment is possible. Chronic kidney failure is rare in kittens or young cats, and when it does occur usually has a congenital (inborn) and possibly hereditary cause. Cats may also suffer acute (sudden) kidney failure – for example, due to an injury or blood clot.

Exact diagnosis of kidney disease is based almost entirely on laboratory examination and tests of urine and blood samples – for example, for urea and protein levels and for the presence of bacteria. Pyelonephritis can be easily treated with antibiotics, but in other cases treatment is difficult as damaged kidney tissue cannot be replaced. The main aim is to keep the cat's fluid intake high and where necessary give vitamin supplements.

Protein-rich foods are used in a form of kidney disease known as glomerulonephritis, which is less commonly recognized than those mentioned above but may occur more frequently than many vets realize. It results in the excessive loss of protein via the urine, leading to a reduction in blood protein levels and the collection of fluid in the tissues known as oedema or dropsy; this is usually most noticeable in the limbs and belly. The cause is believed to be a malfunction of the immune system, the body's defensive mechanism against invading organisms. Vets may use steroid drugs, which suppress the immune response, to treat this form of kidney disease, together with rest and a high-quality diet. Although this can be successful for a period, in the long term the cat may well develop kidney failure of the more common type.

Bladder and urethra problems

The most important disorder affecting the lower part of the urinary system in the cat – and one of the most common serious conditions to afflict cats – is the feline urological syndrome (FUS), otherwise known as urolithiasis or cystitis. (The last term in fact refers to any inflammation of the bladder, such as by bacterial infection, which may or may not accompany the other symptoms of FUS.) These symptoms include blood in the urine and frequent urination. In male cats – particularly neuters – the urethra (the urine passage from the bladder to the outside, which is longer and narrower than in the female) may become blocked by a gritty, paste-like material. As a result, the cat may repeatedly and unsuccessfully strain to pass urine. You may confuse this with constipation, but it is rapidly followed by the depression of kidney failure, and you should seek veterinary help at once.

The vet often needs to insert a catheter (a narrow soft plastic tube) into the urethra to enable the cat to urinate. (Manual pressure on the bladder itself may well rupture it.) The cat may then need an intravenous drip of fluids to overcome the side-effects of the obstruction. After this, treatment – as in straightforward cystitis – may include antibiotics to clear up any infection and dietary measures to increase the cat's fluid intake; possibly combined with substances to make the urine more acidic, these increase urine production and may help to 'flush out' the trouble. You should give the cat moist foods, to which more water may be added, and ensure that fresh water is always available. It is also useful to add small amounts of salt to the diet, and some cats can be encouraged to drink gravy.

However, despite such measures, FUS has a tendency to recur. In a male cat, your vet may be able to prevent repeated obstruction by surgically removing the narrow end part of the urethra. But the bladder inflammation seen in both sexes is much more difficult to control in the long term. The management of cases of FUS is made more difficult by the fact that the condition is poorly understood. It is known that a number of factors – such as neutering (especially in male cats), a diet high in dried foods (probably those with a high magnesium content in particular; see p 150), low fluid intake, obesity and inactivity – seem to make cats more prone to FUS. But the direct cause or causes are not clear.

Other feline bladder problems are less common. Tumours of the bladder are rare in cats, but true bladder stones occur occasionally, usually in queens. They cause irritation to the bladder wall and signs similar to those of FUS: blood in the urine and frequent urination. Treatment is by surgical removal of the stones.

Straining to urinate is a warning sign of urinary trouble. In normal urination **right**, the cat squats down very close to the ground or its litter tray. If the urethra is partially or completely blocked, as in FUS, it adopts a characteristic position **below** with its haunches slightly raised. The pain may make it cry out, and any urine passed is likely to be blood-stained.

Blood and circulatory diseases

The vital importance of the blood's dual main functions – of carrying oxygen and other materials around the body and of fighting infection – means that any disorder in the circulatory system or the blood are potentially extremely serious. In cats, the disorders of the heart and blood vessels that represent such a plague to human health are much less important than diseases of the blood itself and of the associated lymphatic system (see p105). Blood diseases do not, however, normally manifest themselves directly and can be diagnosed accurately only after laboratory analysis of blood samples and sometimes tissues from other parts of the body, such as bone marrow.

Anaemia

The most obvious sign of a malady in the blood system is anaemia – a reduction in the number of red blood cells, or in the amount of oxygen-carrying haemoglobin that gives them their colour. As a result, the cat's mucous membranes – notably the inside of the mouth, the gums and the inside of the eyelids – lose their normal pink colour. Such pallor may also, however, occur in shock (see p180), and in some cats – especially pale-pointed Siamese, such as lilac (frost) points – these areas may normally appear less pink. Since the blood's oxygen-carrying capacity is reduced, anaemic cats breathe more rapidly and deeply than normal. They become lethargic.

Anaemia is not a disease in itself but the result of decreased production or increased loss of the red cells or of their haemoglobin. Rarely, decreased production can be caused by a deficiency of certain vitamins – particularly B_6 and B_{12} – and minerals, especially iron. Kidney failure may also have the same effect, since the kidneys normally produce a substance called erythropoietin that stimulates the bone marrow to produce new red cells. Certain drugs can damage the bone marrow, also reducing production.

Direct loss of red cells can result from bleeding, either internal or external, the former including losses caused by certain intestinal parasites (see p191). Various conditions may cause haemolysis (destruction of blood cells within the body), and in severe cases the resulting build-up of bilirubin – one of the waste products of red cell destruction – causes jaundice (see p193). Causes of this destruction include certain toxins, but the most important is a microscopic parasite called *Haemobartonella* (or *Eperythrozoon*) *felis*, which causes the disease feline infectious anaemia (FIA).

This protozoon (single-celled animal) is found in all parts of the world (though more in some than others), in cats of all ages. The mode of transmission is not known, but may involve biting insects. It is sometimes found in the blood cells of cats with no apparent anaemia, but in certain circum-

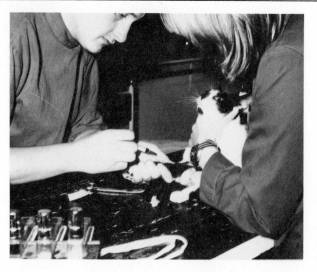

Taking a blood sample, the vet inserts a needle into the cephalic vein on the inside of the front leg **left**. Apart from blood disorders, other diseases may cause a change in blood composition, so this procedure is a routine in many feline illnesses. It is necessary for detecting the presence of the feline leukaemia virus, shown **right** enlarged 125,000 times. This organism causes various other cancers apart from leukaemia, but many cats develop immunity to it. Modern tests depend on identifying the virus under an electron microscope.

stances – particularly if the cat is under stress – it may destroy these cells. Affected cats usually have a high temperature as well as appearing anaemic, but a microscopic examination of a blood sample – or sometimes several samples over a period of days – is needed to confirm the diagnosis.

FIA on its own is rarely fatal in domestic cats as the symptoms usually prompt a visit to the vet long before any permanent damage is done. Once diagnosed, the parasite disappears rapidly in response to oxytetracycline antibiotics, but treatment should be continued for several weeks to prevent recurrence; even then it may reappear. Often, however, FIA is associated with feline leukaemia virus (see below), and in these cases the prognosis is poor.

Some other forms of anaemia may also respond poorly to treatment, which can be hindered by the failure of laboratory tests to reveal the basic cause. In some of these cases, too, the leukaemia virus may be involved. Generally, vets prescribe most anaemic patients dietary supplements of iron and vitamins to ensure that the cat has enough of these to produce new red cells. Anabolic steroids – the body-building drugs used by some athletes – can also promote cell production by the bone marrow. In serious cases, a blood transfusion may be necessary.

Leukaemia and related diseases

Feline leukaemia virus (FeLV) is the main cause of leukaemia in cats – and indeed the most important cause of feline cancer and one of the major feline viral diseases (see p172). It induces cancer in the white blood cells and elsewhere in the body, and is associated with a number of other problems such as anaemia, reproductive failure (see p229) and a general lowering of disease resistance. Common throughout the world, FeLV affects an estimated 1 to 2 per cent of cats, is contagious and, once symptoms appear, is almost always fatal. It is transmitted by saliva, faeces and urine, but cannot live long outside the cat and is easily destroyed by disinfectants. It is not as contagious as some feline viruses, so that it is most prevalent where cats are in close contact – such as breeding and boarding catteries and multi-cat households.

After exposure to FeLV, there are three possibilities: the cat may not be infected at all; it may be infected but successfully develop immunity; or it may develop disease symptoms after an incubation period of anything between a few weeks and several years. These symptoms are very variable, and may include anaemia, fever, vomiting, diarrhoea and laboured breathing. Swift diagnosis, from a blood test, is of little practical value to the diseased cat itself since

The FIA parasite shows up under the microscope **left** as tiny round or rod-shaped bodies on red blood cells. Multiple tests may be needed for positive diagnosis.

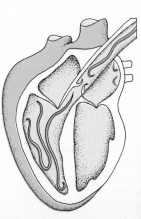

The heartworm infests the right-hand side of the heart **right** and the artery leading to the lungs. Because of the small size of the cat's heart, one or two worms are enough to cause serious heart trouble and often sudden death.

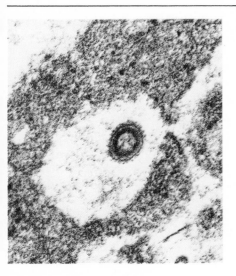

there is no cure, although some drugs can produce a temporary remission. In most cases, however, a vet will recommend that a cat with FeLV that is showing clinical symptoms – whether or not a tumour is detected – be put down. This not only prevents further suffering but reduces the chances of transmission to healthy cats. If euthanasia is not carried out, the cat should certainly be isolated.

The commonest form of organ tumour associated with FeLV is lymphosarcoma, which may occur in tissues anywhere in the body but most commonly the intestines, the thymus gland (which is in the chest) and the kidneys. Apart from the varied signs already mentioned, cats with lymphosarcoma generally lose weight, have a poor appetite and are depressed. The vet may be able to palpate (feel) the tumour, particularly if the lymph nodes are enlarged (see p 105), but positive diagnosis often requires blood tests, X-ray examinations, biopsy (tissue sampling) of growths and bone marrow, and other tests.

With increasing knowledge of the dangers of FeLV, routine testing for the presence of the virus is more common, especially among breeding and show cats. False results very occasionally occur, but if any cat does show a positive result and appears healthy it should be isolated and retested a few months later if symptoms have not developed meanwhile. At the time of the first test it may have been in the incubation stage of the true disease or it may have been developing immunity (see p 173), in which case the second test will prove negative and the cat is no longer a danger to others.

Occasionally, a cat will show consistently positive test results but manifest no disease symptoms; in this case it should be kept out of contact with other cats or destroyed. As long as its FeLV tests are positive it is excreting the virus for other cats to catch. Once a virus-free group of cats is established – especially in a breeding group – it is

wise not to allow contact with any untested cats. For example, stud owners should not accept untested queens – and vice-versa. Unfortunately, no FeLV vaccine is yet available, though veterinary researchers are working to develop one, and this should be available by the mid-1980s.

Although many studies have been made, there is no evidence whatsoever that FeLV can cause disease in humans. However, some vets suggest that, to be ultra-cautious, FeLV-positive cats should not be kept in homes with young children or women of child-bearing age.

Heart and circulatory diseases

Heart disease is not so common in cats as in many other animals, such as dogs. In congenital (inborn) heart disease, a defect, though present since birth, may not become obvious until the cat is quite old. The heart is often quite able to cope at first, but as the cat matures the demands on it grow and signs become apparent. These are mainly due to inadequate oxygen reaching the tissues, and include cyanosis ('blueness') of the mucous membranes. If the oxygen deficiency is so severe that the brain does not receive its full needs, nervous signs such as ataxia and fits (see p 207) may result.

Various forms of congenital heart disorder are occasionally found in cats. The most common of these is the so-called 'hole in the heart' (responsible for human 'blue babies'), in which there is an opening between the two ventricles (the lower chambers of the heart). This allows oxygen-rich and oxygen-poor blood to mix (see p 104), so that the body receives only partially oxygenated blood; the importance of the defect depends on the size of the hole. In another defect, an embryonic blood vessel that, before birth, connects the pulmonary artery (which takes blood from the heart to the lungs) and the aorta (the main artery from the heart to the rest of the body) fails to close; as a result, blood by-passes the lungs, with the same effect as a hole in the heart. Sophisticated X-ray tests are needed to differentiate these and other possible congenital cardiac problems. In most cases surgical treatment is dangerous and the chances of survival poor, so it is normally regarded as inadvisable.

Acquired heart disease – that is, disease that is not inborn – takes a very different form in the cat from that seen in other species. Diseases of the heart valves – so common in dogs – are rare in cats. And, like other domestic animals, they rarely suffer the atherosclerosis (clogging of the arteries) and stroke common in humans. The most common feline heart disease is cardiomyopathy, or failure of the heart muscle. This usually leads to accumulation of fluid in the chest and hence breathing problems. It occurs in cats of all ages, not just old cats.

Blood clots, or thrombi, can form in the heart. In time they may break up, and small fragments, or emboli, lodge in the arteries, blocking them. This is called an embolism or (less accurately) thrombosis. In people, such emboli often block the coronary arteries that supply the heart muscle, causing a coronary thrombosis, or 'heart attack'. In cats, the most usual site of blockage is at the end of the aorta, near the pelvis, where it divides into the two iliac arteries supplying the hind legs. This condition is called iliac embolism (or iliac thrombosis). Affected cats suddenly lose the use of their hind legs, and it may seem as if they have suffered an accident. However, there is no sign of broken bones or dislocations, and since the blood supply to the hind legs is cut off the legs feel cold and have a very weak or non-existent pulse.

Treatment for heart disease in cats often has very disappointing results, although techniques are improving. In severe cases, death occurs rapidly or euthanasia is carried out on humane grounds. In others, the priority in treatment is to relieve the breathing by removing excess fluid with diuretics and to provide cage rest. Unfortunately, some drugs (such as cardiac glycosides) that are valuable in treating heart disease in other species are relatively toxic to cats.

Heartworms

These slim roundworms (*Dirofilaria immitis*) can infest both dogs and cats (though mainly the former) in many parts of the world, including North America, Australia and southern Europe. In fact, cats may be 'accidental' hosts. Transmitted by various types of mosquitoes, the microscopic larvae are sucked from the bloodstream of one animal and, after some development, injected back into that of another. They travel to the right ventricle of the heart and pulmonary artery, where male worms grow to a length of 12–18 cm (5–7 in), females to 25–30 cm (10–12 in). They reach maturity in some six months, after which larvae are shed into the bloodstream and can be detected by microscopic examination of a blood sample.

Because of this maturation time, cats under one year old are rarely diagnosed with this disorder. Symptoms in affected cats vary. Some show no signs; others have breathing trouble or oedema (dropsy – fluid collecting in the tissues), because the worms interfere with the circulation. Sudden death often occurs. Treatment is difficult, since killing the adult worms can result in a fatal blockage of a blood vessel. It is, however, possible to carry out a course of treatment over a period of some weeks, with careful monitoring of the cat's progress. Drugs are also available to kill the larval stages before adult worms develop. In areas where the worm is prevalent, however, you should be sure to protect your cat from mosquitoes.

Rabies

Universally – and rightly – feared as one of the most dangerous animal diseases to humans, rabies is widely distributed around the world. With the exception of Australasia and Antarctica, it occurs on every continent, the British Isles, Hawaii and some other islands currently being – thanks to their isolation by water and strict import controls – among the very few rabies-free places. Where the disease is enzootic (regularly occurring) there is usually a 'reservoir' of infection among wild animals – for example, in foxes in western Europe, in foxes, bats, skunks and racoons in North America, in mongooses in South Africa, India and the Caribbean, and in vampire bats in Central and South America. From these carriers, rabies is transmitted to domestic animals and people mainly through the bite of infected animals, when saliva containing the rabies virus (see p 172) enters a wound.

All warm-blooded animals can be infected, though rabies is more common in carnivores. The dog is the best-known domestic animal to transmit the disease to people, though rabid cat bites can be even more dangerous because the teeth are sharper. The dangers were known nearly 4,500 years ago, a 23rd-century BC Babylonian manuscript stating: 'If a dog is mad and the authorities have brought the fact to the knowledge of its owner; if he does not keep it in, it bites a man and causes his death, then the owner shall pay two-thirds of a mina (40 shekels) of silver.'

An agonizing death is almost inevitable once signs of the disease occur, humans usually developing the characteristic fear of swallowing water known as hydrophobia. (This does not occur in animals.) Because of the danger of rabies to animals and people alike, health authorities in most countries strictly control the transport of domestic animals – particularly carnivores – across frontiers (see p 161).

The course of the disease

Although rabies is normally transmitted by a bite, infective saliva can also contaminate a skin scratch or an existing wound, or enter through the thinner covering of a mucous membrane even if this is not wounded. Very rarely, it can be caught by breathing infective droplets or eating an infected carcass. Once in the body, the virus travels along the nerves to the spinal cord and eventually to the brain, where it multiplies and causes nerve damage that produces the characteristic behavioural changes. The virus travels from the brain along the cranial nerves, and in this way reaches the salivary glands. The saliva can become infective before any clinical signs are obvious – up to 24 hours beforehand in the cat.

The incubation period – from infection to the onset of symptoms – is very variable in all animals, but in general the deeper the

---

IF RABIES IS SUSPECTED

If any animal is suspected of being affected with rabies, every effort should be made to confine it, taking great care to avoid being bitten or scratched. (Wear heavy gloves and other protective clothing if possible.) A cat should preferably be confined in a strong cage or box. Then immediately report the facts of the case to the police or other authorities either directly or via a vet.

IF A PERSON IS BITTEN

Anyone bitten or scratched by an animal suspected of having rabies, or by any animal in a region where the disease is known to exist, should receive medical attention as soon as possible, but immediate first aid can minimize the risk of infection and is well worth while. First flush the wound with copious soap and water, detergent and water, or water alone. Then apply 40 to 70 per cent tincture of iodine or a 0.1 per cent quaternary ammonium compound antiseptic such as cetrimide (see p 178). (With the latter, be sure to thoroughly flush all soap out of the wound first; otherwise it will neutralize the antiseptic.)

---

infected wound and the nearer the head it is, the shorter the period. The amount of virus entering the body and the age of the victim are also factors; young animals are usually more susceptible than old. The normal range in animals is two to eight weeks, and incubation periods longer than six months are rare. Once this period is over, the disease normally follows the same course in cats as in other carnivores, passing through three stages.

The first is called the prodromal stage, and is characterized by uneasiness, anxiousness, irritability and increased sensitivity to noise and light. The only noticeable signs may be a change of temperament: A normally friendly animal may become timid, trying to hide away and becoming resentful if disturbed, whereas a normally timid, shy cat may become unnaturally friendly. In the excitement stage, which follows, restlessness and irritability give way to obvious excitement and aggression. The eyes take on a vacant, staring expression and the cat may have difficulty swallowing, so that it salivates copiously. Early in this stage, bouts of apparent normality and affection may alternate with aggressive phases – the latter often triggered by a sudden noise or movement. The cat may try to escape and run amuck, biting and scratching anything that comes in its path. Finally, the disease passes into the paralytic stage, when the limbs and

---

the rest of body become progressively paralysed; firstly there is lack of co-ordination, then collapse, difficulty in breathing and finally coma and death.

These three 'classical' stages can vary in length and severity, so that the earlier signs may pass unnoticed and only the final stages be observed. If the excitement stage is prolonged and the paralytic stage short, it is commonly known as 'furious' rabies; if the relative length of these is reversed it is said to be 'dumb' rabies. In cats, the furious form is more common. Usually, the period from the first clinical signs to death lasts between two and eight days and only rarely exceeds ten days.

Unlike in humans, in which hydrophobia is a usual symptom, there are no characteristic, conclusive clinical signs by which rabies can be diagnosed in cats or any other animals. Poisoning, foreign bodies lodged in the mouth or throat, brain tumours and certain injuries can all cause suspicious symptoms, and a positive diagnosis of rabies is possible only by carrying out laboratory tests on the animal's brain tissue after death; these include inoculating laboratory mice with this tissue. To facilitate diagnosis, the authorities in some countries require any domestic animal suspected of having rabies to be strictly confined, and the disease allowed to run its course, rather than it being killed outright.

Treatment and vaccination

Once clinical signs of rabies have developed – whether in humans or animals – there is no known treatment and death is more than 99 per cent certain. If given immediately after contact with a rabid animal, however, treatment of humans with anti-rabies serum and vaccine has a good chance of preventing symptoms appearing. In cats (and dogs) living in areas where rabies is enzootic, routine preventative vaccination is generally carried out and gives a high degree of protection. In some countries that are free of the disease (for example, the British Isles), vaccination against rabies is permitted only in special circumstances, such as before an animal is exported or during quarantine after importation.

Broadly speaking, two types of vaccine are available for use in animals, one containing inactivated ('dead') virus, the other modified live virus. Cats can be immunized effectively with any inactivated vaccine and most of the modified live vaccines, but one of the latter – that containing the so-called LEP Flury strain – should not be administered to cats since it has been known to cause actual rabies. National regulations normally govern which vaccines can be used and when they should be administered. In general, however, cats should not be vaccinated until they are three months old and after that should receive a booster vaccination each year.

Nervous disorders

The nervous system – the brain, spinal cord and nerves that radiate to all parts of the cat's body (see p 105) – forms the central control and communications system of the body. So it is not surprising either that nervous disorders tend to be serious or that the nervous system tends to be involved in a wide range of disorders affecting other body systems. For example, such major virus diseases as feline infectious peritonitis (FIP; see p 193) can cause paralysis in their late stages. The protozoan parasite causing toxoplasmosis (see p 191) can also attack the nervous system, resulting in behavioural symptoms. A number of dietary disorders (see p 195) may also cause abnormal behaviour, as do some of the most important feline poisons (see p 184), in both cases because the nervous system is damaged.

All this means that the problems confronting a vet faced with an apparent nervous disorder are usually complex. Not only do the side-effects of such diseases as those mentioned above have to be differentiated from disorders of nervous function themselves, but the part of the nervous system involved has to be located. Some techniques for investigating this are very complicated, involving expensive apparatus and specialized knowledge. As a start, however, and as with human patients, examining such reflexes as the knee-jerk will often indicate which part of the nervous system is working abnormally. Samples of blood or cerebrospinal fluid (the fluid bathing the brain and spinal cord) may reveal clues. X-ray examinations or tests of the electrical function of the nerves or brain may also be needed.

Many nervous diseases tend to produce rather similar signs, such as convulsions or paralysis, and differentiating these is particularly difficult. Paralysis occurs when some agent – it may be a chemical, a micro-organism or an injury – affects the part of the brain controlling bodily movements or the nerves carrying messages to the muscles. Seizures – fits or convulsions – can be caused by a brain infection, tumour, injury or other malfunction. If all other causes are eliminated, there may be true epilepsy, in which bursts of nerve signals from malfunctioning areas of the brain produce violent involuntary movements.

Even if a nervous disorder is diagnosed, in many cases there is no treatment. Unlike other body systems, the brain and spinal cord have little power of regeneration; once a nerve cell is killed by disease or injury, it cannot be replaced. In some circumstances damaged peripheral nerves (that is, those in the outlying parts of the body) can regrow, and even in the brain undamaged parts may be able to take over some of the work formerly done by the part destroyed. In some functional disorders (such as fits) the symptoms may be treatable (for example, by anticonvulsants) even if the cause cannot

be eliminated. In all cases of nervous disorders, careful nursing is essential (see p 178). The cat should be kept in a warm, quiet, dimly lit room and kept under observation but allowed to rest.

Congenital diseases
It is fortunate that inborn nervous disorders are uncommon, since they are generally untreatable and (except in relatively trivial conditions, such as congenital deafness of white cats; see p 31) the kitten must often be destroyed. One of the most important of these disorders is cerebellar hypoplasia or cerebellar ataxia. The cerebellum – the part of the brain responsible for co-ordination – is very small, and affected kittens cannot move their head or limbs in a co-ordinated or controlled way. (These symptoms are known collectively as ataxia.) The usual cause is infection with feline infectious enteritis (FIE; see p 192) before birth.

A second and often fatal condition is hydrocephalus, in which abnormally high fluid pressure within the brain causes the skull to enlarge. Certain tumours and injuries may have a similar effect later in life. Thirdly, and among the most common of these congenital disorders, are various malformations of the spine (for example, spina bifida) that may affect the spinal cord. This occurs most commonly among Manx cats (see pp 42 and 72). Signs may include lack of bowel and bladder control and weakness of the hind legs.

Other physical disorders
The effect of injuries such as street accidents and gunshot wounds (see p 180) depends on the exact part of the nervous system damaged. Brain injury may cause general unconsciousness or partial paralysis, or it may interfere with one or more of the senses. Damage to the spinal cord or to peripheral nerves may also cause paralysis below the site of the injury, with marked wasting of the paralysed muscles within two to three weeks. Depending where the injury is, as explained above, regeneration may or may not take place.

Similar symptoms appearing suddenly without injury, particularly in a middle-aged or elderly cat, can be due to a 'stroke' – cerebral thrombosis (a blood clot in the brain) or haemorrhage (a broken blood vessel). Either results in brain damage and cannot be treated even if diagnosed positively (which may be difficult), though many cats survive with good care. Blockage of the main artery to the hind legs by a blood clot can also cause paralysis and is often mistaken for a nervous disease.

Malignant (cancerous) tumours of the nervous system, in contrast, cause slowly developing and worsening symptoms. These can include behavioural changes, blindness, ataxia or paralysis. The tumour is often difficult to find without highly

complex methods of diagnosis, and treatment (by surgery) is generally not very successful. The final important group of physical disorders affecting the nervous system are degenerative conditions of the spine (for example, arthritis), which may cause pain and weakness in the hind legs. In some cases surgery is possible, but otherwise the symptoms can be treated with pain-killers and other drugs.

Infectious diseases
These include the most dangerous of all diseases of the nervous system, rabies (see opposite), as well as other virus infections (such as FIP) already mentioned. Tetanus (see p 183) is also fundamentally a nervous disease; it is rare in cats but may follow any penetrating wound, particularly if contaminated with soil.

Other bacterial infections may affect the nervous system following infections of the nose, eye or ear, or an injury or bite. Depending where the bacteria attack, they may cause meningitis (inflammation of the covering of the brain and spinal cord, resulting in fever, muscular rigidity and over-excitability), myelitis (inflammation of the spinal cord, resulting in fever and progressive paralysis) or encephalitis (inflammation of the brain itself, causing fever and behavioural symptoms). These diseases can be treated with antibiotics, but this is often difficult since to be effective in some cases the drugs must be able to cross the 'blood-brain barrier'. The patient often recovers, but not always completely.

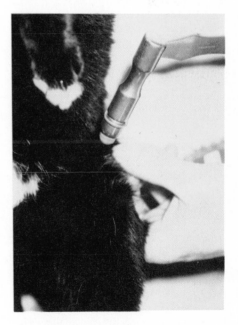

Testing the reflexes is often the first stage in investigating a suspected nervous disorder, as with a human patient. Anything interfering with the transmission of signals in the peripheral nerves will slow down or halt such reflex actions as the knee jerk **above**.

The geriatric cat

Life, it has been said, is an incurable disease. As a cat gets older, the degeneration of its physical mechanisms becomes gradually quicker until, unless it first succumbs to accident or disease, one or more of its vital systems ceases to work and the animal dies. This deterioration is a gradual process, and the cat can make many adaptations to lessen its impact – particularly if helped by a caring owner (see p164). However, one of its effects is to make the old cat vulnerable to many diseases that a younger animal can shrug off with relatively little trouble.

There are also a number of veterinary problems that are special to the elderly cat, and for this reason – and because in very many cases early diagnosis greatly improves the chance of recovery – regular 6- or 12-monthly check-ups by your vet are advisable once your cat passes the age of ten years. This will also enable the vet to ensure that your cat's vaccination programme is up to date – for, although many elderly cats have good immunity against feline infectious enteritis (FIE or panleukopaenia; see p192), this is far from true for respiratory virus infections (cat flu; see p197), immunity to which is relatively short-lived. At the same time, a check can be made on parasite infestation, which can reach serious proportions in some old cats.

Another thing worth checking regularly – say, at three-monthly intervals – is your pet's weight. Progressive weight loss is the most serious problem, other than acute disease conditions, encountered in old cats. It may result from kidney failure (see p203), to which most cats, if they live long enough, are prone. Another major cause of weight loss is a tumour (growth), but in many cases no specific cause can be found, and such cats – although presenting a pitiful appearance – may continue to enjoy life for a number of years.

However, old cats – like old people – are particularly likely to be affected by tumours. Some of these are benign (non-spreading), but malignant (cancerous) tumours gradually supplant normal body cells and spread via the circulatory or lymphatic systems (see p105) to new sites, forming secondary growths. These not only debilitate the body but also interfere with normal organ function, thus eventually causing death. Why cancer occurs is only beginning to be dimly understood, but it seems that 'mistakes' occur in the DNA molecules that control the growth and activity of cells (see p22). The cause of such mistakes may include irritant chemicals, viruses and other agents as yet undetected. Normally the mistakes are rectified by the cell itself but, in time, errors 'slip through' and are transmitted to succeeding generations of cells. As the cat gets older, the chances of such mistakes – which can cause abnormal cell growth – become greater, and thus it is that old animals are more likely to develop cancers.

The most serious and common cancer found in cats in general – and old cats in particular – is lymphosarcoma, which is associated with feline leukaemia virus (FeLV; see p204). One form of lymphosarcoma affects the thymus gland in the chest, often causing laboured breathing as its first symptom (see p199), but this is essentially a disease of young cats. The most serious forms in older animals affect the kidneys or the alimentary canal (gut), in the latter case often causing diffuse thickening that is very difficult to diagnose; the result is to decrease the efficiency of food absorption, resulting in weight loss.

Many other cancers, ranging from skin to liver, bone to lung, can and do occur in old age, but they are often detected too late for effective treatment. In general, surgical removal or destruction of the tumour by X-rays is the only treatment for such growths, and these methods are very traumatic for old cats. There is usually little chance of prolonged survival, so euthanasia is the only reasonable course.

Along with these major problems of old age, the natural degeneration of the tissues will predispose the elderly cat to many other complaints, some serious, some less so. Among them are oral disease such as gingivitis (see p196), heart disease (see p205) and arthritis. This last is less common in old cats than old dogs (and true rheumatism does not occur at all) but degeneration in the joints will sometimes lead to an intermittent lameness which is particularly noticeable after a cat has been lying down for some time. Unfortunately, many painkillers that are helpful to dogs are unsuitable for use in cats because of their toxicity. (Reduction in old cats' liver function lowers their ability to detoxify drugs, a fact the vet has to take into account whenever administering medicines or anaesthetics.) In serious cases of arthritis, anti-inflammatory drugs such as steroids may give some relief, but they can have unpleasant side-effects.

Constipation is perhaps the most common of all complaints encountered in old cats. Several factors may contribute to it, including a depletion in the body's fluid reserves which, combined with an inclination to drink less, increases fluid absorption from the bowel. The faeces become harder and more difficult to pass. Hairballs can also block the bowels (see p194), and loss of muscle tone in the lower intestine contributes to the constipation. Treatment may include giving wetter foods, increasing the bulk of foods and regular dosing with medicinal liquid paraffin (mineral oil). Care must be taken with the latter, however, as it can lead to vitamin and mineral deficiencies if given in excess.

It may seem from all this that getting old is a hazardous and painful certainty. But most elderly cats adapt to their longevity. They seek out warm areas and sleep for longer periods. They adapt to many of the minor diseases of old age. They can and often do live a healthy and contented life well into their teens, and some even into their twenties. Thus, although problems are more likely to develop in old cats, it is by no means certain that they will.

A veterinary examination at regular intervals is particularly necessary for an elderly cat. The vet will check the cat's weight, eyes, ears and mouth, removing any hard tartar that has built up on the teeth. He or she will look for signs of external or internal parasites and will feel for any lumps that might indicate a tumour. A blood sample may be taken for laboratory analysis, and booster shots of vaccines against the common feline ailments given if necessary. The owner will be given advice on coping with the everyday problems of old age, such as constipation, and the vet may prescribe vitamin and mineral supplements.

A tumour, or growth, always needs careful investigation. A biopsy (tissue sampling) is usually necessary to discover if it is cancerous. Tumours in some places – such as an ear **above** – may be easy to remove, but many others are incurable. Such tumours are more common in old age, and may necessitate euthanasia.

Humane destruction

The decision to end the life of an aged, ill or congenitally deformed cat is at best a difficult one. The owner's immediate reaction to the prospect of losing a pet in this way may be one of grief and repulsion, but the welfare of the cat should be the foremost consideration. It must be remembered that this is not the easiest task the vet has to carry out. He or she will not advise this ultimate solution unless it is absolutely necessary. It must also be said that many thousands of cats and other pets are put down every year because they are unowned and unwanted, and no one is able or willing to look after them – the most powerful argument for neutering all cats that are not specifically required for breeding.

Grounds for euthanasia

Disregarding the question of pet population control, the veterinary grounds for euthanasia are fairly clear, but since they depend on a judgement of the cat's condition and prospects of future health, it is reasonable to expect your vet to discuss the pros and cons of a particular case and to offer advice. However, the ultimate responsibility for the decision to put a cat down normally rests with the owner, and vets generally feel that they have a moral, if not legal, obligation to comply with any reasonable request. However, this is not to say that they will not, on occasion, try to persuade the owner to take a particular course of action. And, as a corollary, many vets ask owners to sign a formal request for euthanasia before they will carry it out.

The main veterinary grounds for putting an animal down are that it is so ill that life has become a burden to it and there is no prospect of improvement. Put another way, it is reasonable to destroy a cat if it has a serious illness that is incurable or if the chances of a cure are poor. Euthanasia is also usually valid if a cure is possible only at unreasonable expense, trouble or suffering for the animal, but here there are more difficult judgements to be made.

Kittens born with serious defects – so that they are bound to suffer a crippled existence – should also be destroyed; such conditions are numerous, but include severe hydrocephalus (enlargement of the skull due to excessive fluid pressure; see p207), severe cleft palate, imperforate anus (that is, lack of normal anal opening), spina bifida, a severe umbilical hernia and of course any other gross deformity.

It is always difficult to decide on euthanasia purely on grounds of numbers of kittens in a litter, and most difficult of all in the case of a 'runt' or weakling that may be rejected by its mother but capable, with proper care, of growing up healthily (see pp225 and 227). This is a case where the vet's advice should be sought, for it may have a defect that is not obvious and may never be able to gain adequate strength.

Methods of euthanasia

Euthanasia literally means easy death; for practical purposes this means death with no pain or distress. There may be circumstances when 'physical' methods such as shooting are justifiable – for example, with a rabid cat that cannot be safely captured – but the usual method today is with an intravenous injection of a large overdose of barbiturate anaesthetic in the foreleg. This literally sends the cat to sleep in a few seconds and it will then die peacefully, usually within 30 seconds. In cases where a cat is very feeble, the vet may prefer to inject into an alternative site, since it is often difficult to locate the vein precisely. Occasionally, halothane gas may be administered with a mask. Vets are unanimous in agreeing that old methods, such as drowning and electrocution, cause unnecessary pain, suffering and distress to the animal, and should never be used.

Once it has been decided to euthanize a cat, this should always be carried out by a vet, for only a vet has the training, experience and equipment to perform it in a humane way. Most vets are sympathetic to an owner's request to put a cat down in its home surroundings, but you should remember that at the vet's premises there are trained staff who can assist. At this time it is most important to minimize the psychological upset to the pet. It is a total fallacy that the animal 'knows what is going to happen', but the cat may sense the owner's emotions and become distressed if the owner is grief-stricken. It is much better for comparative strangers such as the vet and nurse to work without the owner present if this will spare the cat unnecessary distress before it dies.

Disposal of the body

This is another question on which the vet's advice may be invaluable, for not only do methods and facilities vary from one locality to another, but so do official regulations. In some places, there is an obligation on local authorities to dispose of an animal's body if requested; elsewhere private arrangements must be made. There may be a local pet cemetery, about which your vet should be able to give information, or cremation facilities. Or you may wish to bury your pet in your own garden – if permitted – in which case the body should be placed at least 1 m (3 ft) deep. Most vets are willing to dispose of the remains, usually via public waste-disposal services or by cremation, and in some localities this is the only permitted method of disposal.

Occasionally, the question may arise of whether or not an autopsy (post-mortem examination) should be carried out. In a few cases this may be required by law – if, for example, a case of rabies is suspected. Or you may yourself want to know the cause of death. Otherwise it is only likely to be requested if the vet wishes to further his or her knowledge, in which case it may benefit future feline patients. It is unlikely that the request would be made for any frivolous reason, if only because of the pressure on the vet's time, but you are nevertheless within your rights to withhold permission and the vet will respect this.

Chapter 5
BREEDING
AND SHOWING CATS

The pros and cons of breeding

Occasionally entering your pet cat – whether it is a pedigree animal or not – in a cat show makes an interesting hobby, but if you embark on both showing and breeding cats, there is a tendency for the hobby to become more a way of life. Most cat shows include a section for 'household pets', and many enthusiastic exhibitors of pedigree animals gained their first insight into the show world by casually entering the family pet in this section. From there it is not a big step to acquiring a pedigree kitten, which, if female, may be 'allowed just one litter'; the results can easily be so fascinating that the feline family rapidly increases in size.

Anyone tempted to set up as a cat breeder should, however, be clear from the start that very few, if any, breeders make a satisfactory living from selling the kittens they raise. An experienced breeder can expect sales to contribute to the cost of feeding, heating and other expenses, but this depends to some extent on which breeds are raised. (Persians command better prices than most short-haired breeds in Britain, but this is not necessarily true elsewhere.) Furthermore, the price that is commanded depends in part on show success, and entering many shows can be costly, especially if long-distance travel and overnight accommodation must be paid for. (The direct rewards of show success are purely nominal – often only rosettes and trophies.)

It is possible for someone who wants to work with cats to make a financial success of running a boarding cattery, but unless the two can be kept physically apart, it is best not to combine this with a breeding establishment. Boarders are bound to intro-duce infection occasionally, and this could devastate a breeding colony.

The practicalities of breeding

If cat breeding is not financially rewarding, at least it is not too labour-intensive. Cats are naturally very clean and self-reliant, so that – apart from arranging planned matings and supervising at births – the only essential tasks are providing the correct diet, grooming, and cleaning the litter tray. The articles that follow explain these practicalities, but there are some basic principles that novice breeders, in parti-cular, need to understand.

If you own an entire female and want her to have kittens, it is advisable to choose her mate rather than to allow her to roam in search of one. This is particularly import-ant, of course, if she is a pedigree animal and you intend to register her offspring (see p 224), since it is normally essential to know the father's pedigree. Furthermore, the sire should have qualities that complement those of the queen if there is to be any hope of top-quality kittens resulting. The answer, particularly for a novice, is to send or take the queen to be mated by a stud male; owners of these may be contacted via the breeder who originally supplied the queen, through a vet or a breed club, or (generally least satisfactorily) through ad-vertisements in cat fancy magazines.

Such journeys to visit a stud are obviously difficult if long distances are involved. For this reason, many experi-enced breeders (in North America particu-larly) keep their own stud males who are mated to a retinue of queens. But keeping a stud successfully – particularly if 'public' – demands many years of experience in hand-ling cats and breeding litters, to say nothing of the need for a regular supply of females to mate, which the novice is unlikely to be able to provide. For these reasons, it is best to start a breeding career with a queen, and – if finding suitable nearby studs promises to be a problem – one belonging to one of the commoner breeds.

Trying for show success

One of the benefits of working with an experienced stud owner is the advice the latter can give the queen's owner on the choice of mates and on which of the off-spring are most likely to produce high-quality kittens in the next generation. If the progeny are of good show standard, it is particularly gratifying if the owner is also the breeder.

Of course, anyone can enter a pedigree kitten in a show, provided that it is healthy and correctly registered, but if success is to be based on anything more than luck, the exhibitor needs to learn about the required standard of the particular breed. This involves studying the winning cats and dis-cussing with more experienced breeders what it is that makes them winners. The second requirement is that the cat should be in peak physical condition, and this demands time and care, both in keeping the cat perfectly fit and also in grooming and presenting it at its best.

With experience, the art of cat breeding and showing can be widened to include the study of genetics (see pp 20–44), possibly leading to experimental breeding and the development of new breeds. Some exhibi-tors sadly become so carried away by their successes or so engrossed in their breeding work that they become both bad losers and terrible bores to friends who are not in-volved with pedigree cats. But, kept in perspective, cat breeding and showing can provide much happiness for both owners and cats, most of which thoroughly enjoy the admiration of their spectators.

A prize-winning feline – plus a good deal of pleasure – may be the reward of persistence in raising litters of your chosen breed, but do not expect substantial financial gain.

How cats reproduce 1

The sexual prowess and fecundity of cats is perhaps better known to most cat owners than the anatomical and physiological details of how they reproduce. Understanding these details does, however, give the owner or breeder a much clearer insight into what is happening and what needs to be done when a female cat becomes pregnant – whether through a planned mating with a prize stud or as a result of a night-time encounter with a neighbourhood tom. And while the reproductive systems of cats do not differ very greatly from those of other mammals – human beings included – they do have a number of unusual features that contribute to cats' success as a species.

The male reproductive system
The main job of the male's reproductive equipment is to make sperm – the male reproductive or germ cells – and to deposit these inside the female's reproductive tract, where they can meet and fertilize her eggs. The first function is performed by the testicles, the second by the penis. Associated with these are various accessory glands, and (as in all sexually reproductive animals) these organs all function under the control of the brain – through both direct nerve signals and chemical 'messengers' called hormones that are carried in the bloodstream.

The penis is essentially an organ of copulation. To remove urine merely needs a suitable external opening, but placing the sperm inside the female's body requires an organ that can stiffen and become erect. For this reason the penis consists largely of spongy tissue with large cavities that become filled with blood during excitement and so give the rigidity needed for penetration. It is also deflected slightly downwards when erect, so that when the queen and tom flex their hindquarters (in opposite directions) during mating the penis can enter the vagina.

In an unborn male kitten, the testicles lie within the abdomen, but shortly after birth they descend into the bag-like scrotum. This is vital because the normal internal body temperature is too high for the development of sperm; if the testicles do not descend the cat will be sterile. The temperature in the scrotum is only a few degrees lower, but this is enough; it is aided by the blood supply to the testicles passing through a network of small blood vessels (called the pampiniform plexus) that allow some of its warmth to escape through the thin skin covering.

Within the testicles are two distinct groups of specialized cells, with different functions. One group – the so-called Leydig or interstitial cells – act under the influence of hormones from the pituitary gland (which lies at the base of the brain) to produce the male sex hormone testosterone. This controls male sexual activity and induces the distinctive male physical and behavioural characteristics – the thick skin of the neck and heavy jowls, the potent urine smell and the habit of spraying to mark territory (see p124).

The second group of cells are organized into convoluted tube-like structures called seminiferous tubules, and these produce sperm. They are lined with spermatogonia – potential sperm cells – which undergo a special form of cell division called meiosis during their conversion into sperm. Meiosis results in a halving of the number of chromosomes per cell and a random assortment of genetic traits (see p22).

The sperm themselves consist of a bulbous head containing the chromosomes (which carry the genetic or hereditary information and are contained in the nucleus) and a small store of food for energy, and a long whip-like tail that can thrash from side to side to propel the sperm forward like a tadpole. Their overall length is about 0.06mm (0.0025in), most of which consists of the tail. When first formed in the tubules, however, the sperm are not fully developed and must lie in the long and convoluted storage tube, the epididymis, undergoing intricate biochemical changes before they are mature. During ejaculation the stored sperm pass along the vas deferens and into the urethra – the central passage of the penis. Along the way, secretions vital to the viability of the sperm are added to the seminal fluid by the accessory glands – the bulbo-urethral (or Cowper's) glands and the prostate gland.

The female reproductive system
In contrast to the male, almost all the female reproductive organs are within the body cavity. The female equivalent of the testicles are the paired ovaries, which lie near the kidneys. Unlike the human uterus, or womb, which forms a thick-walled, roughly triangular organ, that of the cat is distinctly Y-shaped, with two long 'horns' and a quite short central part, or /continued

---

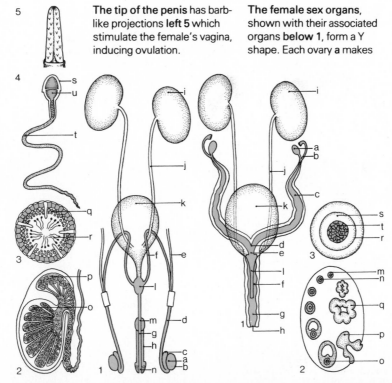

The male sex organs, shown with their associated organs **right 1**, consist of various glands and their connecting tubes. Each testicle **a** lies in the scrotum **b**. Leading from it is the epididymis **c**, leading to the spermatic cord **d** (consisting of the spermatic artery **e** and vas deferens **f**). The latter joins the urethra **g**, which passes along the penis **h**. Other organs include the kidneys **i**, ureters **j**, bladder **k**, prostate **l** and bulbo-urethral (Cowper's) glands **m**. The glans **n** is the part of the penis that enters the vagina. The testicle in cross-section **2** shows the seminiferous tubules **o** and epididymis **p**. The cross-section of a seminiferous tubule **3** shows the spermatogonia **q** from which develop spermatids (immature sperm) **r**. A mature sperm **4** consists of the head **s**, tail **t** and nucleus **u**.

The tip of the penis has barb-like projections **left 5** which stimulate the female's vagina, inducing ovulation.

The female sex organs, shown with their associated organs **below 1**, form a Y shape. Each ovary **a** makes ova (eggs) which pass via the oviduct or Fallopian tube **b** to the horn of the uterus (womb) **c**. The two horns join at the body of the uterus **d**, which opens via the narrow cervix **e** into the vagina **f**. The outer part of the vagina **g** is called the vestibule or urogenital sinus; it opens to the outside at the vulva **h**. As in the male, each kidney **i** empties through its ureter **j** into the bladder **k**, which in turn empties via the urethra **l**. An ovary in cross-section **2** shows a follicle **m** containing an immature egg or oocyte **n**; this develops into an ovum **o** which is released when the follicle bursts **p**. The follicle then develops into a corpus luteum **q**. An ovum greatly enlarged **3** is seen to have a membrane **r**, called the vitelline membrane, surrounding the cytoplasm **s**; this contains the nucleus **t** and also food supplies.

How cats reproduce 2

body. The Fallopian tubes or oviducts, which transport the eggs from the ovaries to the uterus, are also relatively short. The uterus ends in the narrow cervix, or neck, which opens into the vagina – the birth and copulatory passage. The urethra (the urine passage) also opens into the lower part of the vagina, in contrast to the separate openings of the human female. The combined opening is just below the anus.

Puberty – sexual maturity – and all subsequent breeding activity are controlled by a complex interplay between the ovaries, the pituitary gland and the brain. A hormonal chain of command initiates, controls and terminates the various stages of oestrus (the cycle of sexual receptiveness), mating and pregnancy. The sex-controlling part of the brain, the hypothalamus, is sensitive to stimuli from both inside and outside the body, so that many factors – the length of daylight, temperature, presence of other cats and so on – may all influence the reproductive process.

Under instructions from the brain – stimulated in turn by the lengthening daylight and rising temperatures of spring – the pituitary gland produces a 'master' hormone called follicle-stimulating hormone (FSH), which initiates the fundamental cyclic activity of the ovaries, the oestrous cycle. FSH stimulates the growth of small sac-like follicles in the ovaries. These contain incompletely developed eggs, or oocytes, many thousands of which are present in each ovary at birth; like the male sperm, their development involves the process of meiosis, which halves the number of chromosomes in the nucleus.

Apart from producing ova, or eggs, the follicles also manufacture the female sex hormone oestrogen. The main function of this is to prepare the genital tract for mating and fertilization, but it also produces the characteristic behaviour of a queen in heat (see p 130). This may sometimes include spraying, but a vaginal discharge, common in many other oestrous female animals, is unusual. As oestrus develops, the follicles swell and come to the surface of the ovaries. If mating does not take place, then the follicles simply shrivel up in a few days and lie dormant until a renewed surge of FSH starts the next oestrous cycle – generally two to three weeks later, though often sooner in the foreign-type breeds such as Siamese. But if mating does take place a new chain of command is set in motion.

Mating and after

Stimulation of the queen's vagina by the penis during mating (aided by the barb-like projections on the glans or head of the penis) causes her brain to instruct the pituitary to release a second master hormone – luteinizing hormone (LH). This causes the mature follicles to burst open, releasing their eggs in the process known as

The follicular phase of a queen's oestrous cycle begins 1 when the hypothalamus of the brain a signals to the pituitary gland b to produce follicle-stimulating hormone (FSH). This travels through the bloodstream and causes the ovaries to develop follicles 2 containing oocytes (immature eggs). FSH also causes the follicles to release the sex hormone oestrogen, which produces the physical and behavioural changes associated with oestrus or 'heat'. These include extension of the Fallopian tubes around the ovaries 3 so that eggs, when released, are funnelled into the oviducts; preparation of the genital tract for mating and fertilization; and the queen's preparedness to mate. If mated, this lasts about four days; if no mating occurs, the follicles simply shrivel up 4 after about a week and are

absorbed, ceasing oestrogen production, so that the queen comes off heat until renewed FSH production restarts the cycle one to several weeks

later. Cycles recur from late winter until autumn in natural temperate conditions. Indoors, a queen may have oestrus throughout the year.

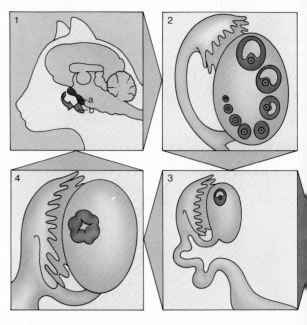

ovulation. Having fulfilled the first part of their task, the follicles are then converted into structures called corpora lutea (singular, corpus luteum), whose job is to produce the second female sex hormone, progesterone. At the same time, production of oestrogen diminishes so that the cat is no longer sexually receptive.

Progesterone's chemical codes prepare the uterus for the arrival of the fertilized eggs and set in motion the complex body changes that are necessary for maintaining pregnancy. The most noticeable effects are changes in fluid balance and body fat distribution, which result in the characteristic enlargement of the abdomen, and a reddening of the nipples about three weeks after mating (known to breeders in Britain as 'pinking up').

Because ovulation, the formation of corpora lutea and the production of progesterone are all initiated by the act (or multiple acts) of mating, cats are classed as induced ovulators. This reproductive feature is not unique – it occurs in other felids and in the rabbit – but it is unusual and has several important implications, for any mating – whether fertile or not – can cause ovulation and progesterone production. As a result, even a sterile mating will produce many of the signs of pregnancy; the queen is then said to be in a state of pseudopregnancy or false pregnancy. However, it is necessary for fertilized eggs to become implanted in the uterus for progesterone production to be prolonged for the full term of pregnancy.

Nevertheless, induced ovulation does

have practical applications, for artificial stimulation of the queen's vagina during oestrus will mimic the action of the penis and trigger the release of LH and cause ovulation. As a result, it is possible with the correct technique to artificially inseminate an oestrous queen, opening up the possibility (as yet little used) of prize studs siring litters without ever meeting the queen. Frozen semen could even be flown over long distances, as it is for many other animals. On the other hand, artificially stimulating an oestrous queen's vagina can curtail the period of 'heat' by inducing pseudopregnancy (see p217).

But perhaps most important is the role played by induced ovulation in the evolutionary success of the cat. Most members of the cat family are solitary, coming together only briefly during the breeding season. The fact that ovulation closely follows mating ensures a high probability that it will result in pregnancy. Most other mammals – humans included – are termed spontaneous ovulators, since they produce eggs (either regularly or just during the breeding season) whether mated or not. Reproductive success with such an arrangement obviously depends on the males and females spending a good deal of time together so that frequent matings can take place; otherwise, either eggs or sperm may deteriorate before fertilization can occur.

Fertilization and implantation

Normally, between three and six eggs will be released by the queen's two ovaries into the funnel-like ends of the Fallopian tubes

The luteal phase of the oestrous cycle begins if mating does occur. Physical stimulation of the queen's vagina during copulation 5 causes her hypothalamus to again signal the pituitary 6, this time to produce LH (luteinizing hormone). This also travels via the bloodstream to the ovaries, triggering the bursting of the follicles 7, so that their mature eggs are released. Once the eggs are released, the follicles are converted into corpora lutea 8, which produce the

second sex hormone, progesterone. This causes various bodily changes characteristic of pregnancy, but most importantly prepare

the uterus for implantation of the fertilized eggs. Meanwhile the tadpole-like sperm propel themselves up the genital tract 9 to meet the eggs

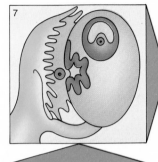

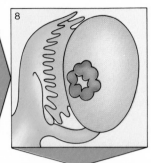

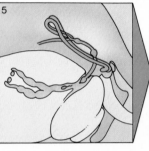

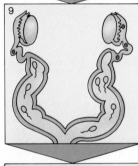

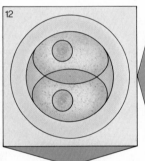

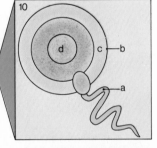

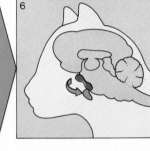

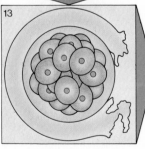

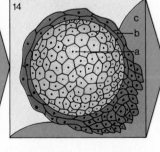

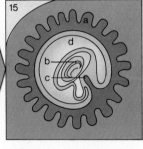

The final stages begin with fertilization 10, when a sperm a penetrates first the outer jelly-like covering b and then the egg itself c to reach the nucleus d. The nuclei fuse 11. As soon as a sperm achieves fertilization, changes in the egg's membrane prevent further sperm entering. The egg grows as it travels down to the uterus. 12 Its single cell becomes two, then four, then eight cells, and so on until it

bursts from its surrounding envelope 13. The cell mass or blastocyst 14 now develops an inner cell mass a, which will form the embryo kitten, and a much larger surrounding layer, the trophoblast b, which will become the placenta. At this stage it implants itself into the thick, spongy tissue lining the uterus c. 15 Finger-like projections a develop from the trophoblast to form the placenta, which will carry

nutrients and oxygen to the rapidly developing embryo and carry away wastes. Now – only a few days after implantation – the embryo proper b is developing from a fold of cells called the primitive streak. The umbilical cord c is developing to connect it to the placenta, and it is cushioned from physical jolts by the amniotic fluid d in the amniotic sac, in which the kitten will eventually be born.

24 to 36 hours after mating. Not all of them may be fertilized, of course, but for those that are fertilization takes place in the Fallopian tubes, up which the sperm propel themselves. The sperm must first penetrate a jelly-like outer layer before entering the egg itself. As soon as one sperm has penetrated an egg, changes occur in the surface layer to block the entry of any more sperm. The nuclei of the egg and sperm then fuse, reconstituting the full set of chromosomes and sealing the future kitten's pattern of inherited traits (see p22).

Although only one sperm can fertilize each egg, an oestrous queen that is allowed free range may well have been mated by a retinue of toms. As a result, every kitten in her litter could have a different father. This phenomenon is called superfecundity. As already mentioned, ovulation and pregnancy normally suppress oestrus, but some queens come into heat during pregnancy and may occasionally even mate. Induced ovulation may then give rise to the development in the uterus of a second set of foetuses (unborn kittens). This is called superfetation. The two litters may subsequently be born at the same time, the second immature litter generally dying. Or, in some cases, the second litter may be born alive a few weeks after the first.

After fertilization, the eggs take several days to pass along the Fallopian tubes to the horns of the uterus. There they at first lie free within the cavity, nourished by the secretions (known as uterine milk) of the uterine glands. Each egg cell begins to divide, and the resulting cluster of cells becomes organized into a layer around the edge of the so-called zona pellucida – the envelope of the original egg – leaving a central cavity. The egg is now termed a blastocyst, and after about eight days the envelope ruptures and the egg 'hatches' out. Very rapid cell division then occurs and the central cavity becomes enlarged, with a thin outer layer called the trophoblast and a smaller inner cell mass.

It is the inner cell mass that will develop into the embryo kitten. The trophoblast will form the placenta, the organ by which the embryo (later termed a foetus) will receive nourishment from its mother's bloodstream. This develops from finger-like projections that grow from the trophoblast after it becomes implanted in the wall of the uterus some 14 days after mating. From this point the cat can truly be said to be pregnant. During the next two weeks, extremely rapid development takes place as the embryonic kitten's body systems and main organs develop and become organized. Growth, in terms of absolute size increase, is not yet very rapid, but by about four weeks from mating the queen's uterus contains foetuses – as yet only 25 to 30mm (about 1 in) long – that are already virtually complete miniature kittens.

Planned feline families 1

The decision to breed pedigree cats is not one to be taken lightly. Planning, patience and a certain amount of work are needed to produce healthy litters of high-quality kittens – ones that are both good examples of their breed and good companions to their owners. Ignorance and mistakes can result at best in financial loss and at worst in suffering and even the loss of feline lives.

Acquiring a brood queen

As explained on page 212, it is best to start off with one or two breeding queens, not a stud. Many breeders find it an advantage to keep two brood queens of similar age; they will generally come into heat within a few days of each other and can therefore be mated and give birth about the same time. Should one of them have difficulties in delivering or feeding her kittens, the other can then usually act as a foster mother.

Ideally, you should acquire a future brood queen while she is still a young kitten, so that a happy relationship can be built before she is mature. You can of course buy an adult queen from a reputable breeder, but make sure that the reason for sale is genuine – that she has not proved unable to carry her litters to full term, for example. If you are a novice breeder you should seek advice – from experienced breeders and owners, cat fancy officials, judges, vets and so on – and visit as many cat shows as possible. In that way, you can get to know the desirable attributes of the breed of your choice and which are the leading bloodlines. An experienced cat fancier may be able to spot the potential in an outsider, but the beginner is well advised to play safe with a well-proven line.

Then, with a definite type of kitten in mind, you should view a number of litters for sale, making contact with their breeders either directly at cat shows, through address listings in cat show catalogues, through a vet or cat club, or by responding to advertisements in cat magazines. An experienced cat fancier is a valuable companion when viewing litters, but the kitten's pedigree (see p 45) is a useful source of information. The kitten's sire and dam may not necessarily be champions, but a good buy will usually have a number of champions among its forebears.

Breeders commonly grade kittens as show, breeding and pet quality (the first being the highest), but you should not necessarily take the breeder's opinion without question. Of course, early success in the kitten classes of cat shows is a good indication of promise, but it will also increase the price. What a breeder – particularly a beginner – needs is not necessarily the best possible example of the breed, but a strong and healthy kitten whose weak points (in terms of the breed standard) can be countered by mating with a stud having complementary qualities. It is impossible to

Stud accommodation varies with climate, space available and number of cats to be housed. If possible, the queen and stud should have separate quarters and runs **below**; otherwise the queen's can be a partitioned part of the stud house **right**. Housing for a 'queen in waiting' should be quite separate **far right**. Key: **a** queen's quarters; **b** stud's quarters; **c** communal or stud's run; **d** queen's run; **e** escape run; **f** queen in waiting.

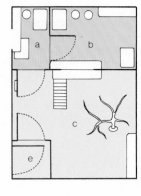
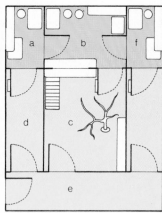

A freestanding stud house is ideal for a mild climate, and can incorporate adjoining sleeping quarters and outside runs for the stud and queen, interconnecting with doors and cat flaps, and reached via a two-door escape run. In areas with harsh winters, the facilities shown here can be adapted to basically indoor accommodation, with or without access to an outdoor run. The problems are much the same as for an indoor boarding cattery (see p 163), but ventilation is particularly important and the quarters, being permanent, should be larger in area.

The outdoor stud house may be of wood or brick, at least 2.5×1.8m (8×6ft), with the queen's sleeping quarters 1×1.8m (3×6ft). The whole building should have a roof high enough for the owner to

walk inside. The walls should be well insulated and finished in the inside with gloss paint or plastic laminate; seal all joints that might harbour parasites. The wooden or concrete floor should be covered with vinyl that extends 30cm (12in) up the walls for easy cleaning. Provide at least two windows which, if openable for ventilation, must have wire mesh to prevent escape. Ideally the division between the stud's and queen's pens should be partly of mesh to allow courtship by sight and scent, and partly solid to allow the queen to relax in privacy. Both houses should have sturdy shelves for exercise, escape and observation. The outside run should total at least 3.5×3m (12×10ft), including the queen's run. The roof should be 2.25m (7ft)

high, and all should be enclosed with strong wire mesh on wooden or metal poles. Concrete is the most easily disinfected flooring; if wood is used, raise it off the ground for water to escape. Fittings inside should include thermostatically controlled heating by tubular heaters or infra-red dull emitters. The absolute minimum temperature should be 8°C (46°F) for long-hairs and 13°C (55°F) for foreign short-hairs, but 20°C (68°F) is the normal minimum in North American catteries. Stout cardboard boxes lined with newspaper and a blanket make good beds; all except the blanket can be destroyed when soiled or when the queen goes home. Use plastic litter trays. Outside, provide exercise shelves and, for the stud, a tree trunk or climbing tower.

name a price for a good breeder quality kitten – this varies widely with breed, location and many other factors – but it will generally range from about £60 ($150) upwards; treat any suggestion of a 'bargain' with suspicion.

The ideal age and health factors to be considered are the same as when acquiring a kitten purely as a companion (see p142), but take one special factor into account: It is mainly the queen, not the stud, that determines the size of the litter, and a female kitten from a large litter is also more likely to prove a prolific breeder.

When the queen comes into heat

Queens vary widely in the age at which they first 'call', or come into heat. Siamese and other foreign-type breeds tend to be sexually precocious, often calling as young as five months or even less. Other shorthairs may first call at about seven months, while most long-haired breeds of Persian type do not call until about ten months old or more. A five-month kitten is certainly too young to be mated. On the other hand, it can be more harmful to allow a queen to call repeatedly without mating than to allow her to mate at a comparatively early age. (A queen that is not mated after more than four oestrous periods may develop ovarian cysts; see p228.) As a general rule, you can mate a queen on her second or third call, when she will probably be 10 to 12 months old.

Of course, it is not always possible to prevent 'accidental' pregnancy unless the queen is confined to the home as soon as she comes into heat. A novice breeder may find it difficult to tell exactly when a young queen's oestrus starts – only the foreign breeds are really vocal, and other signs are not so obvious (see p130) – but the neighbourhood toms will be in no doubt. Should the queen escape for just a few minutes an unwanted mating can occur.

In this case, provided the queen is mature enough, it is best to allow her to bear the litter to full term and then give away the kittens as pets. They will not be pedigree animals, but to destroy them all at birth will not only upset the mother but may also result in mastitis (inflammation of the mammary glands) because the milk is not drawn off. It is now possible for a vet to prevent pregnancy following a mis-mating by giving a hormone injection, but this can upset the queen's hormonal balance so much as to make a subsequent mating infertile. In any case, bearing the 'mongrel' litter will do her no harm – she is certainly not 'ruined for life' and will be perfectly able to breed true to type at her next mating – and the experience can be written off as useful practice. If, however, the litter is large and the queen very young, it may be best to reduce the number of kittens.

How many litters a year a queen should be allowed depends on various factors, but she should not be used simply as a breeding machine. She must be allowed time to build up her strength and fitness between pregnancies; otherwise she will quite soon begin to produce frail and unhealthy kittens, and her life may well be shortened. Generally, Persians and their relatives and the short-haired European and American breeds seem happy when bred once each year, while the more precocious foreign short-hairs thrive on producing two litters in 14 months. If, for any reason, a queen bears only one kitten, she can – barring any disorder – be safely re-mated when the kitten is about three months old.

Whatever the queen's pattern of oestrous cycles and pregnancies, it is vital to record every detail. You should note the dates of all her calls, dates of mating and names of studs, the dates of expected delivery and the dates when she actually does give birth – together with full details of the litters and their subsequent progress. Only then can you keep proper track of her past history and plan for the future.

Choosing a stud

It is best to choose a queen's future mate or mates as soon as possible, and to do this you need to decide into which bloodlines she is to be bred. Once again, the advice of more experienced cat fanciers is invaluable, while stud books maintained by cat fancy organizations are the best source of information on breeding lines. Some of these bodies and some breed clubs also keep lists of cats at stud, while some stud owners advertise in specialist magazines.

The next step is to visit the prospective studs so that you can meet their owners and inspect both studs and premises. No responsible stud owner would object to such an inspection – indeed, it should be welcomed – since the stud should be kept in purpose-built escape-proof accommodation with the highest possible standards of hygiene. (The quarters should be thoroughly disinfected after each queen goes.)

Another purpose of the visit is to establish clearly the terms and conditions of the stud service – many stud /continued

---

CONTRACEPTION FOR CATS

Breeders use contraceptives for female cats as much to suppress calling as to prevent unwanted litters (though the latter use is effectively employed in controlling feral cat populations; see p165). If a brood queen is allowed to call incessantly she will soon lose condition and in time suffer permanent damage to her reproductive system. So contraceptives can be useful to postpone breeding in a queen who first calls when too young, to rest a queen between litters and to plan litters throughout her breeding life.

Two types of contraceptive agent can be used in cats, though they may not be available in all countries. They can generally be used only under veterinary supervision, and are not recommended for long-term use; they are no alternative to spaying.

The first type are synthetic drugs that mimic the natural action of progesterone, the main hormone of pregnancy (see p214), and cause similar side-effects: increased appetite, behavioural changes, retention of fluids and weight gain. These progestagens can be given as tablets – convenient to postpone calling or to suppress a single oestrous period as it starts – or as a longer-term slow-release 'depot injection'. Apart from the side-effects mentioned, they may leave the uterus (womb) more susceptible to infection (see p229).

The second type of chemical contraceptives are relatively new and are called gonadotrophin inhibitors; they stop the release by the pituitary of the hormone FSH, which starts the oestrous cycle (see p214). Early reports suggest they may be less likely to result in uterine infections.

An alternative to either of the above contraceptive drugs is to stimulate the oestrous queen's vagina (see the illustration). This will trigger ovulation, inducing pseudopregnancy (see p214) and a period of sexual quiescence. But make sure that the queen does not mate with even a single tom soon after such stimulation, or she will almost certainly become pregnant.

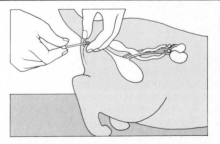

Stopping oestrus A queen can be brought off heat by stimulation of her vagina. An assistant should hold her by the scruff and deflect her tail while you part the lips of the vulva, insert a cotton bud or blunt, smooth-ended glass rod about 1 cm (⅜ in) into the vagina and gently rotate it. The queen will struggle and may call out; this is quite normal. She may show the typical post-coital rolling behaviour. She should cease calling in a few days. The same vaginal stimulation without the risk of pregnancy can be achieved by mating her with a 'teaser tom' – a male with the normal tom's instincts but made infertile by vasectomy.

Planned feline families 2

owners use a standard printed form – and the fee to be paid. This last is as variable as the price of a brood queen, but is likely to range between £25 and £60 in Britain and from $150 upwards in North America. (A grand champion or a top award winner will obviously command a high fee.) Some stud owners may be willing to provide a free stud service to a certain queen in return for the right to choose one of her litter, but you should be aware of the legal problems that can arise with any such arrangement (see p 168). It is normal to pay the stud fee before mating takes place, although some stud owners will defer accepting the fee until they have witnessed a successful mating. It is common (though not universal) to allow a second mating free of charge if the first does not produce results.

Most important of all, however, the visit to the prospective stud should establish his suitability to sire your queen's kittens. In order to judge this, you must know the queen's strengths and weaknesses, and look for complementary qualities in the stud. If, for example, a Siamese queen's head is somewhat rounded, then it is particularly important that the stud's head should be a fine, tapering wedge. Coat and eye colour are important in every breed – though, in terms of points scoring on the show bench, more important in some breeds than others – and this results from the combined effect of major colour genes and of polygenes (see p 27). Thus, for example, you should take into account not only the basic colouring of the stud and queen but also more subtle differences such as the intensity of orange in a red tabby, the quality of a tabby's markings, the degree of shading in a chinchilla, shaded silver or smoke, the shade of eye colour and so on.

The articles on pages 29 to 43 explain the underlying genetics of colour, body type and other features, and should be studied before you start visiting prospective studs. You must, however, be prepared to learn through experience and observation, for the qualities of champion cats are elusive to the inexperienced eye.

Keeping a stud male

Although widely considered – at least, outside North America – to be not for the beginner, keeping a stud male can be very rewarding. But if you are contemplating this step you must be prepared for a greatly increased workload. An active stud male has a natural instinct to spray his territory with extremely strong-smelling urine, so he needs his own spacious quarters, preferably away from the house, with adjacent accommodation for visiting queens. You must be prepared to spend time keeping these quarters spotlessly clean and as sweet-smelling as practically possible. Of course, the stud can easily become lonely and bored in such isolation; he needs human com-

panionship, affection, favourite toys to play with and facilities for exercise.

In moderate climates, such as in the British Isles, the normal accommodation consists of an outdoor run enclosed with wire netting and well-insulated heated sleeping quarters. In many parts of North America the severe winters preclude such arrangements, and the basic accommodation must be indoors – whether or not access to an outdoor run is provided – making cleanliness, hygiene and ventilation doubly important. Many stud owners also keep one or more queens, but their permanent accommodation should be quite separate from the stud's. Certainly, whatever your opinion on whether or not cats in general should be allowed to roam free, a 'professional' stud should always be confined to his quarters to reduce to a minimum the risk of injury or infection and to ensure that he is not missing when needed to service a visiting queen.

Ideally, you should erect the stud-house or other accommodation while the future stud is still a kitten, gradually introducing him to his new home from the age of six months. Give a particularly tasty meal as a reward, and by about ten months he should be ready to take up permanent residence. This of course presupposes that the future stud's qualities are obvious at such a young age. As already mentioned, it is important that the stud be of excellent physique and as true as possible to type, for one of his main uses will be to improve the type of mediocre queens. For this reason, many studs do not embark on their 'career' until they have had some success in major cat shows. An important point to remember is to have the kitten examined by a vet at about six months to ensure that both testicles have descended into the scrotum. A monorchid (a male with only one testicle descended) can sire kittens but cannot be entered in cat shows in Britain, though this is allowed in North America.

The stud should not be used for breeding before the age of 12 months, and even then his first few queens should be experienced.

A queen and stud need supervision, especially if they are strangers. First introductions **above left** should be made with the cats separated by wire. Once the queen starts to act seductively **above** they can be allowed to meet so that mating **above right** can take place. Afterwards, the queen may turn on the tom **far right**, so she needs an escape route.

Nervous, possibly aggressive maiden queens will probably only confuse him, but if he has time to learn what is required of him he will usually develop into a skilled, gentle and popular stud. Once fully mature, a young virile stud who is in demand may service two queens a week – possibly three – but in his later years a lower work rate will give better results.

Taking a queen to stud

Having chosen a suitable stud for your queen and agreed terms, you will need to make a provisional appointment. It is never possible to predict exactly when the queen will come into heat, but knowledge of her past pattern of calling will enable an intelligent guess to be made, to be confirmed by a telephone call to the stud owner when the period of oestrus begins. If possible, you should then take the queen – in a suitable container (see p 160) – to the stud. If this is not possible, she may have to be sent unaccompanied by public transport. Long unaccompanied journeys can upset a queen – especially a novice – even causing her to come off call. But if you make proper provision for the cat's comfort and safety, travel by rail or air poses few problems.

Before being allowed near the stud's quarters, the visiting queen will first be examined for any signs of ill-health, often in an isolation house – a small room or building quite separate from the stud house. If the queen is unaccompanied, a general veterinary health certificate may be required, but in any case you will be expected to produce or send certificates of vaccination against feline infectious enteritis (FIE, or panleukopaenia) and respiratory virus infections (cat flu), and

usually a certificate that the cat is free from feline leukaemia virus (FeLV). (Similar evidence of good health may legitimately be asked of the stud owner.) A copy of the queen's pedigree (if not already provided) and her usual diet sheet should also be supplied. If the examination shows any signs of external parasites, a discharge from eyes or ears, or diarrhoea, a vet will be called in and if any doubt about the queen's health is confirmed the mating will be postponed. This is in the best interests of the queen as well as protecting the stud.

Making introductions

Assuming that the queen is in good health, she should be taken into the queen's pen while still in her travelling container. Many queens seem to go berserk at the first scent of the stud, and she may well twist free and escape if simply carried in the arms. Once inside, she should be released, fussed a little and then left quietly for a while to familiarize herself with her new accommodation. During this settling-in period she will be able to withdraw to her own sleeping quarters or move around the run, making the stud's acquaintance through the wire.

Settling-in time varies greatly. A maiden queen may not stir from her bed for up to eight hours, while an experienced one may do her best to seduce the stud within a few minutes. Great care is needed if this is a first mating for either of the cats; in both cases the partner should be experienced and gentle, for a frightening experience at this time can prove a serious setback to the breeding life of a young animal.

Once the queen has ventured to the dividing wire and begun 'crooning' to the stud, the stud owner should open the gate so that she can join the stud in his own quarters. An experienced tom will watch the queen carefully and usually wait for her to make the first approaches. If this is her first mating, she will probably want to sniff around the stud's quarters before showing much interest in him. Having satisfied herself that all is well, she will then allow him to approach and possibly lick her face before he investigates her genital area. This will usually provide sufficient stimulation for a mature queen to adopt the receptive posture, straddling her rear legs and holding her rear quarters up and tail to one side, while the stud approaches from behind for penetration (see p 130).

The role of the owner

It is essential for the stud owner to remain in attendance during mating as, even with a pair of experienced cats, foreplay, mating and separation can at times be quite violent. Some studs, for example, may become very rough if they have difficulty in getting the queen into position for mounting.

Sometimes a maiden queen may need manual stimulation from the stud owner before becoming sufficiently aroused to accept the stud – though many studs show marked resentment at such intrusion. Again, the breeder may have to hold a particularly small or nervous queen while the stud mounts her. Some queens, on the other hand, will not mate in the presence of humans – in which case observation must be very discreet. Others will only mate if they are allowed to run with the stud for a long period, perhaps even weeks. This last case is rare, but it may be the only way to achieve results and may be worthwhile with a particularly fine queen.

Following a successful mating the queen should be returned to her pen – but only after she has passed the voluptuous rolling-over stage that follows mating. To handle her too soon is to risk a nasty bite or scratch. All queens should be allowed at least three observed matings, after which many breeders allow the queen and stud to run together for a day or two, mating at will. There is no definite rule, but most owners would expect to keep the queen at stud for three or four days. Whatever the period, the need for at least three matings is very important to ensure ovulation and conception (see p214). When the queen has travelled a long distance, arrangements may be made for her to board at the stud's cattery until it is clear that she is pregnant.

The 'difficult' queen

If, as occasionally happens, the journey to the stud causes the queen to stop calling, the stud owner may agree to keep the queen in boarding accommodation on the premises until her next oestrus. Then a daily boarding fee will be charged in addition to the stud fee. Many owners, however, would prefer not to leave a possibly nervous and confused animal in a strange environment for so long a period. Rather more serious is the problem of the queen who, despite good health, fails to conceive even after several matings. These and other breeding problems are discussed on page 228.

Returning home

When the queen is returned to you, the stud owner may provide a certificate of mating (which also states when the kittens can be expected) and – if not already provided – a copy of the stud's pedigree. Normally the queen will settle quickly into her old routine on returning home, though she may seem to sleep more. You should groom her carefully, checking that she has not picked up any fleas, and consult your vet about deworming (see p190). Do not allow her to run free for at least a week even if she normally has access to outdoors, as she will remain sexually attractive to the local toms and superfecundity (see p215) is quite possible.

If conception has not occurred, the queen may start calling again three or four weeks after returning home, and you will have to arrange for her to be re-mated. If mating has been successful, however, the kittens can be expected to arrive some nine weeks later. Remember that records are just as important for a stud owner as for the owner of a queen – probably more so, since a successful stud will service many queens and the owner cannot rely on memory. To complete these records, the stud owner needs to be told the number, colour and quality of the kittens when they are born. Only in this way can a complete picture be built up of the stud's genetic traits and his prowess and success as a breeding sire.

The pregnant cat

The first unmistakable signs of pregnancy occur about three weeks after a female cat has mated: her nipples become quite pink and the surrounding hair recedes slightly. The change – known to breeders in Britain as 'pinking up' – can be most dramatic in a maiden queen, whose nipples have until now been very pale and almost indistinguishable. Caused by hormonal changes in the queen's body, it is a sign that the kittens should arrive in about six weeks (see the gestation chart at the end of this book). During that time, they will have grown from about the size of hazelnuts to a body length of some 12 cm (5 in) and a weight of about 100 g (3½ oz).

In the same period, the queen herself will typically put on 1 to 1.5 kg (2 to 3 lb) in weight – the exact amount varying according to her breed and the number of kittens she is carrying. With a large litter, she will end the nine weeks with a greatly distended abdomen, but with only one or two kittens there will be little increase in size, though her figure will still become more rounded than usual. During the first part of the pregnancy most of the increase consists of the placenta and the membranes and fluid surrounding the foetuses (unborn young). Only during the last three weeks or so do the kittens themselves put on much weight, though the development of their body systems has been rapid since the second week.

Confirming the diagnosis

A veterinary examination is rarely necessary unless the queen has a poor breeding record, but if you are a novice breeder you may feel happier with expert confirmation that your cat is, indeed, pregnant. The ideal time for this is between four and five weeks after mating, when the growing foetuses – about the size of walnuts – can be felt. Be warned not to attempt manual diagnosis – palpation – yourself, however; clumsy groping can seriously damage the young and even cause the queen to abort.

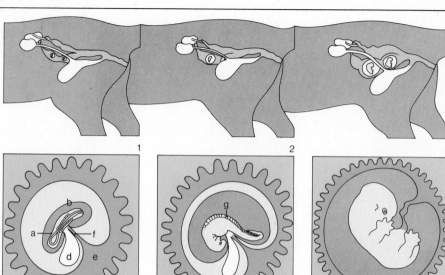

1   2   3

Development of the unborn kittens begins in earnest 16 days after fertilization **1**. The embryo **a**, surrounded by chorionic and amniotic sacs **b**, becomes attached to the uterine wall **c**. A yolk sac **d** provides nutrients until the placenta **e** and umbilical cord **f** have developed sufficiently.

At 18 days **2** the yolk sac is shrinking and an embryonic backbone **g** is developing. Four days later **3** the embryo is receiving life support from its

By about six weeks, the conceptual swellings will have begun to elongate and merge, making them more difficult to feel clearly. But by this time pregnancy will generally be obvious through the general increase in the size of the queen's abdomen. If, by chance, you do not know the date of mating, it is very difficult without expert knowledge to estimate the expected birth date. 'Quickening' (movement) of the foetuses can be felt from the seventh week. If it is vital to know when the queen will give birth, an X-ray of her abdomen taken in the last few weeks before birth may show the number of kittens and their skeletal development (and thus their age). As with human mothers, however, unnecessary X-rays are best avoided as there is a small risk of harming the kittens.

Care of the queen

A queen returning from stud may need to be given roundworm tablets, subject to your vet's advice, but any sign of tapeworms is a matter for serious investigation (see p 191). Otherwise, apart from possibly sleeping more and receiving a boosted diet (see p 150), the pregnant queen should be allowed to lead a perfectly normal life. You can let her go into the garden if she is normally allowed to do so. Do not fuss over her too much; a healthy pregnant cat is in peak condition – usually with a beautiful gloss to her coat – and is quite able to cope with her pregnancy. She can even climb and jump with safety provided that she does not become stranded in some difficult place from where she might jump in panic from too great a height.

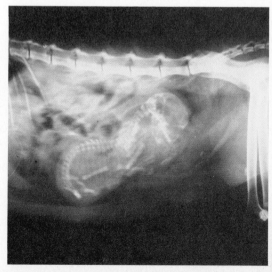

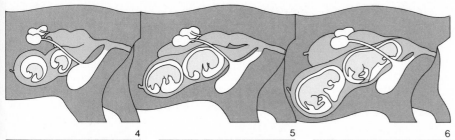

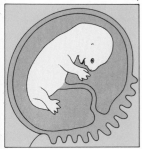 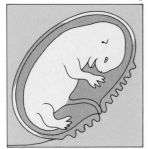 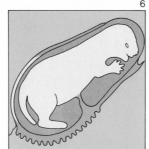

mother via the completed placenta, and its limbs, head and eyes are forming. Four weeks after fertilization **4** a miniature kitten about 2.5 cm

(1 in) long, with all its organs, has developed; from now on it is known as a foetus, and progesterone production is taken over by the placenta.

Now the foetus grows rapidly, and at five to six weeks **5** it is about 6 cm (2½ in) long; this doubles by nine weeks **6**, just before the kitten is born.

difficulty cleaning her anal region; you can help by gently washing the anus and vulva with warm water and patting them dry. Clean her nipples in the same way a few days before the kittens are due, very gently softening and removing any encrustation. At the same time, with long-haired breeds, you can usefully trim away hair from around the genital area and nipples.

Preparing for the birth

About two weeks before the kittens are due, the queen will become restless, searching for a quiet place to give birth. She may need some persuading to choose a convenient spot. It is a good idea to provide newspaper-filled boxes in the various rooms she frequents. She will probably show a preference for one particular place, but as the time for birth approaches she may well tear up the paper in a number of boxes – following an instinct to provide more than one safe kittening nest in case danger should threaten at any time. If you value your clothes and other belongings, keep cupboards (closets), drawers and wardrobes securely shut.

Even if the queen is normally allowed outdoors, you should keep external doors closed as well, so that your queen will not be tempted to run off and perhaps give birth in some secluded but cold place. Cats are great survivors as a species, but the mortality rate at birth and in the first few days is still high. The queen may give birth successfully in a cold garden shed, but her kittens may suffer.

If you offer a well-prepared kittening box, most queens – especially those who have had litters before – will take to it without difficulty. It should be warm, enclosed, lined with material that can be shredded to make a cosy nest and (perhaps most important to the domesticated cat) close to her owner and in familiar surroundings. As the time for birth draws near, the room containing the box should be kept at a minimum temperature of 22°C (72°F). With this steady background heating and perhaps an infra-red dull emitter heater over the box or a heating pad under it, there is no need to place a blanket in the box until after the kittens are born.

You should also have, close at hand, a box or bag containing various other things you may need at the time of delivery: a bottle of diluted antiseptic safe for cats (see p178), petroleum jelly, surgical spirit (rubbing alcohol), cotton wool swabs, several pieces of clean towelling, sharp surgical scissors, and a bulb-ended (rectal) thermometer. Many owners like to have some brandy at hand; two drops in a teaspoonful of water can act as a tonic to an exhausted queen, but more often than not it is consumed by the nervous owner! The queen will normally remain quite calm and eat well right up to the day of giving birth.

Abortion is extremely rare except where a queen has been infected with feline leukaemia virus (FeLV; see p204), though there are certain other occasions when it may occur. The warning sign is bleeding from the vagina; should this occur, keep the cat quiet and warm and obtain veterinary help as soon as possible. Another rare phenomenon that all breeders should be aware of is resorption; something goes wrong after the pregnancy is well established, and the foetuses are absorbed back into the mother's body. If you do suspect trouble of this or any other kind, you should of course consult a vet – and also keep a record for future reference.

In general, no medications should be given, except in an emergency, for the duration of the pregnancy. It is particularly

important that a pregnant queen is not given live feline infectious enteritis (FIE, or panleukopaenia) or respiratory virus (cat flu) vaccine, since both of these can seriously affect the kittens. Also dangerous are any steroid drug and the antibiotic griseofulvin, used against ringworm, which is known to cause deformities, but any drug is potentially harmful.

Constipation may occur in the later stages of pregnancy, and if at all possible you should adjust the queen's diet to provide a natural relief. Milk often helps, as does including in one of her daily meals oily fish such as tuna, herring or pilchard. If constipation persists and causes distress, you can give a teaspoonful of medicinal liquid paraffin (mineral oil). If the queen is carrying a large litter she will have great

A pregnant cat needs very little special care beyond providing a boosted diet, and can live a normal life as part of the family **far left**. This queen shows clearly the prominent nipples and thinning belly hair that begins about the third week. They are caused by the hormonal changes that are necessary to maintain the development of the embryo kittens in her uterus **centre left**. The X-ray of an eight-week pregnant queen **left** shows the position of the foetus in the abdomen and its skeletal development. Only if trouble is suspected will such an X-ray usually be needed.

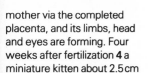

A kittening box should be prepared in good time for the birth. A good one can be made of wood, painted inside and out, measuring about 60×50×50 cm high (24×20×20 in). Or you can use a stout cardboard box, but destroy it after use. Cut an entry hole at one end, about chest-high to the queen. The lid should be removable for observation and cleaning, and part can be cut away if you use an infra-red dull emitter – suspended 1.2 m (4 ft) above the box – for warmth; otherwise provide a heated bed pad (see p144) or underfloor electric heating (in which case the floor must be

absolutely watertight). Wooden rails, 5 cm (2 in) from the floor and walls, will give the kittens some protection from being rolled upon. Newspaper, which the queen can tear up, is a cheap, absorbent lining material.

Giving birth 1

Although 65 days is often quoted as the average length of pregnancy in the cat, you should not be alarmed if your queen starts labour as early as the 61st day after mating or as late as the 70th. Provided there are no other signs of anything wrong, such variation is no grounds for calling in the vet. Many non-essential caesarian deliveries are performed on cats because their owners panic and pressure their vets into operating. If, however, labour begins before the 61st day, you must be prepared to lose all or some of the litter. At this early stage, the premature kittens have little chance of surviving, even if they are born alive.

Once the 61st day has passed, you should watch the queen carefully and not allow her to wander off. Generally her behaviour will indicate when birth is imminent, but a way of checking is to take her temperature rectally (see p174) each day after the 61st. When the temperature has dropped one full degree centigrade (about 2°F) from the normal 38.6°C (101.5°F) – due to hormonal changes – labour should begin within the next 18 hours. Another sign of imminent birth is the start of milk production from the nipples.

The stages of labour

When the first stage of labour starts, the queen's rate of breathing quickens and she may start to breathe through her mouth and purr rhythmically. This stage may last for many hours, and you should not be worried by the frequently-quoted, but quite inaccurate, statement that the first kitten should arrive within an hour of the onset of labour.

Provided the queen is happy, do not fuss over her; she may refuse food, but is just as likely to enjoy a hearty meal shortly before giving birth. The most important point to check at this time is that you have all the things you may need (see p221) and that the room in which the kittens will be born is kept at a temperature no lower than 22°C (72°F). A cold room can cause hypothermia (a drop in body temperature) in the newborn young, which cannot regulate their body heat properly and may quickly 'fade' if they become chilled.

If the queen wants to go off to some hidden, inconvenient spot to give birth, gently put her back in her special kittening box (see p221); she will usually comply if she is relaxed and in good health. Some queens of independent temperament are, however, only happy giving birth in private, in which case all you can do is to keep watch as best you can and make sure that she and her kittens are kept warm.

As labour proceeds there will be some vaginal discharge, colourless at first but later becoming bloodstained. In some cases, the queen may show a clear discharge a day or two before labour starts. This is perfectly normal, but if at any time she shows a discoloured or foul-smelling discharge, or if bleeding is profuse, then this may be a sign of trouble and you should consult your vet immediately.

The second stage of labour begins when the queen experiences contractions of her abdominal muscles and starts to 'bear down'. Initially the contractions may come

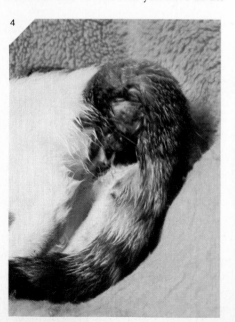

1

2

3

Normal labour The mature foetuses lie within their sacs in the horns of the uterus 1, encircled by their placentas. In the first stage of labour 2 uterine contractions move the first foetus towards the cervix, which dilates. In the second stage 3 further contractions and straining by the mother move the kitten down the vagina or birth canal.

The outer sac will usually rupture before birth, so that this and the placenta follow as the afterbirth. The inner sac may also rupture, but it often still encloses the kitten as it is born. Then the first visible sign of birth is its bubble-like appearance in the vaginal opening 4. With a little more straining the kitten is born 5. If the sac is still intact, the

mother will generally remove it 6 immediately and lick the kitten's face vigorously, stimulating its breathing. If she is not distracted by another birth, she will then sever the umbilical cord 7 and usually eat the afterbirth. She will then clean the kitten all over 8. The kittens may take their first feed 9 even before the last of the litter is born.

4

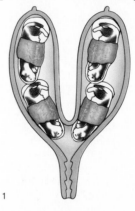

5

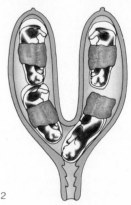

6

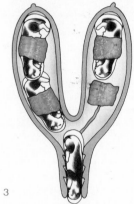

only once an hour, but the rate increases until just before delivery they are occurring about every 30 seconds. The queen will repeatedly lick her genital area and may show considerable signs of agitation. You can help to soothe her by talking to her reassuringly and gently rubbing her belly.

When the contractions are coming regularly and strongly, the vaginal opening will dilate and the first amniotic sac (the fluid-filled bag enclosing a kitten) will come into view. In an ideal birth this sac and the enclosed kitten will be expelled within 15 to 30 minutes. Very often, however, the queen's constant licking will rupture the sac and release the amniotic fluid, leaving the

attempts to release the wedged kitten. She may find it easier to bear down if she can push with her hind legs against the side of her box or against your hand. But even with this help the delivery may take 20 minutes or more.

It can be rather more difficult if the kitten's tail and one of its hind legs have appeared while the other leg remains caught inside the birth passage. Even so, the queen's persistence will probably bring success, but if she should weaken or become distressed you should be ready to help or call the vet. In most births, however, there are no complications at all, and in only a very few do serious difficulties arise.

body. Very often the brownish placenta forming the bulk of the afterbirth will appear at the next contraction. Usually the queen will promptly eat it; this is probably a primitive instinct to avoid attracting potential predators. If she ignores it, you should remove and destroy it, checking that a complete afterbirth is expelled for each kitten; any placental matter allowed to remain inside the body will cause infection. (Bear in mind, however, that identical twins – or even triplets – are sometimes born, and in this case more than one kitten may share the same placenta.)

Occasionally a queen does not attempt to remove the sac from a newborn kitten – she may seem not to know what to do, particularly if she is an inexperienced maiden queen, or may be too busy with the next delivery. In this case, you should allow the queen time to realize what is needed, but if there is no sign of action for more than a minute, act quickly. In gently removing the membrane, take very great care not to pull on the umbilical cord; this can easily cause a nasty hernia of the kitten's navel. If the queen still shows no interest in taking over operations, you should carefully cut or tear the cord. Rub the kitten dry with a clean rough towel to remove the amniotic fluid and to stimulate its breathing and circulation. Very occasionally, more drastic treatment is needed (see overleaf).

After the kitten is clean and breathing well, it may be placed close to the mother's belly. It will usually seize a nipple and begin to suck, and this is generally all that is needed to arouse the queen's maternal instincts enough for her to start licking and fussing over it. If she persists in ignoring the kitten, however, it is best to place it in a warm box in another room, with a hot-water bottle wrapped in a blanket. You should then place each subsequent kitten /continued

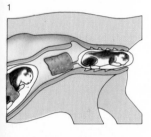

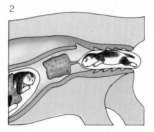

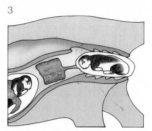

Birth positions Anterior (head-first) presentation is the commonest and is usually very easy. In posterior (legs-

first) presentation, the only problems occur if the queen weakens. The most difficult position is true breech

presentation, the kitten emerging hindquarters-first with one or both hind legs lying along the body.

kitten without its perfectly lubricated 'capsule'. In this case you should remain calm and resist the temptation to interfere; if the kitten is being born head-first a few more contractions will release it.

In about one-third of all births, the hind legs emerge first, and this is only a little more difficult than head-first birth. However, if a true breech birth is imminent – that is, if the kitten is emerging hindquarters- and tail-first – the queen may become agitated and turn around repeatedly in her

Acting as midwife
As soon as the kitten is expelled the queen will generally turn around and start to lick it, rupturing the semi-transparent sac if this is still intact and cleaning the amniotic fluid from its face. The queen's persistent licking stimulates the kitten's breathing reflex and it very soon begins to squirm and cry for the first time.

She will then turn her attention to the umbilical cord, neatly severing it with her teeth 2 or 3 cm (about 1 in) from the kitten's

Giving birth 2

with its fellows in the box and return the whole litter to the mother once the last birth is completed.

There is no way of knowing in advance how long a queen will be in labour. Some queens produce their kittens at intervals of 15 minutes or so. Others may go out of labour for some time and then restart contractions, giving birth at intervals of perhaps one or two hours. In some cases, she may even rest happily for as long as 24 hours, suckling her first kittens, before going back into labour to deliver the remainder. If the litter is large, the queen may show signs of weariness, and here you can again help by offering some easily-digested food such as an egg yolk beaten into a saucerful of evaporated milk or a small amount of some other favourite food. If a kitten has had a lengthy or difficult birth, it too may be weak and in need of help. If its mother's licking brings no response, give it a good overall rubbing with a rough towel as described above.

When to call the vet

Apart from the obviously distressing case of a queen unable to expel a breech-presented kitten, there are two other situations when it is vital to call the vet without delay. The first is when the queen has been having strong contractions for two hours without any sign of kittens appearing; the cause may be two kittens blocking the birth canal. The second is in uterine inertia, when the queen suddenly appears to tire before or after the first kitten is born. Her contractions gradually weaken and cease in spite of the fact that there are obviously more kittens to be born. This is quite different from the resting between births mentioned above; the cat seems generally distressed and exhausted, and veterinary help is obviously needed.

The cause is usually a hormonal or metabolic imbalance or, more rarely, an internal injury. Often a simple injection of the hormone oxytocin will re-establish uterine contractions and enable the queen to continue her delivery normally. Occasionally the problem may be more serious, so that a caesarian delivery is needed (see p 229). The vet's assistant will normally give any help needed during the operation itself, but you can usefully take care of the kittens once healthy breathing has been established. The young are best kept in a warm box as described above. The operation is not a lengthy one, and most vets advise that the kittens should be returned to the queen even before she recovers consciousness; their suckling will reinforce her maternal instinct on waking. However, you should be very careful to make sure that the sedated queen does not roll over on the kittens or act aggressively towards them on waking – a particular possibility with certain anaesthetics.

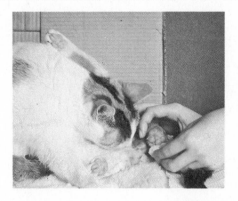

Helping the birth If the queen has difficulty with a breech birth, especially if one leg is trapped within the birth canal, you can help. Thoroughly wash and dry your hands, then lubricate a little finger with medicinal liquid paraffin (mineral oil) or petroleum jelly and insert it very gently between the kitten and the wall of the vagina to ease its passage.
above If the queen becomes exhausted and stops pushing when the kitten is still only part-born, clear the kitten's face, if visible, to prevent suffocation. Then grasp the slippery kitten firmly but gently with a piece of dry towelling and pull gently as the queen attempts to bear down – downwards if the kitten is head first, upwards for a breech birth.
Never interfere unless it is really necessary. Unless the very gentlest help releases the kitten, call veterinary help at once.

Helping the kittens If the queen fails to attend fairly quickly to the newly born kittens, you can again help after carefully washing your hands. If the sac is still in place, feel gently through it to find the position of the head, and then make a small tear with your fingers and gently peel the membranes free. Clear the kitten's face of fluid. Then gently 'milk' the umbilical cord towards the kitten's body before severing it about 5 cm (2 in) from the kitten. If you tear the cord with your fingers it will rarely bleed; if you use sharp scissors **above** – which should be first sterilized in a safe antiseptic (see p 178) or surgical spirit (alcohol) – it is wise to first tie it with thread between the kitten and the cut. Be very careful never to pull on the cord or you may cause the kitten a hernia. A brisk rub-down with clean towelling will next dry the kitten and stimulate breathing

before it is returned to its mother for its first feed. If it fails to breathe strongly within a few minutes, you should hold it on its back or its belly on the palm of your hand, with the head away from you as shown **below**; swing it sharply several times to clear its air passages and stimulate breathing. If this does not work, mouth-to-mouth resuscitation may be needed; remember, however, that the kitten's lungs are minute and you must blow very gently.

REGISTRATION

REGISTRATION
If the kittens are the result of a planned mating between pedigree animals, you should register them when they are a few weeks old. As explained on page 230, in some countries registration with two or more cat fancy organizations may be desirable. The requirements and formalities vary from one organization to another, but the best time is generally at four to six weeks, when in most breeds both the sex and the colour of the kittens should be clear. In some cases, the registration application must be accompanied by a certificate of mating signed by the stud owner; in others, the stud owner countersigns the application. With some bodies each kitten is separately registered – and named – from the start, while with

others the whole litter is registered initially, the individual kittens being registered and given their names later – by the eventual owners, if desired.

In every case, each kitten has to have a unique name that has not been used for any registered cat for a certain number of years. This can be extremely difficult unless you initially register a prefix which becomes the first part of the name of all kittens you breed. For example, the name Blue Boy has almost certainly been used before, but adding the prefix Shawn makes it unique. For more information on registration and prefixes, see page 46. If you are a newcomer to the cat fancy, officials of the relevant association will give you all the information you need on registration.

After the kittens are born 1

The first three weeks after a litter of kittens are born should be a tranquil and happy time for queen and owner alike. You should watch the mother cat carefully, but if she has a healthy appetite and uses her litter tray regularly and normally you can assume all is well. Only if she becomes listless, loses her interest in food or suffers from diarrhoea will she require veterinary attention. Likewise, the kittens will spend their days and nights alternately feeding and sleeping. You should keep an eye on them to ensure that they are well, but their mother will, except in rare cases (see p227), do all that is necessary.

The first few days
Provided that the birth has gone smoothly, the new mother will clean herself thoroughly and then prepare to settle down with her new family. You should carefully remove all soiled bedding from the kittening box, wipe it out if necessary, and place a warm blanket in it. Put the kittens near their mother, and they will probably settle down to a long feed. The first 'milk' produced by the mammary glands is more correctly called colostrum; only produced for the first few days after kittening, it is rich in protein and minerals, and also contains antibodies that protect the kittens from disease. For this reason, it is important to encourage the kittens to suckle as soon as possible.

If the mother has eaten one or more of the placentas, she will probably not want another meal for six hours or so, but some queens feed voraciously soon after giving birth. Her nursing diet should be as varied and nutritious as possible (see p150); the better it is, the better she will be able to feed and care for her family. Include vitamin and calcium supplements if advised by your vet or if not using balanced commercial cat food. If the queen develops diarrhoea, it will usually be cured by adjusting the diet;

Kittens root for a nipple as soon as they are born, and a definite preference soon develops; recognizing its own body scent, a kitten usually returns to the same nipple.

cooked liver or chicken cooked with rice is often effective, though raw liver may have the opposite effect. She may also show a slight discharge of blood from the vaginal opening for a week or so after kittening. Unless this becomes copious, discoloured or unpleasant-smelling – in which case you should consult the vet, as a placenta may have been retained or the uterus (womb) may be infected (see p229) – there is no cause for alarm; simply change the bedding frequently.

If all is well the kittens will put on weight steadily, usually gaining about 15g (½ oz) a day in the initial period of rapid growth. Occasionally one kitten may be pushed out when it tries to suckle and will cry lustily. This is quite normal – especially in a large litter – but if the same kitten is repeatedly kept away from the nipple it will almost certainly lag behind its littermates' weight gain. Careful examination may reveal a defect such as cleft palate (see p196), or it may simply be a 'runt' – an inherently weak member of the litter. It may be possible to foster or hand-rear a rejected kitten (see

p227) or, if the litter is small, reintroduce it to its mother, but a defective or inherently weak kitten should generally be destroyed (see p209) as it will seldom grow into a healthy adult cat.

When the kittens are a few days old, the queen may suddenly decide to move them to a new home, grasping each kitten by the leg, head or (more correctly) scruff of the neck. This is probably a response to a natural instinct to safeguard the young by not staying in one place too long. She will usually settle down again quite contentedly if her bedding is changed and perhaps the kittening box moved to another part of the room or (if convenient) another room. Or you could put the box where she wants it for a few days and then try moving it again.

Discovering the world
The kittens' eyes will start to open when they are five to ten days old, depending on the breed. (Siamese, Burmese and their relatives are, as ever, the early developers.) It usually takes three days for the eyes to open fully. During this time, carefully wash away any sticky discharge with warm water. The discharge usually clears quickly, but if it recurs and the eyes, once open, become sealed shut again, this is a sign of an infection that demands prompt veterinary attention with an antibiotic. (Neglect may lead to abscesses and blindness.) All kittens have blue eyes initially; the adult colours (see p29) do not begin to appear until the kittens are about 12 weeks old.

At the age of 2½ weeks the kittens begin to crawl around their box, and their tiny ears – folded down at birth – will have become erect in the 'alert' position. At about three weeks they can stand, albeit rather unsteadily, their milk teeth begin to develop and they start to look like little cats. This is the age, too, when the kittens can most easily be sexed (see p143), if not already determined at birth.

Weaning the young
If the litter is large, you can start weaning as soon as the kittens can stand, to relieve the burden on the mother. The principle of weaning is to replace the queen's milk with an adult diet gradually and with– /continued

Milestones of development
A newborn kitten 1 has closed eyes and tiny folded-down ears; it may weigh anything from 80 to 140g (3 to 5oz). The stump of the umbilical cord will shrivel and dry, falling off at about five days. The eyes begin to open soon after, this being completed by 8 to 13 days 2. By about 18 days 3 the kitten starts to crawl and the ears straighten; teething begins. By about three weeks

4 it can stand unsteadily and weaning can start. A week or two later 5 it weighs 450g (16oz) or more and can stand and feed from a bowl; it begins to play and to groom itself. By eight weeks 6, now weighing as much as 1 kg (2¼ lb), it is a mischevous,

sturdy kitten with a full set of milk teeth. These start to be shed at 12 weeks 7, when eye colour begins to change. The coat pattern is well defined, though improvement continues and long-hairs show their full beauty only after the first moult.

1   2   3   4   5   6   7

After the kittens are born 2

out upsetting the kitten's digestive system. The first food is therefore milk-based; any reputable proprietary milk for human babies is suitable or better still a proprietary kitten milk substitute, but you can make up an equally nutritious milk by mixing three parts unsweetened evaporated milk with one part boiling water. (All early feeds should be at body temperature.)

After the first day, you can add a little baby cereal, and a week later a meat-based strained baby food can be tried. Then, at about five weeks, you can replace one of the milk feeds with scraped raw beef or steamed fish, or other light solid food, gradually introducing new foods until, by

the age of about eight weeks, the kittens are completely weaned. (Persians and related breeds may be a little slower.) Then they should be taking four or five meals a day, two of which will consist of meat or fish. Vitamin and mineral supplements may also be needed if you are not using complete canned cat food (see p148). Remember that food habits begin young, so avoid 'addiction' to such foods as fish or liver by ensuring plenty of variety.

The feline digestive system is designed to process concentrated foods, so proprietary human baby foods (including milk) should be used at twice the concentration advised for babies. Weak mixes simply put a strain

on the kitten's stomach while giving little nourishment. Similarly, the stomach's small size means that it quickly fills, so feeds must be little and frequent.

Care and grooming

While the queen is still feeding the young she will attend to their toilet, briskly licking the anogenital region to stimulate urination and defecation, and promptly licking away any waste matter. (Young kittens do not spontaneously urinate and defecate.) Once the kittens start to take solid food, however, she will be more reluctant to clean up after them, although she will continue for some time to clean them and thus teach them to groom themselves. They will usually adopt one corner of their box as a toilet area, or – once they can climb out and explore farther afield – use an area some distance from the box.

The time has come to begin toilet-training (see p152), and while the kittens are learning to use the litter tray – whether taught by their mother or owner – the value of an enclosed kitten pen becomes most obvious. Here, the kittening box, litter tray and feeding dishes can be placed conveniently close together within a wire-mesh 'compound'. Such a pen keeps the family safely together while allowing human contact – which is, like play (see p134), a vital part of the 'education' of kittens that are to become household pets.

If there are other cats on the premises apart from the mother, there is always more risk of the kittens picking up infections – particularly respiratory virus infections (cat flu). For this reason, keep the queen and her litter in isolation, out of contact with other cats, until the kittens receive their first vaccinations at the age of about eight weeks. Also make sure that the queen has no contact with an entire tom; some queens come into oestrus (heat) very soon after giving birth, and can easily become pregnant again. Consult your vet about having the kittens dewormed (see p190).

Although short-haired kittens need no special grooming, it is a good idea to clean all kittens' ears once a week from the age of three weeks, keeping a watch for any sign of ear mite infestation (see p202). You should, however, gently groom long-haired kittens every day or two from the age of four weeks (see p155). They then soon become accustomed to this attention – particularly important if the kitten is destined for the show bench, when seemingly endless hours of meticulous grooming will be required. And, as already mentioned, every kitten should have human contact, being picked up and fondled from birth, and played with from the age of four weeks, so that it will grow up to be a companionable cat and one that is, if necessary, willing to be handled and examined by cat show judges.

FEEDING PROGRAMME FOR KITTENS

Age (weeks)	Mother's milk	Number of 'milk' feeds	Number of 'meat' feeds	Size of each feed (teasps)
0–3	Yes	0	0	–
3–4	Yes	3	0	½–1
4–5	Yes	3	1	1–2
5–6	Yes	2	2	2–3
6–8	Yes	2	2	3
8–12	Maybe	2–3	2	3–4
12–16	No	2	2	6–8
16–24	No	1	2	9–12
over 24	No	0	2	c12

Note: 'Milk' feeds refers to proprietary kitten milk, baby milk or evaporated milk made up as described in the text, with cereal added after the first day; 'meat' feeds refers to cooked minced or chopped fish, raw scraped meat, etc, and/or canned cat food. The size of feeds is approximate; generally, feed to appetite; from complete weaning, feed about 60 to 75g per kg body weight (1 to 1.25oz per lb) per day. For feeding after six months, see the article beginning on page 148.

Learning to feed At three weeks, a kitten cannot balance steadily or take food from a saucer, so offer the first feeds from a teaspoon. Support the kitten with one hand, its feet on the floor or your knee, while bringing the spoon to its mouth. Do not hold it with legs dangling, or it will feel insecure.
Within a few days the kitten will begin to enjoy its extra feeds, and by four weeks will be able to stand and take food from a saucer **below** – with a little support at first.

A kitten pen to accommodate the whole family in a confined area while allowing plenty of human contact can be bought or built from wire mesh on a wood frame. Its walls should be about 75cm (2½ ft) tall, so that the queen can come and go but the kittens cannot escape. (Once they are able to

climb, however, a roof may be needed.) Within it are the kittening box (now the family sleeping quarters), litter tray, feeding bowls, toys and so on. Many serious breeders construct permanent indoor quarters along similar lines, in some cases with a cat flap to an outdoor run.

Hand-rearing kittens

The decision to hand-rear a litter of kittens is not one that you should take lightly. It is a very demanding task that will occupy most of your time for at least the first four weeks. It is undoubtedly rewarding, but whenever possible you should try to arrange for a feline foster mother to take over the job.

Sharing the task

If, through illness or injury, the mother cat is unable to feed her young but can care for them in other ways – grooming, toilet training, keeping them warm and contented between feeds, and so on – then the demands on the owner are greatly reduced. It also benefits the kittens psychologically to have feline contact.

If for some reason the queen has totally rejected her kittens, or if she has died or been killed in an accident, then, for the same reasons, fostering should be the first choice. If you have more than one nursing queen, the orphans may be fostered within the 'family'. Cats cannot count and if one or two orphans are added to a young litter in the mother's absence, so that contact mingles the newcomers' scent with that of their new littermates, the queen is unlikely to notice the deception. Provided the existing litter is not too big, she will care for the orphans like her own. (In the case of pedigree young, however, be sure to mark the orphans, if they are not of a distinctive colour, with a non-toxic dye such as gentian violet so that you can later identify which litter is which.)

If you have no potential foster-mother at hand, it is worth asking your vet for help. So many unwanted kittens are brought to most vets for euthanasia that it may be possible to find a local queen which has kittened recently and is still in milk. A sympathetic owner may be prepared to lend her to you for the few weeks needed for the kittens to reach the weaning stage – to the benefit of the deprived queen as well as the orphaned kittens.

Bottle-feeding young kittens

The most important factor in successfully bottle-feeding kittens is hygiene. Kittens fed on their mother's milk acquire antibodies that protect them from many infections (see p 173); hand-reared infants have no such protection, so all feeding utensils must be sterilized each time they are used and fresh food made up each day.

The equipment needed is simple. A small medicinal dropper with a rubber bulb, and a plastic syringe with a short length of 2mm plastic tubing replacing the needle, have both proved useful feeding aids. With the correct technique, it is possible to pass the fine plastic tubing directly into the kitten's stomach, enabling it to be fed even if it seems unable to suck normally. This should be done only after proper instruction from a vet, however, since the tubing can be

passed down the trachea (airway) by mistake, with fatal results. Alternatively, you can use a child's toy baby-bottle, but the best feeding aid is perhaps the specially designed kitten bottle now available from veterinary suppliers and pet stores; its teat is modelled on that of a nursing queen.

The initial basic diet can consist of proprietary milk powder or evaporated milk made up to double the normal human concentration (as explained on page 226), or a special feline milk substitute, if available. You need to feed the kittens every two hours for the first three weeks, although four-hourly feeds are usually adequate at night after the first few days. The amount taken at each feed varies widely, and it is best to gauge this by the kitten's behaviour. As a guide, however, 3 to 5 ml (up to 1 teaspoonful) per feed will be ample at first, rising to about 7 ml after one week and 10 ml at three weeks. At this point, a little baby cereal or dissolved meat jelly (from any good-quality canned cat food) can be mixed in, leading to weaning as with normally-reared kittens (see p 225).

Hand-feeding with a dropper **1**, syringe **2** or feeding bottle **3**, first warm the food to about 38°C (100°F). Hold the kitten in the palm of one hand while placing the feeder tube or teat in its mouth **below**. Squeeze the milk out gently and the kitten (whose natural instinct is to suck) will soon get the idea. It is important not to hurry the kitten.

Fostering is undoubtedly the simplest solution to the problem of motherless or rejected kittens. A queen in milk who has lost her own litter (through accident or euthanasia) will actually be helped by having another's kittens to nurse, while one whose own litter is not too big will usually have a few spare nipples for strangers. Maternal instincts are so strong, in fact, that a mother will often foster young of a different species.

General care

Unless cared for by an adult cat between feeds, the kittens must be kept warm in a cosy, blanket-lined box. An infra-red dull emitter or a thermostatically-controlled under-bed heating pad can be used, but a blanket-wrapped hot-water bottle has the advantage of simulating the natural mother's body for the kittens to snuggle up to. The temperature in the box should be 27 to 30°C (81 to 86°F) at first, reducing gradually to 21°C (70°F) at six weeks.

Kittens entirely hand-raised will need help with their toilet, as maternal licking normally stimulates urination and defecation. The very first faeces (the meconium) may take some time to be passed, but there is no need for veterinary help unless they are delayed more than four days. If any areas of skin become sore with a rash, soothe them with a mild antiseptic cream safe for feline use (see p 178). In other respects, the kittens should be raised much as any others, remembering particularly the importance of play and contact with other cats once they have been vaccinated.

After feeding, help the kitten to urinate and defecate. Gently stroke its lower abdomen to stimulate urination. **below** Bowel movement can be helped by gently massaging the anus with cotton wool moistened with medicinal liquid paraffin (mineral oil). If you suspect constipation after four days, consult your vet.

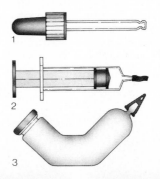

Breeding problems

Preventing cats breeding is more often a problem than failure to reproduce, but breeders of pedigree cats may encounter such troubles, and there are complications that can sometimes arise at various stages when any cat is pregnant. In almost all cases a veterinary investigation is called for, and in some the tests and treatment may be too specialized for a general practitioner, so that the case may need to be referred to an expert in reproductive problems.

Failure to call

Breeds and individual cats vary widely in their onset of puberty (see p130), so you should give due allowance for the possible late development of a young queen. Her environment and the way she is cared for can also affect her sexual cycles. Queens kept in cold, dark, unsuitable housing may fail to call, but day-length seems more important than temperature; indeed many cats kept indoors in artificial lighting will come into heat throughout the year.

Social stimuli are important, too. Females low in the social hierarchy of a large group of cats (see p126) may fail to call, as may isolated queens – who may however show sexual activity if placed with other active queens or near a stud tom. In fact, the oestrus of one queen may induce others in the group to call, so that their cycles become synchronized. If a queen fails to call after a reasonable period in the company of other breeding queens, seek veterinary advice; some abnormality of the reproductive system or hormonal imbalance may be responsible. In some cases, it may be possible to use synthetic follicle-stimulating hormone (FSH; see p214) to induce oestrus, but as with the use of such 'fertility drugs' in human mothers the result may be the production of too many eggs; this is called superovulation.

Failure to mate

The artificial conditions in which pedigree cats are kept and bred – artificial in relation to life in the wild or feral state, or even that of non-pedigree pets allowed to roam outdoors – can result in oestrous queens failing to mate. (The fighting of toms and other courtship rituals help to make a queen sexually receptive.) If a queen has to travel to a stud tom the resulting stress may send her off call; most queens will call again within 24 hours or so, but in some cases may take much longer. Unsuitable housing can have a similar effect. Mate preference is important, too; oestrous queens are not simply sexual robots, and some will mate only with studs of a certain breed or even of a specific colour. Often there is no obvious cause of a queen failing to oblige with a planned mating, when she will mate quite happily with neighbourhood toms on their home ground.

Occasionally a queen may show all the signs of oestrus without yet reaching the peak of sexual receptivity and may therefore refuse to mate. This problem can be solved in other animals by the vet taking a series of vaginal swabs and examining the cells from them; these vary throughout the oestrous cycle, so that the best time to attempt mating can be found. However, taking such a swab from an oestrous queen may result in ovulation (see p217), often making it unsuitable for cats; then the only solution is careful observation combined with trial and error.

A stud tom may show lack of libido, or sexual desire, and this too can result from psychological stress, such as an encounter with an uncooperative queen. In such cases, encouragement and careful selection of gentle queens may help, but in others the cause of the problem is not clear. Unfortunately, a friendly tom – favoured by breeders who want to produce kittens well adapted to human company – may lack the aggressive streak needed of an efficient stud! If a tom who has bred successfully in the past shows a lack of libido, the chances are that the problem will be only temporary. But if a young tom, given adequate time to mature, never displays adult sexual behaviour, the chances of his breeding successfully are poor. Treatment with male hormones may help in some cases.

A converse problem may occur if a queen (particularly a vocal queen of one of the foreign breeds) is allowed to call repeatedly without being mated. This is believed to be one of the causes of ovarian cysts – sacs that develop on the surface of the ovaries and produce abnormal levels of female hormones. As a result, the cat may refuse to mate, or she may mate but fail to conceive, either through failure to ovulate or because the hormone levels prevent implantation of the fertilized eggs in the womb. On the other hand, many queens with spontaneous ovarian cysts seem to breed normally.

Failure to ovulate

A single mating may not provide enough stimulus to cause the release of luteinizing hormone (LH; see p214) and thus ovulation. As a result, of course, there are no eggs for the tom's sperm to fertilize. Multiple matings – which are normal both in planned breeding and among cats 'on the tiles' – usually result in successful ovulation, but not always. As a result, the queen does not show pseudopregnancy (see below) and calls again as if unmated. It is possible to check for ovulation after subsequent matings by checking blood samples for the characteristic rise in progesterone level. If no rise occurs, ovulation has not taken place, and it may be possible to induce it on a later occasion by injecting the queen with an LH substitute soon after mating.

Failure of fertilization

If mating and ovulation occur normally but the eggs are not fertilized, pseudopregnancy, or false pregnancy, results. The pregnancy hormone, progesterone, is produced, just as in a normal pregnancy, so that at three to four weeks the nipples show the characteristic reddening and there will be a weight gain due to the hormone causing fat deposition, fluid retention and increased appetite. Unlike pseudopregnant bitches, queens rarely develop milk and show nesting behaviour, but this may occur. Usually pseudopregnancy lasts about five weeks, and although it is not so obvious as in a bitch you will notice the signs if you are observant.

As a problem in pedigree cat breeding, fertilization failure is not common and more often results in a small litter than in no kittens at all. Its incidence is increased by close inbreeding (see p47), but few people inbreed their cats enough for this to be significant. Ovarian or tubal adhesions, involving the formation of fibrous scar tissue around the ovary or oviduct, may occasionally prevent the eggs passing down to the womb, and in this case no treatment is possible. Remember that older queens produce fewer eggs and thus smaller litters.

Identifying the cause of reproductive failure depends on a series of tests that may need to be performed over several breeding attempts. The cornerstone of diagnosis is detection of pregnancy by palpation (see p220) three to four weeks after mating; this enables the vet to distinguish between resorption and failure at an earlier stage.

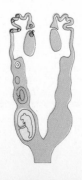

Mating	Negative pregnancy diagnosis	Remate	Negative progesterone assay at five days	Failure of ovulation
			Positive progesterone assay at five days	Failure of fertilization
				Pre-implantation loss
	Positive pregnancy diagnosis	No kittens		Resorption
				Abortion

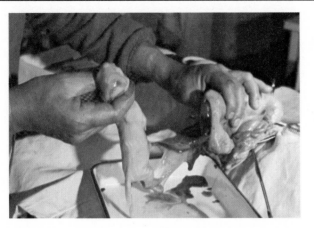

A caesarian section is very rarely needed for delivering kittens. However, if one of the kittens becomes completely wedged in the birth canal, or if there is some other serious complication, the queen must be quickly anaesthetized and prepared for surgery. An incision is made in the abdomen and the wall of the uterus, and the kittens are delivered. Afterwards, hormone therapy may be necessary to ensure that the queen produces milk.

The problem may lie with the stud, whose semen may not be of high enough quality to enable fertilization. The problem can be identified by examining the semen under a microscope, but obtaining a semen sample is difficult. The cause may be the tom's generally poor condition, due to disease or poor diet; in such cases it can in time be reversed. If a male kitten's testicles remain in the abdomen and fail to descend into the scrotum (see p213), they cannot produce viable sperm because of the higher temperature inside the body. This condition is called cryptorchidism. Such cats may show normal (though possibly partly delayed) male behaviour and should be neutered. The same applies to toms with only one descended testicle (generally, though incorrectly, called monorchidism), even though these are normally fertile, since the condition is thought to be hereditary and should not be perpetuated.

Failure of gestation

Loss during pregnancy may take place even before implantation, in which case it may appear to the breeder just like failure of fertilization, resulting in pseudopregnancy. It may be due to death of the fertilized eggs or unfavourable uterine conditions preventing implantation. Such cases are very difficult to diagnose except in a specialized laboratory, and treatment is generally not possible. However, a problem that most experienced breeders come across at one time or another is resorption (or reabsorption). The conceptual swellings can be felt normally at three to four weeks but these disappear over the next few weeks. The dead foetuses (developing kittens) and placentas are simply absorbed back into the mother's body by the uterus (womb). This can happen to a whole litter – when it is obvious – or to one or a few kittens, resulting simply in a very small litter.

Once the foetal skeleton has hardened – by about the seventh week of pregnancy – a dead foetus's tissues can no longer be reabsorbed and it can only be aborted or stillborn. The distinction between abortion and resorption is often not clear, and the queen may pass partially reabsorbed liver-like placental tissue. It may be possible on close inspection to identify a small foetus. Such 'mummified' kittens are often born alongside normal kittens, particularly by foreign-type queens with large litters, and may be due to 'overcrowding' in the womb.

One of the commonest causes of habitual resorption and, to a lesser extent, abortion is feline leukaemia virus (FeLV; see p204). It is particularly important in breeding colonies, and reproductive failure may be the first sign of such infection. At the time of resorption there may be a slight reddish-pink vaginal discharge, and the queen will usually call again within a few days.

Another common cause is chronic endometritis, or infection of the lining of the womb. The condition varies greatly from mild cases (in which the uterus can maintain the foetuses throughout most of the pregnancy, the kittens being still-born) through resorption to total inability to conceive. Often, though not always, there is a vaginal discharge. In some cases the womb may become distended with pus, a condition known as pyometra. In this last case, hysterectomy (removal of the womb) must be carried out, but milder cases are treatable. Antibiotics may be little help, however, even though bacteria are involved, because the basic cause is generally hormonal. The best policy, apart from trying antibiotic therapy, is to leave the queen unmated for one or two calls in the hope that she will clear herself of infection naturally.

There are various other causes of gestational failure in cats, but one that is often blamed by breeders for undiagnosed cases – hormone (particularly progesterone) deficiency – is much less common than is supposed. A poor diet can be a cause, but this is rare among well-cared-for pedigree queens. Undoubtedly you should seek veterinary advice whenever resorption or abortion recurs, however, since precise diagnosis is essential if the more serious causes are to be detected. Many breeders today conduct FeLV tests as a matter of routine, and owners of toms at public stud often will not accept untested queens.

Problems during and after birth

Queens rarely experience difficulty in giving birth to their kittens, even when they are born tail-first, but there are occasions when you may need to help or call in veterinary assistance (see p224). In extreme cases, caesarian delivery may be necessary. Rarely, one or more placentas or foetal membranes may be retained in the uterus after the kittens are born, or the womb may become infected. In all such cases there will be an unpleasant vaginal discharge, together with depression, fever, poor appetite and so on due to toxins (poisons) passing into the mother's bloodstream. Lactation will also usually be affected. The queen will need antibiotic treatment, and in a severe case possibly hysterectomy.

Another uncommon condition that can occur in late pregnancy or while the queen is feeding her kittens is called eclampsia. It is caused by insufficient calcium in the diet – the need for which rises considerably at this time – which leads to stiffening and muscular tremors. Eventually the queen has difficulty walking and may fall over; in untreated cases she may have convulsions. Immediate veterinary attention is needed, entailing a calcium injection, followed by a calcium dietary supplement.

Various problems may also be associated with the feeding of the kittens. The milk glands can become infected with bacteria, a condition known as mastitis, in acute cases becoming hot and swollen, developing abscesses and discharging pus; toxins entering the bloodstream cause serious illness. The vet should be consulted immediately as antibiotics are needed; the nipples will also need gentle bathing. On the other hand, mild cases of mastitis may result in few signs in the queen, but since the kittens are suckling infected milk they soon become ill. They have to be separated from their mother, given antibiotics, nursed and fed by hand (see p227).

In a few cases, a queen may fail to produce milk at all. In maiden queens this may rarely be due to congenital (inborn) abnormalities of the teats. Hormonal imbalances may be involved, particularly in queens who have given birth by caesarian section; in such cases an injection of oxytocin (the birth hormone) may result in 'let-down' of milk. It may also be helpful to put an older, stronger kitten (if available) on the queen for a short time in the hope that the vigorous suckling will induce lactation.

Tumours (growths) of the mammary glands can affect female cats of any age, and are usually malignant (cancerous); fortunately they are uncommon. They may be confused with mammary hypertrophy – massive enlargement of the mammary glands in pregnant cats or those being given chemical contraceptives (see p217). This is hormonal in origin and, unlike tumours, can usually be corrected.

Cat shows I

There have been competitive cat shows for more than a century. They have varied widely in size and organization, but the prime object has always been the same: to display the most beautiful cats and to choose those judged to be the best of their kind. This judgement encompasses not only their colour and form but also their general condition and health.

As a result, shows have become a major part of the lives of serious cat breeders, for it is through show success (or lack of it) and judges' comments on their exhibits that breeders gauge and compare their progress towards producing the 'ideal' cat of their particular breed. Success also increases their status in the cat fancy and the prices their cats can fetch. But shows can be fun for the less dedicated, too, providing social contact with fellow enthusiasts, a chance to see the top cats of all breeds and a competitive edge to their hobby.

The earliest recorded cat show took place in England at the St Giles Fair, Winchester, in 1598. In more modern times, a show was held at a London house in 1861, and later in the same decade the first shows in North America took place in New England, featuring the Maine Coon (see p52), the local breed. Most people consider, however, that cat shows as we know them began with the one organized by Harrison Weir at the Crystal Palace, London, in 1871. In the United States, showing cats became popular after a show was held at Madison Square Gardens, New York, in 1895. The idea later spread to Australia, Canada, New Zealand, South Africa, most countries on the European continent and even to Japan, until there are today, worldwide, many hundreds of cat shows each year. In the United States alone more than 400 major shows are held each year, while some 65 take place in the British Isles.

Organization and regulation

Each country where cat breeding and showing is established has one or more governing bodies or associations which register pedigree cats and regulate cat shows. In Britain there is a single body, the Governing Council of the Cat Fancy (GCCF), but most other countries have more than one. In the United States, for example, there are some nine associations, of which the Cat Fanciers' Association (CFA) is the largest and is international in scope, having affiliated clubs in Canada and Japan. Canada also has its own body, the Canadian Cat Association (CCA). On the European continent, many countries have at least two governing bodies, one of which may be affiliated to the Fédération Internationale Féline (FIFe), the main international association. This also has affiliated clubs in Australia (which has several), New Zealand and South America. Generally speaking, a cat must be registered with the appropriate governing body before it can be entered in the pedigree classes of a cat show. This means that North American breeders and owners have to register their cats with each association in which they intend to exhibit their cats.

The governing bodies do not generally themselves organize shows but license affiliated clubs to hold them. The shows normally (though not invariably) take place at weekends. In Britain, all cat shows are one-day events, but in continental Europe and North America two-day shows are also common, partly because of the long travelling distances involved for many exhibitors. (In Europe, particularly, many exhibitors travel to other countries for important shows.) American cat shows often in fact consist of four 'rings' – each of them a separate competition, often sponsored by a separate club – taking place simultaneously (and with the same cats competing) under the same roof. One or more of these competitions may be restricted to long- or short-haired cats, or even to individual breeds, while others are all-breed shows. Another variation being tried in the United States is a two-day 'back-to-back' show with a separate series of competitions (again sponsored by separate clubs) on succeeding days.

Not all cat shows are large, however. In Britain, small, somewhat informal shows are known as exemption shows. Rather more formal are sanction shows, which can be regarded as rehearsals for full-scale championship shows – which are the only shows at which a cat can gain the challenge certificates needed to become a champion (see below). In North America, all official shows have championship status, but informal, unofficial cat shows may be held in conjunction with county fairs.

But undoubtedly it is the large championship shows that attract most public attention. The largest of all is the National Cat Club show, held in London each December, at which some 2,000 pedigree cats plus (in separate classes) nearly 500 non-pedigree pets take part. Probably the largest in North America is that held in Flushing, New York, which is run jointly by five clubs, while the Cat-Club de Paris holds one of the largest shows on the European continent. Other very big shows take place in Holland and West Germany. Even the biggest shows almost all have special classes for non-pedigree household pet cats, and many children, in particular, derive great pleasure from entering their pets in these. Many shows also have assessment or experimental classes, in which examples of new breeds can be shown and commented upon by the judges without taking part in the competition. /continued

Victorian cat shows became fashionable occasions after Harrison Weir organized the first important one at the Crystal Palace, in London, in 1871. The photograph **far right** is of the judging at a show held at Richmond, on the outskirts of London, about the turn of the century. Then, as now in Britain, the judges examined the cats in or beside their pens and attached prize cards to those of winners. The prize card **right** dates from about the same period; it was won by a white Persian called General White. In those days, before the advent of modern veterinary care and vaccines, showing was much riskier than today, and many cats succumbed to disease.

Judging a cat, a judge assesses two basic things: the overall appearance and condition of the cat, and how closely it approximates to the ideal for its breed and colour. The latter is enshrined in the official show standard (or standard of points) issued by the cat fancy governing body concerned. This standard allocates a certain number of maximum points for each feature, totalling 100.

In some associations (notably the ACFA in the United States) the judge writes down the score awarded for each feature on a judging slip, the show standard specifying precisely the number of points (or fractions of a point) to be deducted for each departure from the ideal. The judge then calculates the total number of points for each cat, the one scoring highest being the winner; only if there is a tie are direct side-by-side comparisons made between different cats.

More usually, the judge makes an overall mental assessment of the cat. In this case, the scale of points in the standard serves more as a guide to the relative importance of different features – such as coat colour, shape of head, coat quality and so on – than as a precise system of scoring. Show standards also often specify faults that – although apparently minor to an outsider – are considered so fundamental as to justify disqualification or the withold of an award.

The allocation of points between different features varies from breed to breed and also, for the same breed, from association to association. Associations differ, too, in the detail of their standards, and this can confuse the beginner. For example, the British standard for some colours of Longhairs (Persians) is much less detailed than for others; there is an unwritten rule that the body type and general features of all Persians should conform to those set out in the show standards for the black or the white.

The system of points and show standards is illustrated below for a red self (solid red) Longhair (Persian), with quotations from the CFA's show standard (US) and that of the GCCF (UK). For more details, refer to the publications of the associations themselves. You should remember, however, that it is always the overall effect that is the most important. In the words of the preface to the CFA show standards: 'The ideal cat is a perfectly proportioned animal, of pleasing appearance and superb refinement . . . If the various parts of a cat are harmoniously balanced and complement each other well, the whole will be greater than the sum of its parts. The total will be a beautiful cat.'

Head

UK (20 points, excluding eyes): Broad and round; small ears well set and well tufted; short broad nose; full round cheeks. (The black is described more fully as follows: Round and broad, with plenty of space between the ears, which should be small, neat and well covered; short nose, full cheeks and broad muzzle. An undershot jaw shall be considered a defect.)

US (30 points, including size and shape of eyes, ear shape and set): Round and massive, with great breadth of skull. Round face with round underlying bone structure. Well set on short, thick neck. Ears small, round-tipped, tilted forward, and not unduly open at the base; set far apart and low on the head, fitting into (without distorting) the rounded contour of the head. Nose short, snub and broad; with 'break'. Cheeks full. Jaws broad and powerful. Chin full and well developed. (See separate description of eyes.)

Eyes

UK (15 points for size, shape and colour): Large and round; deep copper colour. (The standard for the black Longhair adds: Wide apart.)

US (points for size and shape are included with those allocated for head; colour 10 points): Large, round and full; set far apart and brilliant, giving a sweet expression to the face; colour brilliant copper.

Body

UK (15 points): Cobby and solid; short thick legs. (For tail, see description of coat. The standard for the black describes the body more fully, as follows: Cobby and massive, without being coarse, with plenty of bone and substance, and low on the leg.)

US (20 points, including shape, size, bone and length of tail): Of cobby type, low on the legs, deep in the chest, equally massive across the shoulders and rump, with a short, well-rounded middle piece. Large or medium in size; quality the determining consideration, rather than size. Back level. Legs short, thick and strong; forelegs straight. Paws large, round and firm; toes carried close, five in front and four behind. Tail short, but in proportion to body length; carried without a curve and at an angle lower than the back.

Coat

UK (50 points, including colour): Long, dense and silky; tail short and flowing. (The standard for the black describes the coat more fully, as follows: Long and flowing on body, full frill, and brush which should be short and broad.)

US (10 points, excluding colour): Long and thick, standing off from the body; of fine texture, glossy and full of life; long all over the body, including the shoulders. The ruff immense and continuing in a deep frill between the front legs. Ear and toe tufts long. Brush very full.

Colour

UK (points included in 50 for coat): Deep rich red, without markings.

US (20 points): Deep rich, clear, brilliant red; without shading, markings or ticking. Lips and chin the same colour as coat. Nose leather and paw pads brick-red. (For eye colour, see description of eyes).

Other points

UK No specific points given for condition in red Longhair, though in the standards for other colours this may be scored separately or mentioned in combination with coat.

US Balance and refinement are given 5 points each but are not described. The preface to the show standards sets out in general terms the requirements for condition applying to all cats.

Cat shows 2

Classes and awards

Cat associations in different countries vary in the way they organize the classes in which pedigree cats are judged, but as a general rule cats compete on the basis of breed, colour, sex and whether or not they have been neutered. There are separate classes for kittens (four to eight months old in North America, usually three to nine months elsewhere) and adult cats (which may be subdivided into juniors under two years old and seniors). There are also class divisions on the basis of previous show successes, with novice classes for cats that have never won a first prize, classes for champions, grand champions and so on. Some classes may be restricted to cats owned by members of a sponsoring club.

It can all seem very confusing to a beginner, and in fact at British shows and those run on similar lines a cat may be entered in as many as 12 classes, though 5 or 6 is more usual. The most important by far, however, are the open breed classes, in which the cat competes against all other neuters or entire cats of the same breed and colour, adult or kitten. Judging for these always takes place first, while the owners are out of the hall (see below). Later in the day, cats and kittens nominated by the judges of the open classes are assessed by a panel of judges for 'best in show' or 'best of breed' awards.

The system in North America is quite different. There, a cat or kitten is entered initially in one basic colour class (according to its past competition successes) for its breed. The entry is judged in this class in each all-breed and/or speciality competition for which it is eligible – usually a total of four judgings. A colour class may consist of a single colour or, in breeds with relatively small entries, a group of related colours such as solid (self) colours, tabbies and so on. After class judging, the judge announces which cats are the best (and second best) of the colour class, the best champion of the breed and the best (and second best) cat of the breed.

As judging progresses, each judge notes the outstanding cats so that, when all judging is completed (often on the second day), the 'best in show' winners have been decided – together with other awards such as the 'best long-hair'. A 'Finals' ceremony is held by each judge, in which the top five or ten cats are presented to the audience (in reverse order) and commented upon. Separate Finals ceremonies are held in each ring for entire cats, neuters and kittens. At some events, the climax is the 'best of the bests' presentation.

In all countries, the owners of winning cats receive awards of various kinds, but prize money – if given at all – is purely nominal. In Britain, class winners are given prize cards and rosettes (red for a first, blue for a second and yellow for a third), while at

The show hall of a major cat show may have more than 2,000 pens, and is busy from early morning as owners settle their cats and carry out last-minute grooming. In Britain the hall is cleared for the open class judging, but then owners and the general public can view the exhibits during judging of the miscellaneous classes. In countries where ring judging takes place owners remain all day and must be alert for their classes or pen numbers to be called, when the cats must be taken to the ring to be judged. At American shows, there are usually several rings around the hall; in continental Europe, judging may take place in a screened-off area or room.

Judging in North America takes place in a 'ring' where the cats of the class being judged are placed in numbered pens. The judge examines each cat in turn **right**, noting its good and bad points. After each cat in the class has been judged, winners' ribbons are awarded. Because the judges do not visit the pens during judging, these can have name boards and be colourfully decorated **below right** without risk of the judges being influenced.

American shows rosettes and coloured ribbons are awarded – blue for a first prize, red for a second and yellow for a third. 'Best in show' and similar awards may consist of silver trophies or other special prizes.

Apart from these competitive prizes, a cat's success at shows may lead to its gaining such titles as champion and grand champion. Again, the way these titles are won varies. In Britain, the winner of an open adult class at a championship show may, if the judge thinks it is good enough, be awarded a challenge certificate. If it wins three challenge certificates at three separate shows under three different judges, it is eligible for champion status. Thereafter it can compete in 'champion of champions' classes and, if outstanding, be awarded grand challenge certificates, three of which (again under different judges at different shows) are needed to become a grand champion. A similar system operates on the European continent except that cats can also become international champions and international grand champions. In all cases, champions are always entire (unneutered); neuters have a parallel system of titles from

premier up to international grand premier.

North America has the same range of championship and premiership titles (including internationals in Canada), but the system of gaining them is quite different. To become a champion or premier a cat has to win the open class for its breed and colour at least four or six times (depending on the association) under different judges.

Because of the way American shows are run, a cat may be able to achieve this at a single event or two, so that the title does not have as much rarity or status as in Europe. In order to become a grand champion or premier, a cat has to amass a certain number of points at a series of shows, awarded on the basis of the number of other champions beaten, and these titles are much more valuable. Another feature of American cat showing is the award of national, regional and similar prizes based on a cat's wins over the whole of one season.

Penning and judging

Yet another way in which cat shows differ around the world is in the way the cats are penned (caged) and judging takes place. In North America, Japan and most of Europe, ring judging takes place, in which the cats of each class are taken (by the owner or by a steward) from their pens to the 'ring' or judging area. In this case, if an exhibitor has

Cats to be judged are put in a row of special cages behind the judge, and are brought up to the judge's table one at a time. A clerk notes the judge's comments and, in some associations, the points awarded for each feature. (In other associations, the judge makes an overall mental assessment rather than scoring each feature.) Once the judging of the class is finished, the results are announced and the winners' ribbons or rosettes placed on the cages. A variation occurs in Scandinavia, where the judge may explain publicly the reasons for making certain cats winners. With all forms of ring judging, there is an audience around each ring, but the judge should not know who owns which cat.

In the British Isles and several other Commonwealth countries, the judges visit the cats' pens rather than vice-versa. For this reason, no decoration of the cages is allowed, the blanket must be white and there are no name boards, only pen

ing it between each cat), to remove each cat from its pen and hold it for the judge to examine, and then to replace it in the cage. The judge writes down any comments in a book and, once each cat in the class has been seen, compares these assessments and makes the awards. After the open classes have been judged and the results posted on a board, the exhibitors are allowed back into the hall, but the judging continues for the miscellaneous classes. Even in Britain, however, judging of the 'best in show' and similar awards takes place at a central point, a panel of three or five judges passing each contender along the row for examination before deciding on the awards by vote.

Becoming a judge demands extensive knowledge of cats in general and the breeds to be judged in particular, for only experience develops the 'eye' necessary to gauge the subtle differences between a top-class cat and a second-best. Most governing bodies demand that a future judge should

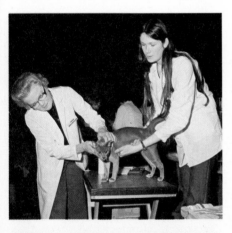

Judging in Britain takes place at the cats' pens **left**. A steward moves the judge's table and holds each cat while it is examined. The pens have only a plain white blanket **below left**, though as the day progresses prize cards and rosettes may be attached. The 'best in show' judging is carried out at a central point by a panel of senior judges **right**; winning cats are then placed in special pens **below** which are decorated with their rosettes and trophies.

have had at least three or five years' experience of breeding and showing the particular breed and in some cases have produced a number of champions. Some associations demand experience as a judge's steward or clerk, followed by personal assessments of the candidate's knowledge and skill; others require written and practical examinations to be taken. In some cases the next stage is to act as a 'probationer' judge, permitted to judge only kittens, for two years before becoming fully qualified to judge one or more breeds. In Britain, judges receive no payment other than hotel and travelling expenses, but many clubs elsewhere pay a fee per show or per cat judged.

Of the many thousands of breeders and exhibitors of pedigree cats, only a very few go on to become judges of their breeds. Most are happy to see their cats presented to the best of their ability on the show bench and enjoying the admiration of visitors. Some owners come to take show success (or lack of it) too seriously, but at its best a cat show provides harmless competition between animals that, most people would agree, are all beautiful.

more than one cat of different colours or even different breeds, they will usually be penned in adjacent cages, which can be (and generally are) decorated gaily with coloured drapes or blankets, trophies won at previous shows and possibly a board giving the name and address of the owner or breeder. This does not matter because the judges do not visit the pens.

numbers. Cats are generally penned in groups according to breed and/or colour, and cats owned by one person may be separated. During judging of the open classes – generally from 10am to noon – owners must leave the hall, so that only the judges and stewards are present.

The steward's job is to move a small trolley or table from pen to pen (disinfect-

Showing your cat

If you are really keen, it is possible to show your cat at intervals of one or two weeks (the latter is enforced in Britain as a health precaution) throughout the year. At the other extreme, you can enter it in the occasional show. It makes little difference whether the cat is a top-grade pedigree animal or a non-pedigree household pet; the formalities are much the same, and it is just as important to ensure that your cat is in good condition and well groomed. The major difference if you show regularly is that the cat needs to be kept in top show condition continuously, since this preparation should ideally begin a month before any show in which it is to appear.

Formalities and entries

As explained on page 230, a cat must have been registered with the appropriate cat fancy organization before being entered in the pedigree classes of any show, but there are of course no such formalities for household pets. Nor is it necessary to belong to a local or breed club to enter a show, though most owners who show at all frequently do so. Shows are generally announced in cat magazines some months ahead. For a beginner, the best place to start is often one of the small shows known in Britain as exemption shows – for example, the cat section of a local agricultural show. Then, if you enjoy your first taste of the show world, you could enter one of the larger sanction or championship shows (only the latter in North America; see p 230).

Write to the show manager for a schedule and entry form (blank) in plenty of time. Study the rules carefully, since they may vary slightly from show to show, and if necessary ask a more experienced cat fancier to help you fill in the application. In Britain, the number of classes that may be entered can cause confusion, but it is much more straightforward in North America (see p 232). Make sure that all the details of your cat's name, registration number, breed, colour, parentage and so on are absolutely correct, as a mistake may result in later disqualification – even after an award has been won. If your cat changes status (for example, becomes a champion) before the day of the show, this makes no difference in Britain; its status at the time of entry is what matters. In North America, however, it will be transferred to the correct class on arrival at the show. It is wise, and in some countries obligatory, to have all cats that are to appear in a show vaccinated against the main feline ailments (see p 172), and you may have to sign a declaration that the cat is in good health.

Send in your entry in ample time, enclosing the correct fee – generally a separate fee of about £1 to £2 for each class entered in the British system, or a single overall fee (typically $15 to $20) in the American. If the show is far from your home or it is a two-day event, arrange overnight accommodation with a friend or a hotel that will accept cats and is as near to the show centre as possible. If, shortly before the show, your cat becomes ill or has contact with a sick cat, it is best to notify the show manager and withdraw your entry; in some cases, fees may be returned.

Show preparation

Even if you plan to show your cat only infrequently, it is important to keep it in good physical condition throughout the year. Principally, this involves giving it a good diet (see p 148) and plenty of exercise, and ensuring that it does not become overweight. Since free outdoor access can result in tangles in the coat of a long-haired cat, many owners who would otherwise be inclined to allow their cats to roam freely confine them to an exercise pen (see p 159) – though this should, if possible, be at least 7 m² (70 sq ft) in area. (In North America, pedigree show cats are commonly confined to the home at all times.)

Each day, starting a month before the show, you should groom your cat (see p 154). Then, about five days before the show, it is a good idea to give a short-haired cat a bran bath. However, with pale-coloured short-hairs and all long-hairs a shampoo is necessary, and many owners shampoo other cats also. It is worthwhile experimenting to find the best time to bath

Training for stardom begins at home. A show cat must be accustomed to being penned for long periods and to being handled by strangers. This can be done by installing a pen at home and encouraging visitors to pick up the cat.

your cat, but in general do not leave this later than five days before the show in the case of a long-hair, or its hair may be too soft on show day. Pale-coloured long-hairs generally need two applications of shampoo. If the cat will tolerate it, an electric hair-drier is a great boon, especially with long-hairs. As the coat dries, you should groom it thoroughly, so that at the end a Persian's coat stands out like a massive brush around the body. With Persians and related breeds, pay careful attention to grooming the head.

The final stage with a pale-coloured cat is to rub in talcum powder once the coat is dry, to be thoroughly brushed out next day, leaving the coat gleaming. This can be repeated just before the show, but no powder must remain in the coat on show day. Many owners of black and other dark-coloured cats apply a final gloss with bay rum or a proprietary cat grooming lotion, but the beginner is well advised to consult a more experienced owner before using these. Short-hairs can be made to look sleek by smoothing the coat with a piece of silk or nylon stocking.

A bran bath is useful for removing all traces of grease and dandruff from the coat of a short-hair; give it about five days before the show. Put 100 g (3½ oz) of bran – the type used for feeding horses and rabbits – on a tray in a warm oven. When it is warm, stand the cat (held by an assistant) on a firm table and rub it into the coat – against the growth – on its back, belly and tail. Leave the bran in as long as possible (though the cat will probably shake itself vigorously), then brush it all out. A pale-coloured cat should then (or alternatively) be powdered with a heavy dusting of talcum powder **right**, which can remain overnight and then be brushed out thoroughly.

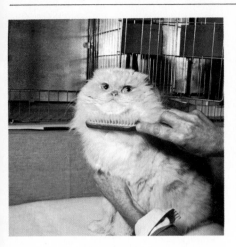

Final grooming takes place in the show hall. It is particularly important with Persians and related breeds, whose thick coat should stand out very fully from the body. Every hair should gleam, with no trace of grooming powder.

The fruits of success for a top-quality, well-trained and carefully groomed pedigree cat: a 'best of breed' rosette and a challenge certificate. Presentation and temperament are as important as quality in a show career.

With all cats, make sure that the claws and teeth are in good condition. If the claws are not kept short by exercise, they should be clipped (see p155). (Declawed cats are banned from shows.) Keep teeth clean and free of tartar, if necessary taking the cat to the vet for this. A small point to remember is not to give your cat fishy or other strong-smelling food just before a show.

Because the cat will be constantly on view at a show, it must be accustomed to being seen and handled by strangers from an early age. Take advantage of any visitors to your home to further this training. Since all show pens are of a similar size, it is worthwhile buying one to keep at home. Then the cat can be trained by being put in the pen for a period each day, with a tasty morsel as reward.

In the weeks before the show, get ready the equipment you will need, preferably in a special case. Basic needs include two or three warm blankets for the pen – white in Britain, coloured if you wish in many other countries – one or two litter trays and litter, feeding and water bowls, material to wipe out the pen if necessary, together with a safe disinfectant (see p178), and grooming equipment. If it is winter and the show premises may not be well heated – and particularly if you are showing a kitten – pack a hot-water bottle.

In North America and some other areas, coloured drapes, cushions and other ornaments and a name board may be included for 'furnishing' the pen. Toys may be taken, too, but in Britain do not give these to the cat until after the main judging. Make sure that the cat's carrying basket or container is clean and ready. Then, on the evening before the show, give the cat its final thorough grooming, prepare food for the next day and get ready for an early start in the morning.

The day of the show

The first formality on arrival at almost all cat shows in Britain is vetting-in, but in many other countries this has been abolished. Where it is still carried out, a queue of exhibitors wait (with the cats in their carriers) for a vet to check that each cat appears to be in good health and free from parasites. In some doubtful cases, a cat may be consigned to the quarantine area for half an hour, to see for example whether a raised temperature is simply the temporary result of the journey. Any obviously ill cat will be rejected and the owner must produce a veterinary certificate of good health before it can enter another show.

Once past any veterinary examination, you can take your cat to its numbered pen, prepare this (with decorations where allowed) and settle it in. This is the time for last-minute grooming and placing the numbered tally on a ribbon or elastic around the cat's neck where these are used. You can fill a water bowl and place it in the pen, but in the British system you should not leave any food during the main judging (when you will have to leave the hall for about two hours). A well-trained show cat will generally sit proudly on its blanket, but if it becomes frightened it may try to hide or even sit in its litter tray. An experienced judge's steward will usually cope with such minor problems, but if the cat should dirty itself the owner will generally be called back into the hall and given a chance to regroom the cat before it is judged.

In shows where ring-judging takes place, you must keep your ears open for your cat's pen number to be called over the public-address system. This may happen a number of times over the two days, since it may be taking part in as many as four separate 'shows' in rings in different parts of the hall. When called, the cat must be taken (in some shows this is done by a steward) to the ring and placed in the appropriate numbered pen behind the judge's table. In between each judging, you may want to do some further grooming or feed your cat, and you should of course clean out the litter tray whenever this is necessary.

As the day progresses, you may accumulate a number of winners' ribbons, rosettes or cards (in Britain, these are placed on the pens after the main judging). On the European continent, judges' comments may be written on cards placed on the pen or given to the exhibitor. In Britain, owners have to wait until these are published in the official show report. American judges do not make comments in writing, but may do so verbally to spectators at their ring. Whatever the system of judging, it is forbidden to try to speak to any judge until judging is completed. Most judges are then prepared to talk to owners, but are under no obligation to do so.

The final climax is always the 'best in show' announcement. In North America, this takes the form of Finals ceremonies for the best entire cats, neuters and kittens. When the judge has decided his or her top cats, these are called up to the ring and placed in the cages behind the judge's table. They are taken out in turn, and the judge displays and praises the cats and announces their awards – usually in reverse order, ending with the 'best cat'.

Returning home

Unless given special dispensation, all cats must remain in their pens until the official closing time. Then owners should pack away their belongings and clean out their pen before returning home. If you have any other cats in the household, keep the returning cat isolated from them for at least a week to 10 days since it is easy to pick up an infection at a show. Give the cat plenty of human company, but watch carefully for any signs of illness. In the case of certain diseases, you may be required to inform the show organizer or governing body concerned. Groom the cat again carefully, too, keeping watch for fleas.

If the cat has qualified at the show for the status of champion, grand champion or other such award, you must write to the proper cat fancy official to claim the appropriate certificate or medal. In some countries, individual prizes are confirmed and prize money sent to owners only after full details of the winners' pedigree registration and so on have been checked. Then, if you are a keen cat fancier, you will want to cut out any show report mentioning your cat from cat magazines and stick it in a scrapbook. But, possibly even before this appears, it may be time for the next show, for which preparation will have already begun. To many people, this kind of 'show business' becomes a way of life.

Postscript
THE CAT IN HUMAN SOCIETY

The cat in human society I

'Cats are a mysterious kind of folk. There is more passing in their minds than we are aware of.' So wrote Sir Walter Scott, and undoubtedly it is this quality of inscrutable mystery that for thousands of years has attracted people to the cat, just as surely as it has repelled others. However, it is logical to suppose that in the beginning it was the cat's special ability to catch vermin that earned it our particular respect, especially in the corn-growing lands of the ancient world, headed by Egypt. And in Egypt the peculiar characteristics of the cat – above all, its aloofness and aura of mystery – ensured that before long this respect became adoration and even worship.

tion wooden cat heads (see p 16). The mummies themselves were bound in bandages of different colours, their faces covered with wooden masks on which eyes, nose, ears and whiskers were all carefully marked. Many more would have survived if archeologists had recognized their immense zoological and historical importance sooner; for example, there was the infamous affair of the 300,000 or so feline mummies excavated at the site of Beni Hassan in the late 19th century, most of which were exported to Liverpool and used as fertilizer on English fields.

In common with similar archeological sites in Egypt, Beni Hassan has however yielded other

The goddess Bast is represented in this Late period Egyptian bronze figure (dated between 600 and 200 BC) as a woman with a feline head. In her right hand is a sistrum, a rattle-like musical instrument, while in her left is an aegis (shield). The special significance, if any, of the kittens at her feet is unknown. The figure was found at Bubastis in about 1892.

Cats' secular role in ancient Egypt is shown brilliantly in the tomb painting **left** found at Thebes and dating from about 1400 BC. In both this and the satyrical papyrus **right**, the cat appears to be a spotted tabby. The papyrus was also found at Thebes, and is believed to have been made by workmen about 1000 BC; it parodies the relationship between the workmen (cats) and the ruling classes (rats).

Egypt – the cat as goddess

From about 1580 BC, a distinctive cat cult in Egypt became firmly identified with Bast, goddess of maternity, fertility and other feminine virtues. (Other names for Bast were Oubastis, Bastet, or Pasht – from which the name puss is said to derive.) The symbolism of Bast and her cult was complex. On the one hand she stood for the light, warmth and life-giving energy of the Sun, whilst on the other the mysterious, night-loving part of the cat's nature led to a connection with Moon worship.

But whatever the complexities of its status as the focus of a religious cult, the cat in ancient Egypt had another part to play as well, for it was looked upon not only as the living embodiment of the goddess but also as a delightful domestic companion. Secure in the reverent affection of its hosts – an affection free, one may be sure, from any hint of that kind of easy-going familiarity that is so distasteful to cats – and in the respect of a community forbidden by law to injure it in any way, it passed its days in peace and comfort, finally at death to be embalmed and entombed with due ceremony and sincere grief.

Some pathetic cat mummies have survived, still in their cases of wood carved to the shape of a cat or in wrappings of plaited and coloured straw with imita-

treasures, among them wall paintings that show cats joining in the daily life and activities of men and women. A well-known example now in the British Museum shows a big tabby accompanying a man on a hunting expedition, pinning down two birds with its feet while trapping the wing of a third between its teeth. This, although the best, is by no means the only such picture of a hunting cat to be found in Egypt; however, it seems probable that these cats did not so much actually hunt or even retrieve game as flush it out of the reeds for the sportsmen's benefit.

After about 350 BC the cult of Bast gradually declined, being finally banned in AD 390 by Imperial decree. It had then existed for almost 2,000 years, and was the source of the many thousands of surviving Egyptian cat images, figurines, amulets and items of jewellery that bear such impressive witness to the enormous popularity of Bast.

The ancient Far East – mixed feelings

The custom of keeping cats was not confined to Egypt and the Middle East in ancient times. They appeared in China some time after Egypt – some authorities even place the cat's complete domestication there as late as AD 400, though a date of 2000 BC is suggested by others. The Chinese attitude to the cat was equivocal. Cats were welcomed for their ability to destroy vermin and were considered suitable pets for women. On the other hand, they were suspected of bringing unwelcome poverty into the household. However, the Chinese believed that this disaster could be averted by the use of ceramic figures of seated cats gazing into the distance. Many of these figures have survived, as have others with hollow eyes used as night-light holders to scare away rats.

Indeed, the need to keep rats at bay was so essential a part of peasant life, depending as it did entirely upon crops, that there is good evidence for a Chinese cat deity called Li Shou which at one time was worshipped by farmers as a kind of divine pest-controller. The cat's powers of seeing in the dark were thought to be especially useful in warding off evil spirits, which were more active at night, and for this reason pictures of cats adorned the walls of Chinese houses, reinforcing the activities of the real

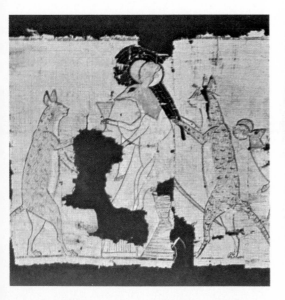

animals. Black cats were unlucky, but the older and uglier a cat the more good fortune it was likely to bring its owner.

More orthodox Chinese especially revered the cat for its powers of self-contained meditation, an attribute greatly valued by Buddhists. Buddhist lands as a whole are rich in cat lore, even though the cat is excepted from the list of protected creatures in the original canons of Buddhism and is excluded from the Chinese and Japanese zodiacs; this (it is said) is either because the cat fell asleep during the Buddha's funeral ceremonies, or else because it so far forgot itself on the same solemn occasion as to attack the rat. Despite this behaviour, the cat has usually received good treatment in Asian lands.

Cats probably arrived on the Indian sub-continent at about the same time as in China. The usual fables and legends associated with them are found in the two great epics, the *Ramayana* and *Mahadharata*, both of pre-500 BC date. A feline goddess Sasti, symbolic of maternity, inevitably invites comparison with Bast. The Hindu and Parsee religions, with their respect for all forms of life, were naturally sympathetic towards the cat, and indeed the feeding and housing of at least one cat is theoretically incumbent upon all orthodox Hindus.

Greece and Rome – cats become commonplace

The domestic cat eventually reached Europe from Egypt. The export of any cat from Egypt was officially discouraged, if not actually forbidden by law, and strenuous efforts were made to see that this rule was obeyed. Nevertheless, some cats were undoubtedly abducted, most probably by Phoenician traders, and so the species spread throughout the whole Mediterranean area. In the religions of the ancient Classical world the personality of Bast survived in the cults of the Greek goddess Artemis and her Roman counterpart Diana, but there is little if any evidence to show that the symbolic creature was in any way linked with the living one, as had been the case in Egypt. The Greeks do not seem to have had any great enthusiasm for cats as pets; they already had an effective antidote to vermin in the form of a semi-domesticated creature thought to have been a species of weasel or marten, and they probably looked on the

cat as a rather exotic importation. Greek representations of cats are confined mainly to coins, although a few are found in vase paintings.

The Romans, like the Greeks, used creatures such as weasels and polecats to catch vermin. But cats were well enough known by the first century AD for the elder Pliny to describe their physical characteristics in his famous *Natural History*, and it seems that their qualities of independence and self-reliance were sufficiently appreciated by the Romans for cats to be used sometimes as pictorial symbols of liberty and freedom. A few relief sculptures found on tombs not only in and around Rome but also in parts of Gaul apparently show the deceased with their pet cats. However, no accredited cat remains have yet been discovered at either Herculaneum or Pompeii, though at the latter site a handful of mosaics showing cats have turned up, notably a fine scene of a large tabby pouncing on a plump pigeon (though even this seems to be the work of Egyptian craftsmen).

As they carried the rule of Rome to the northernmost extremities of her expanding empire, the legions doubtless took with them numbers of cats. After its initial seclusion in Egypt, the domestic cat now spread throughout Europe, but it was not always to find such a warm welcome.   */continued*

Cats in ancient Rome had a much less elevated position than in Egypt, and are not often seen in works of art. However, the mosaic **below** found at Pompeii testifies to their presence; again the cat is a spotted tabby.

A Chinese figurine of a cat in blue porcelain dating from the 18th century illustrates the superstitions surrounding the cat in the Far East. Such figurines were used from early times to ward off evil spirits and also, at a more mundane level, to scare rats.

The cat in human society 2

Medieval Europe – persecution and prestige

The early Christian Church did not much like the cat; the animal had too many connections with paganism. On the other hand, it was not actively persecuted at this time. Both St Patrick late in the 5th century and Pope Gregory the Great a century later are said to have cherished pet cats, and cats are even to be found among the emblems of certain saints, such as St Agatha and St Gertrude of Nivelles. Monasteries and nunneries were probably among the first Christian communities to benefit from the hunting instincts of the cat, and only later was the animal banned from them.

Celtic monks seem to have been especially fond of cats; there are beautiful if stylized illustrations of cats both in the *Lindisfarne Gospels* (about AD 700) and the *Book of Kells* (about 800). There is also the remarkable poem, to be found in most animal anthologies, by an Irish monk of the same period addressed to his own

carved stone capitals, roof bosses, wooden misericord seats and bench ends to be found in medieval cathedrals and churches, in which its prowess as a rat killer and mouse catcher is celebrated with all the earthy humour of the medieval craftsman. These caricatures are supplemented by a number of equally humorous drawings on the same topic in the margins of illuminated manuscripts, invariably the work of monks.

Unfortunately, the cat's renewed popularity was short-lived. The later medieval period in Europe was marred by a revulsion of feeling against the cat expressed in a widespread campaign of extreme cruelty. The persecution seems to have begun in about the middle of the 13th century, and to have been partly triggered off by a revival in the Rhineland of a pagan fertility cult owing allegiance to the Norse goddess of love and fertility, Freyia. Cats figured in the rites of this cult just as they had done in those of

Cats in south-east Asia In Siam (now Thailand) the cat was revered and many colours and patterns prized. The *Cat-Book Poems* **above** illustrates and describes them. Dating from between 1350 and 1750, it may be the oldest book devoted to cats. These are black and white bicolours; others include ancestors of such relatively recent cat breeds as the Siamese, Burmese and Korat.

The medieval cat A cat used as a motif for illumination in the Lindisfarne Gospels **above** and one drawn by an unknown artist in about 1400 in a sketchbook found by the diarist Samuel Pepys **above right** both indicate that, despite later clerical disapproval, the cat was well appreciated in the early Middle Ages.

white cat named Pangur Ban, whom he obviously regarded as a valued companion and friend.

Throughout much of the early Middle Ages the cat, despite official disapproval, seems to have retained the tolerance and even affection of ordinary people, whose attitude towards it no doubt also contained a mixture of lingering superstitious awe and a healthy respect for its skill in controlling vermin. Chaucer, in 'The Maunciple's Tale' from his *Canterbury Tales*, clearly indicates that pampered cats did exist in 14th-century England, while in Italy the celebrated poet Petrarch is said to have been even more devoted in later years to his cat than to the memory of his great love Laura.

General respect for the cat increased sharply when Europe was suddenly invaded by hordes of plague-bearing, corn-eating black rats from the east. These arrived in Europe in the ships of the returning Crusaders (who are also said to have brought with them the first long-hairs to be seen in Europe) from the end of the 11th century onwards, and it was soon found that the only answer to the problem was the cat. The general popularity that the animal enjoyed in consequence is reflected in the large number of

Bast, Artemis and Diana, to each of whom Freyia was closely related. As well as pursuing the human devotees of Freyia with all the rigours of the Inquisition, the Church now also felt fully entitled to launch an all-out attack on the cat – an animal that it had always regarded with the deepest suspicion, noting grimly that cats are not once mentioned in the Bible.

An irrational yet deep-seated popular fear of the cat was now deliberately stimulated and encouraged in the name of religion for the next 450 years or so, during which many thousands of hapless cats perished as agents or symbols of one kind of evil or another; for instance, in the England of both Mary Tudor and Elizabeth I cats were publicly burned as symbols of heresy – that is, of Protestantism and Catholicism respectively. Countless cats were cast in the role of 'familiar' to women who were accused for one reason or another of practising witchcraft, and the cats shared their fate. Moreover, the belief that witches could actually change into cats is a very ancient and widespread one, being found as far distant from Europe as Japan, and must have accounted for the summary execution of many a cat.

Various portions of cat anatomy were also much in demand in medieval Europe as ingredients for making quack medicines.

The particular notoriety of the black cat perhaps originated in the ancient legend of Galinthias, who was turned into a cat and served Hecate, Queen of the Underworld and a synonym for darkness, as a priestess. Though there is some evidence to suggest that the usual 'witch's cat' was more often a mackerel tabby (Shakespeare's witches in *Macbeth* speak of the 'brinded cat', this being another form of brindled, or striped), the black cat is still the supreme embodiment of feline mystery, associated with both good and bad luck in different places and circumstances – the bad unfortunately predominating.

And so religious prejudice played upon popular superstition to produce the general belief in Europe that cats were at best endowed with supernatural powers and at worst direct agents of the Devil.

finally attained Paradise. It is reported that as late as 1926 a cat was ceremonially paraded at the Thai king's coronation, representing his predecessor.

Unlike the Siamese, the Birman cat – another breed seen only comparatively recently at Western shows – does apparently have some claim to be descended directly from the sacred temple cats of Burma. Legend states that its characteristic golden fur and intensely blue eyes were first manifested in the temple cat at the Lao-Tsun monastery, at the moment when it received the soul of the dying saintly Lama Mun-Ha, itself dying seven days later (see p62). But this is only one of the many legends connected with the cats of the Far East, such as those which attribute the typical crossed eyes of many Siamese to its having stared too long and too fixedly at the golden goblet of the Buddha, or the shadowy 'temple mark' on the back of its neck to the hand of the god as he once picked up the animal.

A Cat hung up in Cheapside, habited like a Priest

Medieval Asia – the cat retains respect
The Christian evaluation of the cat contrasted strongly and highly unfavourably with the Muslim attitude, based as it is on that of the great Prophet himself. He is said to have cut off the sleeve of his robe rather than disturb the cat Muezza which was sleeping on it, and to have purified himself with water from the same source as that from which a cat had already been seen to drink.

Cats were also highly regarded in the Far East. Several kinds, not only the seal points now known as Siamese cats, have been prized for centuries in Thailand. They are illustrated in a fascinating Thai manuscript called the *Cat-Book Poems*; this is of uncertain date but could have been written at any time between 1350 and 1750, though a copy was made during the 19th century. Cats were kept as sacred animals in temples, though the probability now is that they were not necessarily seal points. Behind the maintenance of these sacred cats lay the Buddhist belief that the soul of a person who had become very spiritually advanced entered into the body of a cat when that person died, where it remained until the subsequent death of the cat, at which point the soul

Cats were introduced into Japan from China in medieval times, and there is a tradition that the first native Japanese kittens were born in the year 999 at the Imperial Palace in Kyoto. After this momentous event cats were given the utmost consideration and care, to the extent of being kept on leads and pampered like lapdogs. The result of this kindly but misguided treatment was that mice and rats multiplied unchecked, so to combat them likenesses of cats were painted or sculpted on doors and walls. Although, not surprisingly, this had no effect, it was not until the 17th century that Japanese cats were officially released from purdah and allowed to give their natural hunting instincts full play.

The cat reinstated
Happily, even at those times when its general popularity has for one reason or another been at a low ebb, the cat has never lacked champions and friends amongst people of sensitivity, humanity and intelligence, especially artists and men of letters. Moreover there is evidence to show that, during the infamous period of religious persecution in Europe, the Church's attitude to the cat was often   /continued

Cats and the Church   In the later Middle Ages, cats were widely persecuted, suffering for the prejudice of religious factions of all kinds, as is shown in the engraving **above left**, dating from 1554, in which a cat dressed in a priest's vestments is hanged in London as an anti-Catholic demonstration. Much of the Catholic Church, in turn, regarded cats as agents of the devil, but in *The Visitation* by Bernardino di Betto (Pinturicchio) **above**, a white cat is seen with the Virgin Mary.

The cat in human society 3

vigorously opposed by churchmen themselves, among them St Phillip Neri, founder of the Oratorian Order in Rome, and Cardinal Richelieu.

A slow but general change in public attitudes towards the cat first becomes noticeable during the 17th century. As early as 1607 the English naturalist Edward Topsell in his book *The History of Four-Footed Beasts* gives a penetrating description of the cat which shows that he had studied its nature with commendable scientific detachment. Samuel Pepys describes seeing a singed but living cat taken, with evident tenderness, from some smoking ruins after the Great Fire of London (1666), whilst Pepys's contemporary the great scientist Sir Isaac Newton is credited with the invention of the cat door or cat flap for the convenience of his pets. In the field of painting many 17th-century Dutch interiors show cats, and indeed on the evidence of these alone it would seem that in Holland at this period the cat again enjoyed a popularity and respect that it had seldom known since the golden days of Bast.

The rehabilitation of the cat also received an important boost in the literary and artistic circles of France. Here, towards the end of the 17th century, the cat made its most famous appearance in literature, as *Puss in Boots* in the original version by Charles Perrault, while in the 18th century something of a pro-feline cult grew up generally in educated French circles. This was encouraged by the witty yet learned book *Les Chats* (1727) by the courtier François Auguste Paradis de Moncrif. Although Moncrif had to face a certain amount of public ridicule over his book, there were nevertheless many who shared his views on the essential sagacity of cats, among them the Duc de Nivernois, who had the portrait of his favourite long-hair painted on the lid of his snuffbox.

His Grace had a British counterpart in the second Duke of Montagu, who died in 1749 leaving a codicil to his will in favour of his various pets, which included several cats. A famous legal case of the period resulted when the French harp player Mlle Dupuy made a deathbed will leaving two houses and a comfortable allowance to each of her two cats; this legacy was successfully contested in the courts.

The best-known and most comprehensive 18th-century work on natural history is also French, the *Histoire Naturelle* by the Comte de Buffon. The cat appears in volume six (1756), and, although the comments on feline character are basically unsympathetic, the work does contain five interesting engraved plates showing different types of cats (see p51). This is a good indication of the interest then being taken in new and exotic breeds, and is reinforced by other evidence such as the letters passing between the well-known English social gossip Horace Walpole and his friend in France, the blind Mme du Deffand, on the subject of Angora cats and kittens, of which she owned several. She offered two of them to Walpole; his reply is lost, but he is nonetheless one of the notable cat lovers of history. In his collected letters we read among others of Harold, a stray found on the Goodwin Sands (had he perhaps survived a shipwreck?) who lived for a further 15 or so years, and of Selima whose untimely death by drowning in a large goldfish bowl was the subject of a famous poem by Thomas Gray.

The eighteenth century is also the time of Hodge, Dr Johnson's cat, whom he fed with oysters and

Studies of cats in their own right date back to the Renaissance, but the illustrations **top** of cats in action were made about 1800. The engraving **above** after a watercolour by Gottfried Mind displays in its exquisite attention to detail the artist's obsession with the cat.

The Kuniyoshi painting *Catfish* **left** is a play on words, for the cats spell (in Japanese) the title, while the composition suggests the fluid motion of both cats and fish.

treated with the utmost understanding and respect, and of Jeoffry, the subject of a long and appreciative poem by the sensitive mystic Christopher Smart. It is also the period of the Reverend Doctor John Langbourne, who despite his resounding name and titles was not an 18th-century bishop but the best-loved of Jeremy Bentham's many cats, each of which the great philosopher introduced by name to Lord Brougham as the cats sat on individual chairs around the table.

The cat as artist's model

In France the 18th-century interest in cats as expressed in the paintings of artists such as Le Mercier, Boucher and Chardin (though curiously enough the sensuous Fragonard was not a good cat painter) was continued in the 19th century by Géricault, Courbet,

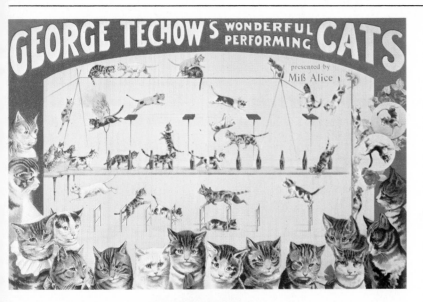

Performing cats of one kind or another are mainly a phenomenon of the 19th and 20th centuries. Sometimes they are treated with reverence, as at the early cat show at London's Crystal Palace **right**, in some cases the opposite, as in the circus display **above**. The use of cats in circuses is rare, however, for most cats will not perform to order.

Cats as decoration The Victorians were also the first to use the beauty of the cat widely for purely decorative purposes, as in the French wallpaper **right** from the period 1825 to 1840. It shows a white long-haired cat in exotic surroundings, pre-echoing the high regard for such cats that was 50 years later to dominate cat breeding and showing.

colony of former strays; these have become famous through Steinlen's posters advertising such things as tea and milk. Steinlen is probably the first artist successfully to show cats in violent motion.

Yet even Steinlen did not concentrate his work as entirely on cats as did two other 19th-century artists, Gottfried Mind of Basle and the Dutch-born Henriette Ronner. Mind's devotion to cats bordered on mania, but his studies of them are nevertheless excellent. Those of Henriette Ronner, on the other hand, while often technically brilliant, are equally often marred by that kind of sentimentality which has ever since been associated with the worst kind of cat art. No such sentimentality spoils the work of the Japanese artist Kuniyoshi, whose passionate devotion to cats surprised even his contemporaries in a country notably well-disposed towards the animal, and is revealed in the large number of his prints and drawings that are devoted entirely to cats.

A further rise in the general popularity of the cat in the Western world may be dated from about 1865 and has been linked, at least in part, to the scientific discoveries of Louis Pasteur, for the natural and fastidious cleanliness of the cat made an immediate appeal to people newly conscious of the nature of diseases and their transmission. Cats became respectable; they were taken from the kitchen to the drawing room, and in Britain this revolution in attitudes was marked by the holding in 1871 of the first National Cat Show at the Crystal Palace, followed in 1887 by the founding of the National Cat Club. The status of cats in society was aided by the fact that Queen Victoria herself was known to be the owner of two blue Persians, and that the Prince of Wales presented prize-winners with signed photographs of himself.

The first large American cat show was held in New York in 1895. This set the seal on a gradual advance into social acceptance which began back in 1749, when the importation of cats into America was officially approved and indeed encouraged. Although there is no doubt that cats had been brought to the New World by the early settlers, none apparently survived, and drastic measures had become necessary to combat the ever-growing menace of the rat. The cat soon proved its worth, though even in America it was not immune from accusations of witchcraft or from superstitious associations.

These last are highlighted at their most dramatic in the work of Edgar Allan Poe, but Poe's treatment of cats in several of his sinister stories contrasts strongly with his affection for Catarina, his large and comfortable tortoiseshell. Later in the 19th century Poe's fellow-countryman, the humorist Mark Twain, was to express the memorable opinion that 'A house without a cat, and a well-fed, well-petted and properly revered cat, may be a perfect house, perhaps, but how can it prove its title?'

Although cat shows began largely as a diversion for the rich, they assumed their more universal appeal after the First World War and have continued to attract ever-increasing interest. One of their important functions is to act as a shop window for new or unfamiliar breeds, though these are not always well received at first. At the 1871 Crystal Palace Show one class of exhibits was described unkindly in a contemporary journal as 'an unnatural, nightmare kind of cat'. Today it is hard to believe that this was the beautiful seal point Siamese. *continued*

Renoir and especially Manet, who loved all cats and liked nothing better than to study them from his windows. From these observations he created a fine series of engravings and posters. Manet's affection for cats in general was shared in French literary circles by such writers of the period as Victor Hugo, Gautier, Baudelaire, Mallarmé, and Champfleury, whose book *Les Chats* (1868) was a worthy sequel to Moncrif's famous work, and for the *de luxe* edition of which Manet provided the illustrations.

Both these important books were paralleled in Germany by the views on life in general which E. T. A. Hoffman wrote in the person of his beloved cat Murr. Also deeply cat-conscious was the Swiss-born artist Théophile Steinlen, whose Paris house was known locally as Cats' Corner and sheltered a large

The cat in human society 4

The cat in modern times

Cats of all kinds continue to fascinate the writers and artists of the 20th century. The tradition first established in France of both keeping cats and writing perceptively about them has been worthily maintained there by great literary figures such as Cocteau and Colette, who once had a famous photograph taken of herself in the typical cat-like pose of the Sphynx, and by specialists such as Dr Fernand Méry.

This tradition has been followed elsewhere by, among others, Lady Aberconway (compiler of the invaluable *Dictionary of Cat Lovers*), Paul Gallico (who in his novel *Jennie* has become perhaps the only writer ever to get so uncannily under the skin of a cat), Michael Joseph, Compton Mackenzie, H. H. Munro ('Saki'), Beverley Nichols and Carl Van Vechten. A number of modern poets have also shown sympathetic insight into the feline nature, including Walter De La Mare, T. S. Eliot (whose *Old Possum's Book of Practical Cats* is a collection of 14 cat poems), Roy Fuller, Thomas Hardy, Ted Hughes, George MacBeth, Don Marquis, Harold Monro, Stevie Smith and W. B. Yeats.

Among artists the French tradition of cat art has continued with the painters Suzanne Valadon, Pierre Bonnard and Jacques Nam, the sculptors Sandoz and Valette, and the designer Erté. In Germany Franz Marc left over 20 portrait studies of cats, while a high proportion of the paintings by the Brazilian-born Leonor Fini contain cats which are large, fluffy and faintly menacing. In Britain an earlier generation is represented by such artists as Gwen John, Vanessa Bell, William Nicholson (whose studies of Sir Winston Churchill's famous marmalade tom are of the highest quality) and Philip Wilson Steer.

An outstanding name among modern British painters is that of Eden Box; through the medium of the commercial colour print her now famous painting *The Co-Existence Tree* has become one of the best-known cat pictures of recent times. The appealing cats of Martin Leman have also recently become widely and deservedly popular. American primitive painting of the 19th and 20th centuries is especially rich in pictures of cats, while the simplistic attraction of genuine folk art cats is especially well conveyed by Russian woodcuts of the same period.

The cat in caricature and children's art

The second President of the British National Cat Club was the artist Louis Wain, whose innumerable caricatures of clothed, semi-human cats in human situations are in a long tradition, the origins of which can be found in Egyptian tomb paintings (see p239). Immensely if rather inexplicably popular in their day, Wain's caricatures do little for the natural dignity of the cat, though there is no doubt that at the time they helped to focus public attention on the animal.

Much more appealing to our modern sense of humour are the swift but affectionate caricatures by Edward Lear of his famous tabby Foss, for whose sole convenience Lear, when moving house in San Remo, had his second villa planned and built as an exact replica of the first. Today's caricature cats *par excellence* are surely those of Ronald Searle, the American artist Saul Steinberg, and the French cartoonist Siné, who with the utmost economy of line wittily illustrates 'catty' words such as catastrophe, catalogue and so on.

In a somewhat different class are cats used both as literary and illustrative material in books intended mainly for children. Perhaps the best-known of all these is the Cheshire Cat in Lewis Carroll's *Alice in Wonderland*, though so many books have appeared over the years (and especially recently) that it is almost impossible here to select specific examples. However, mention must surely be made of the much-loved works of Beatrix Potter and also of the scarcely less famous adventures of Kathleen Hale's creation, *Orlando the Marmalade Cat*.

Two legendary cats that have come to life for generations of children are the pantomime favourites *Puss in Boots* and Dick Whittington's cat. However, in the field of modern entertainment we now have to distinguish between three different classes of cat. In the first come cats which are impersonated by human beings, as in pantomime, ballet (there is a notable

Cats in modern art are breaking away from the centuries-old tradition of realism into a new abstract form. In this painting by the German artist Maria Kloss the figures manage to retain most of the feline character while becoming almost grotesque shapes in an abstract landscape.

Cats in advertising are usually cast in cuddly roles, but in the American army poster **far left**, dating from World War I, the savage side of their nature is enlisted.

Cats in films range from the anthropomorphism of *Felix the Cat, Tom and Jerry* and, more recently, *Fritz the Cat* **left** to the feline star in its own right. Among the doyens of the latter is Solomon, seen **right** in a scene from the James Bond film *Diamonds Are Forever*. Solomon also appeared in *A Clockwork Orange*, but is best known in Britain for advertising carpets.

Cats in caricature range from the sentimentality of Henry Whittier Frees's photographs of kittens in human garb **right**, which were very popular in the 1920s, to the visual puns of such modern artists as Siné and Sara Midda, whose *Catacomb* is shown **far right**. Frees subjected other animals to such treatment, but found kittens to be 'the most versatile actors.'

Cats in research suffer for the advancement of scientific, medical and veterinary knowledge, being subjected to such things as experimentally induced disease, drug tests and dissection by biology students. This cat is being used in neurological research, small electrodes being inserted into the brain so that, by passing minute electric currents, the parts concerned with fear, aggression, pleasure and so on can be found.

perform in front of the cameras, gambolling around at 16 years old as though he were still a kitten. He had a huge following of fans and was that very rare animal, a cat that performs to order because it wants to. This is very important, for anybody who has ever tried to teach a cat to do tricks knows only too well that it will condescend to learn just as much, or as little, as it wishes. However, there can be no doubt that some cats, like some humans, are natural performers. Others have gained nationwide followings simply through walk-on parts on television, such as Morris, star of the American NBC show *Today*, and the late Jason, star of the BBC's *Blue Peter*.

Television has in fact been of considerable benefit to cats. Not only has it endeared individual cats such as Morris and Jason to the public, it has also enhanced the popular image of cats generally by news coverage of cat shows, by separate news items and feature programmes about cats, and by using cats to advertise all kinds of goods ranging from cat foods themselves to coal. Indeed, some cats have in fact reached fame by way of advertising, such as Arthur, whose trick of scooping his food out of the tin with his paw made him the best-known cat in Britain, or Solomon, who languorously promoted carpets. (Solomon, however, was also a film star.)

The use of cats in advertising can be traced back at least as far as Manet and Steinlen, who featured them in their posters. In more recent times advances in photographic techniques have very greatly increased the cat's importance in this field; photographers know that cats, and especially kittens, are eminently photogenic and can be used to sell or promote almost anything. Their use on greetings cards, chocolate boxes, calendars, notepaper and a hundred other

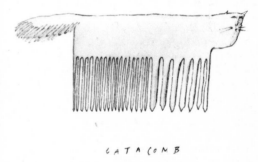

CATACOMB

items is no doubt often a debased form of cat art, but insofar as it promotes general interest in and awareness of the cat cannot be over-criticized.

Today it can safely be said that thanks to modern methods of communication the Western world is more cat-conscious than ever before. In addition to television programmes and films concerning cats in one way or another, all kinds of books and periodicals about them are published. Veterinary knowledge about cats is constantly growing, although it must be pointed out that some of this comes from experiments on living cats that certainly do not benefit. Then there is the plight – largely ignored even by most cat lovers – of the millions of stray cats throughout the world. Their more fortunate brethren, however, continue to act in that inimitable feline way that has endeared them to receptive people for centuries.

pas-de-deux in Tchaikovsky's ballet *The Sleeping Beauty*), or even opera (Ravel wrote a superbly realistic cat duet in his short one-act opera *L'Enfant et les Sortilèges* of 1925). In the second class are the popular cartoon cats of the film industry, beginning with the famous Felix in the 1920s and coming down to our own time with the *Tom and Jerry* series. Unfortunately it has to be said that these cinema cartoon cats, though often amusing, are equally often linked with unpleasant overtones of cruelty and sadism, perpetrated both by and towards the cat.

Cats as stars
In a quite separate class we must place those real-life cats who are stars in their own right, of the cinema or television screen, or both. Doyen of the former was undoubtedly Rhubar, an American tabby who was a natural show–off and liked nothing better than to

Glossary 1

Abdomen: The belly – the part of the trunk below or behind the chest.

Abscess: Collection of pus, usually surrounded by inflammation, forming a lump below the skin.

ACA: American Cat Association, the oldest governing body in North America.

ACFA: American Cat Fanciers Association.

Agouti: The colour between a tabby's stripes. Non-agouti cats lose this background, so that it becomes the same colour as the stripes, resulting in a self (solid) colour (see p 26).

Ailurophile/phobe: Cat lover/hater.

Albino: A creature having little or no coloured pigment in the skin, coat and eyes.

Allele: Any of the alternative genes found at a particular locus (position) on a chromosome that produce alternative physical characteristics (see p 21). (For example, the genes for agouti and non-agouti are alleles, as are those for long and short hair.)

Alter: American term for neuter.

Anaesthetic: A drug that stops pain; may be local, affecting only part of the body, or general, affecting the whole body and causing unconsciousness.

Anoestrus (anestrus): The time between the sexually receptive periods of oestrus.

Antibody: A substance produced by white blood cells in response to 'foreign' protein, such as that of a bacterium, that helps to neutralize and fight the 'invasion' (see p 173).

AOC: Any other colour – that is, any colour other than those specifically recognized in a breed.

AOV: Any other variety – that is, any pedigree cat not specifically recognized as a member of a breed.

Ataxia: Staggering, usually resulting from an ear or brain disorder.

Auditory: Relating to sound or hearing.

Auditory canal: The ear passage leading from the outside to the ear-drum; also called the external auditory meatus.

Awn hairs: The coarser of the two types of secondary hairs, having thickened tips.

Back-crossing: Mating a cat back to one of its parents.

Bacteria: A class of disease-producing micro-organisms, larger than viruses, that can be counteracted with antibiotics or other drugs (see p 172).

BC generation: Back-cross generation, the result of back-crossing.

Bicolour: Having a patched coat of white and another colour.

Bile: A greenish fluid secreted by the liver and stored temporarily in the gall bladder that aids the digestion of fats.

Blaze: A marking down the centre of the forehead.

Bloodline; line: A 'family' of cats related by ancestry or pedigree.

Blue: Colouring ranging from pale blue-grey to slate-grey.

Break: A distinct change in direction of the nose profile.

Breed: A group of cats with similar, defined physical characteristics and related ancestry (see p 44).

Breed number: Classification number under which a breed of cats and its members are grouped by a cat fancy organization.

Brindling: The occurrence of scattered 'wrong'-coloured hairs in the coat.

British: Term used in Britain to describe cobby, non-foreign body conformation.

Brush: Tail (generally of a long-hair).

Calico: American term for tortoiseshell and white.

Calling: A female cat's behaviour during oestrus (see p 130).

Cameo: Chinchilla, shaded or smoke with red or cream tipping to the hairs (see p 35).

Cancer: Any abnormal cell growth or tumour that can spread from one part of the body to another.

Carnivore: Meat-eater. Specifically, a member of the mammalian order Carnivora, to which cats (and dogs, bears, racoons, civets, etc) belong (see p 10).

Carry: In genetics, to possess a recessive gene that is not apparent in the phenotype but can be passed on to offspring. Of disease, to show no symptoms but able to pass it on to other animals.

Castration: Neutering of a male (see p 156).

Cat fancy: A general term for organized cat breeding and showing activities.

Cat flu: Term commonly used in Britain and some other countries for feline upper respiratory virus disease (see p 197).

Catnip; catmint: A perennial plant (*Nepeta cataria*) whose smell gives most cats great pleasure (see p 112).

Cattery: Any place where cats are kept. In Britain the term is mainly used for a boarding establishment, in North America for a breeding establishment.

CCA: Canadian Cat Association.

Cell: The basic structural and functional unit of the body (see p 102).

Cell division: The splitting of a living cell into two 'daughter' cells; it is the basic means by which creatures grow and replace tissues (see p 22).

CFA: Cat Fanciers Association, the largest American cat association, also encompassing Canada and Japan.

CFF: Cat Fanciers Federation (USA).

Champagne: American name for the chocolate colour in Burmese and the lilac colour in Tonkinese.

Champion; grand champion: Awards for excellence given after success at a number of cat shows (see p 232). See also Premier.

Chemoreceptor: Nerve ending, such as a taste bud or olfactory cell, that responds to a chemical stimulus (see also Receptor).

Chequerboard (Punnett square): Method of visualizing the assortment of genetic material from parents to offspring (see p 24).

Chinchilla: Colouring in which only the outermost tips of the hairs are coloured black or another colour, the rest being white or pale (see p 34).

Chocolate: Medium to pale brown; in Siamese distinctly paler than seal.

Chromosomes: The minute rod-shaped bodies in the nucleus of a cell that control the cell's – and the whole cat's – inherited characteristics.

Cobby: Having a short compact body shape, with broad shoulders and rump, a short tail and large rounded head, as in British Shorthair and others (see p 41).

Colostrum: The first 'milk' produced by the queen (see p 225).

Conformation: The particular body form of a cat, encompassing size and shape, and characteristic of a breed. Also called type.

Congenital: Describes a disorder arising before birth, either hereditary or due to abnormal development in the womb.

Cotton wool: Soft wadding known in North America simply as cotton.

Cross: An imprecise term for the mating of two cats, generally implying that they are distinctly different in colour and/or breed, or for their offspring.

CROWN: Crown Cat Fanciers Federation (USA).

Dam: Mother.

Degeneration: Deterioration of an organ or tissue structure due to disease, old age or accident.

Dermatitis: General terms for various inflammatory skin diseases; also commonly called eczema (see p 189).

Differentiation: The process during an embryo's growth in which unspecialized cells develop into tissues and organs.

Digitigrade: Walking on tip-toe, as in the cat.

Dilute: A paler version of a basic colour, such as blue, lilac and cream (see p 29).

Doctoring: Common term for neutering.

Domestic: Term sometimes used in North America for cats of non-foreign body type; equivalent to British.

Dominance: One gene is said to be dominant over its recessive allele when it produces a physical characteristic even when heterozygous (see p 20).

Double recessive: An individual that is homozygous for two pairs of recessive genes (see p 25).

Down (wool) hairs: Short, soft, crimped secondary hairs (see p 106).

Draught: American spelling draft.

Eczema: See Dermatitis.

Egg cell (ovum): The female germ or reproductive cell (see p 214).

Electroencephalogram (EEG): A chart showing the rhythmic electrical activity of the brain (see p 116).

Elizabethan collar: Cone-shaped hood used to stop a cat irritating injured parts of its body (see p 179).

Embryo: The name for an unborn kitten during its early stages of development (see p 220).

Endocrine: Relating to the hormonal system, which consists of glands that secrete hormones (see p 105).

Entire: Not neutered.

Enzyme: A chemical substance produced by the body that causes a chemical change of some kind, such as the digestion of food.

Epistasis: See Masking.

Euthanasia: Painless killing; commonly called destruction, putting down or putting to sleep (see p 209).

FCV: Feline calicivirus; one of the viruses that cause upper respiratory disease (cat flu; see p 197). (See also FVR.)

FeLV: Feline leukaemia virus (see p 204).

Feral: A domesticated animal that has reverted to or has been born in the wild. Feral cats are the same species as domestic cats, unlike true wild cats.

Fertilization: The union of a male sperm and female egg to form a single cell from which an embryo (and thence kitten) will develop (see p 215).

F_1 generation: The first filial generation; the first-generation offspring produced from the mating of two animals at the start of a breeding programme (see p 21).

F_2 generation: The second filial generation; the offspring from a mating of any two of the F_1 generation.

FIA: Feline infectious anaemia (see p 204).

FIE: Feline infectious enteritis, also known as panleukopaenia (see p 192).

FIFe: Fédération Internationale Féline, the main cat fancy organization on the European continent, also encompassing associations on several other continents. Formerly the Fédération Internationale Féline d'Europe (FIFE).

FIP: Feline infectious peritonitis (see p 193).

Flehmen reaction: The characteristic facial gesture seen when a cat's Jacobson's organ is stimulated (see p 112).

Foetus (fetus): An unborn kitten after differentiation of the organs and tissues. From this time, about four weeks after fertilization, growth consists mainly of an increase in size (see p 221).

Follicle: The 'pit' in the skin from which a hair grows. The sac in the female's ovary in which an egg develops.

Foreign: Describes a cat whose body is fine-boned and elegant, as in the Siamese.

FPL: Feline panleukopaenia (see FIE).

Frequency: The number of times a sound wave vibrates in one second; measured in hertz (Hz) and kilohertz (kHz), it determines a sound's pitch.

Frost point: American term for lilac (lavender) point.

FSH: Follicle-stimulating hormone (see p 214).

Fungi: A class of parasitic plants, including moulds, some of which cause skin and other diseases (see p 189).

FUS: Feline urological syndrome (see p 203).

FVR: Feline viral rhinotracheitis, the more serious of the two viral causes of feline respiratory disease (see p 197). (See also FCV.)

Gall bladder: Small sac near the liver that stores bile.

Gamete: See Germ cell.

GCCF: Governing Council of the Cat Fancy, the body controlling cat shows in Britain.

Genes: Units of heredity, which control the growth, development and function of all organisms (see p 20).

Genetics: The study of heredity.

Genotype: The set of genes an individual inherits from its parents.

Germ cell (gamete): A female egg cell (ovum) or male sperm.

Gestation: Pregnancy.

Ghost markings: Faint tabby markings seen in some self (solid) coloured cats, especially when young.

Gland: An organ that produces a chemical secretion, such as a hormone or enzyme.

Guard hairs: Long bristly hairs forming the outer coat.

Haemoglobin: The red colouring matter of blood.

Haemorrhage: Bleeding.

Haematoma: Blood-blister.

Harlequin: A name formerly used by some American breeders for Van pattern.

Haw: Third eyelid or nictitating membrane (see p 110).

Heat: A common name for oestrus.

Hertz: The unit of frequency (of sound, etc) in cycles (vibrations) per second. Abbreviated Hz.

Heterozygous: Having a pair of dissimilar alleles, one from each parent, for a particular characteristic.

Hock: Proper name for the ankle of a cat's hind leg.

Homozygous: Having an identical pair of alleles for a particular characteristic.

Honey mink: The name given to the intermediate brown colour of Tonkinese, corresponding to chocolate (see p 90).

Hormone: A chemical messenger secreted into the bloodstream by a gland in order to affect another part of the body (see p 105).

Host: The animal upon which a parasite lives.

Hybrid: The offspring of a cross between parents that are genetically dissimilar, especially between two different breeds or species.

Hypothalamus: A part of the brain that controls many subconscious functions (see pp 114 and 214).

Hz: Abbreviation for hertz.

ICF: Independent Cat Federation (USA).

Inbreeding: The mating of closely related cats, such as parents to offspring, brothers to sisters.

Induced ovulation: The release of eggs from the ovaries in response to physical stimulation by the male's penis during mating, as in cats, in contrast with spontaneous ovulation (as in humans) which occurs irrespective of such stimulation.

Infertile: Unable to breed.

Jacobson's organ (vomeronasal organ): A sense organ in the roof of the mouth of cats and some other species that responds to chemical stimuli (see p 112).

Karyotype: The characteristics of a set of chromosomes – number, shape, size and so on – represented diagramatically as a karyogram (see p 22).

kHz: Abbreviation for kilohertz.

Kilohertz: The unit of frequency (of sound, etc) in thousands of cycles (vibrations) per second. Abbreviated kHz.

Lactation: Milk production.

Lavender: American term for lilac.

Leucocyte: White blood cell.

Leukaemia: Cancer of the white blood cells.

LH: Luteinizing hormone (see p 214).

Lilac: Pale pinkish-grey, known in North America as lavender.

Liquid paraffin, medicinal: A mild laxative known in North America as mineral oil.

Litter: A family of kittens. Absorbent toilet material.

Linkage: The tendency for a group of genes to be inherited together (see p 23).

Locus: The position of a gene on a chromosome (see p 23).

Lordosis: The crouched, sexually receptive position assumed by a queen in oestrus.

Lymph: The straw-coloured fluid found in lymph vessels. It is similar in composition to blood plasma and contains leucocytes.

Lymphatic system: The system of lymph vessels and nodes (see p 105).

Lymph node: A mass of tissue found at various points on lymph vessels that may become swollen in disease.

Lymphocyte: A type of white blood cell that helps defend against disease.

Lynx point: American name for tabby point.

Mask: The darker-coloured areas of the face, as seen in Siamese and Himalayans (Colourpoint Longhairs).

Masking (epistasis): The effect some genes have of concealing or 'swamping' the presence of others (see p 26).

Melanin: The main pigment that gives colour to skin and hair.

Melanism: Having a very dark or black skin and coat. See also Albino.

Membrane: A thin sheet of tissue.

Mimicry: The occurrence of identical or very similar traits due to different gene mutations.

Modifiers: Polygenes that change the effect of major genes (see p 27).

Mongrel; moggy: A cat of mixed or unknown parentage.

Moult (molt): Periodic shedding of hair (see p 107).

Mutation: A change in a gene – due to environmental influences or a 'mistake' during replication – that results in an abrupt change in hereditary characteristics between two generations (see p 23).

Muzzle: The nose and jaws.

Natural mink: The name given to the darkest colour of Tonkinese, corresponding to seal point Siamese and brown (sable) Burmese (see p 90).

NCFA: National Cat Fanciers Association (USA).

Neurosis: Behavioural abnormality (see p 136).

Neuter (alter): A castrated male or spayed female.

Nictitating membrane: The correct name for the thin opaque membrane that covers the front of the eyeball under the eyelid (see p 110).

Nocturnal: Active at night.

Nucleus: The central part of a living cell that contains the chromosomes.

NZCF: New Zealand Cat Fancy.

Odd-eyed: Having eyes of different colours, usually one blue and one orange or copper (see p 30).

Oesophagus (esophagus): Gullet, the tube leading from the mouth to the stomach.

Oestrus (estrus): Regularly occurring periods of sexual receptivity seen in female cats (see p 130). Commonly known as heat.

Olfactory: Relating to smell.

Olfactory mucosa: The area of the nose responsible for the detection of smells (see p 112).

Omnivore: An animal that eats meat and plant foods.

Organ: A distinct structure found in the body (such as the heart, liver, kidneys and lungs) that has one or more particular functions.

Organism: Any living creature.

Oriental: A term often used interchangeably with foreign, particularly of extreme type. Specifically, relating to the Oriental Shorthair (see p 92).

Ovaries: The female sex glands, which produce egg cells and sex hormones (see p 213).

Ovulation: Release of eggs (see p 215).

Ovum: The correct term for an egg cell.

Pancreas: A gland in the abdomen that produces digestive enzymes and also the hormone insulin, which controls blood sugar levels.

Panleukopaenia: Another term (preferred in North America) for FIE (feline infectious enteritis).

Papilla: A small finger-like tissue projection, as found on the tongue (see p 113) and lining the gut.

Parasite: Any animal or plant that lives in or on another (the host), from which it obtains food and to which it usually does considerable harm (see pp 186 and 190).

Parasiticide: Any substance capable of destroying parasites.

Partial dominance: The occurrence of a pair of alleles where neither is fully dominant to the other, so that heterozygous individuals show mid-way characteristics (as in the Tonkinese, see p 25).

Parti-colour: Term encompassing bicolours, tortoiseshells and tortie-and-whites.

Patched tabby: See Tabby tortoiseshell.

Pedigree: The line of descent of a pure-bred animal, or the document recording this (see p 45).

Pewter: British name for shaded silver.

P generation: The parental generation; the animals that are mated in order to initiate a breed line (see p 21).

Phenotype: An individual's actual physical characteristics – size, shape, eye colour, hair length and so on – representing the physical expression of its genotype (see p 20).

Pheromone: A chemical substance released by an animal that influences the behaviour of another individual of the same species. Pheromones are involved in territorial spraying and sexual attraction.

Piebald: Specifically black and white, but also applied to white spotting with other colours (see p 39).

Pigment: Colouring matter.

Pinking up: A mainly British term for the characteristic colouring of the queen's nipples about three weeks after mating.

Pinna: The ear flap.

Pituitary: A small gland at the base of the brain that is the control centre of the hormonal system (see p 105).

Placenta: The organ by which the unborn kitten is attached to the lining of its mother's womb and through which it receives oxygen and food materials and gets rid of wastes.

Platinum: The American name for a lilac (lavender) in Burmese.

Points: The extremities of a cat's body – the head, ears, tail and feet – which are coloured in Siamese and some other breeds. See also Show standard.

Polygenes: Groups of genes, small in individual effect, that act together to produce bodily characteristics (see p 27). See also Modifiers.

Premier; grand premier: The equivalent of a champion and grand champion for a neuter.

Pricked: Describes ears held up alert.

Primary hairs: The same as guard hairs.

Pseudopregnancy: A condition when all the signs of pregnancy appear after mating but fertilized eggs do not implant in the uterus and no kittens are born; also known as false pregnancy (see p 228).

Psychosomatic: Refers to physical illness with no apparent physical cause.

Puberty: The time when the sex glands become functional and secondary sexual characteristics emerge.

Purulent: Containing pus.

Queen: An un-neutered female cat, particularly one kept for breeding.

Rangy: Describes a cat with long slender legs.

Receptor: A sensory nerve ending that converts information from the environment into nerve impulses which travel to the brain and supply the animal with information about its surroundings.

Recessiveness: The 'opposite' of dominance; the characteristic of a trait or gene that appears only when homozygous.

Recognition: The official acceptance of a breed, colour, etc for show under the rules of a cat fancy organization. There may be different degrees of recognition (see p 45).

Registration: Recording the particulars of a cat's birth and ancestry with an official body.

Roman: Describes a nose with a high, prominent bridge, characteristically seen in some Siamese.

Sable: American name for brown, the darkest coat colour, in Burmese.

Seal: The dark brown colour found at the points of the darkest variety of Siamese.

Secondary hairs: Fine hairs, including awn and down hairs, that form the cat's undercoat (see p 106).

Secondary sexual characteristics: Features that differ between males and females, except the sex organs themselves; include the size and heavy jowls of toms.

Selective breeding: Breeding by planned matings between individuals with behavioural or physical characteristics that the breeder wishes to perpetuate and enhance.

Self (solid): Having a coat of uniform colour (see p 29).

Sex hormone: A hormone unique to males or females that produces sexual characteristics or behaviour, or bodily changes connected with reproduction.

Sex-linkage: The occurrence of a trait exclusively or more commonly in one sex rather than the other (see p 23).

Shaded: Colouring in which the tips of the hairs are coloured, the rest being white or pale, the tipping being intermediate between the chinchilla and the smoke (see p 34).

Shading: Gradual variation in coat colour, usually from back to belly.

Show standard: A descripion of the ideal cat of a particular breed, against which actual cats are judged (see p 231). Also called standard of points.

Silver: Term applied to shaded silver and silver tabby, both tipped colourings (see p 34).

Sire: Father.

Smoke: Colouring in which most of the hairs are coloured, the roots being white or pale (see p 35).

Solid: American term for self.

Spaying: Neutering of a female (see p 156).

Species: The basic unit of biological classification, consisting of similar individuals that are distinctively different from all other species and can breed together to produce fertile offspring like themselves. All domestic cats (of all breeds) belong to one species.

Sperm: The male germ or reproductive cell (see p 214).

Spotting: The occurrence of white patches in the coat (see p 39).

Spraying: The habit of urinating (mainly by toms) to mark out territory.

Standard of points: See Show standard.

Steroid: Any of a number of hormones of a particular chemical type, some synthetic versions of which are used to treat inflammation or as contraceptives.

Glossary 2 / Gestation chart

Stifle: Proper name for the knee of a cat's hind leg.

Stimulus: An occurrence in the environment that evokes a response from a receptor or from the whole animal (see p 152).

Stop: An abrupt change in slope of the nose profile – an extreme form of break.

Stud: A tom kept specifically for breeding.

Tabby: Striped, blotched or spotted (see p 32).

Tabby tortoiseshell: A tortoiseshell with tabby rather than self (solid) black patching; also called patched tabby or torbie (see p 38).

Tapetum lucidum: The mirror-like layer at the back of the cat's eye that produces the characteristic shine (see p 111).

Test cross: A mating carried out in order to investigate an individual cat's genotype.

Testicles: The male sex glands, which produce sperm and male sex hormones.

TICA: The Independant Cat Association (USA).

Ticking: The black 'flecks' seen characteristically on the Abyssinian coat.

Tipped: Having coloured ends to the hairs, the degree of tipping deciding whether a cat is classed as chinchilla, shaded, smoke, etc (see p 34).

Tissue: A mass of cells performing a particular structural or functional role in the body (see p 102).

Tom: An entire (uncastrated) male cat.

Torbie: See Tabby tortoiseshell.

Tortie: Tortoiseshell.

Tortoiseshell: Generally black and orange, but can also include blue-cream (dilute tortoiseshell), lilac-cream, etc (see p 38).

Toxin: A poison, particularly one produced by a micro-organism.

Trait: A discrete inherited feature such as colour, coat length, etc.

True-breeding: Homozygous for all traits being considered. Such a cat, if mated with another similar cat, will produce offspring like itself which, if inbred, will produce yet more offspring with exactly the same traits.

Tumour: Any growth – not necessarily cancerous – caused by abnormal cell multiplication.

Type: Same as conformation.

UCF: United Cat Federation (USA).

Van pattern: Bicolour in which most of the body is white, the colour being restricted to the extremities.

Variety: Strictly, a subdivision of a breed, such as a particular colour form. The term is, however, sometimes used interchangeably with breed.

Vet: Popular term for a qualified animal doctor, in Britain correctly termed a veterinary surgeon and in the United States a veterinarian, used in this book to avoid the above differences in terminology.

Vibrissae: Whiskers.

Viruses: A class of disease-producing micro-organisms, extremely small in size, that cause several of the most serious feline diseases and cannot be treated with antibiotics (see p 172).

Vitamin: A chemical substance needed in the diet in small quantities for proper bodily functioning (see p 149).

Voluntary: Under the brain's conscious control.

Vomeronasal organ: Same as Jacobson's organ.

Wild type: The basic unmutated form of a creature that is found in the wild; in the cat, this is the short-haired brown striped tabby.

Gestation chart If you know the date of mating, it is easy to estimate the date the kittens may be expected by using the chart **below**. The average gestation period is 65 days, but a variation of four days either way is not unusual, so birth may occur any time between the dates shown immediately before and after the average date. An early sign that the queen is in fact pregnant is the 'pinking up' of her nipples (see p220) some 21 days after mating.

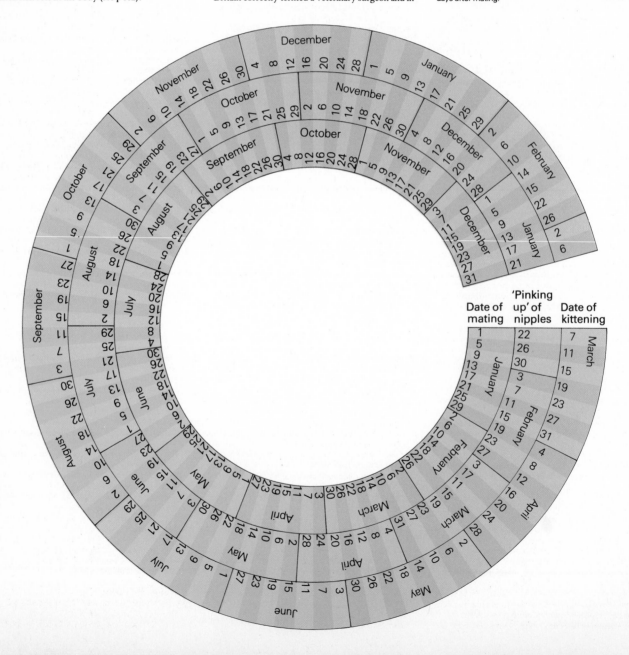

Date of mating	'Pinking up' of nipples	Date of kittening
1	22	7
5	26	11
9	30	15
13	3	19
17	7	23
21	11	27
25	15	31
29	19	4
	23	8
	27	12
	3	16
	7	20
	11	24
	15	28

Bibliography / Useful addresses

BIBLIOGRAPHY
The number of good, reliable and up-to-date books on specialized aspects of cats (as opposed to general, mainly pictorial books) is surprisingly limited. Listed below are a number that readers may find interesting and/or useful for further reading. Of necessity, however, many of these are relatively advanced, being designed for the practising vet or veterinary student. Some others are somewhat outdated. Therefore, inclusion of any book here does not imply blanket endorsement by the editors and contributors. Unless otherwise stated, the publishers are in Britain or have branches in Britain as well as the United States.

Alison Ashford and Grace Pond, *Rex, Abyssinian and Turkish Cats* (John Gifford, 1972); British bias.

J. C. Boudreau and C. Tsuchintani, *Sensory Neurophysiology* (Van Nostrand Reinhold, 1973); advanced, but much information on cat senses not available elsewhere.

Joan McDonald Brearley, *All About Himalayan Cats* (TFH Publications, 1976); includes information on history in Britain and North America.

E. J. Catott, *Feline Medicine and Surgery* (American Veterinary Publications, USA, 1977); a standard textbook.

Catherin Cisin, *An Ocelot in Your Home* (TFH Publications, 1968); some parts may be outdated; American.

J. E. Crouch, *Text-Atlas of Cat Anatomy* (Baillière Tindall, London, 1969; Lea & Febiger, Philadelphia, 1969); for veterinary and biology students.

Mary Dunnill, *The Siamese Cat Owner's Encyclopaedia* (Pelham Books, London, 1974; Howell Book House, NY, 1974).

R. F. Ewer, *The Carnivores* (Weidenfeld & Nicolson, 1973); a standard work on the evolution and natural history of cats' wild relatives.

Michael W. Fox, *Understanding Your Cat* (Bantam Books, NY, 1977; originally published 1974 by Coward, McCann & Geoghegan, NY); chatty, but containing much information on behaviour, etc.

C. A. W. Guggisberg, *The Wild Cats of the World* (David & Charles, 1975).

E. S. E. Hafez (ed), *The Behaviour of Domestic Animals* (3rd edition, Baillière Tindall, London, 1975; Williams & Wilkins, Baltimore, 1975); somewhat academic but readable; includes the cat among other domestic mammals.

Benjamin L. Hart, *Feline Behavior* (Veterinary Practice Publishing Co, California, 1978); reprints of columns from the journal *Feline Practice*, also issued under the title *Behavior of Cats*; some information controversial.

Joan O. Joshua, *Cat Owner's Encyclopedia of Veterinary Medicine* (TFH Publications, 1977; partially revised and expanded edition 1979; originally published by Heinemann as *The Clinical Aspects of Some Diseases of Cats*); a handy-sized text by a British vet originally intended for the veterinary student; some parts may be outdated.

Robert W. Kirk, *First Aid for Pets* (E. P. Dutton, NY, 1978; Pelham Books, London, 1979); clear advice covering most eventualities, with clear photographs. Also deals with dogs and other pets.

George MacBeth and Martin Booth (eds), *The Book of Cats* (Secker & Warburg, 1976; Penguin, 1979); one of the best anthologies of the cat in literature, poetry and art.

Betty Meins and Wanita Floyd, *Show Your Cat* (TFH Publications, 1972); deals with showing in North America, though somewhat outdated.

The Merck Veterinary Manual (Merck & Co, New Jersey, 4th edition 1973); a general reference handbook for practising vets.

Claire Necker, *The Natural History of Cats* (A. S. Barnes, NY, 1970; Delta, NY, 1977); better for anthology and anecdote than for up-to-date factual information.

Nutrient Requirements of Cats (Part 13 of *Nutrient Requirements of Domestic Animals;* National Academy of Sciences, Washington DC, revised edition 1978); the standard reference document.

R. S. Pinniger (ed), *Jones's Animal Nursing* (Pergamon Press, 1966; revised 1976); intended as a textbook for student veterinary nurses, contains much useful information on anatomy, hygiene, first aid, etc.

Robine Pocock, Dorothy Silkstone Richards, Moira Swift and Vic Watson, *The Burmese Cat* (B. T. Batsford, 1975); British bias.

Grace Pond (ed), *The Complete Cat Encyclopedia* (Heinemann, 1972; Crown, NY, 1972); now somewhat outdated, but a comprehensive guide to breeds recognized at the time of publication and their history; cat fancy orientated.

Grace Pond and Muriel Calder, *The Longhaired Cat* (B. T. Batsford, 1974); includes Colourpoint Longhairs (Himalayans), Birmans, Turkish, etc, as well as Persians.

Ivor Raleigh and Grace Pond, *A Standard Guide to Cat Breeds* (Macmillan London, 1979; McGraw Hill, NY, 1979); one of the more recent guides to pedigree cat breeds; cat fancy orientated.

H. L. Reingold (ed), *Maternal Behavior in Animals* (John Wiley, 1963); includes a readable if somewhat academic chapter on the cat; may be outdated in places.

Dorothy Silkstone Richards, *A Handbook of Pedigree Cat Breeding* (B. T. Batsford, 1977); a good beginner's guide based on British practice.

Roy Robinson, *Genetics for Cat Breeders* (Pergamon Press 1971; extensively revised 1977); the best book on the subject, though slightly outdated in a few places.

Godfrey Sandys-Winsch, *Animal Law* (Shaw & Sons, 1978); deals with English law.

Frederic J. Sauter and John A. Glover, *Behavior, Development, and Training of the Cat* (Arco, NY, 1978); deals mainly with training and behaviour modification, with results of laboratory research; little on natural behaviour of feral cats.

Frances Simpson, *The Book of the Cat* (Cassell, 1903); one of the classics; well illustrated.

J. C. Suarès and Seymour Chawast, *The Illustrated Cat* (Harmony Books, NY, 1976; Omnibus, London, 1977) and *The Literary Cat* (Berkley Windhover, NY, 1977); the former a poster book; the latter mainly an anthology of cat prose and poetry but also well illustrated.

Meredith D. Wilson, *Encyclopedia of American Cat Breeds* (TFH Publications, 1978); a reference book of breeds and colours, and which organizations recognize them.

C. E. Woodrow, *The Export and Import of Dogs and Cats* (British Small Animals Veterinary Association, 1975); covers the requirements of most countries, plus IATA and several airlines and shipping companies; inevitably outdated in parts, however, as regulations are constantly changing.

A number of useful (though in some cases outdated in places) offprints of journal articles and pamphlets on specific (mainly veterinary) topics are published by the Feline Advisory Bureau (address on the right) and by the Veterinary Practice Publishing Co, PO Box 4457, Santa Barbara, California 93103, who will supply lists of titles.

Magazines and periodicals
All Cats (Pacific Palisades, California); for the cat lover more than fancier; articles, stories and items of general interest; monthly.

Bulletin of the Feline Advisory Bureau (London); free to FAB members; articles mainly on veterinary problems but also general cat matters; quarterly.

Cats (England); monthly magazine published from 1969 to 1972, interesting historically.

Cats and Catdom Annual (Fur and Feather, Bradford, England); a review of the British cat fancy year; also contains general articles and advertisements.

Cats Magazine (Pittsburgh, Pennsylvania); has the largest circulation of any cat publication; deals mainly with the North American cat fancy (all associations) and sponsors All-American awards; articles, comment, show reports, cattery advertisements; monthly.

Cat World (Phoenix, Arizona); CFA-orientated, but also carries reports and articles from other countries, scientific articles, advertisements, etc; bimonthly.

CFA Yearbook (Red Bank, New Jersey); a massive tome reporting on the CFA year, heavily illustrated with photographs of top winning cats; also general articles and overseas reports, plus extensive cattery advertisements.

Feline Practice (Veterinary Practice Publishing Co, Santa Barbara, California); a veterinary periodical, but written in a readable style and with occasional articles of general interest; reprints of some of these available (see above); bimonthly.

Fur and Feather (Bradford, England); covers cavies, rabbits, fowl, etc, as well as cats; official organ of the GCCF, publishing show reports, breed standard changes, addresses of clubs and so on; also breeders' advertisements; weekly.

Our Cats (England); monthly magazine published from 1952 to 1966; historically interesting breed articles.

Pedigree Digest (Pedigree Petfoods, Melton Mowbray, England); articles on veterinary, behavioural and general matters (dogs as well as cats); quarterly.

USEFUL ADDRESSES
The cat fancy organizations listed below will supply – for a fee – copies of their show standards, show rules and registration rules. Any book you may require should be obtainable through any good bookshop, but those listed specialize in cat books and will supply by mail order. Addresses, unless otherwise stated, are in Britain.

Cat fancy organizations
American Cat Association, 10065 Foothill Boulevard, Lakeview Terrace, California 91342

American Cat Fanciers Association, PO Box 203, Point Lookout, Missouri 65726

Canadian Cat Association, 14 Nelson Street West (Suite 5), Brampton, Ontario L6X 1BY

Cat Fanciers Association, PO Box 430, Red Bank, New Jersey 07701

Cat Fanciers Federation, 2013 Elizabeth Street, Schenectady, New York 12303

Crown Cat Fanciers Federation, 1379 Tyler Park Drive, Louisville, Kentucky 40204

Feline Association of South Australia, PO Box 104, Stirling, South Australia 5152

Fédération Internationale Féline, Friedrichstrasse 48, 6200 Wiesbaden, West Germany

Governing Council of the Cat Fancy, Dovefields, Petworth Road, Witley, Surrey GU8 5QU

National Cat Club, The Laurels, Chesham Lane, Wendover, Bucks

Kensington Kitten and Neuter Cat Club, Fairmont, 78 Highfield Avenue, Aldershot, Hants

Long Island Ocelot Club, PO Box 99542, Tacoma, Washington 98499

New Zealand Cat Fancy Inc, PO Box 3167, Richmond, Nelson, New Zealand

The Independant Cat Association, 211 East Olive (Suite 201), Burbank, California 91502

United Cat Federation, 6621 Thornwood Street, San Diego, California 92111

General
American Humane Association, 5351 S Roslyn Street, Englewood, Colorado 80111

American Society for the Prevention of Cruelty to Animals, 441 East 92nd Street, New York, New York 10028

Cat Action Trust, The Crippetts, Jordens, Beaconsfield, Bucks

Cats Protection League, 29 Church Street, Slough, Berks SL1 1PW

Cat Survival Trust, Marlind Centre, Codicote Road, Welwyn, Herts AL6 9TU

Feline Advisory Bureau, 6 Woodthorpe Road, London SW15 6UQ

Pedigree Petfoods Education Centre, Stanhope House, Stanhope Place, London W2 2HH

Petcare Information and Advisory Service, 254 George Street, Sydney, NSW, Australia

Pet Health Council, 418–422 The Strand, London WC2R 0PL

Royal Society for the Prevention of Cruelty to Animals, The Manor House, Horsham, Sussex RH12 1HG

Society for the Prevention of Cruelty to Animals, Wellington, New Zealand

Cat book specialists
The Cat Book Centre, Box 112, Wykagyl Station, New Rochelle, New York 10804

The Little Bookshop, Farnham Common, Bucks

Genetics index

This index covers references to major genes, coat patterns and colours, and coat types; for general genetic concepts, see the general index. See also the index of breeds. Page references in italics indicate an illustration.

250

Index of cat breeds

Numbers in bold type indicate a major entry, those in italics an illustration.

Page references in italics indicate an illustration. See also the glossary (p 246).

Acknowledgements

The artists and photographers who contributed the illustrations in this book are listed below. Where more than one person was responsible for the illustrations to a two-page spread, these are listed from A to Z starting with the picture farthest to the left and nearest the top of the page, and working down each column in turn.

Front cover: Peter Warner
1–9: Lynn Duncombe
10–11: A: Jacana/Collection Varin-Visage; B: Clem Haagner/Ardea; C: Alan Suttie; D: G. R. Roberts
12–13: A: Jacques Robert/Jacana; B: A. Warren/Ardea; C: P. Wayne/NHPA; D: Picturepoint; E: Eric Hosking; F: Syndication International; G: Tom McArthur
14–15: Ron Hayward
16–17: A: C. M. Dixon; B: Mary Evans Picture Library; C: F. Petter/Jacana; D: Eric Hosking; E: I. R. Beames/Ardea; F: W. A. Newlands
18–19: Lynn Duncombe
20–21: A: Angela Sayer/Animal Graphics; B, C: John Painter
22–23: A, B, D: John Painter; C: Doris H. Wurster Hill/Dartmouth-Hitchcock Foundation; E: Angela Sayer/Animal Graphics
24–25: A: Angela Sayer/Animal Graphics; B, C, E: John Painter; D: Alice Su
26–27: A, D, E, G: Anne Cumbers; B: John Painter; C: Peter Byer/Julia May (owner/breeder); F: Jane Miller
29: John Painter
30–31: A: Barbara Beal (owner/breeder); B: Angela Sayer/Animal Graphics; C: Anne Cumbers; D: Peter Warner, Catherine Harris & Lorna Turpin
32–33: A, D: Peter Warner, Catherine Harris & Lorna Turpin; B: Spectrum Colour Library; C: Peter Warner; E: Angela Sayer/Animal Graphics
34–35: A: Peter Warner; B: Anne Cumbers; C: Peter Warner, Catherine Harris & Lorna Turpin
36–37: A: Peter Warner, Catherine Harris & Lorna Turpin; B, C: Anne Cumbers
38–39: A: Peter Warner; Catherine Harris & Lorna Turpin; B: Anne Cumbers; C, D, E: John Painter
40–41: A: Mr & Mrs H. J. Tomlin (owner/breeders); B: John Painter; C, E, F: Angela Sayer/Animal Graphics; D: Creszentia Allen; G, H: R. R. Ashdown/Royal Veterinary College, London
42–43: A, B: Tim Gruffydd-Jones/Feline Advisory Bureau; C, L: Peter Warner; D: Anne Cumbers; E, G, H, J, K: Creszentia Allen; F: T. Tucker/Mrs J. Seymour (owner/breeder); I: Alice Su
44–45: A: Mansell Collection; B: Roy Robinson & Pat Turner
46–47: A, C: Anne Cumbers; B, D, E: John Painter
48–49: Alan Suttie
50–51: A: Peter Warner; B, D: Sonia Halliday; C: Michael Wilson; E: Anne Cumbers
52–53: A: Peter Warner; B: R. Hoyt/L. E. Sherer; C: Tom B. Jensen; D: Alice Su
54–55: A, D, F: Anne Cumbers; B: Derrick Spear; C: Creszentia Allen; E: Peter Warner
56–57: Creszentia Allen
58–59: A: Peter Warner; B, D, F: Creszentia Allen; C: Sdeuard Bisserôt/Vera Croysdill (owner)/Miss J. Z. Jones (breeder); E: Jane Howard
60–61: A: Peter Warner; B: Jane Howard; C: Vera Croysdill; D, E: Creszentia Allen; F: Anne Cumbers
62–63: A: Peter Warner; B, C: Creszentia Allen; D: Angela Sayer/Animal Graphics; E: Alice Su
64–65: A: Peter Warner; B: Anne Cumbers; C: Creszentia Allen; D: Mrs D. N. Healy
66–67: A: From The Book of The Cat (1903); B: Peter Warner; C: Helen Berryman (owner/breeder); D, E: Angela Sayer/Animal Graphics
68–69: A: Jane Howard/Mr & Mrs Huntington (owner/breeder); B, D, E: Creszentia Allen; C: Peter Warner; F: Chanan Photography
70–71: A: Peter Warner; B: Creszentia Allen
72–73: A: Peter Warner; B, C: Anne Cumbers; D: Alice Su
74–75: A, C: Peter Warner; B: The Brooklyn Museum; D, E: Chanan Photography
76–77: A, D: Peter Warner; B: Angela Sayer/Animal Graphics; C: Alice Su
78–79: A: Anne Cumbers; B: Angela Sayer/Animal Graphics; C, D, F: Alice Su; E: Peter Warner

80–81: A: Peter Warner; B: Daphne Negus/Thai National Library
82–83: A: Peter Warner; B: Daphne Negus/Thai National Library; C: Philip Coffey/Mrs B. Boizard (owner/breeder); D: Angela Sayer/Animal Graphics
84–85: A: Mr & Mrs N. Flowers (owners); B: Peter Warner; C, D, F: Christina Payne; E: Alice Su; G: Creszentia Allen
86–87: A: Daphne Negus/Thai National Library; B: From The Book of The Cat (1903); C: Mansell Collection; D: Peter Warner
88–89: A, B, D, E: Anne Cumbers; C: Creszentia Allen; F: Peter Warner
90–91: A: Alice Su; B, C: Angela Sayer/Animal Graphics; D: Peter Warner
92–93: A: Peter Warner; B: Alice Su; C: Angela Sayer/Animal Graphics; D: Anne Cumbers
94–95: A, B: Angela Sayer/Animal Graphics; C: Creszentia Allen; D, E: Anne Cumbers
96–97: A: Alice Su; B: Creszentia Allen; C, E: Anne Cumbers; D: Mr & Mrs N. Flowers (owners); F: Peter Warner
98–99: A: Rod Williams/Bruce Coleman; B, D: Creszentia Allen; C: Eric Jukes; F: Animals Unlimited; G: Peter Warner
100–101: Lynn Duncombe
102–103: A: Angela Sayer/Animal Graphics; B: Sean Milne
104–105: A: Jacana; B, C, D: Sean Milne; E: Sean Milne and Alan Suttie
106–107: Sean Milne
108–109: A, D: Sean Milne; B: Spectrum Colour Library; C: Chris Forsey
110–111: A–F: Tom McArthur; G: Oxford Scientific Films
112–113: A, F: Tom McArthur; B, C: Angela Sayer/Animal Graphics; D: Priscilla Barrett; E: Zefa
114–115: A: Tom McArthur; B: Picturepoint; C: Creszentia Allen
116–117: A, C: Priscilla Barrett; B: Mr & Mrs D. Bryson (owners); D: Mr & Mrs D. M. Scholes (owners)
118–119: A: Priscilla Barrett; B, F: Alan Suttie; C: Angela Sayer/Animal Graphics; D: Jane Miller; E: Michael Boys/Susan Griggs Agency
120–121: A, B, E: Priscilla Barrett; C, D: Lorna Turpin
122–123: A: Priscilla Barrett; B, C: J. M. Labat/Jacana; D: Oxford Scientific Films
124–125: A: Priscilla Barrett; B: Harry Clow
126–127: A: Mr & Mrs John Lintin Smith (owners)/Mrs Doreen Watts (breeder); B: NHPA; C: Anne Cumbers; D: Creszentia Allen; E: Jerry Cooke/Oxford Scientific Films/Animals Animals; F: Mary Evans Picture Library; G: Marc Henrie
128–129: A, B: Priscilla Barrett; C: Lorna Turpin; D: Raymond Irons; E: Pilloud/Jacana
130–131: A: Priscilla Barrett; B: Anne Cumbers; C: Creszentia Allen
132–133: A: Priscilla Barrett; B: Colin Maher
134–135: A: Priscilla Barrett; B: Anne Cumbers; C: Oxford Scientific Films; D: Angela Sayer; E, G: Spectrum Colour Library; F: Jane Miller
136–137: Priscilla Barrett
138–139: Lynn Duncombe
140–141: A: Raymond Irons; B, C: Popperfoto; D: Lorna Turpin
142–143: A: H. J. Tomlin (owner); B: Mr & Mrs P. Alger (owners); C: Angela Sayer/Animal Graphics; D, E, F, G, I, J: Colin Maher; H: Lorna Turpin
144–145: Vana Haggerty
146–147: A: Keystone Press Ltd; B: Linda Broad; C, D, F: Lorna Turpin; E: Popperfoto; G: Anne Cumbers; H: Angela Sayer/Animal Graphics
148: A, C: Angela Sayer/Animal Graphics; B: Lorna Turpin
150–151: A, B, C, D: Trevor Dolby; E: Vana Haggerty
152–153: A: Vana Haggerty; B, C: Frank Lane
154–155: Linda Broad
156–157: A: Lorna Turpin; B: Mary Evans Picture Library; C, E: Angela Sayer/Animal Graphics; D: Linda Broad
158–159: A: Vana Haggerty; B: Harry Clow; C: Colin Maher; D: Lorna Turpin
160–161: A: Frank Roche/Oxford Scientific Films/Animals Animals; B: Anne Cumbers; C, D: Lorna Turpin; E: Popperfoto

162–163: A: John Moss/Colorific; B: Harry Clow; C: Anne Cumbers; D: Cecil Reilly Associates/Pamela Cross Stern
164–165: A: Angela Sayer/Animal Graphics; B: Alan Suttie; C: Keystone Press; D: The Post Office
166–167: A: Philip Coffey/Mrs B. Boizard (owner); B: Cat Survival Trust; C: Picturepoint; D: Craiglaw Breeding Station; E: Lorna Turpin
170–171: Lynn Duncombe
172–173: A, B, D: Lorna Turpin; C: Marc Henrie
174–175: A: Tim Gruffydd-Jones/Feline Advisory Bureau; B: Lorna Turpin; C: John Painter
176–177: A: Marc Henrie; B, C, D, E: Alice Su
178–179: A, B: Angela Sayer; C, D: Lorna Turpin
180–181: A: RSPCA/Nottingham Evening Post; B, D, E: Lorna Turpin; C: Anthony Self/RSPCA
182–183: Lorna Turpin
184–185: Lorna Turpin
186–187: A–G: Richard Lewington; H: Tim Gruffydd-Jones; I: Lorna Turpin
188–189: A: Angela Sayer: B: A. I. Wright; C, D: Tim Gruffydd-Jones
190–191: A: Alan Suttie; B, C, D, E: Angus Dunn
192–193: A, C: Angela Sayer/Animal Graphics; B: Lorna Turpin; D: Cathy Orr
194–195: A: Tim Gruffydd-Jones/The Journal of Small Animal Practice; B: Lorna Turpin; C: Popperfoto
196–197: A: Tim Gruffydd-Jones/Veterinary Annual; B: Lorna Turpin; C, D: Pitman-Moore, Inc
198–199: A: Alan Suttie; B: Cathy Orr
200–201: A: Marc Henrie; B, D: Frank Startup; C: Tim Gruffydd-Jones
202–203: A, B, C: Lorna Turpin; D: Angela Sayer/Animal Graphics
204–205: A: Marc Henrie; B, C: Lorna Turpin; D: Helen M. Laird/University of Glasgow
206–207: G. Clayton-Jones
208–209: A: Marc Henrie; B: Tim Gruffydd-Jones; C: Anne Cumbers
210–211: Lynn Duncombe
212–213: A: Angela Sayer/Animal Graphics; B: Mr & Mrs P. Alger (owners); C: Jill Della Casa; D: Lorna Turpin
214–215: Alan Suttie
216–217: A: Harry Clow; B, C: Lorna Turpin
218–219: Angela Sayer/Animal Graphics
220–221: A: Angela Sayer/Animal Graphics; B, E: Alan Suttie; C: Tim Gruffydd-Jones; D: Anthony Self/RSPCA
222–223: A, C, D, F, G, H: Angela Sayer/Animal Graphics; B, E: Alan Suttie
224–225: A, B, E: Angela Sayer/Animal Graphics; C: Lorna Turpin; D: Priscilla Barrett
226–227: A, D, F: Anne Cumbers; B: Angela Sayer/Animal Graphics; C: Jane Burton/Bruce Coleman; E: Alan Suttie
228–229: A: Alan Suttie; B: Bernard Rebouleau/Jacana
230–231: A: Pat Turner; B: From The Book of the Cat (1903); C: Peter Warner
232–233: A, C–G: Angela Sayer/Animal Graphics; B: Creszentia Allen
234–235: A: Lorna Turpin; B, C, D, E: Angela Sayer
236–237: Lynn Duncombe
238–239: A: Michael Holford; B, D: C. M. Dixon; C: Snark International; E: Photographie Bulloz
240–241: A: The British Library; B: Samuel Pepys Library, Magdalene College, Cambridge; C: Daphne Negus/Thai National Library; D: Scala; E: Mary Evans Picture Library
242–243: A, D: Hansmann Archiv; B, C: Michael Wilson; E: From The Book of the Cat (1903); F: Cooper Hewitt Museum
244–245: A, C: Snark International; B: Hansmann Archiv; D: Jon Evans; E: United Artists Corporation; F: Ann Bradford; G: Sara Midda
248–249: Jill Della Casa
Back cover: A: NHPA: B: Anne Cumbers; C: Priscilla Barrett; D, F: Linda Broad; E: John Painter; G: Angela Sayer; H: The Brooklyn Museum